INTERDISCIPLINARY
RESEARCH

I dedicate this second edition to Doris, my wife.

INTERDISCIPLINARY RESEARCH

PROCESS AND THEORY

ALLEN F. REPKO

The University of Texas at Arlington

Los Angeles | London | New Delhi
Singapore | Washington DC

Los Angeles | London | New Delhi
Singapore | Washington DC

FOR INFORMATION:

SAGE Publications, Inc.
2455 Teller Road
Thousand Oaks, California 91320
E-mail: order@sagepub.com

SAGE Publications Ltd.
1 Oliver's Yard
55 City Road
London EC1Y 1SP
United Kingdom

SAGE Publications India Pvt. Ltd.
B 1/I 1 Mohan Cooperative Industrial Area
Mathura Road, New Delhi 110 044
India

SAGE Publications Asia-Pacific Pte. Ltd.
33 Pekin Street #02-01
Far East Square
Singapore 048763

Acquisitions Editor: Vicki Knight
Editorial Assistant: Kalie Koscielak
Production Editor: Libby Larson
Copy Editor: Melinda Masson
Typesetter: C&M Digitals (P) Ltd.
Proofreader: Wendy Jo Dymond
Indexer: Terri Corry
Cover Designer: Glenn Vogel
Marketing Manager: Helen Salmon
Permissions Editor: Adele Hutchinson

Printed in the United States of America

Library of Congress Cataloging-in-Publication Data

Repko, Allen F.

Interdisciplinary research : process and theory / Allen F. Repko. — 2nd ed.

p. cm.
Includes bibliographical references and index.

ISBN 978-1-4129-8877-3 (pbk.)

1. Interdisciplinary research. I. Title.

Q180.55.I48R47 2012 001.4—dc23 2011027812

This book is printed on acid-free paper.

11 12 13 14 15 10 9 8 7 6 5 4 3 2 1

Brief Contents _____

Preface	xxi
Acknowledgments	xxxii
About the Author	xxxiii
PART I: About Interdisciplinary Studies	**1**
1. Defining Interdisciplinary Studies	3
2. Mapping the Drivers of Interdisciplinarity	32
PART II: Drawing on Disciplinary Insights	**67**
3. Beginning the Research Process	69
4. Introducing the Disciplines	93
5. Identifying Relevant Disciplines	143
6. Conducting the Literature Search	167
7. Developing Adequacy in Relevant Disciplines	193
8. Analyzing the Problem and Evaluating Insights	225
PART III: Integrating Insights	**259**
9. Understanding Integration	261
10. Identifying Conflicts Between Insights	293
11. Creating Common Ground Between Concepts	321
12. Creating Common Ground Between Theories	355
13. Constructing a More Comprehensive Understanding or Theory	382
14. Reflecting on, Testing, and Communicating the Understanding	409
Conclusion	439
Appendix	445
Glossary of Key Terms	459
References	476
Author Index	496
Subject Index	500

Detailed Contents ____

Preface   xxi

Acknowledgments   xxxii

About the Author   xxxiii

PART I: About Interdisciplinary Studies   1

1. Defining Interdisciplinary Studies   3
   Chapter Preview   3
   The Meaning of Interdisciplinary Studies   3
      Two Conceptions of Interdisciplinary Studies   3
      The "Discipline" Part of Interdisciplinary Studies   4
         Categories of Traditional Disciplines   5
         The Fine and Performing Arts   5
         The Applied and Professional Fields   5
         The Emergence of Interdisciplines   6
         Evolving Constructs   6
      The "Inter" Part of Interdisciplinary Studies   7
         "Inter" Refers to Contested Space   7
         "Inter" Refers to the Action Taken on Insights   7
         "Inter" Refers to the Result of Integration   7
         Aspects of the Prefix "Inter" Summarized   8
      The "Studies" Part of Interdisciplinary Studies   8
         Why Traditional Disciplines Are Not
            Referred to as "Studies"   8
         Why "Studies" Is an Integral Part
            of Interdisciplinary Studies   9
         The Differences Between the Disciplines
            and Interdisciplinary Studies   9
         Why "Studies" Is Plural   11
   A Definition of Interdisciplinary Studies   12
      Reasons for Agreeing on a Definition of
         Interdisciplinary Studies   12

Authoritative Definitions of Interdisciplinary Studies   14

An Integrated Definition of Interdisciplinary Studies   15

What Interdisciplinary Studies Is Not   16

Interdisciplinary Studies Is Not

     Multidisciplinary Studies   16

       Two Metaphors   17

       The Fable of the Elephant House   17

Interdisciplinary Studies Is Not

     Transdisciplinary Studies   20

The Differences Between Multidisciplinarity,

     Interdisciplinarity, and Transdisciplinarity

     Summarized   20

The Premise of Interdisciplinary Studies   21

Competing Impulses Behind the

     Term *Interdisciplinarity*   21

How the Term *Interdisciplinarity* Is Variably Used Today   22

Forms of Interdisciplinarity   22

Interdisciplinarity Is Used to Describe Work   23

     The Work of Integrating Knowledge   23

     The Work of Recognizing and

       Confronting Differences   24

Interdisciplinarity Is Used to Describe

     a Research Process   24

Interdisciplinarity Is Used to Describe the

     Kind of Knowledge Produced   25

Interdisciplinarity Is Used to Describe

     Change in Knowledge Production   25

Metaphors Commonly Used for Interdisciplinary Work   25

The Metaphor of Boundary Crossing   26

The Metaphor of Bridge Building   27

The Metaphor of Mapping   27

The Metaphor of Bilingualism   28

Reflections on These Metaphors   28

Chapter Summary   29

Notes   29

Exercises   30

2.   Mapping the Drivers of Interdisciplinarity   32

Chapter Preview   32

The Primary Drivers of Interdisciplinary

     Research and Education   33

     The Inherent Complexity of Nature and Society   33

     The Desire to Explore Problems and Questions

       That are Not Confined to a Single Discipline   35

     The Need to Solve Social Problems   37

The Need to Produce Revolutionary
  Insights and Generative Technologies   38
The Interdisciplinary Critique of the Disciplines   41
  Specialization Can Blind Us to the Broader Context   42
  Specialization Tends to Produce Tunnel Vision   42
  Disciplinarians Sometimes Fail to Appreciate Other
    Disciplinary Perspectives   43
  Some Worthwhile Topics Fall in the Gaps Between
    Disciplines   43
  Creative Breakthroughs Often Require
    Interdisciplinary Knowledge   43
  The Disciplines Are Often Unable to
    Address Complex Problems Comprehensively   44
  The Disciplines Are Products of a Bygone Age   44
The Formation of the Disciplines and the Origins of
  Interdisciplinarity   45
  The Origins of the University and the Disciplines   46
  The Impact of the Enlightenment and Scientific
    Revolution on the Disciplines   46
  The Consolidation of the Disciplines in the
    Late Eighteenth and Early Nineteenth Centuries   47
  The Professionalization of Knowledge in the Late
    Nineteenth and Early Twentieth Centuries
    and the Rise of the Modern Disciplines   47
  The Emergence of Interdisciplinary Studies and
    Interdisciplinarity   48
    The General Education Movement   49
    The Cold War Era and Interdisciplinarity   49
    University Reforms in the 1960s and the
      Emergence of Interdisciplinary Studies   50
    Interdisciplinary Studies Becomes an
      Academic Field   51
Assumptions of Interdisciplinarity   52
  The Reality Beyond the Academy Requires
    an Interdisciplinary Approach to Research
    and Education   52
  The Disciplines Are Foundational
    to Interdisciplinarity   53
  The Disciplines *by Themselves* Are Inadequate
    to Address Complex Problems   53
  Disciplinary Perspectives are Partial and Biased   55
Cognitive Abilities Fostered by Interdisciplinarity   56
  Develop and Apply Perspective-Taking Techniques   56
  Develop Structural Knowledge of Complex Problems   56
  Create or Discover Common Ground Between
    Conflicting Insights   56

Integrate Conflicting Insights From Two or More Disciplines	57
Produce a Cognitive Advancement or More Comprehensive Understanding of the Problem	57
Reflection on What Interdisciplinary Education Offers	58
Traits and Skills of Interdisciplinarians	58
Traits	58
Skills	61
Reflection on Traits and Skills of Interdisciplinarians	63
Chapter Summary	63
Notes	64
Exercises	65

PART II: Drawing on Disciplinary Insights — **67**

3. Beginning the Research Process	69
Chapter Preview	69
What the Interdisciplinary Research Process Is	69
A Process of Decision Making	69
A Decision-Making Process	70
A Decision-Making Process That Is Heuristic	70
A Decision-Making Process That Is Iterative	71
A Decision-Making Process That Is Reflexive	71
Two Additional Characteristics of the IRP	71
An Integrated Model of the IRP	73
The Benefits of a Map	73
Cautions Concerning These STEPS	74
STEP 1: Define the Problem or State the Research Question	76
Select a Problem or Pose a Question That Is Complex and Requires Insights From More Than One Discipline	76
Define the Scope of the Problem or Question	77
Avoid Three Tendencies That Run Counter to the IRP	78
Disciplinary Bias	78
Disciplinary Jargon	78
Personal Bias	79
Follow Three Guidelines for Stating the Problem or Posing the Question	80
Examples of Statements of an Interdisciplinary Problem or Question	81
Note to Readers	84
STEP 2: Justify Using an Interdisciplinary Approach	84
The Problem or Question Is Complex	85
Important Insights or Theories of the Problem Are Offered by Two or More Disciplines	85
Note to Readers	86

No Single Discipline Has Been Able to Explain
the Problem Comprehensively or Resolve It   86
The Problem Is an Unresolved Societal
Need or Issue   86
*Examples of Statements That Justify Using an
Interdisciplinary Approach*   87
Chapter Summary   89
Notes   90
Exercises   91

4. Introducing the Disciplines   93
Chapter Preview   93
The Structure of Knowledge and Its Reflection in the
Organization of the Academy   93
Disciplines   94
Disciplinarity   94
Categories of Disciplines   94
The Concept of Disciplinary Perspective   96
Disciplinary Perspective   96
Misconceptions About the Term
Disciplinary Perspective   96
Other Problems With the Concept of Disciplinary
Perspective   99
The Concept of Disciplinary Perspective Clarified   100
A Definition of Disciplinary Perspective   101
Using Disciplinary Perspectives   102
The Defining Elements of a Discipline's Perspective   105
Phenomena   105
Phenomena Classified   107
Note to Readers   111
Epistemology   111
*The Nature and Limits of the Truth Claims
Made by Major Epistemological Approaches*   112
Various Epistemologies   113
*Epistomologies of Various
Theories and Schools
of Thought*   117
Note to Readers   119
Assumptions   120
Basic Assumptions   120
Note to Readers   125
Concepts   126
Theory   126
Two Kinds of Theory   127
*The Importance of Theory to
Interdisciplinary Work*   127
Note to Readers   128

Method   128
    The Importance of Disciplinary Methods to
      Interdisciplinary Work   128
    Various Methods   130
    The Correlation Between Epistemologies
      and Method   137
    Note to Readers   137
Chapter Summary   138
Notes   139
Exercises   141

5. **Identifying Relevant Disciplines**   143
  Chapter Preview   143
  STEP 3: Identify Relevant Disciplines   143
  Identify *Potentially* Relevant Disciplines   143
    Identify *Potentially* Relevant Disciplines *Before*
      Conducting the Full-Scale Literature Search   144
      Identify Phenomena Typically of Interest
        to Disciplines   145
      Draw on Disciplinary Perspectives
        in a General Sense   145
      An Example of the Standard Way
        to Proceed   145
    Synthesis of the Perspectival and Classification
      Approaches   147
    Summary of How to Identify Disciplines Potentially
      Relevant to the Problem   148
  Map the Problem to Reveal Its Disciplinary Parts   149
    The Research Map   149
    The Concept or Principle Map   150
    The Theory Map   152
    Systems Thinking and the System Map   152
      Benefits to Students of Using Systems
        Thinking and the System Map   156
      The Similarity of Systems Thinking to
        Problem-Based and Inquiry-Based Learning   157
      How Systems Thinking Promotes
        Interdisciplinary Learning and Facilitates
        the Research Process   158
  Reducing the Number of Potentially Relevant
  Disciplines to Those That Are *Most* Relevant   159
    "Most" Relevant Defined   159
    Three Questions to Ask to Distinguish Between
      Potentially Relevant and Most
      Relevant Disciplines   159
      Applying These Questions to the Disciplines
        Potentially Relevant to Various Topics   160

      Note to Readers   163

      Applying These Questions to the Problem

          of Human Cloning   163

   Chapter Summary   164

   Notes   165

   Exercises   166

6. Conducting the Literature Search   **167**

   Chapter Preview   167

   STEP 4: Conduct the Literature Search   167

   Defining *Literature Search*   167

   Reasons for Conducting the Literature Search   168

   Special Challenges Confronting Interdisciplinarians   170

      There Is Simply More Ground to Be Covered   170

      Interdisciplinary Researchers Risk Being Seduced

         by What Disciplinary Experts Say   170

      Interdisciplinarians Must Place the Insights

         and Theories of Each Relevant Discipline

         Within the Context of Its Unique Perspective   171

      The Methods of Library and Database

         Cataloguing Disadvantage Interdisciplinary

         Researchers   171

   Conducting the Interdisciplinary Literature Search   172

      The Initial Search   173

         The Organization and Classification of

           Books in Libraries   173

         Direct Searching   176

         Search Strategies   179

         Mistakes Commonly Made When Beginning

           the Literature Search   182

      The Full-Scale Literature Search   183

         Note to Readers   184

         Two Challenges of the Full-Scale

           Literature Search   184

         Building on the Connections Discovered

           by Previous Scholars   188

         Consulting Disciplinary Experts   188

         Other Sources of Knowledge   189

   Chapter Summary   190

   Notes   191

   Exercises   191

7. Developing Adequacy in Relevant Disciplines   **193**

   Chapter Preview   193

   STEP 5: Develop Adequacy in Each Relevant Discipline   193

   Comprehending Enough About Each Discipline   193

      How Much Knowledge Is Required From

         Each Discipline?   194

An Undergraduate Example 194
A Solo Interdisciplinarian Example 194
   Examples of the Need for Varying Degrees
   of Adequacy 195
Note to Readers 196
Developing Adequacy in Relevant Disciplines
   Involves Borrowing 196
What Kind of Knowledge Is Required From
  Each Discipline? 197
  Which Disciplinary Elements Are
    Applicable to the Problem? 197
  What Are the Characteristics of the Problem? 197
  What Is the Goal of the Research Project? 198
Developing Adequacy in Theories 198
The Reason to Understand Theories 198
Concepts and How They Relate to Theory 199
How to Proceed 199
  First, Identify Theories Within a
   Single Discipline 199
  Second, Identify Theories Within Each
   of the Other Relevant Disciplines 202
  When to Use a Deductive Approach
   to Theory Selection 203
Developing Adequacy in Disciplinary Methods 204
Defining *Disciplinary Method* 204
Methods Used in the Natural Sciences, the
  Social Sciences, and the Humanities 206
  The Natural Sciences 206
  The Social Sciences 206
  The Humanities 206
The Interdisciplinary Position on Methods 207
  Adequacy in Disciplines Must Include
   Understanding Disciplinary
   Research Methods 207
  Adequacy in Disciplines Includes Knowing the
   Interdisciplinary Position on the Quantitative
   Versus Qualitative Methods Debate 208
  Two Misconceptions About Qualitative Research 209
  Theoretical Implications of Using
   Qualitative Research Methods 209
How a Discipline's Preferred Methods
  Correlates to Its Preferred Theories 210
How to Select Methods 211
  When Conducting Basic Research in
   the Sciences 211
  When Conducting Basic Research in
   the Humanities 212

How the IRP Relates to the Disciplinary
    Method(s) Used in Basic Research   215
The Concept of Triangulation in Research
    Methodology   216
Deciding Which Disciplinary Methods to
    Use in Conducting Basic Research   217
Providing In-Text Evidence of Disciplinary Adequacy   219
Chapter Summary   220
Notes   221
Exercises   223

8. Analyzing the Problem and Evaluating Insights   225
Chapter Preview   225
STEP 6: Analyze the Problem and Evaluate Each
    Insight or Theory   225
Analyzing the Problem From Each Disciplinary
    Perspective   225
How to Analyze a Problem From Each
    Disciplinary Perspective   226
*Examples of Analyzing Problems From
    Disciplinary Perspectives*   228
*Reflections on Analyzing Problems
    From Disciplinary Perspectives*   232
The Problem of Personal Bias   233
Evaluating Insights   234
Disciplinary Perspective in General   234
The Theories Used in Generating Insights   239
*Stating the Theory, Detecting Its Assumptions,
    and Identifying Its Explanatory Strengths
    and Limitations*   239
Asking the "5 W" Questions to Evaluate the
    Appropriateness of Each Theory to the Problem   241
The Data Used as Evidence for Insights   244
*Examples of How Supportive Evidence
    Reflects Disciplinary Perspective*   246
Reflecting on These Examples   246
The Methods Employed   247
The Phenomena Embraced by Insights   251
Checklist for Evaluating Previous Research   255
Chapter Summary   255
Note   256
Exercises   256

PART III: Integrating Insights   259

9. Understanding Integration   261
Chapter Preview   261
What Integration Is   261

A Definition of Integration or Synthesis 262
The Controversy Concerning Integration 263
   The Generalist Critique 264
     Disciplinary Fragmentation 264
     Epistemological Barriers 265
     Conflicting Perspectives and Ideologies 265
     A Variety of Possible Results 265
     Preference for Theory Competition and
       Alternative Integrations 266
   The Integrationist Case 266
     Theories Supportive of Integration
       From Cognitive Psychology 267
     The Development of New Models of the IRP
       That Feature Techniques Demonstrated
       to Achieve Integration 270
The Publication of Groundbreaking Integrative
  Work on a Wide Range of Complex Problems 270
The Insistence on the Centrality of Integration by Leading
  Interdisciplinary and Transdisciplinary Organizations 271
The Advantages of Integration 271
The Readily Available Tests for Selecting the Best
  Comprehensive Understanding 272
   The Goal of Full Integration 273
Conditions Necessary to Perform Integration 274
   Overcoming Monodisciplinarity 274
     Perspective Taking 274
     Balancing Conflicting Views 276
     Holistic Thinking 277
   Triangulating Depth, Breadth, and Integration 278
     Disciplinary Depth 278
     Disciplinary Breadth 279
     Interdisciplinary Integration 280
   Cultivating Seven Qualities of Mind 280
The Model of Integration Used in This Book 281
   What the Model Integrates 281
   How the Model Integrates 281
     Contextualization 282
     Conceptualization 282
     Problem Solving 284
     Summary of How the Broad
       Model Integrates 285
   What the Result of Integration Looks Like 285
     Integration Accommodates Epistemological
       Differences 286
     Integration Is New and More Comprehensive 287
     Integration Is "Larger" Than the Sum of
       Its Parts 288

    The Defining Characteristics of the Result of
       Integration Summarized   288
    Three Fundamental Questions Raised by This
       Discussion of the Broad Model   289
  Chapter Summary   290
  Notes   290
  Exercises   291

10. **Identifying Conflicts Between Insights**   293
  Chapter Preview   293
  STEP 7: Identify Conflicts Between Insights
    or Theories and Their Sources   293
  The Importance of Identifying Conflicts Between Insights   293
    Where Conflicting Insights Are Located   294
      Conflicting Insights Produced by Authors
       From the Same *Discipline*   294
      Conflicting Insights Produced by Authors
       From Different *Disciplines*   295
    Why Insights Conflict   295
      Concepts Embedded in Insights   297
      Assumptions   298
      Organizing Disciplinary Insights   300
  Theories as Sources of Insights and Conflict Between Insights   300
    Theories as Sources of Insights, Concepts,
      and Assumptions   301
      Theories as Sources of Insights   301
      Theories as Sources of Concepts   302
      Theories as Sources of Assumptions   302
      Organizing Information About Theories   303
    Theories From the Same Discipline Can
      Be Sources of Conflict Between Insights   306
    Theories From the Same Discipline Can
      Be Sources of Conflicting Assumptions   309
    Theories From Different Disciplines Can
      Be Sources of Conflict Between Insights   313
  A Note to Readers About Communicating Conflicts
    and Their Sources   316
  Chapter Summary   319
  Exercises   320

11. **Creating Common Ground Between Concepts**   321
  Chapter Preview   321
  STEP 8: Create Common Ground
    Between Concepts and Theories   321
  The Theory of Common Ground as the Basis
    for Collaborative Communication and
    Interdisciplinary Integration   322

A Definition of Interdisciplinary Common Ground   322
Common Ground Is Necessary for Collaborative
   Communication   323
Common Ground Requires Unconventional
   Thinking   324
Common Ground Is Achieved Through the Use
   of Language   326
   Note to Readers   326
Common Ground Must Be Created Whenever
   Concepts or Theories Conflict   327
Common Ground Is Created by Modifying Concepts
   or Theories Directly or Through Their Assumptions   327
Creating Common Ground Is Integral to Preparing
   Concepts and Theories for Integration   328
Creating Common Ground Requires Using Intuition   329
   An Example of How Intuition Helps to Achieve
    Common Ground   330
Creating Common Ground Plays Out Differently in
   Contexts of Narrow Versus Wide Interdisciplinarity   331
Creating Common Ground Is the Interdisciplinarian's
   Responsibility   332
Modifying Concepts and Assumptions   332
  How to Proceed   333
   When to Seek Common Ground   333
   Decide How Comprehensive the Study Will Be   333
   Decide What Common Ground Will
    Be Created From   334
   A Best Practice When Working With
    Concepts and Assumptions   335
  Techniques Demonstrated for Modifying
   Concepts and Assumptions   335
   1. The Technique of Redefinition   336
   2. The Technique of Extension   340
   3. The Technique of Transformation   343
   4. The Technique of Organization   346
   The Value of These Techniques   347
  Creating Common Ground When Assumed
   Values and Rights Conflict   348
   Arguments for the Validity of These Types   349
   How to Know If Insights
    Conflict Over Ethics   349
   Creating Common Ground When Values
    and Ethical Positions Conflict   350
Chapter Summary   352
Notes   352
Exercises   353

12. **Creating Common Ground Between Theories**   355
    Chapter Preview   355
    Disciplinary Theories   355
        A Definition of *Disciplinary Theory*   356
        When Working With Theories Is Necessary   356
    The Relationship of Models, Variables, and Causal
      Processes to Theories   357
        Models   357
        Variables and Relationships   358
        Independent and Dependent Variables   358
        Why a More Comprehensive Theory Includes
          Variables From Other Relevant Theories   359
        Theories May Contain Macro- and/or Micro-Level
          Variables Affecting the Construction of a More
          Comprehensive Theory   359
    Variables and Causality   361
        When Theories Differ Only Minimally and
          Focus Instead on Process   361
    Modifying a Set of Theories   364
        Situation A: One or More Theories in the Set Have
          a Broader Range of Applicability Than Do Others   364
          Identify All Variables or Causal Factors
            Addressed by Each Theory   364
          Reduce These Variables to the Fewest Number
            Possible by Categorizing Them Under a Few
            Broad Headings   365
          Determine How Many of These Categories
            Are Included in Each Theory   366
          If No Theory Encompasses All Categories,
            Determine Which Theory Can Most
            Readily Be Extended to Do So   366
          Modify the Theory by Extending Its Range
            of Applicability   368
    Critiquing Theories   369
        Situation B: None of the Theories in the Set Borrow
          Elements From Other Disciplines   370
          Modifying Concepts Embedded in Theories   371
          Modifying Assumptions Underlying Theories   372
          Modifying Concepts and *Assumptions*   377
    Chapter Summary   379
    Notes   380
    Exercises   380

13. **Constructing a More Comprehensive Understanding**
   or Theory   382
    Chapter Preview   382
    STEP 9: Construct a More Comprehensive Understanding   382

A Definition of *More Comprehensive Understanding*
    and *More Comprehensive Theory*   382
    Unpacking This Definition   383
    The Process Involved   383
Constructing the More Comprehensive Understanding
    From Modified *Concepts*   384
    From the Humanities   384
    From the Social Sciences   386
Constructing a More Comprehensive Theory From
    a Modified *Theory*   387
    Six Strategies to Achieve Causal or
        Propositional Integration   388
        Sequential or End-to-end Causal Integration   388
        Horizontal or Side-by-Side Causal Integration   389
        Multicausal Integration   390
        Cross-level or Multilevel Causal Integration   395
        Spatial and Analytical Integration   403
Chapter Summary   407
Notes   407
Exercises   408

14. Reflecting on, Testing, and Communicating
the Understanding   409
    Chapter Preview   409
    STEP 10: Reflect on, Test, and Communicate
        the Understanding   409
    Reflecting on the More Comprehensive Understanding
        or Theory   409
        Reflect on What Has Actually Been Learned
            From the Project in an Overall Sense   410
        Reflect on STEPS Omitted or Compressed   411
        Reflect on One's Own Biases   411
        Interrogate One's Own Biases   412
        Check One's Work for Biases   413
        Reflect on One's Adherence to
            a Theoretical Approach   413
        Reflect on One's Limited Understanding
        of the Relevant Disciplines, Theories,
        and Methods   414
    Testing the Quality of Interdisciplinary Work   414
        Learning Outcomes Claimed for Interdisciplinarity   415
        Cognitive Abilities Attributable to Interdisciplinary
            Learning Drawn From Research on Cognition
            and Instruction   415
        Develop and Apply Perspective-Taking Techniques   416
        Develop Structural Knowledge of Problems
            Appropriate to Interdisciplinary Inquiry   416

Create Common Ground Between Conflicting
    Disciplinary Insights   417
Integrate Conflicting Disciplinary Insights   417
Produce a Cognitive Advancement or
    Interdisciplinary Understanding of a Problem   417
    Four Core Premises That Underlie the
        Concept of Cognitive Advancement   417
Testing or Assessing the More Comprehensive
    Understanding   418
    The Newell Test   419
    The Tress et al. Test   419
    The Szostak Test   421
    The Boix Mansilla et al. Test   422
    Integrating These Tests   424
Communicating the Results of Integration   425
    A Metaphor   426
    A Model   426
    Examples of Models   427
    A Narrative   429
    Examples of Narratives   429
    Note to Readers   431
    A New Process to Achieve New Outcomes   431
    Examples of New Processes   432
    A New Product   433
    A Critique of an Existing Policy and/or
        a Proposed New Policy   433
    Examples of Critiques   434
    A New Question or Avenue of Scientific Inquiry   435
    The Value of Communicating Back to Disciplines   435
Chapter Summary   436
Note   436
Exercises   437

Conclusion   439

Appendix   445

Glossary of Key Terms   459

References   476

Author Index   496

Subject Index   500

Preface _____

_____ **The Book**

The purpose of the second edition of *Interdisciplinary Research: Process and Theory* is to reflect the substantial research on all aspects of interdisciplinarity that has been published since the appearance of the first edition in 2008. How to do interdisciplinary research is no longer the neglected topic that it once was. This book also reflects feedback from faculty and students who have used the first edition. As in the previous edition, the goal is to provide a comprehensive and systematic presentation of the interdisciplinary research process and the theory that informs it not only for students but also for individual mature scholars and interdisciplinary teams. The book emphasizes the relationship between theory, research, and practice in an orderly framework so that the reader can more easily understand the nature of the interdisciplinary research process.

_____ **New in the 2nd Edition**

The 2nd edition incorporates the following revisions:

- There is now a separate chapter for each of the 10 STEPS in the inter-disciplinary research process, except for STEPS 1 and 2, which are combined in Chapter 3. STEP 8, creating common ground, is divided into two chapters: 11 and 12.
- Chapter 1 (Chapter 1 in the first edition) is revised and includes new material.
- Chapter 2 (Chapter 2 in the first edition) is revised and expanded to include a discussion of factors driving interdisciplinary education and research.
- Chapter 3 (Chapter 6 in the first edition) is revised and introduces the revised research model and STEPS 1 and 2.
- Chapter 4 introduces the disciplines, combines critical material in Chapters 3 and 4 of the first edition, and better explains how this information will be used in performing subsequent STEPS.

- Chapter 5 (the first part of Chapter 7 in the first edition) is mostly new and includes new content on mapping.
- Chapter 6 (the second part of Chapter 7 in the first edition), conducting the literature search (STEP 4), is rewritten and expanded.
- Chapter 7 (Chapter 8 in the first edition), developing adequacy in relevant disciplines (STEP 5), is revised and expanded.
- Chapter 8 (Chapter 9 in the first edition), analyzing the problem and evaluating insights (STEP 6), is revised.
- Chapter 9 (Chapter 5 in the first edition), introducing integration, is revised and expanded.
- Chapter 10 (Chapter 10 in the first edition), identifying conflicts between insights (STEP 7), is revised and expanded.
- Chapter 11 (Chapter 11 in the first edition), creating common ground between concepts (the first half of STEP 8), is revised and expanded.
- Chapter 12 (the second part of STEP 8), Chapter 13 (STEP 9), and Chapter 14 (STEP 10) are new, replacing Chapter 12 in the first edition.
- The Conclusion is revised.
- The Appendix is revised, updated, and expanded.
- Chapters on the STEPS of the research process contain a "Note to Readers" explaining the relevance of certain information to the four audiences that the book is attempting to reach: undergraduates, graduate students, individual mature scholars, and interdisciplinary teams.
- Exercises replace the "Review" questions at the end of each chapter and challenge students to analyze concepts rather than to recall information.
- Several new examples of student and professional work are added to illustrate the STEPS of the research process.
- The Glossary of Key Terms is revised and expanded.

The new edition continues using features that students and instructors have said they find helpful. These include the easy-to-follow step-by-step approach to describe the research process, tables and figures to illustrate aspects of each STEP, and a variety of examples oriented toward students working in the natural sciences, the social sciences, and the humanities. The additions and changes reflect the concerns and developments that have surfaced in the field since the publication of the first edition. The book has benefitted from the constructive criticism offered by instructors and students. Following their advice, I have refined the prose to make it more readable, made key concepts and processes more accessible to students, and reduced the use of in-text quotations except where it is preferable to read the author's own words.

The Need for This Book

This book is needed for four reasons. First, interdisciplinarity is an emerging paradigm of knowledge formation whose spreading influence can no longer be denied, discounted, or ignored. The reason is explicit: "Interdisciplinarity is associated with bold advances in knowledge, solutions to urgent societal problems, an edge in technological innovation, and a more integrative educational experience" (Klein, 2010, p. 2).

Second, this book is a corrective to those who argue that interdisciplinarity is too hard to do, who reject the notion that the field should aspire to its own methodology, or who worry that if the field becomes "disciplined it cannot offer the peculiar kind of insights that our times require" (Frodeman, Klein, Mitcham, & Holbrook, 2010, p. xxxi). There are also those who argue that interdisciplinarity is easy in the sense that it can be done without reflection. This book is also a corrective to them.

Third, those involved in interdisciplinary education have requested this book. As noted by Carol Geary Schneider (2010), president of the Association of American Colleges and Universities, "Interdisciplinarity is now prevalent throughout American colleges and universities" (p. xvi). Faculty are concerned that students learn how to do interdisciplinary research and writing. This is one of the important findings reported in the 2003 volume of *Issues in Integrative Studies* titled "Future Directions for Interdisciplinary Effectiveness in Higher Education: A Delphi Study." The study posed this question to its participants, all of whom are leading interdisciplinary practitioners: "What changes in interdisciplinary studies programs need to take place over the next decade in order to better serve the needs of students whose academic goals are not adequately addressed by traditional discipline-based programs?" Under "Curriculum," the participants recommended a textbook that provides an overview of disciplinary perspectives, theories, and methodologies, and especially integrative techniques, along with concrete examples (Welch, 2003, p. 185). Further evidence that the topic is neglected comes from Klein (2005a), who in *Humanities, Culture, and Interdisciplinarity: The Changing American Academy* criticizes the tendency of scholars to "hover at the level of theory with little or no attention to what is happening on the ground of practice" (p. 7). This book is a response to these concerns. It attempts to apply theory to the "ground of practice" and make the interdisciplinary research process comprehensible and achievable for students.

Fourth, the book enables students to differentiate between interdisciplinary research and disciplinary research. An important contribution of the book is that it surveys the dozen or so research methodologies used by the disciplines and explains how these are foundational to, but different from, the interdisciplinary research process. The book also reflects an emerging consensus about the meanings and operations of important interdisciplinary theories and concepts.

The Intended Audience

The book is aimed at four audiences: undergraduate students, graduate students, faculty, and members of interdisciplinary research teams. The book, because of its extensive discussion of the disciplines and their defining elements, provides students not only with understanding of the interdisciplinary research process but also with useful discipline-specific information that is dispersed. This information on disciplinary perspective, phenomena, epistemology, assumptions, theories, and methods is as necessary for multidisciplinary research as it is for interdisciplinary research. Students in disciplinary majors will find this information helpful as they will likely take courses in different disciplines and will want to know how to tie these together. Graduate students and faculty will appreciate the book's glossary of key terms, endnotes, extensive sources, various teaching aids, numerous examples that demonstrate best practices from professional work, and recommended readings organized by specialty from the field's extensive literature in the Appendix.

Most books on research methods can assume professional consensus about the principles of the field they present. Because the field of interdisciplinary studies has only just reached the point where there is sufficient potential for scholarly consensus on the principles of the field, this book has to point the reader toward a scholarly rationale in the literature for each principle, in addition to explaining the principle itself. In a sense, then, the book is aimed at faculty teaching an interdisciplinary course as much as at students taking that course. Undergraduate and graduate students can learn as much about interdisciplinary studies from the rationale for interdisciplinary principles as from the principles themselves.

The book is intended as either a core or a supplemental resource for undergraduate and graduate courses that are interdisciplinary. More specifically, the book will be useful in a variety of academic contexts: intermediate-level courses that focus on interdisciplinary research and theory; upper-level topics, problems, or theme-based courses that involve working in two or more disciplines; integrative capstone and senior seminar courses that require an indepth interdisciplinary research paper/project; keystone courses that integrate general education for upper-level undergraduate programs; graduate courses in interdisciplinary teaching and/or research; teaching assistant training/ certificate courses in interdisciplinary learning, thinking, and research; first-semester master's-level research courses; and administrators and faculty who wish to develop interdisciplinary courses and programs at their institutions. The book, particularly its early chapters, is being used successfully as a primary text for introductory interdisciplinary studies courses. Multidisciplinary programs calling on students to cross several disciplinary domains will also find this book useful. It is also a useful guide to individual mature scholars and interdisciplinary teams on how best to perform interdisciplinary research.

The Approach Used and Style of Presentation _____

This book's approach to interdisciplinary research is distinctive in at least six respects. (1) It describes how to *actually do* interdisciplinary research using processes and techniques of demonstrated utility whether one is working in the natural sciences, the social sciences, the humanities, or the applied fields. (2) It integrates and applies the body of theory that informs the field into the discussion of the interdisciplinary research process. (3) It presents an easy-to-follow, but not formulaic, decision-making process that makes integration and the goal of producing a more comprehensive understanding achievable. The term *process* is used rather than *method* because, definitionally, process allows for greater flexibility and reflexivity, particularly when working in the humanities, and distinguishes interdisciplinary research from disciplinary methods. (4) The book highlights the foundational and complementary role of the disciplines in interdisciplinary work, the necessity of drawing on and integrating disciplinary insights, including insights derived from one's own basic research. (5) The book includes numerous examples of interdisciplinary work from the natural sciences, the social sciences, and the humanities to illustrate how integration is achieved and an interdisciplinary understanding constructed, reflected on, tested, and communicated. (6) This book is ideally suited for active learning and problem-based pedagogical approaches as well as for team teaching and other more traditional strategies.

Design Features

The book aids student content comprehension by using current learning strategies that characterize the modern textbook. The book's self-contained yet integrated chapters promote flexibility in structuring courses, depending on the individual instructor's needs and interests. Conceptual and organizational approaches include chapter outlines, chapter previews, section headings and subheadings, boldfacing of key concepts, italicizing of key statements, graphics to illustrate key concepts, notes to readers, tables to present content in a concise and coherent way, notes to readers, chapter summaries, a glossary of key concepts with chapter and page references, an author index, and a detailed subject index. Faculty can profitably use chapter components that correspond to their own approach to interdisciplinary research while omitting others.

Contents

The book is divided into three sections, each organized around a theme that addresses a central issue of the field. Part I, which includes two chapters, defines interdisciplinary studies or interdisciplinarity and maps the drivers of this dynamic field. Part II, consisting of six chapters, introduces the model of the interdisciplinary research process and explains how to draw on disciplinary insights and theories. Part III, also consisting of six chapters, explains how to integrate insights by creating common ground between their conflicting concepts or theories, construct a more comprehensive understanding of the problem, and reflect on it, test it, and communicate it.

Part I: About Interdisciplinary Studies

Today, interdisciplinary learning at all academic levels is far more common and there is greater understanding of what it is. Early definitions of interdisciplinary studies were quite general, but the range of meanings has narrowed dramatically over the last decade, though consensus is still lacking. Interdisciplinary learning is more widespread because educators recognize that it is needed, that the disciplines though necessary are insufficient by themselves to address the complex problems that are demanding attention in today's world.

Chapter 1: Defining Interdisciplinary Studies

Chapter 1 answers these questions: *What is interdisciplinarity? How is it different from disciplinarity, multidisciplinarity, and transdisciplinarity?* The popularity of the term *interdisciplinarity* in the academy, the multiplication of interdisciplinary initiatives and programs, and the persistence of exaggerated claims and outdated suppositions about interdisciplinarity heighten the importance of achieving clarity about its meaning that is grounded in authoritative sources. The chapter traces the etymology of *interdisciplinary studies* and *interdisciplinarity;* examines the differences between *interdisciplinarity, disciplinarity, multidisciplinarity,* and *transdisciplinarity;* presents an integrated definition of interdisciplinarity; explains what interdisciplinary studies is *not;* identifies the ways the term *interdisciplinarity* is variably used today; and identifies strengths and limitations of various metaphors used for interdisciplinary work.

Chapter 2: Mapping the Drivers of Interdisciplinarity

Chapter 2 completes the discussion of what interdisciplinary studies is by asking this question: *How did interdisciplinarity become mainstream by the end of the twentieth century?* The chapter begins by mapping the primary drivers of interdisciplinary research and education, presents the interdisciplinary critique of the disciplines, traces the formation of the disciplines and the origins of interdisciplinarity, states the assumptions underlying interdisciplinarity, identifies the cognitive abilities fostered by interdisciplinarity, and reflects on the traits and skills characteristic of interdisciplinarians.

Part II: Drawing on Disciplinary Insights

With definitional issues largely resolved, three more questions follow: *What is the interdisciplinary research process? How is it achieved? What theory or body of theory informs it?* Part II introduces the research model and describes STEPS 1 and 2 (Chapter 3). It introduces the disciplines and the theory of disciplinary perspective (Chapter 4), discusses how to identify disciplines relevant to the problem or research question (Chapter 5), explains how to conduct the literature search (Chapter 6), examines how to develop adequacy in relevant disciplines (Chapter 7), and explains how to analyze the problem and evaluate insights (Chapter 8).

Chapter 3: Beginning the Research Process

Chapter 3 presents an integrated and step-based research model of the interdisciplinary research process. The chapter asserts that the process the model delineates is not linear but a series of carefully considered decision points called "STEPS," which can lead to integration and a more comprehensive understanding of the problem. The process is heuristic and, though steplike, involves a good deal of reflexivity. This chapter begins the process of identifying decision points and research pathways and provides examples of them from published and student work. It stresses the importance of framing the research or focus question in a way that is appropriate to interdisciplinary inquiry. The chapter also emphasizes the importance of justifying the use of an interdisciplinary approach, as opposed to a multidisciplinary or a disciplinary one, that is grounded in theory. This discussion also addresses the need for greater transparency in interdisciplinary writing that would make these decision points and research pathways more explicit.

Chapter 4: Introducing the Disciplines

Interdisciplinary studies is based on the generally held assumption that the disciplines are foundational to interdisciplinarity. If so, then students should know how knowledge is typically structured in the modern academy and how it is reflected in its organization. They should also know how the disciplines usually associated with each major category—the natural sciences, the social sciences, and the humanities—engage in learning and produce new knowledge. There are unresolved questions and significant differences of opinion, however, over precisely what interdisciplinarians should use from the disciplines and how they should use it. The chapter attempts to bridge these differences by clarifying the term *disciplinary perspective* to mean those defining elements of a discipline—the phenomena, epistemology, assumptions, concepts, theories, and methods—that constitute its intellectual "center of gravity" and differentiate it from other disciplines. The chapter unpacks the meaning of these elements and explains how they are used in the interdisciplinary research process. The chapter also presents two approaches to ascertain the relevance of a particular discipline's perspective on the problem: the traditional or "perspectival" approach, which calls for linking the problem to those disciplines whose perspectives embrace it, and the newer "classification approach," pioneered by Rick Szostak (2004), which calls for linking the problem (at least initially) directly to the phenomena typically studied by disciplines. By focusing on phenomena, researchers can broaden their investigation without focusing prematurely on particular disciplines. Chapters 5 to 12 draw heavily from the information provided in this chapter.

Chapter 5: Identifying Relevant Disciplines

Two decision points are the subject of Chapter 5. The first is deciding which disciplines, subdisciplines, interdisciplines, and schools of thought are potentially interested in the problem by applying the perspectival and/or classification approach of phenomena of interest to disciplines. This should be done before conducting the full-scale literature search. Researchers are urged to map the problem to reveal its disciplinary parts. Mapping aids in identifying relevant disciplines by identifying variables and relationships between them that might otherwise escape notice. The second decision point is to reduce the number of "potentially relevant" disciplines to those that are "most relevant." Three questions should be asked to distinguish between potentially relevant disciplines and most relevant disciplines.

Chapter 6: Conducting the Literature Search

After defining "literature search" in an interdisciplinary sense and presenting reasons for conducting the search, the chapter identifies special challenges confronting interdisciplinarians. The chapter differentiates between the initial search, which is conducted at the outset of the project, and the full-scale search, which is conducted later. The chapter discusses the organization and classification of books in research libraries, direct searching, search strategies, and mistakes commonly made when beginning the literature search. The chapter then presents a detailed discussion of how to conduct the full-scale search.

Chapter 7: Developing Adequacy in Relevant Disciplines

This chapter introduces another juncture where several decisions must be made concerning how to develop adequacy in relevant disciplines. These include *how much* knowledge is required from each discipline and *what kind* of knowledge. The chapter discusses how to develop adequacy in disciplinary theories and explains the reason to understand theories, their concepts, and interrelationships. The chapter also discusses developing adequacy in disciplinary methods. Adequacy requires familiarity with the some of the dozen or so methods used in the natural sciences, the social sciences, and the humanities. Adequacy also involves understanding the interdisciplinary position on methods, how a discipline's preferred methods correlate to its preferred theories, how to select methods when conducting basic research in the sciences, how the interdisciplinary research process relates to the disciplinary methods used in basic research, the concept of triangulation in research methodology, and the importance of providing in-text evidence of disciplinary adequacy.

Chapter 8: Analyzing the Problem and Evaluating Insights

Once adequacy in the relevant disciplines is achieved, it is then possible to analyze the problem from each disciplinary perspective and evaluate its insights. How to analyze the problem is illustrated using student and professional work from the natural sciences, the social sciences, and the humanities. Analyzing the problem also includes reflecting on how one's personal and/or disciplinary bias may skew one's understanding of the problem, thus compromising the integrity of the interdisciplinary research process. The chapter explains how to evaluate each insight. This involves identifying the strengths and limitations of each author's perspective and theory, recognizing that each author's approach to the problem may be skewed and understanding the implications of this, recognizing that the data or evidence upon which the insight and theory are based may also be skewed, and recognizing that the methods used by authors may be skewed as well. A checklist by which to evaluate previous research is provided.

Part III: Integrating Insights

Engaging in the interdisciplinary research process raises further questions: *How does one perform the integrative task? What, precisely, is being integrated? What is the understanding that is produced? How should it be tested?* Integration, as presented here, is a process that involves making a series of steplike decisions (Chapter 9). These involve identifying conflicts between insights and locating their sources (Chapter 10), creating common ground between concepts (Chapter 11) or theories (Chapter 12), constructing a more comprehensive understanding (Chapter 13), and reflecting on, testing, and communicating the understanding (Chapter 14).

Chapter 9: Understanding Integration

Integration is the key distinguishing characteristic of interdisciplinary work. After discussing the controversy over integration between generalists and integrationists, the chapter establishes that integration should be the goal of interdisciplinary work though undergraduates, individual research projects, and those working in the humanities may achieve only partial integration. The chapter identifies conditions necessary to perform integration and describes the model of integration used in this book in terms of what the broad model integrates, how it integrates, what the results of integration look like, and three fundamental questions raised by this discussion of the model.

Chapter 10: Identifying Conflicts Between Insights

Beginning the integrative part of the interdisciplinary research process, the chapter addresses the importance of identifying conflicts between insights and locating their source. Conflicts occur either between concepts and/or their underlying assumptions that are embedded in insights *or* between theories that produce insights. Theories from the same discipline can be sources of conflict between insights; theories from the same discipline can be sources of conflicting assumptions; and theories from different disciplines can be sources of conflict between insights.

Chapter 11: Creating Common Ground Between Concepts

The theories of common ground and cognitive interdisciplinarity are the basis for collaborative communication and integration. The chapter defines common ground and explains why it is necessary for collaborative communication, that it is a natural human achievement but requires unconventional thinking, and that it is achieved through the use of language. The chapter establishes what common ground must be created from, that it is integral to the process of integration, that it involves using intuition, that it plays out differently in contexts of wide versus narrow interdisciplinarity, and that creating common ground is the interdisciplinarian's responsibility. The chapter discusses how to create common ground from concepts and/or their underlying assumptions by using various techniques demonstrated to modify concepts and assumptions, and how to create common ground when assumed values and rights conflict.

Chapter 12: Creating Common Ground Between Theories

The chapter defines disciplinary theory and explains when working with theories is necessary. It examines the relationship of models, variables, and causal processes to theories. It describes two situations that researchers working with a set of theories may encounter: The first is when one or more theories in the set have a broader range of applicability than do the others; the second is when none of the theories in the set borrow elements from other disciplines.

Chapter 13: Constructing a More Comprehensive Understanding or Theory

After defining "a more comprehensive understanding" or "more comprehensive theory," the chapter explains the process involved in constructing it. The understanding can be constructed either from modified insights or from a modified theory. For working with theories, the chapter presents several strategies that may be profitably used to achieve causal or propositional integration, including sequential or end-to-end, horizontal or side-by-side, multicausal, cross-level or multilevel, spatial, and analytical.

Chapter 14: Reflecting on, Testing, and Communicating the Understanding

This chapter reflects recent advances in assessing the result or product of the interdisciplinary research process. This involves first reflecting on the understanding or theory by interrogating one's own bias and limited understanding of the relevant disciplines, theories, and methods. Reflection is followed by actually testing the quality of interdisciplinary work. This involves being familiar with the learning outcomes claimed for interdisciplinarity and cultivating the cognitive abilities attributable to interdisciplinary learning drawn from research on cognition and instruction. The chapter introduces four approaches to assessing the quality of the more comprehensive understanding—the Newell (2007a) Test, the Tress et al. (2006) Test, the Szostak (2009) Test, and the Boix Mansilla et al. (2009) Test—and presents an integrated test. Once tested, the understanding should be communicated to appropriate audiences. This may involve using a metaphor, a model, a narrative, a new process, a new product, a critique of an existing policy and/or a proposed new policy, or posing a new question or avenue of scientific inquiry. The chapter concludes with a discussion of the value of communicating back to disciplines.

The field of interdisciplinary studies is beginning to demonstrate its full potential and generate the volume and scope of new knowledge that its founders envisioned. The process of knowledge formation can be accelerated and find a wider audience as its practitioners produce more and better interdisciplinary work. To this end, I offer this second edition with its undoubted limitations to facilitate interdisciplinary education and research.

Professor Allen F. Repko, PhD
Former Director
Interdisciplinary Studies Program
School of Urban and Public Affairs
The University of Texas at Arlington

Acknowledgments ____

Many people have made this book possible. First, my students in the interdisciplinary studies program at the University of Texas at Arlington planted the idea that a comprehensive textbook on the interdisciplinary research process was needed. For years they asked me why I did not provide them with one. Having no good answer, I replied (with a mixture of apology and hope), "Someone will eventually write one."

The seed planted by my students was watered in March 2004 when Stuart Henry and Don Stowe came to our campus to serve as external reviewers of our program. Over lunch, I mentioned that the field of interdisciplinary studies needed a comprehensive textbook. They responded, "Why don't you write it?" After they left, I began transforming class notes into what ultimately became the first edition that was published in 2008. Its wide acceptance has occasioned this second edition.

Several have read the entire manuscript of the second edition including Michelle Buchberger of Franklin University, Andrew T. Arroyo of Norfolk State University, Dave Conz of Arizona State University, Tinola Mayfield-Guerrero at Owens Community College, James Lacey of Franklin Pierce University, Karen G. Bell of Delta State University, Jill LeRoy-Frazier of East Tennessee State University, Rick Szostak of the University of Alberta, and William H. Newell of Miami University.

Others have read one or more chapters and offered helpful suggestions, including Pauline Gagnon of the University of West Georgia and Marilyn Tayler of Montclair State University.

For their encouragement, patient reading of several versions of the manuscript, and many insightful comments, I give special thanks to William H. Newell and Rick Szostak.

Most important, I thank Doris, my wife, for her reading and editing of countless versions of each chapter.

I could not have produced this book without the support and encouragement of the people at SAGE Publications, especially my editor, Vicki Knight, who guided its production.

Ultimately, I assume responsibility for what is lacking in this book. My hope is that it will benefit students, teachers, and administrators and advance the field of interdisciplinary studies.

About the Author _____

Allen F. Repko, PhD, is the former director of the interdisciplinary studies program in the School of Urban and Public Affairs at the University of Texas at Arlington where he developed and taught the program's core curriculum. The program is one of the largest in the United States. Repko has written extensively on all aspects of interdisciplinary studies and has twice served as coeditor of the interdisciplinary journal *Issues in Integrative Studies* and has served on the board of the Association for Integrative Studies. His research interests include strategies for conducting interdisciplinary research, administration, and program assessment. Though just "retired," he remains active writing, consulting, conducting workshops, and speaking at conferences.

PART I

About Interdisciplinary Studies

1 Defining Interdisciplinary Studies

For over a century, universities and colleges throughout the world at all levels have relied on academic disciplines as platforms for imparting knowledge and generating new knowledge. Today, interdisciplinary learning at all levels is far more common as there is growing recognition that it is needed to answer complex questions, solve complex problems, and gain coherent understanding of complex issues that are increasingly beyond the ability of any single discipline to address comprehensively or resolve adequately. As Carole L. Palmer (2001) writes, "The real-world research problems that scientists address rarely arise within orderly disciplinary categories, and neither do their solutions" (p. vii).

This chapter (1) explains the meaning of interdisciplinary studies, (2) presents a definition of interdisciplinary studies, (3) explains what interdisciplinary studies is *not,* (4) discusses how the term *interdisciplinarity* is variably used today, and (5) identifies metaphors commonly associated with interdisciplinary work.

The Meaning of Interdisciplinary Studies

The meaning of interdisciplinary studies or **interdisciplinarity** continues to be contested by its practitioners and critics. But emerging from this debate are key concepts around which consensus is developing and which inform the integrated definition of interdisciplinary studies used in this book. The following discussion unpacks the meaning of these terms and, in doing so, introduces some of the theory undergirding this diverse and growing academic field.

Two Conceptions of Interdisciplinary Studies

A primary focus of the ongoing debate over the meaning of interdisciplinary studies or interdisciplinarity concerns integration. Integration literally means "to make whole." In the context of interdisciplinarity, **integration** is a process by which ideas, data and information, methods, tools, concepts, and/or theories from two or more disciplines are synthesized, connected, or blended.

Generalist interdisciplinarians understand interdisciplinarity loosely to mean "any form of dialog or interaction between two or more disciplines" while minimizing, obscuring, or rejecting altogether the role of integration (Moran, 2010, p. 14).[1]

Integrationist interdisciplinarians, on the other hand, believe that integration should be the *goal* of interdisciplinary work because integration addresses the challenge of complexity. Integrationists point to a growing body of literature that connects integration with interdisciplinary education and research, and are concerned with developing a distinctively interdisciplinary theory-based research process and with describing how it operates (Newell, 2007a, p. 245; Vess & Linkon, 2002, p. 89). They advocate reducing the semantic evasiveness surrounding the term *interdisciplinarity* and point to research in cognitive psychology that shows that integration is both natural and achievable. This book is aligned with the integrationist understanding of interdisciplinarity.

The "Discipline" Part of Interdisciplinary Studies

Inside the academy, the term **discipline** refers to a particular branch of learning or body of knowledge such as physics, psychology, or history (Moran, 2010, p. 2). According to the American Association for Higher Education and Accreditation (AAHEA),

> Disciplines have contrasting substance and syntax . . . —ways of organizing themselves and of defining rules for making arguments and claims that others will warrant. They have different ways of talking about themselves and about the problems, topics, and issues that constitute their subject matters. (Schulman, 2002, pp. vi–vii)

Mary Taylor Huber and Sherwyn P. Morreale (2002) add that "each discipline has its own intellectual history, agreements, and disputes about subject matter and methods" and its own "community of scholars interested in teaching and learning in that field" (p. 2). Disciplines are also distinguished from one another by several factors. These include the questions disciplines ask about the world, their perspective or worldview, the set of assumptions they employ, and the methods they use to build up a body of knowledge (facts, concepts, theories) around a certain subject matter (Newell & Green, 1982, p. 25).

Academic disciplines are scholarly communities that specify which phenomena to study, advance certain central concepts and organizing theories, embrace certain methods of investigation, provide forums for sharing research and insights, and offer career paths for scholars. It is through their power over careers that disciplines are able to maintain these strong preferences. Each discipline has its own defining elements—phenomena, assumptions, epistemology, concepts, theories, and methods—that distinguish it from other disciplines.

These are the subject of Chapter 4. All of these characteristics are interrelated and are subsumed within an overall disciplinary perspective.

History is an example of a discipline because it meets all of the above criteria. Its knowledge domain consists of an enormous body of *facts* (everything that has been recorded in human history). It studies an equally enormous number of *concepts or ideas* (colonialism, racism, freedom, and democracy). It generates *theories* about why things turned out the way they did (e.g., the great man theory argues that the American Civil War lasted so long and was so bloody because President Abraham Lincoln decided to issue the Emancipation Proclamation in 1862), though many historians strive to be atheoretical. And it uses a research *method* that involves close reading and critical analysis of primary sources (i.e., letters, diaries, official documents) and secondary sources (i.e., books and articles on a topic) to present a coherent picture of past events or persons within a particular time and place.

Categories of Traditional Disciplines

There are three broad categories of traditional disciplines[2] (see Table 4.1 in Chapter 4):

- The natural sciences tell us what the world is made of, describe how what it is made of is structured into a complex network of interdependent systems, and explain the behavior of a given localized system.
- The social sciences seek to explain the human world and figure out how to predict and improve it.
- The humanities express human aspirations, interpret and assess human achievements and experience, and seek layers of meaning and richness of detail in written texts, artifacts, and cultural practices.

For the purposes of this book, references to *disciplines* are limited to the traditional disciplines unless otherwise noted. References to specific interdisciplines and schools of thought (e.g., feminism, Marxism) are appropriately identified.

The Fine and Performing Arts

In addition to these categories of the traditional disciplines is the category of the fine and performing arts. These include art, dance, music, and theater. They rightly claim disciplinary status because their defining elements are very different from those of the humanities disciplines.

The Applied and Professional Fields

The applied fields also occupy a prominent place in the modern academy. These include business (and its many subfields such as finance, marketing, and management), communications (and its various subfields including advertising, speech, and journalism), criminal justice and criminology, education, engineering, law, medicine, nursing, and social work. (Note: Many of these applied and profession fields claim disciplinary status.)

The Emergence of Interdisciplines

The line between the disciplines and interdisciplinarity has begun to blur in recent years with the emergence of **interdisciplines** (further defined in Chapter 4). These are fields of study that cross traditional disciplinary boundaries and involve a wide variety of interactions ranging from informal groups of scholars to well-established research and teaching communities. Frequently cited examples of interdisciplines are neuroscience and biochemistry, though the list also includes environmental science, nanotechnology, geobiology, sustainability science and engineering, psycholinguistics, ethnomusicology, cultural studies, women's studies, urban studies, and American studies (Klein, 1990, p. 43; National Academy of Sciences, National Academy of Engineering, & Institute of Medicine, 2005, pp. 249–252). Interdisciplines differ from disciplines in terms of their origins, character, status, and level of development.[3] For example, the interdiscipline of molecular biology developed in response to breakthroughs from the discovery of the structure of DNA and the development of new technologies. Only by bringing together the skills and knowledge of a wide range of disciplinary experts—chemists, geneticists, physicists, bacteriologists, zoologists, and botanists—can many medical problems be solved (Sewell, 1989, pp. 95–96).

Evolving Constructs

The disciplines, applied fields, and interdisciplines are not rigid and unchanging but are evolving social and intellectual constructs and, as such, are time-dependent. That is, today's discipline may well have been yesterday's **subdiscipline** (further defined in Chapter 4) or branch of an existing discipline. An example is the evolution of history, which, prior to the mid–nineteenth century, played a minor role in colleges as a branch of literature but grew rapidly as an independent discipline that absorbed those aspects of politics and economics that had a past dimension (Kuklick, 1985, p. 50). Today, history is a well-entrenched professional discipline that is typically included within the humanities but also has allegiances to the social sciences.

Julie Klein (1996) speaks of the "concealed reality of interdisciplinarity" where interdisciplinarity is flourishing but is not labeled as such, as in, for instance, medicine, agriculture, and oceanography. The pattern by which interdisciplinary studies operates occurs in this way: (1) Researchers detach a subject or an object from existing disciplinary frameworks; (2) they fill gaps in knowledge from lack of attention by the disciplines; and (3) if the research attains critical mass, researchers "redraw boundaries by constituting new knowledge space and new professional roles" (pp. 36–37).

The "Inter" Part of Interdisciplinary Studies

The word *interdisciplinary* consists of two parts: *inter* and *disciplinary*. The prefix *inter* means "between, among, in the midst," or "derived from two or more." **Disciplinary** means "of or relating to a particular field of study" or specialization. So a starting point for the definition of *interdisciplinary* is between two or more fields of study (Stember, 1991, p. 4).

"Inter" Refers to Contested Space

This "in between" space is **contested space**. Most interdisciplinary study examines **contested terrain**—problems, issues, or questions that are the focus of several disciplines. For example, crime in post-9/11 Washington, D.C., is an interdisciplinary problem because it is an economic problem *and* a racial problem *and* a cultural problem. William Newell emphasizes that the test of the interdisciplinarity of a problem is not its distance from each contributing discipline but whether the problem is fundamentally multifaceted or complex (personal communication, June 30, 2004). The important point is that the *disciplines are not the focus of the interdisciplinarian's attention; the focus is the problem or issue or intellectual question that each discipline is addressing.* The disciplines are simply a means to that end.

"Inter" Refers to the Action Taken on Insights

The something "derived from two or more" fields of study is the **insights** or scholarly contributions to the clear understanding of a problem based on research. The *action taken* on these insights by interdisciplinarians is to integrate them. The **integrative process** involves creating common ground between conflicting insights into a particular problem from two or more disciplines. The integrative process is the subject of Part III of this book.

"Inter" Refers to the Result of Integration

The result of integration—and another aspect of the prefix *inter*—is *something altogether new,* distinctive, apart from, and beyond the limits of any discipline and, thus, *a cognitive advancement* or addition to knowledge. This product of the interdisciplinary enterprise is called the *more comprehensive understanding* or *more comprehensive theory,* the subject of Chapter 13. This understanding can be used for a variety of purposes, including formulating new policies, framing new research questions, and producing new artistic creations and technical products. Its being additive to knowledge, however, does not preclude interdisciplinarity critiquing the disciplines or interrogating knowledge structures, government policies, and societal values.

Aspects of the Prefix "Inter" Summarized

Three important aspects of the prefix *inter* may be summarized as follows:

- The contested space between disciplines
- The action taken on disciplinary insights, called integration
- The result of integration that constitutes a cognitive advancement, called a more comprehensive understanding

The "Studies" Part of Interdisciplinary Studies

The word **studies** has had a long and respectable history (since the end of World War II), referring initially to geographical regions (e.g., Soviet studies) and historical eras (e.g., Renaissance studies). In recent decades, however, the term has shifted to cultural groups (including women, Hispanics, and African Americans) and also appears in a host of contexts in the natural sciences and social sciences. In fact, "studies" programs are proliferating in the modern academy. In some cases, even the traditional disciplines (particularly in the humanities) are renaming themselves as studies, such as English studies and literary studies (Garber, 2001, pp. 77–79).

Why Traditional Disciplines Are Not Referred to as "Studies"

Every established discipline has a universally recognized core of knowledge, and this core is subdivided into specific courses called a **curriculum**. The curriculum of each discipline varies from institution to institution in terms of number of courses offered and the titles of courses. Despite this variety, experts in a discipline recognize these courses as uniquely the "territory" of their discipline. The reason disciplines do not refer to themselves as history "studies" or biology "studies" is that their core of study—their curriculum—is well established and is recognized as their research and teaching domain.

This traditional arrangement, however, is being upset by the emergence of multidisciplinary studies programs such as environmental studies and urban studies, and the changing nature and expansion of disciplines. At first, many disciplinary departments simply added "environmental" to some of their course titles, while other departments contributed entire courses to a new environmental studies program, such as environmental geology, environmental psychology, or environmental law. A similar situation developed with urban studies. The problem with these and similar "studies" from an interdisciplinary perspective is that they seldom attempt to engage in integration and, thus, have not coalesced into discrete fields that are unified by general agreement as to their conceptual definition (Klein, 1996, pp. 96–100).[4] For example, after three decades, there is still no definition of "urban" that enjoys general agreement, though most definitions include the interrelation between people and space. An exception is ecology, which, despite these difficulties, has managed to develop a broad field of its own called ecological economics (Rogers, Scaife, & Rizzo, 2005, p. 267).

Why "Studies" Is an Integral Part of Interdisciplinary Studies

Having said that multidisciplinary "studies" programs do not typically engage in integration, it is necessary to explain why the term *studies* is an integral part of interdisciplinary studies. There are two reasons for this. First, the term denotes the activity of drawing on disciplinary expertise relevant to the problem at hand. Second, the term *studies* denotes a "perceived misfit among need, experience, information, and the prevailing structure of knowledge embodied in disciplinary organization" (Caldwell, 1983, pp. 247–249). Studies programs in general represent fundamental challenges to the existing structure of knowledge. These new arrangements share with interdisciplinary studies (as described in this book) a broad dissatisfaction with traditional knowledge structures (i.e., the disciplines) and a recognition that the kinds of complex problems facing humanity demand that new ways be found to order knowledge and bridge different approaches to its creation and communication. Today, there are programs that include a core of explicitly interdisciplinary courses, established interdisciplinary fields such as area studies (e.g., Middle Eastern studies) and materials science, and highly integrated fields such as environmental studies, urban studies, sustainability studies, and cultural studies.

The Differences Between the Disciplines and Interdisciplinary Studies

There are key differences between the disciplines and interdisciplinary studies. The seven main characteristics of the established disciplines are compared and contrasted with those of interdisciplinary studies in Table 1.1. There are three differences (#1, #2, and #3) and four similarities (#4, #5, #6, and #7). The differences explain why the use of "studies" in interdisciplinary studies is appropriate:

- Interdisciplinary studies does not lay claim to a universally recognized core of knowledge as, say, physics does, but rather draws on existing disciplinary knowledge while always transcending it via integration (#1).

- Interdisciplinary studies has a research process of its own to produce knowledge but freely borrows methods from the disciplines when appropriate (#2).
- Interdisciplinary studies, like the disciplines, seeks to produce new knowledge, but, unlike them, it seeks to accomplish this via the process of integration (#3).

Table 1.1 Comparison of Established Disciplines to Interdisciplinary Studies

Established Disciplines*	Interdisciplinary Studies
1. Claim a body of knowledge about certain subjects or objects	1. Claims a burgeoning professional literature of increasing sophistication, depth of analysis, breadth of coverage, and, thus, utility. This literature includes subspecialties on interdisciplinary theory, program administration, curriculum design, research process, pedagogy, and assessment. Most important, a growing body of explicitly interdisciplinary research on real-world problems is emerging.
2. Have methods of acquiring knowledge and theories to order that knowledge	2. Makes use of disciplinary methods, but these are subsumed under a research process of its own that involves drawing on relevant disciplinary insights, concepts, theories, and methods to produce integrated knowledge
3. Seek to produce new knowledge, concepts, and theories within or related to their domains	3. Produces new knowledge, more comprehensive understandings, new meanings, and cognitive advancements
4. Possess a recognized core of courses	4. Is beginning to form a core of explicitly interdisciplinary courses
5. Have their own community of experts	5. Is forming its own community of experts
6. Are self-contained and seek to control their respective domains as they relate to each other	6. Is largely dependent on the disciplines for its source material
7. Train future experts in their discipline-specific master's and doctoral programs	7. Is training future experts in older fields such as American studies and in newer fields such as cultural studies through its master's and doctoral programs and undergraduate majors. Though new and explicitly interdisciplinary PhD programs are emerging, interdisciplinary studies still typically hires those with disciplinary PhDs.

*This column is based, in part, on Jill Vickers (1998, p. 34.)

Why "Studies" Is Plural

"Studies" is plural because of the idea of interaction between disciplines (Klein, 1996, p. 10). Imagine the world of knowledge wherein each discipline is like a box containing thousands of dots, each dot representing a bit of knowledge discovered by an expert in that discipline. Then imagine similar boxes representing other disciplines, each filled with dots of knowledge. Scholars interested in "studies" are excited by the prospect of examining a broad issue or complex question that requires looking inside as many disciplinary boxes as necessary in order to identify those dots of knowledge that have some bearing on the issue or question under investigation. "Studies" scholars, including those in interdisciplinary studies, are in the business of identifying and connecting dots of knowledge regardless of the disciplinary box in which they reside (Long, 2002, p. 14). Interdisciplinarians are interested not in merely rearranging these ever-changing dots of knowledge but in *integrating* them into a new and more comprehensive understanding that is additive to knowledge.

Studies programs recognize that many research problems cannot easily be addressed from the confines of individual disciplines because they require the participation of many experts, each viewing the problem from its distinctive disciplinary perspective. Critics of studies programs charge that they lack disciplinary "substance and good scholarship" (Salter & Hearn, 1996, p. 3). **Scholarship** is a contribution to knowledge that is "*public,* susceptible to *critical review and evaluation,* and accessible for *exchange and use* by other members of one's scholarly community" (Shulman, 1998, p. 5).

"Substance" and "scholarship" are typically code words for disciplinary depth—intensive focus on a discipline or subdiscipline. A contrasting view is that a purely disciplinary focus sacrifices breadth, comprehensiveness, and realism for depth. An integrated view, which this book reflects, recognizes that there is a symbiosis between disciplinary and interdisciplinary research. By building on the disciplines, interdisciplinarity can then feed back new ideas and questions to the disciplines.

Newell speaks for many interdisciplinarians, arguing that interdisciplinary studies is able to achieve as much depth as do the disciplines:

> To the extent that interdisciplinary study harnesses disciplinary depth and rigor, it utilizes similar notions of depth and rigor; but to the extent that it is engaged in a different intellectual enterprise from the disciplines (especially integration), it must have some different notions of depth and rigor in addition. (personal communication, June 30, 2004)

This is not to say that a "studies" program is superior to a disciplinary one. That would be a mistake because the purpose of each is different. Both are needed, particularly in a world characterized by increasing complexity, conflict, and fragmentation.

A Definition of Interdisciplinary Studies

This section discusses reasons for practitioners to agree on a definition, and reviews the prominent definitions of interdisciplinary studies that have emerged in recent years. A definition of interdisciplinary studies that integrates their core concepts is then presented.

Reasons for Agreeing on a Definition of Interdisciplinary Studies

Critics of interdisciplinary studies frequently charge that it has no widely accepted definition. For example, writing in *The Chronicle of Higher Education,* Jeffrey N. Wasserstrom (2006) complains that interdisciplinarity has become "so fuzzy that a university's commitment to it is close to meaningless" (p. B5). For many in the academy, interdisciplinarity is whatever someone says it is.

There are five reasons why the field's practitioners and those who claim to be doing interdisciplinary work—including students—should take the definition of interdisciplinary studies seriously and seek consensus about its meaning.

1. As a maturing academic field, interdisciplinary studies needs to define itself to make the case that interdisciplinarity is, in fact, contributing something distinctive and valuable to the academy and to society at large. Developing a common conception of what interdisciplinary studies is, says Newell (2007c), will enable faculty and students "to show the ways in which they are rigorously following through on the implications of that definition" (p. 2).

2. A common definition will help the field achieve greater depth and sophistication about interdisciplinarity. Learning in most academic contexts is sequential: The subject area is introduced, its theoretical basis and approach to research is explained, and this foundational information is then applied to specific contexts in more advanced courses. The movement is from the most general to the more specific, from breadth to depth. Interdisciplinary studies courses cannot provide more depth and sophistication about interdisciplinarity if each successive course must start over again in presenting the nature of interdisciplinary studies and offer different processes. If courses in the sequence share a common definition of interdisciplinarity and a common understanding of process, then the later courses in the sequences are able to go into more depth about the nature of interdisciplinarity or address conceptual, theoretical, or methodological issues with greater sophistication. "The more explicit the earlier discussions of interdisciplinarity in the sequence," says Newell (2007c), "the more likely students are in later courses to have a clear understanding of it" (p. 3).

3. An agreed upon definition will enable meaningful assessment of student work, program effectiveness, and academic scholarship. Evaluation of student work is made more difficult (for students and instructors alike) where there is confusion about what interdisciplinarity is, what student learning outcomes should be assessed, and which outcomes are distinctive to interdisciplinary learning (Repko, 2008, p. 171). Newell (2007c) argues that where faculty have achieved consensus on a definition of interdisciplinary studies, and thus the nature of interdisciplinary work, it is possible to develop assessment instruments that measure the desired outcomes. Where there is no consensus either on a definition or on the nature of interdisciplinary work,

> it is not possible to assess learning outcomes because there is no basis for agreement on what distinctively interdisciplinary outcomes to look for. As a result, it is effectively impossible for the faculty to provide evidence of value added through interdisciplinary education. (p. 2)

The clarity and quality of interdisciplinary assessment has been improving since research on cognition and instruction has identified learning outcomes that are distinctive to interdisciplinary learning.[5]

4. A common conception of interdisciplinary studies will facilitate communication among faculty and students from different disciplines who are conducting interdisciplinary research and/or applying for grants. If researchers share a common working definition of interdisciplinary studies, says Newell (2007c), "they can much more easily talk with each other about common curricular and pedagogical challenges they face" and perhaps develop joint research proposals (p. 2). If students share a common conception of interdisciplinarity, and if the definition is linked to the same general interdisciplinary process for addressing any complex problem, they are more likely to creatively and habitually apply this process to any complex problem regardless of context.

5. A common definition will also increase student morale. Students in programs or courses where there are different or unspecified conceptions of interdisciplinarity will have much more difficulty explaining what their program or major or degree is than will students in programs that share a common understanding of interdisciplinarity. "Such inarticulateness," says Newell (2007c), "is mildly embarrassing when talking to Aunt Mildred at Christmas, but it has more serious consequences when interviewing with a prospective employer" (p. 2). Students are likely to be more motivated in programs and courses where faculty share a clear understanding of interdisciplinary studies and

> where students focus on issues (especially ones they see as "relevant" to their lives or to the society in which they live, e.g., the

right to privacy in an age of terrorism), and follow an identifiable process (e.g., examine the issue from the perspective of relevant disciplines, draw insights from them, create common ground, and construct a more comprehensive understanding) that leads to more efficacious behavior (e.g., come up with a solution that's responsive to all relevant perspectives). (p. 2)

Authoritative Definitions of Interdisciplinary Studies

Five definitions of interdisciplinary studies have gained wide recognition and express an emerging consensus among practitioners. The first is the definition advanced by Klein and Newell (1997):

[Interdisciplinary studies is] a process of answering a question, solving a problem, or addressing a topic that is too broad or complex to be dealt with adequately by a single discipline or profession . . . and draws on disciplinary perspectives and integrates their insights through construction of a more comprehensive perspective. (pp. 393–394)

The National Academy of Sciences, the National Academy of Engineering, and the Institute of Medicine (hereafter referred to as the National Academies) incorporate this definition into their definition of interdisciplinary research. In *Facilitating Interdisciplinary Research* (2005), they define interdisciplinary research as

a mode of research by teams or individuals that integrates information, data, techniques, tools, perspectives, concepts, and/or theories from two or more disciplines or bodies of specialized knowledge to advance fundamental understanding or to solve problems whose solutions are beyond the scope of a single discipline or area of research practice. (p. 26)

Research, they say, "is truly interdisciplinary when it is not just pasting two disciplines together to create one product but rather an integration or synthesis of ideas and methods" (p. 27).

A third definition is offered by Diana Rhoten, Veronica Boix Mansilla, Marc Chun, and Julie T. Klein (2006) in *Interdisciplinary Education at Liberal Arts Institutions*. They define interdisciplinary education as

a mode of curriculum design and instruction in which individual faculty or teams identify, evaluate, and integrate information, data, techniques, tools, perspectives, concepts, or theories from two or more disciplines or bodies of knowledge to advance students' capacity to understand issues, address problems, and create new approaches and solutions that extend beyond the scope of a single discipline or area of instruction. (p. 3)

A fourth definition is put forth by Veronica Boix Mansilla (2005) in "Assessing Student Work at Disciplinary Crossroads." She is particularly concerned with the product of interdisciplinary work: the "interdisciplinary understanding." Interdisciplinarity, she says, is

> the capacity to integrate knowledge and modes of thinking drawn from two or more disciplines to produce a *cognitive advancement*—for example, explaining a phenomenon, solving a problem, creating a product, or raising a new question—in ways that would have been unlikely through single disciplinary means [italics added]. (p. 16)

Finally, William Newell (2007a) in "Decision Making in Interdisciplinary Studies" offers a fifth definition of interdisciplinary studies (which is a refinement of the 1997 definition). It is, he says,

> a two-part process: it draws critically on disciplinary perspectives, and it integrates their insights into a more comprehensive understanding . . . of an existing complex phenomenon [or into] the creation of a new complex phenomenon. (p. 248)

From these definitions, it is possible to identify key elements that they share and that can form the basis of an integrated definition.

An Integrated Definition of Interdisciplinary Studies

These five authoritative definitions share the following common elements:

- Interdisciplinary research has a particular substantive focus.
- The focus of interdisciplinary research extends beyond a single disciplinary perspective.
- A distinctive characteristic of interdisciplinary research is that it focuses on a problem or question that is complex.
- Interdisciplinary research is characterized by an identifiable process or mode of inquiry.
- Interdisciplinary research draws explicitly on the disciplines.
- The disciplines provide insights about the specific substantive focus of interdisciplinary research.
- Interdisciplinary research has integration as its goal.
- The objective of the interdisciplinary research process is pragmatic: to produce a cognitive advancement in the form of a new understanding, a new product, or a new meaning. (Note: The term **meaning** is important in the humanities, where it is often equated with the intent of the author or artist [Bal, 2002, p. 27].)[6]

From these definitions, it is possible to offer this integrated definition of **interdisciplinary studies**:

> Interdisciplinary studies is a process of answering a question, solving a problem, or addressing a topic that is too broad or complex to be dealt with adequately by a single discipline, and draws on the disciplines with the goal of integrating their insights to construct a more comprehensive understanding.

This definition includes four core concepts—process, disciplines, integration, and a more comprehensive understanding—which are the subjects of later chapters. It is worth noting that this is a "what" definition. Definitions also have a "how" component. For example, when defining an experiment, one almost unavoidably describes how to do one. Since this book is advancing the interdisciplinary research process as an essential component of interdisciplinary studies, the rest of the book can be seen as fleshing out the "how" part of a definition of the field.

Here it is useful to explain the difference between a *disciplinary insight* and an *interdisciplinary insight,* as these terms are used in the discussion that follows. A **disciplinary insight** is an expert's view on a particular problem that is based on research. An **interdisciplinary insight** is produced when the interdisciplinary research process (or some version of it) is used to create an integrated and purposeful result. As used in this book, insights refer to scholarship produced by disciplinary experts, unless otherwise stated.

What Interdisciplinary Studies Is Not

The integrated definition of interdisciplinary studies is further clarified by explaining what it is not.

Interdisciplinary Studies Is Not Multidisciplinary Studies

Regrettably, those who are uninformed and outside the field typically misunderstand the terms *interdisciplinarity* and *multidisciplinarity* as being synonymous and, consequently, have caused much confusion. **Multidisciplinarity** refers to the placing side by side of insights from two or more disciplines. For example, this approach may be used in a course that invites instructors from different disciplines to present their perspectives on the course topic in serial fashion but makes no attempt to integrate the insights produced by these perspectives. "Here the relationship between the disciplines is merely one of proximity," explains Joe Moran (2010); "there is no real integration between them" (p. 14). Merely bringing insights from different disciplines together in some way but failing to engage in the hard work of integration is **multidisciplinary studies**, not interdisciplinary studies. **Multidisciplinary research** "involves more than a single discipline in which each discipline makes a *separate* contribution [italics added]" (National Academies, 2005, p. 27).

Two Metaphors

Two metaphors effectively illustrate the essential difference between multidisciplinary studies and interdisciplinary studies: the fruit salad and the smoothie.

The Bowl of Fruit   Multidisciplinary studies can be compared to a bowl of fruit containing a variety of fruits, each fruit representing a discipline and being in close proximity to the others. The number of fruits used and the proportions of each in the bowl may not be based on anything more than visual appeal.

The Smoothie   This is not so with interdisciplinary studies, however, which Moti Nissani (1995) compares to a "smoothie." The smoothie is "finely blended so that the distinctive flavor of each [fruit] is no longer recognizable, yielding instead the delectable experience of the smoothie" (p. 125). The metaphor of the smoothie, while limited, illustrates four essential characteristics of interdisciplinary studies:

- The selection of fruits (i.e., the disciplines and their insights) is not random but purposeful with the end product clearly in view.
- The blending of fruits (i.e., the process of integration) changes the contribution of each fruit (i.e., disciplinary insight) (Newell, 1998, p. 548).
- The smoothie (i.e., the result of integration), compared to the ingredients used, is something new.
- The activity involved in creating the smoothie (i.e., the interdisciplinary research process) is limited in time and space to the research problem.

The Fable of the Elephant House

Lawrence Wheeler's instructive fable of building a house for an elephant illustrates a typical multidisciplinary approach to solving a complex problem:

Once upon a time a planning group was formed to design a house for an elephant. On the committee were an architect, an interior designer, an engineer, a sociologist, and a psychologist. The elephant was highly educated too . . . but he was not on the committee.

The five professionals met and elected the architect as their chairman. His firm was paying the engineer's salary, and the consulting fees of the other experts, which, of course, made him the natural leader of the group.

At their *fourth* meeting they agreed it was time to get at the essentials of their problem. The architect asked just two things: "How much money can the elephant spend?" and "What does the site look like?"

The engineer said that precast concrete was the ideal material for elephant houses, especially as his firm had a new computer just begging for a stress problem to run.

The psychologist and the sociologist whispered together and then one of them said, "How many elephants are going to live in this house? . . . It turned out that *one* elephant was a psychological problem but *two* or more were a sociological matter. The group finally agreed that though *one* elephant was buying the house, he might eventually marry and raise a family. Each consultant could, therefore, take a legitimate interest in the problem.

The interior designer asked, "What do elephants do when they're at home?"

"They lean against things," said the engineer. "We'll need strong walls."

"They eat a lot," said the psychologist. "You'll want a big dining room . . . and they like the color green."

"As a sociological matter," said the sociologist, "I can tell you that they mate standing up. You'll need high ceilings."

So they built the elephant a house. It had precast concrete walls, high ceilings, and a large dining area. It was painted green to remind him of the jungle. And it was completed for only 15% over the original estimate.

The elephant moved in. He always ate outdoors, so he used the dining room for a library . . . but it wasn't very cozy.

He never leaned against anything, because he had lived in circus tents for years, and knew that walls fall down when you lean on them.

The girl he married *hated* green, and so did he. They were *very* urban elephants.

And the sociologist was wrong too. . . . they didn't stand up. So the high ceilings merely produced echoes that greatly annoyed the elephants. They moved out in less than six months! (Wheeler & Miller, 1970, n.p.)

This fable shows how disciplinary experts usually approach a complex task: They perceive it from the narrow (i.e., monistic) perspective of their specialty and fail to take into account the perspectives of other relevant disciplines, professions, or interested parties (in this case, the elephant).

This story also illustrates how a multidisciplinary approach to understanding a problem merely juxtaposes disciplinary perspectives. The disciplines speak with separate voices on a problem of mutual interest. However, the disciplinary status quo is not questioned, and the distinctive elements of each discipline retain their original identity. In contrast, interdisciplinarity consciously integrates separate disciplinary data, concepts, theories, and methods to produce an interdisciplinary understanding of a complex problem or intellectual question (Klein & Newell, 1997, p. 393).

Multidisciplinarity and interdisciplinarity have this in common: They seek to overcome disciplinary monism. However, they do this in different ways. Multidisciplinarity means limiting activity to merely appreciating different disciplinary perspectives. But interdisciplinarity means being more inclusive of what disciplinary theories, concepts, and methods are appropriate to a problem. It also means being open to alternative methods of inquiry, using different disciplinary tools, and carefully estimating the degree of usefulness of one tool versus another to shed light on the problem (Nikitina, 2005, pp. 413–414).

Research is truly interdisciplinary, states the National Academies (2005), "when it is not just pasting two disciplines together to create one product but rather is an integration and synthesis of ideas and methods" (p. 27). Figure 1.1 shows the difference between multidisciplinarity and interdisciplinarity:

Figure 1.1   Difference Between Multidisciplinary and Interdisciplinary

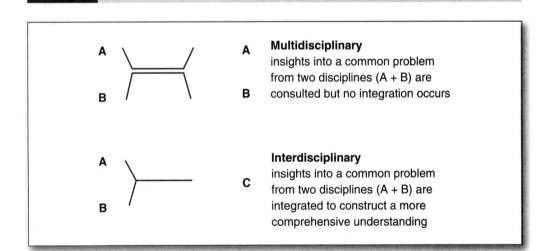

SOURCE: National Academy of Sciences, National Academy of Engineering, & Institute of Medicine. (2005). *Facilitating interdisciplinary research*. Washington, DC: National Academies Press. Page 29.

Interdisciplinary Studies Is Not Transdisciplinary Studies

The contrast between interdisciplinary studies and transdisciplinary studies lies in their differing approaches to the disciplines. Interdisciplinary studies relies *primarily* on the disciplines for their perspectives, insights, concepts, theories, data, and methods in the process of integrating their theories and insights, and constructing a more comprehensive understanding of a *particular* problem, not a class of similar problems. However, interdisciplinary studies uses an overarching research process (the subject of Chapter 3) that subsumes disciplinary methods. While interdisciplinarity focuses on integrating across disciplines, the field is open to voices (i.e., stakeholder views) from beyond the academy.

Transdisciplinary studies takes a very different approach to the disciplines. One variant calls for creating "a total system of knowledge" that is completely "beyond disciplines" (Nicolescu, 2007, p. 1). Quantum physicist Basarab Nicolescu (2007) is promoting the unification of the scientific and the sacred to achieve "unity of knowledge together with the unity of our being" (p. 1). For example, he sees transdisciplinarity aiding holistic health practitioners who are "seeking to promote the understanding of illness as something arising from the interwoven fabric—body, plus mind, plus spirit—that constitutes the whole human being" (p. 1).

The other variant of transdisciplinarity calls for "trans-sector problem solving" where the focus of study is a mega problem or grand theme such as "the city" or "ecological sustainability." Such mega and complex problems require collaboration among a hybrid mix of actors from different disciplines, professions, *and sectors of society* (Klein, 2003, pp. 12, 19).[7] In the United States, reports Klein (2010), transdisciplinarity is conceptualized as a form of "transcendent interdisciplinary research" (p. 24); the transdisciplinary team science movement is "fostering new theoretical frameworks for understanding social, economic, political, environmental, and institutional factors in health and well-being" (p. 24).

The Differences Between Multidisciplinarity, Interdisciplinarity, and Transdisciplinarity Summarized

- Multidisciplinarity studies a topic from the perspective of several disciplines at one time but makes no attempt to integrate their insights. Multidisciplinary approaches tend to be dominated by the method and theory preferred by the home discipline.
- Interdisciplinarity (as defined in this book) studies a complex problem (including mega ones) by drawing on disciplinary insights (and sometimes stakeholder views) and integrating them. By employing a research process that subsumes the methods of the relevant disciplines, interdisciplinary work does not privilege any particular disciplinary method or theory.

- **Transdisciplinarity** concerns that which is at once *between* the disciplines, *across* different disciplines, and *beyond* all disciplines. Its goal is (a) the understanding of the present world, of which one of the imperatives is the unity of knowledge, and (b) the solution of mega and complex problems by drawing on and seeking to integrate disciplinary *and stakeholder views* on the basis of some overarching theory.

The Premise of Interdisciplinary Studies

A major **premise of interdisciplinary studies** is that the disciplines (including interdisciplines) themselves are the necessary preconditions for and foundations of interdisciplinarity.[8] This premise is implicit both in the definition of interdisciplinary studies offered earlier and, as already noted, in the very concept of interdisciplinarity itself. "Precondition" means prerequisite; it also connotes preparation. The disciplines, despite their limitations, are appropriate starting points for doing interdisciplinary research. They have, after all, produced the knowledge that is foundational to advances in education, medicine, engineering, technology, culture, government, and economics.

Furthermore, to ignore the disciplines and the wealth of knowledge that they have generated would severely constrain the interdisciplinarian's ability to research almost any conceivable topic. "Foundation" means the basis upon which something stands, like a house standing on a foundation. The disciplines are foundational to interdisciplinary research because they provide the perspectives, epistemologies, assumptions, theories, concepts, and methods that inform our ability as humans to understand our world. Even with the many shortcomings of the disciplines, interdisciplinarians still need to take them seriously and learn as much as they can from them.

Competing Impulses Behind the Term *Interdisciplinarity*

Interdisciplinarians have differing views on the role of the disciplines. There are, writes Moran (2010), two "competing impulses" behind the term *interdisciplinarity* (p. 13). On one hand, there is the search for a wide-ranging, total knowledge; on the other hand, there is a more radical questioning of the nature of knowledge and our attempts to organize and communicate it. In this sense, says Moran, interdisciplinarity "interlocks with concerns of epistemology—the study of knowledge—and tends to be centered around problems and questions that cannot be addressed or solved within the existing disciplines" (pp. 13–14).

These two differing impulses have implications for the meaning of interdisciplinarity. As Geoffrey Bennington (1999) points out, *inter* is an ambiguous prefix that can mean "forming a communication between" or "joining together." Indeed, the term *interdisciplinarity* is slippery: "It can suggest forging connections across the disciplines; but it can also mean establishing a kind of undisciplined space in the interstices between disciplines, or even attempting to transcend disciplinary boundaries altogether" (p. 104). This ambiguity of interdisciplinarity, says Moran (2010), is a major reason why some critics have come up with other terms, such as *post-disciplinary*, *anti-disciplinary*, and *transdisciplinary*. These terms that are often loosely defined and used interchangeably suggest that being interdisciplinary is not quite enough and that there is another intellectual level where disciplinary divisions can be subverted or even erased (p. 14).

The integrated definition of interdisciplinary studies set out earlier assumes "the existence and relative resilience of disciplines as modes of thought and institutional practices" (Moran, 2010, p. 15). This book agrees with Moran and other practitioners who view interdisciplinarity as complementary to the disciplines. The disciplines and the knowledge they produce in terms of insights, theories, concepts, and methods make interdisciplinary studies possible. This book explores how we can profitably use the disciplines, interdisciplines, and schools of thought to produce new understandings.

How the Term *Interdisciplinarity* Is Variably Used Today

Klein (2005a) cautions that not all interdisciplinarities are the same. "Disagreements about definition," she says, "reflect differing views of the purpose of research and education, the role of disciplines, and the role of critique" (p. 55).

Forms of Interdisciplinarity

There are two dominant forms of interdisciplinarity: instrumental interdisciplinarity and critical interdisciplinarity. **Instrumental interdisciplinarity** is problem-driven. It is a pragmatic approach that focuses on research, borrowing, and practical problem solving in response to the external demands of society. However, borrowing alone is not sufficient for instrumental interdisciplinarity but must be supplemented by integration. For instrumental interdisciplinarity, it is indispensable to achieve as much integration as possible given the insights currently available from the contributing disciplines.

Critical interdisciplinarity is society driven. It "interrogates the dominant structure of knowledge and education with the aim of transforming them, while raising epistemological and political questions of value and purpose" (Klein, 2010, p. 30). This focus is silent in instrumental interdisciplinarity. Critical interdisciplinarians fault the instrumentalists (also known as pragmatists) for merely combining existing disciplinary approaches without advocating their transformation. Rather than building bridges across academic units for practical problem-solving purposes, critical interdisciplinarians seek to transform and dismantle the boundary between the literary and the political, treat cultural objects relationally, and advocate inclusion of low culture (Klein, 2005a, pp. 57–58).

These distinctions between instrumental and critical interdisciplinarity are not absolute or unbridgeable. Research on systemic and complex problems such as the environment and health care often reflects a combination of critique and problem-solving approaches. The integrated definition of interdisciplinary studies used in this book reflects an emerging consensus approach to the field: It is pragmatic, yet leaves ample room for critique and interrogation of the disciplines as well as economic, political, and social structures. This "both/and" approach is reflected in the definition of interdisciplinarity stated earlier: It refers to "answering a question, solving a problem, or addressing a topic," so it reflects an instrumentalist approach. But it also refers to "integrating [disciplinary] insights and theories to construct a more comprehensive understanding." Integrating disciplinary insights (e.g., their concepts and assumptions) or theories typically includes interrogating the disciplines. Similarly, constructing a more comprehensive understanding of a problem (STEP 9) and communicating this understanding (STEP 10) may involve raising epistemological and political questions or proposing transformative policies (see Chapter 3). Interdisciplinarity, then, "has developed from an idea into a complex set of claims, activities, and structures" (Klein, 1996, p. 209). Identification of some of the more important of these follows.

Interdisciplinarity Is Used to Describe Work

The work of interdisciplinary studies has three aspects.

The Work of Integrating Knowledge

According to Veronica Boix Mansilla and Howard Gardner (2003), the principal work of interdisciplinary studies is the integration of knowledge and modes of thinking from two or more disciplines. "Integration," they say, is the "blend[ing] into a functioning or unified whole" (p. 1). The **integration of knowledge**, then, means identifying and blending knowledge from relevant disciplines to produce an interdisciplinary understanding of a particular problem or intellectual question. This understanding is limited in time and to a particular context and would not be possible by relying solely on a single disciplinary approach. For example, a single disciplinary perspective cannot adequately explain the complex phenomenon of terrorism, much less craft a comprehensive solution to it. Understanding terrorism in an interdisciplinary sense calls for drawing on insights and theories from history, political science, cultural anthropology, sociology, law, economics, religious studies, and psychology and integrating these to produce a more comprehensive understanding of it. By drawing on multiple disciplines, says Boix Mansilla (2002), interdisciplinary study "advances our understanding [by explaining complex phenomena, crafting comprehensive solutions, and raising new questions] in ways that would have not been possible through single disciplinary means" (p. 7). The work of integrating knowledge is also about practical problem solving (Boix Mansilla & Gardner, 2003, p. 2).[9]

Interdisciplinary work often leads to the formation of new fields and new interdisciplines. Examples of the growing variety of such fields include ecology; environmental sciences; leadership studies; behavioral economics; resource management; landscape development; industrial ecology; medical ecology; human ecology; social ecology; public health; cancer research; biotechnology; sociology of knowledge; discourse studies; science, technology, and society studies; future studies; conflict studies; cultural studies; media studies; communication studies; information sciences; cybernetics; computer sciences; systems sciences; and knowledge management (Klein, 2003, p. 16).

The Work of Recognizing and Confronting Differences

Interdisciplinarity recognizes and confronts differences, looks for common ground despite those differences, and seeks to produce an understanding that takes those differences into account. "The reality," says Klein (1996),

> is that differences matter. Even if negotiated and mediated, differences do not go away—they continue to create "noise." Misunderstandings, animosities, and competitions cannot be mitigated or glossed over. They must be taken seriously as attempts are made to spell out differences and their possible consequences. Interdisciplinarity . . . does not trust that everything will work out if everyone will just sit down and talk to each other. (p. 221)

The differences that Klein and others say that interdisciplinary studies must recognize and confront include differences over values such as political agendas, cultural traditions, and religious animosities. Klein's straightforward statement is a realistic assessment of the human condition as it is, not as it ought to be. Interdisciplinarity embraces reality. An example of a topic reflecting the reality of political and cultural differences is a study of education for democratic citizenship, which uses political liberalism and civic republicanism to critique each one's assumption and expose each one's overreliance on rights or duties.

Interdisciplinarity Is Used to Describe a Research Process

The interdisciplinary research process (IRP) is the "how" part of the definition of interdisciplinarity. Interdisciplinarity refers to the *process* used to study a complex problem/issue/question, not to the problem/issue/question itself. Chapter 3 introduces the model of this process. As noted in the integrated definition of interdisciplinary studies, the goal, purpose, or result of the research process is to construct *a more comprehensive understanding* (see Chapter 13). This is an umbrella term that refers to a product, policy, technology, poem, or artistic production. A core component of the IRP is integration, the subject of Part III.

Each interdisciplinary research project involves drawing on a different combination of disciplines, insights, and theories because knowledge and problems are contextual and contingent. One practitioner expresses it this way: For interdisciplinarians, the "definition of intellectuality shifts from absolute answers and solutions to tentativeness and reflexivity" (Klein, 1996, p. 214). Chapter 2 discusses the kind of thinking that interdisciplinary studies students should cultivate and ideally exhibit.

Interdisciplinarity Is Used to Describe the Kind of Knowledge Produced

Boix Mansilla, Miller, and Gardner (2000) are concerned with the kind of knowledge that interdisciplinary studies produces. Individuals demonstrate **disciplinary understanding,** they say, "when they use knowledge and modes of thinking in disciplines such as history, science, or the arts, to create products, solve problems, and offer explanations that echo the work of disciplinary experts" (pp. 17–18). By contrast, individuals demonstrate **interdisciplinary understanding** "when they integrate knowledge and modes of thinking from two or more disciplines in order to create products, solve problems, and offer explanations, in ways that would not have been possible through single disciplinary means" (pp. 17–18).

Interdisciplinarity Is Used to Describe Change in Knowledge Production

Knowledge production refers to scholarly research published in the form of peer-reviewed articles and books. The discussion about interdisciplinarity is a dialogue about innovation—that is, *change*—in the means of knowledge production. Disciplinary researchers traditionally are trained to produce knowledge differently than are interdisciplinarians. Interdisciplinarians borrow from the disciplines and integrate this information to produce new understandings and meanings.[10] This activity, which goes against the grain of what many disciplinary researchers have been taught to do and to protect, is needed because knowledge is increasingly interdisciplinary and boundary crossing is commonplace.

Metaphors Commonly Used for Interdisciplinary Work

A **metaphor** is a figure of speech in which a word or phrase, a story, or a picture is likened to the idea that one is attempting to communicate, as shown in the metaphor of the smoothie and the fable of the elephant house.

Metaphors help us visualize an unfamiliar concept (Lakoff & Johnson, 1980, p. ix). They are important to interdisciplinary work and thinking in two ways: (1) They communicate to disciplinarians the nature of interdisciplinary work in an overall sense, and (2) they model the result of a specific research project. Commonly used metaphors descriptive of interdisciplinary work in general include "boundary crossing," "bridge building," "mapping," and "bilingualism."

The Metaphor of Boundary Crossing

Boundary crossing is the process of moving across knowledge formations for the purpose of achieving an enlarged understanding. Boundaries between knowledge units—academic disciplines—are in a continuous, though imperceptibly slow, process of breaking down and reformulating. Indeed, boundary crossing with respect to knowledge production has become the defining characteristic of our age (Klein, 1996, p. 1).

Boundaries exist in many forms, including political, social, economic, religious, and ethnic. Surrounded by boundaries, we are mostly unaware of their existence until we find one blocking our progress. Boundary-related topics include the boundaries between science, religion, and humanist ethics concerning embryonic stem cell research and human cloning; the boundaries between religion, politics, and education concerning appropriate apparel; and the boundaries between politics, business (management), and sociology (race) concerning governmental (at all levels) responses to natural disasters such as Hurricane Katrina and the Haitian earthquake.

Less known but no less important are the boundaries between academic disciplines, or, as Klein (1996) calls them, "specialist domains." "Boundary," she says, "has become a new keyword in discussions of knowledge" (p. 1). Words related to *boundary* include *turf*, *territory*, and *domain*.

The metaphor of boundary crossing is useful to interdisciplinarians because it calls attention to the ways that disciplines have historically staked out their differences, claims, and activities and have built institutional structures to define and protect their knowledge practices (Klein, 1996, p. 1). But *boundary* can also be descriptive of something that is artificial and needlessly obstructive. This is the sense that Steve Fuller (1993) ascribes to the metaphor when he calls disciplinary boundaries "artificial barriers to the transaction of knowledge claims. Such boundaries are necessary evils that become more evil the more they are perceived as necessary" (p. 36).

There are at least two problems, though, with the boundary metaphor. First, it conveys the incorrect notion of a static line or space that fails to acknowledge changes within a discipline or overlapping aims and activities among disciplines. Also, territorial metaphors fail to describe adequately the role of language between disciplines (Lyon, 1992, p. 682). Few boundaries or languages remain fixed—at least not for very long. This is certainly true in the academy.

Reasons for crossing boundaries are several and are discussed in later chapters. For interdisciplinarians, the primary reason for crossing boundaries is to develop a more comprehensive understanding of a problem that would not otherwise be possible by examining it from the perspective of a single discipline.

The Metaphor of Bridge Building

The metaphor of **bridge building** connotes the borrowing of tools and methods from disciplines (Squires, 1975, pp. 42–47). There are two attractions to this metaphor. The first is the idea of showing how interdisciplinary activity, like the spun cables suspended from the piers of the Golden Gate Bridge and firmly anchored in the bedrock on either shore, is something that takes place between two disciplines. The second attraction is the idea that interdisciplinary studies has an applied orientation. Possible bridge building topics include explorations of how environmentalists can work with business and government to sustain the environment while meeting the economic development needs of the indigenous society, and how better communication and understanding can be developed between hostile racial, religious, and other groups.

There is, however, a problem with using bridge building to describe interdisciplinary studies, the interdisciplinary research process, and integration: "Bridge builders do not tend to engage in critical reflection on problem choice, the epistemology of the disciplines being used, or the logic of disciplinary structure" (Klein, 1996, pp. 10–11). In other words, this metaphor suggests that interdisciplinary study is less concerned with the knowledge, perspectives, concepts, assumptions, theories, and methods of those disciplines relevant to the problem or question under investigation than with the construction of a theory (i.e., cable) that would connect the disciplines.

The Metaphor of Mapping

Mapping or mapmaking is a metaphor based on the idea that the carving up of knowledge space is like the practice of cartography or mapmaking. Mapping involves using a "combinational" or integrative method to map or display information that is gathered from a variety of sources (Szostak, 2004, p. 143). European cartographers produced a system of mapping geographical and political space by lines of longitude and latitude forming territorial quadrangles that symbolically represented the world. These divisions were further subdivided into smaller units and, in turn, into still smaller units. In the absence of global positioning systems, inaccuracies abounded and disputes inevitably arose over who owned what sliver of territory (Stoddard, 1991, p. 6).

The classic illustration of this errant approach to mapping was the 1884 partitioning of Africa. Someone has calculated that of the colonial borders that dissected the continent and its peoples, fully 30% were arbitrary (Stoddard, 1991, p. 6). The remapping of the Earth's surface in our own day is occurring at the same time we are remapping knowledge.

Mapping a problem—breaking it down into its component parts and seeing how these parts behave and relate to one another—is an important strategy used by disciplinarians and interdisciplinarians to analyze complex problems. Mapping a problem such as spousal battery or environmental pollution, for example, is likely to require the researcher to seek insights from several disciplines to explain its causes. Chapter 5 introduces various ways to map a problem.

The usefulness of the metaphor of mapping or remapping is that it reveals new interdisciplinary fields and the extent of border crossing between disciplines (Klein, 1996, p. 3). The weakness of this metaphor, however, is that it compares knowledge (which is fluid) to land (which is more stable). Another weakness is that maps necessarily emphasize some aspects over others, and thereby constrain thought and even mislead at times. Szostak (2004) notes that "maps may represent the concerns and interests of the powerful, as when black population centers were ignored on maps of South Africa" (pp. 143–144).

The Metaphor of Bilingualism

Bilingualism is a popular, but inappropriate, metaphor for interdisciplinary work that implies *mastery* of or *proficiency* in two complete languages. Its attraction is that it compares disciplines to foreign languages. For many, developing proficiency in a foreign language is as difficult and time-consuming as developing proficiency in a new discipline. There are two problems with this metaphor. The first is that it assumes that one cannot work in a new discipline without first mastering it. This is not the case. The numerous examples of professional and student work presented in this book (especially Chapter 7) demonstrate that what is required for interdisciplinary work is *adequacy* in relevant disciplines, not mastery of them. This applies both to members of research teams and to individual researchers. The minimal condition for interdisciplinary work (i.e., adequacy) for members of a team of experts from different disciplines, says Klein (1996), must be "communicative competence" (p. 220). The second problem is that a bilingual person speaks in either one language or the other, rather than drawing different insights from each language and then integrating them. Bilingualism involves either/or thinking whereas interdisciplinary studies use both/and thinking.

Reflections on These Metaphors

Lest you feel that you must find just the right metaphor to express visually what you are attempting to do, accept Klein's conclusion that "interdisciplinary activities cannot be depicted in a single image" (Klein, 1996, p. 19).[11] Interdisciplinarians are able to communicate the concept of interdisciplinarity to disciplinarians more effectively when they are mindful of the aspect of interdisciplinarity that each of these metaphors illuminates while being aware of each one's limitations.

Chapter Summary

Interdisciplinary studies and interdisciplinarity are evolving dynamic concepts that are now mainstream in the academy. Still, many disciplinarians use the terms *multidisciplinarity* and *interdisciplinarity* interchangeably and are unaware of the role of integration and of the goal of the interdisciplinary enterprise. This chapter has defined these terms, explained the differences between the disciplines and interdisciplinary studies, examined how interdisciplinarity differs from multidisciplinarity and transdisciplinarity, and identified the ways that interdisciplinarity is variably used today. Lastly, this chapter has identified strengths and weaknesses of various metaphors descriptive of interdisciplinary studies.

Chapter 2 identifies the drivers of interdisciplinary learning and research, presents the etymology of interdisciplinarity, examines the interdisciplinary critique of the disciplines, traces the origins of interdisciplinarity, and describes the interdisciplinary approach to learning and research.

Notes

1. Some generalists such as Moran see the terms *interdisciplinarity* and *integration* as synonymous with *teamwork* as in team teaching and cross-disciplinary communication on research projects (J. R. Davis, 1995, p. 44; Klein, 2005b, p. 23; Lattuca, 2001, p. 12). Other generalists such as Lisa Lattuca (2001) prefer to distinguish between types of interdisciplinarity by focusing primarily on the kinds of questions asked rather than on integration (p. 80). Still other generalists such as Donald G. Richards (1996) go so far as to reject any definition of interdisciplinary studies that "necessarily places priority emphasis on the realization of synthesis [or integration] in the literal sense" (p. 114).

2. For the limited purposes of this book, I am using traditional lists of major disciplines rather than the much fuller contemporary taxonomies.

3. See Klein (1996, pp. 78–84) for a detailed discussion of these differences.

4. However, some argue that some fields of studies have achieved this state.

5. Allen F. Repko (2008) identifies four cognitive abilities that the literature on cognition and instruction suggest are hallmarks of interdisciplinary learning, and shows how these abilities may be expressed in the language of assessment and evaluated on both the course and program levels.

6. In the humanities, students are required to choose a definition of meaning: artist intent, audience reaction, and so on. However, Rick Szostak (2004) argues that the interdisciplinary conception of "meaning" should urge students to embrace all

possible definitions and the causal links they imply. Students "could still choose to specialize with respect to one of these (or not) without needing to assume the others away" (p. 44).

7. For a thorough discussion of the strengths and limitations of transdisciplinarity, see Somerville and Rapport (Eds.) (2000), *Transdisciplinarity: Recreating Integrated Knowledge,* particularly the chapters by Klein and Newell. In the 1990s, reports Klein (2010), transdisciplinarity began appearing more often in the humanities as a label for critical evaluation of knowledge formations. For example, in women's and gender studies, Dölling and Hark (2000) associated transdisciplinarity with critical evaluation of terms, concepts, and methods that cross disciplinary boundaries (pp. 1196–1197).

8. However, as Klein (2005a) notes, interdisciplinarity can no longer be regarded as a single kind of activity framed against a stable disciplinary system (p. 69).

9. They talk about a variety of forms of interdisciplinary work. In their work in total, though, they emphasize epistemic goals that are contingent upon "practical" contexts.

10. Klein (1990) notes, however, that "there are no standards for excellence in borrowing" (p. 94).

11. More recently, Klein (2000a) concludes that "territorial metaphors may be obsolete" and suggests that organic metaphors, such as boundary crossing, that highlight connection may be more useful because "knowledge production is no longer strictly within disciplinary boundaries" (pp. 8–9).

Exercises

Defining for Clarity

1.1   You saw in this chapter the importance of defining the controversial and misunderstood term *interdisciplinary studies* in order to reveal its true meaning. Does the integrated definition fully capture the several aspects of interdisciplinarity advanced by the five authoritative definitions? If not, how might it be improved? Can you think of another controversial or misunderstood term whose true meaning could be clarified by studying its definition?

Claimed and Not Claimed

1.2   This chapter compared and contrasted the field of interdisciplinary studies with the traditional disciplines. What characteristics of interdisciplinary studies are most unlike the characteristics of the disciplines? Why is the field of interdisciplinary studies unlikely to become a discipline?

Reasons for Agreeing

1.3   This chapter presented several reasons for agreeing on a definition of interdisciplinary studies. Which of these would be of greatest interest to (a) university administrators, (b) scholars in traditional disciplines, (c) your family, and (d) employers or prospective employers?

What and How

1.4   Definitions of some terms contain both a "what" and a "how" component. This is true of the integrated definition of interdisciplinary studies that appears in this chapter. What is the "how" component of this definition?

Metaphors

1.5   Metaphors help us visualize complex ideas or concepts. The metaphors of the bowl of fruit and the smoothie help us to visualize two complex concepts, multidisciplinarity and interdisciplinarity, that are mistakenly used interchangeably. Can you think of another metaphor for each of these terms?

Building Houses for Elephants

1.6   The fable of the elephant house is instructive to those who are engaging in a complex enterprise such as building a house. Think of another complex enterprise that is planned or already under way in your community and apply the lessons of the elephant house to it.

1.7   Is there a transdisciplinary aspect to the elephant house project? If so, what is it, or what should it be?

Complementary

1.8   This chapter has argued that interdisciplinarity should be viewed as complementary to the disciplines rather than as a threat to them. In your view, what is the most compelling argument that can be made for a "both/and" rather than an "either/or" position?

More Metaphors

1.9   Of the metaphors commonly used to describe interdisciplinary work (excluding that of the smoothie), which is the most helpful to instrumental interdisciplinarity, and which is most helpful to critical interdisciplinarity?

Reflection

1.10   How has this chapter broadened and/or clarified your understanding of interdisciplinary studies as an academic field?

2 Mapping the Drivers of Interdisciplinarity

Chapter Preview

Before delving into the research process, it is useful to first discuss why interdisciplinary research is so important and identify those factors "driving" it. The problems confronting humanity today are of such magnitude and complexity that new approaches to addressing them are needed. This has sparked renewed interest in interdisciplinarity as a mode of education and an approach to research. Because interdisciplinarity deals with "big questions and real problems," explains Carol Geary Schneider (2010), president of the Association of American Colleges and Universities (AAC&U), "interdisciplinarity is now prevalent throughout American colleges and universities" (p. xvi). In *College Learning for the New Global Century* (2007), the signature report from AAC&U's decade-long initiative on Liberal Education and America's Promise (LEAP), the authors call for making intentional integrative learning a defining feature of liberal education. Brint, Turk-Bicacakci, Proctor, and Murphy (2009) report that interdisciplinary teaching and research is now widely considered a prominent feature of the modern academy. The reason for heightened interest in interdisciplinarity, reports Julie Thompson Klein (2010), is because the word "is associated with bold advances in knowledge, solutions to urgent social problems, an edge in technological innovation, and a more integrative educational experience" (p. 2).

This chapter sets out the four primary drivers propelling the growth of interdisciplinarity in research and education. This discussion is followed by the interdisciplinary critique of the disciplines, a brief recounting of the origins of the disciplines and of interdisciplinarity, and the four key assumptions that anchor this diverse and rapidly evolving field. It concludes by identifying the cognitive abilities that interdisciplinarity fosters and the traits and skills characteristic of interdisciplinarians.

The Primary Drivers of Interdisciplinary Research and Education

The National Academies report *Facilitating Interdisciplinary Research* (2005) identifies four primary and overlapping "drivers" of interdisciplinary research and learning:

1. The inherent complexity of nature and society

2. The desire to explore problems and questions that are not confined to a single discipline

3. The need to solve social problems

4. The need to produce revolutionary insights and generative technologies

Each of these warrants extended discussion.

The Inherent Complexity of Nature and Society

The first driver of interdisciplinary education and research is the need to understand the inherent complexity of nature and society. The complexity discussed here is of two kinds: the complexity of real-world problems that involve natural systems or human society, and the complexity associated with the meaning of cultural artifacts, past and present, such as literature, visual art (e.g., films, paintings, and sculptures), and performance art (e.g., plays, dance, and musical compositions). Real-world problems concerning nature and society are typically complex, ill structured, and not readily solved.

Research in the natural sciences and even more so in the social sciences is increasingly interdisciplinary because the complexity of real-world problems often defies using a single disciplinary approach and requires crossing disciplinary boundaries. Examples of "grand challenge questions" that require scientists to cross disciplinary domains include the following: How did the universe originate? What physical processes control climate? What is the carrying capacity of the biosphere? Complex natural systems such as the Earth's climate cannot be understood comprehensively, they say, "without considering the influence of the oceans, rivers, sea ice, atmospheric constituents, solar radiation, transport processes, land use, land cover, and other anthropogenic practices and feedback mechanisms that link this 'system of subsystems' across scales of space and time" (National Academies, 2005, p. 30).

Human societies are also enormously complex systems. They are affected by myriad influences such as climate, geography, history, cultural traditions, conflict, and systems of sacred beliefs. Examples of high-priority problems that require expert insights from multiple disciplines include world hunger, sustainable resource use, terrorism, and childhood development and learning. For many in the natural and social sciences, "it seems quite clear that the advancement of science in the twenty-first century depends on effective collaboration across disciplinary boundaries. This is so, first and foremost, because of the complexity of issues that must be addressed" (Calhoun & Marrett, 2003, p. v).

The humanities are likewise increasingly interdisciplinary, reflecting what anthropologist Clifford Geertz (1980) describes as the "blurring of the genres" (i.e., disciplinary knowledge domains). Each generation seeks its own understanding of cultural artifacts, as witnessed by the perpetual reinterpretations of Shakespeare's plays, the new biographies of major historical figures, and new forms of artistic expression. Here are examples of topics or themes that require drawing on insights from multiple disciplines in the humanities: How was the Cold War depicted in the films of the 1950s and 1960s? How is the concept of "the gaze" understood in the work of particular artists? How is the rescue motif expressed in hip-hop lyrics? To fully understand any problem, object, work, or system that is complex requires using multiple disciplines. Some problems span the natural sciences, the social sciences, and the humanities.

One aspect of real-world complexity is job complexity. Much of what we actually do at work is becoming more knowledge intensive. "Knowledge—an intangible—is a key ingredient in the success of a tangible product" (Oblinger & Verville, 1998, p. 10). This trend toward job complexity, says noted economist and former U.S. Department of Labor Secretary Robert B. Reich (1991), defines a new type of worker—the *symbolic analyst*—who works with intangible simulations to produce a tangible outcome (pp. 177–180). Research scientists are using simulation techniques to create theoretical molecules that have certain properties for the pharmaceutical industry. Real estate developers conceptualize and market a concept to investors and government officials that may ultimately be transformed into a physical environment. Financial analysts run simulations of how certain combinations of investments will perform under a variety of market conditions. Recent analyses of the future of industry and labor call for persons who can understand, use, and integrate knowledge and methods as well as collaborate with disciplinary teams across industry sectors and cultures (Levy & Murnane, 2004; National Academies, 2005).

For this reason, business is becoming increasingly interdisciplinary because it takes place within an increasingly complex environment that demands interdisciplinary skills to address this complexity. Jan Rivkin (2005), a professor in the Strategy unit of the Harvard Business School, writes that for managers

integrative skills are crucial. Managers who possess them can spot the core of an innovative strategy, grasp the implications for other parts of the company, and build out the idea relentlessly until it comes to pervade a company's entire value chain. They see, for instance, how improvements in a retailer's information system have implications for store locations, store manager autonomy, pricing policy, and vender relations. (p. 42)

Another aspect of real-world complexity is the need to apply systems theory to complex problems. **Complex systems theory** concerns the properties of complex systems in general, including how an overall pattern of behavior is generated, its characteristics, and how it evolves over time or in response to changes in its environment. Examples of complex systems include the environment, the human body, and an urban transportation system. Virtually everything we do takes place within a system. Understanding how a complex system functions and the relationships between the various actors in the system is useful because it improves understanding of system outcomes. For example, if a government widens a congested road, systems theory is able to show that it is likely to become congested again even if the destinations of current drivers, employment patterns, location of entertainment and service venues, and other determinants of driving patterns have not changed (Mathews & Jones, 2008, p. 76).

A complex system that students are perhaps most familiar with is their college or university. Yet, as the American Council on Education reports, those entering a university with its many colleges, schools, and special programs are often unaware of how the many parts of the university relate to the whole (Oblinger & Verville, 1998, p. 78). After completing their general requirements, undergraduates typically specialize in a traditional discipline. As they proceed in their major they are prone to develop a **silo perspective**, meaning that they perceive the university and the larger world through the narrow lens of that major. What is often lacking is context—the context of the whole system—and the ability to view reality or a particular problem through multiple disciplinary or theoretical lenses. Those in an interdisciplinary field such as environmental science, however, are taught to relate the smallest parts of the system they are studying to the whole. Similarly, those in cultural studies learn to discover the meaning of a public space in the broad context of the culture that produced it. A hallmark of interdisciplinary research and learning is relating the particular to the larger whole by drawing on multiple disciplinary perspectives that are relevant to a specific problem.

The Desire to Explore Problems and Questions That Are Not Confined to a Single Discipline

Interdisciplinarity is also driven by the desire to explore problems and questions that extend beyond the confines of a single discipline (National Academies, 2005, p. 16). Interdisciplinarity fills gaps in knowledge created by inattention from the disciplines. From these gaps emerge interdisciplinary spaces and new knowledge formations such as cultural botany, geological information systems, environmental and ecological studies, cognitive science, urban and public policy studies, forensic studies, crime and justice studies, literary cultural studies, sociological cultural studies, area studies of various kinds, word and image studies, cultural analysis, visual culture, ethnomusicology, popular music studies, jazz studies, American cultural studies, and ethnic studies of various kinds (Klein, 2005a, p. 78). Mattei Dogan and Robert Pahre (1990) call this process of gap filling **hybridization,** meaning the integration of specialties across disciplines. Klein (1996) describes hybridization and how interdisciplinarity relates to this ongoing process as follows:

> As older fields have divided into smaller units through fissioning, they have confronted the fragments of other disciplines. The deeper specialization goes, the greater the number of specialties, and the greater inevitability of specialists meeting at the boundaries of other disciplines. . . . Specialization produces narrower and narrower fields, nearly all of which correspond to the intersection of two disciplines. . . . Depending on the case, "interdisciplinarity" may be used as a symbol of crisis, the means of exploding an over rigid discipline, or the foundation for a new discipline. (p. 45)[1]

Noted biologist and philosopher E. O. Wilson (1998) says **consilience**—the "jumping together of knowledge" across disciplines "to create a common groundwork of explanation"—is the most promising path to scientific advancement and human progress (p. 8).

Evidence of increasing boundary crossing is the U.S. National Institutes of Health's (NIH) "road map" for research and funding in 2002. Its former director, Elias H. Zerhouni (2003), declared that the scale and complexity of today's biomedical research problems "increasingly demand that scientists move beyond the confines of their own disciplines." What is needed to understand the combination of molecular events that lead to disease are collaborative teams, new combinations of skills and disciplines, new techniques, and new technologies (p. 3).[2]

This commitment to interdisciplinarity is shared by the American Association for the Advancement of Science's CEO Alan I. Leshner (2004). In "Science at the Leading Edge," appearing in the magazine *Science,* he writes,

> Now many of our papers involve teams of scientists from many specialties, bringing diverse expertise to bear in an *integrated* rather than parallel way. The fact that interdisciplinarity characterizes so much of today's most exciting work may portend the demise of single-discipline science. . . . My greatest concern is that our scientific institutions are not well positioned to promote the interdisciplinarity that characterizes so much of science at the leading edge [italics added]. (p. 729)

Rita Colwell (1998), former director of the U.S. National Science Foundation, adds, "Interdisciplinary connections are absolutely fundamental" because it is "at the *interfaces of the sciences* where the excitement will be the most intense [italics added]."

Perhaps the most fertile ground for the development of interdisciplinary fields in recent decades is at the interfaces among biological, behavioral, social, and health sciences. Other national scholarly associations—from the American Geophysical Union and the American Chemical Society to the American Institute of Biological Sciences and the American Political Science Association—are promoting interdisciplinary analyses and emphasizing interdisciplinary activities at the borders of their represented sciences and disciplines (Rhoten, 2004, p. 8).

Diane Rhoten (2004) finds that the transition to interdisciplinarity and consilience is not a smooth one. What is lacking, she says, is *"systematic implementation"* of interdisciplinarity by university management structures. "The fact is, universities have tended to approach interdisciplinarity as a trend rather than a real transition and to thus undertake their interdisciplinary efforts in a piecemeal, incoherent, catch-as-catch-can fashion rather than approaching them as comprehensive, root-and-branch reforms" (p. 6).

Still, there are notable examples of productive research at the interface of disciplines. One is the International Geosphere-Biosphere Programme (IGBP), "one of the largest interdisciplinary international research efforts ever undertaken." From its inception, "the program reflected all of the major drivers of interdisciplinary research. It begins with the complexity of nature, the interactions between the land mass, the oceans of air and water, and the life forms of Earth" (National Academies, 2005, p. 31). A second example is the Human Genome Project. This highly complex undertaking depended on extensive collaboration across many disciplines (p. 32).

Research at the interface of disciplines, however, is not limited to large public and private projects. Individual researchers are also producing important insights into a wide array of social problems. For example, Barry Blesser and Linda-Ruth Salter (2007) are pioneering the new interdisciplinary field of aural architecture, which involves integrating information from architecture, music, acoustics, evolution, anthropology, cognitive psychology, and audio engineering in the design of public spaces such as concert halls.

Interdisciplinarity is not new, of course. What is new is the determination with which these research initiatives seek to promote connected learning (DeZure, 1999, p. 1). Denise Caruso and Diana Rhoten (2001) remind us that "Great discoveries and shifts in conventional thinking have been traditionally attributed to researchers crossing disciplinary boundaries" (p. 6).

The Need to Solve Social Problems

Certain kinds of problems, increasingly those of general public interest, are not being adequately addressed by individual disciplines. Such high-priority problems include food safety, genetically modified plants and animals, access to affordable education, terrorism, job creation, poverty, community development, and immigration. According to the National Academies (2005),

> Human society depends more than ever on sound science for sound decision making. The fabric of modern life—its food, water, security, jobs, energy, transportation—is held together largely by techniques and tools of science and technology. But the application of technologies to enhance the quality of life can itself create problems that require technological solutions. Examples include the buildup of greenhouse gases (hence global warming), the use of artificial fertilizers (water pollution and eutrophication), nuclear-power generation (radioactive waste), and automotive transportation (highway deaths, urban sprawl, and air pollution). (p. 34)

These complex social problems require drawing on expertise from multiple disciplines. Analyzing and solving such problems, argues Steve Fuller (1993), requires interdisciplinary study (p. 33). Daniele C. Struppa (2002) agrees: The need for interdisciplinary studies "is now stronger than ever because modern objects of investigation require an interdisciplinary approach" (p. 97).

It is often important not only to integrate across disciplines but also to draw on expertise from outside the academy. For example, community development projects in urban and rural areas typically involve workers from various disciplines and institutions who join forces around complex social issues of mutual concern such as poverty, health, peace, housing, the environment, and so forth (Korazim-Korosy & Butterfield, 2007, p. 2). One form of community development is international university-to-university partnerships. For example, three large public universities—George Mason University in the United States, the National Autonomous University of Honduras, and the University of Costa Rica—have established an ongoing relationship with community practitioners in each country to develop a coordinated community response to domestic violence in culturally diverse communities with large immigrant populations. So far, the cross-national, cross-cultural, and cross-disciplinary dialog has reframed domestic violence as a human rights issue and increased cultural awareness among community and university participants (p. 8).

The Need to Produce Revolutionary Insights and Generative Technologies

A fourth primary driver of interdisciplinary research and learning is the need to produce "novel and revolutionary insights" and "generative technologies" (National Academies, 2005, pp. 35, 39). Revolutionary insights are those ideas that have the capacity to transform how we learn, think, and produce new knowledge. **Generative technologies** "are those whose novelty and power not only find applications of great value but also have the capacity to transform existing disciplines and generate new ones" (p. 35). Examples include the Internet, MRI, GPS mapping, the laptop computer, and the iPhone. "Innovation," asserts Carole L. Palmer (2010), "often comes not from the core of a discipline but from the margins where knowledge is more diffuse" (p. 176).

Producing transformative insights and technologies requires what Robert J. Sternberg (1996) calls "successful intelligence." Sternberg, one of the world's leading researchers and authorities on intelligence, says that successfully intelligent people think well in three different ways: creatively, analytically, and practically. **Creative intelligence** is required to formulate ideas and solutions to problems. **Analytical intelligence** is required to solve problems and to evaluate the quality of ideas. **Practical intelligence** is needed to apply the ideas in an effective way, whether in business or in everyday life. What makes for **successful intelligence**, says Sternberg, is balance among these three ways of thinking. It means knowing how and when to use these aspects of successful intelligence rather than just having them (p. 128). The problem with traditional education, he says, is that it appears to privilege analytical intelligence. This kind of intelligence may well be less useful to students in their working lives than are creative and practical intelligence. Education, says Sternberg, needs to be preparing students to live in a world where what matters is successful intelligence, not just inert, analytical intelligence. Outside of the academy, problems are of the real-world variety. For example, in a research lab, scientists do not work on problems whose solutions can be readily discovered simply and mechanistically by applying known formulas. Instead, they tackle problems whose solutions are yet unknown and must be found. Solutions to these real-world problems require different strategies that fall into the realm of **heuristics**, involving intuitive, speculative strategies that sometimes work and other times do not work (p. 172). Innovative companies such as Apple, Google, Microsoft, and Intel value people who are successfully intelligent. As one transformative product is being introduced to the market, another is already under development. Analytical intelligence is required to know the market for a product, but creative intelligence is what produces products in the first place and keeps them coming out (pp. 136, 141).

Interdisciplinary education fosters the development of all three components of "successful intelligence." Marc Spooner (2004) finds that the interdisciplinary research process, as it is generally conceptualized, facilitates the creative process by ignoring or removing or altering disciplinary constraints that otherwise would make interdisciplinary work impossible. In fact, says Spooner, the research process may itself be fruitfully understood as a form of creativity (p. 86). Many interdisciplinarians consciously target the development and interaction of the "thinking tools" identified by the literature on creativity. The creative thinking tools include observing, imaging, abstracting, recognizing patterns, forming patterns, analogizing, body thinking, empathizing, dimensional thinking, modeling, transforming, and synthesiz-ing (Root-Bernstein & Root-Bernstein, 1999). We will, therefore, explore the role of creativity in performing the integrative part of the research process in Chapter 9.

Producing transformative insights and technologies also requires the abil-ity to think integratively. Since the late 1990s, authoritative voices in aca-demia including the Boyer Commission's report, *Reinventing Undergraduate Education: A Blueprint for America's Research Universities* (1998), and the AAC&U's report, *Greater Expectations* (2004), have been advocating increased interdisciplinarity in undergraduate education. The Boyer Commis-sion states,

> As research is increasingly interdisciplinary, undergraduate educa-tion should also be cast in interdisciplinary formats. . . . Because all work will require mental flexibility, students need to view their studies through many lenses. Many students come to the university with some introduction to interdisciplinary learning. . . . Once in college, they should find it possible to create individual majors or minors without undue difficulty. Understanding the close relation-ship between research and classroom learning, universities must seriously focus on ways to create interdisciplinarity in undergradu-ate learning. (p. 23)

Echoing the Boyer Commission, the *Greater Expectations* report calls for higher education to help college students become **intentional learners** who can "integrate knowledge from different sources" (AAC&U, 2004, p. 4). The report criticizes traditional academic departmental structures for atom-izing the curriculum into distinct disciplines. Disciplinary approaches to learning and research, though necessary and valuable, sometimes impede integrative approaches to learning (p. 16).

Joel Podolny, former dean of Yale School of Management, also challenges disciplinary-based education by championing a new curriculum for the school. "We're replacing the disciplinary courses that mapped onto the func-tional silos in organizations with new courses that are actually organized around key constituencies that a manager needs to engage in order to be effective," he writes. The reason, he adds, is this:

> Effective leaders need to be able to own and frame problems . . . then work across organizational boundaries in order to solve those prob-lems. The curriculum in the past was broken down by these disciplin-ary silos and because of that, got in the way of effective management and leadership. . . . The real value to be added is in working across those silos. (*Businessweek*, 2006)

Capping the new integrated curriculum is a course called "The Integrated Leadership Perspective" that brings together all the different perspectives.

The vital need for **integrative thinking**—the ability to knit together information from disparate sources—is a subject of Howard Gardner's *Five Minds for the Future* (2008). Gardner is one of the most influential public intellectuals in the world, a MacArthur Fellowship recipient, and the Hobbs Professor of Cognition and Education at the Harvard Graduate School of Education. The "synthesizing" or integrative mind—the mind able to synthesize and communicate complex ideas—is one of the five minds, according to Gardner, that the fast-paced future will demand. "Against all odds," says Gardner,

individuals seek synthesis. . . . [The] most ambitious form of synthesis occurs in *interdisciplinary work* [italics added]. Biochemists combine biological and chemical knowledge; historians of science apply the tools of history to one or more fields of science. In professional life, interdisciplinarity is typically applied to a team composed of workers who have different professional training. In a medical setting, an interdisciplinary team might consist of one or more surgeons, anesthesiologists, radiologists, nurses, therapists, and social workers. In a business setting, an interdisciplinary or cross-functional team might feature inventors, designers, marketers, the sales force, and representatives drawn from different levels of management. The cutting-edge interdisciplinary team members are granted considerable latitude on the assumption that they will exit their habitual silos and engage in the boldest forms of connection making. (pp. 53–54)

The rapidly changing workplace also highlights the need for integrative thinking. "Workplaces need people educated, generally, in a wide range of disciplines, who know how to integrate knowledge across those disciplines and know how to apply that knowledge to complex problems and issues" (Henry, 2005, p. 11). Because the pace of job destruction and job creation is increasing, students entering the workforce today will need to not only change jobs several times in the course of their working life but also change careers. This means that students need to be flexible and possess a wide range of knowledge and skills that can be adapted and enhanced as their jobs and careers change. Today's employees are expected to question failing practices and offer creative ideas to improve processes and products. Interdisciplinary learning provides students with the competencies to integrate information and synthesize new solutions rather than merely provide formulaic responses based on narrow disciplinary thinking (Gregorian, 2004, pp. 12–14).

The Interdisciplinary Critique of the Disciplines

These authoritative and influential voices clearly emphasize the value of interdisciplinary-based inquiry as a much needed supplement to disciplinary-based research and education. But what is it *exactly* about the disciplines

and the disciplinary approach to research and learning that concerns advocates of interdisciplinarity? The answer to this question is found in the discussion of the interdisciplinary critique of the disciplines. This critique
touches on seven weaknesses of **disciplinary specialization**, the focus on a
particular portion of reality that is of interest to the discipline.

Specialization Can Blind
Us to the Broader Context

Disciplinary specialization can blind us to the broader context. This criticism
is expressed in a bit of dialogue found in *The Little Prince* by Antoine de
Saint-Exupéry (2000)[3]:

> "Your planet is very beautiful," [said the little prince]. "Has it any
> oceans?"
>   "I couldn't tell you," said the geographer. . . .
>   "But you are a geographer!"
>   "Exactly," the geographer said. "But I am not an explorer.
> I haven't a single explorer on my planet. It is not the geographer who
> goes out to count the towns, the rivers, the mountains, the seas, the
> oceans, the deserts. The geographer is much too important to go
> loafing about. He does not leave his desk." (pp. 45–46)

Specialization—that is, "not leaving [one's] desk"—can leave unanswered the larger, more important, and practical issues of life. The fable
of building a house for an elephant referenced in Chapter 1 makes the
same point. Interdisciplinarians believe that specialization alone will not
enable us to master the pressing problems facing humanity today. The
more specialized the disciplines become, the more necessary interdisciplinarity becomes.

Specialization Tends to Produce Tunnel Vision

Interdisciplinarians argue that many (but not all) problems can best be understood by being examined from various disciplinary perspectives and then
integrated to produce more comprehensive understandings. They point out
that disciplinary experts are prone to tunnel vision when it comes to examining important issues. For example, the experts who advocated the damming
of the Columbia and Snake rivers system were certain that building a series
of hydroelectric dams would not harm the many salmon species that spawned
in the rivers' tributaries. But the experts were wrong. Today, despite the
extensive building of fish ladders and other costly efforts to mitigate the
effects of these dams, several species are on the verge of extinction, and an
industry that employed tens of thousands of workers is in ruins. In this world

of specialists, even highly educated persons can be unaware of the social, ethical, and biological dimensions of a policy or an action. Indeed, one may know a great deal about a particular subject but know little about its consequence (Dietrich, 1995).[4]

Disciplinarians Sometimes Fail to Appreciate Other Disciplinary Perspectives

Interdisciplinarians fault the disciplines for sometimes failing to appreciate other disciplinary perspectives. For example, before the terrorist attacks of 9/11, few experts on Middle East policy paid much attention to the central role that religion plays in the region—in particular its role as a motivating force behind much of the organized violence against Western interests there. But since 9/11, scholars are taking a fresh look at how religion, in interdisciplinary combination with other perspectives, informs our understanding of terrorist organizations such as al-Qaeda. The need is to develop a more comprehensive understanding of such terrorist organizations in hopes of learning how to understand them and neutralize their appeal.

Some Worthwhile Topics Fall in the Gaps Between Disciplines

In their critique of the disciplines, interdisciplinarians argue that some problems are neglected because they fall between disciplinary boundaries. An example of a new integrative field is strategic organization, which is an effort to bridge the disciplinary divide between strategic management, usually housed in sociology departments, and organization theory, usually housed in management departments (Baum, 2002, p. 21). According to Giles Gunn (1992), important dimensions of human experience and understanding lie unexplored in the spaces between disciplinary boundaries or the places where they cross, overlap, divide, or dissolve (p. 239). These gaps between the disciplines are being filled by new knowledge formations such as sociobiology and biochemistry that are allowing researchers to address new questions and pursue new topics (Klein, 2000a, p. 16).

Creative Breakthroughs Often Require Interdisciplinary Knowledge

The interdisciplinary critique of the disciplines extends to the need for creative breakthroughs when addressing complex problems. **Creative breakthroughs** often occur when different disciplinary perspectives and previously unrelated ideas are brought together (Sill, 1996, pp. 136–149).[5] Noted British scientist and novelist C. P. Snow (1964) states, "The clashing points of two subjects, two disciplines, two cultures—of two galaxies, so far as that goes—ought to produce creative changes. In the history of mental activity that has been where some of the breakthroughs came" (p. 16). For example, Moran (2010) reports that "interdisciplinarity has produced some of the most interesting intellectual developments in the humanities over the past few decades" (p. 180). Those who wish to speed up the production of knowledge and the solution to pressing problems should promote, or at least tolerate, an interdisciplinary approach.

The Disciplines Are Often Unable to Address Complex Problems Comprehensively

A further problem with the disciplines is their inability to address comprehensively, much less solve, complex problems such as global warming. One might examine global warming from a biological perspective and hypothesize about the effect of increased production of carbon dioxide, a greenhouse gas, on ocean temperatures and coral reefs. One might examine it from an economic standpoint and hypothesize about the effects of climate warming on, say, the supply of freshwater for agriculture and food prices in particular regions. Or one might examine it from the perspective of domestic politics and conclude that partisan political considerations and interest group lobbying are to blame for inaction on the problem.

All these disciplinary contributions may be valuable, but none of them provides the truly comprehensive perspective on the problem that policy makers and the public really need. On too many issues of public importance, the disciplines tend to talk past each other. Disciplinarians act as though the part of the problem they analyze is the whole problem, and simply ignore other aspects.

Most interdisciplinarians do not seek the end of the disciplines, for reasons already discussed in Chapter 1. They believe, however, that although the disciplines are useful for producing, organizing, and applying knowledge, too much specialization narrows and distorts one's view of the world.

The Disciplines Are Products of a Bygone Age

Critics of the disciplines say that they are products of a bygone age that was very different from today's world of increasing complexity and rapid social change. After all, they "were forged in relation to particular historical and social contexts, intellectual problems and achievements, and available methodologies" (Calhoun & Marrett, 2003, p. v). The structure of the disciplines and their silo approach to learning and problem solving reflects the form and the level of knowledge achieved in an earlier historical period. Consequently, it is unreasonable to expect that the disciplines *by themselves* will be capable of providing the comprehensive understandings of, or solutions to, contemporary issues and social problems. There is, then, no reason why the disciplines should continue to enjoy a monopoly on knowledge production.

Conversely, the rise of interdisciplinary research and learning reflects the need to ask new questions, try new approaches, produce new technologies, and develop new intellectual orientations (pp. v–vi). We can never entirely dispense with the disciplines as means of organizing knowledge, says Moran (2010), but we can use them to create new intellectual configurations of knowledge (pp. 181–182). Critics of the disciplines readily admit that interdisciplinarity *by itself* is no panacea for the world's problems. Rather, they believe that a symbiotic relationship between the disciplines and interdisciplinarity holds the promise of producing creative breakthroughs that would otherwise not be possible using traditional approaches.

The Formation of the Disciplines and the Origins of Interdisciplinarity

These concerns about specialization and fragmentation and the drive for integration of knowledge are not new but have a long history extending from ancient Greco-Roman times. The following brief history of the origins of interdisciplinarity shows that they arose in response to a series of cultural and educational challenges that required alternatives.

By the time of the ancient Greeks, knowledge had accumulated to such an extent that Plato's Academy, founded in 387 BC, offered instruction in gymnastics, music, poetry, literature, mathematics, and philosophy. The purpose of this experience was to promote the physical, moral, and social development of the "whole person," a concept foundational to integrative values in modern humanities, liberal education, general education, and many interdisciplinary studies programs (Hirst, 1974, pp. 30–31; Nussbaum, 1985, pp. 6–7).

Aristotle, the great philosopher, began the practice of dividing knowledge into subjects. He established a clear hierarchy of the different academic subjects with the theoretical subjects of theology, mathematics, and physics on top; the practical subjects of ethics and politics in the middle; and the productive subjects of the fine arts, poetics, and engineering at the bottom. Aristotle found this structuring of knowledge necessary but regrettable because it violated the fundamental notion of the unity of all knowledge. To integrate these subjects, he placed philosophy as the universal field of inquiry at the top of his hierarchy, as a way to bring together all the different branches of learning (Moran, 2010, p. 4). Significantly, this **classical division of knowledge** remained intact until the nineteenth century, when a new scheme of disciplinarity arose.

The Origins of the University and the Disciplines

The twelfth century (1100–1200 AD) saw the development of a new institution that was to play a major role in the ascendancy of European civilization and the development of the disciplines: the **university**. The modern university is an institution of higher learning that provides teaching and research and is authorized to grant academic degrees. It evolved from the medieval cathedral schools and "rested on the conviction that there was an essential and universal unity of knowledge and through Christianity, that faith was the highest order of knowledge" (Briggs & Micard, 1972, p. 186). The first recorded appearance of the word *university* is in a letter of Pope Innocent III in 1208 or 1209 (M. Bishop, 1970, p. 266). The first universities appeared in Bologna, Paris, and Oxford, where groups of students and teachers (or masters) would meet, often in rented halls or rooms. Interestingly, the original meaning of the word *university* does not refer to either "universe" or "universal" but rather refers to the totality of a group, as in a group of students (Haskins, 1940, p. 14; Rashdall, 1936, pp. 4–5).

By the thirteenth century and until at least the end of the eighteenth century, university students tended to study a core curriculum of the liberal arts, divided into the trivium (logic, grammar, rhetoric) that addressed things qualitatively and the quadrivium (arithmetic, geometry, astronomy, and music) that addressed things quantitatively (Moran, 2010, pp. 4–5). This curriculum served as the basis of and preparation for the professions. Students went on to specialize in theology, medicine, or law much as students today choose to "major" in a subject. These studies corresponded to modern courses in the arts and sciences (M. Bishop, 1970, p. 267).

The term *discipline*, introduced as *disciplina* by the Romans, was applied to these professions because of the perceived need to relate education to specific economic, political, and ecclesiastical ends (Klein, 1990, p. 20). Interestingly, medieval scholars largely excluded contemporary cultural developments as well as the mechanical arts, including agriculture, navigation, war, weaving, and the theater arts (Saffle, 2005, p. 14). Not until the twentieth century would these fields be absorbed into the academic curriculum of the Western university. The university and the disciplines became an engine of knowledge production that far outstripped any other method of learning devised by any previous civilization.

The Impact of the Enlightenment and Scientific Revolution on the Disciplines

The production of knowledge and disciplinary specialization accelerated during the late seventeenth and eighteenth centuries. Two movements hastened this process. The first was the **Enlightenment**, a Europe-wide intellectual movement that emphasized the progress of human knowledge through the powers of reason and provided justification for the movement known as modernism. The second was the **scientific revolution** that occurred at about the same time and that emphasized greater specialization (i.e., reductionism) and heightened research activity (i.e., empiricism), initially in the sciences and then in all the disciplines. The significance of the Enlightenment and the rise of modern science is that they challenged the idea of the unity of knowledge. The early division of the empirical or natural sciences dates from this period.

Not everyone, however, saw greater disciplinary specialization as a positive development. In the early 1700s, the Italian thinker Giambattista Vico called for a new approach to learning. He claimed that the ascendancy of science and mathematics in the curriculum had led to a neglect of broad education in favor of specialized knowledge. He argued that the "human sciences" such as history, philosophy, and law can achieve knowledge and understanding "from within" and, in fact, were superior to the natural sciences, which can only describe the external phenomena in nature (Moran, 2010, p. 7). Nevertheless, Vico's call for less specialization and a more comprehensive approach to learning largely fell on deaf ears.

The Consolidation of the Disciplines in the Late Eighteenth and Early Nineteenth Centuries

Between 1750 and 1800, the disciplines consolidated their hold on the teaching and production of knowledge by embracing three new revolutionizing techniques: writing, grading, and examination. These practices were introduced in three new teaching settings: the seminar (beginning in the German universities around 1760), the laboratory (beginning in the French *Grandes Écoles* before the Revolution), and the classroom (beginning in Scotland around 1760).

Disciplines also began publishing disciplinary journals and hiring their own PhDs, making it difficult for scholars to cross disciplinary lines. Combined, these practices and settings enabled the disciplines to strengthen their position and accelerate the production of new knowledge (Hoskin, 1993, pp. 275–277). These practices and settings have been so successful that today they are used the world over.

The Professionalization of Knowledge in the Late Nineteenth and Early Twentieth Centuries and the Rise of the Modern Disciplines

The academic disciplines of today and the modern concept of disciplinarity are largely the product of developments in the late nineteenth and early twentieth centuries (Klein, 1990, pp. 21–22; Lattuca, 2001, p. 23). This period saw the formation of disciplines in the physical and natural sciences such as biology, chemistry, and physics, though the division process was under way between the mid-seventeenth century and the late eighteenth century. By the middle of the nineteenth century, the social sciences were fragmenting into anthropology and economics, followed by psychology, sociology, history, and political science. Though the humanities include the oldest subjects, the humanities were the last to assume modern disciplinary form (Easton, 1991, p. 11).

Along with the rise of scientific specialties came increased competition for university resources, so universities began to organize themselves around the disciplines. These new disciplines were accompanied by new professional societies in the United States. National organizations emerged in history in 1884, economics in 1885, political science in 1903, and sociology in 1905 (Hershberg, 1981, p. 23). Disciplinary journals allowed isolated specialists to keep abreast of the latest research and also gave them a forum for presenting their own research. Specialists did not need to consider perspectives other than those of their own specialty (Swoboda, 1979, p. 62).

As the modern university took shape, disciplinarity was reinforced in two major ways, according to Klein (1990). First, industries demanded and received specialists from the universities. Second, the disciplines recruited students to their ranks (pp. 21–22). The trend toward specialization, especially in the sciences, was further propelled by increasingly more expensive instrumentation, elaborately equipped laboratories, and highly trained personnel. "Although the 'Renaissance Man' may have remained an ideal for the well-educated baccalaureate, it was not the model for the new professional, specialized research scholar" (Hershberg, 1981, p. 23).

The proliferation of academic disciplines raised concerns about overspecialization, in particular how these new disciplines were connected to issues of power and self-interest. Late-nineteenth-century German philosopher Friedrich Nietzsche and early-twentieth-century Spanish philosopher José Ortega y Gasset saw the new disciplines as symptoms of a more general phenomenon: the growing interdependence of government, business, and education. Driving this interdependence was an economic system that increasingly depended on the availability of specialists and professionals. Under this system, the disciplines and the universities served two vital functions: They trained persons for careers in government and business, and they gave these new professions legitimacy and status by providing them with academic credentials (Moran, 2010, pp. 11, 12).

The Emergence of Interdisciplinary Studies and Interdisciplinarity

Once the disciplines were established, it was only natural that interest in interdisciplinarity began to develop. For this to be successful it had to appeal to university administrators. It is also notable that pressure for interdisciplinarity came on the teaching side long before it came on the research side. On the teaching side, the notion of interdisciplinarity and the emergence of interdisciplinary studies can be seen as a response to two broad developments in the United States in the twentieth century. The first concerns the general education movement that dates from the early decades of the century. The second concerns the cultural revolution of the 1960s and the resulting reforms in higher education.

The General Education Movement

The **general education movement** that arose after World War I was a response to several problems besetting American culture and education at the time, including the lack of national unity and the eroding cohesiveness of general education (Boyer, 1981, pp. 4–5). The belief animating the general education movement was that these problems could be solved by reemphasizing the arts and the values associated with classical humanism that emphasized wholeness of knowledge and of human nature. These arts and values are "general" in four ways: (1) They apply to all subject areas; (2) they embrace all basic skills; (3) they affect the formation of the whole person; and (4) they provide guidance for all humans (McKeon, 1964, pp. 159, 171–172).

At the heart of the general education movement and of liberal humanism was the implicit notion of interdisciplinarity. There were two differing conceptions of interdisciplinarity at work: **traditional interdisciplinarity** and **pragmatic interdisciplinarity**. The former focused on the classical and secular ideals of culture and liberal education. The latter focused on historically situated problems of society (Hutcheson, 1997, pp. 109–110). What both conceptions held in common, though, was the notion that general education is "the place where all the parts would add up to a cohesive whole" (Klein, 2005a, p. 31). The magnet holding these diverse pieces together was thought to be a common core of great books and ideas based on two millennia of Western cultural development. Requiring students to study this common core of knowledge, advocates believed, would stem the rising tide of "materialism, vocationalism, empiricism, relativism, specialism, and departmentalization" (Graff, 1987, p. 162). Thus, one of the first motivations for interdisciplinary studies in the United States was to unify knowledge (C. Anderson, 2001, pp. 456–457).

The Cold War Era and Interdisciplinarity

After World War II, a second general education reform movement emerged, triggered by the 1945 Harvard report, *General Education in a Free Society.* The report called for a new general education curriculum based on the sciences and writings of the European humanist tradition. Against the backdrop of fascism and communism, proponents intended the curriculum to provide a common core of knowledge, beliefs, and values centered on the ideals of freedom and democracy—in short, a national ideology opposed to communism in the Cold War era (Bender, 1997, pp. 20–21).

At the same time, criticism of the disciplines intensified and focused on two themes. The first was the enormous power that the disciplines had accumulated since the turn of the century. Influenced by Friedrich Nietzsche, French philosopher Michel Foucault argued in the 1960s that the disciplines are not just a way to produce knowledge; they are a sophisticated mechanism for regulating human conduct and social relations. He found the examination to be the "quintessential practice that epitomizes both the modern power of knowledge and the modern practice of meticulous disciplinary control" (Hoskin, 1993, p. 277).

The second criticism focused on the deepening isolation of the disciplines from each other. Tony Becher (1989) uses the anthropological metaphor of tribes to describe the disciplines, each having its own culture and language:

> Men of the sociology tribe rarely visit the land of the physicists and have little idea what they do over there. If the sociologists were to step into the building occupied by the English department, they would encounter the cold stares if not the slingshots of the hostile natives. . . . The disciplines exist as separate estates, with distinctive subcultures. (p. 23)

Echoing Foucault, Moran (2010) complains that the disciplines exercise their considerable power by "permitting certain ways of thinking and operating while excluding others" (p. 13).

University Reforms in the 1960s and the Emergence of Interdisciplinary Studies

This critique of the disciplines was strengthened by the confluence of three major developments in the United States in the 1960s: the Vietnam War, the student revolution, and dramatic changes in social mores. Combined, these served as a catalyst from which emerged new thinking about how the academy should relate to society (Mayville, 1978, p. 3). This new thinking called for radical university reforms, one central element of which was the elimination of the traditional academic disciplines in favor of holistic notions of training that were closer to the practical problems of life (Weingart, 2000, p. xii). The disciplines and the scholarship that they produced had failed to explain, or had ignored, the great social movements and ideological struggles that characterized the period. These included the civil rights, anti-imperialist, antiracist, and women's rights movements. To that generation of students and young faculty, "The disciplines seemed increasingly irrelevant or even obstructionist to their quest to understand, address, and solve the great issues of the day" (Katz, 2001, p. 520). By contrast, *interdisciplinary studies* became a programmatic, value-laden term that stood for reform, innovation, progress, and opening up the university to all kinds of hitherto marginalized publics (Weingart, 2000, p. xii). The radicalism of the 1960s produced new fields such as African American studies, women's studies, and ethnic studies, and new definitions of culture and politics.

But by the late 1970s, when the social struggles had subsided and mundane academic routine had returned to the universities, the call for interdisciplinarity became much less urgent. "What had seemed progressive only a few years earlier appeared outdated, if not quaint" (Weingart, 2000, p. xii). Yet under the surface calm, young interdisciplinarians such as William H. Newell and Julie Thompson Klein were persistently questioning what constituted legitimate subjects of inquiry, and by their work, they began slowly to reconfigure the contours of knowledge and the methods through which such knowledge was produced (Katz, 2001, p. 520).

Interdisciplinary Studies Becomes an Academic Field

In 1979, a group of 50 interdisciplinarians led by Newell decided that they needed to have their own professional organization and journal and formed the **Association for Integrative Studies (AIS)**. Its purpose was to study interdisciplinary methodology, theory, curricula, and administration. In 1982, AIS launched a peer-reviewed journal, *Issues in Integrative Studies*. Within a decade, AIS, under Newell's leadership, became a national voice for interdisciplinary studies and a professional home where several hundred interdisciplinarians could work together to develop the potential of the field.

The founding of AIS converged with a broader development that reflected a fundamental change in the way knowledge is produced. There is, observes Peter Weingart (2000), "a growing pluralism both in the locations of knowledge production and in the patterns of initiation, production, and use of knowledge as well as its disciplinary combinations" (pp. xi–xii). This development is uneven and does not affect all the disciplines in the same way. For example, in the natural sciences, the disciplinary boundaries seem to be more

Figure 2.1 Complementary Ways to Produce Knowledge and Solve Problems

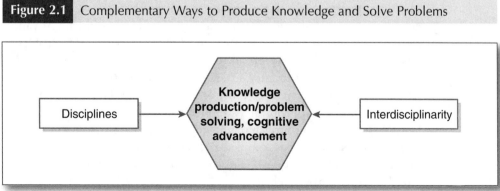

fluid than in the social sciences. Inside the university, where the disciplines command great respect, the goal of knowledge production is to *understand*. However, outside the university, where the goal is to generate practical knowledge in order to *solve practical problems,* the disciplines command less respect and "are even frowned upon as obstacles to innovation or as providing a skewed perspective" (p. xii).

Finally, as disciplinary boundaries are becoming more permeable and as the number of new fields and specialties grows by the day, interdisciplinarity is becoming a fairly common experience. This development, however, does *not* signal the beginning of the end of the disciplines and their replacement by interdisciplinarity. Rather, it shows the limits of the disciplines and the need for interdisciplinarity.

The interdisciplinary research process presented in this book offers a way to apply basic research from relevant disciplines to two types of problems: complex, real-world problems that concern society and science and the need for meaning making that is the focus of the humanities. Both the disciplines and interdisciplinarity are needed and should be viewed as complementary rather than contradictory ways to produce knowledge and solve problems, as shown in Figure 2.1.

Assumptions of Interdisciplinarity

The interdisciplinary approach to research and learning distinguishes this academic field from the disciplines. All disciplines, interdisciplines, and fields of study are based on certain assumptions that provide cohesion to the field. In this regard, interdisciplinary studies is no different. There are at least four assumptions that anchor this diverse and rapidly evolving field, though the extent of agreement on each of them varies.

The Reality Beyond the Academy Requires an Interdisciplinary Approach to Research and Education

Interdisciplinarity reflects the reality that is beyond the academy. It is, according to a recent study by the Carnegie Foundation for the Advancement of Teaching, uniquely able to "address real-world problems, unscripted and sufficiently broad to require multiple areas of knowledge and multiple modes of inquiry, offering multiple solutions and benefiting from multiple perspectives" (Huber & Hutchings, 2004, p. 13). The term *interdisciplinary* is appropriately applied to knowledge of complex problems. A disciplinary approach might suffice to fill gaps in knowledge, and improvements in databases and search engines might suffice to address the fragmentation of knowledge. It's complexity that necessitates an interdisciplinary approach.

The Disciplines Are Foundational to Interdisciplinarity

Speaking for many interdisciplinarians, Deborah DeZure (1999) says, "Interdisciplinarity is not a rejection of the disciplines. It is firmly rooted in them but offers a corrective to the dominance of disciplinary ways of knowing and specialization" (p. 3). We need academic specializations: groups of scholars who share preferences for certain theories, methods, and phenomena of study. But we also need interdisciplinarity to broaden the context and establish links to other ways of constructing knowledge. Indeed, interdisciplinary study, grounded by definition in the disciplines, is both complementary to and critical of them at the same time (Newell, 1992, pp. 212, 220).

Some interdisciplinarians, though, share an **antidisciplinary** view, preferring a more "open" understanding of "knowledge" and "evidence" that would include "lived experience," testimonials, oral traditions, and interpretation of those traditions by elders (Vickers, 1998, pp. 23–26). However, there is a problem with this approach. Without some grounding in the disciplines relevant to the problem, borrowing risks becoming indiscriminate and the result rendered suspect. Moreover, those who reject the knowledge claims of the disciplines altogether may be uncertain how to make knowledge claims other than on grounds of life experience. In academic work, says Klein (2005a), it is still necessary to develop disciplinary adequacy or minimum understanding of the cognitive map of each of the disciplines, interdisciplines, and schools of thought relevant to a particular problem (p. 71). How to achieve adequacy in the disciplines relevant to the problem is the focus of Chapter 7.

The Disciplines *by Themselves* Are Inadequate to Address Complex Problems

Disciplinary inadequacy is the view that the disciplines by themselves are inadequate to address complex problems. Disciplinary inadequacy stems from several factors, beginning with the pressing need for an integrated approach to increasingly complex social, economic, and technological problems. This was one of the findings of the first authoritative national report on interdisciplinary studies published in 1991 by the AAC&U. It confirmed a widely held belief that knowledge is becoming increasingly interdisciplinary. The reasons cited include new developments in research and scholarship, the formation of new hybrid fields, the expanding influence of interdisciplinary methods and concepts, and the pressing need for integrated approaches to complex social, economic, and technological problems (Klein & Newell, 1997, pp. 395–396). Wolfram W. Swoboda (1979) uses even stronger language: "Individual specialties on their own, it is now clear, simply do not have the breadth of perspective nor probably the willingness to assume responsibility for offering extensive and intensive solutions to social problems" (p. 83).

Disciplinary inadequacy stems from a second factor, namely, the claim that the disciplines provide all that is needed to make sense of the modern world. This is so, states Ananta Kuma Giri (2002), observing that there comes a point when disciplinary certainty has to be abandoned in order "to discover the unexpected truths of reality in the borderland" (p. 110). The disciplinary approach fails, she argues, because "whatever categories and concepts we use to make sense of reality, they are not adequate to provide us a total picture" (p. 110). Stanley Fish (1991) notes, "As soon as disciplines are fully established they come quickly to believe in the priority of their own concerns" (pp. 101–102). He complains that the disciplinary boundaries that characterize the university "are not natural but historical" (p. 105). "The problem with disciplinary thinking," says Giri (2002), "is that it fails to realize that its claim to universality needs to be relativized by recognizing the significance of other disciplines in gaining multiple perspectives about the world to which both one's as well as another's discipline contribute" (p. 106).

A third factor explaining disciplinary inadequacy is that the world is undergoing a **paradigm shift**. This refers to a profound and transformative change in the philosophical and theoretical framework that dominates a discipline or an approach to knowledge formation. Accelerating globalization of cultural, technological, economic, and demographic flows is rapidly and profoundly transforming the institutions that produce and disseminate knowledge (Friedman, 2001, p. 504). Interdisciplinarity can aid in this process.

Figure 2.2   Cognitive Decentering

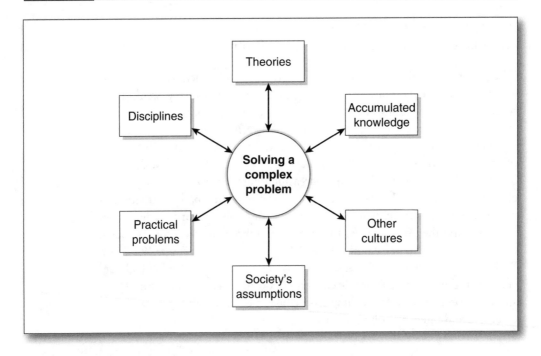

Underlying the calls for an interdisciplinary component to liberal education is the recognition that interdisciplinary study encourages "breadth of vision and the development of the skills of integration and synthesis so frequently demanded by the problems of a culture in the midst of a profound transition" (Newell & Green, 1982, p. 23). Many of the challenges of integrating across disciplines are similar to those involved in integrating across cultures.

As society and its problems become more complex, the traditional academic disciplines will not always be able to prepare students for the complex challenges they will face in the professions (McCall, 1990, p. 1319). Professional education in particular needs to grapple with these social changes (which naturally affect how we conceive law, health, education, etc.). A value inherent in interdisciplinarity is the necessity of preparing future professionals to confront the complex behaviors and problems they will certainly face in a profession.

Disciplinary Perspectives Are Partial and Biased

The insistence on integration by interdisciplinarians rests on the assumption that disciplinary perspectives are partial and biased (Szostak, 2007b, p. 34).[6] Academic disciplines provide their own unique perspective on a given problem, as illustrated in the fable of the blind men and the elephant (see Chapter 4). For example, although "power" is a concept relevant to virtually all the social sciences, each discipline has its own definition of power, and each definition is undergirded by certain assumptions, methods, and so forth that are unique to each discipline. To gain a more balanced and comprehensive understanding of "power" as it relates to a problem, interdisciplinarians must develop adequacy concerning the perspective of each relevant discipline (Hursh, Haas, & Moore, 1983, pp. 44–45).

The ability to do this is called **cognitive decentering**, which is the intellectual capacity to consider a variety of other perspectives and thus perceive reality more accurately, process information more systematically, and solve problems more efficiently. The term *decentering* denotes the ability to shift deliberately among alternative perspectives and to bring each to bear upon a complex problem. This type of thinking allows the student to make connections between disciplines and theories, between practical problems and accumulated knowledge, and between a society's assumptions and those of other cultures, as shown in Figure 2.2.

Above all, cognitive decentering enables interdisciplinarians to evaluate the usefulness of various disciplines to understanding complex problems. The importance of this thinking process is evident in everyday decision making, as well as in scientific pursuits. For example, the cognitive process described above is essential in the search for solutions to such problems as energy depletion, environmental pollution, health care delivery, and urban decay, or in considering aesthetic qualities of line, color, form, and texture from the standpoint of music, art, dance, or theater (Hursh et al., 1983, pp. 44–45).

Cognitive Abilities Fostered by Interdisciplinarity

Interdisciplinary learning fosters the development of at least five cognitive or mental abilities. These include the ability to (1) develop and apply perspective-taking techniques, (2) develop structural knowledge of complex problems, (3) create or discover common ground between conflicting insights, (4) integrate conflicting insights from two or more disciplines, and (5) produce a cognitive advancement or more comprehensive understanding of the problem.

Develop and Apply Perspective-Taking Techniques

Research in cognition and instruction shows that repeated exposure to interdisciplinarity results in students being able to apply perspective-taking techniques. **Perspective taking** or the use of multiple perspectives involves viewing a problem, a topic, or an artifact from alternative viewpoints—including disciplinary-based viewpoints (Baloche, Hynes, & Berger, 1996, p. 3). The difference between disciplines and their perspectives is the subject of Chapter 4.

A core feature of the interdisciplinary research process presented in this book is perspective taking and the ability to draw on disciplinary concepts and theories in order to develop a more comprehensive understanding of a problem, text, or system.

Develop Structural Knowledge of Complex Problems

A second cognitive ability that interdisciplinary learning fosters is the development of structural knowledge of complex problems. Students are challenged to assess critically the relationships among the relevant disciplinary perspectives "and evoke a deeper cognitive analysis of the core theme" of the course (Ivanitskaya, Clark, Montgomery, & Primeau, 2002, p. 99). For example, students studying the roots of animosity between Palestinians and Israelis will need to acquire factual knowledge of their history and religion. But to develop "a deeper cognitive analysis" of the problem, they will need to study how each discipline understands and approaches the problem and how these various perspectives interrelate (p. 99). For this reason, this book emphasizes the importance of mapping the problem that is the focus of study.

Create or Discover Common Ground Between Conflicting Insights

A third cognitive ability fostered by interdisciplinary learning is the ability to create **common ground** between conflicting disciplinary insights or theories (the subject of Chapters 11 and 12). The ability to create common ground is preparatory for performing integration and constructing a more comprehensive understanding of the problem. The research of cognitive psychologist Herbert H. Clark (1996) shows that the activity of establishing common ground is a normal and basic feature of human communication. If it is possible for humans from differing social and other contexts to establish common ground to communicate, then, reasons cognitive psychologist Rainer Bromme (2000), it should also be possible to establish common ground between cognitive constructs such as disciplines and other knowledge formations. Clark's development of common ground theory and Bromme's theory of cognitive interdisciplinarity have important implications for interdisciplinary research and learning. Chiefly, they support the view of interdisciplinarians who argue that integration is fundamental to the notion of interdisciplinarity and that creating or discovering common ground is what makes integration possible. As a result, a growing number of interdisciplinary programs (undergraduate as well as graduate) are applying these theories to their teaching of the interdisciplinary research process. They believe that if interdisciplinarians are self-conscious about process, they should be able to do proactively what people normally do reactively.

Integrate Conflicting Insights
From Two or More Disciplines

A fourth cognitive ability fostered by interdisciplinary learning is the "capacity to integrate conflicting insights from two or more disciplines" (Boix Mansilla, 2005, p. 16). Brain research, says Kathy Lake (1994), "points to interdisciplinary learning [and] thematic teaching" (p. 6). For example, students in an interdisciplinary program are more likely to recall a particular historical period if they have integrated insights from the visual arts, musical expression, cinema, poetry, and philosophical and political events of the period. Of course, the extent and quality of integration achieved will depend on the level of the course and the instructor's command of the interdisciplinary research process. This book argues that integration is a hallmark of interdisciplinary education and research.

Produce a Cognitive Advancement or
More Comprehensive Understanding of the Problem

Interdisciplinary learning also develops a fifth cognitive ability: using integrated knowledge to produce what Boix Mansilla (2005) calls "a cognitive advancement," or what the research model presented in Chapter 3 calls "a more comprehensive understanding." A **cognitive advancement**, explains Boix Mansilla (2005), is the ability to explain a phenomenon, solve a problem, create a product, or raise a new question *"in ways that would have been unlikely through single disciplinary means* [italics added]" (p. 16). Interdisciplinary integration, she says, is a means to an end, not an end in itself. This "end" or result or product of integration is a "cognitive advancement" or a more comprehensive understanding (p. 16). How to construct this advancement or understanding is the focus of Chapter 13, and the core premises that underlie the concept of cognitive advancement are identified and explained in Chapter 14.

Reflection on What Interdisciplinary Education Offers

What interdisciplinary learning offers is a way "to harvest the depth of disciplinary knowledge while *also* moving dialectically across disciplines, noting areas of commonality, areas of difference, and providing a holistic framework for further analysis" (Henry, 2005, p. 13). It seeks to empower students by enabling them to bring together the multiple truth claims of disciplinary experts, acknowledge the contingency of their claims, and recognize the potential of integrating them in order to enhance understanding. Interdisciplinary learning also seeks to empower students by cultivating certain traits and skills that are essential for problem solving, decision making, and research.

Traits and Skills of Interdisciplinarians _____

Interdisciplinary studies is a systematic method of training one's mind and developing one's character. "The effect, if not the purpose, of interdisciplinarity is often nothing less than to alter the way we think about thinking" (Geertz, 1980, pp. 165–166). From the extensive literature on interdisciplinary studies, it is possible to identify no fewer than 15 traits and skills common to interdisciplinarians. Traits are distinguishing qualities of a person, whereas skills are cognitive abilities to use one's knowledge effectively and readily in performing a task.

Traits

Enterprise. The interdisciplinarian is like an entrepreneur in the sense that both are willing to see connections and possibilities that others do not see. And they are willing to assume risk in order to achieve the objective. The interdisciplinarian, like the entrepreneur, sees connections that disciplinarians do not see and the possibility of constructing more comprehensive understandings of complex problems. Cognitive psychologist Rainer Bromme (2000) compares crossing a disciplinary boundary to "moving about in foreign territory" (p. 116). Interdisciplinarians enjoy venturing into unfamiliar places and entertaining new ideas.

Love of Learning. Those drawn to interdisciplinary studies are intensely interested in the world they live in and welcome opportunities to view the world and its problems from differing perspectives (Trow, 1984, p. 15). Since interdisciplinarians often find themselves in new situations, they must also know how to learn and adapt. They need to know what information to ask for and how to acquire a working knowledge of the terminology, concepts, and analytical skills required to understand a given problem (Klein, 1990, p. 183).

Reflection. Learning is a process of cognitive and emotional transformation. Interdisciplinarians are interested in understanding the knowing process. Reflection occurs when students evaluate sources of information, demonstrate lines of reasoning from conflicting perspectives, evaluate complex problems or objects, discuss controversial issues, or justify an important decision. Reflection also occurs when students examine, perhaps in a reflective paper, their responses to an emotionally charged question (C. Myers & Haynes, 2002, pp. 191–192). Consequently, those engaged in interdisciplinary learning develop a strong self-concept (Bromme, 2000, pp. 116–118).

Tolerance for Ambiguity and Paradox in the Midst of Complexity. Interdisciplinarians accept ambiguity and paradox in the midst of complexity. They must be able to see all sides of an issue, reconcile conflicting perspectives by creating common ground among them, and live with ambiguity to the extent that reconciliation proves impossible (Bromme, 2000, pp. 116–118; Hursh et al., 1983, pp. 44–45). Ambiguity can be unsettling, especially for those who demand quick and clear-cut solutions to problems or have deeply held biases. But ambiguity is a fact of life. Real-world problems are often so complicated that it is impossible to know everything that one needs to know to understand them, let alone solve them. Interdisciplinarians accept that understanding any complex problem is an ongoing process, and that complete understanding of it is often elusive. Accepting that there is always something more to know keeps interdisciplinarians from becoming too settled in their understanding of a problem. They remain open to new perspectives and new insights.

Receptivity to Other Disciplines and to the Divergent Perspectives of Those Disciplines. **Receptivity to other disciplines** means being open to information from any and all relevant disciplinary perspectives. This, in turn, means being willing, even eager, to learn about divergent fields of knowledge, gaining both an intuitive and an intellectual grasp of them (Newell, 1992, p. 215). Receptivity to divergent perspectives means recognizing the possibility (or reality) of multiple causes, and being alert to unintended consequences, or to small changes that have large effects. Defined in this way, receptivity to divergent perspectives opens up the possibility of new understandings and surprising insights into complex problems. Receptivity to other disciplines and to their perspectives is essential to developing a more comprehensive understanding of any problem. Understanding a discipline's perspective involves not simply knowing what knowledge the discipline offers, but a willingness to deal with its perspective on its own terms, appreciating its assumptions, epistemology, concepts, theories, and methods (Armstrong, 1980, p. 54; Gunn, 1992, p. 239). In other words, the interdisciplinarian needs to be ready, willing, and able to walk in the shoes of the disciplinarian. Chapter 4 emphasizes the primary importance that interdisciplinarians attach to knowing the commonly used elements of the major disciplines in the sciences, the social sciences, and the humanities. But that knowing must be preceded by receptivity.

Willingness to Achieve "Adequacy" in Multiple Disciplines. Being receptive to multiple perspectives is one thing; successfully understanding them is another. The disciplines have each developed a daunting array of skills and knowledge, and at first glance it seems impossible to comprehend fully, let alone master, any one or two of them in a single lifetime. However, there is a difference between achieving mastery and achieving adequacy in a discipline. Disciplinary mastery means learning a discipline thoroughly in order to practice it, whereas **disciplinary adequacy** means merely comprehending how that discipline characteristically looks at the world in terms of its perspective, phenomena, epistemology, assumptions, concepts, theories, and methods (Klein, 1996, p. 212). The interdisciplinarian needs only to achieve adequacy, meaning knowing the discipline's defining elements and important insights relevant to the problem. How adequacy is achieved is the focus of Chapter 7. This knowledge allows one to have a basic "feel" for the discipline and an understanding of how it approaches the problem. Interdisciplinary learning develops the ability to know the limitations and biases of a discipline, to discover the benefits and perspectives of a discipline, and to understand how a discipline works simply by forcing us to see one discipline in light of another (Carlisle, 1995, p. 10).

Appreciation of Diversity. Appreciating diversity means, simply, having respect for people holding different views, or who are devoted to different faith traditions and different cultures, or who are of different ethnic or racial backgrounds. Interdisciplinarians, acutely aware of their own biases, acknowledge that different points of view are necessary to produce new understanding or new meaning (Newell, 1990, p. 71).

Willingness to Collaborate. Interdisciplinarity is often a collaborative process. No one person, no matter how thoroughly trained, will ever have a complete understanding of any given problem or issue. This includes the interdisciplinarian investigating it. The interdisciplinarian typically draws upon the insights of disciplinary experts. An expert inter-disciplinarian is one who is able to address an issue either by working alone or as part of a team. Willingness to work with others applies espe-cially to interdisciplinarians engaged in technical and scientific research that most commonly involves teamwork. Effective participation in inter-disciplinary teams is not so much a matter of individual traits as it is of learned behavior. People develop intellectual skills, such as dialectical and metaphorical thinking, and patterns of group communication skills that permit them to learn from and be taught by other members of the team (Newell, 1998, p. 551).

Humility. Humility is the one learned behavior that all scholars, including interdisciplinarians, surely need when faced with a problem that exposes the limits of one's training and expertise (Newell, 2001, p. 22). While disciplinarians can take comfort in knowing all there is to know about some sliver of reality that is their specialty, interdisciplinarians cannot hope to achieve this level of mastery of every facet of a complex problem. Instead of experiencing pride of mastery, the interdisciplinarian is hum-bled by knowing how much the relevant domains of knowledge do not know about the complex problem. Practitioners of interdisciplinary stud-ies bring to their craft a humility that comes from knowing what they do not know. Those involved in interdisciplinary investigations quickly dis-cover that they do not know and cannot know everything about the research question. But by using the interdisciplinary research process, they can at least move toward knowing more about the question than they would otherwise be able to learn using a purely disciplinary approach. "Through this process students discover the need for further learning, and they develop respect for different views" (Wentworth & Davis, 2002, p. 17). Interdisciplinarity, according to the Organisation for Economic Co-operation and Development (OECD), "is first and foremost a state of mind" (1972, p. 192).

Skills

Ability to Communicative Competently. Interdisciplinarity is a highly interactive field requiring **communicative competence**, which is the abil-ity to comprehend and translate terminology that is discipline-specific. Each discipline has not only its own set of skills and knowledge but also its own technical language that it uses to describe its assumptions, con-cepts, and theories. Though discipline-specific terminology is effective "shorthand" for experts to use to communicate with each other, it is often incomprehensible to those outside the discipline. This places an additional burden on the interdisciplinarian, who must grasp this terminology and make it accessible to others, regardless of their field of expertise (Klein, 1996, p. 217).

The variety of disciplinary perspectives involved in interdisciplinary research often necessitates the building and coordination of teams of individuals with different training and expertise. An interdisciplinarian must possess keen interpersonal relations skills and be able to engage in productive communication with people who hold a variety of interests, beliefs, and mind-sets, even if some of these sharply conflict.

Interdisciplinarity facilitates communication across disciplinary boundaries. This communication is possible because, despite the differences in jargon, there is overlap among the assumptions, concepts, theories, and methods used by the disciplines as well as underlying recurring patterns in both natural phenomena and human behavior that are perceived across disciplines. In many cases, each of the disciplines is saying something similar about the nature of the world, only in a different language.

Ability to Think Abstractly. **Abstract thinking** is a higher-order cognitive ability that enables one to understand and express an interdisciplinary understanding or meaning of a problem symbolically in terms of a metaphor, or to compare a hard to-understand and complex phenomenon to a symbol that is simple, familiar, and easy to understand. Abstract thinking is an essential skill for many professions and is particularly desirable for the interdisciplinarian, especially when working in the humanities. To achieve the objective of a more comprehensive understanding, the interdisciplinarian has the goal of integrating different disciplinary insights into the problem and, ideally, should be able to express this understanding or meaning symbolically such as using a metaphor. Abstract thinking is an important skill in the interdisciplinarian's toolbox. However, "abstract thinking represents '*an* end, not *the* end' of the thinking process" (Seabury, 2002, p. 47).

Ability to Think Dialectically. In many ways, dialectical thinking is the opposite of disciplinary thinking, but it is an important skill of the interdisciplinarian and a method that underlies interdisciplinary work. **Dialectical thinking** is the ability to view issues from multiple perspectives and to arrive at the most economical and reasonable reconciliation of seemingly contradictory information and positions. It is a method of determining the truth of any assertion by testing it against arguments that might negate it. Composition expert Anne Berthoff (1981) believes that there is a natural dialectic of the mind, "a dialectic of sorting and gathering, of particularizing and generalizing" (p. 105). Indeed, one writer goes so far as to state that dialectical thinking "is *the* underlying method of interdisciplinary work" (W. Davis, 1978). Rather than viewing differences, tension, and conflict as barriers that must be overcome, the interdisciplinarian views these as part of the integrative process.

Ability to Think Creatively. Interdisciplinarity requires creativity. The creative idea is a "combination of previously unrelated ideas, or looking at it another way, a new relationship among ideas" (G. A. Davis, 1992, p. 44). As applied to interdisciplinary work, **creativity** is a process that involves rethinking underlying premises, assumptions, or values, not just tracing out the implications of agreed-upon premises, assumptions, or values. Creativity involves iterative (i.e., repetitive) and heuristic (i.e., experimental) activity (Spooner, 2004, p. 93). Creating common ground among conflicting insights, for example, may well involve iterative and heuristic activity. The techniques and methods useful in creating or discovering common ground, engaging in integration, and producing an interdisciplinary outcome are identified in Part III.

Ability to Think Holistically. **Holistic thinking** involves thinking about the problem as part of a complete system. According to Irene J. Dabrowski (1995), "A holistic perception of reality—*seeing things whole*—requires interdisciplinary focus [italics added]" (p. 3). Aspects of holistic thinking include inclusiveness that accepts similarities as well as differences, comprehensiveness that balances disciplinary breadth and disciplinary depth (disciplinary specialties privilege depth over breadth), ability to associate ideas and information from several disciplines and connect these to the problem, creativity that is dissatisfied with the partial insights available through individual disciplinary specialties and that produces an interdisciplinary understanding, and metaphorical thinking that visually expresses the resultant integration.

Reflection on Traits and Skills of Interdisciplinarians

Some of these skills and traits, such as holistic thinking, typically receive greater emphasis in interdisciplinary contexts than in disciplinary contexts. These skills and traits are arguably desirable for anyone who wishes to lead a meaningful and productive life in any field of endeavor.

Chapter Summary

The drivers of interdisciplinary research and education are formidable and are unlikely to be reversed. What began as a fad in higher education has become a fixture of the modern academy. The interdisciplinary critique of the disciplines is based on seven problematic characteristics of the disciplines, but these limitations in no way justify abandoning them. An examination of the origins of interdisciplinarity and interdisciplinary studies shows that the historical curriculum of European and North American universities was a common core of undergraduate studies deeply rooted in the humanities and the ideals of the generalist model. By the late nineteenth century, however, the generalist model was challenged by a combination of cultural, economic, and educational factors that led ultimately to the modern system of disciplinarity. The negative impacts of knowledge fragmentation, in turn, led to calls for reform of the general education curriculum at the end of both world wars and the rediscovery of interdisciplinarity. The social and political upheavals of the 1960s led to a concerted effort to inject interdisciplinarity into academic culture beyond the confines of general education through the establishment of interdisciplinary courses and programs. This effort continued, though with less intensity, into the 1980s and 1990s. By the turn of the new millennium, the increasing importance of interdisciplinarity was established, and there is now far more agreement on what interdisciplinarity is, what it assumes, and why it is needed. Students are benefiting from the traits and skills inherent in interdisciplinarity research and learning. The commonality undergirding these developments is the growing recognition of the importance of integration to interdisciplinary studies and its ability to produce new knowledge. The integrative process draws on the disciplines and their insights to address problems and questions that require an interdisciplinary approach. This approach is the core feature of the interdisciplinary research model, which is the subject of Chapter 3.

Notes

1. Klein draws from the seminal report *Interdisciplinarity: Problems of Teaching and Research in Universities* resulting from the seminar organized by the Centre for Educational Research and Innovation (CERI) and issued in 1972 by the Organisation for Economic Co-operation and Development (OECD), pp. 44–45.

2. For a more detailed discussion of science and funding priorities for research, see Stuart Henry (2005), "Disciplinary Hegemony Meets Interdisciplinary Ascendancy: Can Interdisciplinary/Integrative Studies Survive and If So, How?" *Issues in Integrative Studies, 23,* pp. 13–15.

3. Source: Harcourt: Excerpt from THE LITTLE PRINCE by Antoine de Saint-Exupery, copyright 1943 by Harcourt, Inc. and renewed 1971 by Consuelo de Saint-Exupery, English translation copyright © 2000 by Richard Howard, reprinted by permission of Houghton Mifflin Harcourt Publishing Company. Egmont: From *The Little Prince* by Antoine de Saint Exupery © Editions Gallimard 1943 and 1971. English translation © 2000 Richard Howard. Published by Egmont UK Ltd London and used with permission.

4. According to Rick Szostak (personal communication, January 2, 2011), the economic methodologist Thomas Mayer has long criticized economists for this. He notes that if A causes B, which in turn causes C, and economists understand how A causes B only, they will just assume that B affects C in the desired manner.

5. Examples of interdisciplinary breakthroughs may be found in R. S. Root-Bernstein and M. Root-Bernstein (1999), *Sparks of Genius: The 23 Thinking Tools of the World's Most Creative People.*

6. Szostak (2007b) adds, "Interdisciplinarians can, do, and should debate just how partial and biased disciplinary insights are and just how optimistic one should be about the possibility of enhanced scholarly understanding" (p. 34).

Exercises

Trends in Education and Research

2.1   Authoritative voices inside and outside the academy have identified several drivers of interdisciplinary education and research. Concerning the profession or academic program you plan to enter, what aspects of it are being impacted by this powerful trend?

Silos

2.2   Consider this situation: A government program was launched to solve a particular social problem. It was well funded and professionally staffed. However, the program produced unintended consequences and ultimately failed to solve the problem it was designed to remedy because it approached it with a silo perspective. Identify a situation with which you are familiar in which a government agency (at any level) attempted to solve a problem but failed because it approached the problem with a silo perspective. How can silo perspectives be identified and corrected in large organizations?

2.3   Why does the development of generative technologies typically require crossing disciplinary domains?

Successful Intelligence

2.4   How does interdisciplinary education foster the development of what Sternberg calls "successful intelligence"? How might interdisciplinary education be improved in this regard?

Privileged Status

2.5   The chapter has made the case for reducing our dependence on disciplinary modes of knowledge production. How is the process of knowledge production inside and outside the academy already challenging the privileged status of the disciplines?

Fundamental Change

2.6   The origin of the university, the development of disciplines, and the emergence of interdisciplinarity are among the most significant developments in human history because they concern how knowledge is produced, applied, and passed on to succeeding generations. What fundamental changes are now at work that are transforming knowledge production, application, and transmittal?

Assumptions

2.7   How are the assumptions of interdisciplinarity reflective of the contemporary human condition?

Decentering

2.8   Consider the profession you plan to enter. How might your ability to engage in cognitive decentering be an asset when dealing with difficult people or a complex situation?

Cognitive Abilities

2.9   Reflect on the discussion of the five cognitive abilities fostered by interdisciplinarity. How might these abilities transform the way you approach problem solving and decision making?

Inventory

2.10 Of the several traits and skills that are associated with interdisciplinary education, which of these do you currently possess?

PART II

Drawing on Disciplinary Insights

3

Beginning the Research Process

_____ **Chapter Preview**

Today there is a vast array of different types of interdisciplinarity being
practiced in the United States, Canada, Europe, and Australia. This reality
prompts this question: Does it make sense to speak of one interdisciplinary
research process? The answer that this chapter and this book provide is this:
Different types of interdisciplinarity can be seen as representing different
choices within an overarching research process. The first section of this
chapter explains what the interdisciplinary research process is, presents the
interdisciplinary research model, and explains its defining characteristics.
The second section introduces the first two "STEPS" or decision points that
the model calls for: Define the problem or state the research question (STEP 1),
and justify using an interdisciplinary approach (STEP 2).

What the Interdisciplinary
Research Process Is

Interdisciplinary research is a decision-making process that is heuristic,
iterative, and reflexive. Each of these terms—*decision making, process,
heuristic, iterative,* and *reflexive*—requires explanation.

A Process of Decision Making

Decision making, a uniquely human activity, is the cognitive ability to choose
after considering alternatives. Decision making is complicated by the prevalence of complex problems in our personal lives, in business, in society as a
whole, and in the international realm. Interdisciplinarity focuses on complex
problems, questions, objects, texts, and systems. A characteristic of these is
that there are many variables involved, each of which may be studied by a
different discipline, subdiscipline, interdiscipline, or school of thought. The
interdisciplinary research process (IRP) is a practical and demonstrated way

to make decisions about how to approach these problems, decide which ones are appropriate for interdisciplinary inquiry, and construct comprehensive understandings of them (Newell, 2007a, p. 247).

A Decision-Making Process

Doing interdisciplinary research, whether performed individually or collaboratively, is characterized by Newell (2007a) as a decision-making process (p. 246). The term **process** means following a procedure or strategy, in this case one that involves integration. Process also entails moment-to-moment interactions as well as interactions over the course of the project (Seabury, 2004, p. 63). The interdisciplinary research process is indeed special compared to the research methods employed by the disciplines because the goal of integration is at the very core of interdisciplinary activity, whereas it is not at the core of disciplinary activity. Disciplinary methodologies usually favor one or a very few theories and methods, whereas interdisciplinarians integrate across these (which involves deciding how much to heed insights from any theory or method). The interdisciplinary research process, then, involves a series of decisions that make possible integration and the construction of a more comprehensive understanding.

A Decision-Making Process That Is Heuristic

A **heuristic** is an aid to understanding or discovery or learning. The heuristic method places the student in the role of the discoverer of knowledge. The student finds how to solve the problem individually or in groups rather than being told about the solution to the problem (Lyman, 1997, p. 304). Hursh, Haas, and Moore (1983) state, "The process of searching, more than the process of finding, is exceedingly important in stimulating cognitive development" (p. 54).

The IRP is heuristic in that it provides a way to understand a problem that otherwise would be impossible using a disciplinary or multidisciplinary approach. The process aids discovery by introducing multiple decision points or STEPS.[1] These provide occasions for students to learn using experimentation or trial and error. The process by which integration is achieved necessitates a two-level approach. The first level focuses on the disciplines and how they approach the topic from their particular perspectives. The second level focuses on integrating the different disciplinary insights (Hursh et al., 1983, pp. 52–53). This two-level approach is used in this book.

In a research process that features decision making and STEP taking, the process is by no means linear, wherein the research proceeds mechanically along a straight, upward-sloping line to the goal. That is, the process is not a simple matter of moving from point "A" to point "B" to point "C" and on to the end. Rather, when the researcher gets to point "B," point "A" may need to be revisited and revised. In fact, revising work performed under earlier STEPS is likely to happen at any given point in the process. The process, for example, of selecting the most relevant disciplines (STEP 3; see Chapter 5) may lead to reformulating the problem identified in STEP 1. The cursory literature search actually begins during STEP 1 and continues over the next STEPS until the full-scale search is completed in STEP 4 (see Chapter 6). As Klein (1990) notes, there is no formula for doing interdisciplinary work (p. 73). Throughout the research process, the researcher should expect to revisit earlier work.

A Decision-Making Process That Is Iterative

The IRP is iterative or procedurally repetitive. Its STEPS or procedures involve repetition of a sequence of operations yielding results successively closer to the desired outcome. For example, one of these procedures, STEP 5 (see Chapter 7), concerns developing adequacy in each of the relevant disciplines. Typically, the procedure used to develop adequacy in one relevant discipline will apply to the other relevant disciplines.

A Decision-Making Process That Is Reflexive

The IRP is also reflexive. This means being self-conscious or self-aware of disciplinary or personal bias that may influence one's work and possibly skew the evaluation of insights and thus the end product. As decisions are made about which insights to use and which to discard, researchers must avoid the temptation to eliminate a perspective or theoretical approach that is unfamiliar to them or that challenges their beliefs. Throughout the research process, the process of challenging one's work must occur. A systematic reexamination process provides the "warning device" that some important information or idea was omitted during the early phases of the project (Hursh et al., 1983, p. 55).

Two Additional Characteristics of the IRP

Two additional characteristics of the IRP warrant comment. For one thing, it requires an act of "creative imagination" (Newell, 1990, p. 74). While researchers must have some grasp of the defining elements of relevant disciplines (introduced in Chapter 4), they must also exercise imagination and creativity to perform several of the STEPS in the process. The term STEP is used to clarify the point of decision or operation that one would normally take in almost any interdisciplinary research project and to differentiate a particular decision or operation from others. Those working in the "softer" social sciences and in the humanities will no doubt wish to stress the elements of creativity, intuition, and art in the research process, more than STEPS. Nevertheless, the IRP, and especially the integrative part of that process (described in Part III), involves intuition *and* method, creativity *and* process, art *and* strategic decision making.

Second, the IRP is very student-friendly. Practitioners in several nations are successfully teaching the material in this book. Students who apply themselves will master this important and new way of approaching complex problems and framing new and creative solutions to them. If some find interdisciplinary research "a tall order," it is probably because so much academic learning is rote learning. This is learning that occurs when the learner memorizes new information without relating it to prior knowledge or understanding the theory underlying it. Rote learning involves no attempt to integrate new knowledge with existing concepts, experience, or objects (Novak, 1998, pp. 19–20). The Western approach to education is so focused on analysis, reductionism, and duality that we lack guides to integration and holism. Consequently, few are prepared to integrate knowledge that requires developing disciplinary depth and breadth (Klein, 1996, p. 212).

In the end, each interdisciplinary research project presents a unique combination of challenges and opportunities. The many examples of professional work and exemplary student projects threaded throughout this book clearly show that there is no one way to do interdisciplinary work. This is not to say that the process is haphazard. Interdisciplinary research has in common with all disciplinary research an overall plan or approach. Reduced to its simplest terms, all research has these three steps in common: (1) The problem is recognized as needing research, (2) the problem is approached using a research strategy, and (3) the problem is solved or at least a tentative solution is devised. Each discipline has developed its own methods and preferred research strategy, as noted in Chapter 4. Likewise, interdisciplinary studies has developed a research process that differs in important respects from disciplinary methods *and subsumes them,* as shown in Figure 3.1. The critical

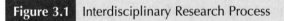

Figure 3.1   Interdisciplinary Research Process

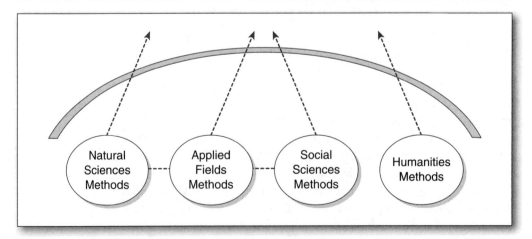

NOTE: The dotted lines connecting the applied fields to the natural sciences and the social sciences show that the applied fields (such as education, criminal justice, communication, law, and business) use research methods drawn from these other disciplinary categories.

differences between interdisciplinary and disciplinary approaches to research are noted along the way.

The IRP is an overarching research process (noted by the arching line) that draws on disciplinary methods (see Tables 4.13, 4.14, and 4.15) that are appropriate to investigating the problem.

An Integrated Model of the IRP

Interdisciplinarians generally agree on the need to specify, at least to some extent, how to draw on disciplinary expertise and, especially, how to integrate disciplinary insights and theories. Those who oppose any greater specificity in research methodology do so reasoning that it might constrain freedom of activity, stifle creativity, or prevent interdisciplinarity from functioning as the antidote to restrictive disciplinary perspectives (Szostak, 2012, p. 4). What these critics overlook is that all research, including interdisciplinary research, uses some method or strategy to approach a problem. Yet, while disciplinary methodologies generally involve a preference for certain theories, methods, and phenomena, the IRP encourages researchers to cast their gaze across *all* relevant theories, methods, phenomena, and insights. The IRP in its most simplified form is shown in Figure 3.2.

Though helpful, Figure 3.2 lacks the detail necessary to proceed from the problem to the understanding. The integrated model of the interdisciplinary research process presented in Table 3.1 describes a proven approach to conducting interdisciplinary research, finding new meaning, and creating new knowledge.

Figure 3.2 From Problem to Understanding

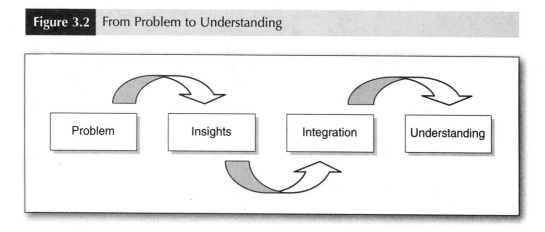

The Benefits of a Map

When driving to an unfamiliar place far from home, a map is essential to avoid unproductive and time-wasting detours. The model of the IRP is like

Table 3.1	An Integrated Model of the Interdisciplinary Research Process (IRP)

A. Drawing on disciplinary insights[a]
1. Define the problem or state the research question
2. Justify using an interdisciplinary approach
3. Identify relevant disciplines
4. Conduct the literature search
5. Develop adequacy in each relevant discipline
6. Analyze the problem and evaluate each insight or theory
B. Integrating disciplinary insights
7. Identify conflicts between insights or theories and their sources
8. Create common ground between concepts and theories
9. Construct a more comprehensive understanding
10. Reflect on, test, and communicate the understanding

SOURCE: Repko (2006, p. 123).

a. The term "disciplinary insights" includes insights from disciplines, subdisciplines, interdisciplines, and schools of thought.

a map in that it provides clear routes on how to journey from a familiar place (the problem) to one that is foreign (the understanding). Furthermore, neither freedom nor creativity is compromised by providing some structure and direction to the research process. In particular, the process encourages inter-disciplinarians to critically engage all relevant theories, methods, phenomena, and disciplines. To this end, Table 3.1 offers a procedural model that integrates the prominent models of the IRP.[2]

While the various research models on which the integrated model is based differ in the number, description, and order of some STEPS, they agree on the need to perform certain essential tasks and make certain critical decisions about how to prepare for integration and then to perform it. Subsequent chapters explain each STEP and provide examples of how the model is being used by students and practitioners.

Cautions Concerning These STEPS

Before describing these STEPS in detail, several cautionary words are in order. First, dividing what is essentially a fluid process into discrete STEPS gives the misleading but unavoidable impression that these STEPS do not overlap. They often do. For example, some researchers begin conducting the full-scale literature search (shown as STEP 4; see Chapter 6) as soon as STEP 1, while others continue the search while performing later STEPS. It is good to consider STEP 4 as a fluid process within the overall research process, especially in its early phases.

Second, numbering the STEPS implies a unidirectional sequence, but this is not the true nature of the IRP. Researchers rely on **nonlinear thinking** to approach a problem creatively, thinking about it "outside the box" without being influenced by solutions attempted in the past and viewing it from different perspectives. The process depicted in Figure 3.2 is much more like an array of **feedback loops** (that require the researcher to periodically revisit earlier activity) than a ladder. **Feedback** is corrective information about a decision, an operation, an event, or a problem that compels the researcher to revisit an earlier phase of the project. This corrective information typically comes from previously overlooked scholarship. Researchers must be careful to recognize the existence of feedback as they perform these various STEPS. Significantly, the integrated model emphasizes the **nonlinearity** of the process, such that along the way the researcher should reflect on, and may need to revisit, or even revise, earlier work. The researcher should periodically ask questions such as the following:

- Have I defined the problem or the question too broadly or too narrowly?
- Have I correctly identified the parts of the problem?
- Have I identified the disciplines most relevant to the problem?
- Have I gathered the most important insights concerning the problem?
- Am I privileging one discipline's literature or terminology over another's simply because I am more comfortable working in the discipline?
- Have I allowed my personal bias to shape the direction of the study?

Third, there is the temptation to avoid difficult STEPS and leap ahead to later STEPS. By keeping in mind the STEPS of the model, researchers are more likely to realize that they have skipped over an important STEP and need to return to complete it. Since each STEP typically requires the completion of previous STEPS, it is important to regularly reexamine the work done in earlier STEPS. For example, one might be tempted not to spend much time developing adequacy in the disciplines relevant to the problem (STEP 5; see Chapter 7) and proceed with analyzing the problem and evaluating disciplinary insights into it (STEP 6; see Chapter 8). This impatience to "get on with the project" can prove costly, however. Unless one knows what specific information to look for when developing adequacy—the discipline's relevant concepts, assumptions, theories, and methods—the time and effort invested may fail to yield the quality information that is needed to perform later STEPS. Ultimately, one has to develop adequacy in each relevant discipline before reading and comprehending the discipline's insights profitably. Avoiding difficult STEPS and decisions will make the task of modifying insights and then integrating them problematic.

Fourth, describing the IRP in terms of STEPS may give the impression that each relevant discipline is "mined separately for nuggets of insights before any integration takes place, and that when integration occurs, it happens all at once" (Newell, 2007a, pp. 248–249). Nothing could be further from actual practice. Researchers should partially integrate as they go, meaning that they should incorporate disciplinary insights or theories into a broader understanding of the problem as they proceed (Newell, 2007a, p. 249).

Step 1: Define the Problem or State the Research Question

Defining the problem or stating the research question is the first and most basic activity that one undertakes in conducting research or engaging in problem solving of any kind. This initial STEP involves making these decisions:

- Select a problem or pose a question that is complex and requires insights from more than one discipline.
- Define the scope of the problem or question.
- Avoid three tendencies that run counter to the IRP.
- Follow three guidelines for stating the problem or posing the question.

Select a Problem or Pose a Question That Is Complex and Requires Insights From More Than One Discipline

A problem is ripe for interdisciplinary study and *researchable in an interdisciplinary sense* when

- it is complex (i.e., requires insights from more than one discipline), and
- it is the focus of two or more disciplines (i.e., authors from at least two disciplines have written on the topic or at least on some aspect of it).

For researchers who may have trouble telling *in advance* if a problem is complex, a useful *initial test* is to ask if there is more than one legitimate way to look at the problem and, if so, if different disciplines would likely be interested in it. (A more detailed discussion of complexity as a criterion for interdisciplinary inquiry follows.)

To decide with confidence if a problem is ripe for interdisciplinary study requires adequacy in the relevant disciplines (the subject of Chapter 7). For undergraduate and some graduate students, adequacy means that they have taken courses in the major contributing disciplines. Solo interdisciplinarians and some graduate students may be able to acquire adequacy in one or two major contributing disciplines that they have not formally studied. For team interdisciplinarians, the question devolves into a question about the feasible composition of the team.

A problem may be complex but for some reason have failed to generate scholarly interest outside a particular discipline. Such is the case with the problem "The Effects of Physician Shortages on Society." The problem is complex and is certainly important to society. But for whatever reason, it has failed to attract much scholarly attention outside the field of medicine (though it is a subject of discussion in multiple arenas that draw on economic, sociological, political, and demographic perspectives). The discovery of such gaps in research opens the door to potentially fruitful interdisciplinary inquiry.

Frequently, the research problem that we would *like* to investigate cannot be the problem that we *can* investigate because the cursory literature search has failed to reveal relevant insights from two or more disciplines on the problem. Consequently, we must revise the problem, question, or topic based on material that the search has revealed.

Define the Scope of the Problem or Question

Once the topic or problem has been identified, the next decision is to define its scope. The scope refers to the parameters of what is included and excluded from consideration. In other words, how much of this problem will be investigated? What are the limits of the investigation? For example, if the problem being addressed is repeat spousal battery, how will this be approached? Will the focus be on the *causes* of repeat spousal battery or the *prevention* of repeat spousal battery? Will it be on the *treatment* of the perpetrator and/or the victim of spousal battery? Or will it be on the *effects* of repeat spousal battery on a particular demographic, say the children? Though all these options are clearly related to the overall problem of repeat spousal battery, narrowing the scope of the problem at the outset, to the extent possible, will facilitate the literature search and provide focus to subsequent STEPS in the research process. The extremes to be avoided are conceiving the problem too broadly so that it is unmanageable, and conceiving the problem too narrowly so that it is not interdisciplinary or researchable.

Two criteria for developing a good interdisciplinary question for students at any level include the following:

1. It must be open-ended and too complex to be addressed by one discipline alone.

2. It must be *researchable in an interdisciplinary sense* meaning that authors from at least two disciplines have written on the topic or at least on some aspect of it (C. Myers & Haynes, 2002, p. 186).

Subsequent STEPS in the research process may require revisiting the statement of the problem or focus question and modifying it in some way. Here is an example of a student transitioning from the very broad topic of ways to prevent domestic violence to a narrower and more focused interdisciplinary statement of the problem:

> The problem of domestic violence is broad, and developing strategies to prevent one of its most insidious manifestations—repeat spousal battery—is a pressing social need. Whereas single disciplinary approaches focus on only a single aspect of repeat spousal battery, an interdisciplinary approach that takes into account all aspects of the problem will hopefully lead to interventions that will mitigate this social scourge.

This transition from broad to narrow was possible after the student had read more widely about the topic of domestic violence and had begun to understand its complexity. This statement, which appeared in the student's introductory paragraph, was the product of several iterations, each of which was made after the student had taken additional STEPS in the IRP.

Avoid Three Tendencies That Run Counter to the IRP

In defining the problem or stating the research question, three tendencies should be avoided that may be acceptable in some academic settings but run counter to the IRP: disciplinary bias, disciplinary jargon, and personal bias.

Disciplinary Bias

The statement of the problem should be free of **disciplinary bias**, using words and phrases that connect the problem to a particular discipline. For example, the problem statement "The Responsibility of Public Education for Sex Education" is biased in favor of education. Stating the problem in *discipline-neutral* terms makes it easier to justify using an interdisciplinary approach. To remove the disciplinary bias in the above example, the problem could be worded like this: "Sex Education in Public Education: An Interdisciplinary Analysis." Adding "An Interdisciplinary Analysis" alerts the reader that the problem is approached from multiple disciplinary perspectives, not just the perspective of education. The exception to this "rule" is when the disciplines involved are so closely related that there is no need for a neutral vocabulary (Wolfe & Haynes, 2003, p. 155).

Disciplinary Jargon

The statement of the problem should be free of **disciplinary jargon**, using technical terms and concepts that are not generally understood outside the discipline. If a technical term or concept must be used in the statement introducing the problem, then it must be defined in the next sentence or two. *A rule* *of thumb is to assume that the reader is unfamiliar with a technical term or concept.* Here is an example of a statement that introduces a problem that is appropriate to interdisciplinary inquiry but contains disciplinary jargon: "The recidivism of domestic batterers is a significant problem in the United States because of the short-term and long-term psychological effects on the victim." This statement of the problem contains three technical terms that are probably unfamiliar to most readers and that require definition: *recidivism, domestic batterers,* and *psychological effects.* (If the researcher wants to limit the investigation to "psychological effects on the victim," then a simple disciplinary approach will do. Otherwise, the statement should omit the term *psychological* to expand the search to other disciplines. Researchers must learn what terms mean and factor them into the interdisciplinary frameworks they construct.[3]) Even disciplinary experts working on interdisciplinary research teams must first develop a common vocabulary before the work of research can begin.

The following are student-written examples of discipline-neutral statements introducing a problem that involves multiple disciplines:

- "Euthanasia is the intentional killing by act or omission of a dependent human being for his or her alleged benefit, be it voluntary or involuntary. The controversy over euthanasia was rekindled in the 1993 case of *Sue Rodriguez v. British Columbia (Attorney General),* which involved a woman in her forties who was suffering from Lou Gehrig's disease and who wanted to choose the time and manner of her inevitable death." From this wording, the reader can readily discern that the three disciplines deemed by the student as most relevant to the problem of euthanasia are ethics, medicine, and law.
- "Recent ACT scores show that a growing number of students are failing to grasp basic scientific knowledge. Science and technology play an integral role in modern society. Without scientifically and technically trained students, there will be a shortage of trained professionals in critical fields such as medicine, biology, engineering, and information technology. Even fields that are not normally thought of as scientific, including business, agriculture, journalism, and sociology, now rely heavily on science and technology." The disciplines that the student found to be most relevant to this topic are biology, psychology, and education.

The statement of an interdisciplinary problem should not privilege any one discipline. Using (perhaps unconsciously) disciplinary jargon or terminology unique to a discipline tacitly favors one disciplinary perspective at the expense of another.

Personal Bias

A third tendency is to inject one's **personal bias,** or point of view, when introducing the problem. While stating a personal opinion before comprehending the research and arguing a point of view selected in advance are appropriate in many academic contexts, they are not appropriate in most interdisciplinary contexts where the goal is quite different: to construct a more comprehensive understanding that includes all (or as many as possible) relevant viewpoints. The trap that some researchers fall into is to marshal evidence from various disciplines to support their personal bias before they identify and evaluate the important perspectives on the problem. Unwittingly, they are simply adding their personal bias to the biased insights of disciplinary authors.

We note the bias in this student's introduction of the problem: "Taxpayer dollars should not be used to finance sports complexes for professional teams." The student obviously believes this and would prefer to write a paper advancing this point of view. However, the interdisciplinarian is not to play the role of prosecuting attorney or defense counsel for the accused. *The role of the interdisciplinarian is to produce an understanding of the problem that is more comprehensive and more inclusive than the narrow and skewed understandings that the disciplines have produced.* This calls for approaching the problem with a frame of mind that is decidedly different from that of the disciplinarian. This frame of mind is one of neutrality (or at least suspended judgment) and objectivity until all the evidence is in. This means openness to different disciplinary insights and theories, even if these challenge one's deeply held beliefs. A defining characteristic of interdisciplinary work should be to mitigate conflict by finding common ground among conflicting perspectives, including one's own.

Follow Three Guidelines for Stating the Problem or Posing the Question

If a problem appears suitable for interdisciplinary inquiry, it should be phrased in conformity to these important guidelines:

- *The problem should be stated clearly and concisely.* This statement demonstrates lack of clarity: "The majority of complaints registered by the Childcare Licensing Agency (CLA) concern unsafe child care facilities." It is unclear what the focus of the investigation is: the complaints (whether or not they are valid), lack of enforcement of safety regulations by the CLA, lack of funding of the CLA by the federal government, or lack of legislation that establishes strict enforcement procedures. Sometimes greater clarity can be achieved by stating the problem as a question.
- *The problem or focus question should be sufficiently narrow to be manageable within the specified limits of the essay.* The problem of "Securing the Southern Border of the United States" was too broad for an essay requiring only three disciplinary perspectives. Upon discovering that the literature on border security was vast, the student narrowed the

problem to the more manageable one of "Perspectives on Securing the Southern Border of the United States Against Human Smuggling: An Interdisciplinary Study."

- *The problem should appear in a context (preferably in the first paragraph of the introduction) that explains why it is important—that is, why the reader should care.* The following introduction places the problem of wife battery in a context that not only engages the reader but, more important, indicates why the problem warrants the reader's interest:

Wife battery is a widespread and growing problem in the United States. It is urgent that a solution be found because of its devastating effects on the victim, including debilitating depression and redirected violence against her children. The wife's extended family and associates also feel the effects of her physical and emotional pain. Most tragically, studies show that children who grow up in abusive homes tend to be abusive to their own children, thus perpetuating a vicious cycle of violence.

Examples of Statements of an Interdisciplinary Problem or Question

The following are examples from published work and student projects of well-written statements introducing the problem that illustrate the above criteria. The student projects are identified by an asterisk (*).

From the Natural Sciences: Dietrich (1995), Northwest Passage: The Great Columbia River

William Dietrich introduces the problem of how dams on the Columbia River system in the Northwest are impacting the salmon populations and the people who depend on them for their livelihood:

To a Pacific Northwest journalist such as myself, the river was inescapable as a subject. Its energy powered the region and its history dictated the region's history. . . . Many of the people I encountered, however, looked at the river from the narrow perspective of their own experience. One colleague said it was as if everyone was looking at the Columbia River through a pipe. . . . Each interest group looked at the Columbia and saw a different river.

That experience dictated the approach of this book. One of the mistakes of the past . . . has been the tendency to focus narrowly on development of some part of a river without considering the consequences for the whole. "When we [whites] are confronted by a complex problem, we want to take a part of the complexity and deal with that," remarked Steve Parker, a fish biologist hired by the Yakima Indian tribe.

The Henry Ford assembly line is an example of this kind of specialization, Parker said. Its economic success is why narrow focus and admiration of specialists became ingrained in American culture. (pp. 23–24)

From the Natural Sciences: Smolinski* (2005), Freshwater Scarcity in Texas

Joe Smolinski introduces the problem of freshwater scarcity in Texas in this clearly written introductory paragraph:

> There is little doubt among experts that freshwater is one of the most valuable natural resources in the state of Texas. Experts, in a variety of disciplines, have not yet been able to reach agreement as to the cause and effect of the widespread freshwater shortages currently experienced across the state. With population predictions calling for a dramatic increase in the number of residents over the next fifty years, the competition between these uses will only become more intense. How we address the use and allocation of water will have a dramatic impact on the environment and the quality of life for all Texans. (p. 1)

From the Social Sciences: Fischer (1988), "On the Need for Integrating Occupational Sex Discrimination Theory on the Basis of Causal Variables"

Charles C. Fischer introduces the problem of occupational sex discrimination (OSD) in the workplace as follows:

> The majority of complaints filed with the Equal Employment Opportunity Commission under Title VII of the Civil Rights Act involve sex discrimination. Complaints of sex discrimination pertain mainly to pay discrimination, promotion (and transfer) discrimination, and occupation discrimination. Occupational sex discrimination (OSD) is particularly serious since other forms of sex discrimination are, to a large degree, symptomatic of a lack of female access to "male" occupations— those occupations that pay good wages, that are connected to long job ladders (that provide opportunities for vertical mobility via job promotion), and that offer positions of responsibility. (p. 22)

From the Social Sciences: Delph* (2005), An Integrative Approach to the Elimination of the "Perfect Crime"

Janet B. Delph introduces the growing problem of unsolved homicides, which she calls "perfect crimes," in these stark terms:

> Modern day criminal investigation techniques do not eliminate the possibility of the "perfect crime." . . . A "perfect crime" is one that will go unnoticed and/or for which the criminal will never be caught

(Fanton, Tolhet, & Achache, 1998). The public is all too aware of these likely outcomes and consequently feels unsafe and vulnerable. Parents experience silent fear each time their child wanders beyond their reach. While "men are afraid women will laugh at them, women are afraid that men will kill them" (DeBecker, 1997, p. 77). Deviant minds should not be allowed to think that they can commit murder without suffering the gravest consequences. (p. 2)

From the Humanities: Bal (1999), "Introduction,"
The Practice of Cultural Analysis: Exposing
Interdisciplinary Interpretation

Mieke Bal's introduction serves two purposes. The first is to decipher the complex meaning of the object she is subjecting to interdisciplinary scrutiny: an enigmatic love note or letter written in yellow paint on a red brick wall (e.g., a graffito) in post–World War II Amsterdam, the Netherlands. The second and closely related purpose is to introduce the reader to the interdisciplinary process of cultural analysis, of which she is a leading practitioner, and illustrate its ability to reveal new meaning in an object or a text like the graffito.

> Cultural analysis as a critical practice is different from what is commonly understood as "history." It is based on a keen awareness of the critic's situatedness in the present, the social and cultural present from which we look, and look back, at the objects that are already of the past, objects that we take to define our present culture. . . .
>
> This graffito, for example, has come to characterize the goals of the Amsterdam School for Cultural Analysis (ASCA). . . . In the most literal translation the text means:
>
>> Note
>> I hold you dear
>> I have not
>> thought you up
>
> This graffito fulfills that function because it makes a good case for the kind of objects at which cultural analysis would look, and—more importantly—how it can go about doing so. (pp. 1–2)

From the Humanities: Silver (2005),* Composing Race
and Gender: The Appropriation of Social Identity in Fiction

Lisa Silver writes an informal personal narrative of how she became interested in her subject, the appropriation of social identity in fiction writing. Her story begins with her trip to Mexico during spring break of her junior year. When she returned, she had a story due in her creative writing class, so she tried writing about the people she met in the mountain villages in Oaxaca, Mexico.

And that's when the interdisciplinarity kicked in. . . . In Mexico we learned it would be offensive for us, as outsiders, to assume we could fix their problems. What could we, carrying our Nalgene bottles, comprehend of the effects of water privatization and pollution? How could we listen to the plight of maquiladora workers while wearing Nikes and stonewashed jeans? How could I understand the lives of the indigenous Oaxacan villagers enough to write about them—especially from their own points of view? I couldn't separate the sociological and political lessons I'd learned in Mexico from my fiction. I ended up writing my story from the first-person peripheral perspective of a white college-aged female looking in at the village. I got good critiques in class, but was never personally satisfied with the story. It felt like I'd written a nonfiction piece. I wanted to create characters with backgrounds unlike my own, but suddenly didn't know how. (p. 2)

Note to Readers

All of these examples conform to the above criteria: They are *appropriate* to interdisciplinary inquiry, they carefully *define* the scope of the problem, and they *avoid the three tendencies* that run counter to the interdisciplinary process: disciplinary bias, disciplinary jargon, and personal bias. They also *follow the three guidelines* for introducing the problem: The problems are stated clearly and concisely, are sufficiently narrow in scope to be manageable (depending on the scale of the writer's project), and appear in a context that explains why the problem should interest the reader.

As further STEPS are taken, students are likely to encounter new information, receive new insights (including intuitive flashes), or encounter unforeseen problems that will require revisiting the initial STEP and modifying the topic. This is a normal part of the research process, especially for interdisciplinary work.

Step 2: Justify Using an Interdisciplinary Approach

Not every problem or question is ripe for interdisciplinary inquiry. There are four criteria commonly used to justify using an interdisciplinary approach:

- The problem or question is complex.
- Important insights or theories of the problem are offered by two or more disciplines.
- No single discipline has been able to address the problem comprehensively or resolve it.
- The problem is an unresolved societal need or issue (National Academies, 2005, pp. 30–35).

The Problem or Question Is Complex

There are multiple but narrowing definitions of complexity. As commonly understood, complexity refers to interactions among multiple variables. Complexity also refers to the behavior of systems. A **system** is any group of interacting components or agents around which there is a clearly defined boundary between it and the rest of the world, but also clearly definable inputs from the world and outputs to the world that cross the boundary (Boyd, 2006, p. 27). (Note: This definition refers to systems in general, but says nothing about the *distinctive characteristics* of systems that are complex. A problem or question is complex when it is composed of multiple components or agents connected through nonlinear as well as linear relationships. Also, a complex system has positive as well as negative feedback loops. The nonlinear relationships and positive feedback loops produce unanticipated consequences to the overall pattern of behavior that is only partly predictable and stable.) *As applied to interdisciplinary research,* complexity *means that the problem has multiple components studied by different disciplines.*

Complexity is a keyword in contemporary descriptions of interdisciplinarity. The definition of interdisciplinary studies appearing in Chapter 1 states that *complexity requires interdisciplinarity.* We know of no way other than interdisciplinarity to study specific complex problems such as global warming, freshwater scarcity, and terrorism. That is, *interdisciplinarity is necessary for the study of complexity.* If the problem is not complex, then it may just as well be investigated in a multidisciplinary manner by merely adding disciplinary insights (Newell, 2001, p. 2). The criterion of complexity also extends to problems that those in the humanities typically examine, such as the contextual meaning of an object or a text.[4]

Examples of complex questions include these: What is consciousness? What is freedom? What is a family? What does it mean to be human? Why does hunger persist? Admittedly, these problems are so fundamental and complex, requiring sophisticated analysis from so many disciplines, that they are beyond the capacity of most undergraduates to address comprehensively. Nevertheless, movement toward a more comprehensive understanding of these questions is possible even if students (most likely undergraduates) are limited to using only a few relevant disciplines.

Confirmation of complexity will be forthcoming as additional STEPS are taken, especially STEP 3, mapping the problem so as to identify relevant disciplines (see Chapter 5), and STEP 4, conducting a full-scale literature search (see Chapter 6).

Important Insights or Theories of the Problem Are Offered by Two or More Disciplines

A problem that is controversial, such as global warming, has likely generated interest from two or more disciplines, each offering its own insights or theories in the form of books and journal articles. This condition makes the problem researchable. Indeed, researchers should be looking for instances of **border disciplinarity**, which exists when at least two disciplines focusing on the same problem create an overlapping area between them. These disciplines, each with its own perspective, insights, concepts, assumptions, theories, and methods, make a productive contribution to understanding the problem because each has studied the problem (Fischer, 1988, p. 37).

Sometimes, however, scholarly work on a controversial problem has not yet been undertaken by one or more of the disciplines one plans to consult. A problem commonly encountered is this: After identifying the disciplines potentially relevant to the problem, the full-scale literature search (STEP 4) reveals that the problem has not yet attracted the attention of some of these disciplines.

Note to Readers

Undergraduates should work on problems that have been studied by more than one discipline. Graduate students and especially senior scholars may be able to project how a hitherto silent discipline might address the problem and what insights it might offer into the problem. In this circumstance, they may choose to conduct basic research on the problem themselves and then integrate their insights or theory with existing disciplinary insights or theories. It would be inappropriate for interdisciplinary teams that are able to include an appropriate scholar from that discipline not to do so.

No Single Discipline Has Been Able to Explain the Problem Comprehensively or Resolve It

A problem is ripe for interdisciplinary inquiry if (a) no single discipline has been able to explain it comprehensively or resolve it or (b) each discipline offers a more or less misleading or biased understanding of it. For example, several disciplines consider terrorism within their respective domains, but no one discipline has been able to create a single comprehensive theory explaining terrorism in all of its complexity, let alone propose a holistic solution to it. For instance, political scientists typically use rational choice theory to explain terrorist behavior, but the theory fails to address religious and cultural variables. Other topics that no single discipline has been able to address comprehensively include illegal immigration, human cloning, and genetically engineered food. The value of an interdisciplinary approach over a single disciplinary approach is that it can address complex problems in a more comprehensive way.

The Problem Is an Unresolved Societal Need or Issue

Societal/public policy problems necessitate what interdisciplinarians call **problem-based research** because it focuses on unresolved societal needs and practical problem solving. Such research is a form of applied research that emphasizes "usefulness, efficiency, and practical results" (Klein, 1990, p. 122). *What distinguishes problem-based research from other applied research is its holistic focus that requires more than one discipline.*

Examples of Statements That Justify Using an Interdisciplinary Approach

The rationale for using an interdisciplinary approach should be made explicit in the introduction to the research project. After all, this rationale distinguishes truly interdisciplinary research from multidisciplinary, not to mention disciplinary, research. Making the rationale explicit even in cases where one does not have choice of topic has the added benefit of alerting one to possible problems with the topic. Spending extra time in carefully screening a potential topic according to these criteria will minimize the possibility of investing in an enterprise that later may prove unprofitable.

Satisfied that the proposed problem or topic meets one or more of the above criteria, it is then possible to present a clear rationale for using an interdisciplinary approach. Common practice is to include this statement of justification in the introduction to the study, as shown in these examples of professional work and student projects noted by an asterisk (*) from the natural sciences, the social sciences, and the humanities.

From the Natural Sciences: Dietrich (1995), Northwest Passage: The Great Columbia River

Dietrich is struck by how narrowly people continue to look at the Columbia River. This narrowness of perspective and the lack of systems thinking provide his justification for taking an interdisciplinary approach, as follows:

> My work as a writer on environmental issues, particularly the old-growth forests of the Pacific Northwest, had introduced me to the idea of ecosystems and the interrelationships of many parts to a greater whole. I wanted a comprehensive understanding of the river embracing history, Earth science, biology, hydrology, economics, and contemporary politics and management. (pp. 23–24)

From the Natural Sciences: Smolinski* (2005), Freshwater Scarcity in Texas

Smolinski is concerned that after years of study, disciplinary experts have not been able to reach agreement on the cause and effect of the worsening problem of freshwater scarcity. This failure provides ample justification for taking an interdisciplinary approach.

The causes and effects of freshwater scarcity across Texas are beyond the ability of any single discipline to explore. A review of the professional literature in political science, Earth science, and biology shows that these disciplines are most relevant to the problem. Each has produced its own well-defined theories about how the shortages impact the state of Texas and its communities. While each of these theories reflects the perspective of its particular discipline, none of these explanations comprehensively addresses the issues posed by the statewide shortage of freshwater. (p. 3)

From the Social Sciences: Fischer (1988), "On the Need for Integrating Occupational Sex Discrimination Theory on the Basis of Causal Variables"

Fischer provides an example of professional work from the social sciences that presents a clear rationale for taking an interdisciplinary approach.

It appears that the problem of OSD is a good candidate for an IR [interdisciplinary] approach. OSD is a problem that a number of disciplines have separately analyzed, yet it is a problem of such complexity and breadth that its division among individual disciplines leads to incomplete and naïve views.

Another important advantage of IR is that it can . . . lead to [a] more complete understanding by providing a dynamic, holistic view of the problem. (p. 37)

From the Social Sciences: Delph* (2005), An Integrative Approach to the Elimination of the "Perfect Crime"

Having introduced the topic and explained its importance, Delph justifies using an interdisciplinary approach.

To achieve the level of expertise necessary to solve more crimes, the criminal justice system must integrate a wide range of skills from multiple disciplines. This synthesis of skills and insights could serve as a strong deterrent to crime and result in safer communities. (p. 2)

From the Humanities: Bal (1999), "Introduction," The Practice of Cultural Analysis: Exposing Interdisciplinary Interpretation

The topic of the graffito is not a societal problem; it is an intellectual one that cries out for interdisciplinary understanding or meaning. Bal (1999) sees cultural analysis as an interdisciplinary practice and the field as a counterweight to critics who charge that interdisciplinarity makes objects of inquiry "vague and methodically muddled" (p. 2). Seeking to correct this mistaken view, she justifies using cultural analysis, an interdisciplinary approach, to find meaning in the graffito.

> As an object, it requires interdisciplinarity [and calls for] an analysis that draws upon cultural anthropology and theology [and] reflection on aesthetics, which makes philosophy an important partner. . . . [T]he humanistic disciplines . . . brutally confront scholars with the need to overcome disciplinary hang-ups. . . . Museum analysis requires the integrative collaboration of linguistics and literary, of visual and philosophical, and of anthropological and social studies. . . . Instead of speaking of an abstract and utopian interdisciplinarity, then, cultural analysis is truly an interdiscipline, with a specific object and a specific set of collaborating disciplines. (pp. 6–7)

From the Humanities: Silver* (2005), Composing Race and Gender: The Appropriation of Social Identity in Fiction

From her fiction class experience, Silver (2005) discovered that she did not know how to write authentically about the people in the Mexican village whose backgrounds were very different from her own. Frustrated and disappointed with the artificial characters she had created for her fiction piece, she decided to use the topic of character appropriation for her senior project. Character appropriation refers to a writer's attempt to write about, or an actor's attempt to assume, another person's identity. As Silver read, she developed "a sense of what different disciplines—sociology, psychology, cultural studies, and creative writing—[said] about the matter" (p. 2). Finding that each of these disciplines offered an important perspective on an important subject, she determined that an interdisciplinary approach was clearly called for (pp. 1–6).

Each of these examples conforms to one or more of the above criteria. In most cases, the writer also identifies the disciplines relevant to the problem.

Chapter Summary

This chapter introduces the interdisciplinary research process (IRP) and examines its initial STEPS. It explains the importance of the research process to interdisciplinarity, describing it as a decision-making process that is heuristic, iterative, and reflexive, and that involves creativity. It introduces an integrated model of the interdisciplinary research process and notes the importance of providing a map for conducting research. The first STEP in this process is to define the problem or the research question. Criteria for developing a good interdisciplinary question at any level include these: (1) It must be open-ended and too complex to be addressed by one discipline alone, and (2) it must be researchable. The chapter alerts students to three tendencies that run counter to good interdisciplinary practice: privileging a particular discipline, using disciplinary jargon without defining it, and allowing personal bias to shape the project.

The second STEP calls for justifying the use of an interdisciplinary approach. Such justification should meet one or more criteria: (1) The problem should be complex; (2) important insights or theories of the problem should have been produced by at least two disciplines; (3) no single discipline has been able to comprehensively explain the problem or resolve it; (4) the problem is an unresolved societal need or issue.

Even after subjecting the proposed problem to these criteria, it is still too early in the research process to know with any certitude that the problem is researchable. This question can be resolved only by taking subsequent STEPS in the research process.

Once the problem is stated (STEP 1) and the justification for using an interdisciplinary approach is stated (STEP 2), students must decide which disciplines are relevant to the problem (STEP 3; see Chapter 5). This decision requires understanding the disciplines and the concept of disciplinary perspective. Disciplinary perspective, a key component of interdisciplinarity, is foundational to the interdisciplinary research process. Chapter 4 unpacks the meaning of several defining elements of perspective.

Notes

1. Nikitina (2005) also uses "STEP" to describe the interdisciplinary process (p. 405).

2. These models include the following: Hursh et al. (1983); Klein (1990), pp. 192–193; Newell (2001), pp. 14–22; Szostak (2002). Klein has moved away from her earlier model, finding it "too linear" (personal communication, April 2005).

3. Comparing these models reveals that scholarly consensus exists on the following STEPS: The problem or focus question should be defined; relevant disciplines and other resources must be identified; information from these disciplines (concepts, theories, methods, etc.) must be gathered; adequacy in each relevant discipline must be achieved; the problem must be studied, and insights into the problem must be located and evaluated; conflicts between insights must be identified, and their sources must be revealed; disciplinary insights must be integrated; and a new understanding must be constructed or new meaning achieved. The models disagree on the number, order, and identity of STEPS, leaving students and instructors alike without a clear road map of the overall interdisciplinary research process. Of special concern is the lack of consensus on how many STEPS are involved in the integrative part of the process. Welch (2003) notes that when the participants in a Delphi Study recommended that students be provided "basic integrational methods," the question arose as to which model and/or which particular STEPS within these models should be provided (p. 185).

4. "What is contested is whether interdisciplinarity studies only complexity, or whether interdisciplinarity can appropriately study problems/issues/questions that are not complex as well. Some practitioners say that interdisciplinarity studies only complexity, but others remain unconvinced. Thus, the debate is not over whether interdisciplinarity is necessary for complexity, but whether complexity is necessary for interdisciplinarity" (William H. Newell, personal communication, January 7, 2011).

Exercises

The Best Approach

3.1   This chapter compared and contrasted the interdisciplinary research process to the disciplinary approach (in a general sense) and argued that both have utility, depending on the problem. Below are short descriptions of a problem, question, or topic. In each case, decide which approach is probably the most appropriate and why:

- The cost of building a high-speed rail system to connect two large cities
- Should the city build a new performing arts center in an area inhabited primarily by persons who are unemployed and on welfare?
- What is the cause of obesity among teens?
- What is the meaning of the science fiction movie *2001: A Space Odyssey?*

The Integrated Model

3.2   The chapter introduced the integrated model of the interdisciplinary research process. What parts of the model are most similar to and different from disciplinary approaches to research?

Is It Researchable?

3.3   The chapter presented criteria for determining if a problem, topic, or question is researchable in an interdisciplinary sense. Which of the following meets one or more of these criteria?

- The psychological dimension of Alzheimer's disease
- The loss of manufacturing jobs to China and India
- The effects of the closing of fine arts programs in public schools

Stating the Problem

3.4   The following is an example of student work on the topic, the underachieving child. Based on the discussion of STEP 1, how could this introduction to the problem be stated differently so that it conforms to the criteria and guidelines set forth?

The Underacheving Child

Many school age children underachieve. Underachievement is when the performance of a child falls below what is expected and the ability of the child. Underachievement means to perform academically below the potential indicated by tests of one's ability or aptitude.

Justify

3.5 The chapter noted that it is common practice for practitioners to justify using an interdisciplinary approach. Compare the various examples and identify their commonalities. What would you change, if anything, in any of the statements?

3.6 In addition to justifying using an interdisciplinary approach, should one argue against taking narrow disciplinary positions on issues?

4 Introducing the Disciplines

This chapter reinforces the claim made in Chapter 1 that the disciplines are foundational to interdisciplinary inquiry. The interdisciplinary research process (IRP) involves integration of insights and theories from disciplines after these have been evaluated with respect to (among other things) disciplinary perspective. Thus, students cannot identify disciplines potentially relevant to a problem and perform interdisciplinary research without a firm grasp of the nature of disciplines and disciplinary perspective.

This chapter presents the structure of knowledge and how it is typically reflected in the organization of the academy. It examines the concept of disciplinary perspective, discusses misconceptions of this key term, defines its meaning, and examines how the perspectives of disciplines may be used in certain situations. The chapter then introduces the defining elements of disciplines (i.e., phenomena, epistemology, assumptions, concepts, theory, and methods). This information, presented in easily accessible tables, is foundational to interdisciplinary research and critical to developing adequacy in relevant disciplines as STEP 5 calls for (see Chapter 7).

The Structure of Knowledge and Its Reflection in the Organization of the Academy

Scholars developed fields of knowledge that exist today as academic disciplines. Most academic departments represent a particular discipline, and clusters of related disciplines form larger units within a university often called **colleges, schools, or faculties** such as the college of science, the school of social sciences, or the faculty of arts. In most university settings, academic departments are foundational to the institution's structure.

Disciplines

Disciplines are academic communities that exhibit a disciplinary perspective (which involves preferences regarding phenomena to study and theories and methods to use, shared terminology called concepts, *and* epistemological and ethical *and* ideological outlooks). Yet crucially, disciplines also involve an institutional structure of PhD programs, departmental hiring, and disciplinary journals. Disciplinary fields and interdisciplines are not truly disciplines until they have their own PhDs and hiring communities.

Disciplinarity

The widely used term **disciplinarity** refers to the system of knowledge specialties called disciplines, which is little more than a century old. *Discipline* is used throughout this book as an umbrella term that also includes subdisciplines and interdisciplines, defined as follows:

- A subdiscipline is a subdivision of a traditional discipline. The discipline of anthropology, for example, has developed several subdisciplines, including cultural anthropology, physical anthropology, anthropology of religion, urban anthropology, and economic anthropology. The formation of subdisciplines is a logical outcome of a cognitive division of labor and is a process driven by research (Bruun & Toppinen, 2004, p. 5).
- An interdiscipline literally means "between disciplines"—that is, between the bodies of knowledge defined by the theories and methods of the established disciplines (Karlqvist, 1999, p. 379). An interdiscipline often begins as an interdisciplinary field, but over time becomes like a discipline, developing its own curriculum, journals, professional associations, and, most important for interdisciplinary studies, perspective. The interdisciplines of biochemistry and neuroscience, for example, emerged as interdisciplinary fields that eventually grew to become their own mainstream disciplines. The transition from interdisciplinary field to interdiscipline is still under way for women's studies (Grace, 1996, pp. 59–86).

Categories of Disciplines

Disciplinary knowledge is produced in the form of books, journals, databases, and conferences—all of which are vetted by the disciplines. Departments and programs structure and organize the passing on of that knowledge to the next generation, create new knowledge, and guide the careers of faculty members who do the teaching and conduct the research in the discipline. Disciplinary departments determine the curriculum or the courses that are taught, oversee what is researched (and often how it is researched), and influence how teaching is done. Departments are organized into broad **disciplinary categories** to form divisions or colleges or schools. Typical categories include the natural sciences; the social sciences; the humanities; the fine and performing arts such as music, theater, and dance; the applied fields such as communications and business; and the professions such as architecture, engineering, law, nursing, education, and social work. (Note: The professions typically involve licensure.)

Table 4.1 presents a conventional classification of the disciplines that includes traditional disciplines (but by no means all of them), but excludes the applied fields and professions.[1] A discipline may be considered part of one category at one university but belong to a different category at another. History, for example, is considered a discipline within the social sciences in some institutions but part of the humanities at others. Though history has elements of both social science and humanities, this book follows the traditional taxonomy of including history in the humanities.

Table 4.1 Categories of Disciplines

Category	Discipline
The Natural Sciences	Biology
	Chemistry
	Earth Science
	Mathematics
	Physics
The Social Sciences	Anthropology
	Economics
	Political Science
	Psychology
	Sociology
The Humanities	Art and Art History
	History[a]
	Literature (English)
	Music and Music Education
	Philosophy
	Religious Studies

a. History can be studied in two broad ways—the social science version that is theory-driven and often quantitative in its scientific testing of hypotheses, and the humanities version that is qualitative, narrative, and nonscientific, painting mental pictures with words rather than testing formal hypotheses, or with a conceptual and methodological pluralism that draws on both approaches.

The Concept of Disciplinary Perspective

Interdisciplinary research requires an understanding of the disciplines. This is consistent with the definition of interdisciplinary studies noted in Chapter 1. According to this definition, interdisciplinarity has a high degree of dependence upon and interaction with the disciplines. Therefore, understanding the role of the disciplines and their perspectives in interdisciplinary work is essential to a full understanding of interdisciplinarity.

Disciplinary Perspective

Disciplinary perspective is each discipline's unique view of reality in a general sense.[2] The first to assert that disciplines have distinct perspectives or worldviews that are pertinent to interdisciplinary understanding, Raymond C. Miller (1982) states that perspective should be "the primary means of distinguishing one discipline from another" (p. 7). A discipline's worldview or "perspective" is a lens through which to view reality. Each discipline acts like a lens when it filters out certain phenomena so that it can focus exclusively on phenomena that interest it. Disciplines such as history and biology are not collections of certified facts; rather, they are *lenses* through which we look at the world and interpret it (Boix Mansilla, Miller, & Gardner, 2000, p. 18). In the sciences, disciplines are most easily distinguished by the phenomena they study. A conventional physicist, for example, would not be interested in studying the declining salmon populations in the Columbia and Snake rivers, but a biologist would. A conventional sociologist would not be interested in theological representation in a fifteenth-century oil painting, but an art historian would. Similarly, a conventional historian would likely not be interested in the regulatory hurdles involved in the building of a new oil refinery, but a political scientist would.

Misconceptions About the Term *Disciplinary Perspective*

There are several misconceptions about disciplinary perspective that have developed over the years. One misconception comes from taking a narrow focus, seeing perspective as referring only to a discipline's overall view of reality. Understood in this limited way, perspective is but one of several elements of a discipline, including its phenomena, epistemology, assumptions, concepts, theories, and methods.[3] Other scholars take a much broader view of perspective, arguing that it is the *source* of all other disciplinary elements.[4] Rick Szostak (2004), for example, explains how disciplinary perspective both reflects and influences a discipline's choice of phenomena, theory, and method. The problem with the narrow conception of perspective is that it is of little use in interdisciplinary work other than to help students generally identify disciplines that are relevant to the problem. *If we cannot define the elements of disciplinary perspective, we cannot readily use disciplinary perspective to identify potentially relevant disciplines and analyze their insights.*

The second misconception about *disciplinary perspective* is that other terms, such as *purview*, can easily be substituted for it. However, *purview*, which means limit or scope of authority, is far from the meaning of *perspective*, which is the capacity to view things in their relationship and relative importance to other things. Intended or not, substituting *purview* for *perspective* emphasizes limitation instead of viewpoint. In the end, attempts to substitute other terms for *perspective* only serve to muddy the definitional waters and make more problematic the operational utility of the term for interdisciplinary work.

Another misconception about the term *perspective* is that it is similar to, if not identical with, *insight*. Interdisciplinary studies, as defined in Chapter 1, is a process of drawing on the disciplines and integrating their insights and theories. It is, therefore, important to clarify the relationship between a discipline's "perspective" and its "insights" and briefly explain how these relate to the objective of the IRP. A discipline's experts produce insights and theories into a problem or class of problems. These insights and theories typically reflect the discipline's perspective. Interdisciplinarians draw on these insights and theories, analyze them (drawing on disciplinary perspectives to do so), identify how they conflict, modify them by creating common ground among them, integrate them, and construct a more comprehensive understanding of the problem.

A fourth misconception about the term *perspective* is that the research process involves integrating perspectives from disciplines relevant to the problem. The interdisciplinary process involves integrating disciplinary *insights and theories*—not perspectives (i.e., a discipline's overall view of reality)—into a particular problem or question. These three examples illustrate the point:

- Earth science views planet Earth as a large-scale and highly complex system involving the four subsystems of geosphere, hydrosphere, atmosphere, and biosphere. When this perspective is applied to a particular problem, say damming a river system such as the Columbia, the insight that Earth science may generate (in the form of a scholarly monograph, journal article, or report to a public agency) is that building the system of dams is feasible given the geological characteristics of the Columbia Basin.
- Sociology views the world as a social reality that includes the range and scope of relationships that exist between people in any given society. When this perspective is applied to a particular problem, say repeated spousal battery, the insight into the problem that sociologists may generate is that it is caused by male unemployment or the desire for patriarchal control.

- Art history views art in all its forms as representing a culture at a given point in time and therefore providing a window into that culture. When this perspective is applied to a specific work of art, say a post–Civil War Currier & Ives lithograph, the insight that art historians may generate concerning the meaning of the work is that it expresses the optimism of a culture that has embraced the concept of progress by conquering nature.

Students must remember that before it is possible to identify disciplinary insights and theories concerning a particular problem, the relevant disciplines (and their perspectives) must first be identified.

Merely examining the same object or phenomenon from different disciplinary perspectives does not *by itself* constitute interdisciplinary work. Without integration, these different perspectives would lead to mere multidisciplinary work (Hacking, 2004, p. 5). The reason is illustrated in a poem by American poet John Godfrey Saxe (1816–1887) based on an Indian fable about six blind men and an elephant. Each of the men thoroughly investigated a particular part of the massive beast, and each emphatically concluded that what he had "observed" was very much like a wall (its sides), a spear (its tusk), a snake (its swinging trunk), a tree (its leg), a fan (its ear), and a rope (its tail). The poem ends,

And so these men of Indostan

Disputed loud and long,

Each in his own opinion

Exceeding stiff and strong,

Though each was partly in the right,

And all were in the wrong! (Saxe, 1963)

The lesson is that simply having six different experts from six different disciplines examine an object will likely yield at least six different insights or theories about the object. This is the nature of multidisciplinarity. What is lacking, of course, is any attempt to integrate these conflicting insights, insofar as this is possible, into one composite description or theory of the object so as to provide a more comprehensive understanding of it. All of the disciplines involved contribute to that integrated understanding, but it is not "owned" by any of them. This analogy can be extended to include a seventh blind person representing the interdisciplinarian who queries the other six about the object. That person then integrates the information provided by the six disciplinarians in an attempt to construct a more comprehensive understanding or coherent "theory" of the elephant.[5]

One of the first tasks of the interdisciplinarian is to ensure that the disciplines are talking about the same thing when they seem to disagree. Also, one

needs to know what the linkages are between the parts of the elephant studied by the other blind men, as well as the perspective of each of them, before
being able to map the insights related to them.

Other Problems With the
Concept of Disciplinary Perspective

In addition to the four misconceptions about the meaning of disciplinary
perspective, there are problems with the term as it relates to the character of
the disciplines themselves. For one thing, the disciplines are heterogeneous
families, not monolithic structures (Lenoir, 1997, p. 61). Also, the overall
nature and content of the disciplines are constantly changing, as are their
external boundaries and their degree of unity. Over time, the changing nature
of disciplinary knowledge domains impacts the identities and cultural characteristics of disciplines and, thus, of their perspectives (Becher & Trowler,
2001, pp. 38, 43).

This point about the changing character of the disciplines themselves is
underscored by the **cognitive discord** that today characterizes so many disciplines (Dogan & Pahre, 1989). This discord consists of disagreement among
a discipline's practitioners over the defining elements of the discipline. Henrik
Bruun and Aino Toppinen (2004) state, "Disciplines are actually quite heterogeneous, from a cognitive and epistemological perspective, and . . . research
seldom follows any strict disciplinary boundaries" (p. 5). The American
Sociological Association (ASA; n.d.), for example, states on its website,
"Sociology provides many distinctive perspectives on the world." These "distinctive perspectives" within sociology, openly acknowledged by the ASA, are
reflective of sociologists having aligned themselves with various theories and
schools of thought that currently inform the discipline. It is the case today,
writes David M. Newman (2004), that most social research, and the insights
it is generating into social problems, "is guided by a particular theory" (p. 72).
Any clarification of disciplinary perspective, then, must include theory as one
of its elements.

Cognitive discord also characterizes art history, a discipline experiencing
divisive theoretical conflicts. Consequently, art historian Donald Preziosi
(1989) says that there is no such thing as "an Olympian perspective" in the
discipline, despite what might be inferred from numerous textbooks (p. xi).
Indeed, some scholars go so far as to claim that a dominant perspective, as
defined in interdisciplinary literature, is lacking in almost every discipline in
the social sciences and humanities (Dogan & Pahre, 1989).

This raises the question of whether some disciplines, such as art history
and sociology in their fragmented states, even have a general perspective on
reality. The answer is yes because the very idea of a discipline as something
entirely coherent, in terms of strict adherence to its defining elements
(assumptions, concepts, theories, methods, etc.), is an idealization. The reality

of disciplinarity, past and present, is ferment and fragmentation.[6] Counterbalancing these centripetal forces to a large degree is an **intellectual center of gravity** that enables each discipline to maintain its identity and have a distinctive overall perspective. As long as disciplines bestow PhDs and make hiring decisions, there will be strong pressure to decide what a suitable sociologist or art historian is.

Compounding this cognitive discord is the well-documented **cognitive fluidity** or phenomenon of boundary crossing and borrowing from other disciplines (Gaff, Ratcliff, & Associates, 1997; Klein, 1999). Studies show two interrelated trends that support this. The first is a "historical reversal" of the long-term trend of growing specialization and proliferation of undergraduate programs and courses (Gaff et al., 1997, p. xiv). The second is an increase in crossing disciplinary boundaries by disciplinarians themselves. Disciplines borrowing concepts, theories, and methods from one another, says Klein (1999), skew the picture of knowledge depicted in conventional maps of the academy. She observes, for example, how textuality, narrative, and interpretation were once thought to belong within the domain of literary studies. Now, she says, they appear across the humanities and the social sciences, including science studies, and the professions of law and psychiatry. Similarly, research on the body and on disease occurs in disciplines as varied as art history, gerontology, and biomedicine. The movement of methods and analytical approaches across disciplinary boundaries, she contends, has become an important feature of knowledge production today (p. 3). However, these new developments do not mean the end of "discipline" in a conventional sense.

Along with the cognitive discord and cognitive fluidity of the disciplines, there is a third characteristic of contemporary disciplines that relates to the concept of perspective. Disciplinarians in the social sciences and the humanities are more apt to use the term *perspective* to reference schools of thought such as modernism and postmodernism that inform their disciplines rather than to associate the term with the disciplines themselves (Agger, 1998, pp. 2–3; Wallace & Wolf, 2006, pp. xi, xii, 5, 7–8). They do so because they look at their own discipline from the inside, not the outside as interdisciplinarians do. One sees the commonalities of a discipline only in contrast to other disciplines. Looking ahead, it is worth noting that theory is only one of several elements of disciplinary perspective, and thus, different disciplines may use the same theory but have quite different perspectives.

The Concept of Disciplinary Perspective Clarified

Clearly, then, the problems with using the term *perspective* are formidable. Narrow conceptions of the term and errant substitutions of other terms for it, combined with the fluid character of the disciplines themselves, have meant that there has been little discussion of the specific elements of this important term and sparse analyses of how they might profitably be used by researchers. The solution is to clarify the term *perspective* in a way that highlights these elements.

The **defining elements of a discipline's perspective** include the phenomena it studies and the kinds of data it collects, its epistemology or rules about what constitutes evidence or "proof," the assumptions it makes about the natural and human world, its basic concepts or vocabulary, its theories about the causes and behaviors of certain phenomena, and its methods (the way it gathers, applies, and produces new knowledge). The defining elements of a discipline's perspective comprise its **cognitive map** (Klein, 2005a, p. 68). Each discipline's community of scholars substantially agrees on what constitutes an interesting and appropriate question to study, what constitutes legitimate evidence, and what a satisfactory answer to the question should look like. These shared emphases also comprise the discipline's perspective, but in a more detailed sense. From its perspective, the discipline frames the "big" questions or "perennial issues and problems" that give the discipline its definition and signature characteristics (Becher & Trowler, 2001, pp. 26, 31).

A Definition of Disciplinary Perspective

A clarified definition of **disciplinary perspective** that takes all of these considerations into account is this:

> Disciplinary perspective is a discipline's view of reality in a general sense which embraces and in turn reflects the ensemble of its defining elements that include phenomena, epistemology, assumptions, concepts, theory, and methods.

The interdisciplinary emphasis on perspective taking is supported by research from cognitive psychology and the emerging cognitive science of interdisciplinary collaboration. This research shows that confrontation of different perspectives is a condition for any kind of cognitive development "both in interdisciplinary dialog and in individual thought" (Bromme, 2000, pp. 115–116). Accordingly, interdisciplinarity aids discovery of new knowledge by juxtaposing different disciplinary perspectives along with their defining elements and by attempting to create common ground among the elements (pp. 116, 119–131).[7] Howard Gardner (1999) contends that a multiple perspective approach can enhance understanding in at least three ways: (1) by providing powerful points of entry to the topic, (2) by offering apt analogies of the problem, and (3) by conveying key ideas (pp. 186–187).

The clarified definition of disciplinary perspective is consistent with the definition of interdisciplinary studies noted in Chapter 1 that emphasizes drawing on the disciplines and integrating their insights and theories to construct a more comprehensive understanding. This clarified definition of perspective also captures the messy reality of what occurs in actual interdisciplinary work—drawing not just on disciplinary perspectives in a general sense, but more particularly on those defining elements of disciplines—for example, assumptions, concepts, and theories—that relate most directly to the problem.

Using Disciplinary Perspectives

Disciplinary perspectives are useful in two circumstances: The first is near the beginning of the research process where the focus is on identifying disciplines that are potentially interested in the problem. (Note: How to identify these disciplines is the focus of STEP 3 and the subject of Chapter 5.) Identifying potentially interested disciplines early on helps to narrow the disciplinary literatures that need to be consulted when performing the full-scale literature search that STEP 4 calls for in Chapter 6.

The disciplinary perspectives in Table 4.2 are separated into the three categories of traditional disciplines and are stated in the most general terms.

Table 4.2   Overall Perspectives of Natural Sciences, Social Sciences, and Humanities Disciplines Stated in General Terms

Discipline	Overall Perspective
Natural Sciences	
Biology	While the other natural sciences focus on the principles that govern the nonliving physical world, biology studies the behavior of the living physical world. When biologists venture into the world of humans, they look for physical, deterministic explanations of behavior (such as genes and evolution) rather than the mental ones (such as the decisions of individuals or groups based on free will or norms) on which the social sciences focus.
Chemistry	Chemistry focuses on the distinctive properties of the elements, individually and in compounds, and their interactions. Chemistry sees larger-scale objects, organic as well as inorganic, in terms of their constituent elements and compounds.
Earth Science	Earth science focuses on the large-scale physical processes of planet Earth and is concerned with both the details and functions of the four subsystems and their interactions: the lithosphere (the Earth's hard, outermost shell), the atmosphere (the mixture of gases that envelop the Earth), the hydrosphere (the subsystems that contain the Earth's water), and the biosphere (the realm of all living things, including humans).
Mathematics	Mathematics is interested in abstract quantitative worlds mathematicians create with postulates, assumptions, axioms, and premises and then explore by proving theorems.

Discipline	Overall Perspective
Physics	Physics studies the basic physical laws connecting objects (atoms and subatomic particles, quanta) and forces (gravity, electromagnetic, strong, weak) that often cannot be directly observed but that establish the underlying structure of observable reality, and cosmology (the form, content, organization, and evolution of the universe).
Social Sciences	
Anthropology	Cultural anthropology sees individual cultures as organic integrated wholes with their own internal logic and culture as the set of symbols, rituals, and beliefs through which a society gives meaning to daily life. Physical anthropology seeks to understand former cultures through the artifacts it uncovers.
Economics	Economics emphasizes the study of market interactions, with the individual functioning as a separate, autonomous, rational entity, and perceives groups (even societies) as nothing more than the sum of individuals within them.
Political Science	Political science views the world as a political arena in which individuals and groups make decisions based on the search for or exercise of power. Politics at all levels and in all cultures is viewed as a perpetual struggle over whose values, not just whose interests, will prevail in setting priorities and making collective choices.
Psychology	Psychology sees human behavior as reflecting the cognitive constructs individuals develop to organize their mental activity. Psychologists also study inherent mental mechanisms, both genetic predisposition and individual differences.
Sociology	Sociology views the world as a social reality that includes the range and nature of the relationships that exist between people in any given society. Sociology is particularly interested in voices of various subcultures, analysis of institutions, and how bureaucracies and vested interests shape life.
Humanities	
Art and Art History	Art history views art in all of its forms as reflecting the culture in which it was formed and therefore providing a window into a culture. Art, and thus art history, has a place for universal aesthetic tastes.
History	Historians believe that any historical period cannot be adequately appreciated without understanding the trends and developments leading up to it, that historical events are the result of both societal forces and individual decisions, and that a picture or narrative of the past can be no better than the richness of its details.
Literature (English)	Literature believes that cultures, past and present, cannot be adequately understood without understanding and appreciating the literature produced by the culture.

(Continued)

Table 4.2   (Continued)

Discipline	Overall Perspective
Music and Music Education	Music educators believe that a critical component of culture past and present cannot be adequately understood without understanding the music produced by the culture.
Philosophy	Philosophy recognizes a variety of limits to human perceptual and cognitive capabilities. Philosophy views reality as situational and perspectival. Reality is not a collection of imperfect representations that reflect an "absolute reality" that transcends all particular situations. Rather, these representations are the reality that is the world.
Religious Studies	Religious studies views faith and faith traditions as human attempts to understand the significance of reality and cope with its vicissitudes through beliefs in a sacred realm beyond everyday life.

NOTE: This **taxonomy** or systematic and orderly classification of selected disciplines and their perspectives raises the question of how students can find perspectives of disciplines, subdisciplines, and interdisciplines not included in this book. Certainly, a good place to obtain leads is this chapter, which has tables that define elements of disciplines (their epistemologies, theories, methods, etc.). Also, the chapter references standard authoritative disciplinary sources. Researchers may also consult content librarians who specialize in certain disciplines. Another strategy is to ask disciplinary experts to recommend sources. This combined approach should produce aids that are authoritative and useful. The issue of finding scholarly research aids is addressed more fully in Chapter 6.

These are not comprehensive generalizations about each discipline, but central tendencies that are a matter of consensus. *The purpose in presenting the following information is to help students decide at the outset of the IRP which disciplines are potentially interested in the problem and thus which disciplinary literatures should be consulted.* Disciplines are defined primarily in terms of phenomena studied because the interdisciplinarian will most often choose disciplines that emphasize the study of phenomena relevant to the question being investigated.

Once a discipline's overall perspective on reality is known, it is relatively easy to apply the perspective to the problem at hand. It is common to work with disciplines within a particular cluster such as the humanities, though some problems require consulting disciplinary literatures from two or more clusters. *A rule of thumb is to let the problem dictate which categories and disciplines within each category are most relevant to it.*

The second circumstance in which disciplinary perspectives are useful is in performing STEP 5, developing adequacy in relevant disciplines (Chapter 7), and STEP 6, analyzing the problem (Chapter 8). In performing these STEPS, disciplinary perspective is used in two ways: in terms of how each discipline's overall perspective influences its understanding of the particular problem under investigation and in terms of which defining elements of disciplines (e.g., their assumptions, concepts, or theories) should be used.

The Defining Elements
of a Discipline's Perspective

As clarified above, disciplinary perspective means not just a discipline's general view of reality but its constituent parts or defining elements as well. The term **elements** is used when referring to the constituent parts of a discipline that provide its essential and formative character. Consistent with this clarified definition, perspective is *not* among the defining elements identified here because it subsumes them. Here the meaning of these defining elements is unpacked.

Phenomena

Phenomena are enduring aspects of human existence that are of interest to scholars and are susceptible to scholarly description and explanation. As Szostak (2004) explains, economic and political institutions evolve and assume different forms in every society, but the classification of possible types of institutions need not change to capture this diversity. Similarly, individuals may differ in terms of personality, but a set of personality characteristics is always with us (pp. 30–31).

The sorting out of distinctions between disciplines in this chapter does not imply that disciplines are static. As already noted, their character is ever changing, and their borders are elastic and porous. This reality and the absence of a logical classification of phenomena to guide the disciplines have produced two unfortunate effects. The first is that several disciplines may share a phenomenon, often unmindful of the efforts of other disciplines to comprehend it. For example, psychology and religious studies share an interest in the phenomenon of terrorism, but one rarely finds in their work references to the theories and research of the other discipline. The second effect is that the disciplines may ignore a particular phenomenon altogether. An example is the cause of economic growth, which is the traditional focus of economists but has not been studied by history or political science.

Interdisciplinary scholars, like their disciplinary counterparts, must identify the phenomena relevant to the research question. They can attempt this in one of two ways: approach the disciplines serially in hopes of locating a particular phenomenon in one or more of them, or focus on the phenomenon itself. Table 4.3 presents the traditional approach of first identifying relevant disciplines and searching their literatures in hopes of finding insights into a particular phenomenon. The success and speed of this search naturally depend on the researcher's familiarity with each discipline. Table 4.3 links the disciplines to illustrative phenomena of interest to them. It is based on the classification of phenomena developed by Rick Szostak (2004). These phenomena are linked to particular disciplines for the purpose of helping students identify which disciplines are relevant to the problem in order to decide which disciplines to mine for insights.[8] The classifications provided in this table and elsewhere in this book should help advanced undergraduate and graduate students see how each discipline's perspective contributes to an overall understanding of a multifaceted problem.

Table 4.3   Disciplines and Their Illustrative Phenomena

Category	Discipline	Phenomena
The Natural Sciences	Biology	Biological taxonomies of species; the nature, interrelationships, and evolution of living organisms; health; nutrition; disease; fertility
	Chemistry	The periodic table of chemical elements that are the building blocks of matter—their composition, properties, and reactions
	Earth Science	Planet Earth's geologic history, processes, and structures; soil types; topography and land forms; climate patterns; resource availability; water availability; natural disasters
	Mathematics	The logic of numbers, statistics, mathematical modeling, computer simulations, theoretical counterpoint to sensitivity analysis
	Physics	Subatomic particles, the nature of matter and energy and their interactions
The Social Sciences	Anthropology	The origins of humanity, the dynamics of cultures worldwide
	Economics	The economy: total output (price level, unemployment, individual goods and services), income distribution, economic ideology, economic institutions (ownership, production, exchange, trade, finance, labor relations, organizations), the impact of economic policies on individuals
	Political Science	The nature and practice of systems of government and of individuals and groups pursuing power within those systems
	Psychology	The nature of human behavior as well as the internal (psychosociological) and external (environmental) factors that affect this behavior
	Sociology	The social nature of societies and of human interactions within them
The Humanities	Art and Art History	Nonreproducible art—painting, sculpture, architecture, prose, poetry—and reproducible art—theater, film, photography, music, dance

Category	Discipline	Phenomena
	History	The people, events, and movements of human civilizations past and present
	Literature	Development and examination (i.e., both traditional literary analysis and theory as well as more contemporary culture-based contextualism and critique) of creative works of the written word
	Music and Music Education	Development, performance, and examination (i.e., both traditional musicological analysis and theory as well as more contemporary culture-based contextualism and critique) of creative works of sound
	Philosophy	The search for wisdom through contemplation and reason using abstract thought
	Religious Studies	The phenomena of humans as religious beings and the manifestations of religious belief such as symbols, institutions, doctrines, and practices

SOURCE: Szostak, R. (2004). *Classifying science: Phenomena, data, theory, method, practice.* Dordrecht: Springer. Page 26–29, 45–50. With kind permission from Springer Science+Business Media.

Phenomena Classified

Until recently, only the **perspectival approach** (i.e., relying on each discipline's unique perspective on reality) was available to interdisciplinarians because no system of classifying all human phenomena existed. Szostak (2004) meets this need in his pioneering work that classifies phenomena about the human world. His **classification approach**, shown as Table 4.4, moves left to right from the most general phenomena to the most specific. A practical benefit of Szostak's approach is that all phenomena can be linked rather easily to particular disciplines, provided that one knows the discipline's general perspective and the phenomena it typically studies.

Using Table 4.4 should facilitate linking most topics readily to one or more of the particular phenomena in the table. For example, the phenomenon of freshwater scarcity concerns the nonhuman environment. Moving from left to right, one can see multiple links to a wide array of subphenomena (center column) that may pertain to the problem. These subphenomena, in turn, provide links to other phenomena identified in the right-hand column that may be of further interest. Reading the literature pertaining to the several subphenomena may lead the researcher to broaden the investigation to include the categories of economics and politics and their respective subphenomena. In short, using Szostak's classification approach should facilitate making connections to neighboring phenomena that may touch on the research question. Making these connections quickly not

Table 4.4   Szostak's Categories of Phenomena About the Human World[a]

First Level	Second Level	Third Level
Genetic Predisposition	Abilities	Consciousness, subconsciousness, vocalization, perception (five senses), decision making, tool making, learning, other physical attributes (movement, eating, etc.)
	Motivations	Food, clothing, shelter, safety, sex, betterment, aggression, altruism, fairness, identification with group
	Emotions	Love, anger, fear, jealousy, guilt, empathy, anxiety, fatigue, humor, joy, grief, disgust, aesthetic sense, emotional display
	Time Preference	
Individual Differences	Abilities: • Physical Abilities • Physical Appearance • Energy Level • Intelligences	 • Speed, strength, endurance • Height, weight, symmetry • Physical, mental • Musical, spatial, mathematical, verbal, kinesthetic, interpersonal
	Personality: • Emotionality (Stable/Moody) • Conscientiousness • Affection (Selfish/Agreeable) • Intellectual Orientation • Other Dimensions? • Disorders? • Sexual Orientation • Schemas • Interpersonal Relationships	 • Contentment, composure vs. anxiety, self-pity • Thoroughness, precision, foresight, organization, perseverance vs. carelessness, disorderly, frivolous • Sympathetic, appreciative, kind, generous vs. cruel, quarrelsome, faultfinding • Openness, imagination, curiosity, sensitivity vs. closed-mindedness • Dominant/submissive, strong/weak, in/dependent, humor, aggression, future/present oriented, happiness • Schizophrenia, psychoticism . . . ? • View of self, others, causal relationships • Parent/child, sibling, employee/r, romance, friendship, casual acquaintance

First Level	Second Level	Third Level
Economy	Total Output	Price level, unemployment, individual goods and services
	Income Distribution	
	Economic Ideology	
	Economic Institutions	Ownership, production, exchange, trade, finance, labor relations, organizations
Art	Nonreproducible	Painting, sculpture, architecture, prose, poetry
	Reproducible	Theater, film, photography, music, dance
Politics	Political Institutions	Decision-making systems, rules, organizations
	Political Ideology	
	Nationalism	
	Public Opinion	Issues (various)[b]
	Crime	Versus persons/property
Culture	Languages	By descent?
	Religions	Providence, revelation, salvation, miracles, doctrine
	Stories	Myths, fairy tales, legends, family sagas, fables, jokes and riddles
	Expressions of Cultural Values:	Rituals, dance, song, cuisine, attire, ornamentation of buildings, games
	• Goals	• Ambition, optimism, attitudes to wealth, power, prestige, beauty, honor, recognition, love, friendship, sex, marriage, time preference, physical and psychological well-being
	• Means	• Honesty, ethics, righteousness, fate, work, violence, vengeance, curiosity, innovation, nature, healing
	• Community	• Identity, family vs. community, openness to outsiders, trust, egalitarianism, attitude to young and old, responsibility, authoritarianism, respect for individuals
	• Everyday Norms	• Courtesy, manners, proxemics, tidiness, cleanliness, punctuality, conversational rules, locomotion rules, tipping
Social Structure	Gender	
	Family Types/Kinship	Nuclear, extended, single parent
	Classes (various)	Occupations (various)
	Ethnic/Racial Divisions	
	Social Ideology	

(Continued)

Table 4.4 (Continued)

First Level	Second Level	Third Level
Technology and Science	Fields (various)	Innovations (various)
	Recognizing the Problem	
	Setting the Stage	
	Act of Insight	
	Critical Revision	
	Diffusion/ Transmission	Communication, adoption
Health	Nutrition	Diverse nutritional needs
	Disease	Viral, bacterial, environmental
Population	Fertility	Fecundity, deviation from, maximum
	Mortality	Causes of death (various)
	Migration	Distance, international, temporary
	Age Distribution	
Nonhuman Environment	Soil	Soil types (various)
	Topography	Land forms (various)
	Climate	Climate patterns (various)
	Flora	Species (various)
	Fauna	Species (various)
	Resource Availability	Various resources
	Water Availability	
	Natural Disasters	Flood, tornado, hurricane, earthquake, volcano
	Day and Night	
	Transport Infrastructure	Mode (various)
	Built Environments	Offices, houses, fences, etc.
	Population Density	

SOURCE: Szostak, R. (2004). *Classifying science: Phenomena, data, theory, method, practice.* Dordrecht: Springer. Page 27–29. With kind permission from Springer Science+Business Media.

a. The table undoubtedly appears daunting at first. Closer examination of it, though, shows that there are only 11 categories of phenomena and relatively small sets of second-level phenomena. The third-level phenomena in the table can be further unpacked into subsidiary phenomena. Szostak (personal communication, May 7, 2007) says that the table was developed using a mix of deduction and induction, and thus can be extended if/when new phenomena are discovered.

b. "Various" here and elsewhere in this table means that there are many subsidiary phenomena. Identifying these will require the student to consult more specialized disciplinary literatures.

only aids the research process, as will be demonstrated in later chapters, but also enables researchers to confirm their selection of potentially relevant disciplines.

Note to Readers

The boundaries of disciplines are evolving, fluid, and overlapping in places while leaving some unexplored territory between themselves and other disciplines. The increasingly common practice of disciplinary scholars borrowing concepts, theories, and methods from other disciplines has implications for interdisciplinary work. The cognitive fluidity that today characterizes the disciplines means that researchers at all levels should not approach disciplines as self-contained repositories of information but be aware that they are open to a wider range of concepts, theories, and methods that transcend their traditional boundaries. That is, researchers should not only examine the characteristic elements of relevant disciplines for insights into the problem but should also search for information from sources that transcend disciplines, such as schools of thought (referenced in Table 4.8) and the categories of phenomena appearing in Table 4.3.

Epistemology

Epistemology is the branch of philosophy that studies how one knows what is true and how one validates truth (Sturgeon, Martin, & Grayling, 1995, p. 9). It has to do with the nature, validity, and limits of inquiry (Rosenau, 1992, p. 109). An epistemological position reflects one's views of what can be known about the world and how it can be known. Literally, an epistemology is a theory of knowledge (Marsh & Furlong, 2002, pp. 18–19). Each discipline's epistemology is its way of knowing that part of reality that it considers within its research domain (Elliott, 2002, p. 85).

Disciplines may differ in terms of ethical, metaphysical, and ideological outlooks. With respect to ethics, disciplines differ in terms of whether they think ethical considerations can or should influence research. (Ethics are discussed later under assumptions.) Readers should be wary of supposedly neutral arguments regarding issues such as euthanasia where ethical attitudes can easily influence research outcomes. Epistemological attitudes will reflect metaphysical attitudes: Scientists who believe they can understand the universe must believe it behaves in an orderly fashion. As for ideology, certain disciplines are naturally more skeptical of the exercise of governmental power than are others. As the discussion of assumptions that follows this section on epistemology shows, assumptions mostly reflect epistemology, but capture elements of ethics, metaphysics, and ideology when these are particularly important.

The **epistemic norms of a discipline** are agreements about how researchers should select their evidence or data, evaluate their experiments, and judge their theories. Science philosopher Jane Maienschein (2000) states, "It is epistemic convictions that dictate what will count as acceptable practice and how theory and practice should work together to yield legitimate scientific knowledge" (p. 123). The experimental approach is based on the epistemological assumption that stresses the value of experimental control and replicability, whereas the field approach is based on the value of studying the "messy, muddled life-in-its-context" (p. 134).

A researcher's epistemological position is reflected in *what* is studied and *how* it is studied. For example, **positivists** are concerned with establishing causal relationships between social phenomena through direct observation, attempting to develop explanatory, and even predictive, models. Positivist researchers believe that (a) the world exists independently of our knowledge of it, (b) social phenomena exist independently of our interpretation of them, and (c) objective analysis is possible. The polar opposite of this position is the interpretivist position. **Interpretivists** believe that (a) the world is socially constructed, (b) social phenomena do not exist independently of our interpretation of them, and (c) objective analysis is impossible (Marsh & Furlong, 2002, pp. 20, 26).

A researcher's epistemological position is reflected not only in what is studied and how it is studied, but also in the status the researcher gives to the findings. For example, a positivist researcher looking for causal relationships will tend to prefer quantitative analyses that are "objective" and "generalizable." By contrast, a researcher in the interpretivist camp is concerned with *understanding* and will, consequently, use qualitative methods to discover the *meaning* that behavior has for agents (Marsh & Furlong, 2002, p. 21).

The Nature and Limits of the Truth Claims Made by Major Epistemological Approaches

Major epistemological approaches inform much of the literature in the natural sciences, the social sciences, and the humanities. Faced with growing epistemological pluralism, interdisciplinarians need to know the nature and limits of the truth claims made by these approaches. **Epistemological pluralism** refers to the diverse approaches that the disciplines use to know and describe reality. Epistemological pluralism exists across the disciplines, but especially those in the social sciences and even more so in the humanities. It is problematic to associate a particular epistemology with a particular discipline because of the deep divide between the modernist and newer critical approaches to knowledge formation. (Note: Disciplinary students are more likely to base their epistemological commitments on their affinity for either modernist [including positivist] or postmodernist [and interpretivist] approaches, rather than on their attachment to some disciplinary grouping [Lattuca, 2001, p. 104].)

In her study of interdisciplinarity at colleges and universities, Lisa Lattuca (2001) finds that professors committed to traditional **modernist approaches** (belief in objective, empirically based, rationally analyzed truth that is knowable) chose theories and methods from different disciplines that were epistemologically consistent with their own way of thinking (p. 105). James A. Bell (1998) agrees, finding that most disciplinary writers tend to fall into one of two epistemological camps. At the one extreme, he says, are the followers of **epistemological positivism** or the "law and order" approach, allied with modernists, who point to any flexibility in matters epistemological as a guise for relativism or at least a mask for being weak or lacking conviction in expressing one's views (p. 101).

At the other extreme are **epistemological interpretivists** who view epistemology as "totally arbitrary, being nothing more than a political power game to legitimize one's favored views" (Bell, 1998, p. 103). This latter conception, says Bell, is at the heart of **postmodernist approaches** that typically operate under the assumption that there is no such thing as objective truth and are skeptical of "metanarratives." As introduced and critiqued by Jean-François Lyotard in his 1984 work, *The Postmodern Condition: A Report on Knowledge*, a **metanarrative** is a comprehensive explanation or totalizing truth embedded in a culture that is created and reinforced by power structures and is therefore not to be trusted. Knowledge, explains Bell (1998), is explained discursively (e.g., proceeding coherently from topic to topic) because the social and political context is a discursive construction, usually as a weapon in the hands of some individuals or groups to dominate and intimidate others (p. 103). Students, he says, are wise to recognize that both extreme positions are harmful because they limit one's own thinking and denigrate the thinking of others.

Various Epistemologies

The statements on epistemologies in Tables 4.5, 4.6, and 4.7 are not definitive but central tendencies. Any way of classifying the epistemological positions of the disciplines can be contested.[9] These tables draw heavily from disciplinary experts, with the recognition that no two scholars may give precisely the same description of their disciplines.

Epistemologies of the Natural Sciences   The characterizations are empiricist. **Empiricism** holds that all knowledge is derived from our perceptions (transmitted by the five senses of touch, smell, taste, hearing, and sight), experience, and observation. Empiricism, as Alex Rosenberg (2000) notes, is the "ruling 'ideology' of science."[10] Empiricism assures us that observation and experimentation make scientific explanations credible, and the predictive power of its theories is ever-increasing (p. 146). However, the epistemologies of the sciences make scientific approaches inadequate for addressing value issues (Kelly, 1996, p. 95).

Table 4.5	Epistemologies of the Natural Sciences

Discipline	Epistemology
Biology	Biology stresses the value of classification and experimental control. The latter is the means of identifying true causes, and therefore privileges experimental methods (because they are replicable) over all other methods of obtaining information (Magnus, 2000, p. 115).
Chemistry	Chemists use both empirics and theory (especially thermodynamics). Even more than physics, chemistry relies on lab experiments, data collection in the field, and computer simulations. Chemistry involves less fieldwork than Earth science and biology do.
Earth Science	In much of Earth science, the theory of uniformitarianism is used. Since geologists are concerned about the history of the Earth but can't directly observe it, they accept that natural laws and processes have not changed over time (L. Standlee, personal communication, April 2005). Geologists stress the value of fieldwork.
Mathematics	Mathematical truths are numerical abstractions that are discovered through logic and reasoning. These truths exist independently of our ability or lack of ability to find them, and they do not change. These truths or forms of "invariance" enable us to categorize, organize, and give structure to the world. These mathematical structures—"geometric images and spaces, or the linguistic/algebraic expressions"—are "grounded on key regularities of the world or what we 'see' in the world" (Longo, 2002, p. 434).
Physics	Like all the physical sciences, physics is empirical, rational, and experimental. It seeks to discover truths or laws about two related and observable concepts—matter and energy—by acquiring objective and measurable information about them (Taffel, 1992, pp. 1, 5).

Epistemologies of the Social Sciences   The disciplines in the social or human sciences, more so than in the natural sciences, tend to embrace more than one epistemology, as shown in Table 4.6. For example, reflecting the growing postmodernist criticism of positivism's empiricism and value neutrality, most social scientists now agree that knowledge in their disciplines is generated by the "continual interplay of personal experience, values, theories, hypotheses, and logical models, as well as empirical evidence generated by a variety of methodological approaches" (Calhoun, 2002, p. 373).

Epistemologies of the Humanities   The humanities, even more so than the social sciences, embrace epistemological pluralism as shown in Table 4.7. This development is explained by the rise of the "new generalism" or "critical humanities" (feminism, critical theory, postcolonial studies, cultural studies, gender studies, postmodernism, poststructuralism, deconstructionism, etc.). The humanities prize diversity of perspective, values, and ways of knowing.

Table 4.6 Epistemologies of the Social Sciences

Discipline	Epistemology
Anthropology	Epistemological pluralism characterizes anthropology. Empiricists hold that people learn their values and that their values are therefore relative to their culture. The rationalist notion is that there are universal truths about right and wrong. Both physical and cultural anthropologists embrace constructivism, which holds that human knowledge is shaped by the social and cultural context in which it is formed and is not merely a reflection of reality (Bernard, 2002, pp. 3–4).
Economics	The epistemological dominance of modernism is being challenged by postmodernism that generates a pluralistic understanding of reality. Postmodernists see reality, and the self, as fragmented. Therefore, human understanding of reality is also fragmented. Nevertheless, the beliefs of economists are still largely determined by empirical evidence in direct relation to the mathematical theories and models they use. Empiricists stress fixed definitions of words, use a deductive method, and examine a small set of variables (Dow, 2001, p. 63).
Political Science	Political science embraces a rationalist epistemology. However, logical positivists in the discipline are trying to cast the "science" of politics in terms of finding some set of "covering laws" so strong that even a single counterexample would suffice to falsify them. But human beings, according to others in the discipline, while they are undeniably subject to certain external forces, are also in part intentional actors, capable of cognition and of acting on the basis of it. Consequently, these scholars study "belief," "purpose," "intention," and "meaning" as potentially crucial elements in explaining the political actions of humans (Goodin & Klingerman, 1996, pp. 9–10).[a]
Psychology	The epistemology of psychology is that psychological constructs and their interrelationships can be inferred through discussion and observation and applied to treatment (clinical) or a series of experiments with slight variations (experimental). A critical ingredient of a good experiment is experimental control that seeks to eliminate extraneous factors that might affect the outcome of the study (Leary, 2004, p. 208).
Sociology	Modernist (i.e., positivist) sociology shares a rationalist epistemology with the other social sciences, but this epistemology is opposed by critical social theory, a theory cluster that includes Marxism, critical theory, feminist theory, postmodernism, multiculturalism, and cultural studies. What unites these approaches in the most general sense is their assumption that knowledge is socially constructed and that knowledge exists in history that can change the course of history if properly applied (Agger, 1998, pp. 1–13).

a. Marsh and Furlong (2002) see the discipline divided among three epistemological positions: positivism, interpretivism, and realism (pp. 22–32).

Table 4.7   Epistemologies of the Humanities

Discipline	Epistemology
Art and Art History	Modernists determine the value of works of art by comparing them with standards of aesthetics and expertise. But practitioners of the new art history who emerged in the 1960s determine the value of works of art in relation to contestation between values of competing groups; that is, it understands them in social and cultural contexts (J. Harris, 2001, pp. 65, 96–97, 130–131, 162–165, 194–196, 228–232, 262–288). Postmodern critics (active from about 1970 to the present) "argue that the supposedly dispassionate old-style art historians are, consciously or not, committed to the false elitist ideas that universal aesthetic criteria exist and that only certain superior things qualify as 'art'" (Barnet, 2008, p. 260).
History	Modernists focus on the authenticity and appropriateness of how an event, a person, or a period is interpreted by evaluating the work in terms of its faithfulness to appropriate primary and secondary sources. "Truth," they believe, "is one, not perspectival" (Novick, 1998, p. 2). Believing that "structure" is fundamental to understanding the past, social historians focus on structure and infrastructure—on material structure, on the economy, on social and political systems—but do not eliminate the individual. More recently, some social historians have begun to employ "micro-history" or the new cultural history (a blend of social history and intellectual history) as a way of studying ideological structures, mental structures (such as notions of family and community), isolated events, individuals, or actions, borrowing from anthropology the ethnographic method of "thick description," which emphasizes close observation of small details, carefully listening to every voice and every nuance of phrase (Howell & Prevenier, 2001, p. 115).
Literature	In general, modernists focus on the text and employ text-based research techniques. Newer approaches see meaning making as a relational process. The close reading of texts is being informed by background research into the context of the text, such as the circumstances surrounding its production, content, and consumption. Other newer approaches abound. For example, notions of auto/biographic writing have shifted from an idea of presenting "the truth" about someone to presenting "a truth." Oral history is viewed as a means of understanding the workings of "literary and cultural phenomena in and on people's imagination." Critical discourse analysis examines patterns in language use in order to uncover the workings of an ideology to see how it exerted control or how it was resisted. Quantitative researchers are using computers to calculate the frequency with which certain words appear in a text so that they can better interpret its meaning (Griffin, 2005, pp. 5–14).
Music and Music Education	For modernists, knowledge is often primarily technical knowledge. They assume, therefore, that empirical investigation produces verifiable and objective "knowledge" and "truth" irrespective of context. Postmodernists embrace a much more pluralistic view of knowledge, viewing it as elusive, fragile, temporary, and conjectural. Postmodernists assert that there are an infinite number of potentially "true" statements that can be developed about

Discipline	Epistemology
	any phenomenon, and that no single form of research can possibly account for the complete "truth" or reality of anything. "The goal of research, then, is continuously to seek relevant descriptions and explanations of a phenomenon based on the best and most complete knowledge we can garner about that phenomenon" (Elliott, 2002, p. 91).
Philosophy	Recently, philosophical questions about perception have become more important. For both empiricist and rationalist positions, one of the major concerns is to ascertain whether the means of getting knowledge are trustworthy. The chief concerns of epistemology in this regard are memory, judgment, introspection, reasoning, "a priori-a posteriori" distinction, and the scientific method (Sturgeon et al., 1995, pp. 9–10).
Religious Studies	Religious studies is concerned about the "assumptions and preconceptions that influence the analysis and interpretation of data, that is, the theoretical and analytical framework, even personal feelings, one brings to the task of organizing and analyzing facts" (Stone, 1998, p. 6). Though all humanities disciplines are concerned about the problem of subjectivity, few are as self-critical as religious studies (p. 7).

Epistemologies of Various Theories and Schools of Thought

In searching for disciplinary insights into a problem, students will inevitably encounter writings that reflect adherence to one of the major epistemological approaches, which are shown in Table 4.8. While authors may not explicitly reveal their epistemological preferences, their writings will often provide clues detectable to the informed interdisciplinarian. Students should know these approaches—their strengths and limitations—so as to be able to recognize and critically analyze insights that use them. The left-hand column identifies theories about how the world works that purport to explain a wide range of phenomena and causal links: modernism, interpretivism, postmodernism, and feminism. The middle column of the table shows the various schools of thought within modernism. Each of these broad theoretical approaches has its own epistemological position shown in the right-hand column. The epistemological position of each theory and school of thought is stated in the right-hand column in general terms.

Postmodernism is of particular interest to those working in the humanities and the social sciences. This critical approach offers a way to understand society by questioning modernism's notion of objective knowledge. The postmodern challenge radiates across the disciplines but more so in the social sciences and the humanities.[11] In political science, for example, it calls into question the authority of hierarchical, bureaucratic decision-making structures, while in psychology it questions the conscious, logical, and coherent subject (Rosenau, 1992). The battle between modernists and postmodernists has been largely settled, but the postmodernist critique of modernism has left a lasting impact.

Table 4.8   Epistemology of Various Theories and Schools of Thought

Theory About How the World Works	School of Thought	Epistemological Position
Modernism		A real world exists independent of our knowledge of it.
	Positivism	External reality is discoverable through empirical observations.
	Realism	Direct observation should not be privileged because deep structures, which cannot be directly observed, have crucial effects on outcomes.
	Behavioralism	General laws about the way things work are discoverable by studying observable behavior.
	Rational Choice	Theoretical models can be constructed that permit us to predict outcomes.
	Marxism	Reality is discoverable by examining the political dimensions of class relations and economic structures.
Interpretivism		The world can be interpreted on an individual basis, but it can never really be known.
Postmodernism		The world is discursively constructed (see **discourse** in the Glossary).
Feminism		Some adherents to feminist theory embrace a modernist (i.e., realist) epistemology while others embrace a postmodern approach.[a]

SOURCE: Based on Elliott (2002, pp. 88–89); Gerring (2001, pp. 11–12); Stoker & Marsh (2002, p. 11).

a. Critics of feminist epistemology such as Cassandra Pinnock (1994) point out that feminist epistemology "should not be taken seriously" because it "is unable to resolve the tension between (a) its thesis that every epistemology is a sociopolitical artifact, and (b) its stated aim to articulate an epistemology that can be *justified* as better than its rivals" (p. 646).

The implication for truth claims of the modernist or positivist and postmodernist or interpretivist approaches is this: Modernist empirical research under the label of positivism assumes an independent reality out there that can be perceived and measured. Based upon the careful design of procedures, the data collected and processed enable empirical research to validate or invalidate a hypothesis about that part of reality under investigation. For positivists, this great faith in data and empirical inquiry is the cornerstone of knowledge production and reliability (Alvesson, 2002, pp. 2–3).

In recent years, **interpretivist approaches** such as postmodernism, feminism, and critical theory are challenging this bedrock assumption, claiming that the perceptions and interpretations of what we perceive are filtered through a web of values, expectations, and vocabularies that influence understanding (Frankfort-Nachmias & Nachmias, 2008, p. 11). Feminists, for example, point to how "male domination has produced a masculine social science built around ideals such as objectivity, neutrality, distance, control, rationality and abstraction" and that these have "marginalized alternative ideas such as commitment, empathy, closeness, cooperation, intuition, and specificity" (Alvesson, 2002, p. 3). Critical theorists charge that knowledge production is grounded in politics and interests. These other critical approaches are calling into question even the possibility of objectivity and the reliability of knowledge.

Note to Readers

Good interdisciplinary work requires a strong degree of **epistemological self-reflexivity** (Klein, 1996, p. 214). Researchers should be aware of the advantages and disadvantages of different epistemological approaches. Also, they should be aware that their epistemological choices tend to influence their selection of research methods that, in turn, influence research outcomes (Bell, 1998, p. 101). Accordingly, interdisciplinarians should take care that their embrace of certain assumptions, epistemologies, theories, methods, and political views do not bias the research process and thus skew the resulting understanding.

Interdisciplinary researchers should be aware of the common criticisms of their favored epistemological approach. The limitations of modernism and postmodernism, for example, are shown in Table 4.9 and are stated in general terms.

Table 4.9   Limitations of Each Epistemology

Theory	Weaknesses
Modernism	1. All forms of human observation are judgmental, conceptual, or theory-laden.
	2. Even a very large number of empirical statements do not add up to "knowledge" in the sense of infallible theories, laws, or general statements (Elliott, 2002, p. 89).
	3. Often there are possible alternative explanations for whatever data scientists gather.
Postmodernism	1. It embraces extreme relativism, arguing that no single interpretation is more defensible than another.
	2. Deconstruction, a postmodern approach to understanding texts, is destructive, not constructive, because it reduces all texts in the same way to the same conclusions.
	3. Postmodernists insist that their way of investigating an issue has more merit than any other and that the social and political agendas they support are superior to others (Rosenau, 1992, p. 124).
	4. Society is fractured into distinct groups of people who cannot meaningfully associate with others outside their group (Elliott, 2002, p. 113).
	5. There are no "right" procedures of investigation because there is no verifiable and universal metasystem of knowledge (Elliott, 2002, p. 96).

Interdisciplinary analysis is possible as long as we back away from the most extreme postmodern arguments (as most postmodernists themselves do).

Assumptions

From each discipline's epistemology (and ethics, etc.) flows a set of assumptions that tend to characterize research in that discipline. An **assumption** is something taken for granted, a supposition. Assumptions are the principles that underlie the discipline as a whole and its overall perspective on reality. As the term implies, these principles are accepted as the truths upon which the discipline's theories, concepts, methods, and curriculum are based. Stated another way, it is the interplay of assumptions and empirical evidence that shapes a discipline's theories, concepts, and insights.

Grasping the underlying assumptions of a discipline as a whole provides important clues to the assumptions underlying its particular insights and theories. Assumptions underlying specific insights are important to the integrative part of the interdisciplinary process that calls for identifying *possible* sources of conflict between them. If conflicts between sets of insights or theories exist, one can then work to modify the conflict(s) by creating common ground among the insights or theories in STEP 8 (Chapter 12). There are two kinds of assumptions: "basic" assumptions that scientists across disciplinary clusters typically make, and more focused or "hallmark" assumptions that are made by scientists working in a particular cluster of disciplines.

Basic Assumptions

There are at least six *basic assumptions* of science:

- Nature is orderly.
- We can know nature.
- All natural phenomena have natural causes.
- Nothing is self-evident.
- Knowledge is based on experience.
- Knowledge is superior to ignorance (Frankfort-Nachmias & Nachmias, 2008, pp. 5–6).

The particular *combination* of assumptions is unique to each discipline, but disciplines can share assumptions. The assumptions in Tables 4.10, 4.11, and 4.12 are not comprehensive generalizations but central tendencies and, thus, can be challenged by disciplinarians who might prefer different representational selections. The purpose in presenting these tables is twofold: (1) to help researchers decide which disciplines are relevant to the problem so that their literatures can be mined for insights and (2) to identify assumptions that will be useful in performing later STEPS, particularly STEP 8.

Hallmark Assumptions of the Natural Sciences The *hallmark assumptions* made by those working in the natural sciences are two. The first is that scientists can transcend their cultural experience and make definitive measurements of phenomena (e.g., things). The second is that "there are no supernatural or other a priori properties of nature that cannot potentially be measured" (Maurer, 2004, pp. 19–20).[12] This assumption is reflected to varying degrees in the characterizations of disciplinary assumptions underlying the natural sciences and mathematics noted in Table 4.10. The sources cited in this and in following tables are good starting points for further reading.

| Table 4.10 | Assumptions of Disciplines in the Natural Sciences |

Discipline	Assumptions
Biology	Biologists assume that the hypothetico-deductive approach (i.e., deductive reasoning used to derive explanations or predictions from laws or theories) based on the principle of falsification (i.e., the doctrine whereby theories of hypotheses derived from them are disproved because proof is logically impossible) is superior to description of pattern and inductive reasoning (Quinn & Keough, 2002, p. 2).
Chemistry	The function of the whole is reducible to the properties of its constituent elements and compounds and their interactions. "All living organisms share certain chemical, molecular, and structural features, interact according to well-defined principles, and follow the same rules with regard to inheritance and evolution" (Donald, 2002, p. 111).
Earth Science	The principle of uniformitarianism leads geologists to assume that the present is the key to understanding the past. Earth processes have not significantly changed during the several billion years that Earth has been a dynamic planet similar in many ways to the other planets constituting the solar system. In the past decade, Earth system scientists have assumed that natural and social systems are strongly coupled and act in nonlinear ways (Steffen et al., 2004, p. 287).
Mathematics	Assumptions (or axioms) in mathematics form the starting point for logical proofs of its theorems. They constitute the "if" part of a statement: "If A, then B." The consequences of the assumptions are found through logical reasoning, which leads the mathematician to discover the conclusion, "then B" (B. Shipman, personal communication, April 2005).
Physics	Logical empiricism assumes the existence of a finite set of laws that governs the behavior of the universe and that there is an objective method for discovering these truths. Natural realism, by contrast, assumes (1) that the universe works in a law-like manner, though the nature of the universe may be extremely complex and much of it may even be unfathomable; and (2) "scientists can build models that approximate nature sufficiently to allow further progress in understanding particular phenomena" (Maurer, 2004, p. 21). This atomistic approach to knowledge further assumes that separate parts together constitute physical reality, that these separate parts are lawfully and precisely related, and that physics events can be predicted.

Hallmark Assumptions of the Social Sciences   The social sciences are grounded in essentially the same set of basic assumptions that characterize the sciences (Frankfort-Nachmias & Nachmias, 2008, p. 5). Assumptions in the social sciences are closely related to the research methods, theories, and schools of thought embraced by members of each discipline's community of scholars. For example, a popular textbook on behavioral research methods (psychology, communication, human development, education, marketing, social work, and the like) states the assumption underlying the scientific approach and systematic empiricism as these methods are applied to the behavioral sciences: "Data obtained through systematic empiricism allow researchers to draw more confident conclusions than they can draw from casual observation alone" (Leary, 2004, p. 9). Modernists share a "grizzled confidence" in such ideas as "progress" and "knowledge" grounded in empirical and replicable data (Cullenberg, Amariglio, & Ruccio, 2001, p. 3). This modernist assumption is present, to varying degrees, in many of the social science disciplines but is being challenged by postmodern notions. Both sets of assumptions—modern and postmodern—are noted in Table 4.11.

Hallmark Assumptions of the Humanities   The humanities are grounded in a set of assumptions that differ greatly from those of the sciences. Over the course of the twentieth century and especially in recent decades, the older assumption of unified knowledge and culture has given way to a pluralistic and even conflicted set of assumptions. Klein (2010) lumps these new assumptions

Table 4.11   Assumptions of Disciplines in the Social Sciences

Discipline	Assumptions
Anthropology	Cultural relativism (the notion that people's ideas about what is good and beautiful are shaped by their culture) assumes that systems of knowledge possessed by different cultures are "incommensurable" (i.e., not comparable and not transferable) (Whitaker, 1996, p. 480). Cultural relativism has been the driving ethic of anthropology for generations, but it is being challenged by feminists, postcolonialists, and advocates for other marginalized groups on the grounds that relativism supports the repressive status quo in other cultures (Bernard, 2002, p. 73).[a]
Economics	Modernist approaches predominate. Modernist economists assume that the same dominant human motivation (rational self-interest) transcends national and cultural boundaries, in the past as in the present. Also, they assume that both usefulness and value are implicit in rational choices (on which they prefer to focus) under conditions of scarcity. Postmodernists assume that all things, including economic motivation and behavior, are intimately bound up with the situatedness (i.e., the cultural, political, and technological context) of those engaged in these activities and thus are not generalizable (Cullenberg et al., 2001, p. 19).

Discipline	Assumptions
Political Science	Political science has been influenced primarily by history, but more recently it is being influenced by theories from sociology, economics, and psychology. Consequently, its assumptions reflect whichever discipline and theory it is drawing from at the moment. Modernists assume rationality: "Human beings, while they are undeniably subject to certain causal forces, are . . . in part intentional actors, capable of cognition and acting on the basis of it" (Goodin & Klingerman, 1996, pp. 9–10). Behavioralists (who are also modernists) assume that political science can become a science capable of prediction and explanation (Somit & Tanenhaus, 1967, pp. 177–178). Proponents of the scientific method of research assume that empirical and quantitative, rather than normative and qualitative, analysis is the most effective way of knowing political reality (Manheim, Rich, Willnat, & Brians, 2006, pp. 2–3).
Psychology	Psychologists assume that "data obtained through systematic empiricism allow researchers to draw more confident conclusions than they can draw from casual observation alone" (Leary, 2004, p. 9). Generalizations about larger populations may be inferred from representative sample populations. Psychologists also assume that group behavior can be reduced to individuals and their interactions and that humans organize their mental life through psychological constructs.
Sociology	Assumptions vary widely in this discipline. Empiricists assume an independent social reality exists that can be perceived and measured through gathering of data. Critics of modernism assume that our perceptions of social reality are filtered through a web of assumptions, cultural influences, and value-laden vocabularies, that individual human behavior is socially constructed, with rationality and autonomy playing modest roles at best; groups, institutions, and especially society have an existence independent of the individuals in them. People, they assume, are motivated primarily by the desire for social status (Alvesson, 2002, pp. 2–3).

a. Cultural relativism does not equate to ethical relativism (that all ethical systems are equally good since they are all cultural products), as Merrilee Salmon (1997) makes clear. Szostak (personal communication, July 7, 2007) notes that there are two distinct issues associated with relativism. The first is incommensurability (which, if true, would challenge the very idea of interdisciplinarity). "The second is that there are no universal standards for evaluating cultural elements. Both issues flow from the idea that cultural elements are tightly bound into a monolithic structure that is best analyzed as a whole (but then it is hard to understand both cultural evolution and subcultures)."

under the heading "the new generalism." This is not a unified paradigm, she explains, but "a cross-fertilizing synergism in the form of shared methods, concepts, and theories about language, culture, and history" (p. 30). The keywords of this new paradigm are *plurality* and *heterogeneity* (replacing *unity* and *universality*), *interrogation* and *intervention* (supplanting *synthesis* and *holism*). The **new humanities**, she says, "interrogates the dominant structure of knowledge and education with the aim of transforming them" with the "explicit intent of deconstructing disciplinary knowledge and boundaries" (p. 30). This trend, Klein asserts, is especially apparent in cultural studies, women's and ethnic studies, and literary studies, where "the epistemological and political are inseparable" (p. 30). She explains that

> As humanities disciplines moved away from older paradigms of historical empiricism and positivist philology [the study of literature and the disciplines associated with literature], increasing attention was paid to contexts of aesthetic works and responses of readers, viewers, and listeners. The concept of culture was also expanded from a narrow focus on elite forms to a broader anthropological notion, and once discrete objects were reimagined as forces that circulate in a network of forms and actions. (p. 30)

These keywords and trends provide important clues to the assumptions of humanities disciplines. Table 4.12 identifies the assumptions of modernism alongside the assumptions of the "new generalism."

Table 4.12 Assumptions of Disciplines in the Humanities

Discipline	Assumptions
Art and Art History	Modernists assume that the intrinsic value of the object is primary. Radical art historians—i.e., Marxist, feminist, psychoanalytical, and poststructuralist—"share a broad historical materialism" of outlook: that all social institutions, such as education, politics, and the media, are exploitative and that "exploitation extends to social relations, based, for instance, on factors of gender, race, and sexual preference" (J. Harris, 2001, p. 264). In general, these critics assume that intrinsic values remain primary, but understanding the social context completes one's grasp of the work (p. 264).[a]
History	Modernist (positivist and historicist) historical scholarship rests on the idea that objectivity in historical research is possible and preferred (Iggers, 1997, p. 9). In general, social history (e.g., Marxian socioeconomic history, the Braudelian method, women's history, African American history, and ethnic history) assumes that those whom traditional history writing had ignored (the poor, the working class, women, homosexuals, minorities, the sick) played an important but unappreciated role in historical change (Howell & Prevenier, 2001, p. 113).
Literature	Literature (broadly defined) or "texts" are assumed to be a lens for understanding life in a culture and an instrument that can be used to understand human experience in all of its complexity. Texts "encompass the continuous substance of all human signifying activities" (D. G. Marshall, 1992, p. 162). Another assumption is that these texts are "alien" to the reader, meaning that "something in the text or in our distance from it in time and

Discipline	Assumptions
	place makes it obscure." The interpreter's task is to make the text "speak" by "reading" the text using extremely complex skills so as to give the text "meaning." *Meaning* is "an intricate and historically situated social process" that occurs between the interpreter and the audience (i.e., reader) that neither fully controls (pp. 159, 165–166).
Music and Music Education	Modernists assume that empirical investigation produces verifiable and objective "knowledge" (i.e., in the sense of infallible theories, laws, or general statements) and "truth" that is context free. Postpositivists (interpretivists, critical theory advocates, gender studies scholars, and postmodernists) deny the possibility of objectivity because human values are always present in human minds (Elliott, 2002, p. 99).
Philosophy	There are two schools of thought about how to get knowledge. Rationalists assume that the chief route to knowledge is the exercise of systematic reasoning and "looking at the scaffolding of our thought and doing conceptual engineering" (Blackburn, 1999, p. 4). The model for rationalists is mathematics and logic. Empiricists assume that the chief route to knowledge is perception (i.e., using the five senses of sight, smell, hearing, taste, and touch and the extension of these using technologies such as the microscope and telescope). The model for empiricists is any of the natural sciences where observation and experiment are the principal means of inquiry (Sturgeon et al., 1995, p. 9).
Religious Studies	Religious studies often queries faith, and the history of religions focuses on understanding man as a religious being. One key assumption of the discipline is that there is something inherently unique about religion, and those who study it must do so without reducing its essence to something other than itself, as sociologists and psychologists tend to do. A related assumption is that even though religion is freighted with human emotion, objectivity is possible (Stone, 1998, p. 5).

a. Marxists assume that class struggle is the primary engine of historical development in capitalist society and that other forms of exploitation are either a product of the basic antagonism of class or peripheral to it. Feminists assume connections and causal links between patriarchal dominance within the society as a whole and its art. Psychoanalytic art historians assume that a full understanding of "the subject" requires inquiry into the complex nature of the embodied human psyche and its conscious and unconscious outworkings (Harris, 2001, pp. 262, 264, 195).

Note to Readers

Assumptions often play an important role in the process of creating common ground among conflicting disciplinary concepts and theories. Chapters 11 and 12 explain how to modify the assumptions underlying concepts and theories to prepare them for integration. For example, in examining theories explaining the causes of suicide terrorism, students in a class whose topic was terrorism found that an important assumption underlying scholarly insights from psychology and political science is that the behavior of the terrorists is rational (as defined by both disciplines), not irrational as many in the class had initially supposed.

Concepts

A **concept** is a symbol expressed in language that represents a phenomenon or an abstract idea generalized from particular instances (Novak, 1998, p. 21; Wallace & Wolf, 2006, pp. 4–5). For example, chairs come in various shapes and sizes, but once a child acquires the concept *chair*, that child will always refer to anything that has legs and a seat as a chair (Novak, 1998, p. 21).

Though *concept* is a key term used throughout this book, examples of concepts favored by each discipline are omitted here for two reasons. First, the term lacks clarity as it relates to other terms such as *phenomena, causal link, theory,* and *method*. Rick Szostak (2004) finds that many concepts can be defined in terms of phenomena, causal links, theory, or method. Some concepts, such as culture, are clearly phenomena. Others, such as oppression, are results of phenomena—in this instance, political decision making. Still others, such as revolution, globalization, and immigration, describe processes of change within or between phenomena (p. 41). But most of these, he observes, can best be understood as illustrating features of causal links—for example, the link between art and human appreciation (pp. 42–43). Humanities scholar Mieke Bal (2002) agrees that concepts "need to be explicit, clear, and defined." She notes, however, that in interdisciplinary humanities, concepts "are neither fixed nor unambiguous" (pp. 5, 22, 23).

In addition to the difficulty of differentiating concepts from phenomena and causal links is the more formidable challenge of dealing with the huge number of concepts that each discipline has generated. Perhaps this is why so few scholars have attempted exhaustive surveys of scholarly concepts in particular disciplines, let alone across entire disciplinary categories. For this reason, this book makes no attempt to associate particular concepts with particular disciplines. Researchers will certainly encounter what are purported to be concepts and should consult Szostak's classification of phenomena presented earlier in this chapter to see whether the concept is, in fact, a phenomenon. If not, the interdisciplinarian should investigate whether the concept is or could be carefully defined in terms of causal links, theory, or method.

Theory

The root meaning of the word *theory* is "looking at or viewing, contemplating or speculating." As generally used, **theory** refers to a generalized scholarly explanation about some aspect of the natural or human world, how it works, and why specific facts are related, that is supported by data and research (Bailis, 2001, p. 39; Calhoun, 2002, p. 482; Novak, 1998, p. 84).

Two Kinds of Theory

There are two kinds of theory: **scientific theory** (about the world), which corresponds to the root meaning of theory just noted, and various types of **philosophical theory** (epistemological, ethical, etc.), which were dealt with in the section on epistemology. Confusion sometimes arises by the fact that some "theories" such as feminism or Marxism or literary theory operate as both scientific theory and philosophical theory: They make not only epistemological arguments, but also arguments about the world.

The Importance of Theory to Interdisciplinary Work

The clarified definition of disciplinary perspective, repeated here, highlights the importance of theory to interdisciplinary research: Disciplinary perspective refers to the ensemble of a discipline's defining elements that include phenomena, epistemology, assumptions, concepts, theory, and methods. Interdisciplinarians need a basic understanding of theory, both scientific and philosophical, for three practical reasons. First, as Janet Donald (2002) emphasizes, for students to work in a discipline, they "must have the vocabulary and the *theory* of the field" because "each discipline requires a different mindset [italics added]" (p. 2).

Second, more than ever before, theory dominates the scholarly discourse within the disciplines and often drives the questions asked, the phenomena investigated, and the insights produced. Klein (1999) notes the increasingly common practice of disciplines borrowing theories and methods from other disciplines and, in some cases, making the borrowed theory or method their own (p. 3). Ben Agger (1998) notes "the ongoing theory explosion across the humanities and social sciences" (p. 10). Lattuca (2001) comments on the "qualitative-quantitative cross currents in the social sciences and the increased use of poststructuralist theories in the humanities and social sciences" as examples of ferment in and among disciplines (p. 3).

Third, since these theories explain particular or local phenomena, they provide many of the disciplinary "insights" into a particular problem, and it is these insights that students need to integrate in order to produce an interdisciplinary understanding of the problem.

Finally, students need to develop a basic understanding of theory because of the interrelationship between theory and disciplinary research methods. In his discussion of how to do interdisciplinarity, Szostak (2002) emphasizes the importance of ascertaining "what theories and methods are particularly relevant to the question at hand. In the conduct of interdisciplinary work," he says, "there are complementarities such that borrowing a theory from one discipline will encourage use of its methods, study of its phenomena, and engagement with its worldview" (p. 106). As with phenomena, he cautions researchers to not ignore theories and methods that may shed some lesser light on the question.[13] He also cautions not to blindly accept the evidence for a theory from the methods preferred by that discipline. Disciplines choose methods that make their theories look good. It is that sort of synergy that makes disciplinary perspective so powerful.

Note to Readers

Understanding each theory, even in general terms, will enable researchers to approach many topics with greater sophistication and depth of insight. Explanation of precisely how theory may actually be used in interdisciplinary work is reserved for later chapters.

To sum up, theory is important to interdisciplinary work for three reasons:

- Theory is a major component of what any discipline is. It is virtually impossible to conduct research in any discipline on any topic without dealing with theory at some level.
- Because theory is so fundamental to disciplinary scholarship, knowing the basics of these theories or schools of thought (including newer theories such as cultural analysis and new historicism) will at least enable the student to detect them when reading the disciplinary literature relevant to the topic.
- Insights are embodied in theories. Theories produce insights into a specific problem.

Method

Method is the final defining element of a discipline and its perspective. Method concerns how one conducts research, analyzes data or evidence, tests theories, and creates new knowledge (Rosenau, 1992, p. 116).[14] Methods are ways to obtain evidence of how some aspect of the natural or human world functions (Szostak, 2004, pp. 99–100). Each discipline tends to devote considerable attention to discussing the method(s) it uses, and it does this by requiring students majoring in the discipline to take a research methods course. The reason is simple: The methods a discipline favors correspond to the theories it embraces. Interdisciplinarians should be aware of this linkage between disciplinary methods and theories. Though a discipline favors one method to investigate a theory, there may be other methods that would shed less favorable light on the method.

The Importance of Disciplinary
Methods to Interdisciplinary Work

The interest of interdisciplinarians in disciplinary methods and the kind of knowledge required of them varies considerably depending on how they work with methods. Advanced undergraduates and graduate students must have some familiarity with the strengths and weaknesses of the methods used by the contributing disciplines in order to evaluate each insight or theory as

STEP 6 calls for (see Chapter 8). Graduate students and even more senior scholars acting as solo interdisciplinarians conducting basic research must have much more knowledge of methods beyond identifying and examining linkages among the insights of contributing disciplines. Interdisciplinary teams conducting basic research must have this same level of knowledge.

Those interdisciplinarians conducting basic research have to decide when and whether to use quantitative (descriptive) or qualitative (relational) methods, or both. Though the furor over this difference is dying down, disciplinary researchers remain divided about which approach is preferable. Interdisciplinarians engaged in basic research should be open to both approaches. The **quantitative approach**, such as the number of molecules and the size of the ozone layer, emphasizes that evidence can be expressed numerically over a specified time frame. The **qualitative approach** focuses on evidence that cannot easily be quantified, such as cultural mannerisms and personal impressions of a musical composition. In reality, the quantitative or qualitative distinction is becoming increasingly blurred. For example, theories in natural science that focus on nonintentional agents—such as the germ theory of disease or cell theory—are inherently qualitative. Interpretivists often quantify by using words such as *most* rather than percentages (Szostak, 2004, p. 111).

Just as researchers must have at least a general knowledge of the theories informing the disciplines relevant to the problem, so, too, must they have a working knowledge of the methods used by these same disciplines. Interdisciplinary programs whose courses cross only a few disciplinary boundaries emphasize, naturally, only a few methods. Interdisciplinary programs or courses that take interdisciplinarity itself as a focus tend toward a much broader coverage of methods, though this coverage is far from exhaustive. The latter kind of program clearly demands that one read widely in the disciplinary literature to develop at least a general understanding of all the standard methods. Fortunately, the number of these is relatively small.

Table 4.13   Method Types Linked to Epistemologies and Their Approaches

Epistemology	Approach	Methods
Positivism	Quantitative	Experiments
		Surveys
		Statistical analysis
		Mathematical modeling
		Classification
		Mapmaking

(Continued)

| Table 4.13 | (Continued) | |

Epistemology	Approach	Methods
		Examination of physical traces
		Careful examination of physical objects (as when geologists study rocks)
Interpretivism	Qualitative	Participant observation
		Interview
		Textual analysis
		Hermeneutics
		Intuition/experience
Postmodernism		Textual analysis

SOURCE: Based on information in Szostak (2004).

Table 4.13 links commonly used quantitative and qualitative methods with the positivist, interpretivist, and postmodern approaches. These correspondences are imperfect and may be contested by practitioners. For example, some researchers who perform structured interviews would not think of themselves as interpretivist.

Analysis of the strengths and weaknesses of each method is reserved for Chapter 7.

Various Methods

Tables 4.14, 4.15, and 4.16 associate particular disciplinary categories with particular methods. The methods associated with each category are not definitive and are stated in the most general terms. Any statement of disciplinary practices can be contested on the ground that it disguises the pluralistic and even conflicted view of disciplinary practice. The following descriptions are written in awareness of the possible criticisms of them. The purpose of these tables is to help researchers decide which research method(s) are appropriate to the problem, or topic.

Methods of the Natural Sciences   There is an underlying logic to how disciplinarians proceed in producing new knowledge, and there's another overlapping but distinct logic to how interdisciplinarians proceed. All the natural sciences use what is often called the "**scientific method**" but is really a methodology.[15] For example, cosmologists or astronomers cannot do experiments; biologists and Earth scientists too often are forced to rely on careful observation.

The methodology, *idealized,* has four steps: (1) observation and description of phenomena and processes; (2) formulation of a hypothesis to explain the phenomena; (3) use of the hypothesis to predict the existence of other phenomena, or to predict quantitatively the result of new observations; and (4) execution of properly performed experiments to test those hypotheses or predictions. The scientific method is based on beliefs in empiricism (whether the observation is direct or indirect), quantifiability (including precision in measurement),[16] replicability or reproducibility, and free exchange of information (so that others can test or attempt to replicate or reproduce).

While the phrase *scientific method* is not closely associated with experimentation, it has been associated with other methods in the past. Interdisciplinarians should be aware that there are more than a dozen legitimate methods used in the scholarly enterprise (see "Methods" in Table 4.13). The scientific method has predominantly followed (with some notable and relatively recent exceptions such as ecology) the strategy of **reductionism**. This is the strategy of "dividing a phenomenon into its constituent parts and studying them separately in the expectation that knowledge produced by narrow specialties can be readily combined into the understanding of the phenomenon as a whole" (Newell, 2004, p. 2).

The scientific method assumes that there is a single explanation of how phenomena that appear to be separate entities are intrinsically unified

Table 4.14   Research Methods Associated With the Natural Sciences

Discipline	Methods
Biology	The epistemological debate between the naturalist or field position and the experimental or laboratory position is also about which methods (i.e., lab or field) produce "good science" (Maienschein, 2000, p. 134). Laboratory (i.e., experimental design and data analysis) methods extract life from its natural ecological setting and examine specimens under controlled conditions using electron microscopy and positron-emission tomography (PET) to produce visual images of the structure of systems (Bechtel, 2000, p. 139). Systems ecologists and developmental biologists insist on studying life in its living, functioning, active form using "philosophical, sociological, anthropological, and cognitive explanatory schemata" (Holmes, 2000, p. 169). For biology, the scientific method must take into consideration ethical limits to experimentation.
Chemistry	One way in which the approach of chemistry differs from that of the other sciences is that it attempts to develop new materials using the foundational principles discovered and developed by chemistry, and chemistry seeks to understand the observed macroscopic properties in terms of atomic and molecular behavior (J. Rogers, personal communication, April 2005). "Understanding the properties of a substance and the changes it undergoes leads to the central theme in chemistry: macroscopic properties and behavior, those we can see, are the results of submicroscopic properties and behavior that we cannot see" (Silberberg, 2006, p. 5).

(Continued)

| Table 4.14 | (Continued) |

Discipline	Methods
Earth Science	Like physics and chemistry, Earth science relies on a variety of quantitative methods of displaying and analyzing data, including statistics, geographic information systems (GIS), computer modeling such as finite elements and discrete elements, X-ray diffraction and florescence, mass spectronomy, emission and absorption spectronomy, gravity and magnetic resonance, acoustic (seismic) wave propagation (reflection and refraction), remote sensing using the electromagnetic spectrum, and well logging techniques that include sonic, electrical resistivity, and neutron absorption. Increasingly, however, geologists are relying more on fieldwork because processes taking place in Deep Time cannot be replicated (J. Wickham, personal communication, August 2006).
Mathematics	Mathematics is totally abstracted from the empirical world, though other disciplines that are empirical apply mathematics. The worlds mathematicians create are rational simply because rationality is a requirement mathematicians impose on themselves. Mathematics uses proven theorems about the properties (e.g., consistency, transitivity, completeness) of the abstract realities they create.
Physics	Like chemistry, physics takes objects apart to study their constituent parts (atoms and subatomic particles, quanta) to see how they are related; but unlike chemistry, it also studies overall characteristics such as mass, velocity, conductivity, and heat of evaporation. The methods of physics are split into theoretical and experimental. "Theoretical" physicists solve problems using mathematical modeling rather than experimentation. Experimental physicists use experiments and computers to measure and quantify objects and phenomena and to test and verify or falsify the theories produced by the theoretical physicists (Donald, 2002, pp. 32–33). In physics, the hypothesis often takes the form of a causal mechanism or a mathematical relation.

(Donald, 2002, p. 32). Similarly, the assumption underlying interdisciplinarity is that conflicting disciplinary insights into a complex problem can be intrinsically unified by modifying or creating an underlying common ground concept, assumption, or theory. This assumption is unlike the assumption underlying the "scientific method," however, in that the resulting general "law" is applicable to all similar phenomena, whereas the resulting interdisciplinary understanding is "local" and limited to the problem at hand.

Not all the sciences use the scientific method in the same way. The physical sciences, such as physics and chemistry, use experimental forms of the method involving experiments to gather numerical data from which relationships are identified and conclusions are drawn. Among the differences that Table 4.14 addresses are what each discipline considers data and how each gathers and processes data. For example, chemistry's approach to research is quite similar to that of the other physical sciences, such as physics and Earth science, in that it seeks to measure and describe observed phenomena. But unlike Earth science, it relies first and foremost on lab experiments.

Methods of the Social Sciences   The social sciences use modernist scientific techniques, such as mathematical models and statistical analysis of empirical data, in conducting much of their research. The more descriptive social sciences, such as anthropology, may use a form of the method that involves gathering information by making visual observations or interviewing and use "thick description" to record this information.

But the modernist and quantitative approach has lost force in recent decades largely because of developments in the philosophy of science and the rise of postmodernism. It is in methodology that postmodernism is having its greatest impact on the social sciences and the humanities by "deflating the confidence previously held in the capacity to identify best practice" (Dow, 2001, p. 66). Today, says H. Russell Bernard (2002), "the differences *within* anthropology and sociology with regard to methods are more important than the differences *between* those disciplines" (p. 3). Consequently, the description of methods in Tables 4.15 and 4.16 reflects both modernist and postmodernist approaches.

Table 4.15   Research Methods Associated With the Social Sciences

Discipline	Methods
Anthropology	Anthropology uses a wide variety of scientific and interpretive techniques to reconstruct the past including experiments, sampling, cultural immersion, fieldwork, interviewing (unstructured and semistructured), structured interviewing (questionnaires and cultural domain analysis), scales and scaling, participant observation, field notes, direct and indirect observation, thick description, analysis of human interaction, language, archaeology, and biology (Bernard, 2002).
Economics	Modernist methods include mathematical modeling and data analysis involving regression analysis, Monte Carlo simulations, plugging the data into systems of large numbers of simultaneous equations, etc. What is distinctive about most economic data sets is that they are generated for other purposes (e.g., governmental policy) and often do not directly measure the variables of interest to economists, so economists end up working with inferential indicators more than direct measurements.
	Mainstream economics, however, is experiencing some degree of methodological fragmentation by postmodernists who oppose the reduction of human behavior and motives to a single purpose: individual gain. Concluding that "an overarching methodology is rendered impossible by the fragmented nature of discourse-based knowledge," postmodernism denies the role of methodology altogether. Recently, a corrective "synthetic" approach has adopted a pluralistic approach to methodology, holding that the methodology of each economic school of thought should be analyzed critically on its own terms (Dow, 2001, pp. 66–67).

(Continued)

| Table 4.15 | (Continued) |

Discipline	Methods
Political Science	Political science does not have a single big methodological device all its own, the way that many disciplines do. Rather, "political science as a discipline is defined by its substantive concerns, by its fixation on 'politics' in all its myriad forms" (Goodin & Klingerman, 1996, p. 7). More specifically, practitioners describe legal governments and examine ideas, normative doctrines, and proposals for social action (Hyneman, 1959, p. 28). Political scientists rely heavily on mathematical modeling and statistical testing. A method distinctive to political science is polling data on voter behavior. Like other social sciences, political science believes that "research should be theory oriented and theory directed," and that "findings [should be] based upon quantifiable data" (Somit & Tanenhaus, 1967, p. 178).
Psychology	Psychology and its many subfields use experiments primarily. Within this method there are many approaches to gaining knowledge, and some of these are more demanding than others. The continuum of demands on the adequacy of information is called "levels of constraint" that focus on precision, structure, and control of the various phases of the research project. These levels of constraint include (from least to most demanding) naturalistic observation, case study research, correlational research, differential research, and experimental research (Graziano & Raulin, 2004, pp. 48–51). There are two primary types of research: basic research to understand psychological processes, the primary goal of which is to increase knowledge, and applied research to find solutions for certain problems such as employee morale. Other applied researchers conduct evaluation research to assess the effects of social or institutional programs on behavior (Leary, 2004, p. 4).
Sociology	The intellectual labor of sociology, not unlike other disciplines, is divided among theorists, methodologists, and researchers. The effect of this cognitive separation in sociology is "that theorists do not deal with the relationship of theory to evidence" and, thus, to method (Alford, 1998, pp. 11–12). Methodologists are usually divided into quantitative and qualitative specialties. "Quants" are further divided between applied and theoretical statisticians. "Quals" are divided into ethno methodologists, symbolic interactionists, grounded theorists, historical methodologists, and ethnographers, each having its own specialized terminology and research techniques. Researchers analyze the substantive problems defined as part of the discipline's subfields of social stratification, political sociology, the family, education, and the sociology of organizations (Alford, 1998, pp. 1, 11). Though sociology has been long dominated by modernist approaches to research, this is being seriously challenged by methodologies inspired by the humanities that are qualitative (i.e., meaning-based), constructionist, interpretative, narrative, and contextualized (situated in power, race, and gender). Qualitative research methods do not rely heavily on mathematical and statistical analysis but "study people in their natural setting and attempt to make sense of phenomena in terms of the meanings that people bring to them" (Dorsten & Hotchkiss, 2005, p. 147).

Methods of the Humanities   Researchers working in the humanities draw on fields of scholarship in which different beliefs hold. Table 4.16 shows that the humanities rarely insist on quantifying observations. Part of the challenge of interdisciplinary integration (introduced in Chapter 9) is reducing conflict between insights by modifying their concepts and/or assumptions. Once these insights are prepared for integration, constructing a more comprehensive understanding is possible. Whereas the natural and social sciences leave the integration of knowledge out of the scientific method altogether and the humanities leave it up to the reader, viewer, or listener to integrate knowledge, interdisciplinary studies strives to achieve integration. The scholarly enterprise needs both specialized and integrative research.

Table 4.16   Research Methods Associated With the Humanities

Discipline	Methods
Art and Art History	Modernist art historians examine art objects in terms of the artists' mastery of appropriate technique, their structure and meaning within particular historical, political, psychological, or cultural contexts. Formalist analysis of a work of art, for example, considers primarily the aesthetic effects created by the component parts of the design, while iconography studies focuses on content rather than form. Two methodological reactions against formalism are Marxism, which studies the economic and social context of art, and feminism, which is predicated on the idea that gender is an essential component to understanding art. Biographical and autobiographical methods rely on texts (if they exist) and approach works of art in relation to the artist's life and personality. Semiotics, a recent methodological approach derived from linguistics, philosophy of language, and literary criticism, assumes that cultures and cultural expressions such as language, art, music, and film are composed of "signs" and that each sign has a meaning beyond, and only beyond, its literal self (Bal & Bryson, 1991, p. 174). Other approaches include deconstruction, which assigns meaning according to contexts that themselves are continually in flux, and the complex psychoanalytic method that deals primarily with unconscious significance of works of art (Adams, 1996). Postmodern critics, who see the artist as deeply implicated in society, "reject formal analysis and tend to discuss artworks not as beautiful objects produced by unique sensibilities but as works that exemplify society's culture, especially its politics" (Barnet, 2008, p. 260).
History	Historians engage in research that involves identification of primary source material from the past in the form of documents, records, letters, interviews, oral history, archaeology, etc., or secondary sources. They also practice critical analysis involving interpretation of historical documents and forming these into a picture of past events or the quality of human life within a particular time and place. To write good history, historians need a combination of well-reasoned arguments based on solid evidence combined with objectivity and

(Continued)

| Table 4.16 | (Continued) |

Discipline	Methods
	interpretive scrutiny. In the twentieth century, the narrative, event-oriented history characteristic of nineteenth-century professional historiography gave way to "various kinds of social science-oriented history spanning the methodological and ideological spectrum from quantitative sociological and economic approaches and the structuralism of the Annales School to Marxist class analysis" (Iggers, 1997, p. 3). As applied to history, postmodernists question whether there are objects of historical research accessible to clearly defined methods of inquiry, asserting that every historical work is a literary work because historical narratives are verbal fictions, the contents of which are more invented than found (pp. 8–10).
Literature (English)	Research methods emphasize the centrality of texts and include auto/biographical, oral history, critical discourse analysis (i.e., analyzing patterns in language) for exploring visual signs (e.g., illuminations of manuscripts, graphic novels, photographs), computer-aided discourse analysis, ethnography (concerns cultural and social practices), quantitative analysis (i.e., how numbers are used as interpretive tools and as a means of calculating the frequency with which certain words occur and the contexts in which they are set), textual analysis that sees meaning making as a relational process (which relies on other research methods such as feminist and deconstructionist ones), interviewing living authors, and creative writing (which must be accompanied by a theoretical piece of writing) (Griffin, 2005, pp. 1–14). Literary theories are also approaches to literature and include New Criticism (that insists on the preeminence of the text itself and its literary properties), psychoanalytic criticism, reader-response criticism, structuralism, deconstructionist criticism, Marxist criticism, feminist criticism, Bakhtinian criticism, Foucaultian criticism, and multicultural criticism that attends to cultural perspectives such as African American or postcolonial (Bressler, 2003).
Music and Music Education	Music education research is multimethod. Positivist scholars use expertise (i.e., mastery of techniques involved in the production of works of art) and criticism (i.e., interpretation of compositions in terms of their aesthetic qualities, techniques employed, and their meaning within specific historical, political, psychological, or cultural contexts). However, the basic trend in music education research methods is on interpretivist forms of inquiry (i.e., phenomenology, action research, ethnography, narrative inquiry that focuses on human actions, beliefs, values, motivations, and attitudes), critical theory (that stresses that teaching and learning are deeply related to social practices and injustices), feminist or gender studies (that argues that gender issues are implicit in all research methods and interpretations, though most in the field reject the idea of a distinctly feminist research methodology), and postmodernism (that rejects the idea of "methods" altogether and holds that there are no rules of procedure that must be followed and no "right" procedures of investigation, though it does embrace introspection, individualized interpretation, and deconstruction) (Elliott, 2002, pp. 85–96).

Discipline	Methods
Philosophy	The method of philosophy is the making and the questioning of distinctions (a distinction is a difference displayed). Philosophy explains by distinguishing between concepts, as, for example, how responsible action is to be distinguished from the irresponsible (Sokolowski, 1998, p. 1). Philosophers use a variety of techniques to examine a written composition including dialectic, syllogism and logic, contemplation, linguistic/symbolic analysis, argument and debate, and also thought experiments.
Religious Studies	Today, there is no real distinction between the methods of science (natural and social) and those of the academic study of religion. Scholars of religion employ a variety of research and analytical methods that cut across disciplinary lines when examining religious phenomena, religious actions, religious groups, and religious ideas. The methods used by researchers are largely dictated by the questions they ask and the issues they seek to explore. The common ground among scholars of religion is their efforts to describe and explain religious phenomena as an aspect of human culture and experience and do this by engaging in self-reflection, self-criticism, self-censorship, and self-control (Stone, 1998, pp. 6–8).

The Correlation Between Epistemologies and Method

Earlier we noted how disciplines choose methods that are good at examining their favored *scientific* theories.

Here we relate methods to the widely divergent epistemologies of positivism, interpretivism, and postmodernism. Interpretivists assume that there are significant differences among individuals in how they perceive the same phenomenon. Postmodernists, by contrast, argue that using any methodology is rendered impossible by the fragmented nature of discourse-based knowledge (Dow, 2001, p. 66). The methods associated with each epistemology are not definitive and are stated in the most general terms. The purpose of Table 4.17 is to aid students in associating methods to these epistemologies.

Note to Readers

Undergraduate interdisciplinarians are highly unlikely to apply disciplinary methods themselves. Their challenge is to critically analyze, interpret, and apply insights produced by disciplinarians wielding those methods. Graduate students and even more senior scholars acting as solo interdisciplinarians may still not apply disciplinary methods themselves other than to identify and examine linkages among the insights of contributing disciplines. However, they would apply disciplinary methods if, as part of their integrative work, they choose to conduct their own basic research. Interdisciplinary teams may well employ such methods as they conduct basic research.

Table 4.17	Positivism, Interpretivism, and Postmodernism: Their Methods Contrasted

Epistemology	Methods
Positivism	1. Study only that which is observable, such as actions, and not attitudes. 2. People are studied independent of their natural environment. 3. Quantification of evidence is essential.
Interpretivism	1. Since humans are intentional and self-reflective, attitudes rather than actions should be studied. 2. People should be studied in their natural environment, seeking to understand rather than to explain. 3. Qualitative analysis is emphasized over quantitative analysis.
Postmodernism	1. It denies both the prescriptive and the descriptive role of methodology because methodology requires some regularity in techniques for acquiring knowledge (Dow, 2001, p. 66).

SOURCE: Based on Szostak (2004, pp. 62–65, 105).

Chapter Summary

This chapter provides information that is foundational to interdisciplinary practice and critical to developing adequacy in contributing disciplines (STEP 5; see Chapter 7) and evaluating their insights (STEP 6; see Chapter 8). It explains the role of the disciplines and clarifies the definition of disciplinary perspective to mean a discipline's worldview as well as its defining elements (i.e., phenomena, epistemology, assumptions, concepts, theory, and method). How perspective is used depends on what STEPS are being performed. The chapter also provides two ways of beginning interdisciplinary inquiry. One is Szostak's classification approach that involves linking the topic to the appropriate phenomena. The virtue of this approach is that it enables researchers to identify more readily neighboring phenomena that may otherwise be overlooked but may well be relevant to the problem. Researchers, then, can broaden their investigation without focusing, at least initially, on particular disciplines. The other, the traditional perspectival approach, involves linking the problem to those disciplines whose perspectives embrace it. Researchers can profitably use both approaches to identify disciplines relevant to the problem to delve deeply into their scholarship, thus countering the occasional criticism that interdisciplinary studies is shallow and lacks rigor. Using both approaches shows that interdisciplinary analysis can be systematic and cumulative.

Armed with this basic knowledge of the disciplines, their perspectives, and their defining elements, students are now able to identify the disciplines relevant to the problem. Making this decision is STEP 3, the subject of Chapter 5.

Notes

1. Among the applied fields and professions, Geertz (1983) includes education, communications, criminal justice, management, law, and engineering (p. 7). Elsewhere, Geertz (2000) characterizes these broad categories as "rather baggy" because of their indeterminacy (p. 156). Mary Taylor Huber and Sherwyn P. Morreale (2002) use the term *disciplinary domains*, referring to the humanities, the social sciences, and the sciences (p. 8). The use of the term *core disciplines* implies a hierarchy of knowledge that many would contest (Salter & Hearn, 1996, p. 6).

2. "Most disciplines tend to think that what they study is the most important part of reality (that is, their worldview isn't just about what they study but [is about] its role in the larger whole" (Rick Szostak, personal communication, January 11, 2011).

3. Early on, interdisciplinarians such as Newell and Green (1982) opted for a narrow definition: "Disciplines are distinguished from one another by the questions they ask about the world, by their perspectives or world view, by the set of assumptions they employ, and by the methods which they use to build up a body of knowledge (facts, concepts, theories) around a certain subject matter" (p. 24). According to this definition, "perspective" is but one of four primary disciplinary elements and is co-equal with the questions that the disciplines ask about the world, the set of assumptions they employ, and the methods they use to build up a body of knowledge (facts, concepts, theories).

4. Newell (1992) now argues that "perspective" should be defined in broader terms, even suggesting that it is the source of all other disciplinary elements. He refers to "perspective" as that "from which those concepts, theories, methods, and facts emerge" (p. 213). He adds, "*The interdisciplinary researcher must understand how the relevant concepts, theories, and methods underlying each discipline's perspective are operationalized* [italics added]" (1998, p. 545). Janet Donald (2002) apparently agrees, emphasizing that "to understand a field of study [i.e., a discipline], students must learn its perspectives and processes of inquiry" (pp. xii–xiii). By "perspective" she means a discipline's epistemology, vocabulary, theory, and methods or processes of inquiry (Donald, 2002, pp. 2, 8). Jill Vickers (1998) states interdisciplinarians "must accept that the different disciplines have different cognitive maps" (p.17). For Hugh Petrie (1976), reliable borrowing from the disciplines requires that the interdisciplinarian know quite a lot about the "cognitive and perceptual apparatus utilized" (p. 35).

5. But Newell (personal communication, January 8, 2011) asserts that interdisciplinarians "must eventually come to terms with linkages between insights, How does the wall connect to the rope, et cetera."

6. Rogers, Scaife, and Rizzo (2005) explain that much of this discord within disciplines "may owe more to internal political agendas than we would like [to admit]" (p. 268). The reason why scholarly disciplines do not become inert and settled, explains Marjorie Garber (2001), is "the disciplinary libido," meaning the ways in which disciplines seek to differentiate themselves from each other while at the same time desiring to become "its nearest neighbor, whether at the edges of the Academy (the professional wants to become an amateur and vice versa), among the disciplines (each covets its neighbor's insights), or within the disciplines (each one attempts to create a new language specific to its objects, but longs for a universal language understood by all)" (p. ix).

7. Three recent studies support Bromme's claim. Svetlana Nikitina (2002) finds that the key elements essential for success in integrative work are "students' and faculties' disposition for boundary-crossing [and] their intellectual breadth and ability to cope with unanswered questions in science" (p. 27). In "Pathways of Interdisciplinary Cognition" (2005), she writes, "interdisciplinary thinking is fundamentally similar to dialogical exchanges occurring in language and in collaborative activities in which epistemological positions are bartered" and argues that "Bakhtin's (1981) theory of dialogic understanding and subsequent linguistic theories of conceptual metaphor and blending serve as a constructive theoretical framework for the understanding of interdisciplinary cognition" (p. 389). The 2005 study by Sharon J. Derry, Christian D. Schunn, and Morton Ann Gernsbacher, *Interdisciplinary Collaboration: An Emerging Cognitive Science*, reflects on the current state of scientific knowledge regarding interdisciplinary collaboration and encourages research that studies interdisciplinary cognition in relation to the ecological contexts in which it occurs.

8. Members of various disciplines will likely find the descriptions of their respective disciplines not comprehensive enough. But experience using these descriptions in interdisciplinary classrooms validates their intended purpose: to point the student to those disciplines that are potentially relevant to the problem. Once these are identified, the student should then consult each discipline's research aids, many of which are cited in tables in this chapter. These include handbooks, companions, journals, and bibliographies to validate the relevance of each discipline to the problem.

9. For example, Alan Bryman (2004) states, "There is no agreement on the epistemological basis of the natural sciences" (p. 439). Competing epistemological values in biology, for example, are fueling the debate over how much can be learned in the laboratory versus how much can be learned in the field—in other words, what constitutes "good science." Admittedly, there is some overlap between assumptions, epistemology, and preferred method in the tables.

10. Empiricism has come under fire from postmodernists, particularly from feminist philosophers of science who identify a role for value judgments in science and advocate tolerance and willingness to encourage a variety of approaches and multiple judgments of significance to the same scientific problem (Rosenberg, 2000, p. 183).

11. For a more complete discussion of postmodernism, see Chris Baldick (2004, pp. 201–202).

12. R. N. Giere (1999) calls this philosophical approach "naturalistic realism" and states that it is closest to the actual mind-set that most scientists take.

13. Polkinghorne (1996) says that philosophers of science, if not practicing scientists, now accept that scientific methods can neither prove nor disprove any theory (or even any narrow hypothesis). Nevertheless, the application of scientific methods to theories provides scientists with invaluable, if imperfect, evidence with which they can judge whether a theory is in accord with reality (pp. 18–19).

14. Szostak (2004), in *Classifying Science: Phenomena, Data, Theory, Method, Practice*, is careful to distinguish methods "from techniques or tools, such as experimental design or instrumentation, or particular statistical packages" (p. 100). Tools and techniques and so on are a subset of methods. His chapter on "Classifying Methods" is indispensable reading for students.

15. Alexander Taffel (1992) states, "The combination of activities in which scientists engage to achieve the understanding they seek is sometimes called the scientific

method. There is however no single method of science, but rather a variety of activities in which scientists use different combinations of these to solve difficult problems. Scientific activities include recognizing and defining problems, observing, measuring, experimenting, making hypotheses and theories, and communicating with other scientists" (p. 5).

16. Modern science relies heavily on statistical methods in the testing of hypotheses (Rosenberg, 2000, p. 112). Taper and Lele (2004) discuss the two schools of statistical thought, frequentist and Bayesian, and how these approaches impact quantitative statements. "There cannot be such a thing as quantification of support for a single hypothesis," they argue. Scientific evidence "is necessarily comparative," meaning that "one needs to specify two hypotheses to compare, and data may support one hypothesis more than the other" (p. 527).

Exercises

Applying Perspective

4.1   This chapter has argued that disciplines tend to view reality, including significant events and behaviors, through their unique perspectives (in a general sense). How might the disciplines of sociology, psychology, and history view (in a general sense) the world economic crisis of 2007–2011?

4.2   How does juxtaposing different or even conflicting perspectives aid one's understanding of a complex problem, event, or behavior?

Phenomena

4.3   Disciplines, we have said, often share interest in the same phenomenon. Which disciplines would likely share an interest in these phenomena?

- Extreme drought in sub-Saharan Africa
- The Israeli-Palestinian conflict
- A performance of Shakespeare's *Hamlet*

4.4   Using Szostak's "Categories of Phenomena About the Human World" (see Table 4.4), identify subphenomena that are likely connected to these problems, topics, or issues:

- Spousal battery
- The disintegration of the Ross Ice Shelf in Antarctica
- The rise of religious fundamentalism around the world

Epistemological Approaches

4.5   How might a positivist and an interpretivist seek to understand King Tut's mummy?

4.6   What are the logical limits of postmodern epistemology?

4.7   What are the strengths and weaknesses of modernist epistemology when it tries to explain the rise of religious fundamentalism around the world? What are the strengths and weaknesses of postmodernist epistemology when it tries to explain the rise of religious fundamentalism around the world?

Assumptions

4.8   What might those working in the natural sciences assume to be the cause of increasing volcanic activity in Indonesia? What might those working in the social sciences assume to be the cause of population decline in the developed nations of the world? What might those working in the humanities and influenced by "the new generalism" assume to be the meaning (in a general sense) of violent lyrics in music?

Quantitative and/or Qualitative

4.9   Here are several research topics that might be addressed by either quantitative or qualitative methods. For each one, describe how you would conduct either a quantitative study or a qualitative study, and explain which approach would most likely lead to a more comprehensive understanding of the topic:

- Legalization of marijuana
- Teen pregnancy
- The threat to personal privacy posed by electronic media

5

Identifying Relevant Disciplines

_____ **Chapter Preview**

Chapter Preview

The fable of building a house for an elephant (referenced in Chapter 1) shows the importance of taking into account *all* relevant disciplinary perspectives when trying to understand complex systems or solve complex problems. Interdisciplinary studies tends to focus on individual complex problems or systems, such as the impact of the system of dams on the salmon populations of the Columbia and Snake rivers, the causes of suicide terrorism, or the meaning of an anonymous piece of graffiti on the wall of a building. These problems are complex because they have many variables (linked nonlinearly as well as linearly), and the disciplines typically study different variables.

After stating the research problem (STEP 1) and justifying an interdisciplinary approach (STEP 2), the next challenge is deciding which disciplines are *potentially* relevant to the problem and then which of these are *most* relevant (STEP 3). Once these are identified, the full-scale literature search (STEP 4; see Chapter 6) can be conducted. This chapter explains how to (1) identify disciplines that are *potentially* relevant to the problem in an overall sense, (2) map the problem so that its constituent disciplinary parts are revealed, and (3) narrow the number of disciplines to those that are *most* relevant.

> **Step 3: Identify Relevant Disciplines**

_____ Identify *Potentially* Relevant Disciplines

In selecting disciplines from which to draw insights and theories, the challenge is to decide which disciplines contribute substantially to the problem or overall pattern of behavior one wishes to study. This challenge can be met by *first* identifying the phenomena related to the problem, and *then* drawing on disciplinary perspectives in a general sense. The movement is from *potentially* relevant disciplines to those that are the most relevant. A **potentially relevant discipline** is one whose research domain includes at least one *phenomenon* involved in the question or problem at hand, whether or not its community of scholars has recognized the problem and published its research. Determining which disciplines are potentially relevant to the problem is a relatively straightforward process, as described in the next section.

Interdisciplinarians also have to work with interdisciplines, which poses a different challenge than working with traditional disciplines. The very nature of an interdiscipline is to focus on complex problems that fall outside traditional disciplinary boundaries. For example, the interdiscipline of environmental studies is (potentially) interested in any problem concerning the environment. So, researching the cause(s) of freshwater scarcity in a particular locale will involve mapping the problem to reveal its constituent parts, and then connecting each part to the appropriate discipline. A *rule of thumb is to simply add the interdiscipline (in this case, environmental studies) to the list of disciplines potentially interested in the problem.* The literature search will reveal if environmental studies has produced insights or theories relevant to the problem.

Identify *Potentially* Relevant Disciplines *Before* Conducting the Full-Scale Literature Search

Interdisciplinarians commonly skim various disciplinary literatures as they attempt to narrow the topic and frame the research question. But skimming is not the same as conducting the full-scale literature search (the subject of Chapter 6). Ideally, one should attempt to identify the disciplines *potentially* relevant to the problem *before* conducting the full-scale search. Why? Disciplinarians usually emphasize conducting the full-scale literature search at the very outset of the research process because they are concerned not to duplicate previous scholarship. Interdisciplinarians, however, are concerned with finding, not duplicating, work done in the discipline on the phenomenon. The challenge is to clarify the problem as much as possible before undertaking the full-scale literature search so as to not waste time searching the wrong or too many disciplines. One strategy is to find one or two prominent studies from each discipline on the problem as initially conceived, just to see if the problem needs to be rethought and/or restated in light of each discipline's approach before proceeding with the full-scale search. Whereas disciplinarians need to conduct only one literature search (that within their discipline's literature), interdisciplinarians need to conduct several—one in the literature of each discipline that is concerned with a particular part of the problem.

Identifying potentially relevant disciplines (before conducting the full-scale literature search) proceeds by taking the following actions. Once these actions are taken, the disciplinary literatures can be systematically searched for insights and theories.

Identify Phenomena Typically of Interest to Disciplines

Interdisciplinarians should logically look at phenomena before perspectives. Recall that looking at phenomena that are typically of interest to disciplines is the focus of "Szostak's Categories of Phenomena About the Human World" introduced in Chapter 4 (see Table 4.4). Also recall the definition of disciplinary perspective in Chapter 4: "Disciplinary perspective is (1) a discipline's view of reality in a general sense (2) which embraces and in turn reflects the ensemble of its defining elements that include phenomena, epistemology, assumptions, concepts, theory, and methods." Here our interest is in the phenomena typically of interest to the discipline. Interdisciplinary researchers must identify the phenomena relevant to the research question. They can attempt this in one of two ways: approach the disciplines *serially* in hopes of locating a particular phenomenon in one or more of them, or focus on the phenomenon itself.

Consulting Szostak's lengthy table of phenomena first, and reflecting on which ones are likely important for the problem at hand, reduces the risk of missing both important literatures (if a phenomenon is studied only a little by a discipline) and, more important, relationships that have been studied by no discipline. The interdisciplinarian can usefully reflect on how to fill such gaps.

Draw on Disciplinary Perspectives in a General Sense

After identifying from Table 4.4 which disciplines study phenomena relevant to the problem, researchers should then consult Tables 4.2 and 4.3, also introduced in Chapter 4, to identify the relevant disciplines and their perspectives. Once identified, the cursory reading in each discipline should confirm that the perspective is applicable, but *final confirmation* will have to wait until the full-scale literature search is completed. Phenomena and perspective are not alternative approaches but complementary approaches.

As used here, the term *perspective* refers to a discipline's unique view of reality in a general sense. Each discipline tends to view a particular aspect or aspects of the problem, not the problem as a whole. Indeed, the interdisciplinarian may initially conceive of the problem too narrowly because of unwitting influence from a particular discipline or disciplines. One reason to cast as wide a net as possible initially is to make sure one's conception of the problem is responsive to all relevant perspectives. Once the entire problem is recognized, then one can shorten the list of the disciplines to those that are essential before conducting the full literature search. The perspectival approach attempts to connect the research problem (as a whole) to disciplines whose unique perspectives on reality include the problem.

An Example of the Standard Way to Proceed

The standard way to proceed by using both approaches in sequence— phenomena, perspective, literature search—is illustrated in this example of a student who was interested in writing an interdisciplinary research paper on the topic of human cloning. After referencing Szostak's table of phenomena (Table 4.4), the student consulted Table 4.2 on perspectives to see if the topic as a whole is included in the phenomena studied by two or more disciplines. Since it is, the student then did some cursory reading, which supported the notion that the topic is ripe for interdisciplinary inquiry, but final confirmation had to wait until the student completed the full-scale literature search. If, however, the student had found that human cloning is embraced by the perspective of only one discipline, then the problem would likely not merit interdisciplinary study, and the topic would have had to be revised or abandoned.

In fact, the student discovered that no fewer than seven disciplinary perspectives embrace the topic of human cloning, as shown in Table 5.1. The characterization of these disciplines as *potentially relevant* is based on the fact that their perspectives embrace some aspect of human cloning. However, just because the problem is embraced by a discipline's perspective does not mean that the discipline's community of scholars has addressed the problem. The information in the right-hand column is derived from the more general information in Table 4.2. For example, Table 4.2 states in the overall perspective for biology that "when biologists venture into the world of humans, they look for physical, deterministic explanations of behavior (such as genes and

Table 5.1	Disciplines Potentially Relevant to the Problem of Human Cloning and How They Illuminate Some Aspect of It (Before the Full-Scale Literature Search)
Discipline, Interdiscipline, and Applied Field	**How Each Illuminates Some Aspect of the Problem of Human Cloning**
Biology	The biological process of human cloning and rates of success or failure
Psychology	Possible psychological impact on the cloned person of a sense of personhood
Political Science	The role of the federal government
Philosophy	Ethical implications of cloning a human life and what it means to be human
Religious Studies	Sanction in sacred writings against the creation of a new form of human life
Law[a]	Legal rights and relationships of the cloned child and its "parents"
Bioethics[b]	Ethical implications of the technical procedures used to clone a human, particularly in the event of failure

a. Law is an applied field in many taxonomies.

b. Bioethics is an interdisciplinary field in many taxonomies.

evolution)." It is reasonable to conclude, then, that biology is likely to be interested in human cloning *as a biological process* and to be concerned with its rates of success or failure.

There are several advantages to creating a table that connects the topic to disciplinary perspectives:

1. It establishes whether or not each perspective is inclusive of the topic and how it illuminates some aspect of it.

2. It may reveal an instance of apparent overlap of perspectives. In the case of human cloning, there is obviously some overlap in perspective between bioethics and philosophy but not enough to warrant ignoring either perspective initially because each may lead to different insights. But one may very well choose to drop one perspective in the narrowing-down process if their insights turn out to overlap too much.

3. It may prompt shifting the focus of the problem or redefining it. Instead of focusing on the problem of human cloning in general, one may wish to narrow the topic and pose a research question such as "What should be the role of government in the development of human cloning technology?" Once again, we see the iterative nature of the interdisciplinary research process (IRP) where performing one STEP may prompt the revisiting of an earlier STEP.

4. It is a convenient resource to consult later in the research process should it be needed.

Identifying potentially relevant disciplines on the basis of whether or not a discipline's perspective embraces the research problem is only a starting point. As noted earlier, broad statements of disciplinary perspectives are typically matters of scholarly contention. For this reason, the results of the perspectival approach should be verified by identifying phenomena that are typically of interest to disciplines.

Synthesis of the Perspective and Classification Approaches

Before Szostak's (2004) classification of phenomena was developed, inter-disciplinarians had to rely solely on the perspective approach (without knowing much about disciplinary perspectives), so the process was hit or miss. But now researchers can consult his classification, consult the perspectives table, and move directly to checking what they learned through those tables by cursory reading in the professional literatures of each discipline identified through that process.

A practical benefit of Szostak's classification approach is that all phenomena can be linked rather easily to particular disciplines, *provided* that one knows the discipline's overall perspective and the phenomena it typically studies. Table 4.3 in Chapter 4 synthesizes the perspectival and classification approaches by connecting individual disciplines to the phenomena they are typically interested in studying. The table's purpose is to help students identify which disciplines are potentially relevant to the problem based on which phenomena are relevant to the problem. The utility of this table depends on the researcher's familiarity with the phenomena each discipline typically investigates. Most phenomena are placed only in the discipline most likely to study them, but most phenomena are studied by more than one discipline.

Summary of How to Identify Disciplines Potentially Relevant to the Problem

Practically, how does one go about identifying the disciplines *potentially* relevant to the problem? Here are some suggestions:

• Think through the problem (before conducting the full-scale literature search) and attempt to identify its various components. Some problems are more complex than others. In any case, one needs to identify relevant phenomena and understand how they interact with each other. The next section explains how mapping the problem helps develop this understanding.

• Refer to Table 4.4, "Szostak's Categories of Phenomena About the Human World," and Table 4.3, "Disciplines and Their Illustrative Phenomena," in Chapter 4 to see which disciplines address the phenomena relevant to the problem.

• Refer to Table 4.2, "Overall Perspectives of Natural Sciences, Social Sciences, and Humanities Disciplines Stated in General Terms," and ask this question of each disciplinary perspective: "Does it illuminate some aspect of the problem or the question?" This questioning process should help the researcher decide which disciplines are potentially relevant to the problem and explain how each illuminates some aspect of the problem.

• Confirm the initial selections of disciplines and their perspectives by reading cursorily in the literature of each potentially relevant discipline. For example, Table 5.1 identifies selected disciplines that are potentially relevant to the problem of human cloning and how each illuminates some aspect of it. The characterization of these disciplines as potentially relevant is based on their embracing some aspect of human cloning within each discipline's research domain or the type of phenomena that the discipline prefers to study. However, just because the problem falls within a discipline's perspective and research domain does not mean that the discipline's community of scholars has addressed the problem. (Note: As STEP 3, this exercise should be done before conducting the full-scale literature search called for in STEP 4, the subject of Chapter 6.)

• Read cursorily to see whether experts in the disciplines have published research on the problem. It is better to err on the side of inclusiveness at the very outset than to conclude prematurely that a discipline is not relevant. If the full-scale literature search reveals that a discipline is not as useful as first supposed, it can be easily removed from the study. (Note: Removing it should occur before conducting a full annotated bibliography or literature review and before developing the requisite disciplinary adequacy as called for in STEP 6, the subject of Chapter 8.)

Map the Problem to Reveal Its Disciplinary Parts

This mapping exercise may well assist in identifying relevant disciplines. After selecting the disciplines potentially relevant to the research question, the next task is to identify the constituent parts of the problem, understand how these relate to each other and to the problem as a whole, and view the problem *as a system*. Mapping the problem as a system and using systems thinking facilitates this understanding.[1] Constructing a map is a valuable exercise because it may reveal a gap in one's understanding of the problem or establish that one is placing too much emphasis on a few disciplinary components at the expense of other equally important components. Whereas the disciplinarian is often satisfied to focus on a single part or on a few "neighboring" parts of the problem, the interdisciplinarian is concerned with achieving an interdisciplinary understanding of the problem as a whole.

Maps that are profitable to interdisciplinary work include the research map, the concept or principle map, the theory map, and the system map. Mapping the problem may occur as early as STEP 1 but should occur before conducting the full-scale literature search (STEP 4; see Chapter 6). The results of the literature search should confirm the completeness and accuracy of the map.

The Research Map

The purpose of creating the research map is to help visualize the problem or question in its complexity. A simple research map can help those new to interdisciplinary research visualize the process from beginning to end. Creating a research map may at first appear as a diversion from the more important business of "getting on" with the project. However, experience shows that investing time in formulating the problem and identifying its various components increases efficiency in performing subsequent STEPS of the research process. An example of a research map is shown in Figure 5.1. The key components of the **research map** are worth noting:

- It states the purpose of the research.
- It identifies what disciplines are *potentially* relevant.
- It states the perspective of each discipline on the problem.
- It identifies the assumptions of each discipline.
- It identifies nondisciplinary sources or interpretations.

| Figure 5.1 | Research Map |

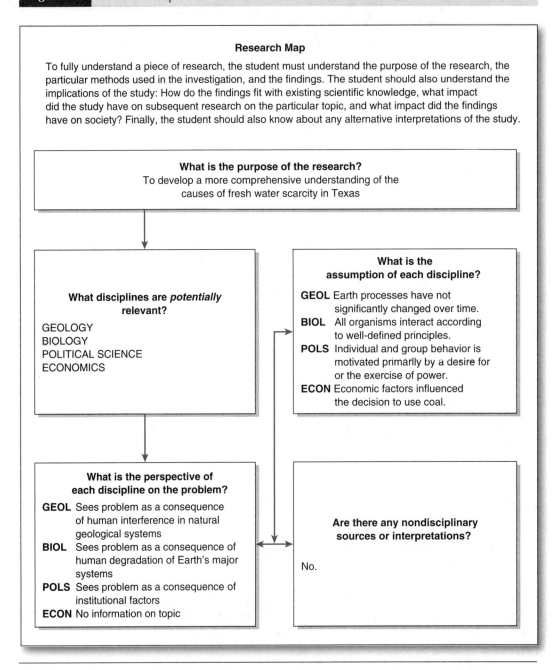

Research Map

To fully understand a piece of research, the student must understand the purpose of the research, the particular methods used in the investigation, and the findings. The student should also understand the implications of the study: How do the findings fit with existing scientific knowledge, what impact did the study have on subsequent research on the particular topic, and what impact did the findings have on society? Finally, the student should also know about any alternative interpretations of the study.

What is the purpose of the research?
To develop a more comprehensive understanding of the
causes of fresh water scarcity in Texas

What disciplines are *potentially* relevant?
GEOLOGY
BIOLOGY
POLITICAL SCIENCE
ECONOMICS

What is the assumption of each discipline?

GEOL Earth processes have not significantly changed over time.
BIOL All organisms interact according to well-defined principles.
POLS Individual and group behavior is motivated primarily by a desire for or the exercise of power.
ECON Economic factors influenced the decision to use coal.

What is the perspective of each discipline on the problem?

GEOL Sees problem as a consequence of human interference in natural geological systems
BIOL Sees problem as a consequence of human degradation of Earth's major systems
POLS Sees problem as a consequence of institutional factors
ECON No information on topic

Are there any nondisciplinary sources or interpretations?

No.

SOURCE: Based on Motes, Bahr, Atha-Weldon, & Dansereau (2003).

The Concept or Principle Map

More advanced students working with more complex or larger-scale problems can benefit from using concept, theory, and system maps to break down the problem into its constituent parts and try to anticipate how the parts may relate to the whole. The **concept or principle map** is a particularly good way to organize information about a problem because it shows meaningful relationships between the parts of the problem. Constructing the concept or principle map requires thinking through all the parts of the problem and anticipating how these behave or function, as shown in Figure 5.2.

Figure 5.2 Concept or Principle Map

Concept or Principle Map

Concepts and principles are ubiquitous in science. To fully understand a concept or principle, the student must be able to describe it and must also know how the concept or principle fits with existing theories and what research has been conducted on the concept or principle. Additionally, the student should know how and why the concept or principle is important to science and society, as well as to any related concepts or principles.

What is the name of the concept or principle?
Implicit memory

What is a good description of the concept or principle?
Memory without awareness

Why is the concept or principle important?
Your thoughts and behavior can be influenced by an event WITHOUT your being aware of the influence!

Are there any related concepts or principles?
Implicit transfer
Covert attention

What theories are related to this concept or principle?
I don't really know:
Ask Professor in
Next CLASS!!

What research has been conducted?
Whole battery of implicit memory tests has been developed:
Verbal, e.g., anagram solving
Nonverbal, e.g., identification of fragmented pictures

SOURCE: Based on Motes et al. (2003).

The Theory Map

Theory is an inescapable part of conducting research in any discipline on an advanced undergraduate and graduate level and is therefore important to interdisciplinary inquiry. The **theory map** describes the theory's supporting evidence, importance, and similarity or competition to other theories. In the following chapters, some of the professional work and student projects used to illustrate aspects of the interdisciplinary research process use theories. For example, a student investigating the causes of freshwater scarcity in Texas discovered that the insights from each of the relevant disciplines are couched in terms of well-known (i.e., within these disciplines) theories. If one or more disciplinary theories are involved in an inquiry, one must develop adequacy in each theory and in each discipline that produced it. Developing adequacy in relevant disciplines is STEP 5 and the subject of Chapter 7. Preliminary to developing adequacy, however, is mapping the problem. The theory map on Piaget's theory of cognitive development shown in Figure 5.3 can easily be modified to focus on additional aspects of any theory.

Systems Thinking and the System Map

Part II of the IRP is designed to deconstruct the complex problem and understand it in all of its complexity. An important and useful tool to accomplish this is systems thinking. **Systems thinking** is a method for visualizing interrelationships within a complex problem or system. It breaks down complex problems into their constituent parts, identifies which parts different disciplines address, evaluates the relative importance of different causal linkages, and recognizes that a system of linkages is much more than the sum of its parts (Mathews & Jones, 2008, pp. 73, 75). Systems thinking adds a powerful dimension to interdisciplinary research, integration, and problem solving.[2]

Though systems thinking is typically associated with the quantitatively oriented fields of engineering, operations management, computer science, and environmental science, it is being applied to a widening range of qualitatively oriented problems. These include the motivation of Shakespeare's Hamlet to avenge the death of his father (Hopkins, 1992), Alice's behaviors during her adventures in Wonderland (Horiuchi, 2003), and the actions of emergency workers at the World Trade Center on September 11, 2001.

A primary analytical tool of systems thinking is system mapping, which enables the researcher to visualize the system or problem as a complex whole. The purpose of constructing the **system map** is to show all the parts of the system (e.g., complex problem) and illustrate the causal relationships among them. Generally, each part of the complex system is studied by a different discipline. Newell (2007a) points out that it may not be fully apparent to those in a discipline how the subsystem they study contributes to the overall pattern of behavior of a system or problem that is truly complex. Constructing the system map will also help reveal disciplinary parts of the problem that

Figure 5.3   Theory Map

Theory Map

To fully appreciate a scientific theory, the student should be able to describe the theory, know evidence for and against the theory, know why the theory is important, and know whether there are any similar and competing theories.

What is the name of the theory ?
Piaget's Theory of
Cognitive Development

What is a good description of the theory?

Our actions are based on our available schemas. Upon encountering new situations, we either assimilate the new information into old schemas (i.e., respond in old ways) or accommodate the new information by creating new schemas (i.e., respond in new ways).

Stages

Sensorimotor - 0–2 yrs: reacts to sensory stimuli through reflexes; seems not to understand object permanence (according to Piaget)

Preoperational - 2–7 yrs: develops language; can represent objects mentally by words and symbols; shows object permanence; lacks concept of conservation

Concrete Operations - 7–11 yrs: understands conservation; can reason logically with regard to concrete objects

Formal Operations - 11 yrs: can reason logically about abstract and hypothetical concepts

---

What evidence is there for and against this theory?

For Piaget's methods of testing each stage (object permanence and conservation tasks) reveal the child's ability or inability to accomplish certain tasks; Piaget found reasoning mistakes made on IQ tests

Against Stages are discontinuous; arguments about age estimates and about reasons for difficulty (e.g., object permanence appears much earlier, and conservation failures may be due to demand characteristics because rewording the questions changes the outcomes)

Conservation of volume is found much earlier if the researcher states a reason for changing from a short fat glass to a tall thin glass; studies of other cultures

---

Why is the theory important?

Major influence on and contributions to developmental and cognitive psychology

Are there any similar or analogous theories?

Neo-Piagetian theories concentrate on scientific or logical aspects Fifth-Stage Theorists

Which theories compete with this one?

Bayley, Gessell Vygotsky zone of proximal development, Info-Processing Theorists

---

SOURCE: Based on Motes et al. (2003).

were not initially obvious (Newell, 2007a, p. 246). The mapping exercise, like other elements, clarifications, or corrections of the IRP, is iterative: The student should sketch the system at the outset but will likely add important elements or clarifications as the research progresses.

Consider, for example, the complex problem of deciding how to rezone a piece of land to change its use. Problems typically associated with land-use change include water-quality degradation created from developed landscapes, rising property values that lead to a lack of affordable housing, loss of aesthetic beauty and productive farmland by converting open spaces to developed areas, and the uncertainties associated with new people, jobs, and ways of life invading an area (Mathews & Jones, 2008, p. 75). Such problems are highly appropriate for interdisciplinary inquiry and require drawing on insights from multiple disciplines to fully understand them. They require *triangulating* or maintaining balance between disciplinary depth, disciplinary breadth, and interdisciplinary integration.

Two types of system maps of particular interest to researchers are causal loop diagrams and stock flow diagrams. These diagrams facilitate our understanding of the interworkings of a system by visualizing the behavior that occurs in the system, as well as the likely outcome(s) that the system will produce. For example, to understand why communities experience traffic congestion on a road system just after it has been expanded requires an understanding of the relationship between the key actors in the system. Figure 5.4 shows a causal loop diagram that illustrates how individuals select driving routes and the relationships between population, driving, air quality, and word-of-mouth communication.

Figure 5.4   Causal Loop Diagram

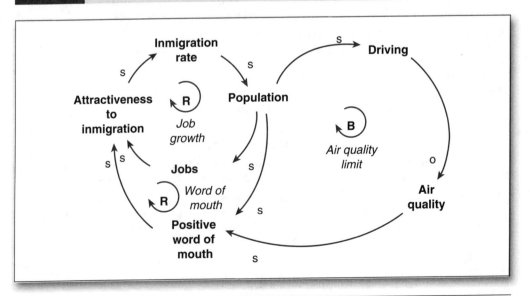

SOURCE: Mathews & Jones (2008, p. 77).

Specifically, Figure 5.4 shows how population affects vehicle traffic in a region that in turn affects air quality negatively. Leah Greden Mathews and Andrew Jones (2008) explain the subscripts:

> The subscripts *s* and *o* on the relationship arrows in a causal loop diagram show whether the two phenomena are moving in the same or opposite direction. Reduced air quality tends to negatively impact public perceptions of a region's livability, which, in turn, has the effect of reducing or even reversing population growth. This type of offsetting relationship is said to be a "balancing loop," and is labeled with a B (for balancing). There are other factors that serve to reinforce the population trend simultaneously which are labeled with an R (for reinforcing) in the causal loop diagram. As population grows, positive word of mouth can also grow as people express enthusiasm about the region to their friends and relatives. The positive "buzz" can lead to "in-migration" which reinforces population growth. (p. 77)

In addition to breaking down a problem into its constituent parts, the causal loop diagram helps identify which parts of the system are likely to be addressed by different disciplines, subdisciplines, and interdisciplines. For example, the disciplines interested in the relationship between a region's road system and its air quality include biology, economics (the economics of transportation), and political science (government agencies at the local, state, and federal levels responsible for monitoring air quality), as well as the interdisciplinary field of environmental science. Knowing the key parts of a system and understanding how they relate to each other and to the problem as a whole enables the researcher to undertake the full-scale literature search with greater focus and efficiency.

Figure 5.5 shows a stock and flow diagram that helps the researcher visualize the flows and accumulations (stocks) in the complex system of diabetes

Figure 5.5   Stock and Flow Diagram Showing the Population-Level Flows of People Through Stages of Diabetes, With the Public Health Interventions

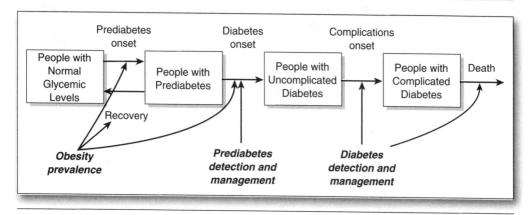

SOURCE: Mathews & Jones (2008, p. 79).

incidence. The usefulness of this diagram is that it makes distinctions between people's physiological condition relative to Type 2 diabetes within a given population.

Mathews and Jones (2008) explain the boxes:

> Each of the boxes represents stocks or accumulations of numbers of people with various diabetic conditions. The arrows represent flows or relationships between the stocks. The flow mapped in Figure 5.5 shows the flow of people through various stages of diabetes. For example, a fraction of *People with Normal Glycemic Levels* will experience prediabetes onset and become part of the population of *People with Diabetes*. Some of these individuals will recover and return to the category of *People with Normal Glycemic Levels*. There is a reverse flow depicted between these two stocks. However, some *People with Prediabetes* will experience diabetes onset and become part of the accumulation of *People with Uncomplicated Diabetes*. (p. 78)

Benefits to Students of Using Systems Thinking and the System Map

There are four practical benefits from using systems thinking and drawing a system map:

- Even if a project is limited to only two or three disciplines, one still needs to understand which parts of the system each illuminates. Researchers may find out as they pursue the research that relationships at first thought to be of secondary importance are of primary importance.
- Drawing a system map and locating the disciplines on it that one believes are relevant enables the researcher to more easily identify other relevant disciplines that may have been overlooked earlier.
- Drawing a system map helps the researcher understand not only how the system operates the way it does but also *why* the system behaves the way it does. For example, simply knowing *how* coal contributes to acid rain does not explain *why* coal was chosen over other materials to fuel electric utilities to begin with. One should be as concerned with knowing the *why* of the problem as knowing the *how*. The system map enables the researcher to see how the disciplinary components of the complex system or problem relate to each other and to the system as a whole (Motes et al., 2003, pp. 240–242).
- A system map can reveal the existence of a system that did not initially seem to be a system. Systems include not only physical phenomena such as roads or climate but also cultural phenomena such as faith traditions and gender roles.

The Similarity of Systems Thinking to
Problem-Based and Inquiry-Based Learning

Systems thinking uses a "scaffolding strategy" that is similar to that used in problem-based and inquiry-based learning. The latter are typical venues for interdisciplinary learning. The **scaffolding strategy** helps structure complex problems to reduce the cognitive load for students while also making disciplinary—and interdisciplinary—strategies explicit (Mathews & Jones, 2008, p. 80). The systems methodology of learning and conducting research is summarized in Figure 5.6.

Figure 5.6   Systems Thinking Methodology

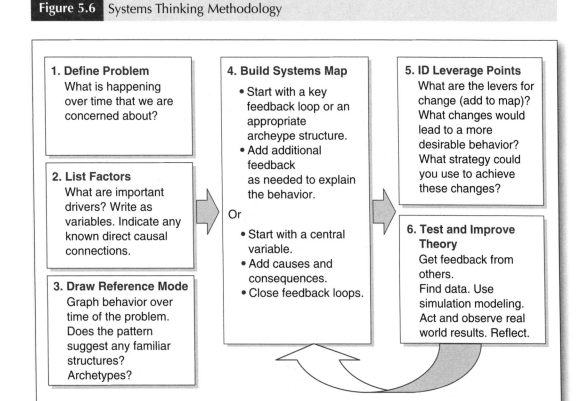

SOURCE: Mathews & Jones (2008, p. 81).

As with the early STEPS of the IRP, disciplinary knowledge is essential to performing the first three steps of the system map. Mathews and Jones (2008) describe the remaining steps:

> [STEP 4] requires the disciplinary skills of systems thinking as well as the interdisciplinary skill of making connections across and between disciplinary knowledge domains. This step may help students identify

cases in which different disciplinary experts appear to be saying different things only because they are talking about different linkages. STEP 5 requires the student to identify [the nonlinear relationships] (e.g., the leverage points, or places where "a small shift in one thing can produce big changes in everything") (Meadows, 1999, p. 1). STEP 6 involves testing and improving theory by seeking feedback from others, testing the model with data, acting and observing real-world results, and reflection. STEPS 5 and 6 require students to integrate knowledge from multiple disciplines to produce a more comprehensive understanding of the system. (p. 80)

How Systems Thinking Promotes Interdisciplinary Learning and Facilitates the Research Process

Using systems thinking and system mapping promotes at least four skills appropriate to interdisciplinary learning and research: perspective taking, nonlinear thinking, holistic thinking, and critical thinking. Perspective taking, as noted in Chapter 4, involves examining a problem from the standpoint of the interested disciplines and identifying the differences between them. Students have to employ perspective taking when asked to identify the potentially relevant disciplines to a problem. For example, in an interdisciplinary course on land use, students were asked to assume the role of an individual experiencing poor air quality who set about to collect data to present to appropriate local, state, and federal agencies.

Systems thinking, as well as system mapping, fosters nonlinear thinking through looking for nonlinear relationships among the phenomena or actors in a system. A small change in one part of the system may lead to big changes elsewhere in the system—what Mathews and Jones (2008) refer to as "leverage points" (p. 80). These nonlinear relationships can be visualized as causal loops. Causal loops include balancing loops—also known as negative feedback loops (where phenomena are in an offsetting relationship)—and reinforcing loops—also known as positive feedback loops (where phenomena are moving in the same direction).[3]

Systems thinking and system mapping promote holistic or comprehensive thinking by asking students to view system parts in relationship to the system as a whole. Comprehensive thinking is required because students must (1) identify a problem, (2) break it down into its constituent parts (so that they connect parts to particular disciplines), (3) identify the causal factors that are important contributors to the problem, and (4) show how these factors relate to each other and to the problem as a whole. "Once students understand the dynamics of the system, they can identify and test hypotheses about where and when to intervene in the system. This will enable them to later propose solutions to the problem" (Mathews & Jones, 2008, p. 78).

Systems thinking also promotes critical thinking by requiring students to examine their assumptions and base their conclusions on evidence. While all disciplines lay claim to critical thinking, such thinking is freighted with added meaning for interdisciplinary students who must examine assumptions (their own as well as those of the disciplines in which they are working) and evaluate and reconcile the conflicting claims of disciplinary experts (Mathews & Jones, 2008, p. 81).

Reducing the Number of Potentially Relevant Disciplines to Those That Are *Most* Relevant

Once the list of disciplines potentially relevant to the problem (i.e., those disciplines that include the problem in their perspective and among the phenomena they are typically interested in) has been drawn up, the next task is to decide which of these are most relevant. This requires conducting at least a cursory search of the literature (but not the full-scale search) of each *potentially* relevant discipline. Once the disciplines *most relevant* to the problem are identified, the student can proceed with the full-scale literature search.

"Most" Relevant Defined

The **most relevant disciplines** are those disciplines, often three or four, which

- are most directly connected to the problem,
- have generated the most important research on it, and
- have advanced the most compelling theories to explain it.

More specifically, these disciplines, or parts of them, provide information about the problem that is essential to developing a comprehensive understanding of it. Students must exercise great care when reducing the number of disciplines to those that are most relevant so as not to neglect important research and thus negatively affect the final product.

Three Questions to Ask to Distinguish Between Potentially Relevant and Most Relevant Disciplines

What is needed is some way to make as sharp as possible the important distinction between the *potentially relevant* disciplines and those that are *most relevant*. To this end, three questions should be asked of each discipline identified as potentially relevant to the problem:

- Does the discipline have a well-defined perspective on the problem? (Note: Perspective in this context refers to the discipline's general view of reality.)

- Has the discipline produced a body of research (i.e., insights and supporting evidence) on the problem of such significance that it cannot be ignored?
- Has the discipline generated one or more theories to explain the problem?

Answering these questions early in the research process will require conducting a cursory literature search (but not necessarily the full-scale literature search of STEP 4).

Applying These Questions to the Disciplines Potentially Relevant to Various Topics

Question 1: Does the discipline have a well-defined perspective on the problem?   At this early phase of the research process, the student should be able to explain how each discipline's overall perspective illuminates the problem or some facet of it. One way to do this (and perhaps gain new insight into the problem) is to recast each perspective in terms of an overarching question about the problem as shown in Tables 5.2, 5.3, 5.4, and 5.5. Compiling this table will likely require cursory reading in each discipline's literature.

Table 5.2	Disciplines and How They Illuminate Some Aspect of the Problem of Human Cloning (Before the Full-Scale Literature Search)

Discipline, Interdiscipline, and Applied Field	Perspective Stated in Terms of an Overarching Question Asked About Human Cloning
Biology	What are the scientific consequences of human cloning?
Psychology	How will the discovery of being cloned affect the cloned person psychologically and the perceptions of others who know this about the person?
Political Science	What should be the role of government concerning this issue?
Philosophy	How will human cloning affect humanity and what it means to be human?
Religious Studies	Does the science of human cloning conform to sacred writings and, more particularly, to the notion of what it means to be human?
Law	What are the legal implications of human cloning, and what are the rights of those who are participants in human cloning experiments?
Bioethics	What are the ethical implications of the biotechnology used in human cloning?

Table 5.3	Disciplines and How They Illuminate Some Aspect of the Columbia River Ecosystem

Discipline	Perspective Stated in Terms of an Overarching Question Asked About the Columbia River Ecosystem
Biology	What are the consequences of the dam system to native salmon populations?
Economics	What are the economic benefits and liabilities of the dam system on the people living in the region?
Earth science	What are the implications of the dams on the region's hydrological system?
History	What does the damming of the Columbia River system tell us about the nation's confidence at this period of history?
Political Science (Politics)	What should be the role of government at all levels concerning the future of the dam system?

Table 5.4	Disciplines and How They Illuminate Some Aspect of Occupational Sex Discrimination (OSD)

Discipline and School of Thought	Perspective Stated in Terms of an Overarching Question Asked About Occupational Sex Discrimination
Economics	What is the economic motivation for OSD?
History	What is the historical context that would help explain OSD?
Sociology	How is OSD a reflection of broader social relationships in society?
Psychology	How does the behavior of the perpetrators and victims of OSD reflect the psychological constructs individuals develop to make sense of their situations?
Marxism	How is OSD a necessary act of preserving capitalism?

Table 5.5	Disciplines and How They Illuminate Some Aspect of a Graffito (i.e., a Wall Writing)

Discipline and Subdiscipline	Perspective Stated in Terms of an Overarching Question Asked About the Graffito
Anthropology (Cultural)	Is the graffito an expression of contemporary "popular" Dutch culture?
Art History	Is the graffito merely illustrative of the text about it?
Linguistics (Narratology)	What does the graffito represent?
Philosophy (Epistemology)	What does the graffito suggest is real and unreal?
Literature	What can the graffito be compared to in Dutch poetry?
Psychology	Is the graffito a text of psychic mourning for love lost?

NOTE: Cultural anthropology, narratology, and epistemology are subdisciplines.

Question 2: Has the discipline produced a body of research (i.e., insights and supporting evidence) on the problem of such significance that it cannot be ignored? Here, the focus is on the significance of each discipline's published research. Since the goal of any interdisciplinary research effort is to achieve the most comprehensive understanding of the problem possible, it is advisable to include those disciplines producing important insights into the problem, whether the number of insights is one or several. In the example of human cloning, the disciplines include biology, psychology, political science, philosophy, religion, law, and bioethics.

Course requirements generally determine how many disciplines and how much reading in their literatures students can reasonably be expected to handle. Some students may need to limit the number of disciplines used to only three or four, based on the *comparative importance of their insights.* Ways to evaluate the importance of insights include

- seeing how often the insight is cited by other writers,
- consulting disciplinary experts, and
- noting the date of publication.

The last factor is particularly important when dealing with time-sensitive issues involving, for instance, rapidly evolving reproductive technologies. Students should focus on research that is published in peer-reviewed journals, by university presses, and by academic presses. There is an abundance of material on the Internet, some of which is peer reviewed but much of which is not.

When determining the relative importance of a discipline and its insights, students should not be influenced by the *quantity* of a discipline's research on the problem. If a discipline has just begun to address the problem, or if the problem is of recent origin, then it is not uncommon to find that its experts have published only one or a few insights. But those few may be extremely important because they are based on the latest research and may advance an important theory. A single treatment of the problem by a leading scholar in a discipline may impact the discussion in such a forceful way that one cannot ignore it. In this event, the student must ask an additional question about the research, and the discipline as a whole, before drawing any conclusions.

Question 3: Has the discipline generated one or more theories to explain the problem? Theories about the causes or consequences (real or possible) of a problem should be part of developing adequacy in each relevant discipline (STEP 5; see Chapter 7) and may be among the possible sources of conflict between disciplinary insights (STEP 7; see Chapter 9). Whether or not theories are involved can be answered only by conducting a full-scale literature search.

Note to Readers

Advanced undergraduates and some graduate students who labor under time and other constraints must somehow reduce the number of potentially relevant disciplines to those that are the most relevant to the problem, and do so quickly and in a way that does not compromise the integrity of the end product. More senior scholars acting as solo interdisciplinarians conducting solo research have considerably more latitude in identifying relevant disciplines and their insights and theories. Reducing the number of disciplines is not as necessary for them as it is for graduate and undergraduate students because professional research is expected to be comprehensive so as not to overlook any important insight or theory. The process of narrowing may occur in collaborative research, where interdisciplinary teams conducting basic research are limited by their budget or by the availability of researchers from particular disciplines. Identifying the most relevant disciplines may involve revisiting the formulation of the research question (STEP 1; see Chapter 3) and undertaking the full-scale literature search (STEP 4; see Chapter 6).

Applying These Questions to the Problem of Human Cloning

Reading the literature on the problem of human cloning with these questions in mind heightened student awareness of not only the amount of disciplinary activity among the relevant disciplines but also the *differing* insights produced by these disciplines. By asking these three questions of each relevant discipline, students were able to reduce their former list of seven to five disciplines that are *most* relevant to the problem of human cloning. These are listed here along with an explanation for their selection:

- Biology: The cursory literature search found that more biologists are writing about human cloning than are scholars from any other discipline. This is understandable because human cloning is itself a biological procedure. Students also found that biologists are advancing some of the most important theories on human cloning and are expressing the greatest diversity of opinion on this issue.
- Bioethics: Essays written by bioethicists contain important bridging concepts and methods. The essays written by bioethicists may appear to be similar to those written by philosophers but differ from them in one important respect: They are science based.
- Philosophy: Though essays written by philosophers appear to overlap those written by bioethicists, there are important differences. For one thing, the essays are not science based but are grounded in humanistic ethics, thus offering a perspective that contrasts sharply with that of bioethicists on this issue. For another, philosophers tend to exclude important bridging concepts and methods that bioethicists tend to include.

- Religious Studies: Religion and the world's major faith traditions are among the most powerful influences in our society today. This explains, for example, why U.S. congressional hearings on "hot button" social issues such as human cloning typically include taking testimony from representatives of the major faith traditions. Therefore, including the perspective of religion seemed appropriate given the amount of attention religious studies scholars have devoted to this issue, the popular interest in their views, and the need to understand value systems that are faith based rather than empirically based.
- Law: Though the amount of legal scholarship on the issue is far smaller than that from the other disciplines, law offers insights that approach the issue from a unique perspective and is therefore pertinent.

In the end, course constraints required limiting the number of disciplines to three. The decision to consider biology, philosophy (i.e., humanistic ethics), and religion as "most" relevant to the problem of human cloning was made on the basis of the criteria noted earlier. Whether these criteria or others are used to differentiate between disciplines that initially appear to be relevant and those that are in fact most relevant, the essential thing is to develop some means by which to identify and justify the disciplines ultimately used and make this decision-making process explicit. Later STEPS in the IRP will validate whether the disciplines selected are in fact the most relevant.

Chapter Summary

STEP 3 of the interdisciplinary research process involves taking three actions: (1) identifying disciplines that are potentially relevant to the problem because it falls within their research domains, (2) applying systems thinking to the problem and mapping it to identify its various disciplinary parts, and (3) reducing the number of disciplines to those that are most relevant. Students are well advised to think through the problem and use both the perspectival and the classification-of-phenomena approaches to identify disciplines potentially relevant to the problem. The STEP of identifying relevant disciplines requires, among other things, that students have a clear understanding of the overall behavioral pattern of the problem they are studying. Students are urged to map the problem to reveal its disciplinary parts and causal linkages. Perceiving linkages and cause-and-effect relationships necessary to deal with complex problems is not possible using a traditional single-discipline approach.

It is in dealing with complex real-world problems that the interdisciplinary research process proves its analytical power and demonstrates its unmatched ability to construct a more comprehensive understanding. A simple research map, for example, can help students new to interdisciplinary research visualize the process from beginning to end. More advanced students working with more complex problems can benefit from using concept, theory, and system maps to break down the problem into its constituent parts and see how the parts relate to the whole. By asking the three proscribed questions of each potentially relevant discipline, students should have little difficulty in identifying those that are most relevant. This process serves three practical purposes: (1) It deepens the student's understanding of the problem, (2) it may reveal the need to refine or restate the research question, and (3) it will make the full-scale literature search more productive.

_____ **Notes**

1. The mental representation of the internal organization of a problem or system may be expressed in a text format or depicted by a visual-spatial technique called concept or knowledge mapping (Czuchry & Dansereau, 1996, pp. 91–96). The knowledge map is composed mainly of nodes of various shapes, sizes, and colors with meaningful links that are labeled to designate the relationships among the nodes. Succinct statements are incorporated in each node, and the links are identified by a letter abbreviation. The links may indicate characteristics, components, consequences, direction of action, outcomes, predictions, subsets, or subtopics; therefore, a legend is included to explain the meaning of the labels for the links. The spatial arrangements of the nodes on the map may be hierarchical, radial (spider), chain, flowchart, or even multidimensional; some map designers have positioned the nodes as trees, ladders, bridges, rockets, or other symbolic shapes for the theme of the map. The most significant purpose of the map's configuration is to depict relationships among the various aspects of the concepts in each node; consequently, the nodes may also be arranged to designate inclusions, exclusions, overlapping concepts, or chronological sequences (C. Atha-Weldon, personal communication, March 2005). Szostak (2004) speaks of mapping the causal links among relevant phenomena to show which phenomena are implicated in a particular research question and how they are related. The researcher might even map which theories are implicated along different links. A useful base from which to sketch such a map when doing work in the social sciences or humanities is his list of phenomena reproduced in Chapter 4 as Table 4.4.

2. Machiel Keestra (2012) presents an example of a particular application of systems thinking. He initiates a promising discussion of the advantages of focusing on mechanisms whereby scholars can engage in intervention, stimulation, or activation experiments with components or operations of individual mechanisms, and look for consequences on that level in a way they usually cannot when testing theories about humans.

3. "When one finds nonlinear relationships, they are normally in reinforcing (i.e., positive feedback) loops, not balancing loops. But not all reinforcing/positive feedback loops involve a nonlinear relationship. Positive feedback loops may merely reinforce or strengthen a relationship (in which case no nonlinear relationship may be involved), but some of them can produce new (not just enhanced) outcomes because the intensified relationship has reached a tipping point (what complex theorists call a bifurcation point) or threshold (in which case a nonlinear relationship is probably involved)" (William H. Newell, personal communication, January 8, 2011).

Exercises _____

Which Strategy?

5.1 This chapter discussed two strategies introduced in Chapter 4, which interdisciplinarians can use to identify disciplines potentially relevant to the problem before conducting the full-scale literature search: focus on phenomena by using "Szostak's Categories of Phenomena About the Human World" (Table 4.4) and/or focus on disciplines by using the perspectival approach. Which strategy would work most effectively concerning the following problems or topics, keeping in mind that you would need to identify potentially interested disciplines so that you could mine their literatures for insights?

- Should the international space station continue to be funded?
- Should the prison camp for alleged terrorists at Guantánamo Bay be closed?
- Should novels with racially pejorative words be used in literature courses in public schools?

Mapping

5.2 This chapter has argued that interdisciplinarians should map the problem as part of the process of identifying relevant disciplines. Identify the kind of map that would best aid one's understanding of each of the following problems and explain why:

- The causes of homelessness
- Why couples divorce
- How to create a new business

Think Systems

5.3 Systems thinking promotes interdisciplinary learning and facilitates the interdisciplinary research process. Create a system map to describe either the causes of a factory closure on a local economy or the effects of a factory closure on a local economy.

Getting Perspective on the Problem

5.4 Using Tables 5.2 through 5.5 as examples, show how the disciplines and their perspectives can illuminate aspects of the problem of teens dropping out of school.

6

Conducting the Literature Search

Chapter Preview

Basic to any research effort is the systematic gathering of information about the problem or topic: the literature search. The integrated model of the interdisciplinary research process (IRP) introduced in Chapter 3 places the full-scale literature search at STEP 4. However, this placement is somewhat arbitrary because the search for information is a dynamic and uneven enterprise that spans multiple STEPS of the IRP. While there is no "right time" to take this STEP for each and every research project, the literature search must begin early on and is often conducted in phases, beginning with (or even preparatory to) STEP 1, defining the problem.

After defining *literature search* in an interdisciplinary sense, this chapter presents reasons for conducting a *systematic* literature search followed by a discussion of the special challenges confronting interdisciplinarians. The primary focus is on how to conduct a library-based interdisciplinary literature search. The search process is divided into two substeps: the initial search and the full-scale search. These are discussed in detail as are the unique challenges that they present to interdisciplinarians and the strategies for overcoming them. Once the search is completed, one can proceed to constructing the annotated bibliography and to writing the interdisciplinary literature review, although these subjects are beyond the scope of this chapter and this book. Detailed descriptions of the process and challenges it poses to interdisciplinarians are found in Newell (2007b).

> Step 4: Conduct the Literature Search

Defining *Literature Search*

The process of gathering scholarly information on a given topic is the domain of the **literature search**, though the term commonly used in the natural and the social sciences is *literature review* (Reshef, 2008, p. 491).[1]

This search carefully examines previous research in journals, books, and conference papers to see how other researchers have addressed the topic. More specifically, the literature search includes identifying the theories that address the topic and what they say, previous research on the topic, whether the findings are consistent or disagree, and if there are flaws in the body of existing research that the student thinks can be remedied (Babbie, 2004, p. 113). The social sciences also conduct a literature search to demonstrate familiarity with the literature on the problem, show the path of prior research and how the current project is linked to it, and integrate and summarize what is known. The literature search in the humanities simply means identifying what has been written on the topic.

Reasons for Conducting the Literature Search

There are several practical reasons for conducting the literature search.

Reason #1: To save time and effort. Discovering what is already known about the problem at the outset will prevent unwitting duplication of work that has already been done, or possibly take the project in a new direction.

Reason #2: To discover what scholarly knowledge has been produced on the topic by different disciplines. **Scholarly knowledge** is knowledge that has been vetted by a discipline's community of scholars through its peer review process. **Peer review** means subjecting an author's scholarly paper or book manuscript to the scrutiny of experts in the field who evaluate it according to academic standards that are viewed as fair and rigorous by the discipline's members. **Scholarly literature** includes journal articles, books (published by university, academic, or commercial presses), and unpublished conference papers. Scholarly literature may also appear on the Internet where an increasing number of scholars and scholarly organizations are posting their research. Students should exercise caution when using online literature because some of it has not been peer-reviewed. The disciplinary nature of much of this literature is easy to identify. However, the growing number of interdisciplines and their journals is complicating the task of neatly dividing scholarly sources by discipline. Students are advised to consult librarians and disciplinary experts to assess the credibility of any site or document.

Reason #3: To narrow the topic and sharpen the focus of the research question. For example, one may be interested in the topic of terrorism but quickly discover that the topic is too broad and the amount of literature on it is too vast to be approached during the time allotted. This does not mean that one should abandon the topic. Rather, the topic will have to be narrowed by focusing on one aspect of terrorism such as a particular form of terrorism, or terrorism in a particular region or historical period, or the causes of one form of terrorism. Narrowing the topic will make the literature search more manageable and rewarding. However, too narrow a focus may remove the topic from an interdisciplinary approach because there is insufficient literature on the topic from two or more disciplines. This is true for undergraduates, less so for graduate students and solo interdisciplinarians, and not very applicable to interdisciplinary teams. The literature search will help students decide whether the topic is ripe for interdisciplinary inquiry. For more advanced students or scholars, a problem may be researchable if two or more disciplines *should have* something to contribute, but for some reason the problem has failed to generate scholarly interest in one or more relevant disciplines.

Reason #4: To identify the factors that have contributed to the development of the problem over time. Every problem has a history. Interdisciplinary writing often traces the historical development of a problem. It is useful to include this "historical development" information in a paper's introduction.

Reason #5: To reveal the paths of prior disciplinary research and how the proposed interdisciplinary project is linked to these and may extend them. Information that is usually included in a literature review includes explaining how the disciplines have approached the problem over time—how disciplinary scholars tried to improve upon previous research by developing concepts, theories, and methods of investigation to better understand the problem—but how these have failed to provide either a comprehensive understanding of the problem or a satisfactory solution to it, thus necessitating an interdisciplinary approach. Reading the literature of each discipline that has addressed the problem also establishes the outlines of that discipline's perspective on the problem and deepens one's understanding of its insights into the problem.

Reason #6: To situate or contextualize the problem. This refers to providing information describing how the problem is connected to other similar problems. In general, situating or contextualizing the problem involves identifying the web of interrelationships in which the problem is embedded. These connections often surface in the process of applying systems thinking to the problem and by drawing a system map as urged in Chapter 5.

Reason #7: To develop "adequacy" in the relevant disciplines (which is STEP 5 of the research process and the subject of Chapter 7). Developing adequacy requires conducting a full-scale literature search and being knowledgeable about the major issues associated with the problem.

Reason #8: To identify the defining elements (i.e., phenomena, epistemology, assumptions, concepts, theory, and methods) used by each discipline's experts in their writing on the problem. This is part of what it means to develop "adequacy" in each discipline. Students should be alert to how the scholarship produced by the relevant disciplines often uses differing terminology (i.e., concepts) and differing explanations (i.e., theories) to describe similar problems. It is critical, therefore, for students to identify the relevant disciplines early on and to investigate their terminology, looking for differences and similarities in meaning and to keep track of these very elements as they read.

Reason #9: To verify that the disciplines identified in STEP 3 as potentially interested in the problem are really relevant. Narrowing the number of disciplines to those that are most relevant is possible only by conducting a literature search.

Special Challenges Confronting Interdisciplinarians _____

Though there are research activities common to disciplinary and interdisciplinary research, special challenges confront interdisciplinarians. Conducting interdisciplinary literature searches is harder than conducting disciplinary literature searches for four main reasons:

- There is simply more ground to be covered.
- Interdisciplinary researchers risk being seduced by what disciplinary experts say.
- Interdisciplinarians must place the insights and theories of each relevant discipline within the context of its unique perspective.
- The methods of library and database cataloguing disadvantage interdisciplinary researchers.

There Is Simply More Ground to Be Covered

With reference to the "ground to be covered," the problems studied by interdisciplinarians are more complex and often broader than those studied by single-discipline scholars. Thus, there is simply more literature to be searched. An interdisciplinary research project requires integration of insights and theories sourced in several disciplines, interdisciplines, or schools of thought. By contrast, a disciplinary research project requires searching the literature of only a single discipline. In fact, the term *literature search* is actually a misnomer because an interdisciplinary research project typically requires several separate literature searches, one for each of the potentially relevant disciplines (Newell, 2007b, p. 92).

Interdisciplinary Researchers Risk Being Seduced by What Disciplinary Experts Say

Novice researchers risk becoming seduced by the existing literature. This seduction may involve accepting a particular discipline's perspective or understanding of the problem to the exclusion of others. Researchers must avoid allowing the existing literature and the views of others, even if they are experts, to disproportionately influence their understanding of the problem. Relying on what others have said at the very outset of the research enterprise risks short-circuiting objective and creative thinking that is essential to good interdisciplinary work.

We must critically evaluate each disciplinary insight with the assumption that it will be only partially correct but also only partly incorrect.

This seduction may lead to being overly impressed by a particular writer's approach *before first developing a clear understanding of how the problem should be approached in an interdisciplinary way.* This would mean concluding at the outset of the project that a particular author or a particular theory holds the key to fully understanding the problem. It may. *But the nature of interdisciplinary work is to suspend judgment and patiently go through the process and let the process reveal if one's earlier assumption is in fact accurate.*

Interdisciplinarians Must Place the Insights and Theories of Each Relevant Discipline Within the Context of Its Unique Perspective

The disciplines assuredly form the foundation of interdisciplinarity and provide much of the information used in the research process. As noted in Chapter 4, disciplines are distinguished from one another by their concentration on different kinds of problems; by the questions they ask about the world; by their perspectives and their defining elements (i.e., phenomena, epistemology, assumptions, concepts, theories, and methods); and by the kind of evidence they consider valid. Unlike disciplinary specialists who take the context of their discipline for granted (to the extent that they are aware of it), interdisciplinarians must place the insights of each discipline they are studying within the context of its unique perspective. This requires not only understanding the defining elements of each discipline, but more generally reading each discipline's insights and theories in light of these elements. This is part of developing adequacy in relevant disciplines (STEP 5, the subject of Chapter 7). The reader must look for possible applications of each discipline's perspective on the problem and be alert to what scholars have overlooked, not just what they have learned. Discovering scholarly silence on a problem is often as important as discovering an important published insight.

The Methods of Library and Database Cataloguing Disadvantage Interdisciplinary Researchers

Students and mature scholars new to interdisciplinary research need to have a "big picture" awareness of the problems with the current methods of library and database cataloguing. The current method of cataloguing in libraries serves the interdisciplinarian poorly because it is organized along disciplinary lines rather than on a comprehensive list of phenomena, concepts, theory types, methods, and so on. Library catalogues are not set up to connect different parts of the problem (or to connect related problems) studied by different disciplines. Nor are they set up to identify the same or similar problems that are given different labels by different disciplines.

The present system of classification also makes it difficult to search by the *name* of the phenomenon. Different terminology is used in different disciplines to describe the same phenomenon. Interdisciplinarians must thus identify the relevant terminology used in each discipline of interest.

Those new to interdisciplinary research may fail to appreciate that a particular discipline is relevant to a particular problem if they search works in that discipline using the terminology of another discipline. To be sure, books may be classified with respect to multiple subjects, as in this example from Miami University's online catalogue that references John Larner's 1999 book, *Marco Polo and the Discovery of the World*. Click on the title and it lists Author(s), Location, Subjects, Formats, Material Type, Language, Audience, Published, LC Classification, Physical Description, and Table of Contents. Under Subjects, one finds

Travels of Marco Polo

Voyages and Travels

Travel, Medieval

Asia—Descriptions and travel—Early works to 1800

Polo, Marco—Travels of Marco Polo

Polo, Marco, 1254–1323? Travels of Marco Polo

If one is interested in Asian history, travel, voyages, or medieval studies, one can see that this book might be of interest. However, without consulting the table of contents or index, one could not tell that it deals with city planning, religion, horsemanship, the invention of paper money, and other issues (William H. Newell, personal communication, January 30, 2011).

Some of these subjects span disciplines, but this only partially alleviates the problem. One way to overcome this limitation is to identify which disciplines are likely to be interested in the problem (STEP 3; see Chapter 5) and then use resources—bibliographies and guides, dictionaries, encyclopedias, handbooks, and databases—specific to each discipline. In this way, the search can proceed systematically and productively across the relevant disciplines. A fuller discussion of the current method of library and database cataloguing and strategies for overcoming their limitations is the subject of the next section.

Conducting the Interdisciplinary Literature Search _____

The literature search is itself a process within the larger interdisciplinary research process, and spans the early STEPS of that process. The literature search is often conducted in two phases: the initial search and the full-scale search. The initial phase begins as one is selecting a topic and deciding if it is **researchable in an interdisciplinary sense**. If it is, then the full-scale search can get under way. The second phase, called the full-scale literature search, precedes and/or coincides with STEP 5, developing adequacy in relevant disciplines (see Chapter 7).

The Initial Search

The first major step in library-based interdisciplinary research is to locate sources on the proposed topic or problem. **Searching** involves deciding where and how to look for information. It may be performed with a single query and may result in retrieving one or more bibliographic sources. But more often, it is a complex and iterative (i.e., repetitive) process (Palmer, Teffeau, & Pirmann, 2009, p. 9). Students new to interdisciplinary research are wise to heed Newell's (2007b) advice: "Even more broadly than with disciplinary research, interdisciplinary scholars need to start broadly and narrow the focus towards more specialized sources as the topic takes shape" (p. 85).

When initiating a literature search, interdisciplinarians have a responsibility to think through the problem in all of its aspects to the best of their ability while (1) avoiding being influenced by what disciplinary experts "see" (i.e., write) and (2) suspending judgment about the problem. One cannot credibly think through a problem without a basic awareness of what others have said about it. However, focusing on only what disciplinary experts have "seen" (i.e., written) risks limiting one's ability to see (Szostak, 2002, p. 106). *Interdisciplinary research involves, among other things, looking for what disciplinarians have failed to see.* Disciplinarians typically focus on one aspect of the overall complex problem to the exclusion of other aspects. One should resist the temptation to form an opinion prior to the initial search and, ideally, before completing the full-scale search. (Admittedly, this is hard to do, especially when working on an issue where one's ethical stance or faith tradition informs one's view.) If one already has an opinion, one should strive not to allow it to influence the search.

Before discussing each search strategy, it is useful to discuss the organization and classification of books in libraries.

The Organization and Classification of Books in Libraries

The appropriate starting point, at least for students and scholars associated with a college or university, is its library collection. Interdisciplinary researchers need to start broadly and then narrow their focus toward more specialized sources as the topic takes shape. In general, this means starting with books and then consulting the journal literature. However, when working in the natural sciences, parts of the social sciences, and some of the newer professional fields such as web design, one needs to begin with journals and online publications because these, not books, are the primary modes of communicating research (Newell, 2007b, p. 85).

The organization and classification of books in libraries reflect the dominance of the disciplines in their approach to producing knowledge. Consequently, libraries serve the needs of disciplinary scholars better than those of interdisciplinary scholars. The two systems of organization and classification in the United States are the Dewey Decimal System and the Library of Congress Classification (LCC) system, though libraries elsewhere in the world utilize different systems. However, all major libraries are grounded in disciplines. Both the Dewey and LCC systems categorize knowledge largely according to how Western academic disciplines divide knowledge, and rely on **controlled vocabulary**. This is a language of descriptors established by librarians to use in subject headings to minimize the use of disciplinary jargon (Fiscella & Kimmel, 1999, p. 80).

The Dewey Decimal and Library of Congress Classification Systems   Of the two systems of classifying literature, the Dewey Decimal System and the Library of Congress Classification, the Dewey system is used primarily in public and small libraries in the United States. It is the older of the two systems, so it is grounded in less current disciplinary knowledge. It organizes hierarchically by disciplinary subject matter (moving from the general to the more specific) into categories, subcategories, specialized topics, and levels of subtopics. The system is designed to facilitate browsing.

Interdisciplinary researchers will likely encounter the Library of Congress Classification system when they use their university's library or log in to its online catalogue, and should therefore be aware of its characteristics. The LCC system used by large U.S. research university libraries has many more categories (by using letters instead of numbers at the most general levels). It is slightly more recent (early twentieth instead of late nineteenth century) and is therefore more reflective of the way knowledge has developed. The LCC system is also enumerative, meaning that it is based on the number of books written in each discipline on particular topics. The system is designed to serve the needs of the disciplines by organizing knowledge according to disciplinary categories. Each category moves from the general to the specific, enabling disciplinarians to easily find books on their specialty. Although many disciplinary books contain information that falls outside disciplinary lines, it is not presently reflected in the LCC system. Knowing this basic information about the LCC system should prompt interdisciplinary students to either browse the physical shelves in the library or conduct a call number search in the online catalogue. Browsing is very useful in the early phase of the literature search, especially when one knows the most basic information about the relevant disciplines (provided in Chapter 4) but has not yet developed adequacy in them.

Interdisciplinarians need to identify not only books that address their topic but also books that reference it cursorily. These latter books are important to the interdisciplinary research process because they may bring out contrasts in disciplinary perspectives that might not otherwise be apparent. These books and their lists of sources may also identify, or at least provide hints regarding, important linkages to other concepts, theories, or information relevant to the topic.

LCC Subject Headings   The purpose of subject headings is to bring together books on the same topic whose authors use different terminology or jargon, including works from different disciplines. Conducting a keyword search on the terms used in a relevant book will likely identify other books on the same topic written from a similar perspective (Newell, 2007b, p. 86). The LCC subject headings and thesauri (e.g., a book of words and their synonyms used by a particular discipline) also provide something of a bridge between the terminologies of different disciplines. Interdisciplinarians seeking a wide range of perspectives on a topic use the subject headings instead of trying to think of all the disciplinary jargon.

Fortunately, catalogue entries for books assigned LCC call numbers often list more than one LCC subject heading to reflect the contents of the book. These subject headings, though far from exhaustive, at least reflect *some* of the topical diversity within the book (Searing, 1992, p. 14). Once the subject headings relevant to the problem or topic are identified, these subject headings may be used to conduct more advanced searches that will yield additional references on the topic.[2]

The Limits of Both Classification Systems   Both the Dewey system and the LCC system permit disciplinary scholars to locate books quickly on the topic of interest, and then to find additional books that may also relate to the topic by browsing nearby shelves (Newell, 2007b, pp. 85–86). However, both systems are less helpful to interdisciplinary scholars (and a growing number of disciplinary scholars) who are interested in topics that cut across disciplinary lines and in the connections among topics addressed by different disciplines. In short, they need to find additional ways beside call numbers to identify relevant books. Newell (2007b) sums up the complaint of these scholars: The "call numbers in both systems are inevitably reductionist in that they reduce the book to a single subject for purposes of locating it on the shelves" (p. 86). The challenge for interdisciplinary scholars, says Newell, is to be able to identify disciplinary books that address, however cursorily, more than one of the subjects (or components) their topic comprises. These books are critical to the interdisciplinarity enterprise because they are likely to bring out contrasts in disciplinary perspectives on the topic, and may also identify, or at least provide hints regarding, linkages among those subjects. "Luckily for interdisciplinarians," says Newell,

> catalog entries for books often list more than one [LCC] subject heading pertaining to the contents of the book [and] unlike call numbers, reflect at least some of the diversity of topics within a book (though they are applied very sparingly . . . and still organize knowledge according to the disciplines). (p. 86)

Once the researcher is able to identify the various subject headings pertinent to the interdisciplinary topic under investigation, advanced subject heading searches will identify a range of relevant books, though likely not all of them.

Books and Periodical Literature   There are various kinds of books: monographs, reports of major research studies, and series of chapters on the problem by different experts. The usefulness of each type of book in interdisciplinary work depends on the problem being investigated, the disciplines involved, and the required depth of the research.

With time-sensitive topics, the material in books may be dated because books require more time to research and publish. Even so, book material often provides pertinent background information that is an important component in research and writing. In starting broadly, one may profitably use "Szostak's Categories of Phenomena About the Human World" (Table 4.4 in Chapter 4). This table conveniently moves (left to right) from the more general to the narrower. It also helps to establish links to neighboring concepts that may be relevant and might otherwise be overlooked. A good way to develop a list of possible sources is to consult the sources used in a recently published book or journal article on the problem, paying attention to which ones are most frequently cited by experts.

Experts consistently report their findings first in periodical literature, including peer-reviewed scholarly journals such as *Social Science Quarterly* and semischolarly professional publications such as *American Demographics*. Experts may also report their findings as papers delivered at professional meetings, dissertations, government documents, or policy reports. Encyclopedia articles may or may not be authoritative, depending on the scholarly credentials of the writer. Like Internet sources, they should be used with great care. Students may profitably consult Chart 5.1, "Types of Publications," in W. Lawrence Neuman's (2006) *Social Research Methods* (6th ed.), which identifies publication types, examples of each type, types of writer, and the purpose, strengths, and weaknesses of each type of publication.

Direct Searching

Direct searching is possible when one has a well-defined problem or question but is not yet certain if the topic is researchable in an interdisciplinary sense. Direct searching is conducted by using *subject* searches and *keyword* searches. Direct searching is also useful for identifying gaps in the literature, verifying facts, and checking for accuracy of quotes and references (A. Foster, 2004).

Subject Searching and Controlled Vocabulary   When searching library catalogues, students should begin by using subject searches rather than keyword searches. While subject searches require a bit of effort to master the correct terminology (though this task is made much easier by online catalogue software), the searcher benefits in two ways: (1) Bibliographers have devoted some effort to classify books according to a few key subject headings, and (2) there is even some effort to ensure that works about the same thing but using different terminology in different disciplines are given the same subject heading.

Subject headings are assigned by librarians who specialize in specific disciplines and who look through books to decide what they are about. The designated subject headings bring together works whose authors use different terminology, jargon, or technical language. A keyword search for the jargon used in a relevant book will likely identify other books on the same topic written from a similar perspective. While helpful to interdisciplinary scholars, it is not sufficient because as Fiscella (1989) points out, "key terms can shift across disciplines" (p. 261). Keyword and subject searches do not entirely obviate the need for interdisciplinarians to be sensitive to disciplinary terminology because reference librarians, though they may attempt to transcend the disciplines in their subject headings, may be only partially successful because they too are influenced by disciplinary thinking. This search strategy, says Newell (2007b), "gets the interdisciplinarian to consider how different people look at these same concepts and think about how the concepts are related" (p. 86).

Keyword Searching   The intellectual challenges of the interdisciplinary research process are matched by the scholarly challenges of using library-based computer searches. Keyword searching is useful primarily *within* a discipline's literature. Since interdisciplinary students often have to identify information that is "intellectually distant" or from unfamiliar disciplines, direct searching must be sensitive to the terminology used in different disciplines so as to not miss important works. Researchers frequently encounter the problem of disciplines using different keywords to describe some aspect of the problem. In the example of human cloning, keywords include *control, legislation,* and *impact* to describe the concept of *power* as it relates to the problem. Disciplinary handbooks, dictionaries, encyclopedias, introductory textbooks, and other sources are tools useful to developing familiarity with the terminology commonly used by each discipline.

Students working online tend to work more quickly but less deeply. When faced with large "retrieval sets," the tendency is to select only items from the first few pages of results. The potential danger of using a "quick and shallow" approach is to overlook an important source. If a keyword search produces a very large retrieval set, this is generally the result of using imprecise terminology (Palmer et al., 2009, p. 11).

Searching Indexes, Databases, and Other Collections   Another category of subject-oriented access to works of particular interest to interdisciplinarians is the indexes, databases, and other collections that organize much of the disciplinary scholarship from which interdisciplinarians must draw. Each of these works has its own thesaurus or classification system based on standardized terminology from that field. The controlled vocabulary of LCC subject headings connects *different* catalogues, databases, and indexes (whether disciplinary, cross-disciplinary, or comprehensive), explains Newell (2007b), "whereas the classification schemes of thesauri connect different disciplines within a particular cross-disciplinary database or index" (p. 87).

> In both cases, they provide a bridge between the terminologies of different disciplines. One can do a keyword search within a particular discipline, but one then needs to expand it through a subject-heading or classification search to find other disciplines and their terminology before conducting a keyword search in another discipline on the same topic. Many databases allow researchers to search a keyword within a particular field, such as a subject heading, when the exact subject heading is not initially known. This is a way to do a more precise search without the knowledge of exact controlled terminology. (Newell, 2007b, p. 87)

Indexes and databases useful for interdisciplinary research are listed in the Appendix. (Note: This chapter emphasizes subject searching whereas the Appendix stresses keyword searching.) These databases are typically available in major research libraries. Students can find out what resources each database offers by referencing its website.

Though many are still restricted to a particular discipline and are organized according to its jargon, new databases are increasingly crossing disciplinary lines, and their thesauri are offering controlled vocabulary connecting works from the contributing disciplines (Newell, 2007b, p. 87). Fortunately for interdisciplinarians, topical databases are now available that cut across disciplines, and referencing these provides a critical source of disciplinary scholarship upon which interdisciplinarians must draw, especially for journal articles.

As interdisciplinarians move from discipline to discipline in search of different insights on the same topic, they need to check the thesaurus or classification system for that collection to find the term(s) to search for. Starting with a good keyword and Boolean search strategy (described in the Appendix) helps locate appropriate descriptors—as subject headings in indexes are often called. Thesauri and subject headings are most useful, says Joan B. Fiscella (1989), where a recognized scholarly community has been established (p. 83). Each time interdisciplinary scholars move to a collection of the work of another discipline in search of a different perspective on the same topic, says Newell (2007b), they need to check the thesaurus or classification system for that collection to find the term(s) to search for (p. 87).

He gives this example in the discipline of psychology, which has done a lot of work on "gender differences":

> A keyword search for it in a thesaurus will yield something like 10,000 hits. But a check of the PsycINFO thesaurus will reveal that it is not a valid subject heading and the use of "human sex differences" instead will produce more like 60,000 hits. (Newell, 2007b, p. 87)

Searching on the Internet   Searching on the Internet is widespread across disciplines, with researchers in science and medicine almost preferring to search using electronic sources (Hemminger, Lu, Vaughn, & Adams, 2007). Search engines, particularly Google and more recently Bing and Wolfram Alpha, allow concurrent searches across a wide and diverse array of sources. However, students are cautioned to be at least skeptical about using nonscholarly sources from the Internet for two reasons: These commercial engines often omit older but still relevant literature, and they tend to focus only on previously cited sources. This results in students using a narrower and more homogenized range of literature (Evans, 2008). Great caution must be exercised when using Internet materials unless these are obtained from a recognized academic website.[3]

Search Strategies

Searching is particularly important at the outset of a research project when one is deciding on a topic and determining if it is researchable in an interdisciplinary sense. The searching activity may begin in a number of ways such as with a reference to the topic in a book or journal article, a suggestion from an instructor, or a keyword aimed at finding specifics or for exploring a new area. The initial phase of the literature search involves browsing, probing, skimming, assessing, and consulting experts.

Browsing   Browsing is an important and widely practiced search technique, and "is especially essential for interdisciplinary researchers working in new and rapidly developing fields" (Palmer, 2010, p. 183). It is open-ended with the searcher looking through a body of assembled or accessible information. For students who are able to select their own topic or problem, browsing will likely begin as part of STEP 1 (see Chapter 3). Students should start broadly and then narrow their search to more specialized sources during the full-scale search described below. Starting broadly generally means skimming books to develop a general understanding of the problem and its parts before consulting the more specialized journal literature. Books often provide more context and history than journal articles can.[4] However, if both the topic or problem and the disciplines to be mined for insights have been preselected, the literature search should be full-scale, not cursory.

Browsing has the potential to result in serendipitous discovery because it tends to be broad and flexible, and to lead researchers to materials that they would otherwise not have found through direct searching or chaining (Palmer et al., 2009, pp. 13–14). Researchers in the arts, humanities, area studies, and languages are more likely to consider browsing printed materials for serendipitous discoveries (Education for Change, Ltd., SIRU at the University of Brighton, and the Research Partnership, 2002, p. 25). Many interdisciplinary researchers report that physical libraries are more conducive to serendipitous discovery than are digital libraries (Borgman et al., 2005; Engel & Antell, 2004; A. Foster, 2004).

Although browsing printed materials on library shelves continues to be important, browsing occurs increasingly with web-based materials. As with other forms of searching, the web has had a profound impact on what and how we browse, and the rate at which we can move through a diverse array of digital sources. Users, according to one study, often engage in "bouncing" or "flicking," moving rapidly from one site to another and occasionally returning to explore material in depth (Nicholas, Huntington, Williams, & Dobrowolski, 2004). For example, the web allows students to easily browse the tables of contents of journals and books. Web browsing can lead researchers to more conventional library resources that otherwise might not have been pursued. Interdisciplinarians working in the humanities and the social sciences engage in some kind of browsing as a normal part of their research process (Spanner, 2001).

Probing   Whereas browsing is often ad hoc in nature, probing is a more deliberate and strategic approach for identifying scattered or remote information. "Researchers probe into peripheral areas outside their expertise," explains Palmer (2010), "to increase breadth of perspective, to generate new ideas, or to explore a wide range of types and sources of information" (p. 183). Interdisciplinarians use probing to locate relevant information that falls outside their discipline or area of expertise when standard searching and browsing techniques are inadequate. As researchers probe the literature of unfamiliar disciplines and encounter new ideas, concepts, theories, and methods that they do not fully understand, they need to develop familiarity with the terminology to carry out their research. Resolving differences in vocabulary and terminology requires "translation work." This work, admits Palmer (2010), "can be the most difficult and laborious part of interdisciplinary research, collaboration, and communication" (p. 183). Nevertheless, it is essential because "valid interdisciplinary research is necessarily based on a deep understanding of how concepts, methods, and results fit in the body of discourse and practice in which they were developed" (p. 183). Interdisciplinary research teams are continually engaged in translation work throughout the project. In fact, says Palmer, "learning enough about the perspectives and problems driving the interests of collaborators appears to be a key factor in the success of interdisciplinary research groups" (p. 183).

Skimming   Skimming is done in the initial phase of the project and seeks to establish if the topic or problem is researchable in an interdisciplinary sense. This is normally true for undergraduates, but solo interdisciplinarians and graduate students may be able to infer how a particular discipline might address the topic or problem; interdisciplinary teams often expect their disciplinary members to do new disciplinary research. However, it is wise to defer a final decision until the full-scale search is completed and one has closely read all authors' insights to see if they are talking about the same thing. A cursory search will provide an initial (though not conclusive) estimate of what and how much has been written about the topic, and enable one to develop a "feel" for the scholarly conversation.

Skimming means reading the document (book, journal article, or online paper) cursorily, not with the intent to fully comprehend the author's argument and findings. Skimming or cursory reading enables one to identify relevant disciplines and insights. It entails flipping through a volume in the library to see if it contains needed information. The action of skimming printed materials involves looking for key components beginning with the abstract (if it is a journal article), preface or introduction (if it is a book), or table of contents (if it is a book), then moving to section or chapter headings, lists, summary statements or conclusions, definitions, and illustrations (Schatz et al., 1999). This process is applicable to digital documents where search features (such as the "Look Inside" function offered by Amazon.com for books) make it easier to pinpoint keywords, theories, and so on (Bishop, 1999). Researchers are making increased use of journal abstracts in full-text databases (Nicholas, Huntington, & Jamali, 2007). However, students are cautioned not to substitute skimming for eventually reading the full publication. Scholars often begin with skimming the preliminary parts of a document such as the table of contents and introduction before printing it for later reading (Tenopir, King, Boyce, Grayson, & Paulson, 2005).

Assessing   As students skim books and journal articles, they must make quick decisions about their relevance and utility. Here are some questions that should be asked about each book and journal article:

- Does it cover the topic as a whole or just some aspect of it?
- Does it have something new to say about the topic or some aspect of it?
- Has the document been published recently?
- Is it peer-reviewed (i.e., does it appear in an academic journal or as a book published by a university, academic, or commercial press that publishes scholarly work)?
- Has it been reviewed (if in book form)?

The more recent the publication, the more valuable its bibliography and endnotes (or footnotes) because they provide authoritative connections to other subsequent work.

Summary of Suggested Strategies   Suggestions about what to do in the initial phase of the literature search are summarized here:

- *Browse* books and journal articles on the topic.
- *Probe* other disciplinary literatures that would possibly be interested in the topic. Consult disciplinary research aids, including bibliographies, encyclopedias, dictionaries, handbooks, companions, and databases, *after* drawing up a list of potentially relevant disciplines (STEP 3; see Chapter 5). For example, an indispensable source of disciplinary references for students working in the social sciences is *Social Science Reference Sources* (Li, 2000).
- *Skim* the literatures of potentially relevant disciplines. (Note: Skimming will minimize the tendency to be unduly influenced by the literature.)
- *Narrow* the topic, if necessary, so that it is manageable, and then restate the problem. Mapping the problem is strongly urged.
- *Decide* if there is sufficient literature on the topic that would justify using an interdisciplinary approach and warrant further searching.
- *Consult* the experts.

Mistakes Commonly Made When Beginning the Literature Search

Those new to interdisciplinary research commonly make two mistakes in the initial phase of the literature search. The first is failing to pay close attention to the disciplinary source of the books and articles being gathered. One unintended consequence of this oversight is to end up with a large number of materials drawn from one or two disciplines at the expense of other equally important disciplines. Interdisciplinary research cannot succeed on this basis. It is important to keep track of which discipline produced which book or article. Rigorous interdisciplinary research involves striking a balance between disciplinary depth and disciplinary breadth. In practical terms, this means identifying the important books and articles and categorizing them according to the writer's disciplinary perspective. In the event this affiliation is not readily evident, a Google or Bing search of the writer's name may provide this information. This ideal balance between disciplinary depth and disciplinary breadth is seldom realized in undergraduate education, however, where students are typically limited to gathering a few publications from only two or three disciplines.

A second mistake those new to interdisciplinary research commonly make is to be unduly influenced by the *quantity* of literature on the problem that a discipline has generated. For example, if the initial search reveals that sociology has contributed only one or two essays on the problem, one may wrongly conclude that sociology is not as relevant to the investigation as other disciplines, each of which has produced several insights. *Quantity of material produced by a discipline should never decide disciplinary relevance.* Why? It may be that the one essay by a cultural anthropologist (and the *only* essay on the problem by any cultural anthropologist) contains information of such importance that an interdisciplinary understanding of the problem would not be complete without it. But what about when, for example, sociology has not addressed the specific topic, say, of rave music? Can one conclude that sociology has nothing to contribute to the discussion? Not necessarily. Sociologists may have addressed house music or punk rock or musical subcultures preceding rave, or investigated some other social phenomenon that influences rave music. Researchers should be open to possibilities that are not initially apparent. Many topics turn out to be subsets of a larger topic. Rather than giving up on sociology upon discovering that it has not examined rave, one should look at the larger context—in this case, what preceded rave. If a discipline has treated a more general category to which a topic or phenomenon is causally related, it would be quite surprising if that treatment does not have some direct applicability to the narrower topic. Indeed, if the more general treatment has no bearing on the narrower topic, then one should reexamine the choice of general category. Graduate students and mature scholars should look to see whether core concepts or theories from a particular discipline might usefully be applied to the topic, even though no one in the discipline has gotten around to making the application.

Students are sometimes surprised to learn that a discipline that initially appears not to be relevant has produced insights into the problem after all. These discoveries are possible only by conducting a full-scale literature search. In this effort, students can again profitably use "Szostak's Categories of Phenomena About the Human World" (Table 4.4 in Chapter 4) to cross-check traditional disciplinary searches.

The Full-Scale Literature Search

In practice, the full-scale literature search should begin as soon as one decides that the topic is researchable in an interdisciplinary sense and one has identified the relevant disciplines. Identifying potentially relevant disciplines, to say nothing of the more demanding task of narrowing these to just the most relevant disciplines, may require extending the literature search until one is confident that all of the relevant disciplines and their important insights and theories are identified. Researchers must avoid limiting their reading to familiar disciplines while ignoring unfamiliar ones. They must check each discipline to see whether it has produced literature on the topic. If it has, then the discipline is relevant. If the full-scale search is hurried, it may not reveal all the relevant disciplines. Those unfamiliar with the interdisciplinary research process are sometimes tempted to end the literature search prematurely after finding a handful of sources produced by a few disciplines or a few experts.

Conducting the **full-scale literature search** involves identifying *all* relevant expert insights and theories on the topic. For undergraduate students, the initial search quickly evolves into the full-scale literature search once one has decided what the project should be about and that it is researchable in an interdisciplinary sense. For graduate students and mature scholars, the full-scale literature search is a way to immerse oneself in the scholarly conversations on the topic and achieve mastery of the problem in all of its complexity. For these and for members of research teams who already know what the project is about, the full-scale literature search provides baseline knowledge about the problem in all of its complexity and allows team members who are going to specialize in only one part of the problem to become knowledgeable about other aspects with which they may be unfamiliar. The full-scale literature search is as interested in disciplinary breadth (i.e., how many disciplines have written on the topic) as it is in disciplinary depth (i.e., the number, quality, and variety of insights produced by a discipline on the topic). Researchers at any level should always err on the side of inclusiveness during the full-scale search. Insights that are marginally relevant will be identified later on and then discarded. But *inclusive* does not mean "open-ended." **Inclusive** refers not to the quantity of disciplinary insights but to the quality and diversity of these published insights. The challenge for the student is to keep these to a manageable number.

Note to Readers

Conducting the full-scale literature search reflects the belief of many interdisciplinarians that there should be a symbiotic relationship between interdisciplinary research and disciplinary or specialized research. As Szostak (2009) notes, interdisciplinary integration is only possible because of the concerted efforts of thousands of scholars across all disciplines. Their insights provide both the disciplinary depth and the disciplinary breadth that makes interdisciplinary integration possible. Therefore, "none of these insights can be taken for granted; each must be carefully evaluated, and compared and contrasted with alternatives" (Szostak, 2009, p. 7).

Conducting the full-scale search is based on an assumption foundational to interdisciplinarity: that no community of scholars has been entirely wasting its time over the past decades or centuries. This assumption should motivate those who are genuinely interested in understanding a particular problem to discover what others have written about it. Interdisciplinary problem solving and scholarship involve integrating insights and theories from multiple disciplinary sources. These deserve to be brought together and organized into a coherent whole in a way that does not privilege any one perspective, theory, or viewpoint (Szostak, 2009, p. 9).

Two Challenges of the Full-Scale Literature Search

Two challenges face the interdisciplinarian who is undertaking the full-scale literature search: (1) *organizing* relevant information about the problem, and (2) closely *reading* this information for specific content. **Relevant information** is information that pertains directly to the problem, that is indispensable to understanding the problem, and that offers distinctive insights into it.

Organizing   Interdisciplinarians face an organizational challenge that disciplinarians do not face. Disciplinarians are responsible for gathering information relevant to their topic primarily from within their discipline whereas interdisciplinarians are faced with the additional demand of gathering information relevant to their topic from multiple disciplines.

For undergraduate and graduate students, the nature of the organizational challenge depends on course requirements. For example, those in an introductory course where the insights (documents, articles, and books) are preselected by the instructor will probably not be faced with the challenge of how to organize this material. However, students in an advanced course that requires them to identify insights into the course problem, or a problem of their own choosing, may face a substantial organizational challenge: how to organize the growing volume of sources in a way that will permit easy access later on.

Table 6.1 is a demonstrated and effective way to organize the books and articles that each discipline has produced on the topic. The table helps one visualize the progress of the search, make decisions about the need for further searching, identify which disciplines are most relevant to the problem, and select which insights should be closely read. (The reader may recall that in the initial phase of the search, books and articles are only skimmed.) In this example, the course required students to identify three disciplines relevant to the course problem, identify at least two insights from each discipline, and show that they are from peer-reviewed sources.

The table reveals that though sociology was a potentially interested discipline, its community of scholars had not yet written about the problem.

For doctoral students and mature scholars working on a solo basis, the nature of the challenge is developing a system that can accommodate a very large number of sources that are organized according to discipline and/or what part of the problem each source focuses on.

As researchers search for information, they build personal collections of those materials that appear relevant to the research problem. These collections,

Table 6.1   Data Table

Data Table		
Disc	**Writer**	**Source of Insight**
PSYC	Smith	Internet (academic site)
	Jones	Internet (academic site)
	Chen	Academic journal
SOCI	No insights found	
POLS	Myers	Academic book
	von Rune	Academic journal

whether physical or electronic or both, range in number from a handful of sources to dozens. Critical to successful research is developing a system to organize the gathered information. Despite the prevalence of digital materials, one university study found that 98% of humanities and social science faculty preferred keeping hard copies of print materials for fear of computer failure, lack of technical skills, and shortage of computer storage space (University of Minnesota Libraries, 2006). Students and faculty often prefer hard copies because they are more accessible and easier to mark up and reread. Those working in the humanities are more likely to develop personalized organizational systems for their collections because so much of their work is based on previous scholarship. Such systems vary from piles on the floor to structured file folder systems and elaborate databases (Palmer & Neuman, 2002). Organizing materials poses a special challenge to interdisciplinarians because of their need to know the disciplinary perspective of each source. Depending on the level of sophistication of the course and the research project it requires, students will likely need to organize their materials by discipline or by theory or by concepts or by research methods, or by some combination of these.

Reading   Interdisciplinarians also face a reading challenge that disciplinarians do not face. Disciplinarians are responsible for reading only their discipline's literature and identifying each author's insight, theory, key concepts, data, and method that are relevant to the problem. By contrast, interdisciplinarians are faced with the responsibility of reading in multiple disciplinary literatures. In addition to identifying each author's insight, theory, key concepts, data, and method, interdisciplinarians must pay special attention to each author's disciplinary perspective. The point of interdisciplinary scholarship is to construct a more comprehensive understanding of the problem by drawing on diverse perspectives of disciplines (as well as interdisciplines and school of thought) and integrate their insights. Good interdisciplinary research, Wolfe and Haynes (2003) remind us, "does not mean that writers must read every source related to their topic that exists, but they should be acquainted with all of the major schools of thought or perspectives on the topic at hand" (p. 135).

A Demonstrated Strategy   A strategy that has demonstrated its utility for undergraduate students working in multiple disciplinary literatures is to read each work closely for specific content as noted in this list:

- The author's disciplinary perspective (in a general sense)
- The author's insight or thesis and its place in the disciplinary literature
- The author's assumptions
- The theory advanced that explains the data presented
- Key concepts
- The author's research method

- The phenomena addressed and their relationships (This is invaluable for mapping the problem and organizing the insights.)
- The author's bias (ethical or ideological)

The full-scale literature search is intensely concerned with thoroughly mining the relevant disciplinary literatures for particular information that is critical to the success of the project. Reading across disciplines and identifying the critical content of each insight is part of what it means to develop adequacy in each discipline, the subject of Chapter 7 (STEP 5). The search may also involve gathering information on the problem that is not of interest to the disciplines or is overlooked by them but is nevertheless relevant to the inquiry.

One way to organize this information is to create a table in Word or Excel as many students are doing. In Table 6.2, students in an advanced undergraduate course were asked to provide information about each author's thesis using the author's own words to eliminate the possibility of skewing the writer's meaning as may occur when paraphrasing. Interdisciplines, schools of thought, and the applied fields should be treated in the same way as one approaches traditional disciplines.

The checklist shows that a literature search that involves working in only a few disciplines and reading only a handful of insights from each perspective still entails gathering, organizing, and comprehending a considerable amount

Table 6.2   Checklist of Things to Look For When Reading

Author	Disciplinary Perspective	Thesis	Assumption	Theory Name	Key Concept(s)	Method	Phenomena Addressed	Author's Bias
Post	Psychology (cognitive)	"Political violence is not instrumental but an end in itself. The cause becomes the rationale for acts of terrorism the terrorist is compelled to commit." (Post, 1998, p. 35).	Humans organize their mental life through psychological constructs.	Terrorist psycho-logic	Special logic (Post, 1998, p. 25)	Case study	Individual human agents	Suicide terrorists are irrational.

NOTE: If constructed using Excel, the table can be easily expanded horizontally to include additional information about any one insight as well as vertically by adding as many insights as necessary. The utility of this table for interdisciplinary work on the undergraduate level will be increasingly evident as the interdisciplinary research process unfolds.

of information. To avoid becoming overwhelmed with information as the reading proceeds, undergraduate and graduate students are encouraged to organize the information in some systematic way so that it can be easily accessed when performing subsequent STEPS of the research process. Experience has shown that the time spent in organizing and recording this critical information will be more than offset by the time saved in retrieving this same information as subsequent STEPS of the research process are performed.

Building on the Connections Discovered by Previous Scholars

In addition to relying on controlled vocabulary to conduct computer searches, interdisciplinarians can "connect the scholarship of different disciplines by building on the connections discovered by previous scholars" (Newell, 2007b, p. 87). Once one has identified a key work on the topic under investigation, one can use a citation index to identify a wide range of subsequent works citing that key work. Citation indexes such as *Science Citation Index* and *Arts & Humanities Citation Index* typically cover an entire academic area. Citation indexes are most useful where an interdisciplinary field such as women's studies has developed a common language. This is because the field is recognized not only by the scholarly community working in it but also by those who identify and index that literature (Fiscella, 1989, p. 83). However, newer interdisciplinary fields such as environment sustainability studies are best searched through a combination of subject headings and citation indexes.

Since interdisciplinary studies explores topics that transcend the disciplines, interdisciplinary researchers end up going back and forth between (a) the Dewey and LCC systems for classifying knowledge, (b) specialized systems developed by the disciplines, and (c) more generic systems developed by librarians and by commercial information providers, including the creators of general indexes such as EBSCO's Academic Search or Gale's Academic OneFile. Disciplinary systems, Newell (2007b) points out, use technical disciplinary terms used by authors in titles and abstracts, and they organize information in discipline-specific databases (for books) and indexes (for journal articles). Those systems can be accessed using keyword searches. However, "the library systems use subject headings, thesauri, and citation systems developed by professional librarians and information managers, and organize information in electronic catalogs as well as in indexes and databases according to classification systems also developed by librarians" (p. 88). These are best accessed using controlled vocabulary searches. "The trick," says Newell, "is to use the library systems to bridge the disciplinary systems" (p. 88).

Consulting Disciplinary Experts

Another method of conducting the full-scale literature search is to consult disciplinary experts. Mature scholars, particularly those conducting solo research, do this regularly. The expert on the topic (or on some aspect of it) is able to provide authoritative feedback on the feasibility of the project, inform the researcher on current research activity under way or nearing completion, and direct the researcher to the most important literature including conference papers and published or soon-to-be-published journal articles and books. Students working on a topic of their choice are well advised to consult faculty who may provide valuable insights concerning the project's feasibility, references to key publications, and practical advice.

Other Sources of Knowledge

Though this discussion on the literature search focuses largely on undergraduate research, it can be quite relevant to graduate students and solo interdisciplinarians who seek to integrate their own basic research with that of previous research on the same topic. Interdisciplinarians know that relevant information sometimes comes from unexpected sources that are nondisciplinary as well as disciplinary. This knowledge has not been produced by trained disciplinary scholars, nor has it been vetted by the disciplines. It may not be of interest to the disciplines or may be overlooked by them but nevertheless may be relevant to the inquiry. Such knowledge may include oral histories, eyewitness testimonies, statistics and tables, artifacts, and artistic creations. The willingness to consider using other knowledge sources is based on the assumption that knowledge accumulates and that people learn from and build upon what others have done (Neuman, 2006, p. 111). Today's knowledge is the product of yesterday's research, and tomorrow's knowledge will be based on today's research.

Interdisciplinarians do not assume that *all* relevant knowledge has been generated by the disciplines. These other sources of knowledge are useful or even necessary to function well in a particular context or to think about a specific concern. However, interdisciplinarians are acutely aware that such knowledge has dramatically different standing in the academic world than does knowledge that has stood the test of expert scrutiny. *All knowledge is not equally valid.* Under certain circumstances, these other sources of knowledge may achieve credibility in the academy and even find their way into the literatures of the disciplines. In women's studies, for example, testimonial or "lived experience" plays a crucial role. In native studies, "traditional knowledge preserved over centuries through oral tradition and interpreted by elders is central" (Vickers, 1998, p. 23). While knowledge produced by the disciplines, compared to these other sources of knowledge, is generally considered the proper focus of the modern academy, Richard M. Carp (2001) urges interdisciplinarians not to limit their search for relevant information to the disciplines, for the simple reason that their knowledge formations are incomplete (p. 98). Interdisciplinarians, he argues, should be more imaginative, more inquiring, and more self-reflective about what knowledge they are willing to use (p. 84). Historians, sociologists, anthropologists, and other disciplinary experts are constantly mining these diverse sources of knowledge for their own disciplinary purposes and often go on to publish their findings. In this way, nonscholarly knowledge finds its way into the academy. Oral histories of migrant workers are a good example of the kind of nonscholarly knowledge that is gathered and presented in a way that disciplinary scholars can accept. Investigating the high cost of health care may include the testimony of health care providers as part of one's study. Interdisciplinary students can attempt to gather and analyze nonscholarly knowledge themselves but should not use it until it has been vetted by experts. Once vetted, it may be used, provided that it is clearly identified and used in a scholarly way. As a general rule, students should be skeptical of insights that have not been carefully tested by experts.

Chapter Summary

The literature search is itself a process within the larger IRP and spans the early STEPS of that process, beginning with STEP 1. This chapter defined the term *literature search* in an interdisciplinary sense, presented reasons for conducting the literature search, and discussed the special challenges confronting interdisciplinarians. The chapter's primary focus was on how to conduct a library-based interdisciplinary literature search. It divided the search process (somewhat arbitrarily) into two substeps: the initial search and the full-scale search. The initial search begins as one is selecting a topic and deciding if it is researchable in an interdisciplinary sense. Once this decision is made, the full-scale literature search can get under way. A successful search will confirm that the topic is researchable and is indeed appropriate to interdisciplinary inquiry. Most importantly to later STEPS in the research process, the successful full-scale search will have identified the most relevant disciplinary perspectives and their insights, though final confirmation will have to await the completion of STEPS 7 and 8 (see Chapters 10 and 11). The chapter warned against limiting one's reading to familiar disciplines while ignoring unfamiliar ones. The chapter urged researchers to categorize insights by disciplinary perspective, which is a research practice distinctive to interdisciplinary studies. The chapter also urged researchers to devise some method of organizing this information so that it can be easily retrieved during later STEPS of the IRP.

If the literature search is hurried, it may not reveal all the relevant disciplines. Those unfamiliar with the interdisciplinary research process are sometimes tempted to end the literature search prematurely after finding a handful of sources produced by a few disciplines or a few experts. Subsequent STEPS in the research process will expose incomplete or careless work done in earlier STEPS. The next chapter advances the research process by explaining how to develop adequacy in the relevant disciplines.

Notes

1. A thorough discussion of the literature review from a social science perspective is in Neuman (2006) and in Hart (1998). *Literature review* is an umbrella term that refers to specialized reviews including context review, historical review, integrative review, methodology review, self-study review, and theoretical review (Neuman, 2006, p. 112). Social scientists typically conduct the literature review at the outset of their research. But see L. G. Ackerson (2007), a leading engineering and science librarian and scholar whose particular areas of expertise are "user information seeking behaviors" and "information resources for interdisciplinary research," who prefers the term *literature search* (p. vii).

2. The best treatment of this topic from an interdisciplinary perspective is Chapter 6 in Fiscella and Kimmel (1999).

3. An excellent discussion of the problem of sources, reliability of sources, and finding and evaluating sources on the Internet is Chapter 5 of Booth, Colomb, and Williams (2003).

4. The disciplines vary in the importance that they attach to books compared to peer-reviewed journal articles. Scholars in the humanities are as likely to publish their research in book form as they are to publish in peer-reviewed journals. This is less so in the social sciences and far less so in the natural sciences.

Exercises

Reasons Evaluated

6.1   Evaluate the nine reasons for conducting the literature search through the lens of researchers from the modernist, interpretivist, and postmodern camps. To what extent does the interdisciplinary approach accommodate these three approaches to research?

Special Challenges

6.2   Concerning the problem or topic that you are interested in investigating, what challenges have you encountered in the initial searching that are discussed in "Special Challenges Confronting Interdisciplinarians"? Is there a challenge that you have encountered that the discussion overlooked?

Initial Searching

6.3   Constructing a quality building depends on two things: using quality materials and having a blueprint or map of its parts and their interrelationship. This applies to constructing the building's foundation. Mapping the problem and stating it (or framing the research question) are critical to constructing the foundation of your research project. Concerning your project, what materials do you need to gather that will enable you to decide if the topic is researchable in an interdisciplinary sense?

6.4   What subject headings and keywords are you using to search for literature on your topic? Are these more helpful when searching your university's databases or when searching through Google or Bing?

6.5   How have the strategies of browsing, probing, skimming, assessing, and consulting experts helped you to decide if your topic is researchable in an interdisciplinary sense? After reflecting on "Mistakes Commonly Made When Beginning the Literature Search," what must you do to make the topic researchable in an interdisciplinary sense?

Going Full-Scale

6.6   How have you addressed the organizational challenges that your project involves? As you proceed with the full-scale search, is your organizational plan able to accommodate the growing number of insights and related bits of information?

6.7   Select the most recently published insight (either a book or a journal article), and read it for the specific content listed under the subheading "A Demonstrated Strategy" and illustrated in Table 6.2. Then, scrutinize the sources/bibliography and notes/endnotes to make connections to other sources related to your topic.

6.8   After mapping your problem and conducting the full-scale literature search, have you discovered a gap in existing research that might be filled if a nondisciplinary source of knowledge was included?

7 Developing Adequacy in Relevant Disciplines

Chapter Preview

Having identified the disciplines that are most relevant to the problem (STEP 3; see Chapter 5) and thoroughly mined their literatures for important insights and theories (STEP 4; see Chapter 6), the next task is to develop adequacy in each of these disciplines (STEP 5). By *adequacy* interdisciplinarians mean knowing enough about the discipline to have a basic understanding of how it approaches, as well as illuminates and characterizes, the problem. Achieving adequacy is essential preparation for successfully performing the latter STEPS of the research process that involve integrating disciplinary insights and theories.

This chapter explains how those new to interdisciplinarity can develop adequacy in the disciplines relevant to the problem. Developing adequacy involves (1) comprehending enough of each relevant discipline to decide which of its defining elements bears on the problem most directly, (2) identifying and understanding relevant theories, (3) identifying and critiquing disciplinary methods, and (4) providing in-text evidence of adequacy.

Step 5: Develop Adequacy in Each Relevant Discipline

Comprehending Enough About Each Discipline

Developing adequacy calls for comprehending enough basic information about each discipline to decide which of its defining elements bear on the problem most directly. Two questions should be asked:

- How much knowledge is required from each discipline?
- What kind of knowledge is required from each discipline?

The first part of the chapter answers these questions and uses examples from student and professional work to illustrate important points.

How Much Knowledge Is Required
From Each Discipline?

This question concerns both depth and breadth in disciplinary knowledge. "How much" refers to the depth of knowledge in the disciplines most relevant to the problem. "How much" also refers to the breadth of knowledge across relevant disciplines. For undergraduates, "how much" is likely to mean that the problem can be adequately illuminated using a handful of insights and introductory-level concepts, assumptions, and theories from each discipline. Students should be able to identify, understand, and apply the perspectives and elements of these few disciplines to the problem. For graduate students and even solo interdisciplinarians, "how much" will likely involve critiquing the perspectives and elements of all relevant disciplines, and identifying and examining linkages among their insights and theories. Interdisciplinary teams engaged in basic research are likely to utilize as well as critique relevant elements.[1]

An Undergraduate Example

The depth and breadth required for undergraduates is usually quite modest and depends on the length and sophistication of the study undertaken. A *rule of thumb is the fewer the disciplines, the more feasible the requirements of developing adequacy.* This is borne out in the example of an undergraduate student paper on the causes of freshwater scarcity in Texas. The three disciplines most relevant to the project included Earth science, biology, and political science. The student's substantial coursework in Earth science and biology provided the necessary disciplinary "depth" for the science component of the project. *Adequacy* in this instance meant that the student had a working knowledge of the major theories, key concepts, and research methods (i.e., how data were collected and used) of these two disciplines. However, the student lacked "depth" in political science, which was needed to develop the policy component of the paper and provide the necessary disciplinary "breadth" to fully understand the problem. Achieving adequacy in political science for this student involved developing a working knowledge of the theories, key concepts, and research methods that informed state regulations concerning freshwater resource management.

A Solo Interdisciplinarian Example

A contrasting example from a solo interdisciplinarian—William Dietrich's (1995) interdisciplinary study of the Columbia River system—involved far greater depth and breadth of disciplinary knowledge. Dietrich, a science reporter for *The Seattle Times,* received the Pulitzer Prize in 1990 for coverage of the Exxon Valdez oil spill. To study the vast and complex Columbia River system comprehensively required Dietrich to develop adequacy in several disciplines and disciplinary specialties, including environmental science (an interdisciplinary field), chemistry, physics, political science, Native American history and culture (an interdisciplinary field), and economics as it relates to his questions about that river system, and integrate their diverse and often conflicting insights.

Students researching much more modest problems than Dietrich's can achieve adequacy in relevant disciplines by reading in their literatures, asking questions of experts, and adhering to the research process.

Examples of the Need for Varying Degrees of Adequacy

What is true for professional interdisciplinarians concerning the need for varying degrees of adequacy in terms of disciplinary depth and breadth is also true for students, as the following examples of undergraduate work illustrate.

Example #1 required the least depth and breadth in relevant disciplines.   A sophomore-level course introducing the field of interdisciplinary studies required students to identify relevant disciplines and their perspectives on the preselected topic of human cloning. Though none of the students had previously researched this particular topic, all had access to Table 4.2 (see Chapter 4) on disciplinary perspectives. From this table, they were able to identify two potentially relevant disciplines, the number required for the assignment. Applying these disciplinary perspectives to the topic, however, proved more challenging as it involved reading two peer-reviewed articles from each discipline and, on the basis of these, ferreting out three defining elements: key concepts, the author's assumption, and the author's theory (if one was advanced). Throughout the exercise, their instructor served as a facilitator and coach rather than "the sage on the stage."

Example #2 required greater depth and breadth in relevant disciplines.   In this junior-level problem-based course on the interdisciplinary research process, students were allowed to research one of three preselected topics: the causes of suicide terrorism, the controversy over euthanasia, or illegal immigration. Students were required to map the problem to help them visualize its complexity and link its parts to particular disciplines. They were also required to consult "Szostak's Categories of Phenomena About the Human World" (Table 4.4 in Chapter 4) to verify their findings and possibly discover linkages to additional disciplines. In addition, students were required to select the three disciplines that they considered most relevant to the problem. For these students, demonstrating adequacy involved identifying a minimum of two peer-reviewed insights on the problem from each discipline, and constructing a data table consisting of each insight's key concepts, underlying assumption, theory, and methodology.

Example #3 required still greater depth and breadth in relevant disciplines. Students entered this senior-level interdisciplinary capstone course with an approved research proposal on a problem or question that related to their professional or academic goal. They had also developed disciplinary depth in two of the three disciplines pertaining to their chosen problem (12–18 credits) and had, in most cases, completed one disciplinary research methods course in addition to completing the interdisciplinary research process and theory course. For these students, demonstrating adequacy involved mapping the problem, consulting "Szostak's Categories," identifying a minimum of three theories on the problem from each relevant discipline (including interdisciplines and schools of thought), and filling out the data table with information drawn from these authors on the defining element of each discipline.

Note to Readers

At every level, from introductory to midlevel to senior project, students, like professionals, must develop adequacy in those disciplines (including subdisciplines, interdisciplines, or schools of thought) that are relevant to the problem. The depth and breadth varies considerably between levels, depending on the complexity of the problem and the requirements of the course. Interdisciplinary research, though challenging, is manageable at all academic levels. What is required is for students to follow a research process that brings them from initial idea to investigation to integration of insights and to the more comprehensive understanding.

This and later chapters will provide numerous examples of interdisciplinary research oriented toward the natural sciences, the social sciences, and the humanities that illustrate this process drawn from student and professional work.

Developing Adequacy in Relevant Disciplines Involves Borrowing

Conducting interdisciplinary research involves **borrowing** from each relevant discipline. What, exactly, is borrowed are the insights and theories and the information that they contain. Borrowing, however, is not indiscriminate; it requires what one practitioner calls the **burden of comprehension**. This means having a minimum understanding of each relevant discipline's cognitive map. The level of comprehension depends on the requirements of the course or research project. Borrowing also calls for careful evaluation of the material borrowed in terms of

- its credibility (is it peer-reviewed?),
- its timeliness (is it time-sensitive?), and
- its relevance (does it illuminate some part of the problem?).

Undergraduates do not need to start out with much specialized knowledge to engage in interdisciplinary research. Just how much depth and breadth is necessary depends, as it does for professional disciplinarians, on the characteristics of the problem, the goal of the research, and the availability of collaborators and their role. If the problem requires sophisticated manipulation of data, or the mastery of highly technical language, or knowledge whose mastery requires formal coursework, then more depth and reliance on disciplinary experts is required. But, says Newell (2007a), if the problem can be illuminated adequately using a handful of introductory-level concepts and theories from each discipline, and modest information readily and simply acquired, then a solo interdisciplinary researcher or even a first-year undergraduate student can handle it. Luckily, one can get some useful initial understanding of most complex problems using a small number of relatively basic concepts and theories from each discipline (Newell, 2007a, p. 253).

What Kind of Knowledge Is Required From Each Discipline?

The kind of knowledge required from each discipline centers, primarily, on the answers to the following questions.

Which Disciplinary Elements Are Applicable to the Problem?

Developing adequacy calls for deciding which disciplinary elements (e.g., phenomena, epistemology, assumptions, concepts, theories, and methods) are applicable to the problem. Some of this foundational knowledge about disciplines is provided in Chapter 4 and should enable researchers to develop a basic "feel" for each relevant discipline. One should ask if the problem can be adequately illuminated by using only a handful of introductory-level elements from each relevant discipline. If far more depth is required, the researcher will have to consult discipline-specific research aids referenced in Chapter 4. The question of what kind of knowledge is required from each discipline, then, can be answered satisfactorily only by engaging in STEP 6 (see Chapter 8), in which the problem is analyzed in detail from the perspective of each discipline.

What Are the Characteristics of the Problem?

If previous STEPS have shown that the problem is complex and researchable, and one has taken the time to map the problem, one should be able to identify the characteristics of the problem: its parts and how these relate to each other and to the problem as a whole. Once the characteristics of the problem are known, it is possible to determine which disciplines, and which elements of each discipline, focus on each part of the problem.

What Is the Goal of the Research Project?

A *rule of thumb is that the more ambitious the goal, the more knowledge (i.e., disciplinary depth and breadth) required.* If the goal of the research project is to integrate only a handful of insights or theories, then the disciplinary knowledge required will be limited, and the understanding constructed will be partial. This is characteristic of undergraduate work. If, however, the goal of the project is to achieve integration and construct an understanding of the problem that is truly comprehensive, then more knowledge will be required. And if the goal of the project is to include one's own basic research and integrate it with existing research on the same problem, then even more knowledge will be required. The specific knowledge called for in this last case is discussed later under the heading "Deciding Which Disciplinary Methods to Use in Conducting Basic Research."

Developing Adequacy in Theories

In interdisciplinary work, developing adequacy in relevant disciplines generally involves identifying relevant theories. Undergraduate students often find theories intimidating, but their apprehension is usually relieved when they understand what theories are and what they are used for. Theories help scholars to understand some aspect of the natural or human world. They explain the behavior of certain phenomena and how parts of a system interact and why. Theories are tested by data and research, and seek to explain the available evidence. Disciplinary experts use theories to produce insights into a specific problem that would otherwise not be possible to achieve. The following discussion extends the discussion of theory that began in Chapter 4.

The Reason to Understand Theories

Researchers need a basic understanding of selected theories for the practical reason that theory is a major source of disciplinary insights. It is virtually impossible to conduct research in any discipline on any topic and not have to deal at some level with theory. This is especially true for insights from the natural and social sciences, and even some of the humanities disciplines such as art history and literature. Because theory is so fundamental to disciplinary scholarship, developing adequacy in relevant disciplines must include knowing about the theories relevant to the problem under study. At a minimum, students should be able to identify the theories while reading these literatures. Advanced undergraduates and graduate students typically work with existing theories; solo interdisciplinarians and especially interdisciplinary teams may well develop new theories.

Concepts and How They Relate to Theory

Each discipline has created a large number of concepts that constitute its technical jargon or terminology. Introductory disciplinary textbooks are excellent sources of concepts and their definitions. Though each discipline has its own specialized vocabulary, it is common to find that a concept in one discipline is also found in the vocabulary of another discipline but has at least a somewhat different meaning. For example, the concept of "rational" in sociology may refer to values and behavior that are normative for the group or for society at large, whereas for religion the concept may be conditioned by one's belief in and behavior governed by the sacred writings of a faith tradition. Interdisciplinarians are interested in concepts because when they are modified, they can often serve as the basis for integrating insights.

In interdisciplinary work, concepts can facilitate making general connections across disciplinary boundaries. For example, the concept of *role* is widely used. Business studies the role of the consumer; sociology studies the role of the individual in social structure; history studies a person's role in some event or process. Other concepts include *area* and *gender*.

How do concepts relate to theory? Concepts are the most elementary "building blocks" of any theory.[2] Some concepts are found in only a single theory, but many are found in a wide range of theories. For example, the concepts of *class, socioeconomic status,* and *social stratification* are found in a wide range of sociological theories. As noted previously, concepts most often describe one or more phenomena or causal links embraced by a theory, but some concepts may address other attributes of a theory.

How to Proceed

Identifying all major theories relevant to the problem is essential to maintaining scholarly rigor and producing an interdisciplinary understanding that is comprehensive. Just as it is necessary to identify all disciplines potentially relevant to the problem before selecting the most relevant disciplines, so too is it necessary to identify all relevant theories before selecting those that are most relevant. The way to proceed is to identify the major theories relevant to the problem in a single discipline and then repeat this process in serial fashion with the other relevant disciplines until all the important theories are identified.

First, Identify Theories Within a Single Discipline

STEP 4 urged categorizing theories by discipline (see Chapter 6). Taking time to do this makes it easier to link, as the following writers do, each relevant discipline with a specific set of theories. The publications in which these theories appear should be read (or reread) with this question in mind: "What theory does each writer advance to explain the problem I am investigating?" This question is applicable to almost any topic, including these:

- The increase in teenage obesity
- Opposition to same-sex unions
- Public funding of professional sports stadiums
- Affordability of prescription drugs
- The development of visual perspective in Renaissance art
- Declining salmon populations in the Columbia and Snake rivers
- Illegal immigration

The following examples are of theories advanced by the same discipline on a particular topic. These are drawn from published work and student projects identified by an asterisk (*) after the surname.

From the Natural Sciences: Smolinski* (2005), Freshwater Scarcity in Texas   Smolinski finds multiple theories within the discipline of Earth science relevant to the problem of freshwater scarcity in Texas, as shown in Table 7.1.

Table 7.1	Theories From a Single Discipline on the Causes of Freshwater Scarcity in Texas
Relevant Discipline	**Theories From a Single Discipline on the Causes of Freshwater Scarcity in Texas**
Earth science	1. Global Warming Theory
	2. Overexploitation Theory
	3. Infiltration Theory

Individual Earth scientists embrace one of three primary theories to explain the growing scarcity of freshwater in any locale: global warming, overexploitation, or infiltration. Deciding that these are the most relevant theories was possible only after Smolinski had grounded himself in the published Earth science literature. To ensure that his research was current and complete, Smolinski worked with an Earth science professor and consulted with professionals employed in the public and private sectors for additional and confirming insights.

From the Social Sciences: Fischer (1988), "On the Need for Integrating Occupational Sex Discrimination Theory on the Basis of Causal Variables"   In introducing his interdisciplinary essay on occupational sex discrimination (OSD), Fischer (1988) writes, "A review of the literature in the fields of psychology, sociology, economics, philosophy and history reveals a wide variety of explanations of OSD, each reflecting the relevant 'looking glass' of the particular discipline (or school of thought)" (p. 22). This statement is appropriate to an interdisciplinary essay for two reasons: (1) It informs the reader that the researcher has conducted an in-depth literature search, and (2) it identifies the disciplines *most* relevant to the problem.

Fischer found that four disciplines and one school of thought (Marxism) had produced important insights into the problem. From these, he began with economics, identifying four important economic theories on OSD, as shown in Table 7.2.

Table 7.2   Theories From a Single Discipline on the Causes of OSD

Relevant Discipline	Theories From a Single Discipline on the Causes of OSD
Economics	1. Monopsony Exploitation Theory
	2. Human Capital Theory
	3. Statistical Discrimination Theory
	4. Prejudice Theory

From the Humanities: Fry (1999), Samuel Taylor Coleridge: The Rime of the Ancient Mariner   Paul H. Fry identifies five literary theories that are used to interpret the meaning of Samuel Taylor Coleridge's complex and ambiguous classic romantic poem, *Rime of the Ancient Mariner.* These theoretical/analytical approaches, noted in some cases as "criticism," are identified in Table 7.3.

Table 7.3   Theories From a Single Discipline on the Meaning of the *Rime*

Relevant Discipline	Theories From a Single Discipline on the Meaning of the *Rime*
Literature	1. Reader-Response Criticism
	2. Marxist Criticism
	3. The New Historicism
	4. Psychoanalytic Criticism
	5. Deconstruction

Summary and Analysis   In each case, the set of theories chosen by the author represents significant explanations of the problem. Each theory makes certain assumptions, expresses itself with certain concepts, and uses a certain method. Interdisciplinarians often have to work with a set of disciplinary theories that offer conflicting explanations of the problem. The temptation to avoid in this situation is to reduce the number of these theories prematurely so as to minimize conflict.

Second, Identify Theories Within Each of the Other Relevant Disciplines

After identifying the relevant theories within a single discipline, repeat the process for the other sets of theories as illustrated in these examples of student and professional work.

From the Natural Sciences: Smolinski* (2005), Freshwater Scarcity in Texas   Smolinski applied the same research process that he used to identify and understand the important Earth science theories to the disciplines of biology and political science, as shown in Table 7.4.

As students take additional steps in the interdisciplinary research process, they will modify and expand this table to keep track of the rapidly proliferating pieces of information that normally accumulate as the research process proceeds.

Table 7.4   Theories From the Relevant Disciplines on the Causes of Fresh Water Scarcity in Texas

Relevant Discipline	Theories From a Single Discipline on the Causes of Freshwater Scarcity in Texas
Earth Science	1. Global Warming Theory
	2. Overexploitation Theory
	3. Infiltration Theory
Biology	4. Single-System Theory
	5. Encroachment Theory
Political Science	6. Market Theory
	7. Border Theory

From the Social Sciences: Fischer (1988), "On the Need for Integrating Occupational Sex Discrimination Theory on the Basis of Causal Variables"   Fischer examines the literature from each of the other relevant disciplines to identify other important theories on the causes of OSD, as shown in Table 7.5.

Summary and Analysis   These tables enable the researcher to keep track of the rapidly proliferating pieces of information that normally accumulate as

| Table 7.5 | Theories From the Relevant Disciplines on the Causes of OSD |

Discipline or School of Thought	Theories From the Relevant Disciplines on the Causes of OSD
Economics	1. Monopsony Exploitation Theory
	2. Human Capital Theory
	3. Statistical Discrimination Theory
	4. Prejudice Theory
Psychology	5. Male Dominance Theory
Sociology	6. Sex Role Orientation Theory
History	7. Institutional Theory
Marxism[a]	8. Class Conflict Theory

a. Marxism is a school of thought.

the interdisciplinary research process (IRP) proceeds. In each case, performing additional STEPS in the IRP will involve revisiting these lists, perhaps modifying or expanding them as necessary.

It is not unusual for a community of scholars to advance two or more theories concerning a particular problem. When this occurs, researchers would be wise to adopt Fischer's (1988) strategy of first identifying the discipline advancing multiple theories before dealing with the other disciplines, each of which may advance only one or two theories. Why is this? Theories from the same discipline are often easier to integrate than are theories from different disciplines, as will become evident in a later STEP.

When to Use a Deductive Approach to Theory Selection

In these examples of research conducted *inductively*, interdisciplinarians were working on problems that had already attracted considerable attention from disciplinary scholars. But what about working on a problem on which little scholarly research has been done, or where only *certain types* of theories have been advanced? Seeing such a gap in the literature, one may wish to advance a theory explaining the problem that disciplinary experts have overlooked. Unless one is already aware of an appropriate theory, selecting a theory from among several *types* or categories of theories will require using a *deductive* approach. This involves (1) selecting an appropriate *theory type* (taking care that it not be the same type that disciplinarians have already used), and then (2) selecting a theory from within the type.

To aid in making this decision, Szostak (2004) provides a "Typology of Selected Theories" reproduced as Table 7.6. He suggests that we begin the narrowing process by asking each theory type the "5 W" questions:

- *Who (agency)?* Who is the agent? Answer: Agents can be intentional or nonintentional, and in each case individuals, groups, or relations.
- *What (action)?* What does the agent do? Answer: Agents may act, react, or express attitudes.
- *Why (decision making)?* How does the agent decide? Answer: Nonintentional agents do not decide, but intentional agents have recourse to five types of decision making.
- *When (time path)?* What time path does the causal process follow? Answer: Causal processes must be in equilibrium, cyclical, unidirectional, or stochastic.
- *Where (generalize)?* How generalizable is the theory? Answer: Generalizability can be evaluated on a nomothetic/ideographic continuum.

Asking these questions has the added benefit of revealing (or confirming) what has been missed in disciplinary research. Also, *answering* the "5 W" questions will reveal source(s) of conflict between theory types. Understanding why theories conflict is preparatory to creating common ground and performing integration.

Developing Adequacy in Disciplinary Methods _____

The disciplinary research methods discussed here are not to be confused with the IRP itself. *The IRP is an overarching research process that subsumes disciplinary methodologies.* Developing adequacy in disciplinary methods varies greatly among the audiences addressed by this book. Undergraduate students must be familiar with the methods used by authors and understand how these methods may skew their insights and theories. Graduate students and solo interdisciplinarians may not apply disciplinary methods themselves (unless they are conducting basic research) other than to identify, critique, and examine linkages among the insights and theories of the contributing disciplines. Interdisciplinary teams, however, may well employ disciplinary methods. This section defines *disciplinary method* and discusses how to develop adequacy in disciplinary methods.

Defining *Disciplinary Method*

Disciplinary method refers to the particular procedure or process or technique used by a discipline's practitioners to conduct, organize, and present research. Method implies an orderly and logical way of doing something.

Table 7.6 Szostak's Typology of Selected Theories

	Questions to Ask of Each Theory				
Theory Type	Who? Agents	What? Action	Why? Decision Making	When? Time Path	Where? Generalize
Most natural science, outside of biological science	Nonintentional agents	Passive	No active decision-making process	Various	Various
Evolutionary biology	Nonintentional general individuals	Active	Inherent	Not the same equilibrium	Nomothetic
Evolutionary human science	Intentional individual (group)	Active	Various	Not the same (any equilibrium)	Nomothetic
Complexity (Describes systems of interaction among phenomena; applied across natural and human sciences)	Catastrophe, chaos	Active and passive	Not strictly rational but must involve adaptive elements	Varies by version	Generally nomothetic
Action (Including theories of praxis)	Intentional individual (relationship)	Intersection of action and attitude	Often rational, but may be subconscious and unpredictable	Various	Generally idiographic
Systems (Recognition that patterns in social life are not accidental)	Various	Action and attitude	Various; emphasize constraints	Various	Generally nomothetic
Psychoanalytic	Intentional individual	Attitudes	Intuition; others possible	Various	Implicit nomothetic
Symbolic Interactionism	Intentional relationships	Attitudes	Various	Stochastic	Idiographic; some nomothetic
Rational Choice	Individual	Action	Rational	Usually equilibrium	Nomothetic
Phenomenology	Relationships (individuals)	Attitudes (actions)	Various	Various	Various

SOURCE: Szostak, R. (2004). *Classifying science: Phenomena, data, theory, method, practice.* Dordrecht: Springer. Page 82–94. With kind permission from Springer Science+Business Media.

NOTE: **Nomothetic** refers to a theory that is applicable to a broad range of phenomena. **Nomothetic theory** posits a general relationship among two or more phenomena, and nomothetic researchers are concerned with showing a broad applicability. **Ideographic** refers to a theory that is applicable only to a narrow range of phenomena and under a constrained set of circumstances. **Ideographic theory** posits a relationship only under specified conditions, and ideographic researchers wish to explain the relevance of a theoretical proposition in a constrained set of circumstances (Szostak, 2004, pp. 68, 108).

In the natural and social sciences, methods are the means by which to obtain evidence of how some aspect of the natural or human world functions (Szostak, 2004, p. 100).[3] Using methods appropriate to the problem, then, serves to bind the interdisciplinary project together.

Methods Used in the Natural Sciences, the Social Sciences, and the Humanities

Fortunately, the number of methods used by the disciplines is quite small compared to the number of theories they favor. Most methods used by the major disciplines in the natural sciences, the social sciences, and the humanities fall into one of the following categories.

The Natural Sciences

The natural sciences generally emphasize quantitative research strategies:[4]

- Experiments (usually in a laboratory setting)
- Mathematical models
- Classification (of natural phenomena)
- Mapping
- Statistical analysis
- Careful examination of physical objects (as when geologists study rocks)

The Social Sciences

The social sciences use both quantitative and qualitative research strategies:[5]

- Experiments (usually in an applied setting)
- Statistical analysis
- Surveys (qualitative)
- Interviews (qualitative)
- Ethnography/unobtrusive measures (qualitative)
- Physical traces (as in archaeology or paleontology)
- Experience/intuition (as used in interpretation of data) (qualitative)
- Classification (of human phenomena)
- Triangulation or mixed methods[6]

The Humanities

The humanities typically emphasize qualitative research strategies:[7]

- Textual analysis (content analysis, discourse analysis, and historiography)
- Hermeneutics/semiotics (study of symbols and their meaning)

- Experience/intuition (as used in interpretation/appreciation of creative works)
- Classification (of periods, schools of thought, etc.) (Berg, 2004, p. 4; Szostak, 2004, pp. 66–130)
- Cultural analysis (a combination of textual and semiotic analysis)

This list of methods raises several important questions:

- What is the interdisciplinary position on disciplinary research methods?
- Should quantitative methods be privileged over qualitative methods?
- What are the theoretical implications of using qualitative strategies?
- How does the interdisciplinarian choose among them?
- What criteria should be used to make these choices?
- How many methods are needed in an interdisciplinary research project?

These are the questions that are now addressed.

The Interdisciplinary Position on Methods

The interdisciplinary position on disciplinary methods is that there are many methods, each with different strengths and weaknesses, and that no one method or overall approach should be privileged over any other in interdisciplinary work. *Interdisciplinarians should not be bound by the theory-method combinations that disciplinarians find convenient.* This view follows from the belief that each discipline relevant to a problem has something to contribute to producing an integrative understanding of the problem. The interdisciplinary position is mainstream, in that there is now philosophical, if not scientific, consensus that no one method, or broad scientific approach such as positivism, animates knowledge formation today (Szostak, 2004, p. 100).

Adequacy in Disciplines Must Include
Understanding Disciplinary Research Methods

Adequacy in disciplines must include understanding disciplinary research methods for this reason: Since the evidence on which insights are based is derived from the application of methods, analysis of these insights must involve a familiarity with the potential weaknesses of those methods.

Generally speaking, most undergraduate research involves integrating insights and theories drawn from published research, though some interdisciplinary courses and senior projects do conduct fieldwork. At this level, the main point in paying attention to methods is to understand how disciplines can and do choose methods that are good at (and biased toward) their favored theories, which, in turn, influence the insights and theories produced. Graduate students can then contemplate how different methods might yield different insights.

Developing adequacy in disciplines must include understanding disciplinary research methods in order to help one decide which methods are applicable to an interdisciplinary research enterprise that includes conducting one's own basic research. While undergraduates should be aware of the importance of the methods used to produce relevant research, attention to and application of method becomes most important in graduate work and professional research, whether solo or team.

Adequacy in Disciplines Includes Knowing the Interdisciplinary Position on the Quantitative Versus Qualitative Methods Debate

Adequacy in disciplines also includes knowing the issues involved in the quantitative versus qualitative methods debate and the interdisciplinary position on it. Historically, disciplinary scholars have been divided over the value of qualitative versus quantitative methods. **Quantitative research strategies** emphasize evidence that can be quantified, such as the number of atoms in a molecule, the flow rate of water in a river, or the amount of energy derived from a windmill. **Qualitative research strategies** focus on the what, how, when, and where of a thing—its essence and its ambiance. Qualitative research, then, refers to meanings, concepts, definitions, characteristics, metaphors, symbols, and descriptions of things or people that are not measured and expressed numerically (Berg, 2004, pp. 2–3). Qualitative research is often most useful for a new problem (or research question) or to frame an old problem or question in a new way. Whereas most of quantitative research relies on numbers, qualitative research tends to rely on words, images, and descriptions.[8]

The quantitative versus qualitative debate is largely over. Today, most authors on methodology stress mixing methods rather than distinguishing between methods (Hall & Hall, 1996, p. 35). Practitioners recognize that the relative importance of the two broad approaches may, nevertheless, vary according to the characteristics of the research problem. Practitioners and students should accept both quantitative and qualitative approaches because each has been long used, accepted, urged, and useful (Tashakkori & Teddlie, 1998, p. 11). This methodological inclusiveness now characterizes many of the leading books on methods in the social sciences, including Bruce L. Berg's (2004) *Qualitative Research Methods,* which is written for students as much as for scholars. He urges researchers "to consider the merits of both quantitative and qualitative research strategies" (p. 3).[9] This is sound advice for interdisciplinary students who are concerned to identify the perspectives of various writers on a problem.

Two Misconceptions About Qualitative Research

There are two common misconceptions about qualitative research. The first is that reliance on numbers results in a more certain and more valid result than qualitative research can provide. Those working in the social sciences are well aware of the tendency to give quantitative orientations more respect. However, qualitative methods are not only fruitful, but they can also provide greater depth of understanding than can be achieved by relying on quantitative methods alone. Though some qualitative research projects have been poorly done, says Berg (2004), qualitative approaches shouldn't be dismissed just because some studies failed to apply them properly. He adds that qualitative methods can and should be extremely systematic and have the ability to be reproduced by subsequent researchers. "Replicability and reproducibility, after all, are central to the creation and testing of theories and their acceptance by scientific communities" (Berg, 2004, p. 7). *Interdisciplinarians, no less than disciplinarians, should be concerned that their research stand the test of having subsequent researchers examine the same problem using the same disciplines, insights, concepts, theories, and methods and achieve the same results.*

The second misconception is the tendency of some to associate qualitative research with the single technique of participant observation, while others extend their understanding of qualitative research to include interviewing as well (Berg, 2004, pp. 2–3). However, qualitative research strategies also include methods such as "observation of experimental natural settings, photographic techniques (including digital recording), historical analysis (historiography), document and textual analysis, sociometry, sociodrama and similar ethnomethodological experimentation, ethnographic research, and a number of unobtrusive techniques" (Berg, 2004, p. 3).

Theoretical Implications of Using Qualitative Research Methods

Research is conducted to discover answers to questions through the application of systematic procedures called research methods or research strategies, or "approaches." Qualitative research focuses on questions concerning various social settings and the persons who occupy those settings. Qualitative researchers, says Berg (2004), "are most interested in how human beings arrange themselves and their settings, and how inhabitants of these settings make sense of their surroundings through symbols, rituals, social structures, social roles, and so forth" (p. 7).

If humans were studied using just quantitative methods, the danger would arise that conclusions—although arithmetically precise—might fail to fit reality or, worse, distort that reality. Qualitative methods provide a way to evaluate and understand unquantifiable facts about actual people or artifacts left by them, such as art, literature, poetry, photographs, letters, newspaper accounts, diaries, and so on. Qualitative techniques explore how people structure their daily lives, learn, and make sense of themselves and others. Researchers using qualitative methods are thus able to understand and give meaning to humans and their activities.[10]

How a Discipline's Preferred Methods Correlate to Its Preferred Theories

(Note: This discussion is geared to those working with disciplinary insights but not necessarily engaged in basic research.)

Adequacy includes understanding how a discipline's preferred methods correlate to its preferred theories. Disciplines consider certain phenomena or problems within their research domains and advance theories to generate insights into these phenomena. *There is a direct correlation between a discipline and the theories it favors to illuminate a particular problem.* In general, when interdisciplinarians identify a discipline as being relevant to the problem, they use one or more of that discipline's theories that address the problem.

Along with the discipline's insights and theories, one is likely (but is not obligated) to use the methods of the discipline. "There are," observes Szostak (2002), "complementarities such that borrowing a theory from one discipline will encourage use of its methods, study of its phenomena, and engagement with its worldview" (p. 106). Berg (2004) agrees, noting that many researchers mistakenly perceive their research method(s) as having little or nothing to do with theory. Because of this, "they fail to recognize that methods impose certain perspectives on reality" (Berg, 2004, p. 4). The tendency of disciplinarians to link theory, method, and phenomena is a source of bias. Interdisciplinarians should be curious about how the theories fare when applied to different phenomena, and especially when tested using different methods.

Berg (2004) illustrates this bias in the example of researchers deciding to canvass a neighborhood and arrange interviews with residents to discuss their views of some social problem. Their decision to use this method of data collection, he says, means that they have already made a theoretical assumption, namely, that reality is fairly constant and stable. Similarly, when researchers make direct observations of events, they assume reality is deeply affected by the actions of all participants, including themselves. Thus, each method—interview and unobtrusive participant observation—reveals a slightly different facet of the same social problem.

There is a direct correlation between the research methods a discipline uses and the insights and theories it produces. Berg (2004) states, "Data gathering . . . is not distinct from theoretical orientations. Rather, data are intricately associated with the motivation for choosing a given subject, the conduct of the study, and ultimately the analysis" (p. 4). The trap that many researchers fall into, he says, is that as advocates of such methodological styles of research as participant observation, they "are frequently more concerned with asserting or defending their techniques than with indicating alternative ways of approaching the study subject" (p. 4).

The relevance of this discussion for interdisciplinary researchers is this: *A discipline tends to link with certain problems that in turn link with certain theories that in turn link with certain methods.* Therefore, concerning any given problem, researchers are confronted not with an extensive list of possible methods but with a short list of those methods commonly used by the disciplines interested in the problem.

If one of the disciplines is from one of the "harder" (i.e., quantitatively oriented) social sciences such as psychology, then methods such as experiments and statistical analysis will likely have been applied by disciplinary researchers, but qualitative methods may be appropriate and may yield quite different insights. On the other hand, if one of the disciplines is from the humanities, then methods such as semiotics or discourse analysis might have been applied, but other methods might prove useful. For *some* scientific questions, one method clearly excels: experiments. Experiments are unrivaled for the analysis of nonhuman agents. Even for scientific questions, though, experiments are fallible. Interdisciplinarians working on a science-oriented topic should supplement experimental evidence with evidence from other methods (Szostak, 2004, pp. 27–28).

How to Select Methods

Sometimes advanced undergraduates and graduate students combine basic research and integrate it with published insights and theories on the same problem. In this event, they have to decide early on how to select a method(s) that is appropriate to the problem and that will best provide new insights that can be integrated with existing insights to generate a superior understanding. *Using a disciplinary method to conduct basic research should not be equated with or substituted for the interdisciplinary research model described in this book but should be used in conjunction with it. The IRP subsumes whichever disciplinary method(s) is used.*

When Conducting Basic Research in the Sciences

Generally speaking, deciding which method(s) is most appropriate to the research question should be comparatively easy, provided that the researcher is conversant with at least the broad outlines of the various methods, their strengths and weaknesses, and the theories informing them. The following touchstone examples of professional work from the natural sciences and the social sciences show how to decide which methods to use when conducting basic research.

From the Natural Sciences: Watson (1968), The Double Helix: A Personal Account of the Discovery of the Structure of DNA   In his personal account of the discovery of the structure of DNA, Watson reveals that the scientific process is seldom straightforward, logical, or linear. This is often true when it comes to selecting appropriate methods when conducting basic research. The methods he and Francis Crick used in their quest to unlock the complex structure of DNA included conducting experiments (involving the combined techniques of chemistry and genetics), designing mathematical models, and manipulating physical models (much like Tinkertoys) based on which chemical elements like to sit next to each other. Their collaborative decisions about which methods to use at various stages of the project were influenced as much by politics, finances, and lab protocol as by purely scientific considerations.

From the Social Sciences: Fischer (1988), "On the Need for Integrating Occupational Sex Discrimination Theory on the Basis of Causal Variables"
The correlation between a discipline, its favored theories, and its preferred methods is illustrated in Fischer's essay on OSD. He makes the important point that a particular method may be currently in or out of favor with disciplinary experts, but that is no justification, by itself, for the interdisciplinarian to use it or not use it. Whatever methods are ultimately used, the interdisciplinarian should at least be transparent about their identity. The example of Fischer, then, shows how the various theories within the discipline of economics link to the problem of the causes of OSD. These economic theories ultimately led him to use a method drawn from economics.

When Conducting Basic Research in the Humanities

Adequacy means knowing how to select methods when conducting basic research in the humanities. To develop a more comprehensive understanding or meaning of a text or art object, the interdisciplinarian working in the humanities would likely choose one of the research methods commonly used by humanities scholars. Selecting a method in the humanities usually involves making two decisions. The first is to think in "both/and," not in "either/or," terms concerning modernist and postmodernist (including cultural analysis and new historicism) approaches. Key distinctions between these two very distinct approaches—that is, modernism and postmodernism—are summarized here in the most general terms:

Modernism

- investigates available written documents about the object and its creator to provide an accurate description or account of them (Fernie, 1995, p. 327), and
- examines the object using visual techniques.

Postmodernism, cultural analysis, or new history

- investigates the social context of the object and its creator, and
- critically evaluates the relevance of prevailing modernist theories of art to the object or text.

Advantages and Disadvantages of Using Modernist or Postmodernist Methods   Achieving adequacy in methods when working in the humanities means knowing the advantages and disadvantages of using either a modernist or a postmodernist approach, as shown in Table 7.7. (Note: What is said concerning the humanities also applies to the qualitative social sciences and the interdisciplinary fields of environmental studies and of science, technology, and society studies [STS].)

Modernism and postmodernism provide insights into the humanities that are not only different but potentially complementary. In art history, for example, modernism connects work to earlier works (i.e., aesthetic traditions) and to universal and timeless aesthetic principles, while postmodernism connects work and the artist who produced the work to the larger society and

Table 7.7   Advantages and Disadvantages of Using a Modernist or Postmodernist Approach

Approach	Advantages	Disadvantages
Modernist	1. Boundaries of inquiry are clearly defined.	1. Boundaries imply exclusion.
	2. Meaning of the object can be clearly stated.	2. Meaning assumes adherence to some universal standard.
	3. The focus of inquiry is the object.	3. Focusing on the object tends to exclude the complex network of political, economic, social, and other cultural factors that provide the context of the object.
Postmodernist, Social, or New History	1. No boundaries	1. The absence of boundaries may mean an open-ended investigation.
	2. Inclusive of scholarly and nonscholarly evidence	2. These approaches show lack of scholarly consensus on what constitutes "nonscholarly evidence."
	3. Opposes "high" definitions of culture and takes seriously popular cultural forms	3. Focusing on popular culture forms may exclude other cultural forms.

culture, especially to its politics (Barnet, 2008, p. 260). Both approaches, if used together, may produce a more comprehensive understanding of an art object than would be possible if only one of these approaches were used. This suggests that the student, who is the integrator of insights drawn from existing scholarship, ought to look for both modern *and* postmodern insights.

The second decision concerns which of the newer (i.e., postmodern) approaches to use: reader response, Marxist criticism, the new historicism, psychoanalytic criticism, deconstruction, or cultural analysis. For the interdisciplinary student, no one postmodern approach is preferable to any other. Why? Because none of these approaches is either inclusive or integrative of *all* of the relevant perspectives. The interdisciplinarian should choose a combination of approaches—modern and postmodern—with an eye to being inclusive of the major relevant perspectives. Only this degree of inclusiveness will enable the interdisciplinarian to achieve the new meaning of the object or text that is truly interdisciplinary.

From the Humanities: Bal (1999), "Introduction," The Practice of Cultural Analysis: Exposing Interdisciplinary Interpretation   The research method Bal chooses is **cultural analysis.** As a critical practice, it draws on a specific set of collaborating disciplines that include disciplines from the humanities as well as from the social sciences: history, psychology, philosophy, literature, linguistics, and art history. Though cultural analysis is inclusive of the perspectives of several disciplines (and thus particularly valuable to the interdisciplinarian), it is dominated by postmodernism and thus misses the advantages of the modernist approach while suffering the disadvantages of the postmodernist approach, as shown in Table 7.8.

Table 7.8	Positivism, Interpretivism, and Postmodernism: Their Methods Contrasted

Theory	Methods
Positivism	1. Scholars should study only that which is observable, such as actions, and not attitudes. 2. People should be studied independent of their natural environment. 3. Quantification of evidence is essential.
Interpretivism	1. Since humans are intentional and self-reflective, scholars should study attitudes over actions. 2. Scholars should study people in their natural environment, seeking to understand rather than to explain. 3. Qualitative analysis is emphasized over quantitative analysis.
Postmodernism	1. It denies both the prescriptive and the descriptive role of methodology because methodology requires some regularity in techniques for acquiring knowledge (Dow, 2001, p. 66).

SOURCE: Based on Szostak (2004, pp. 62–65, 105).

Furthermore, within postmodern scholarship, a particular postmodernist approach typically fails to take into account the scholarship coming out of another postmodernist approach. Thus, *by itself,* cultural analysis does not produce an understanding that is truly comprehensive but produces one that is, nevertheless, interdisciplinary, though imperfectly so.[11]

Cultural analysis, according to Bal (1999), is based on a keen awareness of the viewer's situatedness in the present. "Situatedness" refers to the social and cultural context from which the viewer looks at the object, and the fact that the object is itself part of how we define our present culture. Cultural analysis differs from the historian's attempt to reconstruct the past objectively or to view the past as the culmination of an evolutionary—and thus inevitable—line of development. Instead, cultural analysis seeks to understand "the past as *part* of the present, as what we have around us, and without which no culture would be able to exist" (Bal, 1999, p. 1).

Cultural analysis demands methodological exactness by requiring the object of inquiry to meet two criteria: that it be specific, meaning that it be a recognizable object or text; and that it have precise starting points. Bal (1999) uses the graffito (introduced in Chapter 3) to illustrate the method of cultural analysis that she sums up in the verb *to expose.* Exposing or exposition refers to the action of making public the deepest held views and beliefs of someone or of someone's deeds that deserve to be made public (pp. 4–5).

How the IRP Relates to the Disciplinary Method(s) Used in Basic Research

Adequacy in the relevant disciplines also involves understanding how the IRP relates to the disciplinary approach that one uses to conduct basic research. The main motivation for an interdisciplinarian to conduct basic research is to address potential linkages between phenomena studied by different disciplines. *The IRP is an overarching process that interdisciplinarians use when their goal is to achieve integration and full interdisciplinarity.* As an overarching process, the IRP subsumes whatever disciplinary method(s) that the interdisciplinarian decides is appropriate to conducting basic research on the problem. The interdisciplinarian will then integrate the findings of this basic research with the research conducted by disciplinarians. This section presumes that the basic research is disciplinary. While interdisciplinarians, especially interdisciplinary teams, can appropriately engage in disciplinary research, the key basic research that only interdisciplinarians are included to carry out is to identify and study linkages mentioned above. The results of that research are different from but complementary to the results of research in the disciplines.

Most disciplinary researchers in the social sciences have at least one research strategy or methodological technique they feel most comfortable using, which "often becomes their favorite or only approach to research" (Berg, 2004, p. 4). This is likely true for researchers in the natural sciences as well as the humanities. Interdisciplinarians, however, should not emulate disciplinarians in this regard. *There are important outcome-shaping implications of selecting any research method, and interdisciplinarians must be aware of these implications when they make decisions about which research methods to use.*

The Concept of Triangulation in Research Methodology

The question of how many methods are used in a given research project is directly related to the concept of *triangulation* in research methodology. Understanding this concept is another aspect of what it means for students to develop adequacy in relevant disciplines. Though this term is more commonly associated with surveying, mapmaking, navigation, and military practices, it is also appropriate for conducting research, including interdisciplinary research. Each research method reveals slightly different facets of the same reality, and every method provides a different line of sight directed toward the same point or research problem. By combining several lines of sight, researchers can produce an integrated picture of the problem and have more ways to verify theoretical concepts. Social scientists call the use of multiple lines of sight *triangulation* (Berg, 2004, p. 5).[12]

Triangulation of research methodology involves using multiple data-gathering techniques (usually three) to investigate the same problem/system/process. In this way, findings can be cross-checked, validated, and confirmed. The important feature of triangulation, explains Berg (2004), "is not the simple combination of different kinds of data but the attempt to relate them so as to counteract the threats to validity identified in each" (p. 5). The term *validity* refers to "how well the measurement we use actually represents the true condition of interest—the thing we are trying to measure" (Remler & van Ryzin, 2011, p. 106).[13]

Triangulation involves using varieties of data, theories, and methods. The research literature supports using triangulation or multiple methods in a single research project. Norman K. Denzin (1978) also suggests using multiple data-collection procedures, multiple theoretical perspectives, and multiple analysis techniques (p. 101). The use of multiple methods and theories, Berg (2004) contends, "increases the depth of understanding an investigation can yield" (p. 6).

Regarding the question of how many methods should be used in an interdisciplinary research project, the answer is "It depends on the problem, how it is stated, and how ambitious the investigation is." Ultimately, the number of disciplinary research methods used in a given project depends on many factors, not the least of which is the scope and complexity of the problem and whether or not one decides to integrate one's own findings with those of disciplinary experts.

Deciding Which Disciplinary Methods to Use in Conducting Basic Research

Once one has narrowed the number of possible disciplinary methods to a few, one must then decide which of these should be used. Consider, for example, this student research project, the focus of which is the declining salmon populations in the Columbia and Snake river systems. A topic, as noted earlier, may take any number of research directions. In this instance, the student narrowed the topic to two possible avenues of inquiry:

Option A. Explain the 80% reduction of the salmon populations that has occurred since the system of dams was built.

Option B. Examine the current state of the salmon populations in the Columbia and Snake rivers.

The student decided that the disciplines most relevant to both options were biology, economics, and history (the assignment limited the number of disciplines to three). Consulting Table 7.9, "Research Methods Typically Used by Each Discipline," makes it easy to connect each discipline to its preferred research method(s).

Table 7.9   Research Methods Typically Used by Each Discipline

Relevant Disciplines	Research Methods
Biology	• Experiments • Mathematical models • Classification of natural phenomena • Mapping • Simulations (computer)
Economics	• Mathematical models • Statistical analysis of empirical data
History	• Identification of primary source material from the past in the form of documents, records, letters, interviews, oral history, archeology, etc. or secondary sources in the form of books and articles • Critical analysis in the form of interpretation of historical documents into a picture of past events or the quality of human and other life within a particular time and place

The next task was to decide which of these methods is most appropriate for each avenue of inquiry. Note that each option defines the topic in a way that influences the choice of methods. Option A seeks to explain how the problem developed and who or what was responsible. Table 7.10 shows that the methods most appropriate to Option A are mapping (biology), statistical analysis and critical thinking (economics), and identification and interpretation of historical documents (history).

Table 7.10	Possible Methods to Use in Option A	

Relevant Disciplines	Research Methods	Potential Candidate for Inclusion and Justification
Biology	Experiments	No. The focus of the topic is on what happened in the past.
	Mathematical models	No. It is inappropriate for a historical explanation of how the problem developed.
	Classification of natural phenomena	No. There is nothing concerning the topic that requires classification.
	Simulations (computer)	No. Computer simulations are not appropriate for explaining past decisions.
Economics	Mathematical models	No. It is inappropriate for a historical explanation of how the problem developed.
	Statistical analysis of empirical data	Yes, provided that the statistical information was used to justify the original decision to build the dams.
	Critical thinking	Yes.
History	Identification of primary source materials	Yes. Those supporting and opposing the building of the dams could be interviewed. Original studies and past and present government hearings could be analyzed.
	Critical analysis in the form of interpretation of historical documents	Yes. The historical documents must be interpreted to answer the research questions: "How did the problem develop, and who was responsible?"

Option B seeks a more comprehensive understanding of the current state of the salmon population in the Columbia and Snake rivers. Table 7.11 shows which methods are potential candidates for inclusion in this option. The Option B version of the topic results in a greatly expanded number of possible methods available to the interdisciplinarian.

Deciding which disciplinary research methods should be used depends, primarily, on whether the student is going to conduct basic research on the problem. It also depends on the disciplines interested in it, on the theories producing insights into it, and on the time and resource constraints. The student will decide which methods are most relevant based on the requirements or limitations of the interdisciplinary project.

Table 7.11   Possible Methods to Use in Option B

Relevant Disciplines	Research Methods	Potential Candidate for Inclusion and Justification
Biology	Experiments	Possibly. Experiments recently concluded or in progress may illuminate how the system of dams is impacting various salmon populations.
	Mathematical models	Possibly. Modeling seasonal migrations of salmon under varying conditions would be useful.
	Classification of natural phenomena	No. There is nothing concerning the topic that requires classification.
	Mapping	Possibly. This method can show the progressive impact of past decisions on salmon populations.
	Simulations (computer)	Possibly. Computer simulations are useful to predict various outcomes under variable conditions.
Economics	Mathematical models	Possibly. For reasons stated.
	Statistical analysis of empirical data	Yes. An abundance of recent or current statistical data are likely available.
	Critical thinking	Yes.
History	Identification of primary source materials	Yes. Those presently supporting or opposing the dams could be interviewed. Original studies and past and present government hearings should be analyzed to provide background information and immediate context.
	Critical analysis in the form of interpretation of historical documents	Yes. Documents and sources must be interpreted to answer the research question: "What is the current state of the salmon populations in the Columbia and Snake rivers?"

Providing In-Text Evidence of Disciplinary Adequacy

Adequacy in relevant disciplines involves comprehending enough about each discipline to decide which of its defining elements are relevant to the problem, identifying relevant theories, and identifying appropriate methods. Students are well advised to provide in-text evidence that they have developed adequacy in the disciplines they are using. **In-text evidence of disciplinary adequacy** may be expressed in many ways, such as statements about the disciplinary elements that pertain to the problem, the disciplinary affiliation of leading theorists, and the disciplinary methods used if one is engaging in basic research. It is relatively easy to weave this evidence into the narrative if this confirming information has been collected and organized in an easily retrievable way.

Another way to demonstrate adequacy is to use the most current and authoritative scholarship pertaining to the problem. Interdisciplinary work tends to focus on complex and real-world problems *and* on intellectual problems that are not necessarily real-world. Some problems are time-sensitive. In the case of human cloning, for example, scholarship is being produced from multiple disciplines and interdisciplines in response to procedural breakthroughs, scandals, and legislative attempts to control this reproductive technology. Each of these developments raises new questions and prompts a new round of scholarly comment, often rendering earlier analysis less useful or even obsolete. When working with time-sensitive topics, the most recent scholarship should be consulted.

There are two practical reasons for providing in-text evidence of disciplinary adequacy. First, it demonstrates academic rigor. Interdisciplinary students bear a heavier responsibility than disciplinary students do in their research because interdisciplinarians have to establish adequacy in two or more disciplines. Therefore, students should be concerned to counter possible criticisms of dilettantism and superficiality by doing what more and more professional interdisciplinary writers are doing: Identify those disciplines that pertain to the problem, justify using an interdisciplinary approach, and weave into the narrative an explanation for using certain methods and applying certain theories.

The second practical reason for providing in-text evidence of disciplinary adequacy is to highlight the distinctive character of the research project compared to that of disciplinary research. *Paying attention to the interdisciplinary research process involves not just moving through its various STEPS; it also involves being self-consciously interdisciplinary.* This means reflecting on one's biases (disciplinary and personal), serving as an honest broker when confronting conflicting viewpoints, and all the while keeping in view the end product that prompted the research in the first place.

Chapter Summary

For interdisciplinary students, developing adequacy in disciplines relevant to the problem is usually sufficient. Adequacy means knowing enough information about each discipline to have a basic understanding of how it approaches, illuminates, and characterizes the problem. If students are conducting basic research as part of the IRP, then additional considerations apply. For one thing, the way the problem is stated greatly influences which methods they are likely to use. A consequence of deciding which methods to use is that students may have to restate the problem or reframe the question. In the end, they must make the difficult decision of which theories and which methods are most appropriate in each case. They have not only the freedom to make these choices but also the responsibility to make them transparent. Whether or not students choose to use tables to store and juxtapose data as has been urged, it is important that they develop some method to keep track of the information gathered so that nothing important is lost or overlooked when performing subsequent STEPS.

Clearly, the interdisciplinary student has to engage in far more preparatory analysis than does a disciplinary student. As tedious and time consuming as this is, it must be done in order to perform the later STEPS of the research process that involve integration. Performing these final STEPS satisfactorily is not possible unless these preparatory steps have been completed successfully. The next STEP of the research process (STEP 6, described in Chapter 8) concerns deciding *whether* and *how* the disciplinary elements that have been chosen in STEP 5 (i.e., the insights and their assumptions and theories) adequately illuminate the problem.

Notes

1. Some interdisciplinarians, such as Hal Foster (1998), believe that to be interdisciplinary one must be "disciplinary first," meaning professionally "grounded in one discipline, preferably two" (p. 162).

2. Mieke Bal (2002) argues that concepts constitute interdisciplinary method in the humanities and that their use is inclusive of social science methodology (p. 5).

3. Szostak (2004), in *Classifying Science: Phenomena, Data, Theory, Method, Practice,* is careful to distinguish between methods and "techniques or tools, such as experimental design or instrumentation, or particular statistical packages" (p. 100). Tools and techniques and so on are a subset of methods. His chapter on "Classifying Methods" is indispensable reading for students.

4. Introductory textbooks on the scientific method include Stephen S. Carey's (2003) *A Beginner's Guide to Scientific Method* (2nd ed.) and Hugh G. Gauch, Jr.'s (2002) *Scientific Method in Practice.*

5. Textbooks on social science research methods include Linda E. Dorsten and Lawrence Hotchkiss's (2005) *Research Methods and Society: Foundations of Social Inquiry,* W. Lawrence Neuman's (2006) *Social Research Methods: Qualitative and Quantitative Approaches,* John Gerring's (2001) *Social Science Methodology,* and Chava Frankfort-Nachmias and David Nachmias's (2008) *Research Methods in the Social Sciences* (7th ed.). For research methods of social science-oriented fields, see Frank E. Hagan's (2005) *Essentials of Research Methods in Criminal Justice and Criminology* and William Wiersma and Stephen G. Jurs's (2005) *Research Methods in Education: An Introduction.*

6. Bruce L. Berg (2004) says that triangulation was first used in the social sciences "as a metaphor describing a form of *multiple operationalism* or *convergent validation,*" meaning "multiple data collection technologies designed to measure a

single concept or construct" (p. 5). For many social scientists, triangulation is usually restricted to three data-gathering techniques to investigate the same phenomenon. "The important feature of triangulation," says Berg, "is not the simple combination of different kinds of data but the attempt to relate them so as to counteract the threats to validity identified in each" (p. 5). Alan Bryman (2004) provides extensive discussion of mixed methods in Chapters 21 and 22 of *Social Research Methods*.

7. Though written for the social sciences, Berg's (2004) *Qualitative Research Methods for the Social Sciences* may be used profitably in the humanities. In contrast to the social sciences, humanities books on commonly used research methods are few. These include Catherine Marshall and Gretchen B. Rossman's (2006) *Designing Qualitative Research,* John W. Creswell's (1997) *Qualitative Inquiry and Research Design: Choosing Among Five Traditions,* and Matthew B. Miles and Michael Huberman's (1994) *Qualitative Data Analysis: An Expanded Sourcebook.* Examples of excellent research methods textbooks used in particular humanities disciplines include those by Laurie Schneider Adams (1996), *The Methodologies of Art: An Introduction;* Hong Xio (2005), *Research Methods for English Studies;* Martha Howell and Walter Prevenier (2001), *From Reliable Sources: An Introduction to Historical Methods;* and James J. Scheurich (1997), *Research Method in the Postmodern.*

8. Useful books on qualitative research in all of its aspects include those by John W. Creswell (1997), *Qualitative Inquiry and Research Design: Choosing Among Five Traditions;* John W. Creswell (2002), *Research Design: Qualitative, Quantitative, and Mixed Methods Approaches;* and Norman K. Denzin and Yvonna S. Lincoln (Eds.) (2005), *The SAGE Handbook of Qualitative Research.*

9. Berg (2004) notes that qualitative methodologies have not predominated in the social sciences (p. 2). His chapter "Mixed Methods Procedures" provides a comprehensive summary of this approach and a survey of the literature on the subject.

10. The general purpose of qualitative research derives from the theoretical perspective of symbolic interaction that is one of several theoretical schools of thought associated with the social sciences. It focuses on subjective understandings and the perceptions of and about people, symbols, and objects. Human behavior depends on learning rather than on biological instinct. Humans communicate what we learn through symbols, the most common of these being language. The core task of symbolic interactionists as researchers, Berg (2004) explains, is to "capture the essence of this process for interpreting or attaching meaning to various symbols" (p. 8). By contrast, positivists use empirical methodologies borrowed from the natural sciences to investigate phenomena. Their concern is to provide rigorous, reliable, and verifiably large amounts of data and the statistical testing of empirical hypotheses. Qualitative researchers, on the other hand, are primarily interested in individuals and their so-called life-worlds. "Life-worlds include emotions, motivations, symbols, and their meanings, empathy, and other subjective aspects associated with naturally evolving lives of individuals and groups" (p. 11).

11. In fact, it rejects this posture, typical of new critical forms of interdisciplinarity.

12. Marilyn Stember (1991), among others, also makes this point in "Advancing the Social Sciences Through the Interdisciplinary Enterprise." On triangulation, see pp. 151–153 in R. Szostak (2004), *Classifying Science: Phenomena, Data, Theory, Method, Practice.*

13. For a thorough discussion of "validity" and the difficulties involved in establishing whether a measure is valid or not, see pp. 106–115 in D. K. Remler and G. G. Van Ryzin (2011), *Research Methods in Practice: Strategies for Description and Causation.*

Exercises

Decisions

7.1 What decisions are involved in developing adequacy in disciplines relevant to the problem?

Theories

7.2 Crime statistics are a moving target, sometimes increasing due to certain factors, and at other times decreasing due to other factors. Find out what the crime statistics are in your town or city, and compare the statistics spanning a 10-year time span. Draw upon or formulate two theories that explain the rise or fall of crime (or particular types of crime) in your community, making certain that each theory is from a different disciplinary perspective.

7.3 A related question is this: What theory or theories do local officials use to explain either the rise or the decrease in crime? Does each theory reflect a particular disciplinary perspective? Do the various theories advanced explain the increase or decrease in crime comprehensively?

Gaps

7.4 Let's say you are researching a problem that has generated considerable attention from disciplinary scholars and that they have advanced various theories to explain the behavior of a certain phenomenon or the cause of some behavior. How do you discover if there is a gap in the research? How would you go about advancing a theory to explain the problem (e.g., its cause or the behavior) that disciplinary experts have overlooked?

Methods

7.5 Concerning the above example of crime in your community, would using qualitative or quantitative methods be more helpful in formulating theories to explain the cause of crime, and thus create policies to combat crime?

7.6 What assumption(s) would you be making if you preferred either qualitative or quantitative methods of data collection?

Modernist or Postmodernist Methods

7.7 Which method—modernist or postmodernist—should be used to construct the most comprehensive understanding possible of the following topics:

- Why do Palestinians demand that Jerusalem be the capital of a Palestinian state?
- Should deep water drilling for oil be permitted in light of the BP oil catastrophe in the Gulf of Mexico?
- What is the best approach to reduce the incidence of bullying in public schools?

Adequacy

7.8 Concerning the topic you are researching, how can you provide "in-text" evidence of disciplinary adequacy?

8 Analyzing the Problem and Evaluating Insights

Chapter Preview

Chapter Preview

In STEP 3, we identified the disciplines potentially relevant to the problem and then reduced them to just the most relevant (see Chapter 5). The full-scale literature search conducted in STEP 4 served, among other things, to validate our choices and identify the important disciplinary insights and/or theories (see Chapter 6). Then in STEP 5, we developed adequacy in the relevant disciplines (see Chapter 7). Now, STEP 6 calls for using this disciplinary-specific information to take two actions: (1) Analyze the problem from the perspective of each relevant discipline in a general sense, and (2) evaluate each insight and/or theory.

As discussed in Chapter 4, the disciplines provide different lenses or perspectives (in a general sense) for viewing the same problem and illuminating its parts. The challenge of STEP 6 is to *view* the problem through the lens of each relevant discipline, comparing their perspectives and determining their strengths and limitations, and then *evaluate* each discipline's insights into the problem to reveal their strengths and limitations. Various strategies for evaluating insights are discussed. In STEP 6, the movement is from the general to the particular—from each discipline's perspective on the problem in a general sense to its particular insights into the problem. This work of analyzing perspectives and evaluating the strengths and limitations of insights is foundational to preparing insights for integration, which is the focus of Part III.

Step 6: Analyze the Problem and Evaluate Each Insight or Theory

Analyzing the Problem From Each Disciplinary Perspective

Analyzing the problem from each disciplinary perspective involves moving from one discipline to another and shifting from one perspective to another. Newell (2007a) describes this process of "moving" and "shifting" in rather colorful terms:

> We must take off one set of disciplinary lenses and put on another set in its place as each discipline is examined. A possible initial effect of doing this is "intellectual vertigo" until one's brain can refocus. Experienced interdisciplinarians have developed the mental flexibility that enables them to shift easily from one disciplinary perspective to another. They do this in much the same way that multilingual persons shift easily from English to French to German without really having to think hard about what they are doing. (p. 255)

Analyzing the problem requires viewing it through the lens of each disciplinary perspective *primarily* in terms of its insights and theories. For example, if one wanted to construct a *disciplinary* understanding of the *Rime of the Ancient Mariner,* one would naturally mine the discipline of English literature for insights and interpretive theories. However, if one wanted to construct an integrated and more comprehensive understanding of the *Rime,* one would search for insights generated by authors in disciplinary and interdisciplinary fields that approach the text from different theoretical positions such as reader response, Marxist criticism, new historicism, psychoanalytic criticism, cultural analysis, and deconstruction (e.g., Fry, 1999). When working in the humanities, one typically works with a mix of disciplinary and interdisciplinary fields.

How to Analyze a Problem From Each Disciplinary Perspective

The problem of acid rain was a classroom exercise designed to illustrate disciplinary perspective taking. Table 8.1 views the problem from the perspective of each relevant discipline stated in terms of an overarching "what" or "how" question that can be asked of any problem.

The overarching question posed by each relevant discipline or interdiscipline reflects its perspective (in a general sense), as noted in Table 4.2 in Chapter 4 (excluding law, environmental studies, and science and technology studies, which were not examined). There are two benefits of asking overarching "what" or "how" questions framed in each discipline's perspective: The question can deepen an existing line of inquiry and possibly initiate a new line of inquiry, and the question can help draw out interrelationships among phenomena. Table 8.1 reveals disciplinary bias in terms of the questions asked; the disciplines may also be biased in the answers they provide.

The very premise of interdisciplinary studies is that disciplines can rarely explain all aspects of a complex problem. When dealing with a problem that is complex, such as acid rain, no single discipline is equipped to approach it comprehensively. Readers can discover how involved a problem really is by mapping it (see Chapter 5) and by connecting the problem to

| Table 8.1 | Disciplines and Their Perspectives Stated in Terms of Overarching Questions Asked About the Problem of Acid Rain |

Discipline and Interdiscipline	Perspective Stated in Terms of the Kinds of Overarching Questions Asked
Physics	What are the fundamental physical principles underlying electrical power production that lead to acid rain?
Engineering	How does the design of the power generation process lead to acid rain?
Chemistry	What molecular changes lie behind the creation of acid rain and its effects?
Biology	How does acid rain affect flora and fauna?
Economics	What public policies could encourage firms to produce less acid rain?
Political Science	How could those public policies be adopted and implemented?
Law	How could those policies be enforced?
Environmental Studies	How is the problem of acid rain part of a complex environmental system?
Science and Technology Studies	How is the problem of acid rain a reflection of the relationship between scientific and technical innovations and social, political, and cultural values of society?

NOTE: Environmental studies and science and technology studies are interdisciplines.

the perspective of each relevant discipline, as Table 8.2 does. The table was constructed by taking each discipline's general perspective (provided in Table 4.2) and applying it to the specific problem of acid rain.

For example, the general perspective of economics, as stated in Table 4.2, is that it "emphasizes the study of market interactions, with the individual functioning as a separate, autonomous, rational entity, and perceives groups (even societies) as nothing more than the sum of individuals within them." In other words, almost any problem is viewed as a "rational" (and therefore predictable and quantifiable) outworking of "market interactions." As applied to the complex problem of acid rain in the United States, therefore, economics sees it as a market problem resulting from decisions made by rational actors.

But the focus of our interest is not on the problem of acid rain in its entirety (i.e., its causes and effects) but only on its causes. A system map of the problem (not shown) reveals the various parts of the problem including the power plants that produce the electricity; their power source, which is predominantly coal; the chemical properties of power plant emissions; federal and state regulations; and so forth. So, the perspective of economics applied to the problem of acid rain is that it is caused by the behavior of that portion of the economic system that drives decisions about the use of coal in power plants. This "telescoping down" strategy of applying a general disciplinary perspective to a particular complex problem or part of it is not possible without first mapping the problem and understanding how its parts interact with each other. Table 8.2 shows how each discipline's unique perspective allows it to focus narrowly on only one aspect of the complex problem of acid rain.

Examples of Analyzing Problems From Disciplinary Perspectives

Analyzing problems from various disciplinary perspectives is demonstrated in several multithreaded examples from published and student (marked by an asterisk) work. The categorization of these examples refers to the area of the researcher's training and the orientation of the topic, more than to the disciplines from which insights are drawn.

From the Natural Sciences: Watson (1968), The Double Helix: A Personal Account of the Discovery of the Structure of DNA   Watson appropriately identifies all of the relevant disciplines early on in his study. One of his purposes

Table 8.2   Disciplinary Perspectives Relevant to the Problem of Acid Rain

Relevant Discipline or Interdiscipline	Perspectives on Acid Rain in a General Sense
Physics	May see acid rain as a consequence of basic thermodynamic principles underlying the operation of an electricity-generating power plant
Engineering	May see acid rain as a power plant design problem
Chemistry	May see acid rain as the result of a series of chemical processes
Biology	May see acid rain as posing a biological problem for downwind flora and fauna
Economics	May see acid rain as the result of the behavior of that portion of the economic system that drives decisions about the use of coal in power plants
Political Science	May see acid rain as a regulatory problem
Law	May see the destructive effects of acid rain on property as a question of who is responsible and thus liable
Environmental Studies	May see acid rain as complex physical, chemical, and biological interaction caused by human activity
Science and Technology Studies	May see acid rain as an example of how embedded social, political, and cultural values affect scientific research and technological innovation and how these, in turn, affect society, politics, and culture

NOTE: Environmental studies and science and technology studies are interdisciplines.

| Table 8.3 | Disciplinary Perspectives Relevant to the Problem of the Structure of DNA |

Discipline or Subdiscipline Most Relevant to the Problem	Perspective on Problem Stated in General Terms
Physics	Sees the problem of DNA as a structural problem solvable by using X-ray diffraction photography as the principal tool of research
Microbiology	Sees the problem of DNA as a genetic problem solvable by discovering how genes act
Biochemistry	Sees the problem of DNA as solvable by working out DNA's chemical structure

NOTE: Microbiology is a subdiscipline of biology.

in presenting this case study is to establish a historical timeline of how his work in the relevant disciplines led him and Crick to make critical decisions about which disciplinary insights to use and which to discard. These disciplines are identified and their perspectives stated in general terms in Table 8.3.

From the Natural Sciences: Smolinski* (2005), Freshwater Scarcity in Texas   Smolinski has already identified the disciplines most relevant to the complex problem of freshwater scarcity in Texas in STEP 3 (Chapter 5). These are listed in the left-hand column in Table 8.4. Using the information on disciplinary perspective provided in Table 4.2 and information gathered in the literature search, he is able to apply the general perspective of each relevant discipline to the specific problem of freshwater scarcity in Texas and then state these narrowed perspectives in general terms. This is possible even though each discipline embraces two or more conflicting theories explaining why the problem exists and offering possible solutions.

| Table 8.4 | Disciplinary Perspectives Relevant to the Problem of Freshwater Scarcity in Texas |

Discipline Most Relevant to the Problem	Perspective on Problem Stated in General Terms
Earth Science	Sees the problem as a consequence of human interference in natural geological systems
Biology	Sees the problem as a consequence of human degradation of the Earth's major systems: atmosphere, biosphere, geosphere, and hydrosphere
Political Science	Sees the problem as a reflection of institutional and interest group factors

These general statements of each discipline's perspective applied to the problem provide a glimpse into how it will be possible to eventually integrate conflicting theories within each discipline.

From the Social Sciences: Fischer (1988), "On the Need for Integrating Occupational Sex Discrimination Theory on the Basis of Causal Variables" Fischer is grappling with a complex social problem involving several disciplines—and a school of thought (i.e., Marxism)—and their perspectives. While it is unlikely that undergraduate or even graduate students would be required to work with as many disciplines and theories as Fischer does, his approach is instructive because of the way he simplifies the process for us by briefly describing each perspective in a concise narrative. Once again, the general perspective of each relevant discipline is applied to the problem, and Fischer states these narrowed perspectives in concise statements, as shown in Table 8.5.

From the Social Sciences: Delph* (2005), An Integrative Approach to the Elimination of the "Perfect Crime" In her senior project Delph uses one interdiscipline (criminal justice) and two subdisciplines (forensic science and forensic psychology) in the study of how "perfect crimes" (i.e., the criminal is not caught) can be eliminated or, at least, greatly reduced. An interdiscipline brings together aspects of other disciplines to focus on a complex phenomenon such as crime. As an interdiscipline, criminal justice brings together the subdisciplines of forensic science (biology) and forensic psychology (psychology) along with elements of sociology that focus on criminal behavior. Criminal justice generates its own theories and uses a variety of research methods borrowed

Table 8.5 Disciplinary Perspectives on the Problem of Occupational Sex Discrimination (OSD)

Discipline or School of Thought Most Relevant to the Problem	Perspective on Problem Stated in General Terms
Economics	OSD is caused by rational economic decision making on the part of males and females (Fischer, 1988, pp. 27–31).
History	OSD is caused and perpetuated by longstanding institutional forces (pp. 32–34).
Sociology	OSD is caused by a process of female socialization different from men which, in turn, is directly reflected in their occupational structures (p. 34).
Psychology	OSD is caused and perpetuated by males to maintain the traditional male-female division of labor (pp. 35–36).
Marxism	OSD is a necessary act in preserving the institutions of capitalism (p. 32).

NOTE: Marxism is a school of thought.

from biology, psychology, and sociology. Early on, Delph decided to limit her study to the interdiscipline and subdisciplines listed in Table 8.6. Their perspectives, as they apply to the problem, are stated concisely in general terms.

| Table 8.6 | Disciplinary Perspectives Relevant to the Problem of Eliminating the "Perfect Crime" |

Interdiscipline or Subdiscipline Most Relevant to the Problem	Perspective on Problem Stated in General Terms
Criminal Justice	Sees the persistence of "perfect (i.e., unsolvable) crimes" as a result of inefficient investigatory processes
Forensic Science	Sees the persistence of "perfect crimes" as a result of improper application of forensic science to criminal investigations
Forensic Psychology	Sees the persistence of "perfect crimes" as a result of insufficient attention to the art of criminal profiling

NOTE: Forensic science and forensic psychology are subdisciplines.

From the Humanities: Bal (1999), "Introduction," The Practice of Cultural Analysis: Exposing Interdisciplinary Interpretation   Bal, befitting an interdisciplinary approach, is able to state, in general terms, each relevant discipline's overall perspective on the meaning of the art object, a graffito, which is her focus of study. A table such as Table 8.7 is useful in keeping track of

| Table 8.7 | Disciplinary Perspectives on the Meaning of a Graffito |

Discipline or Interdiscipline	Perspective on Problem Stated in General Terms
Art History	Sees the graffito as an autographic art object reflective of a period of Dutch culture and thus providing a window into that culture
History	Sees the graffito as a product of Flemish history and a window into Flemish culture
Linguistics	Sees the graffito as self-referential
Literature	Sees the graffito as allographic literature
Philosophy	Sees the graffito as an epistemological argument
Psychology	Sees the graffito as an expression of psychic mourning
Cultural Analysis	Sees the graffito as a "text-image" that embodies the program of cultural analysis

NOTE: Cultural analysis is an interdiscipline.

the several perspectives involved in the analysis. Juxtaposing these perspectives in this way enables the researcher to more readily identify possible areas of overlap and points of conflict among them, which is called for in STEP 6.

From the Humanities: Silver* (2005), Composing Race and Gender: The Appropriation of Social Identity in Fiction   Silver studies the ethics of appropriation of social identities by fiction writers, a topic that has been practically ignored, especially by fiction writers themselves. "Appropriation" refers to the practice commonly used by actors, filmmakers, and fiction writers to assume another person's social identity, although the ethics of doing so is rarely discussed. Appropriation, or "putting oneself in another's shoes," helps the artist or author to gain a more personal understanding of those people who are being appropriated. Among the examples of appropriation she cites is that of John Howard Griffin who wrote *Black Like Me* to call attention to racial injustice. By appropriating the skin of a black man, Griffin became the first known white person to experience directly the kind of treatment known only to black people. Silver explores this topic from the perspectives of three disciplines: sociology, psychology, and literature. She applies the general perspective of each discipline to the problem of appropriation, as shown in Table 8.8.

Reflections on Analyzing Problems From Disciplinary Perspectives

Analyzing a problem from the perspectives of only a few disciplines may reveal that the problem is too broad and needs to be narrowed further. If so, STEP 1 will have to be revisited and the statement of the problem reworded to reflect the narrowed focus (see Chapter 3). Analyzing the problem of acid rain reveals that it is a very broad problem that requires consulting quite a few disciplines if a truly comprehensive understanding of its causes is to be achieved. Deciding which part of the problem to focus on

Table 8.8	Disciplinary Perspectives on the Problem of the Appropriation of Social Identity in Fiction

Discipline Most Relevant to the Problem	Perspective on Problem Stated in General Terms
Sociology	Sees the problem arising from socially constructed power dynamics and guilt feelings that impact race and gender relations
Psychology	Sees the problem arising from writers attempting empathetic arousal of their audience
Literature	Sees the problem as arising from authors' need to achieve a sense of authenticity

would most likely result in reducing the number of disciplines to those that are the most relevant to the narrowed focus. *The progression of the research is from defining the problem to identifying its parts to identifying the disciplines that specialize in those parts.*

Applying each discipline's general perspective to the problem and stating this perspective concisely is worthwhile for three reasons. First, the "telescoping down" strategy forces us to think deductively, to move from the general to the particular. Second, the strategy of "telescoping down" or applying a general disciplinary perspective to a particular complex problem, or part of it, requires that we map the problem and understand how its parts interact with each other. We may well identify gaps between disciplinary perspectives. Third, the action of writing each discipline's narrowed perspective in a concise statement is integrative in this sense: If a discipline has produced two or more conflicting insights or theories about the causes of a problem, these conflicting insights or theories will still probably share the discipline's general perspective as well as the narrowed statement of that perspective. Fourth, focusing so intensely on perspective enables us to verify whether or not the disciplines selected earlier are as relevant to the problem as we thought they were.

Creating tables is a worthwhile activity because their juxtaposition of disciplinary perspectives reveals similarities and differences that otherwise might be overlooked. It is easier to compare things that are close together than to compare things that are far apart. Juxtaposing the perspectives of the relevant disciplines makes it easier to see the narrowness of each perspective and the necessity of pushing on with the IRP. *Integration cannot proceed unless we first identify similarities and differences (and sometimes gaps) between perspectives and their insights.* Clearly, the disciplines, by themselves, are unable to explain a complex problem comprehensively.

The Problem of Personal Bias

In addition to the bias inherent in disciplinary approaches to complex problems, personal bias can also skew interdisciplinary work. How should one ultimately decide which disciplinary information to include or exclude from the study? The answer is by progressing from the topic to its parts to the disciplines that specialize in those parts. In other words, the parts of the problem that one wants to focus on largely determine which disciplines one ends up using. This, again, points up the value of mapping the problem. But there is an additional factor that may influence one's decision.

Individual scholars, interdisciplinary as well as disciplinary, often bring their personal biases or settled prejudices to certain problems. For example, sociology, since its founding, has been more liberal than is economics, and "studies" of any sort (e.g., women's, environmental, and even religious) tend to be more liberal than are their disciplinary counterparts. It bears emphasizing that interdisciplinarians value diversity of perspective and seek out conflicting viewpoints with which they disagree. They can live with ideological diversity and tension. They also value difference and ambiguity. The trap that they should avoid falling into is drawing disproportionately from disciplines or schools of thought (i.e., from their insights and theories) with which they agree or are more familiar, whether this is done consciously or unconsciously (Newell, 2007a, p. 252).

Throughout the entire interdisciplinary research process (IRP), the goal must be kept in mind: to construct a more *comprehensive* understanding of the problem. The understanding cannot be truly comprehensive if it excludes certain views or is dominated by certain views. If the scales of scholarship are prejudiced, then the rigor, comprehensiveness, and intellectual integrity of the project will be seriously, or even fatally, compromised.

As with previous steps, performing STEP 6 *may* involve revisiting earlier steps. Here, it is important to connect each part of the problem with those disciplines that are interested in it and that have produced important insights and theories on it. Performing STEP 6 thoroughly and with integrity will enable one to identify which perspectives are the most compelling and which ones are (possibly) missing.

Evaluating Insights

The first part of STEP 6 involves analyzing the problem through the lens of each discipline's unique perspective (in a general sense). The second part of STEP 6, discussed here, involves evaluating the insights produced by disciplinary perspectives. These insights should have been identified by the end of the literature search conducted in STEP 4 (see Chapter 6) and their relevance confirmed in STEP 5 (see Chapter 7). Evaluating insights involves using different strategies. These are organized under the following headings: disciplinary perspective in general, the theories used in generating insights, the data used as evidence for insights, the methods employed, and the phenomena embraced by insights. This structure is guided by the definition of disciplinary perspective presented in Chapter 4. These five strategies should be seen as complements rather than substitutes. While researchers should understand how each works in isolation, they will often find that evaluation proceeds best when these strategies are employed in concert. Indeed, while the examples below were each chosen to illustrate the working of one particular strategy, the reader will often note that other strategies are in evidence as well.

Disciplinary Perspective in General

Insights, we have said, are scholarly understandings of a specific problem produced by disciplinary authors. Disciplinary authors produce insights that typically reflect their disciplinary perspective in a general sense.

The purpose of this exercise is to recognize how each author's understanding of the problem may be skewed. The term **skewed understanding** means the degree to which the insight reflects the biases inherent in the discipline's perspective and thus the way the author understands the problem. Skewed understanding results from the author's deliberate decision or unconscious predisposition to omit certain information that pertains to a problem.

Rick Szostak (personal communication, January 24, 2011) advises researchers to query the epistemological, metaphysical, ethical, and ideological elements of a discipline's perspective (the other elements of disciplinary perspective will be treated below).

> A discipline that is pessimistic of the potential for scholarly understanding, or that doubts the existence of an external reality, will likely produce more ambiguous insights than a discipline that is confident of progressing toward precise understandings of a fixed reality. A discipline that thinks a particular outcome is good will likely study it differently than a discipline that thinks it bad. Last but not least, policy implications may influence scholarly conclusions (generally subconsciously).

In the following example, Repko (2012) evaluates three important insights into the causes of suicide terrorism produced by psychology. Before identifying each author's understanding of the problem, Repko queries the disciplinary perspective of psychology along the lines urged by Szostak:

> Psychology typically sees human behavior as reflecting the cognitive constructs individuals develop to organize their mental activity. Psychologists also study inherent mental mechanisms, both generic predispositions as well as individual differences. Psychology is confident of progressing toward understanding this phenomenon, and has produced insights marked by precise (though at times conflicting) understandings of *individual* terrorist behavior. As applied to suicide terrorism, psychologists generally understand the problem in terms of individuals whose behavior is the product of mental constructs and cognitive restructuring. Psychologists attempt to identify the possible motivations behind a person's decision to join a terrorist group and commit acts of shocking violence, and are consciously aware that their findings have policy implications. They tend to agree that there is no single terrorist mindset, a finding that greatly complicates attempts to profile terrorists groups and leaders on a more systematic and accurate basis. (p. 130)

He then identifies the major authors from the discipline of psychology who are considered experts on the causes of suicide terrorism based on how frequently they are cited by other authors: Jerrold M. Post, Albert Bandura, and Ariel Merari. Table 8.9 shows Repko's evaluation of each insight in terms of (a) its understanding or explanation of the problem, (b) its underlying assumption, and (c) its strength and limitation.

Table 8.9　Evaluation of Each Insight/Understanding From Psychology

Author	Insight/Understanding	Assumption	Strength/Limitation of Insight
Post	Terrorists reason logically but employ what he calls "a special logic" or "psycho-logic."	Terrorists are born, not made.	Strength: It challenges other research that shows that most suicide attackers are psychologically normal. Limitation: It fails to account for external influences such as culture.
Bandura	Terrorists rationalize their acts of violence using various techniques.	Terrorists are made, not born.	Strength: It addresses causal factors external to the individual attacker including political factors, the influence of culture on one's sense of identity, and the influence of sacred beliefs. Limitation: It is silent concerning a person's cognitive predisposition and personality traits that may influence decision making.
Merari	Terrorists need a specific mind-set to carry out suicide attacks that is shaped by various factors.	Terrorists are made, not born.	Strength: It takes into account personality factors, especially the psychological impact of a broken family background, but attributes primary responsibility to recruiting organizations and their charismatic trainers. Limitation: It fails to address the causal factors of politics, culture, and religion that research outside of psychology has shown to be highly influential in the development of a suicide attacker.

This strategy accommodates any combination and number of insights. The table can be expanded and lines can be drawn to divide one set of insights from another. Placing this information in a table has two practical benefits. It enables the researcher to keep track of the growing amount of information that performing each STEP generates. And it juxtaposes each critical piece of information so as to reveal similarities and differences between them. At a minimum, this strategy will enable one to perform STEP 7 in the IRP more efficiently (see Chapter 10).

Evaluating insights in this manner requires close reading to detect the author's understanding, explanation, or argument. Evaluating insights may also involve evaluating the assumptions made in generating each insight. This is often challenging because authors typically do not make their assumptions explicit. It is possible to discover an author's assumption from the author's disciplinary perspective by applying that perspective to the problem at hand. In the above example, none of the psychology authors stated their assumption, so Repko applied the disciplinary assumption of psychology to each author's approach to the problem of suicide terrorism. This process did not produce a uniform result as demonstrated by two very different assumptions noted in the center column. But underlying these different assumptions, the larger and more basic assumption of the discipline is evident, and this assumption can serve as the basis for integrating the insights produced by psychology.

Identifying the strength and limitation of each insight and what it assumes to be true about the problem can be done only after carefully reading each insight and comparing them to each other. Newell (2007a) observes, "Each discipline has its own distinctive strengths," and "the flip side of those strengths is often its distinctive weaknesses" (p. 254).

> A discipline such as psychology that is strong in understanding individuals is thereby weak in understanding groups; its focus on parts means that its view of wholes is blurry. A discipline such as sociology that focuses [primarily] on groups doesn't see individuals clearly; indeed, at the extreme it sees individuals as epiphenomenal—as little more than the product of their society. Empirically based disciplines in the social and natural sciences cannot see those aspects of human reality that are spiritual or imaginative, and their focus on behavior that is lawful, rule-based, or patterned leads them to overlook human behavior that is idiosyncratic, individualistic, capricious and messy, or to lump it into unexplained variance. Humanists, on the other hand, are attracted to those aspects and tend to grow restive with a focus on behavior that is predictable, feeling that it misses the most interesting features of human existence. (p. 254)

In the humanities, the object is to analyze, for instance, how Greek tragedies reflect the gender and class relations of the time as well as to expose the multiple meanings of an object or a text. Upon entering this realm of the academy, the number and diversity of insights produced by disciplinary perspectives expands considerably.

From the Humanities: Bal (1999), "Introduction," The Practice of Cultural Analysis: Exposing Interdisciplinary Interpretation   In the following example, Bal draws on the perspectives of various critical approaches to objects and texts to develop the most comprehensive understanding of the graffito (e.g., note or letter painted on a wall) possible. These approaches and their perspectives stated in general terms include Reader Response, Marxist Criticism, New Historicism, Psychoanalytic Criticism, Deconstruction, and Cultural Analysis and are shown in Table 8.10.

The next task is to apply each perspective to the graffito to expose its meaning.

| Table 8.10 | Critical Approaches and Their Perspectives Stated in General Terms |

Critical Approach	Perspective
Reader Response	The reader of the graffito is to cite direct references in the text to show that the world of the text corresponds to the one in which the reader is situated.
Marxist Criticism	The graffito is a product of work and, as such, is to be understood as the product of a complex web of social and economic relationships as well as the prevailing ideology to which the majority of people uncritically subscribe.
New Historicism	The critic/reader of the graffito is to be highly conscious of and even discuss preconceived notions before situating the text in its historical/literary context.
Psychoanalytic Criticism	The graffito, as an invention of the mind, provides a psychological study of the writer, and of the reader.
Deconstruction	The graffito is an ambiguous text consisting of words from the many discourses that inform it, the meaning of which is ultimately indeterminate.
Cultural Analysis	The graffito heightens one's awareness of one's situatedness in the present, the social and cultural present from which one looks at the graffito.

This humanities example of Bal's graffito raises the issue of how to handle a large number of insights and theories. The possible insights and theories from just one discipline have to be multiplied by the number of disciplines relevant to the topic. In the Bal example, this means six disciplinary literatures multiplied by the number of insights and theories generated by each discipline relating to the graffito—a formidable challenge even for graduate students and senior researchers. One solution is to focus not so much on each critical approach but on how the perspective of each approach reveals new meaning when applied to a particular object and/or text as Bal does.

The example of the graffito shows that when it comes to conducting interdisciplinary work in the humanities, one must be flexible in developing research strategies that balance disciplinary depth with disciplinary breadth while keeping in clear view the ultimate goal of the enterprise—in this case, a more comprehensive and fully integrated understanding of the meaning of the graffito in all of its complexity.

From the Natural Sciences: Watson (1968), The Double Helix: A Personal Account of the Discovery of the Structure of DNA   Watson's account of the discovery of the structure of DNA provides a good example of the importance of recognizing the strengths and limitations of relevant disciplines and their perspectives into a particular problem. In this case, the disciplines are biology and its subdiscipline of genetics, chemistry, biochemistry, and physics and its subdiscipline of X-ray crystallography. Each brought what initially appeared to be certain strengths to the problem of the structure of DNA, but each strength was counterbalanced by critical weaknesses.

For example, geneticists had supposed that the best way to learn how genes control cellular heredity was to study viruses because they are a form of naked gene and thus might provide important clues to the structure of DNA. Watson discovered, however, that genetics was unable to describe the structure of a gene and therefore unable to describe its behavior (p. 23). Watson realized that working out DNA's chemical structure might be the essential step in learning how genes duplicated. This realization forced him to turn to biochemistry for answers.

Watson soon learned that the solid chemical facts known about DNA were meager and that the chemists who did work on DNA were almost always organic chemists with no interest in genetics. So he went to a lab in Copenhagen that was combining techniques of chemistry with genetics (p. 24). There, he began to consider the possibility that physics and the new field of X-ray diffraction photography could provide a three-dimensional picture of DNA and thus reveal important clues about its structure. Watson also learned from Maurice Wilkins, a physicist who had turned to biochemistry to understand the structure and properties of genes (p. 33).

Watson's work illustrates the importance of the researcher knowing the strengths and limitations of each relevant discipline and its perspective. Once limitations are discovered, the researcher can overcome them, as Watson did, by quickly developing alternative strategies.

The Theories Used in Generating Insights

A second strategy to evaluate insights is to evaluate the theories that produce them. Theories, we have said, are generalized scholarly explanations that are supported by data and research about some aspect of the natural or human world, how it works, and why specific facts are related. Theories also produce insights into problems. Our interest here is to evaluate theories and identify their strengths and limitations. There are two ways to evaluate theories. One is to use the strategy used in evaluating insights: state the theory, detect its assumptions, and identify its explanatory strengths and limitations. The other is to ask the "5 W" questions to evaluate the appropriateness of each theory to the problem. We begin with the first strategy.

Stating the Theory, Detecting Its Assumptions, and Identifying Its Explanatory Strengths and Limitations

We have said that disciplinary authors produce insights that typically reflect their disciplinary perspective in a general sense. In the natural sciences and social sciences, authors typically use theories to explain cause or behavior; these theories also reflect their disciplinary perspective. Moreover, these same theories also produce insights into a problem. So, when working in the natural or social sciences, one should expect to work with theories as well as the insights they produce. The progression of evaluation, then, is from disciplinary perspective to disciplinary theories. In order to evaluate insights that are produced by theories, one must evaluate the theories themselves, as Watson and Fischer do in the following examples.

From the Natural Sciences: Watson (1968), The Double Helix: A Personal Account of the Discovery of the Structure of DNA   In his research, Watson first drew on all relevant disciplinary perspectives on the problem of DNA to learn their strengths and limitations. He then recognized that he must also draw on their theories and evaluate their ability to explain the problem, as shown in Table 8.11.

Table 8.11   Disciplinary Theories and Their Strengths in Explaining the Structure of DNA

Discipline or Subdiscipline	Theory	Strength of Theory
Physics	Structure of Molecules	To learn how the genes controlled cellular heredity, the chemical structure of the virus (gene) would first have to be cracked open (pp. 15, 23).
Microbiology	Phage Theory (the multiplication of bacterial viruses called bacteriophages, or phages for short)	Viruses may be a form of naked genes. Therefore, the best way to find out what a gene is and how it duplicates is to study the properties of viruses (p. 22).
Biochemistry	Molecular Theory	DNA is "the most golden of all molecules" (p. 18).

From the Social Sciences: Fischer (1988), "On the Need for Integrating Occupational Sex Discrimination Theory on the Basis of Causal Variables"   Fischer, liker Watson, analyzes the problem of occupational sex discrimination (OSD) from the perspective of each of the relevant disciplines in terms of the theories that each discipline advances to explain the problem. Note that the insight of each theory appearing in Table 8.12 reflects the unique and narrow perspective that produced it.

Table 8.13 shows the explanatory strengths and limitations of each cluster of theories. Fischer obtained this information by closely reading (or rereading in some cases) the various theories he had earlier identified as most relevant to the problem of OSD.

Simply the fact that a theory has explanatory limitations should not disqualify it from being used. However, these limitations *do* mean that the insights are skewed by the way the theory understands the problem, and interdisciplinarians should acknowledge this, as Fischer does.

Table 8.12	Disciplinary Theories and Their Strengths in Explaining the Problem of OSD	

Discipline or School of Thought	Theory	Strength of Theory
Economics	1. Monopsony Exploitation	1. OSD is caused by rational decision making that focuses on the demand for labor.
	2. Human Capital	2. OSD is caused by rational decision making that focuses on the supply of labor.
	3. Statistical Discrimination	3. OSD is caused by rational decision making that focuses on the higher turnover "costs" associated with female employees.
	4. Prejudice	4. OSD is the result of some employers indulging their own sexual prejudices.
History	Institutional Development	OSD is caused and perpetuated by longstanding institutional forces.
Sociology	Sex Role Orientation	OSD is caused by a process of "female socialization different from men which, in turn, is directly related in their occupational structure" (p. 34).
Psychology	Male Dominance	OSD is caused and perpetuated by males to maintain the traditional male-female division of labor.
Marxism	Class Conflict	OSD is a necessary act in preserving the institutions of capitalism.

NOTE: Marxism is a school of thought.

Asking the "5 W" Questions to Evaluate the _____ Appropriateness of Each Theory to the Problem

To determine the appropriateness of each theory to the problem at hand, the reader may ask of it the "5 W" questions (introduced in Chapter 7). For example, the first question is, "Who is the agent?" If each of the theories operates at the level of individuals, but one feels that group processes are important to the problem, then one needs to ask how the insight might change if group agency were considered. A theory on group agency would need to be included with the theories to be integrated.

Another of the "5 W" questions is, "How does the agent decide?" The decision in the Fischer example is whether or not to engage in OSD. The example illustrates how to query the decision-making processes that are addressed by each of the theories. Concerning the economic theories,

Table 8.13 Explanatory Strength and Limitation of Each Theory on OSD

Discipline or School of Thought	Theory	Insight of Theory	Explanatory Strength of Theory	Explanatory Limitation of Theory
Economics	1. Monopsony Exploitation	1. OSD is caused by rational decision making that focuses on the demand for labor.	1. It explains economic motivation of employers.	1. Economists have not decided upon a single explanation of OSD.
	2. Human Capital	2. OSD is caused by rational decision making that focuses on the supply of labor.	2. It explains economic motivation of employers.	2. Economic motivation fails to account for prejudice, sex role socialization, and "tastes" adverse to hiring women.
	3. Statistical Discrimination	3. OSD is caused by rational decision making that focuses on the higher turnover "costs" associated with female employees.	3. It explains economic motivation of employers.	3. It assumes that individuals are rational and self-interested.
	4. Prejudice	4. OSD is the result of some employers indulging their own sexual prejudices.	4. It is open to factors extending beyond economic motivation.	4. It assumes that individuals are rational and self-interested.

			Strengths	Weaknesses
History	Institutional Development	OSD is caused and perpetuated by longstanding institutional forces.	1. It identifies historical trends that may have produced the problem. 2. It places the problem in a broad context.	1. It is unable to analyze the behavior of groups. 2. It is unable to account for psychological motivation of individuals.
Sociology	Sex Role Orientation	OSD is caused by a process of "female socialization different from men which, in turn, is directly related in their occupational structure" (p. 34).	1. It identifies conflict among social groups and institutions. 2. It accounts for differences between adult men and women in terms of how they were raised.	Its focus on groups fails to account for individual behavior motivated by complex psychological factors or genetic predisposition.
Psychology	Male Dominance	OSD is caused and perpetuated by males to maintain the traditional male-female division of labor.	It explains individual behavior and decision-making processes.	It is unable to study group behavior.
Marxism	Class Conflict	OSD is a necessary act in preserving the institutions of capitalism.	It explains macro trends and developments.	Economic considerations fail to explain behavior of all groups or individuals.

NOTE: Marxism is a school of thought.

Fischer (1988) comments, "'Economic man' supposedly makes economic decisions in a predictable and exact way, always acts intentionally and deliberately, never acts impulsively or altruistically, knows the consequences of her or his actions, and acts to maximize economic benefit to herself or himself" (p. 24). The value of asking this question is this: If a theory posits a form of decision making, but one thinks other forms of decision making are vital to the problem, then one needs to reflect on how the insight might be changed by integrating insights from theories that posit different types of decision making. (Note: Here is an instance of where one "integrates as one goes," performing some integration while looking ahead to the integrative phase of the IRP.) Insights from the discipline of economics that presume individuals are rational and self-interested may need to be reassessed when the problem involves social, religious, or cultural behavior (as in the case of OSD) that is based on other motivations as well. "In using skewed insights," says Newell (2007a), "interdisciplinarians need to maintain some psychological distance from the disciplinary perspectives on which they draw, borrowing *from* them without completely buying *into* them [italics added]" (p. 254).

After surveying the four major economics theories in his study of OSD, Fischer (1988) concludes that economists define the problem largely (but not exclusively) in terms of the economic motivation of employers. He correctly concludes that each of these economic theories is appropriate to the problem even though each "offers a highly restrictive and incomplete explanation of the causes of OSD" (Fischer, 1988, p. 31). Therefore, Fischer asserts, it is necessary to "broaden the analysis to include other prominent theories of OSD" (p. 31). This phrasing alerts the reader to the overall limitations of the economic theories and explains why Fischer finds it necessary to examine theories advanced by the other relevant disciplines.

The strategy of evaluating insights by evaluating the theories that produce them as illustrated in the Watson and Fischer examples is applicable to any situation where one has identified two or more theories from two or more disciplines. However, merely evaluating theories from multiple disciplines does not constitute full interdisciplinarity but only constitutes multidisciplinarity. Full interdisciplinarity is achieved only by continuing the IRP and actually integrating the most important theories and constructing a more comprehensive understanding of the problem. This is the subject of Part III.

The Data Used as Evidence for Insights

A third strategy for evaluating insights is to focus on the data that authors use as evidence for their insights. Interdisciplinarians must be keenly aware that the data presented by disciplinary experts may also be skewed. Each discipline has an epistemology, or way of knowing, and it collects, organizes, and presents data in a certain way that is consistent with this knowing.

To say that the data presented by disciplinary experts may be "skewed" is not to allege that the data are falsified or sloppily gathered or presented in a biased way (though the latter is sometimes the case). Rather, it is to say that experts *may* omit or fail to collect certain kinds of data for various reasons. This is because experts are interested in certain kinds of questions and amass data to answer these questions without consciously realizing that they may be excluding other data that would, if included in the study, modify or even contradict the study's findings. Part of the task in identifying conflicts in insights (Chapter 10) is to identify and evaluate the different kinds of evidence used by each discipline or theory to support its insights. What one discipline counts as evidence may be discounted or considered inappropriate by another. Therefore, the interdisciplinarian should be alert to possible conflicts arising over the different kinds of evidence used by each discipline or theory.

As noted earlier, the sciences and the harder social sciences employ the methods of experiments, models, and statistics, all of which constitute what are thought to be convincing evidence. For Watson, experiments and models provided the convincing evidence that the DNA molecule has an α-helical structure. Different disciplines consider evidence in terms of what makes one piece of knowledge persuasive and other pieces of knowledge not persuasive. In women's studies, for example, the testimonial (i.e., "lived experience") is considered persuasive, and "in native studies, traditional knowledge preserved over centuries through an oral tradition and interpreted by Elders is central" (Vickers, 1998, p. 23). Neither kind of evidence would be considered valid by those adhering to a positivist/empiricist epistemology and using quantitative evidence.

Historians, on the other hand, count a wide array of artifacts as evidence, including diaries, oral testimony, and official documents, none of which are accepted or considered appropriate by the sciences. Evidence for literary criticism consists of the imaginative application of theory—including the five theories discussed earlier—to the text. For Bal (1999), what counts as evidence is the discovery *in the text*, using the technique of close reading, of traces of each theory's imprint. These may be summarized in the meaning of the verb "to expose." One example makes the point. A close reading of the word "Note," with which the text of the graffito begins, "shows" a speech act in its purest form: direct address to the reader in the present but loaded with "pastness" (pp. 7–8). The student working with a theory (or series of theories) must be sufficiently grounded in the theory to identify the evidence that the writer advances to support it.

In reading and thinking about the sources one gathers, one should ask these two questions:

- What counts as evidence in this discipline?
- What kind of evidence is this disciplinary author omitting that would shed additional light on the problem?

Examples of How Supportive
Evidence Reflects Disciplinary Perspective

The close connection between disciplinary perspective and the kind of supportive evidence typically used by practitioners in the discipline is illustrated by
examining essays by scholars from two disciplines and a profession that grapple with this question: Should schools adopt computer-assisted education?

Essay #1: Discipline: Communications/Information Technology   Clifford
Stoll (1999) argues in *High-Tech Heretic: Why Computers Don't Belong in
the Classroom and Other Reflections by a Computer Contrarian* that schools
should not adopt computer-assisted education. His expertise in the field of
information technology extends to the business aspect of it, and this is
reflected in the kind of evidence he presents to support his case: the hidden
financial costs of computers, reference to supportive essays in the disciplinary
journal *Education Technology News,* examples of schools having to make
hard choices between making needed repairs and buying technology, and
careful examination of the mythical cost savings derived from automating
education administration.

Essay #2: Discipline: Psychology (Learning Theory)   The National Research
Council (NRC) is the research arm of the National Academy of Sciences, a
private, nonprofit scholarly society that advises the federal government in
scientific and technical matters. Its influential study, *How People Learn:
Brain, Mind, Experience, and School,* argues that computer-assisted education
can enhance learning (Bradsford, Brown, & Cocking, 1999). The supportive
evidence used by the NRC includes references to state-of-the-art learning software and several experimental projects such as GLOBE, which gathered data
from students in over 2,000 schools in 34 countries (Bradsford et al., 1999).

Essay #3: Profession: Education   In 1999, the Alliance for Childhood, a
partnership of individuals and organizations, issued the report *Fool's Gold:
A Critical Look at Computers in Childhood* that subsequently appeared in a
leading education journal. The report argues that computer-assisted education does not benefit young children. This view, a matter of heated debate
within the teaching profession, was nevertheless included in the Education
Department's own 1999 study of nine troubled schools in high-poverty areas,
as well as in extensive references to studies by leading education experts,
including Stanford professor (of education) Larry Cuban, theorist John
Dewey, Austrian innovator Rudolf Steiner, and MIT professor Sherry Turkle
(Alliance for Childhood, 1999).

Reflecting on These Examples

These examples show how each discipline or profession amasses and presents
evidence that reflects its epistemology. However, in all three cases, the experts

omit evidence that they consider outside the scope of their discipline or profession. "Facts," then, are not always what they appear to be. They reflect what the discipline and its community of experts are interested in.

It is easy for students and the public to be seduced by data produced by "experts" on the problem, mistakenly assuming that the data must surely be "correct" and objective because they came from an authoritative source. It is particularly important for interdisciplinarians "to be attuned to the subliminal message of facts, and keep track of the complex problem that interests them without being sidetracked by the narrower, value-laden interests of the disciplines on which they draw" (Newell, 2007a, pp. 254–255). The lesson here is that the reader must evaluate carefully the kind of evidence used by disciplinary authors, understand how they use that evidence, and ask whether other types of data might possibly alter the insight.

The Methods Employed

A fourth strategy that is useful in evaluating insights is to focus on the methods employed. Chapter 7 introduced the dozen or so distinct methods employed by scientists (often in combination) to conduct research and produce new knowledge. The focus here is on the importance of recognizing how these methods may be skewed. As with theories, says Szostak (2004), there are key questions that should be asked of any method used.

Question 1: Who is being studied? Is the focus of the method on intentional agents or nonintentional agents? Some disciplines—and, therefore, their methods—pay more heed to individuals than to groups. As with theories, the interdisciplinarian should query how appropriate a particular method is to the type(s) of agency inherent in the problem at hand. A subsidiary question here involves the number of agents that a method investigates. For example, surveys deal with numerous people, interviews deal with few, and observation (especially participant observation) deals with fewer. The problem with these methods, Szostak (2004) says, is that if any subset (from one to many) of the relevant population is examined, researchers will face questions of sampling: "Is the sample biased, or does it represent the average of the larger population, or perhaps the most common attributes of the larger population (which can be quite different from the average)?" (p. 104).

Question 2: What is being studied? Some methods study actions (and some especially reactions), while others study attitudes (Szostak, 2004, p. 105). For example, strict interpretivists would argue that scholars should study only attitudes and not actions. This point of view flows from two assumptions: that there are significant differences between individuals and how they perceive apparently similar situations, and that people can only be studied in their natural environment. Flowing from these beliefs is the interpretivist emphasis on qualitative versus quantitative analysis (see Chapter 7). Strict positivists, Szostak says, take the opposite view on all three issues (p. 105).

Question 3: What sorts of decision making can the method examine? As in the case of theory, the focus of this question is on the decision-making process used by agents, including the passive decision making of nonintentional agents. Particular methods, observes Szostak (2004), "prove to be best suited to answering one type of question, but methods are differentially applicable to different types of decision making" (p. 107).

Question 4: Where is the place or setting of the phenomenon or process to be studied? Phenomena can be analyzed in one place or as they are in motion. Analysis can be performed in a natural setting or in an artificial setting. The latter allows the researcher to control variables and thus isolate a particular cause-effect relationship but at the risk that agents behave differently than they would in a natural setting (Szostak, 2004, p. 108).

Question 5: When (at what time) can the phenomena be studied? Some methods are biased toward a conclusion that a particular sort of time path is at work. Szostak (2004) asks, do researchers

> analyze a set of phenomena at one point in time, continuously through time, or at several discrete points in time? Do they analyze all phenomena at the same time(s) or at different times? The advantage of continuous time is that the researcher can study the process of change, but analysis at particular points of time is easier. (p. 109)[1]

Strengths and limitations of selected methods (not exhaustive) noted by Szostak (2004) are shown in Table 8.14 and should be used only as a starting point for further study. Students wishing more detail should consult Chapter 4 of his book.

| Table 8.14 | Strengths and Limitations of Disciplinary Methods (Not Exhaustive) |

Method	Strengths	Limitations
Experiments	Experiments are primarily a deductive tool whereby the subject is manipulated in a particular way and results are measured. They are potentially highly reliable because "they can be easily repeated with all sorts of subtle changes to research design." Experiments are best at identifying simple cause-effect relationships, and "can illuminate some aspects of decision making, such as the degree to which people are swayed by the views of others" (pp. 119–121).	Analysis of group behavior is generally, but not always, unfeasible. Since experiments involve control and manipulation, advocates of qualitative research, including feminists, have often been hostile to them. "With intentional agents, researchers must worry about signaling the desired result to subjects" (pp. 118, 120–121).

Method	Strengths	Limitations
Surveys	Focus is on the individual level with results often broken down on a group basis. Results "speak to average tendencies of group members rather than group processes themselves" (p. 135). They can point to important differences among group members. They can provide quantitative data on attitudes at a point in time (p. 135).	They may contain too few causal variables and usually speak only directly to relationships (but network analysis can identify relationships by surveying people with whom they interact) (p. 135).
Statistical analysis (secondary data analysis)	This most popular single method in social science involves analysis of statistics collected by others, including those generated by surveys or experiments. Data are often available for huge numbers of people, can be aggregated to show group tendencies as well as differences within groups, and are available for both nonintentional and intentional agents (p. 131). This method can establish correlations extremely well.	"Secondary data cannot provide detailed insight into how any intentional agent forms attitudes." When a correlation is established, researchers must use judgment and rely on theory in inferring causation (Silverman, 2000, pp. 6–9). McKim (1997) states that statistical analysis should only be taken as evidence of a causal relationship if reinforced by plausible theory and direct evidence from other methods (p. 10). Szostak (2004) notes that researchers "must also worry about the strength of a relationship; researchers often celebrate the 'statistical significance' of a result without taking the necessary—and inherently qualitative—step of asking if the relationship is important. They may thus too easily embrace a theory with limited explanatory power, or reject a theory with great explanatory power because their sample size was small and thus statistical evidence not established" (p. 131). Researchers "must look at how data are recorded, and ask whether either those reporting or those recording had likely biases" (p. 134).
Content or textual analysis	This method includes "a variety of techniques . . . often grounded in different theoretical understandings of the meaning of a text." Texts speak most directly to the intentions of the author and "can provide valuable insights into the author's perception of groups, relationships,	Theorists disagree whether, and to what degree, the core message of any text can be identified. Though texts can provide a diversity of interpretations, there are limitations to the insights that can be drawn from any text. "No text can be understood fully in isolation from other texts, since language is symbolic."

Table 8.14 (Continued)

Method	Strengths	Limitations
	and nonintentional agents." Authors often reveal why they or others made decisions as they did, though they may be incorrect or purposely biased (pp. 136–137).	A further limitation is that researchers can only build upon the information that the author (consciously or not) provides (pp. 136–137). Szostak cautions researchers that authors may bias their understanding of events. "Content analysis, by which quantitative analysis is performed on how often particular ideas or phrases appear in a text, is one technique which can potentially identify intentions of which the author was not even aware" (p. 137).
Participant observation (PO) (including ethnographic fieldwork)	PO is the most common form of observational analysis, though discreet observation is also used. PO researchers focus on intentional agents and emphasize attitudes, but may also study actions as well as constraints/incentives. PO follows subjects over a period of time as they make decisions and often ask subjects to explain why they acted as they did. PO may be the best way to study certain or unique events and identify idiosyncrasies that prevent a rule from operating (pp. 127–128). Palys (1997) notes that PO is almost always used in conjunction with interviews, surveys, and/or textual analysis, allowing researchers to compare what people say and do, and reducing the problem of researcher bias.	Only a small number of individuals and relationships can be studied at one time (p. 127). Goldenberg (1992) notes that the very presence of an observer may cause participants to behave differently and feign different attitudes. He also says that many researchers believe that the method is better for exploration/induction than hypothesis testing (p. 322). Though PO research is inherently inductive, it is possible for researchers to ignore evidence that conflicts with their desired conclusions (Szostak, 2004, p. 128). Szostak notes that protocol analysis (whereby participants are asked to perform a task and describe verbally their thoughts while doing so) "effectively combines elements of PO and interviewing. It is more inductive than other types of PO. It is also more artificial, and thus raises questions of whether participants will both do and think as they would in a less artificial environment" (p. 129).
Interview	Interviews are more costly than surveys and thus tend to involve fewer people. Interviews are good for identifying attitudes that encouraged certain actions (but often people do not know why they act as they do). Questions can elicit insights into constraints/incentives imposed by impersonal	Interviews can speak only indirectly to relationships and group processes. "They are limited in their ability to identify temporal priority . . . and dependent on the researcher asking appropriate questions" (p. 122). Interviewees may be misled about why they acted/thought as they did/do, either purposefully or through faulty memory (p. 122). Because

Method	Strengths	Limitations
	agents (p. 122). Narrative analysis overcomes problems of researchers biasing results through their questions by asking people to tell their own stories (p. 123).	interviews necessarily involve small numbers of people, "generalizations require integration of results across many studies" (p. 123).
Case study (a mixed method generally incorporating textual analysis, observation, and/or interviews)	Case studies provide insight into a particular issue or theory in rich detail (while statistical analysis tends to seek patterns across numerous cases). Case studies can be quantitative and/or qualitative (p. 140).	"Researchers should be careful not just to report those observations that seem to lend themselves to generalizations; other information may encourage the development of alternative theories or the recognition of limits to existing theories" (p. 141).

SOURCE: Szostak, R. (2004). *Classifying science: Phenomena, data, theory, method, practice*. Dordrecht: Springer. With kind permission from Springer Science+Business Media.

The Phenomena Embraced by Insights

A fifth strategy used to evaluate the appropriateness of an insight to the problem at hand is to focus on the phenomena that each discipline considers within its research domain. The authors' insights are skewed by the way they define the problem (i.e., those parts of the problem they overlook). Their insights are also skewed in the way that they look at what they *do* see. This is due to the phenomena or the behavior they choose to investigate. Overall their choice of phenomena influences their choice of method, which in turn influences their choice of theory. Focusing on phenomena points up the importance of first mapping the problem in order to see which parts of it are covered by the disciplines. The examples by Watson, Fischer, and Bal illustrate, to varying degrees, how mapping the problem (either consciously or unconsciously) helped them to identify relevant disciplines, theories, and the insights they produced concerning the problem at hand.

From the Natural Sciences: Watson (1968), The Double Helix: A Personal Account of the Discovery of the Structure of DNA   Watson discovered early on that each discipline's way of defining the problem of the structure of DNA was skewed, and he understood the implications of this. Biology and its subdisciplines of genetics and microbiology defined the problem as a cellular problem. Geneticists and microbiologists believed that studying viruses would eventually reveal how virus genes controlled cellular heredity.

This line of reasoning led biologists to overlook the importance of identifying the chemical structure of virus genes (p. 23).

The few chemists interested in the problem (most ignored the problem altogether) believed that it had something to do with the metabolism of nucleotides. Watson succeeds here by at least subconsciously mapping the problem and connecting each major part to an appropriate discipline. As it was, scientists were limiting their focus to the chemical process of nucleotide metabolism without first knowing the three-dimensional configuration of a nucleic acid molecule (p. 31).

Physicists, principally X-ray crystallographers, were not interested in the problem of the structure of DNA specifically. However, they were interested in perfecting X-ray diffraction pictures of molecular structures in general. The implication of their pursuit of this new method of revealing structures was to point Watson and Crick in the right direction of applying this technology to solving the structure of crystallized genes.

From the Social Sciences: Fischer (1988), "On the Need for Integrating Occupational Sex Discrimination Theory on the Basis of Causal Variables" Fischer, like Watson, is explicit in identifying the strengths and limitations of relevant disciplines based on the phenomena that each one typically investigates. Rather than discuss all five disciplines that Fischer considers relevant to the problem of OSD, he limits his discussion to economics and history. As a trained economist, Fischer has a professional mastery of his discipline. The strength of economics, he says, is that it views the problem of OSD as having to do with economic behavior. But that strength is also its weakness. The problem with economics, he says, is that its theories and methods are skewed. At one time, political economists, as they called themselves, believed that social, cultural, psychological, and political factors were as much a part of their discipline as were economic factors. But since 1900, the desire of orthodox economists to transform the discipline into a science has resulted in their whittling down political economy to "economics proper," meaning that economists focus narrowly on the behavior of "economic man" (or woman—sex was not an issue), the assumptions of perfect competition, and the exclusion of normative issues (e.g., epistemological issues).

After mapping the problem (subconsciously in Fischer's case), Fischer asked which phenomena are excluded from certain insights. He concluded that the economic theories on OSD ignore many of the key causal dimensions of the problem and offer an "incomplete and unpersuasive explanation" of it (p. 26). This skewed approach, says Fischer, explains why a major sex discrimination case involving Sears Roebuck and Company and its employees used expert witnesses who were historians rather than economists. Historians, Fischer notes, "understand the importance of long-run institutional forces causing and perpetuating OSD, an area neglected by most economists" (p. 26).

When a discipline focuses on a complex problem such as occupational sex discrimination, it immediately redefines the problem in a way that allows the discipline to make use of its distinctive elements. The result is that authors offer powerful but limited (and sometimes skewed) theories and insights on the problem. This is not surprising because, as previously noted, disciplines specialize in different kinds of problems and on certain parts of the problem.

Fischer's explanation of how a discipline can so easily skew its approach to a problem is instructive for interdisciplinarians. By not mapping the problem to reveal its key parts, even professionals can easily buy into their discipline's skewed perspective. If this is true for professionals, it is likely to be equally true for students. This emphasizes the importance for inter-disciplinarians to map the problem and connect each part to a discipline that studies that part. This also points up the need to develop adequacy in each relevant discipline (in this case, the phenomena that they typically study), yet to avoid being impressed with its skewed perspective, theories, and insights.

Notably, Fischer, a trained economist who knows well the strengths and limitations of his discipline, is not a trained historian. Yet, he took the time to develop adequacy in history to the extent that he knows its perspective on the subject of OSD.

From the Humanities: Bal (1999), "Introduction," The Practice of Cultural Analysis: Exposing Interdisciplinary Interpretation   Bal uses cultural analysis because it is an interdisciplinary field with its own theory and method that enables the practitioner to explain more comprehensively than traditional disciplinary approaches can the enigmatic meaning of a complex object such as the graffito. For example, cultural analysis differs from a traditional historical approach in its focus on the viewer's situated-ness in the present and its seeking to understand the past as part of the present in which the viewer is immersed (p. 1). History tends to view the past, whether person, event, or object, as the product of evolutionary trends and developments leading up to it, societal forces, and individual decisions, which it seeks to describe in rich detail. Using history as it is usually practiced, then, would skew one's understanding of the graffito by ignoring the silent assumptions that historians consciously or uncon-sciously impose on the past.

The strength of art history (which is increasingly interdisciplinary in orientation) is its ability to study an art object in terms of concepts such as quality, its visual appeal, how the artist fits into the canon of great artists, the social context of the object, the uses and misuses of stylistic analysis, and the relationship of art history and movements such as postmodernism and feminism (Fernie, 1995). Though there is much that art history can contribute to one's understanding of the graffito, there is much that it is not equipped to deliver. For one thing, the graffito is unique and the author is unknown, making it impossible to fit it into the canon of great art and artists. Nor can art history comment on the graffito's philosophically profound message, evaluate its poetic structure, or explain how it embodies the concept of "culture."

Philosophy and its subdiscipline of epistemology concern how we can know what is real and what is not real. Relying on epistemic philosophy in the case of the graffito, however, would skew our understanding of the text:

Note

I hold you dear

I have not

thought you up

The text contains a statement of nonfiction, "I have not thought you up." However, this statement appears to be contradicted by the address— "Note"—that changes a real person, the anonymous writer's beloved, into a self-referential description of the note; that is, a referential "dear" becomes a self-referential "Note" or short letter. This changes the note into a piece of fictional prose (Bal, 1999, p. 3). If the note is fiction, then epistemic philosophy is of little use to deepen our understanding of the text's meaning. Instead, we would turn to literature because it quite easily suspends ontological questions (i.e., concerning the kinds of things that have existence), and it has no trouble distinguishing between fiction and reality.

Literature's strengths in evaluating the graffito are its enabling one to approach it from different theoretical perspectives and situate it biographically, critically, and historically. These strengths, however, are balanced by literature's limitations: its inability to situate such an evaluation culturally, understand it as an art object, explain it semantically, and probe it epistemologically and ontologically.

The strength of psychology is to probe the recesses of a person's psyche, whether artist or viewer of the art object. However, psychology is not equipped to situate an art object in a cultural and historical context, examine its poetic form and narrative mode, or understand it as an aesthetic and ethical expression.

Unfortunately, some authors who purport to engage in interdisciplinary work do not talk as self-consciously about their methodology as Bal does. One way to fathom an author's methodology is to read reviews of the writer's book(s). Another way is to read the author's article on the topic closely, paying particular attention to the footnotes (or endnotes) that may contain important methodological clues. A third way is to consult disciplinary experts, who should be called upon in any event to confirm one's understanding.

Checklist for Evaluating Previous Research

Readers can profitably use this checklist to evaluate previous research (i.e., insights and theories) on the problem before identifying conflicts in insights and theories and locating their sources (Chapter 10):

- Reflect self-critically on the bias that one may be bringing to the problem. Szostak's (2002) insight is worth noting here: "While disciplines are an important source of bias, human nature, individual psychologies, and the diverse roles that people play in society are also sources of bias" (pp. 112–113).
- Identify the disciplinary background of each scholar (if this was not done during the literature search). The theory or method used by an author will generally reflect the general perspective of the discipline. One should question how this perspective influenced the question that the author raised, the theory and method used, and the understanding produced.
- Question whether nonscholarly information (i.e., the "other knowledge" discussed in Chapter 7) can possibly provide further perspectives. Both Klein (2001) and Carp (2001) urge students to look beyond the scholarly literature for evidence, but rely on experts to vet it. Newell (2001) also urges students to avoid the extreme postmodernist view that there is no difference between scholarly and nonscholarly research.
- Determine whether some key phenomena (i.e., parts of the problem) were excluded from previous analysis and the impact of this (Szostak, 2002, p. 112).
- Identify the evidence that each scholar's discipline typically considers as valid. Analyze the evidence for possible clues concerning its source(s).
- Identify the epistemology that each scholar's discipline typically embraces using the information in Tables 4.8, 4.9, and 4.10. (The challenge here may be in discovering whether the author is assuming a modernist stance or is embracing one of the newer critical stances.)
- Identify the theory that informs each writer's insight (if it is theory-based) and be familiar with its strengths and limitations. Ask how the expert applied the theory to the problem.
- Identify the research method that each scholar uses and be familiar with its strengths and limitations.

Chapter Summary

In order to analyze a problem and evaluate the insights and theories on it, we must appreciate the strengths and corresponding limitations of each discipline's perspective (in a general sense) and be aware that these strengths and limitations flow primarily from differences in phenomena studied and theories and methods used. Limitations in phenomena are best identified by mapping the problem. Limitations in theories and their insights are best identified by asking the "5 W" questions. Limitations in methods are best identified by asking a second series of questions. Only then is it possible to evaluate the insights and theories generated by each discipline's community of authors and assess the relevance of these to the problem.

In this STEP of the IRP, one may decide to replace one of the relevant disciplines with a discipline that seemed only marginally relevant in earlier STEPS. Fischer (1988), for example, found that Marxism was only marginally relevant to explaining the causes of OSD compared to the more nuanced theories advanced by modern economists. At this juncture, one may realize the need to extend the literature search to learn more about what additional insights, concepts, or theories a particular discipline or school of thought has to offer. One may decide that the wording of the problem that once looked neutral (i.e., did not appear to privilege any one discipline) now seems too much indebted to the perspective of one of the relevant disciplines. Or one may realize that the very conception of the problem is overly reflective of a particular discipline.

At the end of STEP 6, one will have finally decided which parts of the problem to investigate and thus which disciplinary insights and theories are truly relevant to the problem. By completing this STEP and reflecting on previous work, one is now ready to engage in the integrative part of the IRP. This is the focus of Chapters 9 to 13 of Part III.

Note

1. For a fuller discussion of these five questions, see Szostak (2004), Chapter 4.

Exercises

The Location of a Wind Farm

8.1 In response to public pressure to reduce its dependence on coal and switch to renewable energy sources, a public utility is proposing to build a large wind farm in shallow water within view of prime beachfront property, exclusive resort hotels, and private luxury condos whose taxes are a significant source of revenue to the local economy. Assuming that disciplinary experts from a nearby university will be asked to conduct studies on the proposal by the local governing council, what disciplinary perspectives should be included to enable public officials to make a fully informed decision to approve or not approve the construction of the wind farm? The problem should first be mapped in order to reveal the parts of the problem and identify relevant disciplines.

The Problem of Homelessness

8.2   Say you are participating in a service learning course that is focusing on the problem of homelessness in a particular area of town. Before going out into the "field," you are to write a brief background paper on the subject. Having had extensive coursework in business, you prefer to examine the problem from a business perspective.

   a. Is this possible in an interdisciplinary course?

   b. How might you make use of your business background in a way that is appropriate to interdisciplinary inquiry?

   c. How could you state the research problem in a way that does not privilege any one disciplinary perspective?

The Progression of Research

8.3   Referencing one of the problems above, explain the progression of research. If you are limited to working with only two or three disciplines, which perspectives would contribute to the fullest understanding of the problem and why?

The "Telescoping Down" Strategy

8.4   Let's assume that the problems referenced above are too general to research in a short time frame and that you have to focus on one of the problems and then on only one or a few of its parts. How could you apply the "telescoping down" strategy to the problem?

Personal Bias

8.5   You have deeply held beliefs concerning the issue of euthanasia, and you believe it is ethically permissible, or even desirable, in certain situations. How can you remain true to your deeply held convictions and yet engage in interdisciplinary inquiry concerning this issue when evaluating insights?

Limits of Perspectives

8.6   Select one of the above problems and identify the limits that three disciplinary perspectives impose on developing a more comprehensive understanding of it.

8.7   Given the limits of disciplinary perspectives and the fact that they are skewed, how does viewing a complex problem through disciplinary lenses help us to understand the problem?

Evaluating Theories

8.8   How does Bal's work illustrate the importance of being flexible in developing research strategies that balance disciplinary depth with theoretical breadth?

How Supportive Evidence Reflects Disciplinary Perspective

8.9   In the above example of the proposed offshore wind farm project, what kinds of data/evidence would be considered valid by each contributing disciplinary expert? More generally, what are the ways that factual information may be skewed by the very nature of disciplinarity?

How Methods May be Skewed

8.10 From Table 8.13, select a method and subject it to the "5 W" questions. How can asking these questions of any disciplinary method provide important insights into an expert's analysis of the problem?

Phenomena Embraced by Insights

8.11 Referencing the above problem of homelessness, what phenomena are omitted from the discussion of possible causes when only the disciplines of economics and psychology are considered? The problem should first be mapped in order to reveal the parts of the problem and identify relevant disciplines.

8.12 How is cultural analysis, though an interdisciplinary approach, limited in its approach to understanding an object such as the graffito?

PART III

Integrating Insights

9   Understanding Integration

In 2000, an interdisciplinary team of cognitive psychologists, curriculum specialists, teacher educators, and researchers updated Bloom's classic taxonomy of levels of intellectual thinking important to learning. They identified six levels within the cognitive domain, from the simple recognition or recall of facts at the lowest level through increasingly more complex and abstract mental levels, leading ultimately to the highest-order ability, creating, shown in Figure 9.1.

The significance of this taxonomy for interdisciplinarity is that it elevates the cognitive abilities of creating and integrating to the highest level of knowledge. Creating involves combining elements—integrating them—to produce something that is new, coherent, and functionally whole.

This chapter introduces the second part of the interdisciplinary research process (IRP): integration (STEPS 7 to 9). The chapter explains what integration is, discusses the controversy concerning integration and its place within interdisciplinary studies, and describes the conditions necessary to perform integration. The chapter also introduces the broad model of integration used in this book in terms of what it integrates, how it integrates, and what the result of the integration looks like. The chapter concludes by raising and answering three fundamental questions concerning integration.

What Integration Is

Interdisciplinarians generally agree on the centrality of integration to interdisciplinarity and the interdisciplinary research process,[1] and they are moving toward consensus about what integration should encompass. "Integration," asserts Klein (2010), "is widely viewed as the litmus test of interdisciplinarity" (p. 112). Though integration is not easy, it is possible, even for those new to the field.

Figure 9.1	The Updated Bloom's Taxonomy

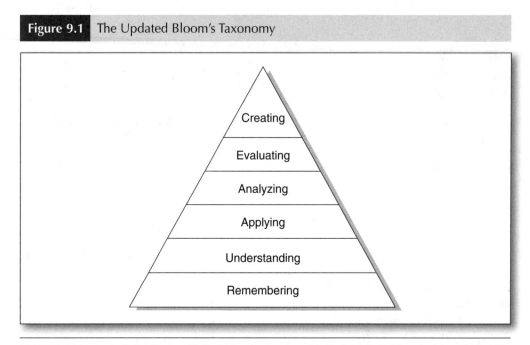

SOURCE: Anderson, Lorin W.; Krathwohl, David R.; Airasian, Peter W.; Cruikshank, Kathleen A.; Mayer, Richard E.; Pintrich, Paul R.; Raths, James; Wittrock, Merlin C., *Taxonomy for Learning, Teaching, and Assessing, A: A Revision of Bloom's Taxonomy of Educational Objectives, Complete Edition,* 1st Edition, © 2001, p. 28. Reprinted by permission of Pearson Education, Inc. Upper Saddle River, NJ.

NOTE: One of the features of the L. W. Anderson et al. (2000) taxonomy that differentiates it from Bloom's 1956 taxonomy is that it reverses the order of evaluation and synthesis or integration, placing "creating," which involves integration, at the highest level of cognitive activity. For a comparison of Bloom's taxonomy with Anderson et al.'s revision of it, see the useful discussion by Leslie Owen Wilson (2006) at www.uwsp.edu/education/lwilson/curric/newtaxonomy.htm.

A Definition of Integration or Synthesis

A good way to start defining a word is to look at its etymology or historical beginnings. The English word *integration* can be traced back to the Latin word *integrare,* meaning "to make whole." As a verb, *integrate* means "to unite or blend into a functioning whole." Over the centuries, says Klein (2012), "the idea of integration was associated with holism, unity, and synthesis" (p. 284).

From the literature, two important ideas about integration emerge that should be included in its definition. Practitioners repeatedly refer to interdisciplinary integration as a *process* as opposed to an *activity.* This is deliberate. Process conveys the notion of making gradual changes that lead toward a particular (but often unanticipated) result, whereas *activity* has the more limited meaning of vigorous or energetic action not necessarily related to achieving a goal.

Additionally, practitioners refer to the result of the integrative process as culminating in a new and more comprehensive understanding.[2] This understanding is sometimes called "the integrative result," "the new whole," "the new meaning," "the integrative product," "the extended theoretical explanation," "the conceptual blend," or "the cognitive advancement." Though these terms have similar meanings, the one generally used in this book is "more comprehensive understanding." Achieving the new understanding requires combining expert insights and knowledge from disciplines, subdisciplines, interdisciplines, and schools of thought, and sometimes from perspectives beyond the academy. The premise of interdisciplinary studies is

> **Interdisciplinary integration**, then, is the cognitive process of critically evaluating disciplinary insights and creating common ground among them to construct a more comprehensive understanding. The understanding is the product or result of the integrative process.

that the disciplines themselves are the necessary preconditions for and foundation of interdisciplinarity.

Integration is something that we must create. It does not derive from a pre-determined pattern or a universal template that is applicable beyond the specific problem, issue, or question being addressed in a particular course or research project.

A synonym of integration is the noun **synthesis**. Klein (1996) states, "Synthesis connotes creation of an interdisciplinary outcome through a series of *integrative actions* [italics added]" (p. 212). What these "integrative actions," decisions, or steps involve is the subject of Chapters 10 to 13.

Several traits attend the terms *integration* and *synthesis*:

- They are synonyms.
- They convey the meaning of goal-driven behavior to solve a problem, answer a question, or resolve an issue.
- Central to integrative activity is critically evaluating.
- What gets critically evaluated are disciplinary insights.
- The nature of the integrative process is creative combining or uniting.
- What is combined, united, or blended are the disciplinary concepts or theories used to generate their insights.
- The result of integration is valid only for a particular problem and context.
- The object of this process is the creative formation of something new and greater than (and different from) the sum of its parts—a more comprehensive understanding. (Note: The distinctive characteristics of the understanding are discussed elsewhere in this chapter.)

Because the terms *integration* and *synthesis* are so close in meaning, many practitioners use them interchangeably. This book uses *integration* because it appears in the prominent definitions of interdisciplinary studies noted in Chapter 1. This chapter examines both the *process* and the *product* of integration.

The Controversy Concerning Integration

Practitioners take one of two positions concerning the place of integration within interdisciplinary studies. These positions can be described as "generalist" and "integrationist" (Repko, 2007, p. 2).

The Generalist Critique

Generalists or critics of integration reject the notion that it should be *the* defining feature of genuine interdisciplinary research and teaching. They understand interdisciplinarity loosely to mean "any form of dialog or interaction between two or more disciplines" while minimizing, obscuring, or rejecting altogether the role of integration (Moran, 2010, p. 14).

Some generalists see the terms *interdisciplinarity* and *integration* as synonymous with *teamwork* as in team teaching or cross-disciplinary communication on research teams. Other generalists prefer to distinguish between types of interdisciplinarity by focusing primarily on the kinds of questions asked rather than on integration and leave "the question of integration open" (Lattuca, 2001, pp. 4, 78, 80). Still others go so far as to reject any definition of interdisciplinary studies that "necessarily places priority emphasis on the realization of synthesis [or integration] in the literal sense" (Richards, 1996, p. 114).

The core of the generalist case is that in most cases integration is simply not achievable. Generalists identify at least five factors that complicate, retard, or even prevent integration: (1) disciplinary fragmentation, (2) unbreachable epistemological barriers, (3) conflicting perspectives and ideologies, (4) a variety of possible results, and (5) the preference for theory competition and alternative integrations.

Disciplinary Fragmentation

Each discipline is fragmented, say critics, and "the fragments, too, are fragmented" (Dogan & Pahre, 1990, p. 5). While specialization can advance knowledge, it can also isolate subfields from each other. Psychologist Elaine Hatfield and historian Richard Rapson (1996) point to hundreds of specialized subdisciplines, each "speaking their own languages, adopting their own definitions and methodologies, asking their separate questions, and rarely addressing one another" (p. viii). The result is "incommensurability of concepts, different units of analysis, differences in worldviews, expectations, criteria, and value judgments" (Rogers, Scaife, & Rizzo, 2005, p. 268).

One result of disciplinary fragmentation, according to critics, is that scholars can produce "two incompatible theories, each consistent with all actual and possible observational evidence." When this occurs, explains philosopher Robert Klee (1997), theory is said to be "*under*determined by observational evidence, meaning that the evidence cannot by itself determine that [one] of the . . . competing theories is the correct one" (p. 66). So we can never have good empirical grounds for choosing one of these theories over others. When underdetermination occurs, says Fuchsman (2009), any attempt at integrating disciplinary insights can meet an equally good but incompatible integration. In such cases, "there can be more than one comprehensive perspective, but it will not lead to a single coherent entity" (p. 78).

Epistemological Barriers

Critics point to a second factor that makes integration problematic: unbreachable epistemological barriers between disciplines. Some types of knowledge are so qualitatively distinct, claims Richards (1996), that they will not permit integration under any circumstances. This problem is said to occur when, for example, one attempts to combine insights from the sciences (natural and/or social) that are analytical-deductive with those from the humanities, which are subjective-evaluative. In such cases, he asserts, "there would seem to be unbreachable epistemological barriers preventing genuine integration" (p. 122). These barriers also render developing a common vocabulary or basis for common communication between disciplines problematic. Critics doubt the efficacy of seeking common ground "as a way to uniformly resolve all-important differences" because "in choosing some common ground over others, there can be competing versions of what is held in common" (Fuchsman, 2009, p. 79).

Conflicting Perspectives and Ideologies

A third obstacle to integration is conflicting perspectives and ideologies within disciplines and across disciplines. Hyland (2004) stresses conflict *within* disciplines. "Most disciplines," he says, "are characterized by several competing perspectives and embody often bitterly contested beliefs and values" (p. 11). Szostak (2002), on the other hand, stresses conflict *across* disciplines because authors typically use the theories and methods that their home disciplines favor (p. 111). This fact, explains biologist Ernst Mayr (1997), makes consensus within and across disciplines hard to achieve because "disagreeing scientists adhere to different underlying ideologies, making certain theories acceptable to one group which are impossible for another group" (p. 103).

A Variety of Possible Results

A fourth objection to integration is that when the conditions for interdisciplinarity exist, a variety of possible results also exist. There can be **full integration** when all relevant disciplinary insights have been integrated into a new, single, coherent, and comprehensive understanding or theory that is consistent with the available empirical evidence (but note the following two exceptions below); **partial integration** when only some insights have been integrated and it applies to only some part(s) of the problem; *multiple integrations* when two or more investigations of the same problem and working with the same materials produce different understandings; or *no integration* when the problem cannot be addressed by drawing on two or more disciplinary literatures and the conditions for using an interdisciplinarity approach cannot be satisfied. Critics charge that an increasing number of interdisciplinary combinations will simply produce a plurality of more comprehensive understandings, or competing metatheories, and that these will result in theoretical confusion. Given these possible outcomes, epistemological barriers, and ideological preferences, one critic concludes that "the concept of integration as a single coherent entity no longer fully applies" (Fuchsman, 2009, pp. 79–80). Consequently, generalists see no justification for including integration in any definition of interdisciplinary studies.

Preference for Theory Competition and Alternative Integrations

Critics prefer offering readers a menu of competing theories, each of which responds to a different but overlapping set of questions, instead of presenting one integrative theory that combines elements of several competing theories. For example, some criminologists argue that criminology theories should remain separate and unequal and that "theory competition" is preferable to theory integration (Akers, 1994, p. 195; Thornberry, 1989, p. 54).

This criticism is analogous to the position taken in the fine and performing arts, and often the humanities that study them, where scholars prefer setting up a range of alternative integrations for readers or viewers to consider rather than providing one. Rationales for doing this perhaps include the desire to engage others in the issue, the feeling that it would be presumptuous to take a stand, the sense that declaring one integration "best" is premature, or the feeling that the best integration depends on the particularities of each situation. The strongest rationale for not pursuing integration further is the recognition that works of art and literature are inherently ambiguous.

The Integrationist Case

Integrationists regard integration as *the key distinguishing characteristic* of interdisciplinarity and *the goal* of fully interdisciplinary work. The core of their position is that integration is achievable and that researchers should come as close to achieving integration as possible given the problem under study and the disciplinary insights at their disposal. They point to four developments that make integration achievable: (1) theories from cognitive psychology that are supportive of integration, (2) new models of the interdisciplinarity research process that feature techniques demonstrated to achieve integration, (3) the publication of groundbreaking integrative work on a wide range of complex problems, and (4) the insistence of leading interdisciplinary and transdisciplinary organizations on the centrality of integration. Integrationists make two additional arguments: (5) Competition for the best explanations is inherently unequal if the integrative explanation is omitted from theory competition, and (6) theoretical confusion already exists.

Theories Supportive of Integration
From Cognitive Psychology

Integrationists assert that critics are overlooking important theories developed by cognitive psychologists on common ground and cognitive interdisciplinarity and how these theories support the goal of integration. The definition of integration noted earlier includes the idea that integration is a cognitive process. Indeed, that is the theoretical premise underlying interdisciplinary integration. Understanding the theory underlying integration will advance our understanding of integration as a process involving various actions. It is the appropriate starting place for a mental journey.

The Theories of Clark and Bromme   Noted cognitive psychologist Herbert H. Clark (1996) defines common ground as the knowledge, beliefs, and suppositions that each person has to establish with another person in order to interact with that person (pp. 12, 116). Central to Clark's common ground theory is its emphasis on the *context* of language. He finds, for example, that all people take as common ground aspects of human nature such as physical senses, communal lexicons (i.e., sets of word conventions in individual communities), and cultural facts, norms, and procedures (pp. 106–108). Clark explains that when it comes to coordinating a joint action, "people cannot rely on just any information they have about each other. They must establish *just the right piece of common ground,* and that depends on them finding a *shared basis for that piece* [italics added]" (pp. 93, 99). As applied to interdisciplinary work, Clark's theory of common ground means that the interdisciplinarian should expect to find latent linguistic commonalities (i.e., common ground) between insights from different disciplines that could provide the basis for integration.

Building on the work of Clark, cognitive psychologist Rainer Bromme (2000) has developed the theory of **cognitive interdisciplinarity.** Whereas Clark developed common ground theory to explain everyday interactions, Bromme and others are applying it to communication across academic disciplines, especially the natural sciences. A significant finding of Bromme is that in **interdisciplinary communication,** differences in common ground are frequently "discovered" only when the partners of cooperation—that is, the relevant disciplines—"find out that they use the same concepts with different meanings, or that they use different codings (terms, symbol systems) for approximately the same concepts" (p. 127).

Bromme's theory has direct applicability to the interdisciplinary research process developed by integrationists. This process calls for interdisciplinarians, whether they are developing a collaborative language or trying to integrate conflicting disciplinary insights, to *first* identify the concepts with different meanings or the theories providing different explanations *before* attempting to discover common ground. Once these are identified, the interdisciplinarian can then proceed with creating the "**common ground integrator**"—that is, the *one or more assumptions, concepts, or theories*—by which these conflicting insights (whether disciplinary or stakeholder) can be integrated.

Other significant aspects of the theory of cognitive interdisciplinarity that pertain to interdisciplinary integration and the creation of common ground include the following:

- Common ground can be realized in the form of *terminology common to two or more disciplines or knowledge domains.* (Interdisciplinarians are also interested in different concepts that appear to have the same or similar meanings.)
- Common ground can be realized in the form of *common terminology that does not dissolve all the differences between disciplinary perspectives.* (How to modify conflicting disciplinary assumptions and concepts is addressed in Chapter 11 under "Techniques Demonstrated for Modifying Concepts and Assumptions.")
- Common ground can be created from *knowledge that is distributed among or is common to disciplines* (i.e., in the form of concepts, their underlying assumptions, or theoretical explanations).
- Common ground can also comprise *agreement on what is not part of the shared knowledge* (Bromme, 2000, pp. 128–129).

Clark's common ground theory and Bromme's theory of cognitive interdisciplinarity inform the debate over the role of integration in interdisciplinary work in at least four ways:

1. Both theories claim that the activity of establishing common ground is a normal and basic feature of human communication and, therefore, is *natural* and *achievable.* What integrationists assert is possible, cognitive psychologists have discovered that everyday people do routinely.

2. If it is possible for humans from differing social and other societal contexts to establish common ground and to communicate, then it should also be possible to establish common ground between disciplines, which are human constructs, as well as between stakeholders. Clark and Bromme agree that what integrationists seek is, at bottom, part of normal human discourse. If the easiest form of integration (i.e., that which occurs between conversants) is already part of humanity's collective social repertoire, then perhaps more challenging cases may be tractable as well, provided that close attention is paid to process and technique. In fact, "even the most challenging cases may yield to the skilled use of refined techniques within a practical process" (William H. Newell, personal communication, May 27, 2007).

3. If common ground is natural and achievable, then so should be the result of integration—a more comprehensive understanding—because that is what results from common ground in everyday conversation.

4. And if integration is natural and achievable, then there is no reason to divorce integration from a definition of interdisciplinarity as generalists feel compelled to do. The difference between cognitive psychologists and integrationists is the latter's assertion that if interdisciplinarians are self-conscious about process, they should be able to do proactively what people normally do reactively.

Integration, then, involves a normal set of cognitive activities that may be explained in terms of distinct and recurrent mental operations.

Nikitina's Work on Interdisciplinary Cognition   In her pioneering work on interdisciplinary cognition, Nikitina (2005) reports that there is an important similarity—and possibly a fundamental connection—between interdisciplinary integration "and other mental operations that involve internal and external dialog such as metaphoric thought, collaborative work, and other forms of negotiating of differences and merging of ideas" (p. 392). Interdisciplinary thinking, she says, "is fundamentally similar to dialogical exchanges occurring in language and in collaborative activities in which epistemological positions are bartered" (p. 389).

What "yields the deepest understanding of the workings of the mind and its cognitive operations in performing integration," says Nikitina (2005), "is viewing disciplines as languages in the broad sense of the word." As used here, language signifies more than the rules of grammar and syntax. Rather, language is a carrier of belief systems and a representation of ideological positions (pp. 395–396). This finding is especially instructive to those involved in collaborative research because it points up the need to begin the process of integration at the outset of the project. That is, interdisciplinary team members first have to create some common "language" before they can even agree on the guiding research question.

Nikitina finds the linguistic theories of Bakhtin (1981) on conceptual blending particularly useful. They capture the two core features of interdisciplinary work: its rootedness in deep disciplinary knowledge (what Bakhtin calls individual voice), and the substantive exchange and transformation of disciplinary perspective (or voice) in the course of interacting with other disciplines (or voices). For Bakhtin, dialogue is achieved when one can hear and comprehend all voices simultaneously, creating something similar to a musical chord. In a chord, Nikitina (2005) explains,

> voices remain different, but they form a different type of music, which is in principle unachievable by a single voice. The idea that dialogue is being continually crafted and depends on the individuality of each note provides a powerful parallel to what happens at the interface of disciplines or in inquiry-based classrooms. (p. 406)

A musical chord is an excellent metaphor for integration.

In fact, says Nikitina (2005), "the parallel between interdisciplinary thought and language may be more pronounced at the point of merger" because a move toward integration involves explicit blending of disciplinary ideas and language. In conceptual blends or integrations, the composite meaning emerges at the point where different verbal inputs merge (p. 406).

Nikitina (2005) relates how physics and astronomy professor Burke and philosophy professor Provence came to see color "as some sort of cooperative thing between brains and world" (p. 406). They arrived at a view of color as "a psychophysical unity, informed both by physics and by individual perception, with neither perspective being definitive" (p. 406). Their mental journey moved from appreciating each other's disciplinary perspective, to sorting out the strengths and weaknesses of philosophy and physics as ways to account for the phenomenon of color, to active learning from each other and attempting a merger of perspectives (p. 406). *Integration, then, is a cognitive process involving collaboration and language.*

The Development of New Models of the IRP That Feature Techniques Demonstrated to Achieve Integration

Second, the integrationist case rests on the development of new models of the IRP that feature techniques and strategies demonstrated to achieve integration. Though these models differ on several points such as the number, order, and identity of certain steps, they agree on four key points:

- Integration should be the *goal* of the interdisciplinary research enterprise.
- Integration is a *process*.
- Integration is *achievable* if one pays careful attention to process.
- Integration is something that we must *create* using techniques demonstrated to achieve the goal of integration (Repko, 2007, p. 13).

These models—including the integrated model used in this book—understand interdisciplinary integration as a cognitive process. They feature integrative moves or "STEPS" that use techniques and strategies demonstrated to create common ground, integrate theories, and construct a more comprehensive understanding of the problem. Chapters 10 through 13 demonstrate how to perform these STEPS by applying these techniques and strategies to a wide range of problems. *Critics may view integration as an ideal that is almost impossible to realize, but it is, in practice, very achievable.*

The Publication of Groundbreaking Integrative Work on a Wide Range of Complex Problems

The third development that supports the integrationist case is the growing number of publications that view integration as the primary methodology of interdisciplinarity. These include Rick Szostak's (2004) *Classifying Science:*

Phenomena, Data, Theory, Method, Practice; the National Academies' (2005) *Facilitating Interdisciplinary Research*; Sharon J. Derry, Christian D. Schunn, and Morton Ann Gernsbacher's (2005) *Interdisciplinary Collaboration: An Emerging Cognitive Science*; John Atkinson and Malcolm Crowe's (2006) *Interdisciplinary Research: Diverse Approaches in Science, Technology, Health and Society*; David McDonald, Gabriele Bammer, and Peter Deane's (2009) *Research Integration Using Dialogue Methods;* Rick Szostak's (2009) *The Causes of Economic Growth: Interdisciplinary Perspectives*; and Allen F. Repko, William H. Newell, and Rick Szostak's (2012) *Case Studies in Interdisciplinary Integration*. These books provide a number of examples, several rather detailed, of successful interdisciplinary integration. They and a large number of journal articles offer a variety of insights into interdisciplinary research, share a common conception of interdisciplinarity, and appreciate that integration is the best way to address complex problems that confront us. The examples they showcase do not fully address concerns about the difficulties of interdisciplinary integration, but they stand as convincing counterexamples to claims that barriers of fragmentation, epistemology, ideology, and perspective make integration infeasible.

The Insistence on the Centrality of Integration by Leading Interdisciplinary and Transdisciplinary Organizations

A fourth development that integrationists look to is the insistence on the centrality of integration by leading interdisciplinary and transdisciplinary organizations. The *Handbook of Transdisciplinary Research* calls integration "the core methodology underpinning the transdisciplinary research process" (Pohl, van Kerkhoff, Hadorn, & Bammer, 2008, p. 421). In the field of landscape research, for example, the issue is not whether to integrate but "how to apply new and specific interdisciplinary and/or transdisciplinary techniques" (Tress, Tress, & Fry, 2006, p. i). The Swiss Academies of Arts and Sciences Network for Transdisciplinary Research (td-net) devoted an international conference to the topic in 2009. The Australian-based Integration and Implementation Sciences network provides an academic base for synthesizing pertinent knowledge, concepts, and methods in order to address complex problems (Bammer, 2005). And the Association for Integrative Studies (AIS) has long promoted integration as the distinctive characteristic of interdisciplinarity and the goal of interdisciplinary studies.

The Advantages of Integration

Concerning critics' charge that an increasing number of interdisciplinary combinations will simply produce a plurality of more comprehensive understandings, or competing metatheories, and that these will result in theoretical confusion, integrationists respond that theoretical confusion already abounds in cases where multiple theories offer conflicting explanations of a particular behavior or phenomenon. Integrationists in the field of criminology, for example, see several distinct advantages in integrating existing discipline-based theories. Integration, they argue,

- facilitates the development of central concepts that are common to several theories,
- provides coherence to a bewildering array of fragmented theories and thereby reduces their number,
- achieves comprehensiveness and completeness, and thereby enhances their explanatory power,
- advances scientific progress and theory development, and
- synthesizes ideas about crime causation and social control policy (Henry & Bracy, 2012, p. 261).

What is needed, say integrationists, is not more granular and conflicting explanations but a synthesis of these explanations.

Concerning the preference of critics for presenting a menu of competing theories and meanings rather than one comprehensive theory or meaning, integrationists make two counterarguments. First, competition for the best explanations is inherently unequal if the integrative explanation is omitted from theory competition. We need to move beyond debate between disciplinary theories to discussion and critical evaluation of more comprehensive understandings produced through interdisciplinary integration (especially when they form the basis for public policy). Second, while it is useful to have some scholars working to promote further discussion of complex issues, many interdisciplinarians are eager to move beyond talk to action, which needs to be based on full integration. In some cases, we are talking about complex societal problems and policy issues that cannot wait longer to be addressed. Policy makers need a specific recommendation, though this may be very nuanced (and might even involve: Try X; if that doesn't work, try Y).

The Readily Available Tests for Selecting the Best Comprehensive Understanding _____

Critics' concern over "integrational confusion" is overblown, say integrationists, because it presumes that there is no way to adjudicate between competing integrative theories. First, there is always some basis for choosing one theory over another (its simplicity, elegance, compatibility with other theories, etc.), and thus, our earlier evaluative efforts should not yield a tie between competing theories. Second, our main purpose is not to choose between theories but to generate an even better theory by integrating the best elements of competing theories. As shown elsewhere in this book, there are, in fact, multiple ways to adjudicate between competing theories. One test is to ask, "Which understanding is most consistent both with the contributing concepts and the theories *and* with the available empirical evidence?" If more than one comprehensive understanding passes the consistency test, then the second test can readily distinguish between/among them: "Which one produces the more desirable solution when applied to the complex problem under study?" The problem, however, is not an abundance of integrative explanations but a scarcity of them. *We need to move beyond debate between disciplinary theories to discussion and critical evaluation of more comprehensive understandings produced through interdisciplinary integration (especially when they form the basis for public policy).*

The Goal of Full Integration

The integrationist case establishes that epistemological and ideological barriers can be overcome. And thus, we can aspire to push past partial integration (though this is better than nothing), setting the stage for fuller integrations. This brings to mind a question that Richards (1996) raises in "The Meaning and Relevance of 'Synthesis' in Interdisciplinary Studies": Must one *achieve* integration to qualify as doing *fully* integrative work? The answer is that the product of the interdisciplinary research process should be tested empirically against the objective of the particular research project. That objective may be to achieve full interdisciplinarity or partial interdisciplinarity.

When the research is carried out by an interdisciplinary team, full interdisciplinarity refers to the research conducted by the team as a whole. Individual members would be considered to be engaged in fully interdisciplinary work even though they do not carry out every step of the process themselves (Newell, 2012, p. 302).

A second exception is made to the definition of full interdisciplinarity concerning those in the fine and performing arts and related humanities who do not even attempt to do fully interdisciplinary work. For these scholars, partial integration may be the best one can do because the creative works being analyzed are themselves conflicted. These scholars are conscientious objectors, not failed interdisciplinarians. They prefer to prepare readers or observers or listeners to evaluate alternative more comprehensive understandings rather than to present a single or best understanding, though they can be faulted for not exploring the ways in which some more comprehensive understandings are preferable to others.

Interdisciplinarians need to embrace integration as the *goal* of fully interdisciplinary work, and should come as *close* to achieving it as possible, given the problem under study and the disciplinary insights at their disposal. Thus, for work that does not achieve integration to be accorded the status of fully interdisciplinary, other interdisciplinarians vetting the work would have to agree that the work came as close to achieving integration as was possible under the circumstances. This allows for the interdisciplinary result to take the form "In situation A the best explanation is X, but in slightly different situation B the best explanation is Y." This book (and almost all interdisciplinarians outside the fine and performing arts and related humanities) makes the case for pursuing the goal of full integration.

Conditions Necessary to Perform Integration

Three conditions are necessary to perform integration: (1) overcoming monodisciplinarity; (2) triangulating depth, breadth, and integration; and (3) cultivating six qualities of mind.

Overcoming Monodisciplinarity

The first condition necessary to perform interdisciplinary integration is overcoming **monodisciplinarity**. This is the tendency to view a problem primarily from the perspective of the discipline in which the researcher is grounded while discounting or rejecting other disciplinary perspectives. For example, a researcher grounded in economics is most likely to view the problem of road congestion as primarily an economic problem and fail to appreciate (or even be aware of) its sociological and political contexts. Overcoming monodisciplinarity involves three cognitive abilities: perspective taking, balancing different disciplinary views, and holistic thinking.

Perspective Taking

Perspective taking is viewing some problem, object, or phenomenon from a standpoint other than one's own. In interdisciplinary work, perspective taking involves appreciating alternative disciplinary perspectives. It may also involve role taking.

Appreciating Alternative Disciplinary Perspectives   Integrating insights from outside one's home discipline is arguably impossible without some degree of appreciating alternative disciplinary perspectives. Appreciating other disciplinary perspectives does not mean abandoning one's own disciplinary beliefs to the views of another discipline. It does mean being aware of more than one way to account for natural and social phenomena and processes. For example, in *Catching the Light: The Entwined History of Light and Mind*, historian of science Zajonc (1993) describes how philosophical and psychological arguments influenced the understanding of the nature of light waves:

> Light . . . has been treated scientifically by physicists, symbolically by religious thinkers, and practically by artists and technicians. Each gives voice to a part of our experience of light. When heard together,

all speak of one thing whose nature and meaning has been the object of human attention for millennia. During the last three centuries, the artistic and religious dimensions of light have been kept severely apart from its scientific study. . . . The time has come to welcome them back, and to craft a fuller image of light than any one discipline can offer. (p. 8)

But, interdisciplinary openness to other perspectives is of a special nature. It involves, says Nikitina (2005), "deeper exploration of the epistemological roots of one's understanding, critical comparison of different disciplinary methods, and substantive transformation of views as a result" (p. 404). This "deeper exploration" of the roots of conflict between disciplinary insights is the focus of STEP 7, the subject of Chapter 10. At its cognitive core, it "bears resemblance to the best disciplinary work . . . which involves attending to differences and extending a respectful regard to clashing views" (p. 403). In practice, says Nikitina, appreciating alternative disciplinary views also means realizing the limits of one's own disciplinary expertise. "Thus, the interdisciplinary dialog is not just about general receptivity to alternative views. It involves active selection and critical judgment" (p. 403).

The point to be stressed is that the interdisciplinary mind tends to go beyond mere *appreciation* of other disciplinary perspectives (i.e., multidisciplinarity); it *critiques* their capacity to address a problem, or even assesses their relevance. The interdisciplinary mind attempts to creatively fuse those insights together into a coherent whole (Nikitina, 2005, p. 409).

Role Taking   Another type of perspective taking is **role taking**, which is used especially by interdisciplinary research teams. This is the act of temporarily adopting a set of perspectives associated with a person or a culture. The literature from social psychology and its research on role taking offers insights that are applicable to interdisciplinarity. The first is that people's judgments are biased in the direction of their own knowledge. This was one of the important findings of a series of studies conducted by Susan G. Fussell of Carnegie Mellon University's Human-Computer Interaction Institute and Robert Kraus of Columbia University. Their studies found that judges are prone to "false consensus bias," meaning that they assume that others are more similar to themselves than they actually are (Fussell & Kraus, 1991, 1992). The implication of Fussell and Kraus's research for both the solo researcher and those working on interdisciplinary teams is that they need to be aware of their own biases, including disciplinary biases, so that these do not color (consciously or unconsciously) the integrative outcome.

Other insights on perspective taking come from research on leader-member exchange (LMX) theory, an approach to understanding leader-member relationships in the workplace (Martin, Thomas, Charles, Epitropaki, & McNamara, 2005, p. 141). Central to this theory are the three role-taking aspects of perspective taking. Each of these aspects is pertinent to interdisciplinary integration. The first role-taking aspect is that role takers must accurately perceive how others see and understand the world. This finding of the Society for Industrial and Organization Psychology (1998) echoes the research by Fussell and Kraus on "false consensus bias." Interdisciplinarians and particularly members of a research team need to see themselves as role takers. To integrate differing insights, interdisciplinary researchers must consciously assume in turn the role, if only briefly, of a disciplinarian researching in each of the disciplines relevant to the problem.

LMX theory also calls for role takers to have "large role-taking ranges." This simply means that role takers should be able to view a situation from diverse perspectives (Martin et al., 2005, p. 141). The implications for integrative work are obvious: Students must not limit their inquiries to only those disciplines with which they are familiar or those insights with which they agree.

A third role-taking aspect is that role takers "should be able to perceive the other's perspective in depth and have a full understanding of the other's perspective" (Martin et al., 2005, p. 141). In interdisciplinary work, achieving depth of understanding sufficient for full understanding of another's (i.e., another discipline's) perspective refers to developing adequacy in the discipline, the focus of Chapter 8.

Summary of Key Points   The key points of perspective taking as it pertains to interdisciplinary integration are summarized here:

- Interdisciplinarians must reflect on their biases, disciplinary as well as personal.
- Researchers must assume the role of disciplinarian, though briefly, as they mine each discipline for insights into the problem.
- Researchers must not limit their inquiries to only those disciplines with which they are familiar or those insights and theories with which they agree.

Balancing Conflicting Views

Overcoming monodisciplinarity involves a second cognitive ability: balancing different disciplinary views.

Integration or conceptual blending is a constant balancing act. Interdisciplinary work is often an unsettling process of sorting out strengths and weaknesses in different positions that argue against each other while at the same time keeping these positions in balance.[2] Sometimes this leads to realizing that one's own disciplinary grounding and tools cannot quite handle the problem, and sometimes one begins to see clearly the weakness in the other disciplines' perspectives (Nikitina, 2005, p. 403).

Nikitina (2005) illustrates this point by describing how professors involved in teaching an interdisciplinary course on the nature of light and color carefully considered alternative disciplinary arguments and attempted to keep these in balance:

> Working side by side with a philosopher, Burke begins to see the filters that his disciplinary assumptions as a physicist impose on his approach to the understanding of color. He has never questioned the broad concepts of mass, energy, and material reality because they seemed "obvious" to him as a physicist. It took philosopher Provence to point out to him how "sloppy" and "grubby-hands-on-whatever-works" were his answers to these fundamental questions. . . . Working side by side with the humanities faculty. . . , Burke and [geoscientist] Pestrong come to realize that scientific answers to the question of color, mass, and energy are not powerful enough. (p. 404)

At the same time that Burke discovered the failings of physics in its ability to understand color, he realized that philosophy, too, does not have all of the answers.

> "Philosophy has really ceased in large measure to be informed by the physical sciences," whereas physics is weak in its definitions of mass, energy, and reality. In a similar fashion, [biologist] Gilbert . . . exposed the weaknesses and strengths of both biology and critical theory [from the humanities] by bringing them into close contact. He used science "to limit interpretations" with experimental data while at the same time turning to the humanities to prevent simplification of an issue and to remind science of its social responsibility. (Nikitina, 2005, p. 404)

This vignette illustrates that appreciating alternative disciplinary perspectives goes hand-in-hand with critically comparing and carefully balancing different disciplinary toolkits. This process of sorting, weighing, and balancing is a crucial step toward integrating ideas.

Holistic Thinking

The third cognitive ability that is involved in overcoming monodisciplinarity is holistic thinking, a characteristic of interdisciplinarians described in Chapter 2 and discussed more fully here. Holistic thinking is the ability to understand how ideas and information from relevant disciplines relate to each other and to the problem (Bailis, 2002, pp. 4–5). Holistic thinking differs from perspective taking in this important respect: Whereas perspective taking (the subject of Chapter 4) is the ability to understand how each discipline would typically view the problem, holistic thinking is the ability to see the whole problem in terms of its constituent disciplinary parts. In holistic thinking, the focus is on the relationships of parts to the whole and on the differences between and similarities to other parts. The object of holistic thinking is to view the problem inclusively in a larger context rather than under controlled or restrictive conditions favored by disciplinary specialists. But "larger context" does not mean the most encompassing context possible. One actually wants the narrowest context possible that still encompasses everything needed to address the problem *as a whole*. Holistic thinking allows for seeing characteristics of a problem that are not apparent when studying the problem in disciplinary isolation. For example, an interdisciplinary study of community art, usually seen as separate from urban economic development, may show how the community benefits socially, culturally, and economically (i.e., more holistically) from various kinds of art. The goal or the product of holistic thinking is a more comprehensive understanding of the problem (discussed below). Overcoming monodisciplinarity involves deciding that other disciplines—their perspectives, epistemologies, assumptions, theories, and methods—are worth considering when studying a particular problem. Indeed, interdisciplinarians eventually come to value and seek other perspectives.

Triangulating Depth, Breadth, and Integration

The second condition necessary to perform interdisciplinary integration is the ability to triangulate (or keep in equilibrium) disciplinary depth, disciplinary breadth, and interdisciplinary integration. Integration, explains Klein (1996), does not result from "simply mastering a body of knowledge, applying a formula, or moving in linear fashion from point A to point B. . . . It requires active triangulation of depth, breadth, and synthesis [i.e., integration]" (p. 212). The concept of **interdisciplinary triangulation** is shown in Figure 9.2.

Disciplinary Depth

Whereas disciplinary research values depth over breadth, interdisciplinary research values depth *and* breadth. **Disciplinary depth** refers to the **disciplinary knowledge** that one must draw upon. This includes (1) an understanding of the overall perspective of each relevant discipline and (2) adequacy in each discipline's defining elements as they pertain to the problem. These elements and the discipline's perspective in a general sense are usually reflected in the discipline's literature, from which insights into particular problems are drawn. The movement here is from the most general knowledge of a discipline—its perspective in a general sense—to more specific knowledge about the discipline's defining elements, to still more specific knowledge of how each of its elements informs its theories and insights into the problem. The movement, in short, is from understanding a discipline's general perspective on reality, to more focused reading on the defining elements, to intensive "digging" into the discipline's scholarly literature.

| Figure 9.2 | Triangulation of Disciplinary Depth, Disciplinary Breadth, and Interdisciplinary Integration |

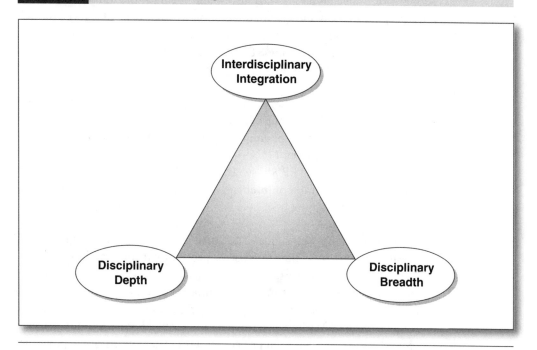

NOTE: In her discussion of the metaphor of the triangulation of "depth," "breadth," and "synthesis," Klein (1996) uses the term *synthesis* because, as she explains, it "connotes creation of an interdisciplinary outcome through *a series of integrative actions* [italics added]" (p. 212). Her preference for *synthesis* over *integration* in this context is understandable. However, the graphic that attempts to depict this metaphor substitutes the term *integration* for *synthesis* because it is the term used in the definition of interdisciplinary studies that this book embraces. See the Association of American Colleges (1991, p. 74) for an early reference to the notion of interdisciplinary triangulation.

Disciplinary Breadth

Disciplinary breadth refers to disciplines, subdisciplines, and interdisciplines interested in the problem and whose experts have produced the most relevant insights into it. These disciplines may be epistemologically distant (e.g., a natural science discipline and a humanities discipline) or near (e.g., physics and chemistry). Clearly, the burden on the interdisciplinary researcher is far greater than the burden on the disciplinary researcher.

What is required for successfully engaging in the first half of the IRP (i.e., drawing on disciplines and their insights) is developing *adequacy* or sufficiency in each relevant discipline (the subject of Chapter 7). The **interdisciplinary breadth** required for engaging in the second half of the research process (i.e., integrating theories and insights) involves knowing enough about all the relevant disciplines so that one can work with their theories and insights and integrate them.

Interdisciplinary Integration

Along with achieving disciplinary depth and breadth, the interdisciplinarian must keep the process and goal of integration constantly in view (even though one does not yet know what the result is going to look like). The integrative part of the IRP calls for taking STEPS 7, 8a and 8b, and 9, each of which is the subject of one of the following four chapters:

- Identify conflicts between disciplinary theories and insights and locate their sources (STEP 7; see Chapter 10).
- Modify concepts and assumptions through creating common ground (STEP 8a; see Chapter 11).
- Modify theories (STEP 8b; see Chapter 12).
- Construct a more comprehensive understanding of the problem (STEP 9; see Chapter 13).

Throughout this process, adequacy must be maintained. Adequacy does not mean that one can claim expertise or professional command of the disciplines used; rather, **adequacy** means that one acquires a *sufficient* understanding of each discipline's cognitive map and is thus able to identify its perspective, epistemology, assumptions, concepts, theories, and methods in order to understand its insights into a particular problem. How much adequacy is required depends on what each project requires. The notions of "depth" and "rigor," says Klein (1996), are usually associated with disciplinarity. However, in interdisciplinary work, they are redefined: "Depth in interdisciplinary work derives from competence in pertinent knowledges and approaches, [and interdisciplinary] rigor derives from attention to integrative process" (p. 212).

Cultivating Seven Qualities of Mind

The third condition to successfully performing integration involves cultivating these seven qualities of mind:

- Seeking what is useful even if it is problematic
- Thinking inclusively and integratively, not exclusively
- Being responsive to each perspective but dominated by none (e.g., not allowing one's strength in a particular discipline to influence one's treatment of other relevant disciplines with which one is less familiar)
- Striving for balance among conflicting disciplinary perspectives and insights
- Maintaining intellectual flexibility
- Thinking both inductively and deductively
- Thinking about the whole while simultaneously working with parts

These internal dispositions correspond to several of the traits and skills of interdisciplinarians identified in Chapter 2.

The Model of Integration
Used in This Book

This section introduces the broad model of integration used in this book. The discussion addresses three key questions: (1) What is integrated? (2) How is it integrated? (3) What does the result of integration look like? In discussing each of these questions, reference is made to other integrative approaches used in certain sectors of the academy for the purpose of identifying their limitations compared to the broad model. The term *broad model* is used because it is flexible enough to subsume these more narrowly focused approaches to integration and overcome their limitations.

What the Model Integrates

The broad model integrates insights concerning a particular complex problem that are produced by disciplines, subdisciplines, interdisciplines, schools of thought, professional fields, and one's basic research. Some of these theories and insights may be from disciplines that are epistemologically distant. Insights are not limited to those produced inside the academy and may include expertise from interested stakeholders outside the academy. This expertise may be from government agencies, private industry, or not-for-profit organizations. Such expertise often reflects the disciplinary background of the stakeholder and/or the disciplinary orientation of the organization that the stakeholder represents. This expertise is expressed in the form of insights into the problem. Theories and the insights they produce along with their concepts and assumptions constitute the "raw material" used in integration. Depending on the combination of disciplines that produced them, these theories and insights do not usually fit together naturally or easily (with exceptions in the natural sciences), though they may be somewhat complementary.

The flexibility of the broad model enables it to work with disciplinary theories and their key concepts in the natural and social sciences. The model is also able to work with specific objects such as text, photos, film, or other objects that are the focus of the humanities and applied arts, and use tools from a specific set of collaborating disciplines to analyze them. Moreover, the model can integrate any disciplinary material in the fabric of time, culture, and personal experience and address timeless questions concerning the human condition.

How the Model Integrates

The broad model uses a process approach to achieve integration. It proceeds in a steplike fashion but also involves reflecting on and possibly revisiting earlier STEPS. It has three components: (1) identifying conflicts in insights and theories and locating their sources (STEP 7 and the subject of Chapter 10),

(2) creating common ground between conflicting disciplinary concepts (STEP 8a, the subject of Chapter 11) or theories (STEP 8b, the subject of Chapter 12), and (3) constructing a more comprehensive understanding of the problem (STEP 9 and the subject of Chapter 13). Though these STEPS can usefully be understood separately, each one is closely connected to those that immediately precede and follow it.

A helpful way to clarify how the broad model integrates is to compare it to other approaches to integration used in some sectors of the academy. These approaches include contextualization (used in the humanities), conceptualization (used in mathematics and the natural sciences), and problem solving (used in various interdisciplinary and applied fields). Each of these is examined in terms of its approach to integration, how its approach is incomplete, and how its limitations are overcome by the broad model.

Contextualization

Contextualization, in an interdisciplinary sense, connects disciplines that are epistemological neighbors by embedding any disciplinary material in the fabric of time, culture, and personal experience (Nikitina, 2006, pp. 252, 257). Contextualization is used to interpret cultural artifacts, such as art works, in order to uncover their meaning (Bal, 2002, p. 134). The disciplines of the humanities differ in the specific tools they use and the contexts they rely on. History, for example, "uses time; cultural studies uses both time and space; philosophy mines the fundamental and possibly timeless questions of [the] human condition" (Nikitina, 2006, p. 257).

Contextualization is incomplete in its approach to integration in three ways. First, it typically includes only those disciplines that the humanities comprises. Second, the process of integration is not explicit, which makes it difficult for the reader to parse. Third, the process fails to critically examine crucial elements of the relevant disciplines, such as their methodological and philosophical cores, and explain how these elements may be relevant to the research question.

The broad model subsumes the contextualization approach and overcomes its limitations by (a) being open to integrating insights from disciplines that are epistemologically distant (e.g., outside the humanities), (b) making the process of integration explicit, and (c) critically examining the methodological and philosophical roots of relevant disciplines and explaining their relevance to the research question.

Conceptualization

Conceptualization takes "scientific and mathematical thinking beyond the facts and singular theories to the level of underlying concepts" (Nikitina, 2006, p. 261). Nikitina (2006) explains how contextualization in the humanities differs from conceptualization in the sciences: "The goal of conceptualization is not to interpret human experience as contextualization does, but to understand essential laws of the world that operate regardless of our perception and interpretation" (p. 261). With science as a guiding epistemological paradigm, conceptualizing connections in the natural sciences are anything but metaphorical or suggestive (as they tend to be in the humanities).

The conceptualization approach uses concepts such as *linearity, change,* and *scale* to effectively tie together disciplines in mathematics and the natural sciences such as algebra, geometry, physics, and biology. These conceptualizations need to meet a stringent standard of verification, replication, and mathematical expression. They "are not philosophical suppositions, but a common denominator in the form of empirical data stripped to their core mathematical base, a common denominator that defies difference in symbolic and notational systems" (Nikitina, 2006, p. 261). The process of integration by conceptualization begins with a question, as in this example:

> To answer the question of how the atmosphere acts as a radiation filter, students bring together chemistry (how bonds between the oxygen molecules in the ozone can be broken), physics (how ray energy makes molecules vibrate similar to string action), and mathematics (to calculate the frequency of these vibrations or oscillations per second) in order, as one student explained in her paper, "to find the wavelength necessary to break the bond between two atoms." This figure is then translated back into chemical terms helping to conclude that the "free oxygen atom (the result of an ozone split)" could potentially bind with an oxygen molecule ClO and release into the atmosphere an unstable and polluting gas Cl_2. The implication of this chemical reaction for the environment is deduced from that: "Since the chlorine ends up unbonded at the end, it continues to destroy ozone." (Nikitina, 2006, pp. 261–262)

This example shows that integration by conceptualization is not just a collection of chemical, physical, and biological ideas, but "a tight mathematical matrix of relationships" that are constructed using the tools of different scientific disciplines (Nikitina, 2006, p. 262). The end product of this effort, explains Nikitina (2006), is a strong correlation between the chemical reactions and the probability of the preservation or destruction of ozone. A major strength of this integrative approach is its rigorous correlation of related (e.g., not too epistemologically distant) knowledge, and rich exchange in discipline-specific content (e.g., facts, theories, methods) (p. 262).

However, the conceptualization approach is incomplete in three respects. First, it limits the breadth of disciplinary connections to the natural sciences. Second, it obscures the process by which integration occurs. And third, though it properly emphasizes achieving integration at the start of the project (in terms of establishing a common language among disciplinary experts), it neglects to identify points along the way where taking additional integrative actions is likewise essential.

The broad model incorporates the strengths of the conceptualization approach and overcomes its limitations by (a) connecting disciplines that are epistemologically distant, (b) identifying discrete steps in the integrative process, and (c) recognizing that these integrative actions occur throughout the project, *not just at its start.*

Problem Solving

The approach of **problem solving** uses critical issues of public debate, product development, or an intervention such as one designed to improve health and well-being as focal points for making connections between disciplines. For example, the Center for Bioethics at the University of Pennsylvania brings together all the disciplinary tools it can to bear on such complex and vital issues as human cloning, stem cell research, and organ transplantation. Unlike contextualization and conceptualization, which focus on promoting self-understanding or building coherence among concepts, problem solving is aimed at generating tangible outcomes and change. This approach is attractive to the applied sciences, business, technology, and the fields of applied social science that aim to create new products, improve on existing conditions, or develop policies for social change. Natural users of this model include such interdisciplinary fields as bioethics and public health (Nikitina, 2006, p. 263). The epistemological goal of this model is not so much to make knowledge personally meaningful (as in contextualization), or to advance fundamental knowledge (as in conceptualization), but to attack a pressing problem by drawing on all available disciplinary tools in order to resolve it. In its focus on the human predicament, the problem-solving approach may seem similar to the humanities-based contextualization approach. However, they approach human concerns in a different way. In contextualization work the goal is to attain a deeper understanding of the human condition, whereas in problem-solving work "the fundamental metaphysical questions of 'who we are' and 'why are we here' are distinctly secondary to the primary goal of finding causes and cures for human calamities" (pp. 265–266).

The problem-solving approach emphasizes the development of a solid understanding of the relevant disciplines with an activist view of how to put the disciplines at the service of the problem and other human concerns. The approach does not hesitate to draw on disciplines that are epistemologically distant as long as these are relevant to the problem.

The problem-solving approach is incomplete in at least three ways. First, the disciplinary "tools" that it uses are primarily methodological (i.e., quantitative or qualitative) and tend to exclude other tools that may be equally relevant to the problem such as each contributing discipline's perspectives, assumptions, concepts, and favored theories. Second, the problem is seldom deconstructed (or mapped) to reveal its complexity and causal links. This omission tends to obscure difference or conflict between disciplinary perspectives on the problem. Third, the process of how integration occurs tends to be obscured by the primary focus of the approach, which is on blending viewpoints (in an additive way), articulating the author's personal stand on the issue, and formulating a policy or recommending legal action (Nikitina, 2006, p. 264).

The broad model reflects the instrumentalist focus of the problem-solving approach. It overcomes its limitations by (a) using all "disciplinary tools" including assumptions, concepts, theories, and methods; (b) mapping complex problems to reveal their complexity and causal links; (c) critically evaluating expert and/or stakeholder views (i.e., insights) by seeking to discover how these may reflect disciplinary thinking; and (d) seeking to create commonalities (i.e., common ground) between views on the basis of their shared understanding of one or more key assumptions, concepts, or theoretical explanations.

Summary of How the Broad Model Integrates

How the broad model integrates is summarized here:

- It makes the process of integration explicit and transparent by breaking it down into discrete STEPS that require reflecting on earlier STEPS.
- It maps complex problems to reveal their complexity and causal links.
- It connects disciplines that are epistemologically distant or close.
- It uses all disciplinary methodological and philosophical tools that are relevant to the problem.
- It draws upon all relevant disciplinary theories and insights, including those derived from one's own basic research and those of stakeholders outside the academy, and critically evaluates these to locate sources of conflict.
- It uses various techniques (see Chapters 11 and 12) to modify insights and theories to create common ground on the basis of shared concepts or assumptions.
- It melds insights concerning a particular phenomenon until the contribution of each becomes inseparable.
- The cognitive process involved in performing integration is both compelling and elusive. It is compelling because the idea of integration is heavily supported by theory; it is elusive because other than the broad model, none of the specialized approaches delineates explicit actions, operations, or steps that make it possible (but not inevitable in every case) to achieve integration in a wide range of contexts.

What the Result of Integration Looks Like

Interdisciplinarians have not always been clear about how to achieve integration; they have been even less clear about the result of integration. The definition of integration stated earlier specifies that the integrative process should produce a result possessing certain characteristics. Newell (1990) relates how he and other practitioners used to think of integration as analogous to completing a jigsaw puzzle (p. 74). For a time, this analogy was commonly used. However, comparing the result of integration to a completed jigsaw puzzle is problematic in at least three critical respects. Discussing these will deepen our understanding of integration both as a process and as a result.

Integration Accommodates Epistemological Differences

The first characteristic of the resulting integration is that it *accommodates* (but does not fully resolve) epistemological differences. The pieces of a jigsaw puzzle are finely milled to fit together as tightly as possible. This is not so with disciplinary insights, which pertain to a particular problem or object and thus "fit" to some degree on that limited basis. The problem of fit is minimized in the natural sciences where fit is achieved merely by reconciling alternative conceptualizations of the same phenomenon. For example, when addressing the energy crisis, physics may focus on how a power plant works (i.e., the alternative formulations of thermodynamics) and chemistry on how energy is released from chemical bonds in coal. The insights may be fully complementary but require using the technique of redefinition (see Chapter 11), perhaps to address differences in scale (Newell & Green, 1982, pp. 25–26). However, when an issue connects the natural sciences to the humanities or social sciences as in the embryonic stem cell research controversy, insights become less complementary, so the problem of fit becomes more challenging (Kelly, 1996, p. 95).

The reason why fit is so challenging when investigating a problem such as human cloning that spans the natural sciences, the social sciences, and the humanities is that there are deep epistemological fissures between these disciplinary categories. Although the sciences are "geared up to tell us what the facts are," says Kelly (1996), science does not ascribe value or morality to these facts. "The only recognized epistemological powers operative in the scientific realm are those of the five senses. And we do not (literally) see, hear, smell, touch, or taste wrongness or rightness" (Kelly, 1996, p. 96). Kelly calls this understanding of interdisciplinarity *narrow interdisciplinarity* because it focuses on factual situations and structures in need of modification, not on the rightness or wrongness of the activity, which is the realm of the humanities. This conception of interdisciplinarity would, therefore, focus on cloning techniques, not on the rightness or wrongness of cloning. Instead, Kelly argues for practicing a *wide interdisciplinarity*, which enables interdisciplinary practitioners from the sciences and the humanities to work together to identify, solve, or resolve normative problems, both practical and theoretical, having to do with the satisfaction of human needs (p. 96). This book reflects Kelly's "wide" conception of interdisciplinarity.

Integration Is New and More Comprehensive

The second characteristic of the resulting integration is that it is new and more comprehensive. The jigsaw puzzle pieces, when assembled, form a picture that is not new because it existed before the pieces were assembled (e.g., the picture on the puzzle box). With disciplinary insights, however, there is no predetermined pattern that one can consult to see if one is "getting it right." In fact, working with disciplinary theories and insights is comparable to working with puzzle pieces from different puzzles mixed together with no picture for guidance. The absence of pattern is particularly challenging when working in the social sciences and the humanities where theories and insights from different disciplines tend to conflict more sharply. For example, in examining the meaning of the Temple Mount in Jerusalem to Judaism, Christianity, and Islam, religious studies scholars may focus on the sanctity of the Mount based on the sacred writings of these faith traditions, whereas political scientists may focus on the political implications of physical and administrative control of the site. Because the disciplinary insights conflict, they make the task of creating common ground difficult, though not impossible. Once common ground is created and integration is performed, one can see whether the new understanding is consistent with or can accommodate the conflicting disciplinary insights.

When disciplinary insights are integrated, they generally form something that is truly new—a new understanding, a new meaning, or extended theoretical explanation.[3] When a disciplinary expert produces an insight into a problem and the insight appears as a book aimed at a disciplinary audience or as an article published in a peer-reviewed journal, the insight is considered new, complete, and authoritative in the view of the discipline. It is not perceived as missing some piece from another discipline. From an interdisciplinary standpoint, however, the same insight is only partial and only one of many possible explanations of the problem or interpretation of the object, especially if other disciplines have produced insights into it.

This resulting integration or more comprehensive understanding is "new" in four ways:

- It is the result of an explicit, reflexive, and iterative integrative process.
- It is inclusive of the relevant disciplinary insights but not dominated by any one of them.
- It did not exist prior to the integration of the separate disciplinary theories and/or insights.
- It is not merely a combination of the separate disciplinary insights or a juxtaposition of them in a multidisciplinary fashion.

Though new, the integrated result should be viewed as only provisional until it is tested according to criteria presented in Chapter 14.

Integration Is "Larger" Than the Sum of Its Parts

The third characteristic of the resulting integration is that it is "larger" than the sum of its constituent parts, not in spatial terms but in *cognitive* terms. The puzzle picture before it was cut up encompassed a predetermined area expressed in square inches or centimeters. When the pieces are fitted together, the completed puzzle is not larger (or smaller) than the sum of its pieces. By contrast, the new understanding created by the activity of integration constitutes what Boix Mansilla (2005) calls, "a cognitive advancement," meaning that it would have been unlikely through single disciplinary means (p. 16). The new whole or more comprehensive understanding is larger than its constituent parts in another way: It cannot be reduced to the separate disciplinary insights from which it emerged (Newell, 1990, p. 74). Consequently, the understanding is cognitively "larger" compared to what could be achieved by merely gathering up individual specialty insights and using them to view the problem from a series of disciplinary perspectives the way multidisciplinarity does. The understanding is likewise "larger" in that nothing relevant has been excluded. Disciplinarity tends to exclude, whereas interdisciplinarity strives for inclusion.

The Defining Characteristics of the Result of Integration Summarized

The defining characteristics of the result of integration are summarized here:

- It is motivated by the instrumentalist goal of using the resulting integrative understanding to solve a real-world problem, better understand the human condition (past and present), and open new pathways of research.
- It is formed from disciplinary and stakeholder insights that do not fit together naturally or easily, though they may be somewhat complementary.
- It is created without benefit of a preexisting integrative pattern (though a recognized approach to achieve integration is used).
- It has characteristics that differ from any of those of the contributing insights.
- It is inclusive of relevant information.
- It may be partial or full.
- It cannot necessarily be used as a template to solve other similar problems because the resulting integration takes the form of insights into the specific problem that transcend disciplinary insights, and their integration is valid only for that specific context.
- It may assume an infinite variety of forms.
- It is often messy with all sorts of caveats.

The result of integration is valued not as an end in itself but for the more comprehensive understanding, cognitive advancement, or new product it makes possible. Marsha Bundy Seabury (2002), an expert in interdisciplinary pedagogy, writes of her hope that students will *move toward integration,* and thus reach a more comprehensive understanding. The metaphor of "moving toward integration" does *not* mean "a graph-like progression whereby students gradually move from lower forms of thinking on up to more holistic, abstract thinking, ending in the upper-right quadrant of the page" (Seabury, 2002, p. 47). Sometimes the "'goal' may be *not a position but a motion,* meaning that students should be able to move among levels of abstraction and generalization [italics added]," which is part of the integrative process (p. 47). Perhaps the most accessible metaphor for how the new understanding should "look" is Nissani's smoothie noted in Chapter 1.

Three Fundamental Questions Raised by This Discussion of the Broad Model

The first question is, "What does integration change?" Does integration change only the contribution of each discipline, or are the disciplines themselves somehow changed? The answer to the first half of the question is that the contributions of each discipline are changed because one cannot integrate insights before they have been modified to create common ground. Most practitioners agree that disciplinary contributions—that is, assumptions, concepts, and theories—must change for integration to succeed. Precisely how this occurs will be demonstrated in Chapters 11 and 12. Interdisciplinary and disciplinary research are symbiotic: Interdisciplinary insights resulting from integration can feed back into disciplinary research; encourage new questions; change concepts, theories, and methods; and pay attention to a wider range of phenomena. The answer to the second half of the question is that the feedback effect on the contributing disciplines themselves is neither inevitable nor essential though it can happen.[4]

The second question is, "Must integration result in a clear-cut solution to a problem for a study to be 'successful' and truly interdisciplinary?" The answer is not necessarily. Those in the humanities and in the fine and performing arts resist the impulse to provide a single best integration (or best meaning), preferring instead to respect the ambiguity inherent in the art objects they critically examine and *lay out the range of possibilities for integration.* Interdisciplinarians in the natural and social sciences, by contrast, seek to integrate on behalf of others, presenting their new, more comprehensive understanding as a finished product or "clear-cut solution." To conclude that the integrative effort has "failed" because of the absence of a feasible solution, even though the effort revealed a new understanding or new areas to be investigated, would be a mistake. As long as the integration results in *something* "new" to the understanding of a complex problem, even an increased appreciation of its complexity, or the range of possibilities for integration, or of new avenues for research, the work should be viewed as successful. Assessing interdisciplinary work is the focus of Chapter 14.

The third question is, "Will integration always resolve all conflict?" Here again, the answer is not necessarily. Seipel (2002) cautions students and teachers alike that we should not expect that the process of integration will always result in a neat, tidy solution in which all contradictions between the alternative disciplinary insights are resolved. "Interdisciplinary study," he writes, "may indeed be 'messy'" because the problems it studies are messy (Seipel, 2002, p. 3). Differing insights into a problem and accompanying tensions between disciplines may not only provide further understanding, he says, but should be seen as a "healthy symptom" of interdisciplinarity. The richest interdisciplinary work is that resulting from a research process that works through these tensions and contradictions between disciplinary systems of knowledge with the goal of integration, the creation of new knowledge (p. 3). One such example of integrative work is William Dietrich's (1995) *Northwest Passage: The Great Columbia River*, which was introduced earlier and will be referenced in later chapters to illustrate certain steps of the integrative process.

Chapter Summary

This chapter has examined both the process and the product of integration. As a defining characteristic of interdisciplinarity, integration is what differentiates interdisciplinarity from multidisciplinarity. This chapter discussed the controversy between generalists and integrationists over the role that integration should play in interdisciplinary work as well as the three conditions necessary to perform integration. These include overcoming monodisciplinarity; triangulating depth, breadth, and integration; and cultivating seven qualities of mind. The chapter introduced the broad model of integration used in this book and compared it to three approaches to integration used in certain sectors of the academy. The chapter concluded by identifying the defining characteristics of the integrative result and answered questions raised by the discussion of the broad model.

Moving forward, Chapters 10 to 13 explain STEPS 7 to 9 of the IRP. STEP 7 calls for identifying conflicts between insights and locating their sources; STEP 8 calls for modifying insights and/or theories through the creation of common ground between their concepts and/or assumptions; and STEP 9 calls for constructing a more comprehensive understanding of the problem.

Notes

1. Some interdisciplinarians continue to object to the notion of process with respect to integration. Postmodernist interdisciplinarians are typically committed to integration but object to step-based models that specify how to conduct interdisciplinary research on the grounds that this might constrain freedom of activity or suggest objectivist modernism. On the matter of integration, then, postmodernists appear to be closer to the generalist position which objects to integration as a defining characteristic of interdisciplinarity. Other interdisciplinarians, such as Ken Fuchsman (2009), are troubled by the variety of results that are possible including full integration, partial

integration, no integration, and multiple integrations. He argues that "the concept of integration as a single coherent entity no longer fully applies" because of "the epistemological questions raised by multiple integrations" (pp. 79–80).

2. The concept of balance in interdisciplinary work is still undergoing development and therefore lacks precision. William H. Newell (personal communication, September 20, 2010) comments, for example, that "balance like beauty is in the eye of the beholder; one person's balance is another's imbalance." He asks, "Against what objective standard is balance determined? What characteristics of these positions are, in principle, being balanced?"

3. Recent interdisciplinary work has shown that the more comprehensive understanding is not *inevitably* new or novel. For example, the more comprehensive understanding that Marilyn Tayler (2012) achieves is that one of the positions was correct all along, only now we can appreciate (in a way even that its advocates could not) *why* it is correct. Her understanding is "new" in the limited sense that it casts an old position in a new light.

4. William H. Newell (personal communication, February 6, 2011) points out that "whether there is a feedback effect (and how great that effect is) depends on a number of factors: whether others in the discipline pay attention to those modifications, which may in turn be influenced by the prominence of the researcher(s) from the discipline and the visibility of the study; the frequency with which these shortcomings are revealed through other interdisciplinary projects; the reactions of researchers in the disciplines to the shortcomings of the discipline revealed through these modifications; the ease with which those shortcomings can be overcome within the discipline; and the interest of the discipline in participating in future interdisciplinary research.

Exercises

Defining Integration

9.1 Compare the definition of integration to the definition of interdisciplinary studies presented in Chapter 1. What insight(s) does the definition of integration add to your understanding of interdisciplinarity and to the interdisciplinary research process?

Generalists

9.2 What is the strongest argument that generalists make for understanding interdisciplinarity "loosely"?

9.3 Explain how a *generalist* interdisciplinarian would go about developing a policy recommendation for combating homegrown terrorism.

Integrationists

9.4 What is the strongest argument that integrationists make for insisting that full integration be the goal of interdisciplinarity?

9.5 Explain how an *integrationist* interdisciplinarian would go about developing a policy recommendation for combating homegrown terrorism.

Supportive Theories

9.6 How do Clark's and Bromme's theories complement Nikitina's, and how do all three theories strengthen the theoretical basis of interdisciplinarity?

Perspective Taking

9.7 What does the discussion on perspective taking and role taking add to our understanding of perspective as it is presented in Chapter 4?

Holistic Thinking

9.8 What is the difference between holistic thinking and perspective taking?

Triangulating

9.9 How might a triangulated approach help us better understand the cause of rising budget deficits on the local and/or national level?

To Contextualize or to Conceptualize

9.10 Which approach, contextualization, conceptualization, or problem solving, should be used in approaching the following:

a. Smog attributable, in part, to diesel exhaust emissions from trucks/lorries

b. Application to rezone 100 acres of farmland and woodland that would permit the building of residential housing (single and multifamily) and commercial buildings that would increase employment in an economically depressed area

c. Proposed legislation that would ban religious garb that obscures the identity of the person wearing it

d. The meaning of *The Kite Runner*

What are the strengths and limitations of each approach?

9.11 How might the broad model of integration described in this book approach each of the situations described in 9.10?

10 Identifying Conflicts Between Insights

_____ Chapter Preview

The first part of the interdisciplinary research process (IRP), in summation, involves drawing on insights from relevant disciplines and making two kinds of decisions: disciplinary and interdisciplinary. Disciplinary decisions include determining which disciplines are relevant to the problem, which disciplinary elements (i.e., phenomena, epistemologies, assumptions, concepts, theories, and methods) pertain to the problem, how many and what kind of sources to collect, how to develop adequacy in each of the relevant disciplines, and how to analyze the problem and critically evaluate each insight into it. Interdisciplinary decisions include determining whether the disciplines have skewed their data and findings in their approach to the problem, and considering the possibility that one's own disciplinary and personal bias may have crept into the work. The interdisciplinarian must also be alert to the possibility that the problem is not about conflicts between insights but gaps between them.

This chapter explains the importance of identifying conflicts between disciplinary insights and locating their sources of conflict. It concludes with a note to readers about how to communicate this information to their respective audiences. Throughout the chapter, professional and student work is used to illustrate aspects of this STEP. Identifying conflicts and locating their sources (STEP 7) is preparatory to creating common ground (STEP 8; see Chapters 11 and 12), and constructing a more comprehensive understanding of the problem (STEP 9; see Chapter 13).

> ### Step 7: Identify Conflicts Between Insights or Theories and Their Sources

The Importance of Identifying
_____ Conflicts Between Insights

The immediate challenge for interdisciplinarian is to identify conflicts between disciplinary insights concerning the problem. (The term *insights* includes those produced by theories and concepts unless otherwise noted.)

This is necessary because these conflicts stand in the way of creating common ground and, thus, of achieving integration. One cannot integrate two things that are exactly alike or that have identical properties. Integration can be achieved only between things that are different, whether those differences are seemingly small or seem impossibly large. In other words, integration arises out of conflict, controversy, and difference. Without them, integration would be unnecessary.

The existence of conflict is not some inconvenience that somehow keeps popping up when reading the literature on a problem; rather, it is endemic, inevitable, and central to the interdisciplinary enterprise. Conflict is what one typically discovers when viewing a complex problem from the perspective of several disciplines and reading their insights. Conflict between the insights produced by scholars from different disciplines should not be surprising, explains Newell (2007a), because the disciplines reflect "the irreducibly different, conflicting, or even incommensurate principles" by which that part of reality they study operates (p. 256).

Conflicts between insights are often discovered when conducting the full-scale literature search. The nature and extent of conflict in insights may depend on whether they are drawn from the natural sciences, the social sciences, or the humanities (Newell, 2007a, p. 256). Two questions face the student at this juncture in the IRP: Where are the conflicting insights located, and why do they conflict?

Where Conflicting Insights Are Located

Insights into the same problem may be produced by authors from the *same* discipline or from *different* disciplines.

Conflicting Insights Produced by Authors From the Same Discipline

Conflicting insights into the same problem may be produced by authors from the same discipline. In the threaded problem of suicide terrorism, the literature search revealed three insights from cognitive psychology, a subdiscipline of psychology. (The relative importance of these insights is determined, in part, by how often other writers cite these insights and by how much scholarly debate they generate.) Though these insights are from the same discipline, the insights of each author clearly conflict, as Table 10.1 shows.

Students may be tempted to gloss over the differences in these insights in the literature search, but doing so risks overlooking important clues to how each author's insight differs from others' insights. Oftentimes these differences are nuanced rather than stark because they are from the same discipline, reflecting the discipline's perspective (in a general sense) and its basic assumptions. Consequently, it is often more challenging to detect sources of conflict

Table 10.1	Conflicting Insights into the Causes of Suicide Terrorism From the *Same* Discipline

Subdiscipline	Insight of Author
Cognitive Psychology	Individuals are driven to commit acts of violence that "they are psychologically compelled to commit" (Post, 1998, p. 25).
	"Self-sanctions can be disengaged by cognitively restructuring the moral value of killing so that the killing can be done free of self-censuring restraints" (Bandura, 1998, p. 164).
	"In most cases, the perpetrators sacrificed themselves in the name of a nationalistic rather than a religious idea" (Merari, 1998, p. 205).

between insights from the same discipline than it is to detect sources of conflict between insights from different disciplines. Only by closely reading each author's phrasing (reproduced here) is it possible to detect these differences.

Conflicting Insights Produced by Authors From Different Disciplines

Conflicting insights into the same problem may be produced by authors from different disciplines. In this situation, interdisciplinarians encounter a new challenge: determining if the authors are all talking about the same thing. The way to make this decision is to map each author's argument. Bal's (1999) study of the enigmatic graffito, introduced in Chapter 3, is an example of insights from different disciplines and how these can easily conflict. For example, history's focus on the graffito's "pastness" conflicts with art history's view that the writing is subservient to the image itself and the wall on which it was painted. Similarly, linguistics's focus on the graffito's utterance "Note" (thus creating a subject/object dichotomy) conflicts with rhetorical analysis's broader focus of helping us "read" not just the graffito but the wall as well (Bal, 1999, pp. 8–9).

In general, there is far more opportunity for conflicts to arise between insights from different disciplines because their perspectives and assumptions differ. This is shown in the study of the causes of suicide terrorism in Table 10.2.

Once the important disciplinary insights are located, the next task is to explain why these insights conflict.

Why Insights Conflict

Establishing that the relevant disciplinary insights conflict is not enough: The interdisciplinarian must ferret out the sources of conflict, and this involves focusing on referent concepts and assumptions. If authors advance

| Table 10.2 | Conflicting Insights Into the Causes of Suicide Terrorism From the Same Discipline and From Different Disciplines |

Discipline or Subdiscipline	Insight of Author
Cognitive Psychology	Individuals are driven to commit acts of violence that "they are psychologically compelled to commit" (Post, 1998, p. 25).
	"Self-sanctions can be disengaged by cognitively restructuring the moral value of killing so that the killing can be done free of self-censuring restraints" (Bandura, 1998, p. 164).
	"In most cases, the perpetrators sacrificed themselves in the name of a nationalistic rather than a religious idea" (Merari, 1998, p. 205).
Political Science	"Terrorism can be understood as an expression of political strategy" (Crenshaw, 1998, p. 7).
	"The principal difference in means between sacred terror and secular terror derives from the special justifications and precedents each uses" (Rapoport, 1998, p. 107).
Cultural Anthropology	Suicide terrorists act out of a universal heartfelt human sentiment of self-sacrifice for the welfare of the group/culture (Atran, 2003b, p. 2).

NOTE: Cultural anthropology is a subdiscipline of anthropology.

different theories to explain the cause or behavior of some event or process, then the interdisciplinarian will also focus on theories and the insights that they produce. *The three possible sources of conflict between insights then, are concepts, assumptions, and theories.* Readers will recall that concepts are technical terms that represent a phenomenon or an idea and are basic components of insights. Assumptions underlie both concepts and theories. Here we are referring to the guiding philosophical assumptions of a discipline. **Philosophical assumptions** are the assumptions underlying or inherent in philosophical theories (and thus disciplinary perspectives) while theoretical assumptions are the particular assumptions made within a particular theory.

The three types of assumptions we discuss below are philosophical assumptions. Theories, which increasingly dominate the scholarly discourse within the disciplines, heavily influence the questions asked, the phenomena investigated, and the insights produced. Advanced students and professionals often find themselves having to deal with insights from one or more theories and determine why these theory-based insights conflict.

Theory-based insights are insights informed by or advancing a particular theory or theoretical perspective. Given their importance to interdisciplinary work, a more extended discussion of theories will follow this section.

Concepts Embedded in Insights

Because disciplinary insights are largely expressed in language, conflicts in insights may involve embedded terminology or concepts. (However, those in the fine and performing arts are quick to point out that insights are not exclusively expressed in language but may also be expressed in form, movement, and sound.) Interdisciplinarians commonly encounter four problematic situations concerning concepts.

One problematic situation arises when *the same concept masks different contextual meanings in the relevant disciplinary insights* (Bromme, 2000, p. 127). When the same concept is used by two disciplines to describe some aspect of the problem, the researcher needs to look closely for differences in both connotative as well as denotative meaning. Concerning the example of acid rain in Chapter 8, the alert interdisciplinarian will discover that the concept of "efficiency" has related but different meanings for biologists and physicists (energy out/energy in), economists (dollars out/dollars in), and political scientists (influence exerted/political capital expended) (Newell, 2001, p. 19). Creating common ground when the same concept masks different contextual meanings is relatively easy because the integrative concept (in this case, "efficiency") already exists and merely awaits discovery.

Another problematic situation involves semantic disagreements that arise *when different concepts are used to describe similar ideas.* In the threaded example of suicide terrorism, Table 10.3 shows that the subdiscipline of cognitive psychology uses the concept of "special logic" that has a similar meaning to the political science concept of "strategic logic."

Importantly, both concepts share the same assumption: The agents (i.e., terrorists) are rational. In other words, the basis for common ground already exists between these two concepts, and thus between the insights in which they are embedded and the theories that produced them. This is an example of "integrating as we go." However, this partial integration should

Table 10.3   Differing Concepts Used by Disciplinary Theories to Address the Causes of Suicide Terrorism

Discipline or Subdiscipline	Theory	Concept
Cognitive Psychology	Terrorist Psycho-logic	Special logic
	Self-Sanction	Displacement
	Suicidal Terrorism	Indoctrination
Political Science	Collective Rational Strategic Choice	Strategic choice
	"Sacred" Terror	Strategic logic
Cultural Anthropology	Kin Altruism	Religious communion

be viewed as *provisional* because at this point, we do not know if the assumption of rationality applies equally to the other concepts, their insights, or their theories. This will not become clear until STEP 8 is completed (see Chapters 11 and 12).

A third problematic situation involves real disagreements that arise *when different concepts are used that cannot be overcome by clarifying or modifying their meaning.* This is the case between the concepts of "displacement" and "religious communion," which also appear in Table 10.3. The former concerns an individual's psychological state of mind in a given context, while the latter concerns a communal commitment to a faith tradition. In this case, differences in meaning cannot be overcome by clarifying or modifying definitions. Some other technique will have to be used to create common ground between their insights and thus the theories that produced them.

A fourth problematic situation involves only a few authors using concepts. For concepts to be a credible source of conflict between the relevant insights into the same problem, all of the authors must use one or more concepts that pertain to the problem. Otherwise, the interdisciplinarian will have to work with assumptions underlying each of the insights.

Assumptions

Interdisciplinarians work with assumptions when they find that concepts are not the fundamental source of conflict between all of the relevant insights. Chapter 4 establishes that every discipline makes a number of assumptions. These assumptions include what constitutes truth, what counts as evidence or proof, how problems should be formulated, and what the general ideals of the discipline are (Wolfe & Haynes, 2003, p. 154). Disciplinary scholars seldom feel the need to make these assumptions explicit in their writings, much less justify them. Undergraduates majoring in a discipline absorb these assumptions by taking advanced coursework in the discipline and becoming enculturated in the discipline. However, interdisciplinary students who have not had much coursework in a particular discipline need to ferret out these assumptions in order to achieve integration.

According to Newell (2007a), assumptions can be of three kinds:

a. Ontological (regarding the nature of reality): For example, each social science makes an ontological assumption about the rationality of individuals: whether they are rational, irrational, or rationalizing. If, for example, the student is trying to develop an interdisciplinary understanding of those persons carrying out suicide bombings, the student will likely encounter a variety of scholarly assumptions about the bomber's state of mind, ranging from rational to irrational to rationalizing. Other ontological assumptions by the social sciences concern whether persons who act autonomously or as a product of their culture are self-centered or other-regarding.

b. Epistemological (regarding the nature of knowledge of that "reality"): Epistemology basically answers the question, "How do and can we know what we know?" In essence, epistemology is a way of testing any belief or assertion of truth. Each discipline tests for truth in different ways. In biology, for example, the assumption that all plants need sunlight may seem obvious. However, in order to establish that this is true, the biologist must conduct experiments to demonstrate consistently and conclusively that plants die without sunlight. Experiments often lead to new knowledge, for instance, that forms of artificial light can cause plants to grow or that some plants are not very dependent on light. In the humanities, by contrast, epistemology becomes much more subjective. A poem may acquire validity not because it is liked by a large number of people, but because its meaning has stood the test of time.

c. Value-laden: The social sciences make value assumptions about diversity, justice, and truth; the humanities often deal quite directly with questions of value; and the natural sciences make value judgments about which problems are worth studying and what knowledge is worth developing (p. 256).

Each discipline brings its time-tested assumptions to bear as it focuses on the part of the problem in which it specializes. While the insights into a problem generated by each discipline necessarily share some assumptions (otherwise the discipline would dissolve), they may differ on other assumptions. Where these differences are relevant to the problem at hand, they will lead to controversy within the discipline (Newell, 2007a, pp. 256–257). Assumptions may vary somewhat within a discipline, but they vary much more from discipline to discipline.

Examining an object like Bal's (1999) graffito that spans many disciplines illustrates how ontological, epistemological, and value-laden assumptions can easily conflict. Concerning ontological assumptions, just as disciplinary communities differ over the state of mind of a person who carries out a suicide bombing, so, too, will scholars differ over the state of mind of the person who wrote the graffito. This person's state of mind, like that of the suicide bomber, can range from rational to irrational to rationalizing. Another ontological assumption that may be disputed by scholars from the relevant disciplines concerns whether the writer was acting autonomously or merely as a product of the culture.

The epistemological assumptions brought to bear by the relevant disciplines are no less problematic. As applied to the graffito, one cannot establish that it has a singular meaning by conducting an experiment. Epistemology is much more subjective in the humanities than in the social sciences or the natural sciences.

Making value-laden assumptions about the graffito is also problematic because these, too, are likely to generate conflict. As Bal (1999) says, "an exposition is always also an argument" (p. 5). What, then, are researchers to do in such circumstances? They should recognize that conflicting assumptions are a natural feature of the interdisciplinary landscape.

Students at all levels should be mindful of disciplinary assumptions in order to more easily identify conflicts between disciplinary insights. One effective way to probe the assumptions of a discipline is to step back from the disciplinary insights into the problem and ask the simple question, "How does this writer see the problem?" By stepping back from the insights of economists on occupational sex discrimination (OSD) as shown later in Tables 10.8, 10.11, and 10.13, for example, one can see clearly that economics views OSD as an economic problem and the result of rational decision making.

An author's assumptions are typically implicit, and identifying them requires close reading of the text. Table 10.3 also shows how it is possible for insights produced by a discipline (in this case, by cognitive psychology and political science) to share the discipline's basic assumptions even though the insights conflict somewhat.

Consulting Tables 4.10, 4.11, and 4.12 on disciplinary assumptions is useful for probing the assumptions of insights. Also, juxtaposing these differences will prove invaluable for performing STEP 8 (the subject of Chapters 11 and 12).

Organizing Disciplinary Insights

As information is gathered on each disciplinary insight, the challenge is to organize this information in some systematic way so that it can be easily retrieved when performing subsequent STEPS of the IRP. This information should include its perspective (in a general sense), its key concepts, *and its assumptions*. For students at all levels, gathering this information is necessary whether one is dealing with insights from the same discipline or insights from different disciplines. Table 10.2 is an example of a taxonomy of relevant insights organized by discipline. Their close juxtaposition makes it easier to identify points of conflict that might otherwise escape one's notice.

Theories as Sources of Insights and Conflict Between Insights _____

Theories are the third possible source of conflict between insights. This discussion on theories focuses on the important role that theories play in the integrative phase of the IRP. This section discusses (1) theories as sources of insights, concepts, and assumptions; (2) theories from *the same discipline* as sources of conflict between insights; (3) theories from *the same discipline* as sources of conflict between assumptions; and (4) theories from *different disciplines* as sources of conflict between insights.

Theories as Sources of Insights, Concepts, and Assumptions

Depending on the problem, researchers are likely to encounter multiple theories from one or several disciplines that provide causal explanations of some aspect of the problem. As always, researchers are well advised to first map the problem and conduct a full-scale literature search so as not to overlook any relevant theory. Omitting one or more relevant theories will likely skew the more comprehensive understanding produced and call into question its validity. Theories are themselves sources of insights, concepts, and assumptions about the problem.

Theories as Sources of Insights

Theories, as stated earlier, produce insights into particular problems. Picking up the threaded example of suicide terrorism, Table 10.4 shows the relevant theories and their insights into the causes of suicide terrorism.

   These theories and their insights clearly conflict, but it is difficult to locate the *sources of conflict* without probing more deeply into each theory. This involves focusing on each theory's concepts and assumptions.

Table 10.4   Theories and Their Insights Into the Causes of Suicide Terrorism

Theory	Insight of Theory
Terrorist Psycho-logic	Individuals are driven to commit acts of violence that "they are psychologically compelled to commit" (Post, 1998, p. 25).
Self-Sanction	"Self-sanctions can be disengaged by cognitively restructuring the moral value of killing so that the killing can be done free of self-censuring restraints" (Bandura, 1998, p. 164).
Suicidal Terrorism	"In most cases, the perpetrators sacrificed themselves in the name of a nationalistic rather than a religious idea" (Merari, 1998, p. 205).
Collective Rational Strategic Choice	"Terrorism can be understood as an expression of political strategy" (Crenshaw, 1998, p. 7).
"Sacred" Terror	"The principal difference in means between sacred terror and secular terror derives from the special justifications and precedents each uses" (Rapoport, 1998, p. 107).
Kin Altruism	Suicide terrorists act out of a universal heartfelt human sentiment of self-sacrifice for the welfare of the group/culture (Atran, 2003b, p. 2).

Theories as Sources of Concepts

Theories are sources of concepts. For example, Table 10.3 shows that *special logic* is a technical term that describes the basic idea of Terrorist Psycho-logic Theory. Therefore, understanding this concept is essential to developing a full understanding of the theory.

Theories as Sources of Assumptions

Theories are also sources of assumptions about the problem. These focused assumptions typically reflect the more general assumption(s) of the discipline that produced the theory. Picking up the threaded example of suicide terrorism, the right-hand column in Table 10.5 shows how each theory's

Table 10.5	The Assumptions of the Relevant Theories on the Causes of Suicide Terrorism Reflecting the More General Assumption of the Discipline That Produced It

Discipline or Subdiscipline	General Assumption of Discipline or Subdiscipline	Theory	Assumption(s) of Theory
Cognitive Psychology	Group behavior can be reduced to individuals and their interactions, and humans organize their mental life through psychological constructs (Leary, 2004, p. 9).	*Terrorist Psycho-logic*	Humans organize their mental life through psychological constructs.
		Self-Sanction	
		Martyrdom	
Political Science	Individual and group behavior is motivated primarily by a desire for or the exercise of power. "[H]uman beings, while they are undeniably subject to certain causal forces, are . . . in part intentional actors, capable of cognition and acting on the basis of it" (Goodin & Klingerman, 1996, pp. 9–10).	*Collective Rational Strategic Choice*	"Terrorism may follow logical processes that can be discovered and explained" (Crenshaw, 1998, p. 7).
		Identity[a]	There is no separation between religion and politics. Religious identity explains "political" behavior.
Cultural Anthropology	Cultural relativism (the notion that people's ideas about what is good and beautiful are shaped by their culture) assumes that systems of knowledge possessed by different cultures are "incommensurable" (i.e., not comparable and not transferable) (Whitaker, 1996, p. 480).	*Fictive kin*	Personal relationships shape people's ideas about what is good.

SOURCE: Repko (2012).

a. Identity theory is already an interdisciplinary theory, though imperfectly so.

assumption tends to reflect the more general assumption of the discipline that produced the theory.

Organizing Information About Theories

Once again, the problem arises as to how to systematically organize the rapidly accumulating data. The approach used here is the same as the approach used earlier for insights: develop a taxonomy of the most relevant theories whether they are from a single discipline or from several disciplines. This taxonomy should include each theory's name, its insight into the problem stated in the author's own words (so as to avoid skewing its meaning), its key concepts that express the theory, and its core assumption(s) about the problem. Experience has shown that condensing and juxtaposing this critical information in a taxonomy similar to Table 10.5 greatly facilitates drawing on this information when performing subsequent STEPS of the IRP. As a rule of thumb, it is better to err on the side of including too much information than too little for the simple reason that it is impossible to know with certainty what information will ultimately prove critical to creating common ground and performing integration. Basic information about the theories and insights relevant to the problem of suicide terrorism is shown in Table 10.6.

It is worth pointing out that Table 10.6 consists largely of quotations rather than paraphrases of each writer's words. This is good practice for undergraduates who may be tempted to summarize the author's phrasing and thereby overlook important nuance. Paraphrasing a carefully crafted statement runs the risk of unintentionally distorting the author's meaning or skewing definitions of complex and unfamiliar concepts. Also, the systematic juxtaposing of each theory's defining elements in a taxonomy makes it easier to detect sources of conflict as well as latent commonalities. Locating these elements in each book and article requires skill in the technique of **close reading**. This is a fundamental method of modern criticism that calls for the careful analysis of a text and close attention to individual words, syntax, and the order in which sentences and ideas unfold (Baldick, 2004). Given the necessity of careful textual analysis across disciplinary literatures in interdisciplinary work, close reading is an indispensable skill that undergraduates must develop. They should approach each insight with an agenda of particular things to look for and then organize this information in a systematic way that is easily retrievable for future use.

Readers may not use every feature of the IRP presented in this book on any given research project. For example, Watson (1968), Fischer (1988), and Bal (1999) use most of these features, but not all of them. Since there are no conflicting theories *within* the disciplines used in Watson's natural science example, we revisit the student paper (marked by an asterisk) *Freshwater Scarcity in Texas*. To broaden coverage of approaches used in the humanities, we look at the critique on the British Romantic poem *Rime of the Ancient Mariner* by Samuel Taylor Coleridge.

Table 10.6 Taxonomy of Relevant Theories on the Problem of Suicide Terrorism

Theory	Insight of Theory Stated in General Terms	Insight Into the Problem	Concept	Assumption
Terrorist Psycho-logic	"Political violence is not instrumental but an end in itself. The cause becomes the rationale for acts of terrorism the terrorist is compelled to commit" (Post, 1998, p. 35).	"Individuals are drawn to the path of terrorism to commit acts of violence . . . as a consequence of psychological forces, and that their special psycho-logic is constructed to rationalize acts they are psychologically compelled to commit" (Post, 1998, p. 25).	Special logic (Post, 1998, p. 25)	Humans organize their mental life through psychological constructs.
Self-Sanction	"Self-sanctions can be disengaged by reconstruing conduct as serving moral purposes, by obscuring personal agency in detrimental activities, by disregarding or misrepresenting the injurious consequences of one's victims, or by blaming and dehumanizing the victims" (Bandura, 1998, p. 161).	"Self-sanctions can be disengaged by cognitively restructuring the moral value of killing so that the killing can be done free of self-censuring restraints" (Bandura, 1998, p. 164).	Moral cognitive restructuring (Bandura, 1998, p. 164)	
Suicidal Terrorism	"Terrorist suicide . . . is basically an individual rather than a group phenomenon; it is done by people who wish to die for	"Perpetrators of suicidal attacks . . . are not the exclusive domain of religious fanaticism in general. . . . In most cases, the	Indoctrination (Merari, 1998, p. 199)	

Theory	Insight of Theory Stated in General Terms	Insight Into the Problem	Concept	Assumption
	personal reasons" (Merari, 1998, p. 206). "Personality factors seem to play a critical role in suicidal terrorism. . . . It seems that a broken family background is an important constituent" (p. 207).	perpetrators sacrificed themselves in the name of a nationalistic rather than a religious idea" (Merari, 1998, p. 205).		
Collective Rational Strategic Choice	"This approach permits the construction of a standard that can measure degrees of rationality, the degree to which strategic reasoning is modified by psychology and other constraints, and explain how reality is interpreted" (Crenshaw, 1998, pp. 9–10).	"Terrorism can be understood as an expression of political strategy" (Crenshaw, 1998, p. 7).	Collective rationality (Crenshaw, 1998, pp. 8–9)	"Terrorism may follow logical processes that can be discovered and explained" (Crenshaw, 1998, p. 7).
"Sacred" Terror	"Holy" or "sacred" terror is "terrorist activities to support religious purposes or terror justified in theological terms" (Rapoport, 1998, p. 103).	"Holy" or "sacred" terrorists justify the means they use on the basis of sacred writings and/or on certain theological interpretations of these writings (Rapoport, 1998, pp. 107–130).	"Holy" or "sacred" terror (Rapoport, 1998, p. 103)	
Kin Altruism	"A sense of religious sharing and empowerment motivates suicide terrorists" (Atran, 2003b, p. 6).	Suicide terrorists act out of a universal heartfelt human sentiment of self-sacrifice for the welfare of the group/culture (Atran, 2003b, p. 2).	"Religious communion" (Atran, 2003b, p. 6)	People's ideas about what is good and beautiful are shaped by their culture (Whitaker, 1996, p. 480).[a]

a. This expression of cultural relativism does not equate to ethical relativism (that all ethical systems are equally good because they are all cultural products), as Merrilee Salmon (1997) makes clear.

Theories From the Same Discipline
Can Be Sources of Conflict Between Insights

Theories from the *same* discipline are likely to have far less conflict because they typically reflect the discipline's perspective (in a general sense), its epistemology, and other defining elements. Nevertheless, theories and their insights from the same discipline typically conflict in important ways because each discipline differs considerably in its internal coherence, varying from tight unification as in economics to fragmentation among a host of theoretical approaches as in English literature. The following examples of interdisciplinary work from the natural sciences, the social sciences, and the humanities each show theories as sources of conflict into a particular problem.

From the Natural Sciences: Smolinski* (2005), Freshwater Scarcity in Texas   Table 10.7 illustrates the conflicting insights from three geological theories relevant to the problem of water scarcity in *global* terms. These theories are then applied to the *local* problem of freshwater scarcity in Texas. In the absence of prior discussion of these theoretical approaches, the insight of each theory is conveyed in general terms before being applied to the problem.

Table 10.7   Conflicting Theories and Their Insights into the Problem of Freshwater Scarcity in Texas From the Same Discipline

Discipline	Theory	Insight of the Theory Stated in General Terms	Insight of the Theory Applied to the Problem
Earth Science	Global Warming	The production of greenhouse gases has caused, and will continue to cause, the planet's temperature to rise, and this negatively impacts freshwater availability.	Global warming will significantly increase the rates of evaporation, exacerbating an already critical freshwater shortage in Texas.
	Overexploitation	Too much water is taken from aquifers (water-bearing rock formations), and this practice is seriously degrading the quality of the remaining volume of water in these aquifers.	Increased rates of water removal from the Ogallala Aquifer under Texas coupled with decreased rates of recharge have led to an overall drawdown of the water table (the uppermost limit of the water contained in the Ogallala Aquifer).
	Infiltration	There is more than enough water in the nation's groundwater systems to satisfy demand, but saline water is increasingly contaminating it.	In Texas, saline and brackish water is infiltrating and contaminating the remaining groundwater.

From the Social Sciences: Fischer (1988), "On the Need for Integrating Occupational Sex Discrimination Theory on the Basis of Causal Variables" Table 10.8 identifies four major economics theories that provide insights into the causes of occupational sex discrimination (OSD).

For each theory, conflict between the insights is noticeably sharpened when it is applied to the particular problem of OSD.

From the Humanities: Fry (1999), Samuel Taylor Coleridge: The Rime of the Ancient Mariner Coleridge's *Rime* illustrates the importance of identifying

Table 10.8 Conflicting Theories and Their Insights into the Problem of OSD From the Same Discipline

Discipline	Theory	Insight of the Theory Stated in General Terms	Insight of the Theory as Applied to the Problem
Economics	Monopsony Exploitation	"The profit-maximizing monopsonist . . . hires labor up to the point of where marginal labor costs equal marginal revenue (or marginal value) . . . [and thus] pays workers a wage less than their value contribution to the firm" (p. 27).	Focuses on the demand side of OSD, explaining it as "the result of collusive behavior of male employers in discriminating against females" (p. 31)
	Human Capital	"Each worker [human capital] is viewed as a combination of native abilities and raw labor power plus specific skills acquired through education and training" (p. 28).	"Focuses on the supply side of OSD, characteristics of females—particularly their education and training levels" (p. 31)
	Statistical Discrimination	"Statistical discrimination exists when an individual is evaluated on the basis of the average characteristics of the group to which he or she belongs, rather than on his or her personal characteristics" (p. 29).	"Emphasizes group (rather than individual) characteristics of female job applicants. It is female group characteristics that make women a poor choice for risk adverse employers" (p. 31)
	Prejudice	This model is "based on the notion that some employers indulge their own sexual prejudices (or the prejudices, real or perceived, of their employees and customers) in making hiring and other personnel decisions" (p. 30).	Says that "the male employer doesn't hire women because of his own tastes or preferences for female discrimination" (p. 31)

SOURCE: Fischer (1988).

conflicting theories and their insights into a text or work of art. In literature, critical essays on a text typically begin work using different theoretical approaches (p. v). These are of great interest to the interdisciplinarian because they are informed by a set of coherent assumptions that can be articulated and also modified and extended through comparison as the process of integration proceeds. Table 10.9 shows five theoretical approaches and their insights into the text.

Examining a text from the stance of two or more theoretical approaches, while valuable, is not, by itself, interdisciplinary. Nor is juxtaposing them and leaving it up to the reader to somehow perform the integration and create

Table 10.9	Conflicting Theoretical Approaches and Their Insights Into the Meaning of *The Rime of the Ancient Mariner* From the Same Discipline

Discipline	Theoretical Approach	Insight of the Approach	Insight of the Approach as Applied to the Text
Literature	Reader-Response	The meaning of a work is not inherent in its internal form but rather is cooperatively produced by the readers (what they bring to the text) and the text (Murfin, 1999c, p. 169, 1999e, p. 108).	The major issue of the poem is not its implied moral values but the process of arriving at moral values, and that process is about reading (Ferguson, 1999, p. 123; Murfin, 1999e, p. 108).
	Marxist Criticism	Literature is a material medium that reflects prevailing social and cultural ideologies and also "transcends or sees through the limitations of ideology" (Murfin, 1999b, p. 144).	*The Rime* is susceptible to an historical approach that reveals an early instance of ecological concern, an emerging interest in hypnotism, and that raises Protestant issues regarding free will, choice, election, and damnation, as well as broader, philosophical questions regarding "epistemological consensus" (Simpson, 1999, pp. 152, 158).
	The New Historicism	"Literature is not a sphere apart or distinct from the history that is relevant to it" (Murfin, 1999c, p. 171).	Reconstructing the historical context of a literary text like *The Rime* is, by itself, treacherously difficult to achieve, and all the more so because we have been conditioned by our own place and time (Murfin, 1999c, p. 171).

Discipline	Theoretical Approach	Insight of the Approach	Insight of the Approach as Applied to the Text
	Psychoanalytic Criticism	"A work of literature is a fantasy or a dream, and psychoanalysis can help explain the mind that produced it" (Murfin, 1999d, p. 225).	*The Rime* is a constructed world unified by language and symbols and is, in fact, "a reaction against the horrifying loss of a boundariless, pre-oedipal world in which the infant, mother and natural world are one" (Murfin, 1999d, p. 232).
	Deconstruction	"A text is not a unique, hermetically sealed space but is perpetually open to being seen in the light of new contexts and has the potential to be different each time it is read" (Murfin, 1999a, p. 268).	*The Rime* should be seen in terms of its "linguistic strangeness, as a 'series of dislocations—translations, displacements, metonymies'— that 'dares its audience to make sense of it'" (Eilenberg, 1999, p. 283).

new meaning. What is needed for the analysis of the text to be fully interdisciplinary is the creation of a theory, concept, or assumption that can be modified and used as the basis for integrating these conflicting interpretations. How to do this is the subject of Chapters 12 and 13.

Theories From the Same Discipline
Can Be Sources of Conflicting Assumptions

Theories from the *same* discipline are likely to have far less conflict because they typically share the discipline's basic assumptions. Each theory is undergirded by one or more assumptions that typically reflect its disciplinary origin. Admittedly, these assumptions are more difficult for those new to a particular discipline to discover because detecting them requires a greater knowledge of the discipline and the skill of close reading. Though relatively easy for graduate students and mature scholars, the task is not impossible for undergraduates and may simply involve using the tables of disciplinary assumptions in Chapter 4 and asking a disciplinary expert for help.

From the Natural Sciences: Smolinski* (2005), Freshwater Scarcity in Texas   Even though theories from the same discipline tend to share its underlying assumptions, Table 10.10 illustrates that when these theories focus on a particular problem, their assumptions about the problem can still differ significantly. Such is the case with the theories explaining the reasons for freshwater scarcity in Texas. This situation makes more challenging the student's task of creating common ground between them.

| Table 10.10 | Conflicting Theories and Their Assumptions and Insights Into the Problem of Freshwater Scarcity in Texas From the Same Discipline |

Discipline	Theory	Assumption of the Theory	Insight of the Theory as Applied to the Problem
Earth Science	Global Warming	Global warming is the result of rapid agricultural and technological advances.	Global warming will significantly increase the rates of evaporation, exacerbating an already critical freshwater shortage.
	Overexploitation	Strict conservation legislation aimed primarily at agriculture will solve the problem.	Increased rates of water removal from the Ogallala Aquifer coupled with decreased rates of recharge have led to an overall drawdown of the water table (the uppermost limit of the water contained in the Ogallala Aquifer).
	Infiltration	Freshwater scarcity already exists, as a result of either global warming or overexploitation.	In Texas, saline and brackish water is infiltrating and contaminating the remaining groundwater.

From the Social Sciences: Fischer (1988), "On the Need for Integrating Occupational Sex Discrimination Theory on the Basis of Causal Variables"   Fischer's study is an example of how a professional interdisciplinarian may see the need to make explicit the conflicting assumptions of theories advanced by a particular discipline, in this case, economics. After identifying the four major orthodox or mainstream economic theories that address OSD, Fischer states the assumptions of each one. He says, for instance, that Monopsony Exploitation Theory "*assumes* that men, in their role as husbands, employers, workers, consumers, and legislators, have power over female occupational choices [italics added]" (p. 26). These economic theories, their assumptions, and corresponding insights into the problem of OSD are summarized in Table 10.11.

Since these theories are from the same discipline, they share the discipline's overall perspective that the world is a rational marketplace and its fundamental assumption that humans are motivated by rational self-interest (see Table 4.4). However, when these theories address the causes of OSD, it is clear that they conflict more than they overlap, even though they are from the same discipline. It is appropriate for researchers to explain, as Fischer does, why there is need to go beyond these particular theories: Each of them, he says, offers an "incomplete explanation of the causes of OSD,"

Table 10.11	Conflicting Theories and Their Assumptions and Insights Into the Problem of OSD From the Same Discipline

Discipline	Theory	Assumption of the Theory	Insight of the Theory as Applied to the Problem
Economics	Monopsony Exploitation	OSD is an economic demand problem.	Focuses on the demand side of OSD, explaining it as "the result of collusive behavior of male employers in discriminating against females" (p. 31)
	Human Capital	"OSD is an economic supply problem: Women make rational choices regarding home responsibilities and career commitment" (p. 29).	"Focuses on the supply side of OSD, characteristics of females—particularly their education and training levels" (p. 31)
	Statistical Discrimination	OSD is an economic demand problem: "Discrimination exists because . . . its benefits to the employer overweigh its costs" (p. 30).	"Emphasizes group (rather than individual) characteristics of female job applicants. It is female group characteristics that make women a poor choice for risk adverse employers" (p. 31).
	Prejudice	OSD is an economic demand problem: "Sex role socialization helps form [employer] tastes . . . For example, . . . employers tend to believe that women can not and should not do hard physical work . . . [and] 'can't handle responsibility'" (p. 31).	Says that "the male employer doesn't hire women because of his own tastes or preferences for female discrimination" (p. 31)

SOURCE: Fischer (1988).

requiring that the analysis be broadened to include the "relevant work in related disciplines if an interdisciplinary understanding is to be achieved" (Fischer, 1988, p. 31).

From the Humanities: Fry (1999), Samuel Taylor Coleridge: The Rime of the Ancient Mariner The theories of reader-response, Marxist criticism, New Historicism, psychoanalytic criticism, and deconstruction shown in Table 10.12 are prevalent in literary criticism (Fry, 1999, pp. v–vi). They are not monolithic schools of thought but, rather, umbrella terms, each of which covers

| Table 10.12 | Conflicting Theories and Their Assumptions and Insights into the Meaning of *The Rime of the Ancient Mariner* Within the Same Discipline |

Discipline	Theory	Assumption of the Theory	Insight of the Theory as Applied to the Text
Literature	Reader-Response	*The Rime* is about its author and the deluded reader.	The major issue of *The Rime* is not its implied moral values but the process of arriving at moral values and that process is about reading (Ferguson 1999, p. 123; Murfin, 1999e, p. 108).
	Marxist Criticism	"*The Rime* is driven by an 'agenda' of remystifying the world and thus undermines the reader's confidence in rationality and rationalist theories" (Simpson, 1999, p. 158).	*The Rime* is susceptible to a historical approach that reveals an early instance of ecological concern, an emerging interest in hypnotism, and that raises Protestant issues regarding free will, choice, election, and damnation, as well as broader, philosophical questions regarding "epistemological consensus" (Simpson, 1999, pp. 152, 158).
	The New Historicism	"*The Rime* reflects and challenges any number of ideologies or value systems, ranging from Christianity to the radical political standpoints on the French Revolution to the slave trade" (Modiano, 1999, p. 215).	"Reconstructing the historical context of a literary text like *The Rime* is, by itself, treacherously difficult to achieve, and all the more so because we have been conditioned by our own place and time" (Murfin, 1999c, p. 171).
	Psychoanalytic Criticism	"The 'horror' at the heart of *The Rime* is a symptom of the not yet self's casting off the maternal and semiotic (loosely associational) in favor of the paternal and symbolic" (Murfin, 1999d, p. 231).	*The Rime* is a constructed world unified by language and symbols and is, in fact, "a reaction against the horrifying loss of a boundariless, pre-oedipal world in which the infant, mother and natural world are one" (Murfin, 1999d, p. 232).
	Deconstruction	"All texts, including *The Rime,* are ultimately unreadable (if reading means reducing a text to a single homogenous meaning)" (Murfin, 1999a, p. 269).	*The Rime* should be seen in terms of its "linguistic strangeness, as a 'series of dislocations—translations, displacements, metonymies'—that 'dares its audience to make sense of it'" (Eilenberg, 1999, p. 283).

a variety of approaches to textual criticism. The insights associated with each theory, therefore, are not definitive but expressive of each critic's way of applying the theory to the text.

Theories From Different Disciplines Can Be Sources of Conflict Between Insights

Once the theories from the same discipline are identified and their sources of conflict are located, the interdisciplinarian must continue the process of locating sources of conflict between those theories from the other relevant disciplines. When moving from one discipline to another, one must be sure that authors are talking about the same thing. Locating the sources of conflict between theories from all relevant disciplines is critical to performing STEP 8 (see Chapters 11 and 12). The following examples of threaded work illustrate how theories from different disciplines are sources of conflict between their insights into a particular problem.

From the Natural Sciences: Watson (1968), The Double Helix: A Personal Account of the Discovery of the Structure of DNA   Theories from different disciplines were prominent in the story of the discovery of the structure of DNA. Watson's account of the process by which he and Crick discovered the structure of DNA is useful to interdisciplinarians because it illustrates the value of consulting all relevant theories, including those that conflict significantly. The "suspicion" (i.e., theory) among geneticists, Watson recalls, was that viruses are a form of "naked gene." If true, the best way to find out what a gene is and how it duplicates was to study the properties of viruses, beginning with the phages, or simplest viruses. So, Watson joined the growing number of scientists who studied phages in hopes that they would eventually learn how the genes control cellular heredity (pp. 22–23). Soon, however, he began to realize "deep down" that "it is impossible to describe the behavior of something when you don't know what it is" (p. 23). This realization led him to consider Wilkins's method of X-ray crystallography (physics) that Watson hoped would provide a picture that showed DNA having a crystalline structure. He realized that no single discipline or theory would, by itself, solve the mystery of the structure of the DNA molecule, but that the solution would involve integrating theories and research techniques from chemistry, genetics (biology), and physics. Interdisciplinarians are interested in theories because they generate insights into problems.

From the Social Sciences, Fischer (1988), "On the Need for Integrating Occupational Sex Discrimination Theory on the Basis of Causal Variables" Table 10.13 is an extension of Table 10.8 and includes theories from the other relevant disciplines on the causes of OSD. The conflict between economic theories and theories from the other relevant disciplines becomes stark when they are juxtaposed in this manner.

Table 10.13	Conflicting Theory-Based Insights and Their Corresponding Assumptions on the Problem of OSD Within and Between Disciplines		

Discipline or School of Thought	Theory	Assumption	Insight of the Theory as Applied to the Problem
Economics	Monopsony Exploitation	OSD is an economic (supply and demand) problem.	Focuses on the demand side of OSD, explaining it as "the result of collusive behavior of male employers in discriminating against females" (p. 31)
	Human Capital		"Focuses on the supply side of OSD, characteristics of females—particularly their education and training levels" (p. 31)
	Statistical Discrimination		"Emphasizes group (rather than individual) characteristics of female job applicants. It is female group characteristics that make women a poor choice for risk adverse employers" (p. 31)
	Prejudice		Says that "the male employer doesn't hire women because of his own tastes or preferences for female discrimination" (p. 31)
History	Institutional Development	OSD is a historical problem.	"Sex segregation at entry to firms is perpetuated over time, and done so without the need for further overt sex discrimination" (p. 34).
Sociology	Sex Role Orientation	OSD is a social problem.	"Female socialization encourages the acceptance of responsibility for domestic work, and a nurturant and helping orientation for child care. . . . Female socialization, on the other hand, discourages authoritativeness or aggressiveness, physical prowess, and quantitative or mechanical aptitude. It is argued that sex role orientation produces different traits in females, and employers use their knowledge of these traits to decide what jobs should be 'female jobs'" (p. 34).

Discipline or School of Thought	Theory	Assumption	Insight of the Theory as Applied to the Problem
Psychology	Male Dominance	OSD is a male problem.	"Men have socio-economic incentives to continue monopolizing their privileged status in the labor market, and that they can best do this by maintaining the traditional male-female division of household production" (p. 36).
Marxism	Class Conflict	OSD is an ideological problem.	"Some workers—women in particular—are channeled into less desirable jobs and segregated from other workers to keep workers in general from developing a class consciousness and acting collusively to overthrow capitalism. Here, OSD is seen as a necessary act in preserving the institutions of capitalism" (p. 32).

SOURCE: Fischer (1988).

Insights of theories from different disciplines, but focused on the same problem, are likely to conflict even more because the basic assumptions of each discipline conflict. Having identified all relevant theory-based insights into the problem of OSD, Fischer is ready to proceed with STEP 8b, modifying theories, the subject of Chapter 12.

From the Humanities: Bal (1999), "Introduction," The Practice of Cultural Analysis: Exposing Interdisciplinary Interpretation At several points, Bal's discussion of the graffito reveals conflicts between the relevant theoretical approaches used by different disciplines. For one thing, by stressing the methodological explicitness of cultural analysis, Bal is implicitly challenging postmodernism, with its disdain for explicitness and method (p. 4). Also, cultural analysis's emphasis on self-reflexivity places this theory at odds with the modernist emphasis on the object and/or text as opposed to the viewer and/or reader (p. 6). For Bal, what counts as evidence is the discovery in the text of layered meanings using the technique of close reading. One example of layered meaning is the word "Note" at the beginning of the graffito, which, on one level, is a direct address to the reader in the present, but, on another level, is an address to a past someone (pp. 7–8).

Those working with a complex theory such as cultural analysis, or even a series of theories, must be sufficiently grounded in the theory to identify the evidence that the writer advances to support it. The sciences and the harder social sciences employ the methods of experiments, models, and statistics, all of which constitute convincing and seemingly incontrovertible evidence. For Watson (1968), experiments and models provided the convincing evidence that the DNA molecule has an α-helical structure. What one disciplinary scholar counts as evidence may be discounted or considered inappropriate by a scholar from another discipline. Therefore, interdisciplinarians should be alert to possible conflicts arising over the different kinds of evidence the various authors use.

A Note to Readers About Communicating Conflicts and Their Sources

Once interdisciplinarians have identified all of the relevant insights and theories and have located their sources of conflict, they should communicate this information to the appropriate audience. For undergraduates, a paragraph that concisely summarizes the results of STEP 7 is often sufficient. For graduate students, mature researchers, and members of research teams, a more detailed accounting may be called for. There are multiple ways to do this, as evidenced in the touchstone examples by Watson (1968), Fischer (1988), and Bal (1999). These examples offer three different types of interdisciplinary literature, each of which is aimed at a somewhat different audience.

From the Natural Sciences: Watson (1968), The Double Helix: A Personal Account of the Discovery of the Structure of DNA   Watson's book-length recollection informs the general reader of how he and Crick made one of history's greatest scientific discoveries. Ever the scientist, Watson is careful to identify each theory as he and Crick encountered it, explain each one in language that the general reader can easily understand, and show how it conflicted with other major theories about the DNA molecule. Two of these conflicting theories are Avery's gene theory and Bragg's theory of X-ray diffraction. Concerning Avery's theory and the role that scientists supposed DNA played in passing on hereditary traits from one cell to another, Watson writes,

> Given the fact that DNA was known to occur in the chromosomes of all cells, Avery's experiments strongly suggested that future experiments would show that all genes were composed of DNA. If true, this meant to Francis [Crick] that proteins would not be the Rosetta Stone for unraveling the true secret of life. Instead DNA would have to provide the key to enable us to find out how the genes determined,

among other characteristics, the color of our hair, our eyes, most likely our comparative intelligence, and maybe even our potential to amuse others. (p. 14)

Watson introduces Bragg's theory of X-ray diffraction with equal clarity:

For almost forty years Bragg, a Nobel Prize winner and one of the founders of crystallography, had been watching X-ray diffraction methods solve structures of ever-increasing difficulty. The more complex the molecule, the happier Bragg became when a new method allowed its elucidation. Thus in the immediate postwar years he was especially keen about the possibility of solving the structures of proteins, the most complicated of all molecules. (p. 8)

Later, the reader learns that it is not the structure of proteins that holds the key to unlocking the mystery of the complex helical structure of DNA, but X-ray crystallography.

From the Social Sciences: Fischer (1988), "On the Need for Integrating Occupational Sex Discrimination Theory on the Basis of Causal Variables"
Fischer's peer-reviewed journal article on OSD illustrates the interdisciplinary research process to a professional audience. Theory is central to his purpose and his discussion of it dominates the essay, but in clearly defined ways. First, Fischer is concerned to describe concisely each theory and its underlying assumption. Consider, for example, his description of human capital theory:

The human capital theory of OSD focuses on the relatively high mobility and intermittent nature of employment women tend to experience.... Because of domestic responsibilities, women tend to be in and out of the labor force more frequently than men and thus acquire less on-the-job training (OJT) than their male counterparts. This, it is argued, adversely affects female occupational opportunities in two ways. First, fewer women than men acquire sufficient human capital for jobs which require substantial previous experience. Second, while women are out of the labor force, their job skills depreciate. It is thus rational for women who anticipate intermittent employment to choose occupations which require relatively little time to acquire the necessary job skills and which require job skills that do not depreciate rapidly from nonuse. The combined impact of reduced job experience and the incentive to minimize depreciation of job skills results in women being concentrated in service, sales, clerical and labor jobs and underrepresented among operators, managers, and professionals. (pp. 28–29)

Second, Fischer contrasts each theory with the theory that precedes it. Contrasting differences precedes comparing differences. In what follows,

Fischer contrasts monopsony theory (the first economic theory) with human capital theory (the second economic theory):

> While monopsony theory focuses on the demand side of OSD, human capital theory offers a supply-side explanation of OSD. Each worker is viewed as a combination of native abilities and raw labor power plus specific skills acquired through education and training. The latter is commonly referred to as human capital. (p. 28)

Third, Fischer applies the theory specifically and clearly to the problem of OSD. He concludes that "In summary, the human capital theory of OSD holds that economic incentives lead women to segregate themselves into female occupations. It is economically rational for women to continue to pursue traditional female jobs" (p. 29).

Finally, Fischer briefly critiques each theory. Concerning human capital theory as applied to the problem of OSD, he says that "it is bound to be controversial since it implies that OSD is largely the result of choices that women make regarding home responsibilities and career commitment; that is, it tends to 'blame the victim' for OSD" (p. 29).

From the Humanities: Bal (1999), "Introduction," The Practice of Cultural Analysis: Exposing Interdisciplinary Interpretation   Bal's interdisciplinary essay differs from Watson's and Fischer's work in two ways. First, unlike Watson and Fischer, who assume that the reader has little prior knowledge of the topic or theories relevant to it, Bal assumes that the reader is already familiar with the theory and concepts of cultural analysis. Second, Bal, in contrast to Watson and Fischer, privileges the theory of cultural analysis over other approaches. Watson is concerned to show how he and Crick avoided the trap of privileging any particular theory, as most scientists investigating DNA were doing. Fischer tries not to privilege one discipline over the others, but he nonetheless ends up organizing them in a framework that is essentially economic and that uses economic concepts such as demand, supply, and labor market. Bal, however, privileges cultural analysis because "it is an interdisciplinary practice" (though imperfectly so) (p. 1). She uses the graffito to demonstrate what cultural analysis can and should be, and to answer critics who fault cultural analysis for its lack of "methodological explicitness" (p. 4).

She contrasts other approaches with cultural analysis, beginning with history:

> Cultural analysis as a critical practice is different from what is commonly understood as "history." It is based on a keen awareness of the critic's situatedness in the present, the social and cultural present from which we look, and look back, at the objects that are always already of the past, objects that we take to define our present culture. (p. 1)

Once she explains this basic contrast, Bal is able to expand the contrast, emphasizing three differences. The first is that cultural analysis probes "history's silent assumptions in order to come to an understanding of the past that is different" (p. 1). The object, of course, is not merely to have an understanding that is just different but that is different because it is integrative and, thus, interdisciplinary. Her second point is that cultural analysis does not attempt to project on the past, and thus on the object in question, what she calls "an objectivist 'reconstruction'" (p. 1). She means that cultural analysis accepts that there will remain, even after one has undertaken the most comprehensive examination of the moment in time and of the object in it that is possible, an element of ambiguity and mystery. Bal's third point of contrast is that cultural analysis, in contrast to much history writing, does not seek to impose on the past "an evolutionist line," meaning that the object was an inevitable product of knowable historical "developments."

These examples by Watson, Fischer, and Bal show how interdisciplinarians, writing for different audiences, approaching different problems, and using different methods, go about describing conflicting theories. Fischer's four actions can profitably be applied to theories relating to almost any problem.

Chapter Summary

STEP 7 calls for identifying conflicts between insights and theories and locating sources of conflict. Experts in the *same* discipline often study the same problem but produce insights concerning it that differ. Art critics, for example, study the same painting but arrive at very different understandings of its meaning. This tendency is even more pronounced when experts in different disciplines approach the same problem. These insights typically conflict. However, it is not enough to say that insights differ or even conflict. Interdisciplinarians must probe more deeply and discover *why* they conflict; they must also identify the *particular source(s)* of conflict. The discussion of STEP 7 noted two possible sources of conflicts between disciplinary insights: their embedded concepts and underlying assumptions. The discussion of STEP 7 also explained that theories are sources of conflict between insights produced either by the same discipline or by different disciplines.

One important insight of this chapter is the great diversity of interdisciplinary work, as is evident in the touchstone examples by Watson (1968), Fischer (1988), and Bal (1999). Different audiences, different problems, and different purposes for writing are inevitably reflected in different approaches to the interdisciplinary task. Using a combination of narrative and tables is helpful when dealing with many variables (i.e., insights and theories). While professionals may not use every feature of the interdisciplinary research process described in this book, they typically deal with conflicting insights and theories. Identifying these conflicts and their sources is foundational to STEP 8 of the integrative process: creating common ground among insights and theories by modifying their concepts and assumptions.

Exercises

Concepts Embedded in Insights

10.1 Identify two insights from academic journals or books, each from a different disciplinary perspective, that focus on the topic *sustainable* or *sustainability*. Compare and contrast how each author defines this term and the context in which it is used. Decide which of the following problematic situations apply here:

   a. Though the concepts are the same, they mask different contextual meanings.

   b. The concepts are used to describe similar (but not exactly the same) ideas.

   c. The concepts, as used, are so different in meaning that differences cannot be overcome without modifying their meaning.

Assumptions

10.2 Determine from each author's insight into sustainability the kind of assumption(s) each makes.

   a. Ontological

   b. Epistemological

   c. Value-laden

Theories

10.3 Identify two theories from the same discipline on the topic of sustainability and answer the following questions:

   a. What concepts does each author use?

   b. What assumption(s) does each author make?

   c. What insight or argument does each theory advance?

10.4 Repeat the exercise of 10.3 using two theories from two different disciplines and answer the same questions.

Conflicting Theoretical Approaches

10.5 According to the chapter, can drawing on multiple and conflicting theoretical approaches from within the same discipline constitute interdisciplinarity? Explain why or why not.

11 Creating Common Ground Between Concepts

_____ **Chapter Preview**

STEP 8 of the interdisciplinary research process (IRP) calls for creating common ground between conflicting concepts or theories. This process plays out differently depending on whether one is working with concepts or theories. Whether one is focusing on concepts or theories, common ground is created by modifying them directly or via their underlying assumptions. In both cases, common ground must be created so that the insights in which they are embedded (and the disciplinary authors that produced them) can "talk to each other."

Though creating common ground between conflicting concepts or theories is the focus of a single STEP, the discussion is split between two chapters because by this point in the IRP, readers know whether they are working with a set of concepts alone _or_ with theories as well. Consequently, STEP 8 is divided into two sub-STEPS: the first addressing the creation of common ground between concepts (the subject of this chapter), the second dealing with the creation of common ground between the theories themselves (the subject of Chapter 12).

_____
Step 8: Create Common Ground Between Concepts and Theories
_____

This chapter is divided into two sections: Section 1 discusses the theory of common ground as the basis for collaborative communication and interdisciplinary integration; section 2 explains how to create common ground between conflicting insights either directly by modifying their concepts or indirectly by modifying their underlying assumptions. Techniques used to modify concepts or assumptions are illustrated from student and professional work. While there is no guarantee that common ground can be achieved in every case, this chapter and the following chapter are guided by the idea that conflicting disciplinary insights and theories are potentially complementary if their concepts and/or assumptions are sufficiently modified.[1]

In interdisciplinary work, creating common ground is undoubtedly the most challenging task that one faces. This is probably because it requires a combination of original thought, close reading, analytical reasoning, creativity, and intuition. But it is achievable if one takes a systematic approach, pays attention to the nature of the challenge, and chooses an appropriate technique.

The Theory of Common Ground as the Basis for Collaborative Communication and Interdisciplinary Integration _____

The basis for collaborative communication across disciplines and integration of their conflicting concepts or theories is the creation of common ground. From the earliest conceptions of interdisciplinarity, researchers have recognized the need for a common or collaborative language. Joseph J. Kockelmans (1979) was the first to use the term *common ground*, seeing it as the basis for collaborative communication—"a common ground"— among research scientists from different disciplines working on large government and industry projects. Common ground, he says, is the fundamental element of all interdisciplinary investigation because without it, "genuine communication between those who participate in the discussion would be impossible" (Kockelmans, 1979, p. 141). Kockelmans was also the first to connect integrating disciplinary insights with developing common ground (pp. 142–143). In explaining how to teach interdisciplinary research practice, Szostak (2007a) stresses the importance of first creating common ground among different disciplinary insights (p. 2).

A Definition of Interdisciplinary Common Ground

Interdisciplinary common ground is one or more concepts or assumptions through which conflicting insights or theories can be largely reconciled and subsequently integrated, thus enabling collaborative communication between disciplines. Common ground is not the same as integration, but it is integral to the process of integration. The creation of common ground is a necessary but not a sufficient condition for integration. Common ground is achieved through the use of language.

Two metaphors, though imperfect, depict what common ground is like: the bridge and the golden thread. Creating common ground is like building a bridge in order to span a deep chasm. The near side is the place of conflicting insights and the lack of a common language (STEP 7; see Chapter 10); the opposite side is the product of the process of integration: the more comprehensive understanding (STEP 9; see Chapter 13). Unless the interdisciplinarian first builds the bridge of common ground to connect the two sides (STEP 8; see also Chapter 12), the integrative enterprise cannot succeed. The bridge metaphor is useful because it shows how, in operational terms, the steps in the integrative process (identifying conflicts, creating common ground to reconcile them, and producing a more comprehensive understanding) are connected yet discrete. Another metaphor descriptive of common ground is that of the golden thread, which connects many different textures, shapes, and colors of cloth.

This definition and description of common ground is foundational to the core ideas developed in the first section of this chapter:

- Common ground is necessary for collaborative communication.
- Common ground requires unconventional thinking.
- Common ground is achieved through the use of language.
- Common ground must be created whenever concepts or theories conflict.[2]
- Common ground is created by modifying concepts or theories directly or through their assumptions.
- Creating common ground is integral to preparing concepts and theories for integration.
- Creating common ground requires using intuition.
- Creating common ground plays out differently in contexts of narrow versus wide interdisciplinarity.
- Creating common ground is the interdisciplinarian's responsibility.

Common Ground Is Necessary for Collaborative Communication

The purpose of creating common ground is to develop collaborative communication among disciplinary scholars and reconcile (to the extent possible) their different insights and theories on a particular problem. The term *common ground* is not just academic; it has entered the mainstream media. According to a report from the Associated Press, "Seeking elusive *common ground* on abortion, prominent activists and clergy on both sides of the debate are throwing their support behind a bill aimed at preventing unintended pregnancies and supporting pregnant women [italics added]" (*USA Today,* 2009). A headline by National Public Radio (NPR) reporter Liz Halloran (2009) reads, "Gay Activists, Black Ministers Seek Common Ground." On such controversial and emotionally charged issues, creating common ground between differing or opposing views is often difficult, but not impossible.

Sometimes attempts are made to communicate across disciplines without realizing the necessity of first creating common ground among them. Eugenia P. Gerdes, former dean of liberal arts at Bucknell University, illustrates this point in the story of her efforts to revise the general education curriculum and expose students to multiple disciplinary perspectives. Her challenge was to communicate this noble vision to her faculty in language that they would all understand and rally behind. Instead, she inadvertently "stepped on the toes" of one discipline by using language appropriate to her discipline but that struck some in the creative arts as "discordant." She said to the faculty, "I want our students to be able to get outside their own *intuitive perspective*—to recognize where they are situated in nature, in history, among the world's cultures, and in a pluralized American society [emphasis added]" (Gerdes, 2002, p. 50).

To Gerdes (2002), a social psychologist, "'intuition' represents the unexamined biases of self-interest, stereotypes, prejudices, etc." (p. 50). To her shock and embarrassment, an indignant studio artist informed her, "a professor in the arts not only values, but also seeks to put students in touch with, the intuitive!" (p. 50). Unfortunately, she confesses, "in attempting to espouse [that] all students [be] exposed to a variety of disciplinary perspectives, I excluded one type of perspective as legitimate because of my ignorance of other disciplines" (pp. 49–50).

Common ground is required in at least two circumstances. The first is when people (or disciplines) use different concepts or terms to describe the same thing. For example, the terms *city* and *suburb* have different meanings across disciplines. The second is when people take opposing positions on a particular issue stemming from conflicting assumptions or values. If these are the sources of difference or even outright conflict, then the solution must be to create common ground. Common ground is *not* needed, however, in cases where authors *seem to be disagreeing* but may not be because they are talking about different things—altogether different phenomena or variables. Mapping their arguments will reveal if this is so.

There are at least five additional occasions when creating common ground is required. These include when (1) research scientists trained in different disciplines need to develop a collaborative language, (2) planners need to develop a comprehensive approach to community development, (3) business needs to produce a comprehensive strategy to produce and market a new product, (4) counselors need to reconcile partners who are contemplating divorce, and (5) policy makers need to develop broad support for a particular legislative action.

But what about issues that involve diametrically opposed ethical values, deeply held religious beliefs, or sharply conflicting political ideals? Such issues are often emotionally charged, supposedly reducing notions of common ground to mere wishful thinking. But even when dealing with such issues, it is often possible to create common ground.

Common Ground Requires Unconventional Thinking

Chapter 1 emphasizes that interdisciplinarity requires altering the way we think about thinking. Achieving common ground, and indeed the whole interdisciplinary research process, requires that we engage in unconventional thinking about how to approach problems and their solutions. In this connection, it is worth contrasting our *natural* thinking process with our *learned* thinking process. While unconventional thinking may seem challenging, in reality we are naturally able to pursue common ground but are commonly educated not to do so.

Psychologists tell us that the human brain is designed to process information integratively. This is evident from the many complex activities that a person engages in every day. People seldom even realize the extent to which they are thinking and acting in an integrative way when they play an instrument, plant a garden, cook a meal, or drive to work. A person's ability to make a series of complex decisions without consciously reflecting on all the components of those decisions is an example of a person's natural capacity to process information integratively.

But a person's *natural* thinking process stands in sharp contrast to a person's *learned* thinking process. Much of modern education teaches students to think in three nonintegrative ways:

- *Disciplinary categories.* From kindergarten onward, students are taught to think in disciplinary categories. They are told that knowledge is found in clearly marked "boxes" or disciplines called math, social studies, English, and art (though this is slowly changing). Learning, students discover, occurs through a process of knowledge fragmentation, compartmentalization, and reductionism.
- *Right or wrong answers.* We are trained to think in terms of answers to questions as being either right or wrong. Standardized tests that promote a focus on facts over reasoning lead to education that, for example, asks students to read a novel like *Tom Sawyer* and choose whether Huck Finn is a good or bad influence on Tom, even though most of us recognize that humans are a mixture of good and bad, and that mixture can change with the circumstances, and that the very concepts of "good" and "bad" are contested.
- *For or against something.* Though debates on controversial topics are effective ways to engage students and teach debating techniques, they reinforce the idea that the point of it all is to win and that the purpose of confronting alternative perspectives is to choose one and reject the rest.

However, the interdisciplinary enterprise is not like prosecuting a case, defending a client, or just adding another pro or con opinion to the many pro or con opinions already offered on the issue. Rather, the interdisciplinary enterprise is about building bridges that join together rather than erecting walls that divide. It is about creating commonalities rather than sharpening differences. It is about inclusion rather than exclusion. It is about producing understandings and meanings that are new and more comprehensive rather than those using a single disciplinary approach. And this requires a different kind of thinking and mode of analysis, one that draws (critically but sympathetically) on most, if not all, available disciplinary perspectives and their insights. So, instead of asking if Huck was a good or bad influence on Tom, the interdisciplinarian would ask about the whole package of Huck's influences (positive, negative, and mixed) on Tom, and probably about Tom's influences on Huck as well.

Common Ground Is Achieved
Through the Use of Language

Common ground is achieved through the use of language. In everyday communication, we encounter people who have different perspectives than we have on a wide range of matters. Our everyday perception of facts and events depends on the categories we bring to a certain situation, raising the question of how we are able to comprehend so many different perspectives.

Cognitive psychology explains successful communication between individuals having different perspectives by exploring the way our brain subjectively constructs perceiving, seeing, and acting. Common ground theory says that "every act of communication presumes a common cognitive frame of reference between the partners of interaction called the common ground" (Bromme, 2000, p. 119). The phrase "common cognitive frame of reference between the partners of interaction" simply refers to everyday social interaction where two individuals enter into each other's frame of reference, attempt to discuss a problem, try to identify sources of disagreement concerning it, and arrive jointly at a resolution of it. Common ground theory postulates further that "all contributions to the process of mutual understanding serve to establish or ascertain and continually maintain this common ground" (p. 119). This theory applies to both oral and written communication.

The theory assumes that any successful verbal encounter represents an act of cooperation by both parties. When we communicate, we do so to attain a certain goal or to respond to a certain question, whether verbalized or unspoken. According to cognitive psychologist Rainer Bromme (2000),

> all contributions to communication are formulated and understood on the basis of background assumptions we make about the situation in question, the object of conversation and its goal: "Two people's common ground is, in effect, the sum of their mutual, common, or joint knowledge, beliefs, and suppositions" (Clark, 1996, p. 93). . . . One's own assumptions on which the conversation is based are designated as one's own perspective and that of the other person as [the] perspective of the other. (p. 120)

Though common ground theory was developed to explain everyday interactions, cognitive psychology is now applying it to communication across academic disciplines, especially the natural sciences.

Note to Readers

The process of integration and creating common ground between conflicting concepts involves adjudicating disciplinary disputes over their meaning. For undergraduates, creating common ground involves closely reading definitions of concepts and identifying differences in their meaning. For graduate students, mature scholars, and members of research teams, creating common ground necessarily involves drawing on the intellectual skills of philosophy (using abstract thinking to make fine distinctions about the gradations of meaning).

Common Ground Must Be Created Whenever Concepts or Theories Conflict

Since common ground is achieved through the use of language, creating common ground requires modifying definitions of key concepts and/or their underlying assumptions, or modifying theories. (Both concepts and theories are sources of insights.) Here, we discuss common definitions of concepts.

In most cases, if not all cases, common definitions must be created since different disciplines have different definitions—connotative if not denotative—for the same concepts. For example, disciplines have different understandings of "sustainability" and "social justice" that are rooted in their overall perspectives on reality and the phenomena they typically study. Creating common ground involves identifying one or more latent commonalities that are embedded in the concepts from two or more disciplines. Authors communicate their insights using concepts based on assumptions that typically reflect the assumption(s) and perspective of each author's home discipline. Newell (2007a) says that the step of creating common ground can be carried out either directly or indirectly: *directly* by modifying the concepts, or *indirectly* by modifying the assumptions. In either case, he says, "the challenge is to decide how to modify concepts or assumptions as little as possible to bring out latent commonalities" (p. 257). How to modify concepts and assumptions is explained in the second section of this chapter.

Common Ground Is Created by Modifying Concepts or Theories Directly or Through Their Assumptions

The nature of the challenge of creating common ground varies with *what* common ground is created *from. Common ground is created from conflicting concepts or theories.* Both concepts and theories are sources of insights. (Theories can be thought of as specifying relationships among concepts—more accurately variables—and those concepts or theories can be modified either directly or indirectly through assumptions in which they are grounded. How to do this is the subject of Chapter 12.)

Whether working in the natural sciences, the social sciences, or the humanities, one typically creates common ground by modifying concepts directly. (Note: Concepts refer not just to things but also to the processes that these are involved in and the influences exerted by one thing on another.)

But what about situations where insights conflict because of conflicting values? *Values manifest themselves in common ground creation as assumptions.*

Rick Szostak (personal communication, January 2010) urges us to appreciate that conflicts are generated not just from the assumptions made within a theory but from a broader set of philosophical assumptions: the epistemological, ethical, religious, and ideological views that may inform theory construction. These philosophical assumptions may or may not be clearly stated by the scholar.

Common ground, it must be emphasized, is created *not* from a discipline's perspective (in a general sense), but from the concepts or assumptions embedded in the insights or theories themselves. Consequently, when working with insights in which theories are not present, one must decide what to create common ground from: concepts or the assumptions underlying them.

Creating Common Ground Is Integral to Preparing Concepts and Theories for Integration

Creating common ground is integral to the process of integration (Kockelmans, 1979, pp. 142–143; Repko, 2007). The purpose of performing integration, as noted in Chapter 9, is to develop collaborative communication across disciplines and reconcile different or conflicting insights. The connection between creating common ground and performing integration is established by a study conducted by the Interdisciplinary Studies Project (Project Zero), Harvard Graduate School of Education. It examines exemplary practices of interdisciplinary work at the precollegiate, collegiate, and professional levels. The study finds that there exists

> an important similarity—and possibly a fundamental connection!— between the interdisciplinary efforts and other mental operations that involve internal or external dialogue such as metaphoric thought, collaborative work, and other forms of negotiating differences [i.e., creating common ground] and merging [i.e., integrating] ideas. (Nikitina, 2005, p. 392)

According to the study, interdisciplinary thinking occurs as the mind performs a *complicated chain of cognitive operations* in which it integrates disciplinary ideas. At the juncture of disciplines, the mind is involved in two cognitive activities: (1) overcoming internal monodisciplinarity (i.e., the preference for a single and simplistic disciplinary perspective), and (2) *attaining integration*. A key finding of the study is the possibility that there exists "a central cognitive process," expressive of the *dialogical tendency of the human mind,* that manifests itself in interdisciplinary thinking (Nikitina, 2005, p. 414). This "central cognitive process," which is a natural tendency of the human mind, involves creating common ground.

Creating Common Ground Requires Using Intuition

Any discussion of common ground and its underlying theory must include the role of intuition.[3] **Intuition** is the natural ability to understand or perceive something immediately without consciously using reason, analysis, or inference (Welch, 2007, p. 3). This definition may be satisfying to students working in the humanities where creativity and spontaneity are prized, but it may be disconcerting to students working in the natural sciences and hard social sciences where rational or logical methods are highly valued. In the sciences, intuition is typically seen as a form of common sense. In fact, science advances not so much by incremental expansion of knowledge but more often by discontinuous leaps of creative or intuitive thought (Csikszentmihalyi & Sawyer, 1995, p. 242; Kuhn 1996). Historians of science generally agree that both logic and intuition are involved in scientific discovery. Scientists work hard on a problem and gather relevant information. But the insight often comes while they are taking a break from work, allowing their subconscious mind to do its work while they are walking in the park or taking a bath.

Intuitive understanding is experienced in a number of modes. It may occur as

- a moment of instant assessment of a complex situation or object;
- a "gut instinct"—visceral, emotional, and empathetic—in a social situation (D. G. Myers, 2002, pp. 33–38);
- the result of mulling over a problem that is "on the back burner" of our mind, "where insight into a persistent conundrum that had been dismissed from consciousness comes to light 'out of the blue'" (Welch, 2007, p. 3);
- a "common sense" insight into "the complexity of ordinary decision-making, which is embedded in collective cultural standards" (Gerber, 2001, p. 72);
- creativity, which is entwined with the process of inspiration, imagination, artistic expression, and symbolic understanding (D. G. Myers, 2002, pp. 59–61); or
- insight, which is understanding the underlying structure of a problem and attaining a more holistic synthesis of the relationships among its disparate elements (Csikszentmihalyi & Sawyer, 1995, p. 329; Dominowski & Ballob, 1995, p. 38; D. G. Myers, 1995, p. 28).

Intuition has been the subject of extensive research in cognitive psychology. According to James Welch (2007), the unconscious mind is now seen as a kind of reality processor that in many ways is superior to the processes of consciousness. The unconscious mind is not merely cataloguing discreet packets of experiential information, but accumulating an adaptive multidimensional matrix of associations (p. 6).

Intuitive insights do not just happen. They are, says Arthur Miller (1996), the inevitable result of a process of mental gestation—a highly trained mind has been purposefully focusing on a particular problem for a length of time (p. 419). This finding has important implications for interdisciplinary research, which features an "iterative process that works toward solution through an interweaving of generative and cognitive processes, not a big bang that comes all at once, then not again" (Sill, 1996, p. 144).

Interdisciplinarians are conflicted concerning the role of intuition in interdisciplinarity research. Some argue against an uncritical acceptance of intuitive insight, arguing that any valid understanding of reality must be based upon logic and empirical methods. Others assert that interdisciplinarity, seen from the perspective of postmodernism, "must be highly individual, unspecifiable, and institutionally anarchical" (Welch, 2007, p. 5). Szostak (2002), however, views this dichotomy between structure and intuition as essentially false. In good interdisciplinary fashion, he argues that *both structure and intuition* are necessary for developing new integrative approaches (pp. 131–137). Welch (2007) agrees and argues for what he calls *equilibrium between intellect and intuition*. This equilibrium is expressed in what he calls "integrative wisdom." This he defines as the synthetic interaction between "inspiration, intellect, and intuition" (p. 149).

Wisdom is the synthesis of all avenues of insight—rational, experiential, intuitive, physical, cultural, and emotional. [It] breaks down all boundaries between categories of knowledge and returns them [to] holistic understanding. Wisdom creates equilibrium among these faculties, minimizing their individual weaknesses and achieving synergy. (Welch, 2007, pp. 149–150)

This book reflects Szostak's stress on balance and Welch's call for equilibrium between intellect and intuition. When it comes to intuition, says Welch (2007), interdisciplinary studies, "with its emphasis on practical problem solving, cannot afford to dismiss such a potentially powerful [cognitive] faculty for integrative understanding" (p. 148).

Also, adherence to a steplike research process cannot automatically resolve all problems, including the challenging problem of creating common ground. That is why students are well advised to leave room, in some cases a great deal of room, for an "intuitive leap" or a "eureka moment" when, after a period of struggle, reflection, and analysis, they suddenly discover how to create common ground.

An Example of How Intuition Helps to Achieve Common Ground

The story of Helen Keller provides an example, though imperfect, of how intuition helps achieve common ground between two persons who have been unable to communicate with each other. Helen, after an illness in infancy, was left unable to see or hear, and thus unable to speak or communicate with anyone. Though everyone had given up on Helen, her young teacher, Anne Sullivan, did not, believing that she could find a way to communicate with Helen. For some time, Anne's best efforts proved fruitless, and Helen grew more and more incorrigible—until one day when they were at the well outside the cabin where they were staying, and Helen knocked over the bucket of drinking water that Anne had just drawn. In that moment, water became more than water. In an intuitive flash, Anne realized that she could use the spilled water to make the sign for "water" in the palm of Helen's wet hand. It worked. Helen understood. Anne had achieved common ground with Helen. Water became the key that ended Helen's terrible isolation and enabled her to comprehend and communicate with her world. The result was a new and an amazingly productive life. (Note: This example overlooks the fact that one usually has to redefine disciplinary concepts to create or even discover common ground. And without using redefinition or some other integrative technique discussed in this chapter, common ground, and thus integration, can seldom be achieved.)

Creating Common Ground Plays Out Differently in Contexts of Narrow Versus Wide Interdisciplinarity

Creating common ground plays out differently in contexts of narrow versus wide interdisciplinarity. Narrow interdisciplinarity draws on disciplines that are epistemologically close (e.g., physics and chemistry). Wide interdisciplinarity draws on disciplines that are epistemologically farther apart (e.g., art history and mathematics). The epistemological presuppositions of the natural sciences promote a focus on facts—on what something is and how it works. Scientific presuppositions do not allow us to assign value (in a moral or ethical sense) to facts as do the epistemological presuppositions of the humanities that give us access to moral reality. This means that it should be easier to discover commonalities between insights produced by the natural sciences concerning a problem (given their more narrow epistemological focus) than it is to find commonalities between insights produced by disciplines spanning the natural sciences and the humanities, whose epistemologies differ widely. In general, *the greater the epistemological distance between disciplines, the more difficult it is to create common ground between their insights.*

Creating common ground is possible in contexts of narrow *and* wide interdisciplinarity. As noted, creative insight is dependent upon mental gestation. Regardless of the epistemological distances between the relevant disciplines, students must immerse themselves in each discipline's insights, concepts, assumptions, theories, and so forth, concentrate on the problem, and not be in a rush to "get it done."

Creating Common Ground Is
the Interdisciplinarian's Responsibility

There is an abundance of opinion (scholarly and otherwise) but a scarcity of understanding of the many complex problems that bedevil our society and characterize our world. *Interdisciplinary study is not about who can win the argument but about who can bring together the best ideas of all stakeholders to get the job done.* The task of the interdisciplinarian is to achieve this much needed understanding in a way that is similar to the role played by a marriage counselor.

The marriage counselor knows that nothing lasting will be achieved if the parties remain focused on the differences that divide them, much as the interdisciplinarian knows that common ground will not be created if the focus remains on the differences between disciplinary insights. Marriage counselors try to get behind the conflicting positions of the parties to find out what commonalities exist, much as the interdisciplinarian tries to get behind the conflicting insights to find the commonalities that they share. Marriage counselors try to find common ground by identifying interests that are

- shared or overlapping (analogous to common meaning revealed through redefinition, explained later in this chapter);
- similar or related (analogous to common ground achieved through extension, explained later in this chapter);
- compatible (analogous to common ground achieved through organization, explained later in this chapter); or
- negotiable (analogous to common ground achieved through transformation, explained later in this chapter).[4]

Though instructive, the example is not truly interdisciplinary in that the conflicting issues straining the relationship cannot be neatly categorized in disciplinary or theoretical terms.

The interdisciplinarian looks at the conflicting insights and asks, "Where can I narrow the conflict or make concepts or assumptions more commensurate, and how can I get these folks to stop talking past each other?" Interdisciplinarians cannot promise that if we create commonalities between disciplines (and stakeholders outside the academy) integration will result; but we can promise that if we fail to create commonalities between disciplines so they can talk to one other, integration cannot occur.

Modifying Concepts and Assumptions

The first section of the chapter established that creating common ground between conflicting concepts and theories is the basis for collaborative communication and a focus of integration. This next section explains how to actually create common ground between conflicting concepts by modifying them and/ or their underlying assumptions. This discussion assumes that the reader has had little or no formal experience in attempting to create common ground. It begins by discussing how to proceed with creating common ground between conflicting concepts and then introduces techniques for modifying them. Each of these techniques is illustrated from professional and student work.

How to Proceed

Deciding how to proceed with creating common ground calls for asking this question: What is necessary for integration? The answer to this question involves (1) knowing when to seek common ground, (2) deciding how comprehensive the study will be, (3) and deciding what common ground will be created from.

When to Seek Common Ground

Researchers should seek common ground only when different concepts and their insights are in conflict regarding the *same* problem or process. Logically, then, they seek common ground *after* having mapped the problem in order to determine that different authors are in fact talking about the same thing. Mapping the problem and each author's insight into it enables one to distinguish real conflicts (over the same thing) from apparent conflicts (when authors talk about different things). In the course of mapping each author's insight, the researcher looks for concepts that are the source of the insight. In other words, mapping helps us make sure that creating common ground is even necessary. If authors seem to be disagreeing, it may be not because common ground is lacking but because they are talking about two different things—altogether different phenomena or causal relationships.

One only needs to find common ground between authors who are disagreeing about the same "something," not between those who are talking about two different things. If the authors are talking about completely different aspects of a complex system such that they have no concepts or processes in common, the place to address that is in Chapter 13 on constructing a more comprehensive understanding. If they share at least one "something" in common, however, then one needs to create common ground for it.

The order, then, is this: First, map the problem to see if authors are talking about the same thing. Second, if they are, see if they use concepts the same way. Third, create common ground between concepts; and only if there are still conflicts work with assumptions.

Decide How Comprehensive the Study Will Be

Researchers need to decide how *comprehensive* their study will be. Most undergraduates and even some graduate students will find themselves limited in the number of disciplines on which they can draw. But these students can and should seek to *integrate fully the insights* of the disciplines from which they draw. For individual mature scholars and members of interdisciplinary research teams, their studies will be comprehensive: They will draw on all relevant disciplines and all relevant insights and seek full integration.

Decide What Common Ground Will Be Created From

Researchers must also decide what common ground will be created from: concepts and/or assumptions. A situation typically encountered is after locating a number of important insights on the topic, the student finds that some authors refer to concepts and others present theories, but few, if any, refer explicitly to their assumptions. How should one proceed when facing a patchwork quilt of approaches? A best practice is to begin with concepts before working with assumptions.

1. *Begin looking for concepts.* One needs to return to the data table created earlier (see Chapter 6, Table 6.1) to see which insights make explicit reference to one or more concepts. One may discover that only a few authors reference one or more concepts while others do not reference any. *To create common ground using concepts, all the authors must use one or more concepts that reference the problem in some way, even though these concepts may have different (apparent or real) meanings.* For a concept to be used as the basis for creating common ground, it must be applicable to all, not just a few, of the insights. Examples of how to modify concepts for this purpose appear below.

2. *Work with assumptions when this seems more promising.* One needs to consult the data table to identify the assumptions of each author's insight. If this information was not collected earlier, it will have to be now. Identifying assumptions is often challenging to undergraduates because authors seldom state them explicitly. Assumptions, it will be recalled, are what each author assumes or believes to be true about the problem. One strategy for ferreting out assumptions is to identify the discipline that has produced each of the insights and refer to the tables on disciplinary assumptions in Chapter 4, applying each relevant discipline's overall assumptions concerning the problem. This often requires close *rereading* of the insight to see how it reflects the overall assumptions of the discipline that produced it. For example, Martha Crenshaw (1998), a political scientist, writes that her approach to understanding the cause of suicide terrorism "permits the construction of a standard which can measure degrees of rationality, the degree to which strategic reasoning is modified by psychology and other constraints, and explain how reality is interpreted" (pp. 9–10). As a political scientist, Crenshaw is likely to share one of the discipline's major assumptions that are noted in Table 4.11. Her statement about the importance of measuring "degrees of rationality" (as well as other statements that she makes in her essay) appears to reflect the modernist and secular assumption that "human beings are . . . in part intentional actors, [and] capable of cognition and

acting on the basis of it" (Goodin & Klingerman, 1996, pp. 9–10). Thus, from the text of Crenshaw's insight and from the assumption statements concerning political science in Table 4.11, it is relatively easy to construct an assumption statement as follows: "Suicide terrorists follow logical processes that can be discovered and explained." The same assumption may be stated even more succinctly like this: "Suicide terrorists are rational actors."

3. *Work with theoretical explanations only when all authors use them to explain the cause of the behavior in question.* Authors in the social sciences typically base their insights on theoretical or causal explanations. How to integrate different theoretical explanations of the same problem is the subject of the following chapter.

Another situation commonly encountered is working with insights by authors from applied fields (such as education or business) and/or interdisciplinary fields (such as bioethics or women's studies). The defining elements of these fields are not included in Chapter 4. Consequently, the researcher will have to carefully examine each insight and look for statements that reveal the author's assumption (i.e., what the author believes to be true about the problem).

A Best Practice When Working With Concepts and Assumptions

A best practice when working with concepts and assumptions is to follow the **principle of least action**. This means making sure that the changes made in them are the smallest possible to still create sufficient common ground on which to construct the more comprehensive understanding. The rationale for using this principle is essentially grounded in the conservative laws of thermodynamics: Nature finds the path that requires the least expenditure of energy. It will also make it easier to communicate back to disciplines.

Techniques Demonstrated for Modifying Concepts and Assumptions

Having decided what common ground will be created from, the next decision concerns which technique to use when modifying concepts and assumptions. This decision should be based on the nature and extent of the conflict. There are three possible situations:

- Concepts and assumptions do not conflict at all, though commonality is still obscured by discipline-specific terminology or context.
- Concepts and assumptions of two disciplines are different but not opposing; they really represent alternatives.
- Concepts and assumptions are diametrically opposed (Newell, 2007a, p. 258).

For most complex problems, says Newell (2007a), "the challenge of creating common ground confronts the interdisciplinarian with more than one of these situations; for problems that require input from the social sciences and humanities, all three are likely to be involved" (p. 258). Of the four techniques discussed here, some are useful in more than one situation, so the interdisciplinarian needs to understand the range and applicability of each technique.

Four techniques are used for creating common ground: *redefinition*, *extension*, *transformation*, and *organization*, or possibly some combination of these. Students, especially those new to the interdisciplinary research process, will almost always use redefinition (whether it takes the form of a new term or a new meaning for an old term). But whether they also use the technique of extension, transformation, or organization depends on the challenges posed by those concepts and assumptions.

Examples of each modification technique are drawn from problem-based course projects, published literature, and student papers that are explicitly interdisciplinary. An asterisk (*) after the surname identifies the student examples. As with the touchstone examples written by professional interdisciplinarians, the problem-based course project and student papers illustrate many, but not all, of the possible features of an interdisciplinary research paper. The categorization of these examples refers to the area of the researcher's training and the orientation of the topic more than to the disciplines from which insights were drawn.

1. The Technique of Redefinition

Redefinition concerns what we call something—its label. It concerns language. Redefinition applies only to concepts, not assumptions. The technique of redefinition involves modifying or redefining *concepts* in different texts and contexts to bring out a common meaning. In interdisciplinary work, the technique of redefinition is sometimes referred to as "textual integration" (Brown, 1989, cited in Henry & Bracy, 2012, p. 264). As noted earlier, each discipline has developed its own technical vocabulary to describe the phenomena it prefers to study. Since every discipline has its own vocabulary expressed as concepts, it is necessary for the interdisciplinarian to create a common vocabulary to facilitate communication between disciplines—that is, to "get them on the same page." This new vocabulary may amount to only a few key terms, just enough of them to enable disciplinary specialists to communicate effectively with each other (Wolfe & Haynes, 2003, p. 155). Since most disciplinary concepts and assumptions are couched in discipline-specific language, the technique of redefinition is used in most efforts to create common ground, in conjunction with other techniques as well as by itself (Newell, 2007a, p. 258). The trick is to modify terms as little as possible while still creating common ground on which to construct a more comprehensive understanding (Newell, 2001, pp. 19–20). *Redefining a concept might also involve some modification of the assumption(s) underlying the concept.*

Example of the Admission, Review, and Dismissal (ARD) Meeting The importance of finding common ground when trying to achieve coherent understanding of a complex problem is illustrated in the example of an Admission, Review, and Dismissal (ARD) meeting in special education. The purpose of this meeting is to develop a comprehensive approach to providing individualized instruction for a student with learning disabilities. Those attending the meeting include administrators, various specialists, the student, the student's parents, and the facilitator whose job it is to move the discussion toward an integrated plan for the student's educational needs for the coming year. The facilitator asks each person—the speech pathologist, the social studies teacher, the neurologist, an assistant principal—to propose a solution designed to meet the student's ongoing educational needs for the coming year. The specialists commonly use highly technical concepts or language to describe the student's disability. Perhaps sensing that the parents do not understand what the specialists are saying, the facilitator asks the specialists to "translate" the technical jargon into language that the parents, and indeed all in attendance, can understand. The facilitator attempts to find common ground among the various proposals offered by the specialists and the parents. These proposals are typically grounded in theory. Then, building on that, the facilitator proposes an integrative solution.

The facilitator's role in the ARD meeting is similar to that of the interdisciplinary student who is attempting to produce an integrative understanding of, say, the causes of the high rate of obesity among adolescents. Each discipline interested in the problem brings its perspective to the table. And experts in each of these disciplines attribute the causes of the problem to various factors. The task of the student working on this problem, like that of the ARD facilitator, is to allow each viewpoint to be expressed, identify conflicts and their sources, and then encourage one or more points of agreement to surface. This latter activity is creating or finding common ground.

Two lessons can be drawn from the above narrative. The first is the role of technical language (i.e., concepts) in establishing common ground. The second is the importance of recognizing that underneath the technical language used by the various professionals are disciplinary perspectives (i.e., theories, concepts, and assumptions) on how to treat a child with learning disabilities. In interdisciplinary work, one must take into account not only disciplinary terminology but also disciplinary perspectives.

Working With Concepts Concerning concepts, then, researchers should do two things. First, pay close attention to how the *same concept* may have different meanings when used by different disciplines within the context of the *same* problem. As mentioned before, the concept "efficiency" has quite different meanings for economists (money out/money in), biologists (energy out/energy in), and political scientists (influence exerted/political capital expended) (Newell, 2001, p. 19).

Second, one should be alert to how experts from different disciplines use *different concepts* in their discussion of the same problem. Also, one should be able to distinguish between cases in which these different concepts refer to *quite different things,* and cases where different concepts have *overlapping meanings.* Both are common occurrences. From these, it is often possible to identify one concept that can be modified by using the technique of redefinition.

When redefining a concept, one should avoid using terminology that tacitly favors one disciplinary approach at the expense of another. Using the technique of redefinition can reveal commonalities in concepts that may be obscured by discipline-specific language. Once this language is stripped away, the concept can be redefined, enabling it to become the basis for creating common ground between the conflicting insights. Sometimes this occurs in conjunction with other integrative techniques, as shown in these threaded examples.

From the Humanities: Silver* (2005), Composing Race and Gender: The Appropriation of Social Identity in Fiction   Creative writing, says Silver, like all other disciplines, sees the world through its own "peephole" or perspective. "I love this peephole deeply," she confides, "but I also want to see the entire truth [because] *truth* is fundamental to fiction" (p. 75). For Silver, seeing the "entire truth" as a writer of fiction involves crossing disciplinary boundaries. One way fiction writers do this is by appropriating (i.e., assuming) social identities, which are reflected in their characters. Silver uses the modification technique of *redefinition* to resolve an ethical dilemma that exists when fiction writers, actors, and filmmakers regularly and uncritically appropriate a person's identity. That dilemma is how to engage in this practice in an ethical, by which Silver means truthful or authentic, way. The disciplines that Silver finds most relevant to the topic are sociology, psychology, cultural studies, and creative writing. The challenge for Silver was identifying a concept that these disciplinary insights shared concerning this common practice. This concept, she concluded, was "implicature," which denotes either (a) the act of meaning, implying, or suggesting one thing by saying something else, or (b) the object of that act (*Stanford Encyclopedia of Philosophy*, 2010). By redefining "implicature" to mean "the ultimate level of empathy that one person can have with another," Silver makes it possible to practice appropriation in a way that is ethical rather than hypocritical.

From the Natural Sciences and the Social Sciences: Delph* (2005), An Integrative Approach to the Elimination of the "Perfect Crime"   Delph questions whether advances in criminal investigatory techniques are able to eliminate the possibility of the "perfect crime." She defines a "perfect crime" as one that goes unnoticed and/or as one for which the criminal will never be caught (p. 2). Of the several disciplines and subdisciplines that are relevant to crime investigation, the three that Delph finds most relevant are criminal justice, forensic science, and forensic psychology. Delph identifies the current theories of these rapidly evolving subdisciplines and finds that the source of conflict between them is their preference for two different investigatory methods and reliance on two kinds of evidence. Forensic science analyzes physical evidence, whereas forensic psychology analyzes behavioral evidence. Each approach constructs a "profile" of the criminal, with forensic science using physical evidence and forensic psychology using a combination of intuition informed by years of experience and information collected from interviews and other sources.

Delph creates common ground between the conflicting approaches by redefining the concept of profiling to include both forensic science, with its emphasis on physical evidence, and forensic psychology, with its emphasis on "intuition" born of extensive experience and insights derived from crime scene analysis. This redefinition of criminal profiling enables her to bridge the physical (i.e., forensic science) and behavioral sciences (i.e., forensic psychology and criminal investigation). Forensic scientists do not need to use profiling as long as they have adequate evidence to analyze. But in the absence of such evidence, profiling can move the investigation forward by using a combination of "intuition" born of extensive experience and insights derived from crime scene analysis (p. 29). In this way, the redefined concept of profiling serves as common ground between the specialized knowledge that criminal investigation, forensic science, and forensic psychology offer.

From the Social Sciences: Schoenfeld* (2005), Customer Service: The Ultimate Return Policy   Schoenfeld draws from the disciplines of psychology, sociology, and management to address an all-too-often overlooked and underappreciated aspect of consumerism, customer service. She defines customer service as "anything we do for a patron that embraces their experience" (p. ii). The goal of her study is to probe "the deeper levels of providing customer service," which is another way of saying "to develop a holistic approach to the customer experience" (pp. 3–4). Schoenfeld distinguishes between the concept of customer service (any steps that are taken to satisfy and retain customers' loyalty while they are in the store) and the concept of customer relationship management, or CRM (any steps taken to satisfy and retain customers when they are not in the store), and seeks to create common ground between them (p. 6). Her approach is to identify theories generated by psychology, sociology, and anthropology—including social exchange theory, expectancy theory, reasoned action, role theory, and attribution theory—that explain customers' expectations, behaviors, and habits. Schoenfeld observes that these theories describe the concept of customer service in two different ways: from the perspective of the customer and from the perspective of the merchant or store owner instead of from just one or the other. To create common ground, she redefines the concept of customer service so that it includes both perspectives. The focus of the concept is unaltered, or altered only slightly.

2. The Technique of Extension

Extension in an interdisciplinary sense refers to increasing the scope of the "something" that we are talking about. Whereas the focus of redefinition is linguistic, the focus of extension is conceptual. It involves addressing differences or oppositions in disciplinary concepts and/or assumptions by extending their meaning beyond the domain of the discipline that originated them into the domain(s) of the other relevant discipline(s) (Newell, 2007a, p. 258).

Example of Extending Concepts   The following is an example of a concept that was birthed in one disciplinary domain and later extended into other disciplinary domains. In the threaded example of the graffito, Bal extends the concept of exposure so that it includes three different perspectives on a note or letter written on a brick wall (i.e., graffito).

From the Humanities: Bal (1999), "Introduction," The Practice of Cultural Analysis: Exposing Interdisciplinary Interpretation   The challenge Bal faces with the graffito is how to expose its fullest meaning while not privileging any single disciplinary perspective. Her strategy is to analyze it from three perspectives (but not disciplinary ones) simultaneously: from the perspective of its author, from the perspective of the subject (i.e., the author's beloved), and from the perspective of one who is reading the graffito and pondering its meaning. Bal uses the technique of extension to create a common vocabulary centered on the verb *to expose,* to which she connects three nouns: *exposition, exposé,* and *exposure.* These are the three meanings or insights that this close reading of the graffito brings together. The verb refers to making a public presentation or to "publicly demonstrating"; "it can be combined with a noun meaning opinions or judgments and refer to the public presentation of someone's views; and it can refer to the performing of those deeds that deserve to be made public" (pp. 4–5). The graffito, as an exposition, brings out into the public domain the deepest held views and beliefs of the author. Exposition, says Bal, "is also always an argument. Therefore, in publicizing these views the author objectifies or exposes himself as much as the subject. This makes the graffito an exposure of the self. Such exposure is an act of producing meaning, a performance" (p. 2).

Example of Extending Assumptions   Concepts as well as assumptions can and often are extended (e.g., the concept of sustainability has been extended in recent decades from economic development to include the ecology, culture, and political system of a country). The example of extending assumptions that follows addresses the assumption of rationality, which some authors make explicit and others leave implicit.

From the Social Sciences and the Humanities: Repko (2012), "Integrating Theory-Based Insights on the Causes of Suicide Terrorism" In previous STEPS, Repko identifies the relevant insights (noting that all of them explicitly espouse a particular theoretical explanation) and the sources of conflict between them. Given the great diversity of concepts used and their conflicting meanings, he concludes that common ground cannot be created by redefining any one of these concepts. So, unable to work with concepts, he decides instead to work with assumptions. He begins by reflecting on the taxonomy of theory-based insights he developed earlier, shown here as Table 11.1.

Table 11.1   Insights Into the Causes of Suicide Terrorism

Theory	Insight of Theory Stated in General Terms	Concept	Assumption
Terrorist psycho-logic	"Political violence is not instrumental but an end in itself. The cause becomes the rationale for acts of terrorism the terrorist is compelled to commit" (Post, 1998, p. 35).	Special logic (Post, 1998, p. 25)	Terrorists are rational actors who organize their mental life through psychological constructs.
Self-sanction	"Self-sanctions can be disengaged by reconstruing conduct as serving moral purposes, by obscuring personal agency in detrimental activities, by disregarding or misrepresenting the injurious consequences of one's victims, or by blaming and dehumanizing the victims" (Bandura, 1998, p. 161).	Moral cognitive restructuring (Bandura, 1998, p. 164)	
Martyrdom	"Terrorist suicide is basically an individual rather than a group phenomenon; it is done by people who wish to die for personal reasons. . . . Personality factors seem to play a critical role in suicidal terrorism. . . . It seems that a broken family background is an important constituent" (Merari, 1998, pp. 206–207).	Indoctrination (Merari, 1998, p. 199)	

(Continued)

Table 11.1   (Continued)

Theory	Insight of Theory Stated in General Terms	Concept	Assumption
Collective rational strategic choice	"This approach permits the construction of a standard that can measure degrees of rationality, the degree to which strategic reasoning is modified by psychology and other constraints, and explain how reality is interpreted (Crenshaw, 1998, pp. 9–10).	Collective rationality (Crenshaw, 1998, pp. 8–9)	"Terrorism may follow logical processes that can be discovered and explained" (Crenshaw, 1998, p. 7).
"Sacred" terror	"Holy" or "sacred" terror is "terrorist activities to support religious purposes or terror justified in theological terms" (Rapoport, 1998, p. 103).	"Holy" or "sacred" terror (Rapoport, 1998, p. 103)	
Identity	"Religious identity sets and determines the range of options open to the fundamentalist. It extends into all areas of life and respects no separation between the private and the political" (Monroe & Kreidie, 1997, p. 41).	Identity	Religious identity explains "political" behavior.
Fictive kin	Loyalty to an intimate cohort of peers who are emotionally bonded to the same religious and political sentiments (Atran, 2003a, pp. 1534, 1537).	"Religious communion" (Atran, 2003a, p. 1537)	Personal relationships shape people's ideas about what is "good."
Modernization	Explains the process of historical and cultural change and why some cultures "modernize" or transform themselves politically, economically, and technologically following the Western model while others do not (B. Lewis, 2002, p. 59).	Modernization	Terrorists behave rationally in response to these exogenous factors.

Repko observes that insights from the same discipline usually share the same assumption. For example, the political science theories of collective rational strategic choice and sacred terror share the assumption that terrorists are rational actors who follow logical processes that can be discovered and explained.

He also observes that conflicts exist between the assumptions of different disciplines:

The assumption underlying self-sanction theory (from cognitive psychology) is that understanding the behavior and motivation of suicide terrorists requires studying *primarily* the mental life and the psychological constructs of *individual* terrorists. By contrast, the assumption of identity theory (from political science) is that understanding the behavior and motivation of suicide terrorists requires studying their cultural as well as their religious identity, but not at the expense of taking into account personality traits (inherent and acquired). (p. 145)

A deeper probing of the assumptions of these theories reveals a commonality that both share, namely the *goals* of suicide terrorists. These are understood not in terms of self-interest as rational choice advocates would have it, but rather as "moral imperatives" or "sacred duties." It so happens that this deeper—and extended—assumption is also shared by the theories of fictive kin, strategic rational choice, "sacred terror," martyrdom, terrorist psycho-logic, and modernization. He concludes that the common ground assumption shared by all of the theory-based insights to varying degrees is this: *The goals of suicide terrorists are "moral" and "sacred"—and, thus, rational—as defined by Islamic fundamentalism* (p. 145).

3. The Technique of Transformation

The technique of **transformation** is used to modify concepts or assumptions that are not merely different (e.g., love, fear, selfishness) but opposite (e.g., rational, irrational) into continuous variables (Newell, 2007a, p. 259). For example, Amitai Etzioni (1988) in *The Moral Dimension: Towards a New Economics* addressed the problem of how to overcome diametrically opposed concepts and assumptions about the rationality (economics) or irrationality (sociology) of humans. His solution was to transform them by placing them on opposite ends of a continuous variable called "the degree of rationality." By studying the factors that influence rationality, he found that it is possible to determine in principle the degree of rationality exercised in any given situation. Similarly, Etzioni treated trust and governmental intervention as continuous variables, making it possible to explore and estimate determinative influences in any particular context rather than as dichotomous assumptions to accept or reject.

The value of transformation in creating common ground is this: Rather than forcing us to accept or reject dichotomous concepts and assumptions, continuous variables allow us to push back assumptions and extend the scope of theory. The effect of this strategy is not only to resolve a philosophical dispute but also to extend the range of a theory (Newell, 2007a, p. 260). Transforming opposing assumptions into variables allows the interdisciplinarian to move toward resolving almost *any* dichotomy or duality, as illustrated in these examples.

From the Social Sciences: Englehart* (2005), Organized Environmentalism: Towards a Shift in the Political and Social Roles and Tactics of Environmental Advocacy Groups   Englehart is concerned that antienvironmentalism was becoming institutionalized in American politics during the G. W. Bush administration. To ensure that environmental responsibility becomes an integral part of our society, she proposes that environmental advocacy groups integrate their social and political agendas. These groups assume various active roles in society: They challenge and pressure the government with an environmental ethic; they are actors in the political arena who influence policy making by lobbying and campaigning in election cycles; and they are what sociologists call "social movement organizers" who mobilize the public to take action on pressing environmental issues. To better understand the roles and tactics of environmental groups, Englehart examines them in light of relevant theories, including social movement theory (in its several variations), rational choice theory, collective identity theory, and structural network theory. By comparing these theories and the insights they have generated, she finds that for environmental groups to grow and recapture the political initiative, they must change their approach to what they do and how they do it.

Creating common ground among the various theories and insights requires that she use the technique of transformation. This involves transforming opposing theoretical assumptions so as to extend the scope of social movement theory. This resulted in transforming the "I" of self-interested economics and political advocacy and the "We" of collective identity in social movements into a jointly maximized "I" and "We" for environmental advocacy. Englehart advocates using face-to-face relationships within an environmental organization to shift members along the continuum from "I" to "We," and then to extend the "We" (for the purposes of interorganizational networking) to include those with differing environmental values. Practically, this will cause environmental organizations to concentrate their efforts on educating and politicizing the social arena and creating their own political opportunity structures through innovative mobilization strategies so as to challenge current antienvironmental political action. Integration via transformation of these theoretical and disciplinary insights, Englehart argues, would result in a bottom-up, grassroots, coalition-driven social emphasis that, when combined with the traditional top-down, legislative-driven political pressure, will help environmental advocacy groups recapture the political initiative (pp. 58–63).

From the Natural Sciences and the Humanities: Arms* (2005), Mathematics and Religion: Processes of Faith and Reason   Arms compares faith and reason, which are often seen as polar opposites. "People think," she says, "that religion finds its home in the heart and faith, while mathematics belongs in the brain and reason" (p. i). The disciplines of her focus are mathematics, philosophy (i.e., logic), and religion. Logic, she finds, is the fulcrum discipline for mathematics *and* religion because both rely on it. Religion employs logic, albeit according to its own rules and within its own frame of reference. Logic is also used in determining the provability of mathematics, and this requires that one employ deductive reasoning. Gödel's Incompleteness Theorems, says Arms, show that we cannot prove necessary truths in mathematics. But by his Completeness Theorem, we know that first-order logic, sometimes called mathematical logic, is complete, and therefore at least trustworthy (p. 5). She also draws upon sociology and Durkheim's theory of religion and extracts from the latter his definition of religion as a socially constructed belief system, which she employs in her study.

The belief in the existence of a Christian God and the belief in the completeness and consistency of mathematics are not only belief systems, Arms says, but faith-based belief systems, and very different ones at that (pp. 66–67). She uses the concept of faith to continue the idea that mathematics and religion still have the possibility of certainty. Her reasoning runs as follows:

> We take it on faith that reason is a good thing. Since reason is an object of faith, it is reasonable to assume than an object of reason can become an object of faith. Faith is justifiable in keeping belief in the certainty of mathematics. Mathematics has made it clear to us that we cannot depend on it purely through reason. And even if Gödel and his Incompleteness Theorems had never come about, there would still be things in mathematics that are not provable. There are plenty of problems that have never been solved, and many that may never be solved. It took mathematicians over 300 years to solve Fermat's Last Theorem, but they had faith that it was true and that they would find a solution. In mathematics, it is common to prove something using an idea that we do not know is true, but assume it is. (p. 76)

To find common ground between faith and reason, Arms transforms the dichotomies of faith and reason and, by implication, the dichotomies of mathematics and religion. In the end, she confesses that she had been under the impression that her logic could "go anywhere"; that "science trumped religion, and [that] logic trumped science." Therefore, logic was obviously stronger than faith. Then she learned that her "dear logic," while complete, could not prove even mathematics. This rude awakening kept faith "afloat" and enabled her to accept "the complementary nature of reason and faith" (p. 80).

From the Social Sciences: Boulding (1981), A Preface to Grants Economics: The Economy of Love and Fear Boulding's study of research grants involved him probing the complexities of human behavior that motivates grant bequests. More particularly, Boulding sought a way to transform the debate about whether human nature in general is selfish or altruistic, as described in Newell's (2007a) summation:

Boulding (1981) recognized that both benevolent behavior (studied by sociologists) and malevolent behavior (studied by political scientists) can be understood as other-regarding behavior (positive and negative, respectively). He then arrayed them along a continuum of other-regarding behavior. The self-interested behavior studied by economists became the midpoint on that continuum because its degree of other-regarding behavior is zero. Thus, he set out a way to transform the debate about whether human nature in general is selfish or altruistic into a choice of where on the continuum of motivations people are likely to fall in the complex problem under study. By combining into a single continuum with self-interest the motivations of love and hate/fear that support or threaten the integrative mechanisms binding societies and politics together, Boulding used the technique of organization to integrate the differing conceptions of human nature under economics, sociology, and political science. (p. 259)

4. The Technique of Organization

The technique of **organization** creates common ground by clarifying how certain phenomena interact and mapping the causal relationships. More specifically, organization (1) identifies a latent commonality in the meaning of different concepts or assumptions (or variables) and redefines them accordingly and (2) then organizes, arranges, arrays, or maps the redefined concepts or assumptions to bring out a relationship between them (Newell, 2007a, p. 259). Organization focuses on the overall relations between distinct variables or clusters of distinct variables (but not the precise explicit relationships set out by a particular theory).

At this point in the IRP, the map created earlier may need to be refined so as to show all causal relations (some of which may have been overlooked when the map was first drawn). In effect, *the revised map of causal relations depicts the common ground.* (This may be true in the sciences but not in the humanities, which often do not stress causation at all.) Sometime we may already have used organization without realizing it earlier when we first mapped the problem. *What we are doing here that is new is appreciating that each discipline tends to make assumptions that privilege its own phenomena.* So economists stress individual rational decisions, and sociologists stress the influences of other people, but we can see how the latter shapes the former. Thus, we are indeed coping with the core assumptions of these disciplines. What we tend to address with organization is the type of assumption that limits the phenomena engaged by a particular discipline by stressing the influence of other phenomena (Rick Szostak, personal communication, February 11, 2011).

For example, organization enables us to see cultural values as providing a context within which rational decisions are made. Culture might influence both individual goals and the acceptable means by which those goals can be pursued. Individuals, then, rationally choose how best to achieve their goals using acceptable means in a particular situation. In this case, rationality is contained within the envelope of culture and is also permeated by it. The map of an individual's decision in a particular cultural context would show the variables of cultural influences and how these influence the choices the person faces, with the person making the best choice given the person's beliefs (Rick Szostak, personal communication, 2010).

From the Social Sciences: Etzioni (1988), *The Moral Dimension: Towards a New Economics*   We turn again to Etzioni's book, this time to show how the technique of organization can be extended from individual concepts and assumptions to large-scale models, major theoretical approaches, and even entire disciplines. Etzioni's use of organization is summarized here by Newell (2007a):

> Etzioni argued that there are several identifiable large-scale patterns of interrelationships between the "rational/empirical" factors studied by economics and the "normative/affective" factors studied by sociology. One such pattern I call an envelope. Here the rational behavior studied by economics is bounded, limited, or constrained by the normative factors studied by sociologists. Thus, rational economic behavior functions within a normative sociological envelope. Another pattern might be called inter-penetration. Some sociologic factors directly influence economic behavior, while some economic factors directly influence social behavior. Thus, social relationships can have an effect on how economic information is gathered and processed, what inferences are drawn, and what options are considered. And a third pattern can be referred to as facilitation. Etzioni points out that the "free individuals [studied by economics] are found only within communities [studied by sociologists], which anchor emotions and morals" (xi). Thus, sociological factors such as communities can actually facilitate individual economic behavior. (p. 259)

In this example, the technique of organization can make macro-level applications to bring out the relationship among commonalities of meaning within contrasting disciplinary concepts or assumptions.

The Value of These Techniques

The value of these techniques is that they enable us to create common ground when working with concepts (and their underlying assumptions). They replace the either/or thinking characteristic of the disciplines with both/and thinking characteristic of interdisciplinary integration. Inclusion, insofar as this is possible, is substituted for conflict. Creating common ground *does not* remove the tension between the concepts and the insights they produce; it *does* reduce this tension and make integration possible (but does not guarantee it).

Creating Common Ground When Assumed Values and Rights Conflict

Students commonly work with issues that involve conflicting values and rights. Examples include the value of an unborn's life versus the value that the mother assigns to her freedom of choice, the value of equality for women versus the value of a cultural tradition that denies such equality, the right of the terminally ill to end life with dignity versus the right of society to sustain life, and the value of using fertilizers to increase crop production versus the value of using organic (i.e., sustainable) farming techniques.

Values and rights involve ethics (a subdiscipline of philosophy) and call for students to make ethical evaluations of the relevant insights. Ethics (a type of philosophical theory) is concerned with how the world *should* work rather than how it *does* work (which is the function of scientific theory). Ethical evaluations are made at two points in the IRP. The first occurs during the literature search. Here students should strive *not* to allow their personal views to skew the *selection* of insights concerning the issue. As noted earlier, such skewing is a common practice but has no place in quality interdisciplinary work where all relevant viewpoints should be accorded equal voice. The second is made when analyzing the problem (STEP 6, the subject of Chapter 8). Here students should strive *not* to allow their personal views to skew their *evaluation* of insights with which they may disagree.

A proven way to work with insights that conflict because their ethical positions conflict is to use Szostak's (2004) classification of five broad types of ethical analysis and decision making:

1. *Consequentialism:* where an act is judged in terms of whether its consequences are good or not

2. *Deontology:* where an individual's act conforms to certain rules such as the Golden Rule (i.e., "Do unto others as you would have others do unto you"), the Kantian categorical imperative (i.e., "An act is ethical if and only if it is in accord with general principles that everyone would want to live by"), and arguments from rights

3. *Virtue:* where individuals are urged to live in accord with one or more virtues, such as honesty

4. *Intuition/experience:* where unique insight into an act, person, relationship, group, or decision is based on "knowing" from experience and reliance on one's subconscious mind (An act is thus judged to be good if it feels right.)

5. *Tradition:* where a behavior, relationship, group, or decision is judged based on its conformity to a historical cultural or societal practice (pp. 124, 194)

These five types of decision-making processes, says Szostak (2004), are mutually exclusive and exhaustive. They "are the five ways in which *any* person might make *any* decision. In terms of ethics," he says, "these five processes describe the five ways in which any person might evaluate *any* act or outcome" (p. 195).

Arguments for the Validity of These Types

Szostak (2004) advances three arguments for the validity of these five broad types of ethical analysis.

1. They each start from valid premises. It makes sense to judge acts by consequences. But it also makes sense to judge acts in terms of virtues or some predetermined rules. And it makes sense to respect (albeit critically) a society's traditions, for there is good reason to suspect these have been (imperfectly) selected to serve the society. And it makes sense to not do things that make us feel guilty.

2. Each of us uses these five types of decision making all the time: We rationally evaluate big decisions (going to university), follow certain rules (be nice to strangers, say), identify ourselves as kind or courageous or honest, do what others do (say, when buying clothes), and act on intuition (when dating). Indeed, we usually do and should use more than one type when making particular decisions: A little rational evaluation of dating choices is a good idea, for example.

3. Philosophers constantly justify only one type of analysis through appeals to others. Rule utilitarians, for example, justify following rules by arguing that we don't have the time or cognitive capacity to rationally evaluate each decision, and thus should follow rules that generally lead to good outcomes. In turn, utilitarians, when asked why we should focus on happiness as the consequence we care about, argue that our intuition tells us that humans want to be happy. Indeed, as much as philosophers like to downplay the role of intuition, the fact is that individuals have an incentive to behave ethically (in situations where nobody will know), only because they will feel bad if they don't (Rick Szostak, personal communication, November 16, 2009).

How to Know If Insights Conflict Over Ethics

Students can determine if insights conflict because of ethical disagreements (rather than because of conflicting theories, concepts, or assumptions) by asking certain questions of each insight. Note that these questions correspond to the five broad types of ethical analysis and decision making. The following questions are designed to help the student identify which type of analysis—consequences, rights, and so on—is at issue:

- Do the insights differ on the desired *consequences* of individual actions?
- Do the insights differ on the *rights* that should be accorded an individual or group?
- Do the insights differ over the choice of which *virtues* should be appreciated or established (i.e., either at the group level, at the individual level, or by adherence to some universal code)?
- Do the insights differ in their beliefs about human *intuition* (e.g., "If one believes that human intuition is grounded in genetics or 'the gift of god' one will expect universal intuitive behavior; if it is thought that intuition is grounded in experience one will not" (Szostak, 2004, p. 195)?
- Do they differ over the role that *tradition* should play when evaluating an act or attitude?

Creating Common Ground When Values and Ethical Positions Conflict

There are at least two possible ways to create common ground when working with dichotomous ethical views. One is to develop a continuum as described in the discussion of transformation and illustrated in the work of Englehart and Etzioni. Readers will recall from their works that they created common ground (though Etzioni did not use this term) between conflicting ethical views. For example, one could develop a continuum between one's right to act and one's right not to be hurt by the actions of others. This strategy works when authors employ different versions of the *same type of ethical analysis*. However, when different types of ethical analysis are employed, a different strategy needs to be employed. For example, when different ethical perspectives focus on different parts of a problem (such that consequentialism stresses results while virtue ethics stresses how we achieve them), it may be useful to redefine terms or employ the technique of organization.

A second possible way to create common ground when identifying and analyzing the potential ethical impacts of decisions is to use the ethical matrix developed by Mepham (2000) for rational ethical analysis. The components of the matrix are based on the work of Beauchamp and Childress (2001) on bioethics that has gained wide support in medicine and medical ethics. They introduced the "four principles approach" through which decision makers were guided to consider four core values: nonmaleficence (doing no harm), beneficence, autonomy, and justice. As an analytical tool, the matrix

> has the three principles (wellbeing, autonomy and justice) on the horizontal axis. On the vertical axis one lists the interest groups— that is, the people, organizations, communities, and so on—who stand to be affected by the decisions being made. The task then is to identify and document the ethical impacts of the matter under consideration in each cell of the matrix. While this task can be undertaken through desk-based research, it is also a dialogue tool when undertaken through group discussion. (McDonald, Bammer, and Deane, 2009, p. 110)

The matrix is particularly useful in situations where, for example, decision makers are concerned that their diverse or conflicting values have the potential to influence their decision on a particularly sensitive matter such as the ethical impacts of introducing a proposed technology (Mepham, 2000, p. 168). "Once the cells of the matrix are filled in," explain McDonald et al. (2009),

> its users weigh the relative importance of the issues identified. Different people might give different weights to a given potential ethical impact on a particular interest group. Through discussion, the users of the matrix reach agreement about how the options under consideration, if implemented, will affect different interest groups with respect to their wellbeing, autonomy and entitlement to justice. (p. 110)

McDonald et al. (2009) identify four primary strengths of the matrix as an approach to prepare for integration:

- It is able to anticipate what the values of different stakeholders might be and how they will be differently impacted by the options available for implementing the initiative.
- It raises the salience of values and conflicts.
- It is grounded in people's own ways of seeing values.
- It is conceptually straightforward. (p. 113)

However, they point to this critical limitation: The matrix fails to provide any clear guidelines on how to move toward a consensus on (i.e., integrate) the values it identifies (p. 113).

In the end, the researcher should evaluate any ethical statement about reality employed in an ethical argument just as one would with any other argument. Assuredly, it is doubtful that common ground can be created in all ethical disputes.

Chapter Summary

This chapter has argued that the process of creating common ground plays out differently depending on whether disciplinary concepts or theories are in view. If concepts, then these are the objects of modification (or the assumptions underlying them); if theories, then the objects of modification are the theories themselves. The first section of the chapter defined common ground, explained that creating common ground requires unconventional thinking, established that it is necessary for collaborative communication across disciplines, and pointed out that common ground is achieved through the use of language. This section also established that common ground is created from concepts and/or assumptions embedded in disciplinary insights, is integral to performing integration, requires using intuition, and plays out differently in contexts of narrow versus wide interdisciplinarity and that creating common ground is the interdisciplinarian's responsibility. The second section detailed how to modify conflicting concepts and assumptions by using one or more modification techniques. These were illustrated from student and professional work. The section also explained how to create common ground when assumed values and rights conflict.

The discussion of STEP 8 in this and in the following chapter is guided by the idea that disciplinary insights are potentially complementary if their concepts or theories are sufficiently modified. But there is no guarantee that common ground can be achieved in every case. Chapter 12 continues the discussion of STEP 8 by focusing on how to modify disciplinary theories.

Notes

1. This belief is opposed to the belief that disciplines are different worlds capable of being understood only from the inside. Weingast (1998) agrees that disciplinary insights are potentially complementary: "In the past, interaction among scholars using different perspectives has tended to emphasize their seeming irreconcilability, as if Kuhn's 'competing paradigms' provides the unique program for interaction among different approaches in the social sciences. In recent years an alternative program has emerged, emphasizing the complementarities among different approaches. This new program acknowledges differences not as competing paradigms but as potentially complementary approaches to complex phenomena. This suggests a more fruitful interaction among scholars of different approaches, where not only the tools and techniques of the other become relevant, but also too do the phenomena under study" (p. 183).

2. That common ground has to be created is especially true in the social sciences and the humanities. William H. Newell (personal communication, January 25, 2010) says, "While many if not most differences are turning out to be

differences in degree, not in kind, I still see at least one difference in kind (or to such a degree that it may as well be a difference in kind) between the social and natural sciences, namely that humans have mental capacities that lead them to exhibit behaviors that are qualitatively different from those of the rest of the natural world (including the overwhelming majority of other living species). Because humans can think systematically, anticipate the future, imagine alternative futures and how they might be achieved, and distinguish between what is and what is not desirable, they can eventually see when there are undesirable unanticipated systemic consequences of their behavior and sometimes change it by deliberately and systematically manipulating, changing, or adding feedback loops within the system."

3. Several interdisciplinary practitioners—including Klein (1996), Repko (2008), Szostak (2004), and Welch (2007)—agree that intuition deserves a place in interdisciplinary theory and methods.

4. I am indebted to William H. Newell (personal communication, April 2005), who gave me the idea to link the four interests in marriage counseling to these techniques.

Exercises

Definition

11.1 How does the definition of common ground complement and extend the definitions of interdisciplinary studies and interdisciplinarity?

Common Ground Theory

11.2 How does common ground theory explain how we are able to comprehend so many different perspectives? What are the implications of the theories of Clark and Bromme for dealing with conflict of all kinds, including values?

Intuition

11.3 How is the story of Helen Keller an example of how intuition helps achieve common ground, and what does this story overlook?

Roles

11.4 How is the role of a marriage counselor similar to the interdisciplinarian's responsibility?

11.5 How is the role that the facilitator plays in an Admission, Review, and Dismissal meeting in special education similar to the role played by the interdisciplinarian in attempting to create common ground among conflicting disciplinary insights?

Best Practice

11.6   How should one proceed with creating common ground in the following situations?

   a. Some of the authors make explicit reference to one or more concepts, but the authors of other insights do not.

   b. All of the authors reference the problem using concepts that have different (apparent or real) meanings.

   c. Some authors use theoretical explanations, but others do not.

Techniques

11.7   What technique(s) might be used in the following situations?

   a. Some of the authors use concepts, and some use theories.

   b. All of the authors use the same concept but use different language to define it.

   c. Authors employ concepts or assumptions and generate insights without formulating theories.

   d. Authors have conflicting conceptions and assumptions about whether behavior is rational or irrational.

11.8   How is Bal's approach to the graffito an example of extending concepts?

11.9   Why did Repko decide to work with assumptions?

12

Creating Common Ground Between Theories

So far our discussion of STEP 8 has established that creating common ground plays out differently depending on whether one is working with a set of concepts *or* a set of theories. Insights produced especially by the social and physical sciences generally rely on theories to explain the phenomena they study. Many theories have concepts embedded within them (e.g., consumer theory has the concepts of preferences or tastes, marginal utility or marginal rate of substitution, trade-offs, and personal income embedded within it). And many social science analyses make use of both theories and concepts (e.g., the economic analysis of international trade makes use not only of the theory of comparative advantage but also of the concept of a production function). So, readers working with a set of theories will have to create common ground by modifying them directly through their concepts or indirectly via their underlying assumptions. The modification strategies commonly used are the subject of this chapter.

The first section of this chapter discusses disciplinary theories and their role in integration. The second section explains the relationship of disciplinary theories to models, variables, and causal processes. The third section presents strategies for preparing a set of disciplinary theories for integration under various conditions.

Disciplinary Theories

Here we define the term *disciplinary theory*, discuss the positions that interdisciplinarians take concerning theory integration, and specify the conditions that require our working with theories.

355

A Definition of *Disciplinary Theory*

As noted in Chapter 1, a **disciplinary theory** explains a behavior or phenomenon that falls within its traditional research domain and *may* have a specified range of applicability.[1] Theories are generally built up from concepts, or kernels of ideas, that theorists then link together into explanations for behavior or events. This feature is one reason why it is necessary to treat concepts separately from theories.

Disciplinary theories have four parts: concepts, assumptions, variables, and processes. Ideally, a theory should "specify in a logically consistent manner agency, action, decision-making processes, location, and time path, with respect to any (posited) causal relationship" (Szostak, 2004, p. 75). Unfortunately, not all disciplinary theories specify these things.

The social sciences, like their natural science counterparts, typically see theories as assertions about relationships among variables. Disciplinary theories provide insights into the cause or effect of a behavior or phenomenon. Each discipline uses its preferred method(s) to judge whether a theory seems to accord with reality.

When Working With Theories Is Necessary

We are obligated to work with theories when they dominate disciplinary discourse concerning a particular problem. More particularly, we must work with theories when the literature search has identified insights that are produced by theories.

By now it should be clear that we are primarily interested in solving complex problems, creating more comprehensive meanings and interpretations, and developing comprehensive understandings of complex processes and systems. Szostak (2009) reminds us that expert insights into these problems and theoretical explanations of them can only be understood within the context of a discipline's theories, methods, subject matter, and overall perspective. "It cannot be stressed too much that disciplines choose a mutually compatible set of theories, methods, and phenomena: methods that are good at investigating their theory, and phenomena that lend themselves to the application of that theory and method" (Szostak, 2009, p. 15).

Disciplinary theories are developed to explain how some aspect of the world works. They explain particular aspects of complex social problems such as the causes of economic growth. Since each theory focuses on only a particular aspect of a problem, any one theory will provide incomplete understanding. That is, different theories will illuminate different aspects of the question of, say, the causes of economic growth.

BOX 12.1

These scientific theories must be distinguished from a variety of philosophical theories regarding ethical, epistemological, and metaphysical questions. For example, ethical theories help to decide whether or not economic growth is good. While scientific theories are the more common focus of integration, we discuss in Chapter 13 how to cope with philosophical theories. Given the centrality of theories in explanation outside the humanities, a key substep in this part of the interdisciplinary research process (IRP) should be to check the impact of any change in concept or assumption (made to create common ground) on the relevant theories that use variables based on the assumption or concept.

The Relationship of Models, Variables, and Causal Processes to Theories

Having established when working with theories is necessary, we next discuss the relationship of models, variables, and causal processes to theories.

Models

A model serves to visualize and communicate a theory. "It is a representation that is specific and clear in the same way that a model of a building represents clearly and precisely what an architect plans to build" (Remler & van Ryzin, 2011, p. 30). Models are very helpful in making sense of complex processes and depicting cause-and-effect relationships.

Models may be either graphical (a picture) or mathematical (an equation).[2] In this book, graphical models, such as path models, are used to express theory. Figure 12.1 is a path model that depicts "the broken window theory of crime." It communicates the idea that seemingly trivial acts of disorder (like broken windows) trigger more serious crime (p. 31).

Figure 12.1   Path Model of the "Broken Windows" Theory

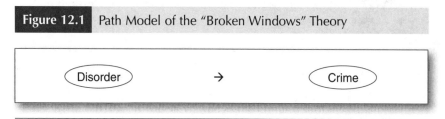

SOURCE: Remler & van Ryzin (2011, p. 31).

Variables and Relationships

A model such as that shown in Figure 12.1 is made up of two elements: variables (the ovals) and the relationship(s) between them (the arrow). The relationship between crime and disorder is represented by the arrow pointing from disorder to crime. The arrow shows the direction of the relationship: Disorder triggers crime.

Here a variable means the same thing as a phenomenon and is consistent with how it is defined in Chapter 4. A **variable** "is something that can take on different values or assume different attributes—it is something that varies" (Remler & van Ryzin, 2011, p. 31). For example, the broken windows theory is based on empirical evidence demonstrating that the murder rate takes on different values over time and across cities—so murder rate is a variable. The theory attempts to explain this variation between high and low murder rates by way of another variable—disorder. It should be stressed that in saying that one variable influences another, it need not be asserted that only that variable does so.

Theories explain causal relationships (hence the unidirectional arrow). A **causal relationship** refers to how a change in one variable produces or leads to change in another variable. The purpose of science, says Szostak (2004), is to understand causal relationships or links. For this reason, "each theory needs to carefully express which causal links it addresses, and under what circumstances the theory holds along those links: that is, its **range of applicability**" (p. 75). According to the broken windows theory, cracking down on vandalism and graffiti produces a reduction in more serious crime (p. 31). The social sciences, like their natural science counterparts, typically see theories as assertions about relationships among variables, or (in the language of the humanities) about how some things influence others.

Independent and Dependent Variables

Figure 12.2 shows the cause-and-effect relationship of *disorder* (the **independent variable**) and *crime* (the **dependent variable**). The independent variable

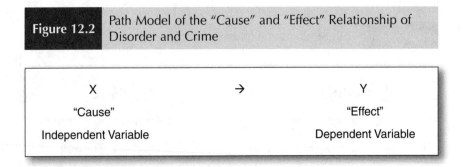

Figure 12.2   Path Model of the "Cause" and "Effect" Relationship of Disorder and Crime

X	→	Y
"Cause"		"Effect"
Independent Variable		Dependent Variable

SOURCE: Remler & van Ryzin (2011, p. 31).

is the *cause* and the dependent variable is the *effect,* so the model asserts that crime "depends" on disorder. By convention, the independent variable is symbolized by *X,* while the dependent variable is symbolized by Y. Remler and van Ryzin (2011) explain: "Just as cause comes before effect, and X comes before Y in the alphabet, the independent variable comes before the dependent variable in the causal order of things" (p. 31).

As these authors note, two of the most fundamental yet often confusing terms in research are *independent variable* and *dependent variable.* Unfortunately, researchers in different disciplines use different terms to describe independent and dependent variables. For example, in health science research, the independent variable is often called a *treatment* and the dependent variable an *outcome.* Other terms for an independent variable include *explanatory, predictor,* and *regressor;* other terms for a dependent variable include *response, predicted,* and *regressand.* Therefore, one should think carefully about the sequence of the variables and ask which is the presumed "cause" of the problem and which is the "effect" (Remler & van Ryzin, 2011, p. 32). Our use of the word *cause* allows for multiple causes. To be a "cause" the independent variable needs only to exert *some* effect on the dependent variable.

Why a More Comprehensive Theory Includes Variables From Other Relevant Theories

A disciplinary theory such as the broken windows theory typically explains the relationship between only a few variables as shown in Figure 12.1. Interdisciplinarians, however, must work with a set of theories from two or more disciplines *and their corresponding variables* in order to construct a more comprehensive theoretical explanation of a problem, process, or system. Therefore, the comprehensive theoretical explanation will have to include more variables than does any single disciplinary theory. Because disciplines look at a complex phenomenon from different perspectives, they must of necessity use at least somewhat different variables to explain its different aspects. Otherwise, it would be a simple phenomenon. The interdisciplinarian may also decide to develop a model of the complex system that is consistent with the theoretical disciplinary insights. If so, the model will have to show the relationships among the variables drawn from multiple theories.

Theories May Contain Macro- and/or Micro-Level Variables Affecting the Construction of a More Comprehensive Theory

A set of theories may contain variables (e.g., micro or macro from different levels). The most common distinction in the social sciences is between the micro and macro levels—that is, between the level of individuals and the level of society—though there are plenty of theories that operate at the mezzo (or "in between") level of groups or communities, and theories that operate at the international level. In a two-level analysis (as in the following example), *macro* may be used generally to refer to any level larger than individuals. Some theorists choose to use different terms for some levels, and some layer reality differently depending on their focus (e.g., subcultural, cultural, cross-cultural). Since the terminology of levels is not consistent from author to author, much less from discipline to discipline, interdisciplinarians need to exercise care in identifying the level of each variable.

Criminologists Stuart Henry and Nicole Bracy (2012) provide this example: "We might want to look at the range of variables from different theories that have empirically demonstrated to correlate with the propensity of juveniles to join gangs" (p. 263). One set of theories may include variables such as "neighborhood housing density, age, criminality of parents or siblings, degree of neighborhood disorganization, or neighborhood transience rates" (Henry & Bracy, 2012, p. 263). Note that these variables operate at the macro level of the community or society and are external to the juvenile. Another set of theories may include variables that operate at the micro level and are internal to the person such as the biological or psychological development processes of juveniles.

These sets of variables, explain Henry and Bracy (2012), may be interconnected in different ways:

> Theories that see community as shaping the opportunities available for adolescents to make more or less delinquent decisions present a different set of interconnections than those that see such opportunities in the environment only being acted on by juveniles who are predisposed to sensation-seeking behavior through biological or psychological development processes. In this individual-level predisposition case, we might be including variables such as adolescent brain development, domestic abuse, traumatic brain syndrome, high sugar consumption, addictive personality, etc. (p. 263)

Clearly, then, a different theoretical explanation of the problem of why juveniles join gangs would emerge based on whether (a) we integrate variables located at the micro level of analysis (at the level of the individual), or (b) we integrate elements of theory based at the macro level of analysis (i.e., at the level of the community and society) since the latter are influenced by the former, and vice versa. Henry and Bracy's (2012) point is this: "*The decision about the nature of the interconnections between variables affects which concepts are integrated from the different discipline-based theories* [emphasis added]" (p. 263). Therefore, a more comprehensive theory (one that has been extended in STEP 9, the subject of Chapter 13) will include a wider array of variables (e.g., both macro and micro) and provide a much different explanation than do any of the individual disciplinary theories and their corresponding variables (Henry & Bracy, 2012, p. 263).

BOX 12.2

Henry and Bracy (2012) seem to suggest that different sets of criminologists focus on different *directions* of causation. However, the presumption that causation only operates in one direction limits the comprehensiveness of the understanding. For example, economists often assume that societies can be understood entirely in terms of individual decision making, and sociologists often imagine that individuals are mere creatures of societal roles. Interdisciplinarians should urge the integration of these approaches.

Variables and Causality

Theories express causal relationships. Therefore, a change in the independent variable is presumed to cause change in the dependent variable. *How* this happens is what researchers call a **causal process** that underlies this relationship. For example, disorder in a neighborhood evidenced by broken windows and graffiti signals that no one cares and that rules are not enforced. According to the broken windows theory, criminals read these signals and become emboldened to commit crime. This is the causal process theorized in the broken windows theory (Remler & van Ryzin, 2011, p. 32).

Though the causal process noted here is a critical component of the broken windows theory, it does not appear in the model shown in Figure 12.1. So, to provide a full description of the theory, we need to add to the model a statement of the process that explains *how* change in the independent variable causes change in the dependent variable. And, we need to make this causal process explicit by adding what is called an "intervening variable" to the model. An **intervening variable** is a step(s) in the causal process that leads from the independent to the dependent variable (Remler & van Ryzin, 2011, p. 33).

When Theories Differ Only Minimally and Focus Instead on Process

There are cases when different disciplinary authors have developed theories that overlap more than they differ. They focus primarily on how the process identified in one theory sets the stage for the process identified in others, which in turn influences others. These cases involve multiple interactions and feedbacks. In these cases, the map showing these interactions and feedbacks depicts the common ground. Student work is identified by an asterisk (*).

From the Social Sciences: Foisy* (2010), Creating Meaning in Everyday Life: An Interdisciplinary Understanding In this threaded example, Michelle Foisy studies the problem of how people create meaning in their everyday lives. She draws on the perspectives of two disciplines, psychology and philosophy (at least indirectly), because they both have produced widely accepted theories on "meaning" in a general sense. She also draws on a non-disciplinary pop psychology perspective popularized in the movie *The Bucket List*. From these, she identified four theories: Flow Theory and Goal-Setting Theory from psychology (more specifically, positive psychology, a recent offshoot of humanistic psychology); Logotherapy from a philosophically based form of psychoanalysis; and "Bucket List" Theory from a nondisciplinary source that was vetted by her instructor.

Foisy compares these theories using Szostak's (2004) 5 Ws, and developed Table 12.1 to juxtapose them and discover their similarities and differences. The table reveals minimal conflict between these theories: They all focus on the individual and overlap in terms of the range of decision-making strategies they promote. Foisy writes, "It is likely that when investigating the topic of meaning, all five decision-making strategies could be appropriate, and the *most* appropriate strategy might vary depending on the nature of the problem and the personality of the individual" (p. 16). The theories differ only in terms of *what* the individual is doing (acting, thinking, or reacting), and *where* and *when* the process occurs.

Table 12.1　A Summary of Flow Theory, Goal-Setting Theory, Logotherapy, and "Bucket List" Theory Using Szostak's 5 Ws

	Flow Theory	Goal-Setting Theory	Logotherapy	"Bucket List" Theory
Who?	Individual	Individual	Individual	Individual
What?	Act	Act Think	*React*	Think
Why?	Emotional/ intuitive	Rational Traditional Emotional/intuitive Value-based Rule-based	Rational Value-based	Rational Traditional Emotional/intuitive Value-based Rule-based
Where?	Universal	Universal	Universal	*Culture-specific*
When?	Change in one direction	Change in one direction	Change in one direction	*Cyclical*

SOURCE: Foisy (2010).

NOTE: *Red* text identifies conflicts between theories.

The challenge for Foisy is to create common ground between theories that conflict minimally and that focus on process. Her narrative first addresses how the theories differ:

> Logotherapy is the only theory that focuses on the individual *reacting*. . . . "Bucket List" Theory is culture-specific and cyclical, whereas the other three theories are universal theories that promote change in one direction. A third conflict that is not identified in Table 12.1 is the issue of semantics. Lastly, there are also gaps between all four theories that need to be addressed. (p. 18)

More problematic, she continues, was that these theories "all seem to address *different parts* of my research question": "Bucket List" Theory focuses on explicitly identifying life goals; Flow Theory focuses on the process of becoming engaged in an activity; Logotherapy discusses people's reactions to their current situation; and Goal-Setting Theory focuses on setting clear goals that the individual can reach (p. 18). The solution to the problem of how to create common ground in this case was for Foisy to map the problem as shown in Figure 12.3.

In this case, the map of the causal processes at work depicts the common ground.

Figure 12.3   Meaning Construction Model: An Interdisciplinary Answer to the Question, "How Can People Create Meaning in Their Lives?"

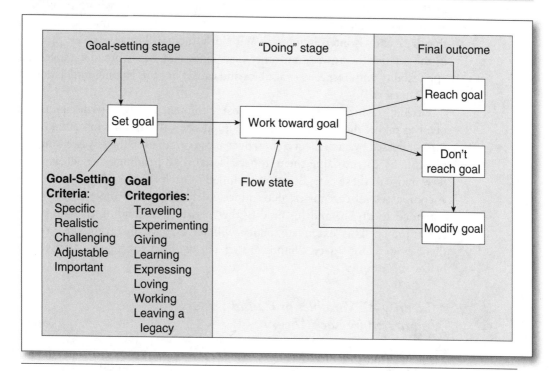

SOURCE: Foisy (2010).

Modifying a Set of Theories

When working with theories, two situations are commonly encountered. The first is discovering that some theories in the set have a broader range of applicability than do others (Situation A) and, thus, may already be narrowly interdisciplinary. In this case, one has to decide which of these broader range theories requires the smallest changes to make it more comprehensively interdisciplinary.

The second situation is discovering that none of the theories in the set borrows elements from other disciplines (Situation B). In this event, one will have to decide on an appropriate modification strategy involving either each theory's concepts or its assumptions. *When modifying a theory in any way, the principle of least action should be followed: making sure that the changes are the smallest possible.*

In either situation, one should make certain that the different authors are in fact talking about the same thing. Mapping their arguments enables the researcher to distinguish real conflicts (over the same thing) from apparent conflicts (when authors talk about different things).

Situation A: One or More Theories in the Set Have a Broader Range of Applicability Than Do Others

In this situation, there are one or more theories in the set whose range of applicability is already broad (i.e., it borrows from other disciplines), and/or that are narrowly interdisciplinary. With luck, there will be at least one theory in the set that borrows from other disciplines and has a broader range of applicability with respect to variables and causal links (including interactions between causes).

Deciding which theory is the most comprehensively interdisciplinary involves taking the following substeps: (a) identify all variables or causal factors addressed by each theory; (b) reduce these variables to the fewest number possible by categorizing them under a few broad headings; (c) determine how many of these categories are included in each theory; (d) if no theory encompasses all categories, determine which theory can most readily be extended to do so; and (e) modify the theory by extending its range of applicability. This extended theory will be used to integrate the other theories in STEP 9 (see Chapter 13). Each of these substeps is discussed below more fully.

Identify All Variables or Causal Factors Addressed by Each Theory

These variables should have been identified when the problem was mapped in STEP 3 (see Chapter 5). In the threaded example of the problem of suicide terrorism, Repko (2012) identifies eight variables that theories claim are likely causes of suicide terrorism: (a) cognitive constructs that may predispose a person to become a suicide terrorist; (b) influences on a person's mental development; (c) "justification" (an even stronger, more compelling, moral claim that overrides one's natural repugnance to engage in suicide terrorism); (d) "emotion" triggered by traumatic memory, or regret for not exacting vengeance on an enemy; (e) the influence of institutions, both domestic and foreign, that may trigger or exacerbate a collective or an individual sense of political oppression and/or historical loss; (f) a shared sense of place, and identification with a race, an ethnic group, a history, a nation, and/or a religion; (g) emotional bonding to a way of life, traditions, behaviors, values, and symbols; and (h) a fundamentalist faith tradition that relies on sacred writings and charismatic leadership to determine an individual's motivations and actions and a belief that religion must struggle to assert (or reassert) its control over every facet of life.

Reduce These Variables to the Fewest Number Possible by Categorizing Them Under a Few Broad Headings

Next, reduce these variables or causal factors to the fewest number possible by categorizing them under a few broad headings derived from Szostak's table of phenomena introduced in Chapter 4 (see Table 4.4). Repko (2012) creates four categories: *personality traits, power seeking, cultural identity,* and *sacred values. Personality traits* refers to cognitive constructs that may predispose a person to become a suicide terrorist as well as influence a person's mental development. These traits include "justification" (an even stronger, more compelling moral claim that overrides one's natural repugnance to engage in suicide terrorism) and strong "emotion" (triggered by traumatic memory or regret for not exacting vengeance on an enemy) (Reisberg, 2006, pp. 465–470). *Power seeking* refers to the influence of domestic and foreign institutions on individuals, on particular groups, and on society as a whole. Such influence may include the policies and activities of Western corporations, UN agencies, foreign military forces, Western support of oppressive regimes, American support of Israel, and the countervailing influence of terrorist organizations such as al-Qaeda. Each and any of these influences may trigger or exacerbate a collective or an individual sense of political oppression and/or historical loss. *Cultural identity* refers to having a shared sense of place and identification with a race, an ethnic group, a history, a nation, and/or a religion. Cultural identity may also include emotional bonding based on a way of life, traditions, behaviors, values, and symbols. *Sacred values* refers to a fundamentalist faith tradition that relies on sacred writings and charismatic leadership to determine an individual's motivations and actions. This factor includes the idea that religion must struggle to assert (or reassert) its control over every facet of life. The perspective of history is subsumed under culture, politics, and religion (Reisberg, 2006, pp. 146–147).

Determine How Many of These Categories Are Included in Each Theory

The next substep is to determine how many of these categories are included in each theory. The result of this evaluative process is shown in Table 12.2.

The table shows that all of the theories (listed vertically on the left) focus on at least two of the causal factors (listed horizontally across the top). The theories of "sacred" terror, self-sanction, and identity attribute the causes of suicide terrorism to three of the four factors. The value of this process is that it narrows the number of possible candidates for theory modification from eight to three: "sacred" terror, self-sanction, and identity theory. The next challenge is to decide which of these three theories should be modified.

If No Theory Encompasses All Categories, Determine Which Theory Can Most Readily Be Extended to Do So

When working with a large number of theories, it is necessary to continue the process of narrowing until the theory that is the most comprehensive is revealed. The most comprehensive interdisciplinary theory is one that requires the least possible modification so that it includes all variables.

Table 12.2	Theories on the Causes of Suicide Terrorism (ST) Showing Key Causal Factors

Theory of ST	Variables or Causal Factors Broadly Stated			
Theory	Personality traits	Power seeking	Cultural identity	Sacred beliefs
Terrorist psycho-logic	Yes	No	No	No
Self-sanction	No	Yes	Yes	Yes
Martyrdom	Yes	No	No	No
Collective rational strategic choice	Yes	Yes	No	No
"Sacred" terror	No	Yes	Yes	Yes
Identity	Yes	Yes	Yes	Yes
Fictive kin	No	No	Yes	Yes
Modernization	No	Yes	Yes	Indirectly

SOURCE: Repko (2012, p. 147).

What follows is Repko's (2012) description of the process he uses to determine which of the three theories he identifies as interdisciplinary meets this standard:

• Rapoport's (1998) theory of "holy" or "sacred" terror: Though the theory explains suicide terrorism as a political problem caused by terrorist political aspirations, it takes into account how culture and religious values may motivate a person to become a suicide terrorist. But, because the theory does not borrow from psychology, it is unable to explain how a person's mind may be predisposed [to], susceptible to, or shaped by these complex influences and motivated to commit such a horrific act. So rather than force the theory to explain what it was not designed to explain—that is, the shaping of a person's personality and cognitive development—it is better to consider the possibilities offered by the other two.

• Bandura's (1998) self-sanction theory: The theory explains how terrorist organizations convert "socialized people" into dedicated combatants by "cognitively restructuring the moral value of killing, so that the killing can be done free from self-censuring restraints" (p. 164). The process of moral cognitive restructuring involves using religion, politics, and psychology to construe suicide attacks narrowly. This involves using (a) religion to justify such acts by invoking "situational imperatives," (b) the political argument of self-defense to show how the group is "fighting ruthless oppressors" who are threatening the community's "cherished values and way of life," and (c) the psychological device of dehumanization to justify killing "the enemy." . . . Though the theory does not borrow from other disciplines, it explains how cultural and political factors are integrated into the mental process of construal and inform individual decision making. One weakness of the theory is its silence concerning individual personality factors that may influence the would-be terrorist's decision-making process. But since the theory is a psychological theory, this weakness can be overcome by borrowing from other psychology theories so that it would be able to include the influence of personality traits and dispositions.

• Monroe and Kreidie's (1997) identity theory: Identity theory is already interdisciplinary (though narrowly so) because it borrows from other disciplines. Identity theory already addresses three of the four factors—cultural identity, sacred beliefs (i.e., religion), and power seeking (i.e., politics). The theory draws from religious studies by showing that the Islamic fundamentalist conception of religion is, in fact, an all-encompassing ideology that erases all lines between public and private. This theology-based ideology is grounded in religious writings and commentaries on these writings that are viewed by its most devoted followers as sacred, inviolable, nonnegotiable, and worth dying for. As a "sacred ideology" (Marxism never achieved this lofty status) Islamic fundamentalism redefines politics and power. As Monroe and Kreidie show, politics for Islamic fundamentalists is subsumed under an all-encompassing religious faith, and is sought and exercised for the purpose of extending the faith. Achieving, maintaining, and extending power is a sacred duty that has priority over all other obligations, including family. Because the theory holds that the self is culturally situated, it is able to explain how culture influences identity formation. (Repko, 2012, pp. 147–148)

From his analysis of the three theories, Repko (2012) concludes that Monroe and Kreidie's (1997) identity theory, which is already interdisciplinary, will require the smallest changes.

Modify the Theory by Extending Its Range of Applicability

Once the theory that is the most comprehensive interdisciplinary theory is identified, the next task is to extend its range of applicability by using the technique of **theory extension**. Extending a disciplinary theory calls for taking well-known facts normally treated as exogenous (i.e., external) to it (such as organisms altering their environment) and making them endogenous (i.e., internal) to and mutually interactive with it. This commonly used technique enables a theory to encompass other relevant theories or combine the best parts of them. When extending a theory, the principle of least action should be followed: making sure that the changes are the smallest possible.

In the present example, it is appropriate for Repko (2012) to use theory extension because identity theory already has parts that come from other disciplines. Here, he explains how he extends identity theory to make it fully interdisciplinary:

> For the theory to include the fourth causal factor of personality traits would require the least amount of "stretching and pulling" (i.e., extending). This is because identity theory, as already noted, is based on the psychological concepts of cognition and perspective. These concepts address personality traits in a way that is inclusive of the psychology theories already examined. Monroe and Kreidie [1997] use the concept of cognition in a developmental way, meaning that they are concerned to show how persons are influenced by factors external to themselves—namely culture and societal norms—rather than focusing on individual cognitive abnormalities as Post [1998] does to argue that some persons are psychologically predisposed to commit acts of suicide terrorism. Only slight "stretching" or extending is necessary to have identity theory include personality factors intrinsic to the individual suicide terrorist. Monroe and Kreidie's application of "perspective" to explain suicide terrorist behavior is also helpful in this regard because it effectively delineates the options that terrorists perceive as being available to them. . . . The act of committing a suicide attack in the service of a fundamentalist conception of *jihad* "emanates primarily from the person accepting their identity which means that they have to abide by the tenets of their religion." . . . By borrowing these

concepts from psychology, identity theory offers an understanding of human behavior that is based on the interplay of mental constructs in tandem with the exogenous variables of politics, culture, and religion. (Repko, 2012, pp. 148–149)

Once extended, identity theory is of sufficient generality to include the causal factors from psychology.

Ideally, an extended theory that is fully interdisciplinary will incorporate all relevant causal factors, propositions, and parallel interactive processes from the other theories in the set. Propositions are "the interconnections or relationships between two or more variables, or among a specific (and usually small) set of variables" (Henry & Bracy, 2012, p. 265). Theory extension is used most often in causal or propositional integration (discussed in Chapter 13).

Critiquing Theories

Earlier we said that theories tend to be partly right and partly wrong. Theories thought to be relevant to the problem should be evaluated, and not just when they conflict. So far, the examples used here *appear* to presume that the theories identified as most relevant are all incomplete but correct. This gives readers the false impression that interdisciplinarity is only about combining and not about critiquing and rethinking. However, the authors referenced here critiqued their theories during earlier STEPS of the IRP.

What follows are ideas on *how* to critique theories:

- Theories that seem sensible (and fit the available data) within one disciplinary perspective when applied to one aspect of a complex phenomenon may need to be revised as well as extended when applied to the complex phenomenon as a whole.
- One tests each theory against the available empirical data for the complex phenomenon as a whole. Remember that van der Lecq (2012) evaluated theories "by testing them against the pool of information to which research from all the perspectives contributed" (Newell, 2012, p. 308).
- One revises and integrates theories by "go[ing] back and forth between parts and whole [between partial theoretical insights and overall empirical information], asking how disciplinary insights might be modified or postulating additional interdisciplinary linkages, so that the behavior they predict is consistent with the observed behavior of the complex system" (Newell, 2007a, p. 261).

Undergraduate students are less likely to be asked to critique each theory to the same extent as graduate students. It is expected that mature scholars and members of interdisciplinary research teams will thoroughly critique each theory.

Situation B: None of the Theories in the Set Borrow Elements From Other Disciplines

It may be that none of the theories in the set has a broader range of applicability than do the others. In this event, the researcher will have to decide what *parts* of the theories in the set to modify: their concepts or their assumptions. When working with theories, one must be certain that the different authors are in fact talking about the same thing.

In interdisciplinary work, concepts and assumptions are the elements most commonly modified. *Concepts* are the most basic building blocks of any theory. A concept, it will be recalled, is a word or symbol that represents a phenomenon (a label we use to name and classify our perceptions of reality and our experiences) or an abstract idea generalized from particular instances. Theories are generally built up from concepts, or kernels of ideas, that theorists then link together into explanations for events or phenomena. Earlier we said that a disciplinary theory includes variables and describes relationships between them. A variable may be a concept or, more often, a way of operationalizing a concept. Henry and Bracy (2012) explain how the social disorganization theory of gang formation is built up from concepts:

> High levels of immigration into cities combined with profit-seeking landlords leads to poor quality, low rent multi-family inner-city housing with high resident turnover; the resultant neighborhood instability fragments communities, resulting in a breakdown of informal networks of social control. Fearful of being victimized, youth band together for self-protection forming subcultures that can form into territorial gangs that protect their own members by exerting fear on non-gang or other gang members and maintain their autonomy by engaging in a variety of delinquency such as vandalism and drug dealing (social disorganization theory of gang formation). (p. 264)

The second component of a disciplinary theory is its underlying *assumptions*. Assumptions may concern human nature or the physical environment. For example, sociologists differ in whether they view human behavior as essentially determined (and so in principle predictable) or they emphasize human creativity. An explicit philosophical statement of the first view is found in George C. Homan's work where he emphasizes the role played by individual choices and decisions. But his whole approach is based on the assumption that human behavior has causes, and so is predictable (Wallace & Wolf, 2006, p. 6). Disciplinary theories make assumptions (often implicit as well as explicit) about each variable and each relationship. In short, a disciplinary theory specifies what affects what (variables) and how (processes).

Modifying Concepts Embedded in Theories

The objective of concept modification is to develop a common language across disciplines. Concept modification involves (a) finding concepts that have similar meanings in different theories, (b) modifying the concepts so that they have the same meaning across all the theories, and (c) paying attention to disciplinary perspective when redefining concepts. Differences in terminology may mean that disciplinary authors are talking about different causal processes, even if they appear initially to be talking about the same thing and disagreeing. Nagy's (2005) study of anthropogenic forces degrading tropical ecosystems in a Latin American country is an example of how to modify concepts that appear to be similar but have different meanings in different disciplinary theories.

Concepts That Have Different Meanings in Different Disciplinary Theories   Nagy (2005) draws on theories from biology, anthropology, and economics to explain the ecological and environmental problems facing Costa Rica. She finds a dichotomy between theories dealing with the environment and those dealing with economics. Nagy explains that the region's economic and environmental problems are linked in a mutual feedback loop: Growing population requires increased economic development, which causes environmental degradation of tropical ecosystems, which worsens living conditions for the poor and widens the income gap between the rich and the poor. Purely disciplinary approaches (of which there are many) suggest that the choice is between economics and environmental science. That is, Costa Rica (or a similar nation) must choose between increasing economic development to help raise living standards (and thereby worsen environmental degradation) and restricting development to protect fragile tropical ecosystems (and thereby reduce living standards).

The challenge for Nagy is to reduce the conflict between these irreconcilable disciplinary stances. While reflecting on the possible reasons for this conflict, she realized that the basic values of the two perspectives are in conflict. These conflicting values express themselves in how each discipline defines "wealth." For environmental scientists, wealth refers to the health of an ecosystem (excluding humans) and to the diversity of species within it. For economists, wealth is accumulated assets derived from development.

Modifying the Concept So That It Has the Same Meaning Across All the Theories   One way to modify a concept in preparation for modifying the theories that use it is to redefine it. (Note: The technique of redefinition is discussed in Chapter 11.) Another way is to extend its meaning. Nagy (2005) does both. She redefines the concept of "wealth," enabling it to include both economic development and ecosystem health. She also extends the redefined meaning of wealth from assets valued solely by the marketplace (the result of development) to include assets valued by society as a whole (a healthy and diverse environment). By freeing herself from the marketplace, she can also extend "wealth" from a short-term (economic) to a long-term (environmental) concept (Nagy 2005, pp. 104–108).

Paying Attention to Disciplinary Perspective   Henry and Bracy (2012) urge us to pay attention to disciplinary perspectives when redefining concepts. In modifying concepts, the separate disciplinary "languages" (really, definitions of terms) reflect the differences as well as the similarities in meanings of related concepts. Those differences, say Henry and Bracy, reflect what distinguishes one discipline from another, most generally, its *perspective or worldview*. Concept modification, then, is not the simple task of focusing on similarities and ignoring differences. Rather, it entails figuring out how to utilize those similarities in a way that retains the integrity of the original concept (Henry & Bracy, 2012, p. 264).

These authors take the position that, much like the integration of insights, each redefined concept should be responsive to the perspective of each contributing discipline, but dominated by none of them. They illustrate their point with this example:

> Akers's (1994) "conceptual absorption" approach takes concepts from social learning and social control theory (among others) and merges these together. The control theory concept of "belief," which refers to a person's moral conviction for or against delinquency, is equated to learning theory's "definitions favorable or unfavorable to crime" (differential association). Interestingly, there are parallels here to the theory of human cognitive practice known as "conceptual blending" in which humans subconsciously integrate elements and relations from diverse situations to create new concepts, a process seen by some as being at the heart of the creative process. (Henry & Bracy, 2012, p. 264)

Modifying Assumptions Underlying Theories

A second strategy to prepare theories for integration when none of the theories borrows from other disciplines is to modify their underlying assumptions. When speaking of assumptions, we mean assumptions regarding how a particular influence or causal relationship operates. One has to get *behind* the conflict itself to bring out the *source(s)* of the conflict. One has to dig into the text of each theory in the set and juxtapose their insights to discover why their explanations, arguments, concepts, and use of data conflict.

Assumption modification involves (a) critiquing each theory, (b) identifying the assumption of each theory, (c) determining which assumptions are shared by the other theories, and then (d) modifying these assumptions so that all the theories in the set share a bedrock or common assumption.

Critique Each Theory   Critiquing each theory means checking to see if it is merely different from others in the set or conflicting. Differences in language may mean that disciplinary authors are talking about different things, even if they appear initially to be talking about the same thing and disagreeing. Creating common ground among the assumptions of disciplinary theories is possible only if the different authors are talking about the same thing.

Identify the Assumption(s) of Each Theory   Disciplinary theories typically reflect the assumption(s) of the disciplines that produce them. The assumptions of each theory should be available from the mapping of the problem and from the data table that one developed earlier (see Chapter 6). While performing earlier STEPS, Repko (2012) found that some authors used concepts (in some cases multiple concepts) while others did not use any. He concluded that he could not create common ground by redefining any of these concepts because they would not (indeed could not) apply to all of the theories. So, unable to work with concepts, he decided to work with assumptions. The assumption(s) of each theory are identified in Table 12.3. Readers will note that these assumptions are primary-level assumptions because they are derived directly from the theory itself.

Table 12.3   Theories and Their Assumptions on the Causes of Suicide Terrorism

Theory	Assumption(s) of Theory (Primary Level)
Terrorist psycho-logic	Suicide terrorists are born, not made. Understanding the behavior and motivation of suicide terrorists requires studying primarily the mental life and the psychological constructs of individual terrorists.
Self-sanction	Suicide terrorists are made, not born. Understanding the behavior and motivation of suicide terrorists requires studying primarily the mental life and the psychological constructs of individual terrorists.
Martyrdom	Suicide terrorists are made, not born. Understanding the behavior and motivation of suicide terrorists requires studying primarily the mental life and the psychological constructs of individual terrorists.
Collective rational strategic choice	Suicide terrorists follow logical processes that can be discovered and explained. The primary focus of research should be on terrorist groups rather than on individuals.
"Sacred" terror	Suicide terrorists follow logical processes that can be discovered and explained. The primary focus of research should be on terrorist groups rather than on individuals.
Identity	Suicide terrorists are made, not born. Religious identity is (at least in this instance) an effective way to explain the "political" phenomenon of suicide terrorism. Terrorist behavior is essentially rational.

(Continued)

Table 12.3	(Continued)

Theory	Assumption(s) of Theory (Primary Level)
Fictive kin	Suicide terrorists are made, not born. Suicide terrorists are largely the product of identity with and loyalty to a culturally cohesive and intimate cohort of peers that recruiting organizations often promote through religious indoctrination.
Modernization	Suicide terrorists are made, not born. Poverty, authoritarianism, and diminishing expectations inevitably breed alienation and violence. Suicide terrorism is the inevitable result of Islam's failure to embrace Western institutions and values.

Identify Which Assumptions Are Shared by the Other Theories   The next substep is to identify which assumptions are shared by other theories. Table 12.3, which Repko (2012) constructed while performing STEP 7 and has reproduced here, provides this information. It lists the relevant theories concerning the causes of suicide terrorism (left column), their parent disciplines (center column), and the assumption that each group of disciplinary theories shares (right column). These assumptions are secondary-level assumptions.

Juxtaposing the assumptions of each theory as Table 12.4 does reveals that some of these assumptions are shared by more than one theory. For example, the psychology theories of terrorist psycho-logic, self-sanction, and martyrdom share the assumption typical of psychology: Understanding the behavior and motivation of suicide terrorists requires studying the mental life and psychological constructs of individual terrorists.

The theories of collective rational strategic choice, "sacred" terror, and identity share two assumptions of political science that suicide terrorists follow logical processes that can be discovered and explained and that the primary focus of study should be the behavior of terrorist groups rather than the behavior of individual terrorists. But note that only "sacred" terror theory and identity theory assume that a terrorist's religious affiliation is an effective way to explain the "political" phenomenon of suicide terrorism.

Fictive kin theory is grounded in cultural anthropology and therefore reflects its assumption that the determining factor in shaping the development of a suicide terrorist is the terrorist's loyalty to an intimate cohort of peers, all of whom share an intense devotion to religious dogma. This theory (as shown in Table 12.5) shares with identity theory (introduced in Chapter 10 as an interdisciplinary theory grounded in political science and religious studies) the assumption that religion is an important factor in understanding the development of a suicide terrorist. Finally, modernization theory from history rests on the assumption that suicide terrorism is the result of Islam's failure to embrace Western institutions and values.

Table 12.4	Sources of Conflict Between Relevant Theories in Terms of Their Underlying Assumptions	

Theory	Discipline	Assumption(s) of Theory (Secondary Level)
Terrorist psycho-logic	Cognitive Psychology	Understanding the behavior and motivation of suicide terrorists requires studying primarily the mental life and the psychological constructs of individual terrorists.
Self-sanction		
Martyrdom		
Collective rational strategic choice	Political Science	Suicide terrorists follow logical processes that can be discovered and explained. The primary focus of research should be on the behavior of terrorist groups rather than on the behavior of individual terrorists.
"Sacred" terror		
Identity		
"Sacred" terror		Religious identity is (at least in this instance) an effective way to explain the "political" phenomenon of suicide terrorism. Terrorist behavior is essentially a rational outworking of one's religious identity.
Identity		
Fictive kin	Cultural Anthropology	Suicide terrorists are largely the product of identity with and loyalty to a culturally cohesive and intimate cohort of peers that recruiting organizations often promote through religious indoctrination.
Modernization	History	Poverty, authoritarianism, and diminishing expectations inevitably breed alienation and violence. Suicide terrorism is the inevitable result of Islam's failure to embrace Western institutions and values.

Continue to Modify Assumptions Until All Relevant Theories Share the Same Bedrock Assumption By the end of STEP 8, the number of assumptions should be reduced to one "bedrock assumption" that is shared by all the theories in the set. Table 12.5 demonstrates how to "drill down" from the secondary-level assumption shared by each group of disciplinary theories to a third level of assumptions shared by theories from other disciplines, and ultimately to the bedrock assumption that all the theories share.

This bedrock assumption is that suicide terrorists view their behavior as "moral" and "sacred"—and, thus, rational—as defined by Islamic fundamentalism. This common ground assumption, then, can serve as the basis for integrating these theories and producing the more comprehensive theory in STEP 9 (see Chapter 13).

	How "Drilling Down" Into Disciplinary Assumptions Reveals a Bedrock Assumption
Table 12.5	

Theory	Secondary-Level Assumptions	Third-Level Assumptions	Bedrock Assumption
Terrorist psycho-logic Self-sanction Martyrdom	Understanding the behavior and motivation of suicide terrorists requires studying primarily the mental life and the psychological constructs of individual terrorists.	Suicide terrorism is a rational outworking of the mental life and psychological constructs of individual terrorists.	Suicide terrorists are rational, not in the Western understanding of the term, but as defined by their culture and faith tradition.
Collective rational strategic choice "Sacred" terror	Suicide terrorists follow logical processes that can be discovered and explained.		
Identity	Religious identity is (at least in this instance) an effective way to explain the "political" phenomenon of suicide terrorism. Terrorist behavior is essentially rational.	Suicide terrorists are "rational" in the sense that their behavior is consistent with adherence to their cultural and religious values.	
Fictive kin	Suicide terrorists are largely the product of identity with and loyalty to a culturally cohesive and intimate cohort of peers, whom recruiting organizations often promote through religious indoctrination.		
Modernization	Poverty, authoritarianism, and diminishing expectations inevitably breed alienation and violence. Suicide terrorism is the inevitable result of Islam's failure to embrace Western institutions and values.	Suicide terrorism is a rational response to exogenous factors.	

For undergraduate students who have little experience working with assumptions of theories, there are two practical benefits of comparing the assumptions of these disciplinary theories in this manner. The first is that it reveals which assumptions are shared by two or more theories in the set, thus reducing the number of assumptions that require modification. The second benefit is that it begins the *partial* integration of the theories by working with assumptions from the "bottom up." Graduate students and mature scholars, who are experienced in working with theories and their assumptions, are more likely to arrive at a bedrock assumption intuitively.

Modifying Concepts and *Assumptions*

Sometimes it is necessary to modify concepts *and* assumptions. This is required when working with theories that are based on a grand theory such as evolution (macro level) but are divided on their understanding or application of the grand theory (micro level). A case in point is Ria van der Lecq's (2012) study of the origin of language where theories are traditionally divided between those that emphasize genetic evolution and those that emphasize cultural evolution. "Even if all these theories are coherent (i.e., internally consistent)," she says, "they cannot be valid at the same time in the same respect if the conflicting elements remain unresolved" (p. 216). These "conflicting elements" are two concepts that are central to all four theories, evolution and communication, and their underlying assumptions. Her challenge, then, is to prepare these two sets of theories for integration.

Modifying Concepts   Van der Lecq (2012) begins with concepts and notes that though the four theories have different assumptions, they nevertheless share a common understanding of the concept "evolution":

> The [theory-based] insights into the problem of the primary function of language have one thing in common: they take the Darwinian theory of evolution as their point of departure. Although some of the details may be open to interpretation, the outlines of this theory are common knowledge and function as a point of common ground for all four theories. Although GG [grooming and gossip theory (social-brain hypothesis)] and RSt [relevance for status theory (political hypothesis)] have different assumptions regarding the question *how* language developed (continuous versus discontinuous), they use the term *evolution* in its biological sense, and agree that natural selection is its cause. (p. 216)

In effect, the theories of GG and RSt have modified themselves based on their common understanding of the concept "evolution."

Not so with theories of niche construction (NCt) and complexity (Ct) which have conflicting notions of evolution. As van der Lecq (2012) explains,

> NCt extends the Darwinian theory of evolution to include cultural developments in so far as they induce changes in the environment over generations. Ct appears to compare the evolution of languages with the evolution of other cultural constructs: Their evolution is not the result of natural selection but of a "natural" tendency to evolve towards more complexity. (pp. 216–217)

To bridge these opposing conceptions of evolution, van der Lecq (2012) turns to medieval philosophy:

> Medieval philosophers used to solve this kind of terminological problem, which they often encountered when they had to reconcile philosophical insights with religious truths, by making a distinction between a strict (or literal) sense and a broad sense of a term. In our case, we could solve the conflict by making a distinction between a strict sense of the term "evolution," meaning evolution-with-modification-by-natural-selection, and a broad sense for the evolution of knowledge, cultures, societies and institutions. The evolution of language towards more complexity would be an example of evolution in the broad sense. This technique of "distinguishing," as it was called in the Middle Ages, is probably best described as a combination of . . . redefinition and extension. (p. 217)

A second source of conflict between the theories was their different understanding of the concept "communication." Van der Lecq (2012) proceeds in a similar way, but in the opposite direction. She redefines communication to cover both its social and its cognitive function: "the cooperative sharing of information by producing knowledge in the minds of hearers" (van der Lecq, 2012, p. 217). After all, she says, "it is hard to imagine that the exchange of social information succeeds if the partners in the conversation do not understand each other's messages" (p. 217).

Modifying Assumptions   With the conflict over terminology resolved, van der Lecq's next challenge is to reconcile the conflicting assumptions underlying the four theories: *Man is a social animal* versus *Man is a political animal*. She proceeds by raising two questions: (1) "Is sociality a prerequisite for communication (GG and NCt), or is it just a by-product of communication (RSt)?" (2) "Is man a social (GG and NCt) or a political (RSt) animal?" To answer these questions, van der Lecq (2012) draws on another perspective, that of computer science and the work of Luc Steels:

> Based on the evidence of language game experiments with robots, Steels (2008) argues that one of the factors that make communication successful is a strong social engagement ("joint attention") of speaker and hearer. Another aspect of sociality is the ability to adopt the perspective of the other. Without this power of perspective reversal no communication system is possible, according to Steels. Thus, if we adopt Steels' conclusions, sociality is a necessary condition for the emergence of language. (p. 217)

Van der Lecq (2012) explains how Steels's work makes it possible to reconcile the conflicting assumptions that "man is a social animal" and that "man is a political animal":

> Again, we may find some inspiration in medieval philosophy, this time in the work of Thomas Aquinas (14th century). Entrusted with the task of reconciling Aristotle's political philosophy with Christian values, he silently extended Aristotle's claim that "man is a *political* animal" to "man is a *political and social* animal." Aquinas' motive must have been that for him man is not only a citizen with civic duties, but also an individual with Christian duties. Applying this technique to our case, we could argue that humans use linguistic communication in the context of their family and friends mainly for social reasons, but on the level of the larger community they need language to make coalitions. Thus the common ground assumption is that man is a social *and* political animal. (pp. 217–218)

For van der Lecq (2012), the result of STEP 8 is the creation of two common ground concepts and one common ground assumption. The common ground concept of "evolution" encompasses Darwinian as well as natural evolution. The common ground concept of *communication* refers to the cooperative sharing of information by producing knowledge in the minds of hearers. The common ground assumption is that man is both a social *and* a political animal. The challenge of STEP 9, discussed in the next chapter, will be to construct a new theory that distinguishes between them when necessary.

Chapter Summary

This chapter concludes our discussion of STEP 8 (spanning Chapters 11 and 12) concerning how to create common ground when working with conflicting disciplinary concepts or theories. For concepts, common ground can be created either directly by modifying the concepts themselves or indirectly by modifying their underlying assumptions; for theories, modification involves using various strategies depending on whether (a) one or more theories in the set already have a broader range of applicability than do the others, or (b) none of the theories in the set borrows from other disciplines. The modification strategy used in the first situation involves identifying the theory that is already the most comprehensive interdisciplinary theory (though narrowly so) and then extending its range of applicability. The strategy used in the second situation depends on whether we are working with the theory's concepts or assumptions. Working with concepts involves (a) finding concepts that have similar meanings in different theories, (b) modifying the concepts so that they have the same meaning across all the theories, and (c) paying attention to disciplinary perspective when redefining concepts. Working with assumptions involves (a) critiquing each theory, (b) identifying the assumption(s) of each theory, (c) determining which assumptions are shared by the other theories, and then (d) modifying these assumptions so that all the theories in the set share a bedrock or common assumption. Once these preparatory measures are complete, the insights and theories are ready for integration in STEP 9.

Notes

1. Concerning theories in the social sciences, William H. Newell (personal communication, February 15, 2011) comments, "Way too many theories in the social sciences *ought* to be restricted in their range of application but are not. Indeed, one of the contributions of interdisciplinarians critiquing disciplinary theories is to point out appropriate restrictions on their range. That is, disciplinarians—typically thinking that their discipline is most important—have a tendency to overreach when they theorize. Famously, psychologists for decades couched their theories in universalist terms, ignoring cultural (and, earlier, sex or racial) differences. It is by playing one discipline off against another that these needed restrictions in range of applicability become evident."

2. Mathematical modeling is also a method. Such a model can be seen as not only representing but even clarifying and establishing the consistency of a theory.

Exercises

Models

12.1 Create a model of one of these problems/topics that shows the variables and the relationship(s) among them.

a. Litter

b. Labor strike

c. Child abuse

Variables

12.2 Using the same problem/topic chosen in Exercise 12.1, identify in your model independent and dependent variables.

Macro- and/or Micro-Level Variables

12.3 This chapter states that a set of theories may contain variables from different levels. Construct a model that shows the levels and the variables that my be operative at each level concerning one of the following problems/topics:

a. Plant/factor/business closing

b. Rising food prices

c. Rising anti-immigration sentiment

Causality

12.4 To provide a full description of a theory and model it, add to the model developed in Exercise 12.1 and expanded in Exercise 12.2 a statement of the process that explains how change in the independent variable causes change in the dependent variable.

The Most Comprehensive Interdisciplinary Theory

12.5 Why is identity theory the most comprehensive interdisciplinary theory of the set of theories that Repko (2012) is working with?

Extending a Theory

12.6 How, exactly, does one go about extending a theory?

Situation B

12.7 If none of the theories in the set of theories you are working with has a broader range of applicability than do the others, what should you do?

13

Constructing a More Comprehensive Understanding or Theory

Chapter Preview

The process of integration that began with identifying conflicts between insights in STEP 7 (Chapter 10) progressed in STEP 8 (Chapters 11–12) to creating common ground between conflicting concepts *or* theories embedded in them. Only after concepts and theories are modified can we turn our attention to the possibilities for constructing a more comprehensive understanding that is opened up as a result. This is STEP 9 of the research process and the subject of this chapter. Whether one is working with concepts or theories, it is important to engage in full integration, or at least attempt to do so.

This chapter is divided into three sections. Section 1 defines the term *more comprehensive understanding* and unpacks its meaning. Section 2 explains how to construct a more comprehensive understanding from concepts that were modified and from which common ground was created. Section 3 explains how to construct a more comprehensive theory, using illustrations of student and professional work. This discussion will be especially useful to those working in the natural sciences and social sciences where theoretical explanations dominate disciplinary discourse concerning a particular complex problem.

Step 9: Construct a More Comprehensive Understanding

A Definition of *More Comprehensive Understanding* and *More Comprehensive Theory*

A **more comprehensive understanding** is the integration of insights to produce a new and more nuanced whole.[1] This definition is consistent with the definition of interdisciplinary studies used in this book that says *insights* get integrated. *The integration of concepts or theories is an objective in service of the goal of integrating disciplinary insights, a means to the end of integrating insights.* Concerning the term *more comprehensive understanding*, authors use a variety of other terms that have similar meanings such as *complex understanding, holistic understanding, interdisciplinary understanding, integrative understanding, integrated result, new meaning,* and *interdisciplinary product.* What one chooses to call the understanding that results from integration is a matter of preference.

Unpacking This Definition

Unpacking this definition deepens our understanding of it and of STEP 9:

- "More comprehensive" refers to the defining characteristic of the understanding or theory: that it combines more elements than does any disciplinary understanding or theory.
- "Integration" refers to the process used to construct the understanding or theory.
- "Insights" get integrated, not the contributing disciplines themselves or their perspectives.
- "New" references the improbability of any one discipline producing a similar result, and that no one (other than the interdisciplinarian) takes responsibility for studying the complex problem, object, text, or system that falls between the disciplines or that transcends them.
- "Nuanced" refers to the understanding or theory often needing more clarifications than do disciplinary understandings.
- "Whole" refers to the comprehensiveness of the research result such that the understanding is responsive to the perspective of each contributing discipline but not dominated by any one of them. This "whole" may refer to a theory. Theory references authors in the natural sciences, the social sciences, and the humanities who rely on the development of theories to explain the phenomena they study. In such cases, the theories themselves are the focus of integration.

To be clear, the more comprehensive understanding or theory is something that one must construct from a set of modified concepts or theories. STEP 9 completes the process of integration by constructing this understanding or theory.

The Process Involved

Constructing a more comprehensive understanding or a more comprehensive theory requires drawing on the skills and abilities listed at the end of Chapter 2 (especially creativity). Also required is a lot of shuttling back and forth between the overall observable pattern of the behavior of the phenomenon as a whole and the contributing disciplinary theories to construct the more comprehensive theory or interdisciplinary theory. *The best theory is the one that jointly maximizes its fit with the overall pattern on the one hand, and with the disciplinary theories on the other hand.* Researchers may well find that they end up having to adjust their map of the problem, having failed to appreciate at the outset the full set of linkages between variables studied by different disciplines. It is always helpful to have a map at first to guide one's thinking and then modify it later.

How one actually integrates concepts or theories and then their insights in STEP 9 largely depends on whether one is working primarily in the humanities, the fine and performing arts, and the applied fields, *or* in the natural and social sciences. Since theories do not dominate the former, interdisciplinarians typically integrate conflicting concepts and the insights they produce after common ground has been created between them. However, since the natural and social sciences rely on the development of theories to explain the phenomena they study, interdisciplinarians typically integrate conflicting theories.

Sections 2 and 3 of this chapter carry forward the threaded examples of student (*) and professional work used in previous chapters. Each example briefly summarizes the common ground created in STEP 8 before demonstrating how the author achieves integration and constructs the more comprehensive understanding or more comprehensive theory in STEP 9. Completing this STEP, or at least attempting to do so, is what constitutes full interdisciplinarity.

Constructing the More Comprehensive Understanding From Modified *Concepts*

Constructing the more comprehensive understanding is carried out by using the common ground created in STEP 8 to integrate the various parts or subsystems that compose the complex problem as a whole. This action is usually described in a written narrative, the purpose of which is to explain *how the modified concept, assumption, or theory is inclusive of the others and fits best with the available evidence.* Since each part or subsystem is disciplinary in nature and is the subject of a particular insight, this combining or integrating also applies to the insights themselves. The narrative may also include a model or a metaphor to help the reader visualize the understanding.

From the Humanities

In these examples from the humanities, Lisa Silver and Mieke Bal construct their understandings from the insights they modified earlier. It is worth noting that these understandings are framed as practical applications of concepts that were redefined or extended when common ground was created. That common ground is summarized in each example.

Silver* (2005), Composing Race and Gender: The Appropriation of Social Identity in Fiction Silver's purpose is to develop "a cohesive set of guidelines concerning the fictional appropriation of race and gender" (p. ii). Appropriation refers to a person's attempt to take possession of another person's identity for literary, artistic, or entertainment purposes (p. 7).

STEP 8 Summarized: Silver's challenge in STEP 8 was to create common ground between insights from psychology, sociology, and literature concerning the practice of appropriation. These insights defined appropriation in accordance with their particular disciplinary perspective and conflicted substantially. Silver decided that the best way to create common ground between these conflicting meanings of "appropriation" was to redefine it so that its broadened meaning could apply to the professions of acting and filmmaking not normally associated with it.

STEP 9: The broadened meaning of appropriation enabled Silver to integrate "the [literary] 'rules of fiction' with the social and historical implications of appropriation" (p. 11). This, says Silver, makes it possible

> to arrive at a cohesive set of guidelines concerning the fictional appropriation of race and gender. These guidelines require that authors have: (1) an awareness of the implications associated with appropriating a social identity, (2) a valid reason or desire to appropriate despite the implications, and (3) an ability to implicate themselves within the social identity being appropriated. (p. ii)

Silver's more comprehensive understanding of the concept of "appropriation" is appropriately nuanced. "Implicature," she says, "usually occurs through an awareness of one's own ethnocentric feelings, extended and meaningful contact with the group being represented, and hyper connective thinking" (p. ii). She adds, "Following these guidelines does not guarantee successful appropriation; however, examples of successful and ethical appropriation in fiction tend to meet these guidelines" (p. ii).

Bal (1999), "Introduction," The Practice of Cultural Analysis: Exposing Interdisciplinary Interpretation Bal's challenge is to expose the fullest possible meaning of an enigmatic note or letter painted in yellow on a red brick wall in Amsterdam after World War II:

Note

I hold you dear

I have not

Thought you up (p. 2)

STEP 8 Summarized: Bal's strategy is to analyze or "expose" the meaning of this note or letter from three perspectives (although not disciplinary ones) simultaneously: from the perspective of the note or letter's author, from the perspective of the subject of the note or letter (i.e., the author's beloved), and from the perspective of one who is viewing the note or letter and pondering its meaning. She does this by extending the meaning of the verb *expose* from a specific and literal definition (i.e., to make a public presentation) so that it is broader, more ambiguous, and metaphorical. She combines the verb's meaning with the triple meaning of the noun *exposé*: "opinion" or "judgment," "the public presentation of someone's view," and/or "the public presentation of those deeds that deserve to be made public" (p. 5).

STEP 9: Bal uses the broadened meaning of the verb/noun *expose/exposé* to construct a more comprehensive understanding of the note or letter that focuses on its three aspects or dimensions. As an exposition, the note or letter

> makes something public, and that event of showing involves articulating in the public domain the most deeply held views and beliefs of a subject. . . . In publicizing these views, the subject of exposing objectifies, exposing himself as much as the object [i.e., his lost love]; this makes the exposition an exposure of the self. (p. 5)

Second, as an exposition, the note or letter is also an argument. The word *Note* has something to say about love and its public discourse, and it argues against oppositions such as public versus private, romantic belief in unique individuality versus the masses, and truth versus fiction.

Third, the note or letter is partly a metaphor of present culture, "a present that carries the past within itself. The present is a museum in which we walk as if it were a city" (p. 5). The note or letter's author brings the past into the present and engages the viewer in both.

From the Social Sciences

In this example, Delph decided to work not with theories but with concepts because not all of the most relevant insights came from theories. Consequently, her understanding is conceptual and practical rather than theoretical.

Delph* (2005), An Integrative Approach to the Elimination of the "Perfect Crime"   *STEP 8 Summarized:* Delph's task is to create common ground between two sharply contrasting approaches to criminal investigation and profiling: that used by forensic science (which analyzes physical evidence), and that used by forensic psychology (which analyzes behavioral evidence). She creates common ground between them by *redefining* the meaning of the concept of "profiling" so that the broadened term includes the specialized kind of knowledge that criminal investigation, forensic science, and forensic psychology all privilege in their approach to profiling.

STEP 9: What is actually integrated, explains Delph, is "the unique knowledge possessed by each of these areas of expertise" and how they apply this knowledge to developing a profile of the perpetrator (p. 30). Criminal profiling, she writes, could achieve its greatest potential if profilers from forensic psychology and forensic science blended their analytical techniques and shared them with local criminal investigators. If achieved, this integrated approach would produce four likely outcomes: (1) quickly reduce the list of possible suspects, (2) predict the prime suspect's future behavior, (3) offer investigative avenues that have been overlooked by police, and (4) empower local law enforcement agencies to use these integrated profiling techniques themselves (p. 32).

Constructing a More Comprehensive Theory From a Modified *Theory*

Most propositions involve some sort of causal assertion. A **proposition** makes a truth claim. Such claims generally involve an argument about how one or more variables affect one or more others, though they may refer only to the internal workings of a variable. Here is an example of a proposition: "Children cared for in day care facilities as opposed to their own homes develop social awareness that serves them well upon entering public schools." This proposition also makes a causal argument: that day care facilities cause children to develop social awareness. **Causal arguments** examine the underlying cause for any particular situation or argument, and analyze what causes a trend, an event, or a phenomenon. Thus propositional integration cannot be distinct from causal integration. As noted elsewhere, our use of the word *cause* allows for multiple causes.

Causal or propositional integration refers to combining truth claims from disciplinary theoretical explanations to form an integrated theory—that is, a new proposition that is interdisciplinary and more comprehensive (Lanier & Henry, 2004, p. 343). Propositional integration, explain Paternoster and Bachman (2001),

> is a more formal effort [at integration] because it entails *linking the propositions* and not just the concepts of two or more theorists into a combined theory. . . . Rather than simply usurpation, a propositionally integrated theory must actually meaningfully connect or relate the propositions of different theories into the new theory [emphasis added]. (p. 307)

Critics of causal or propositional integration warn that it can produce an exponential number of variables, making the testing of the resulting integrative theory impractical because of the large sample size required (Shoemaker, 1996, p. 254). Henry and Bracy (2012) counter that proliferation of variables is not inevitable:

> Interdisciplinarians may come to realize that some variables from one discipline are being used without much success to explain an aspect of crime that is much better explained by another discipline. Those variables

would then be supplanted in the more comprehensive theory by variables from the other discipline or disciplines. (p. 265)

The key challenge in constructing a comprehensive theory is how causal arguments or theoretical propositions are logically related to each other. There are several causal or propositional strategies demonstrated to achieve integration of a set of conflicting theories and construct a more comprehensive theory.

Six Strategies to Achieve Causal or Propositional Integration

There are at least six strategies demonstrated to achieve causal or propositional integration and construct a more comprehensive theory:

1. **Sequential or end-to-end**, which implies a sequential causal order

2. **Horizontal or side-by-side**, which implies overlapping influences

3. **Multiple causality**, wherein several variables combine to produce an effect

4. **Cross-level or multilevel**, wherein different behaviors occur on different levels

5. **Spatial**, wherein theoretical explanations of why the causes or effects of problems are not distributed evenly in space

6. **Analytical**, wherein different analytical perspectives are used to evaluate a highly complex process involving multiple factors such as metropolitan formation

These strategies are the focus of the following discussion and are illustrated by examples of student (*) and professional work. Noted along the way are the lessons that each strategy holds for interdisciplinary practice.

Sequential or End-to-End Causal Integration

Sequential or end-to-end causal integration links the immediate cause of the problem (in this case, crime) to a more distant cause, and then links that to an even more distant cause (Henry & Bracy, 2012, p. 266). This type integrates *fully complementary explanations of aspects* of the problem into an explanation of the problem as a whole: A causes B, and B causes C, as shown in Figure 13.1.

Figure 13.1 Sequential or End-to-End Causal Integration

A → B → C = Comprehensive explanation

A general rule when performing sequential or end-to-end integration is that the common ground will have to be either some shared assumption or the causal process itself. Henry and Bracy (2012) describe the causal chain approach to constructing a more comprehensive causal theory of gang violence:

> For example, an arrest for gang violence might be the outcome of the following process of sequential causes over time. Biological defects at birth may lead to low IQ, which leads to learning disabilities in early childhood, which may lead to an inability to follow social norms, which may lead to group and institutional exclusion, which produces reduced self-esteem and [increased] alienation, which generates anger and hostility that results in affiliations with similarly alienated peers, which leads to delinquent peer or gang formation, which leads to law violation, which is reacted to by authorities producing criminal justice intervention and stigmatization and results in an arrest for gang violence. (pp. 266–267)

In this example, an arrest for gang violence is explained by a series of theoretical propositions drawn from several disciplinary theories including labeling theory, subcultural theory, learning theory, cognitive theory, and biological or genetic theory. In sequential integration, no one theory explains the whole sequence. Only when the relevant theories are linked end-to-end in a causal chain may they do so (Henry & Bracy, 2012, p. 267). It is possible that C can have some effect on A, making for a feedback loop.

Horizontal or Side-by-Side Causal Integration

There are two distinct categories of horizontal or side-by-side causal integration and a spectrum of possibilities between them. One is where the explanations are fully complementary but focus on separate aspects of the complex problem. The explanations can be completely non-overlapping or some of them may share common variables. Here the challenge of performing horizontal integration is to figure out the relationships among the different causal explanations (or at least some of their variables) in order to construct a more comprehensive theory. The other category (and the focus of the discussion below) is where the explanations have the same focus but are fully competing. Here the challenge is to make use of the common ground between the competing theories developed in STEP 8 to construct a more comprehensive theory. Competing explanations from different disciplines usually disagree on the nature of the causal relationship between those variables. Agreement on the same causal relationship but disagreement on the mechanism by which it operates is found primarily in the natural sciences, or within a single discipline. (Note: Some sets of side-by-side theories may fall in between these two categories by being complementary in some ways and competing in others, and by focusing on different aspects to some extent but also on some overlap between them. Between the two categories, researchers will face a combination of the two challenges.)

Figure 13.2 describes the second category of side-by-side causal integration where the explanations have the same focus but are fully competing.

Figure 13.2   Horizontal or Side-by-Side Causal Integration

Explanation A of Causal Relationship 1 + Explanation B of Causal Relationship 1 + Explanation C of Causal Relationship 1 = More Comprehensive Theory of Causal Relationship 1

Here we face conflict, but perhaps only a trivial conflict. If the different causes act independently, we can add them together. The only conflict is the "my variables matter most" assumption of each discipline. Presumably, though, some common ground has been created between these conflicting explanations in STEP 8 (see Chapters 11 and 12), perhaps by drilling down into their respective assumptions and discovering a deeper assumption that the theories share. The challenge here is how to build a more comprehensive theory on that common ground.

Horizontal or side-by-side causal integration is illustrated in the following example where competing theories explain the link between individual psychology and different types of sexual assault:

> Some acts of sexual assault may be explained by *self-control theory* which argues that such crimes are the result of a predisposition to sensation seeking and the desire for immediate gratification; but sexual assault may also be explained by *social learning theory* and *low self-esteem [theory]* as a result of the offender being a victim of childhood sexual abuse. Of course the question this raises is whether two acts defined by law as the same crime are actually the same or different behaviors. If different, then each theory would be explaining a different act, even though the law classified them as the same with regard to the harm and consequences for the victim [italics added]. (Henry & Bracy, 2012, p. 267)

An integrated theory, then, would combine these three conflicting causal explanations of sexual assault into a more comprehensive theory. A general rule in performing horizontal integration is that the common ground must involve some idea of how the different causal explanations are related so that this relationship can form the basis of the more comprehensive theory.

Multicausal Integration

This and the preceding strategy, though closely related, are treated as separate strategies because multicausal integration sees the subject phenomenon as *the outcome of several different independent variables.* This strategy addresses the common case in which a more comprehensive explanation is achieved by combining different propositions or causal variables regarding the same *effect* or behavior.

One cannot know whether different explanations are *complementary* or *conflicting* until one has mapped the process under investigation. And then one needs to ask: "Does Explanation 1 logically preclude Explanation 2?" As noted above, when a discipline assumes that only its variables matter, its conflict with another discipline's insights may be considerable. *Only if there is some logical conflict—some element of Explanation 1 precludes the operation of Explanation 2—do we really have a conflict that requires the search for a common ground other than the map of causal relationships itself.* Economists once stressed investment as the primary cause of economic growth, but later came to emphasize technological innovation. The integrative researcher can recognize the value in both explanations, and also that the biggest cause of growth may occur when new technology is embodied in new investment. We thus see the causes as *interdependent* but not really in conflict.

Multiple causation explains the phenomenon or behavior by creating a theory of sufficient generality that it incorporates multiple propositions or causal factors from relevant theories, each of which explains only a part of the phenomenon or behavior: A + B + C + D cause E, which in turn causes Y, as shown in Figure 13.3.

Figure 13.3	Multicausal Integration

A (control theory = weak parental attachment)

+

B (social learning theory = underachievement in school)

+

C (conflict theory = conflict with family)

+

D (developmental theory = alienation from family)

cause E (identification with peers), which

causes Y (gang-related delinquency)

In their study, Henry and Bracy (2012) present theories on the causes of gang-related delinquency that are interdependent:

Several different theories offer explanations of why adolescents engage in delinquent acts. *Control theory,* for example, has a key concept of parental attachment which is inversely related to delinquency (assuming parents are themselves moral and law-abiding). Combined with other elements such as low commitment to convention and lack of involvement in conventional activities, an adolescent may do poorly in school. *Conflict theory* as well as *developmental theory* argues that family conflict can arise from a variety of internal family dynamics or external societal pressures and can produce alienation of the adolescent from their family. Low commitment to convention can also lead to underachieving at school, which in turn can exacerbate conflict and alienation in the family. Social disorganization also contributes to the alienation of some adolescents from their parents, through a lack of identification, and *social learning theory* shows how alienated and underachieving students can identify more directly with underachieving peers, which in turn can create more alienation and further under-achievement as well as lead to deviant and law breaking activity. (p. 268)

Since no one theory explains the causes of gang-related delinquency com-prehensively, a more comprehensive theory is needed to identify the way the theories are interdependent. For example, parental attachment (from control theory) may be related to the dynamics of family conflict. An example of arriving at such a theory regarding another complex social phenomenon, suicide terrorism, is shown below.

From the Social Sciences and the Humanities: Repko (2012), "Integrating Theory-Based Insights on the Causes of Suicide Terrorism"   In this threaded example, Repko focuses on the causes of suicide terrorism, arguing that this form of terrorism is best understood using the strategy of multiple causal explanation. His study is an example of a problem that has been examined narrowly through single disciplinary frameworks rather than through an integrative paradigm.

Repko's purpose is to construct a comprehensive theory explaining this phenomenon from a set of eight prominent theories on the causes of suicide terrorism. These are rooted in the disciplines of cognitive psychology, politi-cal science, cultural anthropology, and history. Of these, only one theory—identity theory advanced by Monroe and Kreidie (1997) and rooted in political science—attempts to cross disciplinary boundaries. Other than Monroe and Kreidie, no author has recognized the value of taking an explic-itly interdisciplinary approach to understand this complex phenomenon or has attempted to develop a multiple causation theory that integrates these conflicting explanations. Consequently, this phenomenon is typically viewed through narrow disciplinary lenses. This produces fragmented and conflicting understandings, which result in conflicting, unrealistic, and fragmented pub-lic policies.

Repko's strategy is two-pronged: to work from the "bottom up" with assumptions (in STEP 8) while working from the "top down" with theories (in STEP 9). The goal is a comprehensive theory that combines all salient causal factors addressed by the set of theories and that rests on a commonly held assumption.

This example shows how STEP 9 flows from STEP 8 (see Chapters 11 and 12). *A general rule when using the strategy of multiple causal explana-tion is that the common ground will have to be some shared understanding of the proximate cause* (e.g., seeing one's goal as sacred). In this case, the common ground could be in the form of either a written narrative or a map depicting causal relationships.

STEP 8 Summarized: The challenge that Repko faced in STEP 8 was two-fold. First, he had to identify a theory from the set of eight theories whose range of applicability was already broad and could be extended further. He identified the multiple variables or factors causing suicide terrorism. He then compared each theory-based insight and its theoretical explanation to a list of four causal factors to see which one(s) each theory included. The result of this evaluative process was that of all the theories under review, only three attributed the causes of suicide terrorist behavior to three of the four factors. Next, he narrowed the possible theories from three to one on the basis that Monroe and Kreidie's (1997) *identity theory* would require the least amount of modification or extending since it was already interdisciplinary, though imperfectly so. This decision was guided by the principle of least action, making sure that the changes would be the smallest possible.

The second challenge was to identify an assumption that was common to all of the theories and thereby reduce the conflict among them. Repko identified the assumptions of each theory and compared them to each other. By drilling down more deeply into their assumptions, he was able to reduce the number of conflicts between the theories to only a few. By drilling down even more deeply into these, he discovered a more basic assumption that all eight theories shared: that the terrorists considered their *goals* as "moral imperatives" and "sacred duties," and thus rational, as defined by Islamic fundamentalism (p. 145). This common ground assumption, then, served as the basis for the more comprehensive explanation of suicide terrorism constructed in STEP 9. By identifying a common assumption, Repko in effect conducted a *partial* integration.

STEP 9: To develop a multicausal explanation of suicide terrorism involves taking two actions: broaden identity theory's range of applicability still further by using the technique of extension, and construct a comprehensive multicausal explanation that reflects the bedrock assumption created in STEP 8.

When working with theories, there are two possible approaches. The first approach is to piece together the "good parts" from each of the relevant theories to form a more comprehensive theory. The "good parts" are determined by their compatibility with the overall patterning behavior (i.e., the full ranging available empirical evidence). (Note: this applies as well to the selection of parts of theories.) This approach is appropriate when each theory is deeply rooted in the discipline from which it emerges because it avoids the problem of either/or thinking—of having to choose one theory and reject the others.

The second approach (and the one Repko uses) is to add parts from several theories to extend the explanatory range of one of the theories, in this case, identity theory. The integrative technique of extension is used when one of the theories already has parts that come from more than one discipline, as identity theory does. Best practice is to use the former approach and avoid the latter, *except when one of the theories is already interdisciplinary, though imperfectly so, as in the present case.* "Already interdisciplinary" means that parts of the theory are borrowed from other disciplines. What is missing, and what theory extension provides, is one or more additional parts—that is, causal factors—from the other relevant theories that will enable it to account for all the known factors causing the problem.

Identity theory, says Repko, possesses two strengths that make it ideal for extension:

> First, it already addresses three of the four factors—cultural identity, sacred beliefs (i.e., religion), and power seeking (i.e., politics). Identity theory includes religion by showing that the Islamic fundamentalist conception of religion is, in fact, an all-encompassing ideology that erases all lines between public and private. This theology-based ideology is based on religious writings and commentaries on these writings that are viewed by its most devoted followers as sacred, inviolable, nonnegotiable—and worth dying for. As a "sacred ideology" . . . Islamic fundamentalism redefines Western notions of politics and power. As Monroe and Kreidie [1997] show, politics for Islamic fundamentalists is subsumed under an all-encompassing religious faith, and is sought and exercised for the purpose of extending the faith. Achieving, maintaining, and extending power is a sacred duty that has priority over all other obligations, including family. Because the theory holds that the self is culturally situated, it is able to explain how culture (and religion is a key component of culture) influences identity formation. (p. 248)

A second strength compared to the other theories is that it requires the least amount of "stretching and pulling" to extend its explanatory range to include personality factors intrinsic to the suicide terrorist.

> Extending the theory so that it includes the causal factor of personality traits is possible because identity theory . . . is based on the psychological concepts of cognition and perspective. These concepts address personality traits in a way that is inclusive of the psychology theories already examined. Monroe and Kreidie [1997] use the concept of cognition in a developmental way, meaning that they are concerned to show how persons are influenced by factors external to themselves—namely culture and societal norms—rather than focusing on individual cognitive abnormalities as Post [1998] does to argue that some persons are psychologically predisposed to commit acts of suicide terrorism. (p. 248)

Monroe and Kreidie's (1997) application of the concept of "perspective" to explain suicide terrorist behavior is also helpful in this regard because it effectively delineates the options that terrorists perceive as being available to them. Repko explains that

The act of committing a suicide attack in the service of a fundamentalist conception of *jihad* "emanates primarily from the person accepting their identity which means that they have to abide by the tenets of their religion" ([Monroe & Kreidie] 1997, pp. 26, 36). By borrowing these concepts from psychology, identity theory offers an understanding of human behavior that is based on the interplay of mental constructs in tandem with the exogenous variables of politics, culture, and religion. (p. 149)

The extended theory, combined with its underlying assumption, enables Repko to construct a comprehensive multiple causation explanation of suicide terrorism stated here:

> Suicide terrorism is caused by a complex interaction of variables that are both endogenous and exogenous to the individual. Endogenous variables include psychological predispositions and cognitive constructs developed over time; exogenous variables include the combined influences of culture, politics, and religion, with Islamic fundamentalism providing the perceptual framework that determines an individual's identity, motivation, and behavior. Suicide terrorists manifest varying degrees of rationality in pursuing goals that they consider "moral" and "sacred" according to a theologically based cost/benefit calculus. (p. 153)

Lessons for Interdisciplinary Practice   This example demonstrates the utility of first establishing common ground before attempting to integrate the major theoretical causal explanations and construct the multicausal explanation. Students may not need to identify a bedrock assumption underlying all of the theories as Repko does in STEP 8 in order to arrive at a more comprehensive theory. But more advanced students and practitioners are encouraged to do so for the simple reason that it anchors the comprehensive explanation in a bedrock assumption that is inclusive of all the theories, which in turn enhances the credibility of the explanation itself. This example also demonstrates the utility of theory extension as an effective way to integrate several conflicting causal explanations. Undergraduate students working with only a few theories will find it far easier to perform this integrative task than will graduate students, mature scholars, and interdisciplinary teams who are working with numerous theories as Repko does.

Cross-Level or Multilevel Causal Integration

Cross-level or multilevel causal integration refers to different levels on which behavior takes place. There is constant interaction between each level with the other levels, creating a fluid causal process with multiple feedback loops. This strategy differs from any other multiple causation strategy only if there are emergent properties at one level that act causally at another. Otherwise we are just talking about causal links between variables or theories at different levels. An **emergent property** is defined as a characteristic "of a system that cannot be understood by reference to its constituent elements (phenomena and causal links) but only at the level of the system as a whole" (Szostak, 2009, p. 43). For example, consciousness may be an emergent property of human beings that cannot be understood by reference to the details of our biology (Szostak, 2004).[2]

Cross-level or multilevel causal integration involves combining theories from one level with theories from the other levels. Deciding which levels to integrate may require returning to STEP 1 of the interdisciplinary research process (IRP) and rethinking the kind of complex problem to be studied (see Chapter 3). It may be that the problem, as first framed, is too broad and needs to be narrowed to make the study more manageable. Mapping the problem (if this was not done earlier) should reveal the levels involved. For example, factors contributing to the delinquent behavior of juveniles take place on multiple levels as shown in Figure 13.4.

Figure 13.4   Cross-Level or Multilevel Causal Integration

Level 5. Culture of materialism with limited moral direction

Level 4. The community and neighborhood

Level 3. Institutionalized educational practices

Level 2. Peer group pecking orders

Level 1. Relations in the family

A family is a primary group that operates at a micro level of society, whereas a school is an institution that operates at a more macro level in society than primary groups do. Relations in the family are part of the relations in school, relations between peers are part of the relations of school and family, and so on. In this situation, the more comprehensive theory of delinquency would be constructed from theories that focus on the different levels on which the behavior takes place and that account for the constant interactions between the family and each of the other levels. In other words, interdisciplinarians are urged to extend their gaze over the widest range of theories that bear on the problem.

The following examples of multilevel causal integration presented by Stuart Henry (2009) and Ria van der Lecq (2012) are from the natural and social sciences and demonstrate the use of theories to explain the phenomena they study. Interdisciplinary work in both areas has typically drawn on theories to produce more comprehensive explanations of complex phenomena. In each case, the resulting comprehensive explanation takes the form of a theory that has undergone extension.

From the Social Sciences: Henry (2009), "School Violence Beyond Columbine: A Complex Problem in Need of an Interdisciplinary Analysis" Henry argues that understanding the cause of school violence is best achieved using interactive/reciprocal causal explanations rather than single or multiple independent causality. He also believes that a comprehensive understanding of school violence requires examination of causation across multiple levels of society. Henry works with 12 different theories rooted in a cluster of social and behavioral disciplinary fields: economics, biology, psychology, geography, sociology, political science, Marxist philosophy, feminism, and, most recently, postmodernism. His purpose is to combine these theoretical explanations into a single integrated theoretical model that has greater comprehensiveness and explanatory value than any one of its component theories (p. 1). What is crucial, says Henry, are the ways that these causal factors converge over time and culminate in a dramatic eruption of mass violence, or remain bottled up.

His study shows how STEP 8 flows into STEP 9. A *general rule when performing any integrative strategy*, including this one, *is to create common ground among the conflicting theories*. In this case, the goal is to seek a common ground proximate cause, which might be that there is some threshold level of aggravation that triggers school shootings. And then we show how a variety of causes interact to get us there.

STEP 8 Summarized: The challenge facing Henry in STEP 8 is to show that the incidents of violence in schools are not only cumulative between victim and offender, but also operate across multiple levels of society. Of the five levels he examines, only Levels 1 and 2 are presented here.

> Level 1 violence includes much student-on-student violence, such as predatory economic crimes in which students use violence and threats to extract material gain from other students. It can also include physical violence, such as fighting between students because of disputes about girlfriends or boyfriends or because of verbal challenges to manhood, reputation, or insults. Much interpersonal violence occurs around proving issues of gender dominance and masculinity. Level 1 violence can also include the relatively rare but dramatic serious rampage homicides, where an individual attacks the whole school or collective elements in it, such as fellow students, teachers, and/or administrators in suicidal-homicidal explosions of hate, rage, or depression. However, the more recent evidence generally shows that when these incidents occur, the "individual" source of violence has previously been the victim of violence over time, and the extent of the extreme violent event is the outcome of the effects of reciprocal victimization at multiple levels rather than at just one. (pp. 11–12)

After the 1999 massacre at Columbine High School, says Henry, critically important Level 2 violence became evident when the role of collective policing of peer group pecking orders through violence, bullying, and exclusion became apparent.

> Such peer group policing rejects those who are different from or less accomplished, good-looking, or datable than those at the top of the school social hierarchy. . . . Newman et al. (2004) point out that "among adolescents, whose identities are closely tied to peer relations and positions in the pecking order, bullying and other forms of social exclusion are recipes for marginalization and isolation, which in turn breed extreme levels of desperation and frustration" (pp. 229–230). . . . Indeed, [their] research reveals that four out of five offenders in rampage school shootings had been socially marginalized into outcast cliques (p. 239), and between half and three quarters of shooters (depending on the data source) had been victimized in a variety of ways, including being bullied, threatened with physical violence, persecuted, or assaulted or having their property stolen, for a considerable period of time, in many cases, for years, prior to the decision to commit mass violence (pp. 241–242). The authors say that "very few of these boys seem to meet the physical and social ideals of masculinity—tall, handsome, muscular, athletic, and confident" and that "in three out of five cases, the shooters had suffered an attack on their masculinity . . . by being physically bullied, mercilessly teased or humiliated, sexually or physically abused, or having recently been rejected by a girl." Unable to protect themselves from attacks on their manliness, they found a bloody way to "set the record straight" (p. 242). (p. 12)

After showing that the incidences of violence in schools not only are cumulative between victim and offender but also operate across multiple levels of society, Henry identifies a common ground proximate cause: There is some threshold level of aggravation that triggers school shootings.

STEP 9: The construction of a comprehensive multilevel causal explanation of school violence must reflect the complex and systemic nature of the problem. This explanation, says Henry, will enable us to better see the interconnected processes that produce school violence. Given the complexity of the problem involving multilevel causal factors, it is to be expected that stating this more comprehensive explanation will reflect this complexity. He begins with a propositional statement that reflects the theoretical explanations of the lower levels of causation examined in STEP 8: "Lower-level and more diffuse harm production can produce victims who, over time, can come to resent their victimization and react violently against it" (p. 17). Henry then explains how this process works, noting in particular that "social exclusion can occur in multiple ways that are both evident and concealed" and that such exclusion "can be the product of social hierarchies in the social networks of peers, bolstered by societal-cultural discourses of masculinity and violence and supported by school systems through their own hierarchies of power" (p. 17).

If the focus of Henry's analysis were limited to Levels 1 and 2, this causal explanation would be sufficient. As it is, however, there are three additional levels of causation (not described earlier) that he must integrate into his multilevel causal explanation if it is to be fully interdisciplinary. This means that he must take into account "the wider framing discourses" that operate in and across all five levels and explain how these function as a system that is conducive to producing violence. Henry continues his comprehensive causal explanation:

> Although we can examine the psychological processes and situational explanations for why students acted violently, we need to step outside of the microcontexts to explore the wider framing discourses of gender and power, masculinity and violence, and social class and race that produce social exclusion, victimization, anger, and rage. We need to see how these discourses shape the school curriculum, teaching practices, the institution of education, the meaning of "school," and its associated educational policy. How do parents, both in their absence and in their presence, harm the lives of students? We need to proactively engage in the deconstruction of hierarchies of power that exclude, and in the process create, a wasted class of teenagers who feel hopeless, whose escape from hopelessness is blocked, and whose only way out are violent symbolic acts of self-destruction and other-destruction. We also need to challenge the ways in which the economic and political structure of American society reproduces and tolerates hierarchies of exclusion and structural violence. This needs to go beyond cultural causes of school violence to see how these cultural forms are integrated with structural inequalities. Any adequate analysis of school violence, therefore, has to locate the microinteractive, institutional practices and sociocultural productions in the wider political economy of the society in which these occur. Ignoring the structural inequalities of power in the wider system reduces the cause to local and situational inequalities of power, suggesting that policies can be addressed to intervene locally, such as at the level of peer subculture or school organization. Although these levels of intervention are important, they alone are insufficient. (pp. 16–17)

Lessons for Interdisciplinary Practice   The cross-level or multilevel causal strategy that Henry uses may involve conflicting theories at one or more levels of causation. If so, common ground will have to be created at each level where these theories conflict before a comprehensive theory involving all levels can be constructed. A further possible complication is how many variables there are among the levels and how much they interact. It seems that what Henry is saying here with his talk of thresholds is that school shootings are an "emergent property" of a system of interactions: It is hard to trace them to one particular cause; rather they must be traced to the reinforcing effects of multiple causes. Once identified, this emergent property will form the basis for the more comprehensive theory.

From the Natural Sciences: van der Lecq (2012), "Why We Talk: An Interdisciplinary Approach to the Evolutionary Origin of Language"   In this example of cross-level or multilevel integration, van der Lecq's aim is to formulate a coherent and testable theory that answers the question, "What was the primary function for which language emerged?" Her strategy is to construct an interdisciplinary model that integrates four theories (identified in Chapter 12). The model is cross-level because it connects theories from one level with theories from other levels. Since the model seeks understanding that is as comprehensive as possible, all theoretical levels need to be addressed simultaneously and show parallel interactive processes.

STEP 8 Summarized: Van der Lecq creates common ground—actually three layers of common ground—among relevant theory-based explanations of why humans talk. The result of STEP 8, she explains, is that we have created two common ground concepts and one common ground assumption.

> The common ground concept of *evolution* is a complex concept, because it encompasses "Darwinian" as well as "natural" evolution. The new comprehensive theory will have to distinguish between the two aspects when necessary. The common ground concept of *communication* refers to the cooperative sharing of information by producing knowledge in the minds of hearers. The common ground assumption is that man is a social and political animal. (p. 218)

Van der Lecq notes that a further common ground concept (evolution) pulls these causes together. The result of STEP 8 is a common ground proximate cause: We need to talk because we need to communicate. And then she talks about how various phenomena interact to increase our need to communicate.

STEP 9: Rather than creating a new theory from pieces of existing theories, van der Lecq begins constructing her model from a base theory that already incorporates both/and thinking in an interdisciplinary sense, such as niche construction theory. She explains her selection of niche construction theory as the base theory as follows:

> Niche construction theory enables us to see linguistic communication as one of the activities that may modify more conventional sources of natural selection. Group living, the theory says, depends on social and communicative niche construction. A *social* niche is a subset of natural selection pressures in an evolutionary niche that are induced by interactions with other organisms in the group (e.g., grooming). The construction of a *communicative* niche depends on the ability of living organisms to exchange meaningful information. Communication with evolutionary consequences typically involves learning and cognition. The fact that only humans use speech to communicate is explained by

assuming that human language is a component of human culture. Cultural practices change rapidly and with the generation of more cultural variants better ways of communicating were selected for. (pp. 218–219)

Van der Lecq extends the explanatory range of the base theory by connecting a second theory, grooming and gossip theory, to it. Adding this theory helps to explain one of the base theory's key elements (niche construction).

> Using Dunbar's grooming and gossip theory, we may add that better ways of communicating were also necessary for humans to communicate in larger groups with complex networks. This theory says that language evolved to replace social grooming when group sizes increased. Accepting the idea that grooming contributes to the construction of a social niche makes it possible to include grooming and gossip theory in niche construction theory. From grooming and gossip theory we also take the social brain hypothesis and the continuity hypothesis. Together these hypotheses propose that language (both learning and performance) evolved gradually out of primate social intelligence. Research in neurology corroborates this idea by showing that there is an overlap in the brain between the language centers and the location of social intelligence (Worden, 1998). (p. 219)

She then connects a third theory, relevance-for-status, to the base theory to help it explain how another of its key elements (communication) operates.

> Accepting the common ground assumption that man is a social *and* political animal and using the common ground concept of communication as a social *and* cognitive activity, it is possible to partially integrate Dessalles' relevance-for-status theory. This theory sees language (performance) as a way of "showing off," its primary function being communication of salient features. Integration of this theory is possible if we accept the idea that the (primary) function of language may have been (and still is) different for different individuals. (p. 219)

Finally, van der Lecq connects a fourth theory, complexity theory, to explain the base theory's prediction that language becomes more complex over time:

> Niche construction theory suggests that growth in cultural complexity made better ways of communicating necessary. In addition complexity theory explains *how* languages evolve in complexity over time, often becoming more complex, sometimes being simplified. We must consider the possibility that in the beginning there was no selection pressure for complexity, but that once language existed it quite "naturally" evolved in complexity like other cultural institutions and then more complex language abilities were selected for. This idea is compatible

with niche construction theory, when we assume that complex languages make communication about complex environmental problems and the solution of these problems possible. Language can induce changes in the environment to which organisms will adapt. (p. 219)

Thus, based on the common ground concepts of evolution and communication and the common ground assumption that humans are social and political, it is possible to extend niche construction theory such that it includes Dunbar's (1996) grooming and gossip theory and the political hypothesis exemplified by Dessalles's (2007) relevance-for-status theory. "The new theory," says van der Lecq, "is the result of niche construction theory, which in turn is an extension of conventional evolutionary theory" (p. 219).

What remains is for van der Lecq to state the more comprehensive theoretical explanation in a way that answers the question that motivated the study: What was the primary function for which language emerged? The understanding, she says, must answer three subquestions: (1) Why did language emerge? (2) Why only with humans? and (3) What (and how) did language evolve into such a complex system? The complexity of these questions is reflected in the complexity (and length) of her integrative model and resultant understanding:

> The emergence of our natural predisposition to speech can be seen as the result of gene-culture interaction. Humans belong to the family of primates. For primates, living in social groups is advantageous because it increases the fitness of individual members of the group. In other words, groups construct a necessary social context (social niche) for existence. The formation and maintenance of a social group depends on communication. Our ancestors were able to handle social problems by grooming, but when group sizes increased and social relations became more complex, grooming became time consuming. Moreover, it was advantageous to be able to share "displaced" information. This explains the emergence of language, because with language more individuals can be reached with less effort. Moreover, human group sizes and the complexity of human networks require more than grooming for social bonding. Social bonding is the most likely *original* function of language.
>
> Once the possibility of linguistic communication had emerged, it may have served multiple purposes for different individuals, including mating, childcare, tool making, and hunting. For language to have an evolutionary impact in the Darwinian sense, a certain amount of learning and cognition must have been involved. So, most probably, it evolved as a means of advancing the social and cognitive transmission of life-skills to young hominids. But for some (male?) individuals, it may also have played a role in the "coalition game." As we know from election campaigns, language can be used as a way of showing our talent for

leadership and strong leaders benefit all the members of the group. Thus, the primary function of language may differ for individuals in different situations and is not necessarily the same as the original function for which language emerged, social bonding.

Like other cultural constructs and knowledge, languages have a "natural" tendency to evolve in complexity over time. Language complexity does not seem to be advantageous in itself, but when environmental problems become more complex, we need complex linguistic skills (scientific reasoning) to solve them. But when we use language for "social grooming," one or two simple words may be enough. (p. 220)

Lessons for Interdisciplinary Practice   Van der Lecq and Repko used a similar process to identify their "base theories": Both niche construction theory and identity theory are already interdisciplinary (though imperfectly so) and incorporate both/and thinking. Therefore, they were prime candidates for extension. In making their selections, van der Lecq and Repko adhered to the principle of least action, making sure that the required changes would be the smallest possible.

Spatial and Analytical Integration

Spatial explanation and analytical explanation are additional (and complementary) strategies that can be employed when investigating problems relating to urban history, the new suburban history, public affairs, public policy, and many other problems. Spatial integration refers to combining theoretical explanations of why the causes or effects of problems are not distributed evenly in space. This strategy is useful, for example, when trying to explain why and how residential location ties individuals and families to spatial patterns of distribution. Local living environments greatly affect opportunity and "influence life chances, shape perceptions, political views, and values, and structure political, economic, social, and ecological conflicts" (Connor, 2012, p. 53). For a wide variety of problems, it is important to understand and map how causal processes operate across space, and understand that disciplines may differ in the spaces they emphasize. Analytical integration refers to synthesizing theoretical perspectives on a highly complex process involving multiple factors such as a metropolitan formation. Connor (2012) uses it as a counterpoint to "spatial integration" to refer to considering the metropolitan area as a unity consisting of "city" and "suburbs."

From the Humanities and the Social Sciences: Connor (2012), "The Metropolitan Problem in Interdisciplinary Perspective"   Michan Connor employs these complementary strategies to explain the process of metropolitan formation in the United States: *spatial explanation* at the metropolitan or regional (as opposed to urban or suburban) level, and *analytical explanation* concerning the legal, political, and cultural dimensions of relationships between metropolitan areas. His objective is to construct a comprehensive theory that fully integrates "explanatory constructs" (i.e., theories) of history, metropolitics, public choice theory, and critical legal studies concerning the complex problem of metropolitan formation (p. 71).

STEP 8 Summarized: Connor's task in STEP 8 is to leverage the theoretical insights of history, public choice theory, metropolitics, and critical legal studies by identifying a theory, already interdisciplinary but imperfectly so, that could be extended "across disciplinary domains to address the spatial assumptions of each perspective," which he summarizes here:

> Although particular academic disciplines may use the concepts of spatiality and place overtly, and others implicitly, traditional disciplinary approaches fail to integrate the multiple, overlapping, and occasionally conflicting elements of the essential relationship between places and social life. In the U.S. context, suburbanization and home ownership have connected individuals and families to historical changes in social class, racial differentiation, and political interest. However, historians have typically been limited by a spatial framing of social processes that seldom transcends the presumed division between urban and suburban places. Metropolitics and public choice theory approaches in the social sciences supply frameworks for assessing social processes that cross municipal boundaries but provide starkly different assessments of which social mechanisms—politics or the market—best account for differentiation between metropolitan places. The field of critical legal studies provides a systematic critique of municipal boundaries as political, symbolic, and economic dividers between places and people. Because research in this field focuses very diligently on the processes by which legal principles of local control have evolved in legal doctrine, critical legal studies points to the need to consider the way that policy or legal doctrines have emerged in particular historical contexts and influenced the course of events in those times. (p. 84)

In spite of what he sees as its shortcomings, he selects Lefebvre's (1991) theory of the social production of space for modification because of its "mutually reinforcing patterns of ideas (ideologies, values, ideals), political power (over institutions and over the validation of particular ideas), and social practices" (p. 74). One of the tests he uses for gauging the appropriateness of a theory is that it must recognize (or be compatible with) "historical contingency": the way things happen to play out, and how this constrains and shapes what is possible or at least likely thereafter.

STEP 9: Theory extension for Connor involves "extending the theoretical notions of the spatial and temporal nature of social life into the domain of multiple disciplines where it is differentially acknowledged" (p. 72). Here, he explains how the extended theory increases its explanatory range or "pays attention" to additional factors:

Integrating the theoretical insights of these fields also requires expanding the characteristic methods of local history. A more spatially and analytically open case study methodology employed here addresses the qualities of individual places, but it also pays attention to the nonlocal factors, like ideology, law, and public policy, affecting metropolitan places. In addition, it pays attention to the ways in which local places are not separate but affect each other. (p. 84)

The basis of Connor's study is his own primary research on how the theory of public choice informed the Lakewood Plan, which shaped the formation of modern-day metropolitan Los Angeles County. Connor's more comprehensive theoretical explanation of why Los Angeles County has developed in the way it has is in two parts. The first part explains the effect of the Lakewood Plan:

The Lakewood Plan . . . shaped the metropolitan area, but that influence depended on the very particular qualities of Lakewood as a symbol of the positive values of local autonomy. Public choice theory ideas, because they have been influential in governing as well as in scholarship, merit special scrutiny in this framework. The history of metropolitan formation in Los Angeles demonstrates the partial validity of these ideas. Under the conditions of the rule of homes, suburban residents in the Lakewood Plan cities acted in ways that were consistent with rational self-interest: advocating for low taxes, demanding better services, and seeking to exclude neighbors or land uses that threatened the value of property. Under the political and cultural conditions that have prevailed in the United States and in Los Angeles in particular, it has also been rational for relatively affluent suburban areas to reject common obligations with other metropolitan places. However, this rationality is neither an inherent part of human nature nor a complete explanation for the political and social patterns of metropolitan formation. Rather, it was formed in the context of historically produced legal, social, and political frameworks that made certain behaviors, orientations, and outlooks productive. . . . Public choice theory ideas have, in fact, been more important as shapers of public life than descriptors of it. (p. 84)

In the second part of his comprehensive explanation, Connor particularizes the "behaviors, orientations, and outlooks" resulting from these frameworks of economic incentives and political justifications:

These frameworks of incentives and justifications are not inevitable, but they are powerful, and they have been constructed and reinforced over time through the political rationality they support. In Los Angeles County, homeowners, local and state officials, judges, realtors, bankers, and builders produced new places in the county, attached certain social privileges to favored places, and protected those privileges against claims that they were unfair or unjust. These agents worked through institutional and cultural channels at local, metropolitan, and state scales to create what was visible in hindsight: a white middle class, multiple municipal jurisdictions that could insulate portions of that class from taxation or service obligations, and perhaps most important, the sense that this division was a legitimate component of politics that reflected not exclusion or segregation but "choice." (pp. 84–85)

Connor concedes that because Los Angeles County has its own particular history, making generalizations about other metropolitan areas is problematic. Even so, he contends that it should be possible to use a case study method involving Los Angeles to propose a methodology for evaluating the particular factors influencing metropolitan development elsewhere.

Metropolitan areas nationwide exhibit comparable political division, social inequality, and privilege for affluent homeowners, regardless of the particular path of development, and researchers should devote attention to the ways that institutions, ideas, and experiences (in their particular local incarnations) have interacted to shape development. It is beyond the scope of this essay to recommend policy changes that can promote greater metropolitan equity, though metropolitics scholars offer many suggestions. Rather, by demonstrating that inequality is part of a long process of metropolitan formation with roots in many dimensions of social life, this essay suggests the limits of narrow policy solutions, which are likely to provoke intense opposition and unlikely to secure political legitimacy in the current metropolitan climate of the United States. As Gerald Frug (1999) observes, a fragmented metropolitan area is "perpetuated by the kind of person this fragmentation has nurtured" (p. 80). Reform proposals for regional equity are unlikely to succeed without substantial efforts to unravel dominant values and ideals about place and community in metropolitan America, ideals which have coalesced around the priority given to local interests and the rule of homes. (p. 85)

Connor's integration and more comprehensive theory produces an analysis that is spatially integrated at the metropolitan (or regional) scale and analytically integrated through its attention to the legal, political, and cultural dimensions of relationships between metropolitan places.

Lessons for Interdisciplinary Practice   Connor's study demonstrates that using a combination of integrative strategies may be necessary when working with highly complex processes such as metropolitan formation. Critical to such integrative efforts is first recognizing, as Connor does, the inability of disciplinary theories and their corresponding methodologies to explain the system in its complexity. This involves developing a base theory that can integrate these theories of spatial framings of metropolitan issue, and integrating these with the their legal, political, and cultural dimensions.

Chapter Summary

This chapter explains STEP 9, constructing a more comprehensive understanding or theory. It defines both terms, unpacks their meaning, and explains how this STEP relates to previous STEPS in the integrative process. STEP 9 reflects the two intellectual tendencies within the academy: those disciplines that work primarily with concepts and those disciplines that rely on the development of theories to explain the phenomena they study. Consequently, STEP 9 reflects this bifurcated approach to knowledge formation by laying out two pathways by which the understanding may be achieved. The first pathway, explained in Section 2, is applicable to the humanities, the fine and performing arts, and some applied fields where the focus of integration is directly on concepts and indirectly on their underlying assumptions. In these contexts, achieving full interdisciplinarity involves consciously choosing to construct an understanding that is comprehensive and nuanced.

The second pathway, explained in Section 3, is applicable to the natural and social sciences, sometimes to the humanities, and to some applied and multidisciplinary fields where the focus of knowledge formation is on the development of theories to explain the phenomena of interest. Six strategies demonstrated to achieve integration and construction of a more comprehensive theory are identified and illustrated by student and professional work. The examples by Repko (2010), Henry (2009), van der Lecq (2012), and Connor (2012) illustrate how authors creatively apply these strategies to achieve integration. Once the more comprehensive understanding or theory is constructed, the final task is to reflect on it, assess it, and communicate it. This is the subject of Chapter 14.

Notes

1. The more comprehensive understanding is similar to Boix Mansilla's (2006) "complex explanation" where "aspects of the phenomenon, typically studied by different disciplines, are considered in dynamic complementary interaction" (p. 14). For a detailed discussion of the term *understanding* from a social science perspective, and an explanation of the difference between the *verstehen* (and the more recent interpretive) approach and the predictive approach, see Frankfort-Nachmias and Nachmias (2008, pp. 10–11).

2. For a detailed discussion of emergent properties and their relation to a system of causal links as a whole, see Szostak (2009, pp. 43–45).

Exercises

Defining Terms

13.1   How is the definition of *more comprehensive understanding* consistent with and an extension of the definition of *interdisciplinary studies* as a whole (see Chapter 1)?

Constructing Understandings

13.2   If you are working with concepts, explain what the understandings by Silver (2005), Bal (1999), and Delph (2005) have in common.

13.3   If you are working with theories, decide which strategy for achieving causal or propositional integration is most appropriate to the problem. Create a figure depicting the various causes, including feedback loops where these may exist.

13.4   How many levels of causality can you identify concerning the problem of the rising cost of university education, and how should they be labeled? Is there an "emergent property" involved?

13.5   What must Henry (2009) do to make his understanding of school violence fully interdisciplinary?

13.6   How is van der Lecq's (2012) "base theory" similar to Monroe and Kreidie's (1997) identity theory in Repko's (2012) example?

13.7   How would you apply spatial explanation and analytical explanation to the complex problem of constructing a high-speed rail system somewhere in the countryside near or where you live?

14

Reflecting on, Testing, and Communicating the Understanding

Having constructed the more comprehensive understanding, what remains is to reflect on, test, and communicate it. Since interdisciplinarians recognize that no method is perfect, this book advocates using multiple ways of evaluating the understanding constructed in STEP 9. This book also challenges readers at all levels to communicate the understanding by feeding back integrative knowledge into the scientific community. "To contribute to progress in science, integrative knowledge, theories, and methods need to be transformed from tacit into explicit knowledge" (Tress, Tress, & Fry, 2006, p. 22).

This chapter is organized in three sections. The first discusses the importance of reflecting on the understanding and the utility of the interdisciplinary research process (IRP) to its development. The second identifies distinctive cognitive abilities that the literature on cognition and instruction asserts are fostered by interdisciplinary education and research, and how these can form the basis for testing or assessing the quality of interdisciplinary work. The section also identifies four approaches to assessment that practitioners have recently developed and then presents an approach that integrates them. The third section discusses the importance of communicating the new understanding in a variety of manners.

> Step 10: Reflect on, Test, and Communicate the Understanding

Reflecting on the More Comprehensive Understanding or Theory

Research of any kind, including interdisciplinary research, involves reflection. In one sense, the interdisciplinary researcher is like the brick mason who periodically steps back from the wall one is building or the artist who steps back from the canvas one is painting to contemplate the character and quality of the work as it develops. **Reflection in an interdisciplinary sense is a self-conscious activity that involves thinking about why certain choices were made at various points in the research process and how these choices have affected the development of the work.** Interdisciplinarians, Szostak (2009) suggests, may well have to be more reflective than disciplinary specialists for this reason: Interdisciplinarians must be able to demonstrate the ability to enter the specialized scholarly discourse (i.e., disciplinary literatures) on the problem in an interesting and persuasive manner, and explain those elements of their own research that may cause concern among the intended audience (p. 331).

While reflection should be pursued throughout the research process, reflection toward the end of the research process serves two broad purposes. Most obviously, reflections should guide researchers to add material to their conclusions. Scholarly papers generally include "suggestions for further research" in their concluding sections, and even undergraduates may find it useful to reflect on what they or others might do next to further the research. Ideally, researchers will also want to revisit earlier STEPS in the research that their reflections suggest could have been performed better.

The second reason for reflecting here is more personal but arguably more important. Undergraduate students in particular should ask themselves what they have learned from applying the interdisciplinary research process that they can apply in future research projects, and indeed in tackling the complex problems that they will inevitably face in life. Every course in university might well close with some reflection on what the student should take out of it. This is especially the case with the interdisciplinary research process, and its many strategies for solving complex problems.

Szostak (2009) identifies four sorts of reflection that are called for in interdisciplinary work: (1) what has actually been learned from the project, (2) steps omitted, (3) one's own biases, and (4) strengths and weaknesses of the insights, theories, and methods used, including the IRP itself (pp. 331–334).

Reflect on What Has Actually Been Learned From the Project in an Overall Sense

Students at all levels should reflect on what they have actually done and learned from the project, including its probable benefits for their careers and/ or for society. More specifically, this includes reflecting on the *contents* of the project (i.e., what was learned about the subject of the project) and on the *process* used. By "process" is meant how the project was organized, how it proceeded, the positive and negative experiences, and the utility of the research process described in this book. For example, if the research project was a group project, participants can reflect on their goal to integrate different knowledge cultures and decide the ways and the extent to which this goal was achieved, as well as the ways that integration was incomplete or its results were less than fully satisfied. Participants can also reflect on when and under which circumstances common learning took place and what can be done to stimulate such moments. Another point for students to reflect on is how disciplinary and interdisciplinary knowledge were shared, and how that sharing influenced the development of the resultant understanding. Boix Mansilla, Duraisingh, Wolfe, and Haynes (2009) suggest that students ask, "Do the conclusions drawn indicate that understanding has been advanced by the integration of disciplinary views?" This question essentially asks, "Was it worth the effort? Did it yield a new, richer, deeper, broader, or more nuanced understanding of the problem?" (p. 345).

Reflect on STEPS Omitted or Compressed

The research process delineated in this book involves making a series of decisions, which are conveniently characterized as "STEPS." Some undergraduate or graduate students may have omitted one or more STEPS for various reasons, or may not have been able to perform each STEP in the way described in this book. Or, they may have compressed some STEPS. For example, some programs and courses may view STEP 2, justifying using an interdisciplinary approach, as something that can be folded into STEP 1 or eliminated entirely. Others may compress STEP 3, identifying relevant disciplinary insights and their insights and theories, with STEP 4, conducting the literature search. Still others may compress STEP 5, developing adequacy in each relevant discipline, with STEP 6, analyzing the problem and evaluating each insight into it. And still others may view STEPS 8 and 9 as two parts of a single STEP.

For most complex problems even grad students and academic teams do not always perform each STEP. There is always more literature that could be read, for example. And thus even advanced researchers should reflect on what they did not do. If the researcher decides to omit or change the order of certain STEPS, then these omissions or alterations to the research strategy should be explained and their possible cumulative effect on the final product described. Typically, these effects surface in glaring ways near the end of the research process. For example, failure to develop adequacy in each relevant discipline may result in certain theories and methods being overlooked or misunderstood.

Reflect on One's Own Biases

Researchers at all levels should reflect on their own biases that they consciously or unconsciously bring to the problem they wish to research. Szostak (2009) makes a compelling case for why reflecting on one's own biases is necessary and should even be mandatory in interdisciplinary work:

> A key guiding principle of interdisciplinary analysis is that no piece of scholarly research is perfect. If we accept that no scholarly method can guide a researcher flawlessly towards insight, then it follows that scholarly results may reflect researcher biases. This does not mean that results only reflect such biases, as some in the field of science studies have claimed. But it does mean that one way of evaluating the insights generated by research is to interrogate researcher bias. (p. 331)

In this statement, Szostak makes two points: (1) Researchers should reflect on their own biases concerning the problem, and (2) researcher bias is one way of evaluating the researcher's insights.

Interrogate One's Own Biases

Practically, students should interrogate their own biases. One way is to ask these questions:

- "Why was I drawn to the problem in the first place?" Typically, students—as well as practitioners—select a topic that they have strong views on or personal experience with. For example, one student in a senior capstone course wished to examine the causes of alienation that teens often experience. She admitted that what drew her to the topic was her own experience with alienation and now, as a mother of a teen, watching her daughter experience the same struggle. Selecting a research topic on this basis need not skew the research process or its result.
- "Did I select expert views based on whether or not I agreed with them?" Selecting insights on this basis is a common trap that many students fall into. They mistakenly believe that interdisciplinary research is similar to research papers that they have written for other courses in which they are urged to argue a particular viewpoint and support it with expert testimony. This mode of "research," of course, is antithetical to interdisciplinary work, which involves taking into account expert insights regardless of whether they run counter to the student's point of view. As noted elsewhere in this book, the role of the interdisciplinary researcher is similar to that of a marriage counselor who is attempting to bridge differences, not ignore them.
- "Did I select insights based solely or primarily on my familiarity with particular disciplines and their literatures?" The answer to this question is usually yes for undergraduates because they are generally limited to using two or three disciplines to make the research project manageable. The answer may be yes or no for graduate students depending on course requirements and the scope of the paper or thesis. Regardless of the level, students at all levels should be able to justify the disciplines

and their insights chosen and articulate in STEP 10 how any omission or limitation has affected the final understanding. For mature scholars and members of research teams, insights should be chosen without regard for familiarity with any particular discipline and its literature.

Check One's Work for Biases

Students may check their work for bias. In the following composite example, an undergraduate student reveals personal bias concerning the qualities of an ideal manager in this opening paragraph to the paper's introduction.

> ## The Ideal Manager: An Interdisciplinary Model
>
> Good managers must have at least two essential qualities. They must be fully knowledgeable of the products that their unit is responsible for, and they must understand that a single error can produce unforeseen consequences resulting in a very dissatisfied customer. Constantly, one sees reports of higher management going terribly bad. Whether it's a case of lying, cheating, or stealing, the number of unfaithful or unreliable management keeps increasing.

The problem with this introduction is that the student has already decided (based on her experience working under several poor managers) that an ideal manager should have these particular qualities *even before* conducting the in-depth literature search. The student's bias was also revealed (not surprisingly) in the literature search itself by preferring insights that reflected her preconceived notions of an ideal manager.

Reflect on One's Adherence to a Theoretical Approach

Reflecting on one's own bias should include reflecting on one's adherence to one of the theoretical approaches noted earlier in this book. For example, it may be that as a postmodernist one prizes personal freedom over structure and therefore objects to the very notion of following an interdisciplinary research process of any kind. In this case, one can reflect on these questions:

- How has your experience using the process changed or tempered your bias?
- Have you become more self-consciously interdisciplinary, and if so, how has this happened?
- Have you concluded that interdisciplinary studies needs some structure in order to dissuade scholars from using superficial forms of interdisciplinary analysis?
- Are you more aware that scholarly results reflect some combination of the influence of personal biases and of external reality?

Reflect on One's Limited Understanding of the Relevant Disciplines, Theories, and Methods

Students should reflect on the simple fact that all humans have limited perceptual and cognitive capabilities. Even if one has achieved adequacy in understanding the relevant insights, theories, and methods pertaining to the problem, one can hardly claim to have practitioner-level understanding of every insight produced and every theory and method used by the authors who have written about the problem. It is appropriate, therefore, to do what practitioners often do in their concluding remarks: state the ways in which you may have overestimated or underestimated the importance of some insights, theories, and methods and therefore the ways your results may reflect this possibility. Academic writing, say Boix Mansilla et al. (2009), is strengthened when authors are aware of the limitations of their work (p. 346).

Reflecting on one's limited understanding extends to one's awareness of the limitations and benefits of the contributing disciplines and how the disciplines intertwine (Boix Mansilla et al., 2009, p. 345). Interdisciplinary work, say Boix Mansilla et al., requires "a deliberate intertwining of disciplinary perspectives" and careful "evaluation of disciplinary insights for their potential contributions and limitations" (p. 345). Instead of dividing students into undergraduates and graduates, Boix Mansilla et al. categorize students according to their level of reflection. Novice-level students, they say, may limit their reflection "to a pro forma critique such as 'More research is needed on this topic.'" "Apprentice-level students" they say, "may weigh the merits and limitations of the selected disciplines in turn [i.e., serially] against alternative selections available" (pp. 345–346). Novice-level students are satisfied to name the disciplinary perspectives used and may only fleetingly refer to how each could potentially limit or advance the argument. But to move from a novice to an apprentice level, students should explicitly consider the limitations of the relevant disciplinary understandings and explain how using an interdisciplinary approach has enlarged and strengthened understanding (pp. 345–346).

Testing the Quality of Interdisciplinary Work _____

A pundit has compared testing and assessing the quality of interdisciplinary work to being marched to the Chinese countryside during Mao's Great Cultural Revolution to dig onions, and then spending the rest of one's time confessing how much one has learned by digging onions. According to the authors of the Teagle Foundation White Paper (Rhoten, Boix Mansilla, Chun, & Klein, 2006) on interdisciplinary education at liberal arts institutions, "the biggest challenge to interdisciplinarity, particularly at the undergraduate level," is "the lack of generalizable methods for judging interdisciplinary education and its direct impacts on student learning" (Executive Summary). Veronica Boix Mansilla (2005), principal investigator of the Interdisciplinary Studies Project at Project Zero, Harvard Graduate School of Education, points to a related problem: the "lack of clarity" about interdisciplinary learning outcomes and "indicators of quality" (p. 16).

Learning Outcomes Claimed for Interdisciplinarity

Researchers at any level should think about what skills they take away from the project that they can employ both in future formal research projects and in life more generally. The learning outcomes typically claimed for interdisciplinarity include tolerance of ambiguity or paradox, critical thinking, a balance between subjective and objective thinking, an ability to demythologize experts, increased empowerment to see new and different questions and issues, and the ability to draw on multiple methods and the knowledge to address them (Cornwell & Stoddard, 2001, p. 162; Field, Lee, & Field, 1994, p. 70). Notably, interdisciplinarians substantially agree that integration is "fundamental to any 'successful' interdisciplinary program" and consider "the ability to synthesize or integrate" as the "hallmark of interdisciplinarity" (Rhoten et al., 2006, pp. 3–4).

Some of these outcomes are also claimed for disciplinary and multidisciplinary learning. Disciplines in the liberal arts and the humanities typically claim "critical thinking" as an important outcome, as do the natural sciences and the applied fields. This collective claim to critical thinking raises a question: How do interdisciplinary approaches contribute to the development of this key cognitive skill in ways that are different from or superior to single-subject approaches? "For [an interdisciplinary] learner to be truly empowered through critical thinking," says Toynton (2005), "more than one context or one discipline needs to be encountered" (p. 110). If interdisciplinarians insist on including "critical thinking" in the learning outcomes at the program level, he asserts, they should make clear that the development of this skill requires viewing "the approaches, products, and processes" of relevant disciplines "from a detached and comparative viewpoint" (p. 110).

While *critical thinking* is a broad term, few would deny that key elements include distinguishing assumptions from argument and assumption from evidence, evaluating the quality of argument and evidence, comparing conflicting arguments and evidence, and reaching a reasoned conclusion regarding which argument or combination of arguments is best. These elements may (or may not) be addressed in a disciplinary education, but each lies at the heart of the interdisciplinary research process. Most if not all of the topics addressed in the next section may be thought of as particular critical thinking skills.

Cognitive Abilities Attributable to Interdisciplinary Learning Drawn From Research on Cognition and Instruction

The literature on cognition and instruction identifies five cognitive abilities that interdisciplinary learning fosters. These include the ability to (1) develop and apply perspective-taking techniques, (2) develop structural knowledge of problems that are appropriate to interdisciplinary inquiry, (3) create common ground, (4) integrate conflicting insights (i.e., expert views) from two or more disciplines, and (5) produce a cognitive advancement or interdisciplinary understanding of the problem. Each of these abilities, introduced in Chapter 2, is examined here.

Develop and Apply Perspective-Taking Techniques

One result of repeated exposure to interdisciplinarity is the ability to apply perspective-taking techniques. This critical ability, discussed in Chapter 4, involves understanding differing and conflicting views on a given issue (Baloche, Hynes, & Berger, 1996, p. 3). Perspective taking is an approach commonly suggested for assembling new sets of potential solutions to a given problem (Halpern, 1996, pp. 1, 21). Interdisciplinarity helps students to

> move developmentally from a clear understanding of the differences between disciplines and their perspectives on a problem to distinguishing the essential characteristics of disciplines—to understanding their discrete domains of usefulness, what kinds of questions they ask, and their rules of evidence. (Baloche et al., 1996, p. 3)

By contrast, discipline-specific and multidisciplinary approaches to learning frequently fail to demonstrate how particular disciplines interface with one another when they focus on the same problem (Ivanitskaya, Clark, Montgomery, & Primeau, 2002, p. 96). Researchers caution that students presented with information in disciplinary isolation tend to acquire knowledge in disparate categories (Humpreys, Post, & Ellis, 1981). The result, they say, is that they "may fail to perceive, or even question, the overlapping values or questions raised by different disciplines" or knowledge formations when addressing a particular problem (Ivanitskaya et al., 2002, pp. 96–97).

Develop Structural Knowledge of Problems Appropriate to Interdisciplinary Inquiry

By focusing on a problem or core theme as is typical of interdisciplinary courses, interdisciplinary learning readily facilitates the development of the ability to structure knowledge in terms of higher-order relationships and organizing principles (Goldsmith & Johnson, 1990). This ability is developed by acquiring *declarative knowledge* (factual information) and *procedural knowledge* (process-based information) that is used for problem solving or step-by-step task completion (J. R. Anderson, 1982). In interdisciplinary terms, this ability is derived from developing adequacy in different knowledge domains as students focus on a particular problem or topic. But students will also have to develop adequacy in the procedural knowledge of relevant disciplines whose experts have written on the subject. These constructs represent a central tenet of cognitive science: that the organization of knowledge is at least as important as the quantity of knowledge acquired in helping the individual to determine when and how a set of declarative facts applies to a particular situation (Dorsey, Campbell, Foster, & Miles, 1999, p. 32). Structural knowledge of problems is demonstrated by mapping the problem.

Create Common Ground Between Conflicting Disciplinary Insights

A third result of interdisciplinary learning is the ability to create common ground between conflicting disciplinary insights. As discussed in detail in Chapter 11, creating common ground is an essential STEP that the interdisciplinarian must take in order to prepare insights for integration and construct the more comprehensive understanding.

Integrate Conflicting Disciplinary Insights

A fourth result of interdisciplinary learning is that it "enhances students' capacity to integrate" conflicting insights from two or more disciplines (Boix Mansilla, 2005, p. 16). As a distinctive approach to learning, interdisciplinarity guides students beyond simpler forms of knowledge acquisition to "a deeper assimilation of cross-disciplinary concepts" (Ivanitskaya et al., 2002, p. 97).

Produce a Cognitive Advancement or Interdisciplinary Understanding of a Problem

A fifth result of interdisciplinary learning is that it develops students' ability to use integrated knowledge and modes of thinking to "produce a cognitive advancement," or what this book calls a more comprehensive understanding.

Four Core Premises That Underlie the Concept of Cognitive Advancement

According to Boix Mansilla (2005), four core premises underlie the concept of cognitive advancement:

- "It builds on a *performance* view of interdisciplinary understanding—one that privileges the capacity to use knowledge over that of simply having or accumulating it [italics added] . . . From this perspective, individuals understand a concept when they are able to apply it—or *think with it*—accurately and flexibly in novel situations" (pp. 16–17). Using knowledge also involves effectively communicating it to others.

- "The understanding is highly *disciplined*, meaning that it is *deeply informed by disciplinary expertise* [italics added]" (p. 17). This refers to the distinction between genuine disciplinary insights and common sense. "Interdisciplinary understanding differs from naïve common sense precisely in its ability to draw on disciplinary insights" (p. 17).
- "The understanding is achieved through the *integration* of disciplinary views [italics added] . . . "In interdisciplinary work," says Boix Mansilla, "these perspectives are not merely juxtaposed" but "actively inform one another, thereby leveraging understanding" (p. 17).
- The interdisciplinary understanding "is *purposeful*" leading to a "*cognitive advancement*—e.g., a new insight, a solution, an account, an explanation [emphasis added]" (p. 17). Examples of cognitive advancements include explaining a phenomenon, creating a product, raising a new question, generating a new insight, proposing a solution, providing an account, or offering an explanation (pp. 16–17). Like all research results, the cognitive advancement must be communicated for it to be useful.

The interdisciplinary understanding, then, is new knowledge that is useful, disciplined, integrative, and purposeful. These core premises are the primary indicators of quality interdisciplinary work and form the basis for testing or assessing the quality of the understanding produced. Approaches to testing the understanding and examples of understandings are discussed elsewhere in the chapter.

Testing or Assessing the More Comprehensive Understanding

Reflecting on the more comprehensive understanding or theory is quite different from assessing or testing it, though arguably assessment may involve reflection. The meanings of *test* and *assess* are practically synonymous. For the purposes of this discussion, the term *test* is used.

Test has different meanings in different disciplinary contexts. Testing in a discipline usually means applying the method(s) favored by the discipline to the data favored by the discipline. These tests will be flawed to the extent that the methods and data used are imperfect. Interdisciplinarians face a challenge but also an opportunity: They cannot rely on just one method but can by triangulating among different methods aspire to a less biased test. The undergraduate is unlikely to do any formal testing but can reflect on what different methods might produce (and might refer back to the earlier discussion of strengths and weaknesses of methods in doing so).

There are also four holistic approaches to testing an interdisciplinary understanding. Three of these look at the results and ask in turn whether there seem be useful policy implications (Newell, 2007a, and part of Szostak, 2009), whether others find the results interesting (Tress et al., 2006), and whether the interdisciplinary understanding seems to provide enhanced understanding (Szostak, 2009). The fourth test looks at the process used to produce the result, and asks whether this was appropriate (Boix Mansilla et al., 2009). This fourth test bears some similarity to the practice within disciplines of judging whether disciplinary methods were applied properly in generating a certain result.

The Newell Test

Newell's (2007a) concern with the *utility* or applicability of the understanding is balanced by his concern with the *process* used to produce the understanding. He identifies three of the most common sources of "failure" or "inadequacy" in producing the understanding. The first is failure to perform each step adequately. The second is doing insufficient work in identifying connections between the aspects of the problem studied by different disciplines, and thus the connections between the variables or concepts used by those disciplines. Relatively little is known about connections, he says, because most scholars are disciplinarians and are not interested in other aspects of the problem or how other disciplines explain them. The third common source of failure or inadequacy is overlooking one or more perspectives. Depending on the shortcoming, "the nature of the inadequacy may suggest which steps need to be examined" (Newell, 2007a, p. 262). Students may test their understanding by responding to one or more of Newell's questions:

- Does it allow for more effective action?
- Does it help solve the problem, resolve the issue, or answer the research question?
- Is it useful to practitioners, the public, or policy makers who are concerned with that particular complex problem, issue, or question? (p. 262)

The value of these questions, he says, is that they serve as a bridge between the ivory tower of the academy and the real world.

If the pragmatic judgments of practitioners are that the more comprehensive understanding

lacks utility, or if it has limited value because of a serious weakness, then the interdisciplinarian must correct the weakness by revisiting the earlier steps in the interdisciplinary process. (Newell, 2007a, p. 262)

The Tress et al. Test

Another test of an interdisciplinary understanding's utility is whether others are interested in it. Tress et al. (2006) emphasize the importance of communicating one's research to the scientific community. By "research," Tress et al. mean "original investigation undertaken specifically to gain knowledge and under-standing" (p. 21). Gathering data, recording observations, collecting expe-riences, developing plans, discussing with stakeholders, and even solving real-world problems, though valuable, are not necessarily research. Rather, integrative "knowledge creation becomes research when all data and infor-mation we have gathered are systematized, analyzed and *fed back* into academic communities [italics added]" (Tress et al., 2006, p. 21). Theories of organization learning stress the importance of researchers developing formal and informal mechanisms to engage in information exchanges within their institutions. "If knowledge remains implicit and is not integrated and shared at the institutional level, it can easily get lost" (p. 23).

Integrative research, they say, requires creating new knowledge, which must be transformed from **tacit knowledge** (not directly accessible to others) into **explicit knowledge** (accessible to others). Explicit knowledge "is fixed on some kind of medium such as a book, scientific journal, CD, video or a web site that moves it into the wider context of the public domain" (Tress et al., 2006, p. 22). Subjecting the new knowledge to peer review and publishing it is one of the main pillars of scientific progress (p. 22). Only when this hap-pens, they say, can we "speak of research activity, since it is through this . . . feedback that generic knowledge is created." Scientific reflection "considers the assumptions/hypotheses and whether they were confirmed or rejected" (p. 23). It also considers the selection of method(s), their advantages and limitations, and consequently what needs to be developed. One of the most important topics for reflection concerns the results of the project and particularly how these results relate to previous findings. Practitioners may ask, "Does the new understanding support existing theories or challenge them so that the new theory development becomes necessary?" Of course, the most common way of feeding such reflections back into science is through peer-reviewed publication (p. 23).

Though Tress et al. (2006) have in mind students, mature scholars, and interdisciplinary teams, undergraduates can also communicate their research in these ways:

- *As feedback into the academy:* Students can share the results of their research inside the academy. Commonly used communication strategies include public poster sessions, student panels, symposia, student journals, and student portfolios. Some graduate programs host an annual inter-disciplinary research conference that involves outside speakers, poster sessions, and other activities to highlight interdisciplinarity and the quality of their work.
- *As feedback into the community:* Students can share their research with appropriate public or private entities and solicit their feedback. Students at one undergraduate program have been successfully leveraging their senior research projects to secure professional positions and gain entry into graduate programs.

The Szostak Test

Szostak (2009) offers a two-part approach to testing the understanding. The first part asks two questions of the understanding:

1. Does it give us better insight into the problem than if there was no new understanding (i.e., is something better than nothing)? If so, how is it better? (Note: This is a low-level question that asks the student, "Is the new understanding better than no new understanding?")

2. Does it explain some aspect of a causal relationship better than any alternative explanation? If so, how (p. 335)? (Note: This is a higher-level question that asks the student to compare the understanding [or some part of it] to the various alternative [disciplinary] understandings and explain how the student's understanding is better than each of these.)

If the new understanding seems to provide some sort of insight but it turns out that some other understanding explains everything captured by the new understanding *and more* (and/or seems to provide a more plausible explanation), then, says Szostak (2009), we should be very wary of attributing any importance to the new understanding. But a more likely result is that the new understanding will explain the problem (or at least some aspects of it) better than other (i.e., disciplinary) understandings (Szostak, 2009, p. 335). If so, the student should make this contribution clear.

The test of the understanding, he says, generally should be to see *not* whether particular disciplinary insights were "right" but whether the student has accorded them too little or too much emphasis in the new understanding. Szostak (2009) admits that such a test "may seem both more difficult and more arbitrary," especially for undergraduates. Still, "no method or piece of scholarly research is perfect, and thus no test of any hypothesis is perfect. Scholarly judgment always has to be exercised in determining how important a particular argument is" (p. 336).

The second part of Szostak's approach to testing the new understanding is to subject it to what he calls "the holistic test." This test is appropriate in situations where new understanding is aimed at shaping public policy. The understanding passes the "holistic test" if it proves useful to policy makers. In this respect, it is similar to Newell's (2007a) utility test that relies on the pragmatic judgment of practitioners. Szostak (2009) cautions against neglecting the possible negative side effects of any policy-oriented understanding. "Interdisciplinary analysis," he says, "naturally tends to highlight the potential weakness of each theory or disciplinary perspective. Attention to the full range of causal relationships should further reduce the probability of this type of error" (Szostak, 2009, p. 337).

More advanced students, as well as mature scholars and interdisciplinary teams, may wish to subject their understanding (if it is policy-oriented) to

Szostak's (2009) more demanding "holistic" test. This involves submitting the understanding to a second set of questions that are broader and more probing:

1. Does the interdisciplinary analysis neglect possible negative side effects of the understanding if it is implemented?

2. Does the interdisciplinary analysis pay attention to the full range of causal relationships involved?

3. Is the understanding and the problem it addresses adequately contextualized?

4. Do policy makers find the understanding and the insights the study provides useful? (p. 337)

The Boix Mansilla et al. Test

Veronica Boix Mansilla, Elizabeth Dawes Duraisingh, Christopher Wolfe, and Carolyn Haynes (2009) have developed a rubric to test or assess the quality of interdisciplinary work. Their approach differs from the approaches offered by Newell (2007a) and Szostak (2009) in two important respects: (1) Whereas Newell's and Szostak's focus is on *students testing their own work,* the focus of Boix Mansilla et al. is on *faculty evaluating student work;* (2) whereas Newell's and Szostak's focus is on *the utility of the understanding,* the focus of Boix Mansilla et al. is on *showing developmental differences* between the interdisciplinary writing produced by upper- and lower-division undergraduate students. However, faculty can adapt the Boix Mansilla et al. rubric so that students can judge the quality of their own work and reflect on ways in which they can develop it further (Brough & Pool, 2005; Huber & Hutchings, 2004; Walvoord & Anderson, 1998).[1]

The Boix Mansilla et al. (2009) rubric identifies four defining qualities that apply to student work at any level and that students can use to assess their own work. These qualities (which are identical to the core premises noted earlier) include the work's *purposefulness,* its *disciplinary grounding,* its *integration,* and its *critical awareness.* Each quality is connected to one or more of the STEPS in the IRP. Producing a quality interdisciplinary understanding requires that students demonstrate the following:

- *Purposefulness:* Have clarity about the purpose of their inquiry and the intended audience (STEP 1) and an explicit rationale for taking an interdisciplinary approach (STEP 2). Two questions relating to purposefulness are these:

  (1) "Does the student's framing of the problem invite an interdisciplinary approach? (2) Does the student use the writing genre effectively to communicate with his or her intended audience?" (Boix Mansilla et al., 2009, p. 342)

- *Disciplinary grounding:* Show understanding of the chosen disciplinary insights, modes of thinking, or disciplinary perspective (i.e., the discipline's preferred concepts, units of analysis, methods, and forms of communication in a discipline). This is similar to STEPS 3, 4, and 5. Two questions relating to disciplinary grounding are these:

  (1) "Does the student use disciplinary *knowledge* accurately and effectively (e.g., concepts, theories, perspectives, findings, examples)?

  (2) Does the student use disciplinary *methods* accurately and effectively (e.g., experimental design, philosophical argumentation, textual analysis)?" (Boix Mansilla et al., 2009, p. 343)

- *Integration:* Identify "points where insights from different disciplines are brought together and articulate the cognitive advantage enabled by the combination of these insights" (Boix Mansilla et al., 2009, p. 338). This involves STEPS 8, 9, and 10. Four questions to be asked that relate to integration are these:

  (1) "Does the student include selected disciplinary perspectives or insights from two or more disciplinary traditions that are relevant to the purpose of the paper? (2) Is there an integrative device or strategy (e.g., a model, metaphor, analogy)? (3) Is there a sense of balance in the overall composition of the piece with regard to how the student brings the disciplinary perspectives or insights together to advance the purpose of the piece? (4) Do the conclusions drawn by the student indicate that understanding has been advanced by the integration of disciplinary views?" (Boix Mansilla et al., 2009, pp. 344–345)

- *Critical awareness:* "Engage in a process of considered judgment and critique: weighing disciplinary options, making informed adjustments to achieve their proposed aims, recognizing the limitations of the work produced" (Boix Mansilla et al., 2009, pp. 338–339). A question relating to critical awareness is this:

  (1) "Does the student show awareness of the limitations and benefits of the contributing disciplines and how the disciplines intertwine?" (Boix Mansilla et al., 2009, p. 346)

For each criterion, Boix Mansilla et al. (2009) describe four qualitatively distinct levels of student achievement: *naïve, novice, apprentice,* and *master.* These levels are described here:

- *Naïve:* "A project can be characterized as naïve if it lacks clarity of purpose and audience, is built primarily on common sense or folk beliefs about the topic at hand, fails to draw on disciplinary insights, and makes no effort to integrate them because disciplinary perspectives themselves are not considered as such. These students may benefit from discussions about why the topic matters, what would be gained by understanding it in depth, how the topic connects with and expands personal experience, or how their intuitions or beliefs about the topic may be challenged" (Boix Mansilla et al., 2009, pp. 339–340).

- *Novice:* "A project exemplifies a novice understanding when it exhibits a superficial understanding of the nature of interdisciplinary academic work. The purpose of the project may be too broad or unviable, disciplinary concepts and theories are uncritically presented as matters of fact, and integrative language may be mechanistic and pro forma. These students grasp the nature of and differences between disciplinary work and the distinctive process of interdisciplinary inquiry. Students at this level may benefit from analyzing examples of work by experts in which the process of knowledge construction in and across disciplines is apparent as well as to reflect critically on the strengths and weaknesses of the different disciplinary insights" (Boix Mansilla et al., 2009, p. 340).

- *Apprentice:* Projects at this level approach professional interdisciplinary work. It "exhibits a clear and viable purpose and a sense of the multiple audiences for the work." These students adequately use disciplinary elements (e.g., concepts, theories, assumptions) and modes of thinking, and support key claims with examples and sources. "Integration is reached through a metaphor, conceptual framework, causal explanation, or other device that contributes to a deepening understanding of the topic" (Boix Mansilla et al., 2009, p. 340). Student projects that fall within this category may still fail to strengthen an argument or critically probe an insight's benefit or shortcoming. Nevertheless, they attain "a robust understanding of disciplinary foundations" and understand "how and why integration can deepen understanding of the topic at hand" (p. 340).

- *Master:* Projects at the master level are characterized by their creativity, analytical sophistication, and self-reflection. Students "demonstrate comfortable understanding of disciplinary foundations and interdisciplinary integration" (Boix Mansilla et al., 2009, p. 341). Their work exhibits a clear sense of purpose and the need for an interdisciplinary approach. Students at this level "have mastered multiple expressive genres," introduce "new insightful examples to support disciplinary claims," and integrate insights "elegantly and coherently" while not overlooking opportunities to advance the argument. Undergraduate students performing at this level are ready to move to a new topic. Graduate students are ready to consider new criteria "such as originality, potential impact of the work, and whether scholarly precedent and contributions have been accounted for" (p. 341).

Integrating These Tests

Newell (2007a), Tress et al. (2006), Szostak (2009), and Boix Mansilla et al. (2009) offer varying approaches to testing an interdisciplinary understanding. From these approaches, it is possible to identify seven key indicators of quality. Each of the following indicators, with the exception of "communication," which only Tress et al. advocate, is supported by at least two authors. Scholars all advocate communication; we just don't think of it as a test (but should). The decision as to which indicators are most appropriate for a particular project must be made locally on the basis of a course's academic level, purpose, and content.

- Usefulness: Applicability to practitioners who are concerned with the problem (Boix Mansilla et al., Newell, Szostak).
- Disciplinary grounding: Adequacy is achieved in relevant disciplines; linkages between disciplines are identified; careful evaluation is made of disciplinary insights for their potential contributions and limitations; all relevant perspectives, insights, and theories are addressed; balance is achieved in using disciplinary insights; strengths and weaknesses of author's insight(s) and understanding are addressed; personal bias is recognized and suspended so as not to skew analysis (Boix Mansilla et al., Newell, Szostak, Tress et al.).
- Integration: Synthesis of varying or conflicting viewpoints is explicit (Boix Mansilla et al., Newell, Szostak, Tress et al.).
- Process: Which steps proved advantageous or problematic and why, which steps were modified or not followed and why, and which steps proved most necessary to producing a better understanding (Newell, Szostak, Tress et al.).
- Comparison: Insight(s) into the problem are better than any alternative explanations (Boix Mansilla et al., Newell, Szostak).
- Self-reflection: Author is aware of the limitations of his/her work (Boix Mansilla et al., Szostak, Tress et al.).
- Communication: Subject to peer review feedback (Tress et al.).

Communicating the Results of Integration

Advanced undergraduate or graduate courses typically encourage or even require students to use metaphors, models, and narratives to capture creatively the new understanding in all of its richness. However one chooses to communicate the new understanding, it should be inclusive of each discipline's insights but beholden to none of them. That is, each relevant insight, theory, or concept should contribute to the understanding but not dominate it. The objective of this part of STEP 10 is to achieve unity, coherence, and balance among the disciplinary influences that have contributed to the understanding (Newell, 2007a, p. 261). In effect, the use of metaphors, models, and narratives to communicate the understanding constitutes a test of whether it is coherent, unified, and balanced and, thus, truly interdisciplinary. The understanding, theory, product, or meaning may be communicated in one of several forms, or some combination of these, as shown in the following examples of student (noted with an *) and professional work.

A Metaphor

A metaphor "brings out the defining characteristics of the understanding without denying the remaining conflict that underlies it" (Newell, 2007a, p. 261). The value of metaphors is that they allow readers to connect new information to what they already know. Metaphors are particularly useful in the humanities, where meaning cannot be adequately expressed using quantitative and empirical approaches. The social sciences and even the natural sciences also make use of metaphors. Metaphors help us to understand one thing in terms of another (Lakoff & Johnson, 1980, p. 5). An interdisciplinary understanding has been reached when the metaphor is consistent with (1) the contributing disciplinary insights as modified to create common ground, (2) the interdisciplinary linkages found, and (3) the patterns observable in the overall behavior of the complex system (Newell, 2007a, p. 261).

Visual or physical metaphors can be effective and powerful integrative devices. They "frame reality in terms of similarities between constructs pertaining to different realms" (Boix Mansilla, 2009, p. 10). A visual metaphor combines a *"vehicle concept"* with the *topic*. An example of a visual metaphor is Maya Lin's Vietnam Veterans Memorial in Washington, DC. She uses the vehicle concept of a scar—a cut in the earth to be healed by time—to highlight certain features of the topic—the devastating consequences of the Vietnam War on American society. Boix Mansilla (2009) explains Lin's approach:

> Framing the Vietnam War as a scar sheds light on the personal emotional experience of war and its long-lasting impact. It does not illuminate, for instance, the political and military connundra that the war presented to American administrations at different points in time. To the extent that the mind can explicate the tacit analogy presented by a [visual] metaphor, the metaphor offers parsimony and impact in our representation of reality. (p. 10)

Visual metaphors "create a holistic synthesis and operate in a physical medium—in this case, the landscape, the stone, the engravings [of names]" (Boix Mansilla, 2009, p. 10). As an integrative device, the visual metaphor itself constitutes the more comprehensive understanding of the topic or event. The metaphor brings out the defining characteristics of the understanding without denying the remaining ambiguity or conflict that underlies it (Newell, 2007a, p. 261).

A Model

A model, such as a pattern, an archetype, or a prototype, can be set before one for guidance or imitation. Serving as a visual aid to comprehension, it may capture the unity, coherence, and balance contained in the interdisciplinary understanding. The model may be a Tinkertoy-like depiction of the DNA molecule that Watson (1968) and Crick built or Nagy's (2005) description of sustainable development for Costa Rica.

Examples of Models

An example, whether real or imagined, can bring home to the reader how the comprehensive understanding works in practice. Two examples of models are those by Nagy (2005) and Foisy (2010).

From the Natural Sciences: Nagy* (2005), Anthropogenic Forces Degrading Tropical Ecosystems in Latin America: A Costa Rican Case Study   Nagy produces a model of "sustainable development" for the Costa Rican coastal region that is designed to meet the immediate needs of the people, but in a way that will not mortgage the ability of future generations to secure their basic needs. Sustainable development, she says, considers not just the environment and economic development, but social and cultural aspects as well. The components of her model, though she does not map relationships among them, include "resource conservation, ecosystem protection, economic motivation, cultural celebration and protection, and social considerations" (p. 107). Nagy believes that her integrative model *makes it easier to* incorporate cultural diversity and protection of indigenous peoples for the simple reason that the practices of these groups, often linked myopically to endangered ecosystems, are also in need of economic development to ensure their survival. Within her continuum, indigenous culture (and thus the needs of indigenous peoples) would fall between economic development and environmental protection. Perhaps, she says, by focusing on conservation rather than preservation, sustainability could be achieved for these people as well. This insight is drawn from recognizing that it is unlikely that countries like Costa Rica, which need more economic development in order to meet the needs of their growing populations, will continue to set aside large tracts of land for these small groups as they have been doing. *"Rather than emphasizing the preservation of land in a pristine and untouched condition, it is more realistic that activities allowing for multi-purpose land use (for ecosystem and cultural protection and economic development) will progress towards sustainability* [italics added]" (p. 108).

From the Social Sciences: Foisy* (2010), Creating Meaning in Everyday Life: An Interdisciplinary Understanding   In this threaded example, Foisy refers to the Meaning Construction Model (introduced in Chapter 12) that she developed as the basis for integrating the various theories on how to create meaning in everyday life. In the conclusion to her paper reproduced here, she applies the Meaning Construction Model to the case of Andrew the Volunteer.

Conclusion: A Return to the Case Study of Andrew the Volunteer

I will conclude by illustrating the usefulness of the Meaning Construction Model, and I will do so by returning to the case study of Andrew presented at the start of this book. Andrew's first step (according to the Meaning Construction Model) was making the conscious decision to volunteer in Africa (goal-setting stage). He made his goal specific ("I want to volunteer in Moshi, Tanzania") and realistic ("I will spend one year planning this trip and will double-check that I am able to get the time off work"). Andrew's goal was challenging, adjustable, and personally important (for example, he originally wanted to volunteer for six months, but could not get that much time off work, so he adjusted the length of his volunteer position to three months). His volunteer trip fell into several different "goal categories": traveling, giving, loving, and working.

Once Andrew set his goal, he began working towards it by booking his plane ticket, fund-raising, getting vaccinated, and speaking with his boss to get time off work. One year later, Andrew's plane landed in Africa: He had reached his goal.

Upon arrival, Andrew began working towards several *new* goals, one of which was to "ensure that every child I treat makes a full recovery." Andrew eventually found himself in many situations where the child did not get better, and he had to acknowledge that his goal was not realistic. Andrew therefore modified his goal to the following: "treat every child with compassion and respect while giving them high-quality medical care."

Now, because Andrew's goal is realistic, he is able to fully immerse himself in the moment and dedicate his full attention to each child. Andrew spends much of each day in a state of flow, where each moment is meaningful in and of itself. Because he is actively engaged in work that he finds meaningful, he is also able to provide better medical care.

When Andrew returns home at the end of his volunteer period, he will likely feel a sense of accomplishment and purpose. The sense of meaning that Andrew felt in Africa will likely transfer to his own medical practice, and he might find himself experiencing a state of flow while treating patients in his home country. Upon his return, Andrew might decide to set entirely new goals ("teach my daughter to ride her bike this summer"), or he might set a goal that *builds* from his volunteer experience ("send monthly care packages to the clinic where I volunteered"). It is likely that he will make both kinds of goals and pursue them concurrently.

Because of its interdisciplinary nature, the Meaning Construction Model can account for a variety of real-life goals that Andrew could set for himself. While this model is by no means flawless, it takes important concepts from four separate theories and integrates them into a practical model that can be applied to everyday situations.

The Meaning Construction Model is by no means the one correct answer to the question, "How do people create meaning in their lives?" If three other students along with myself had researched this same topic, it is likely that the

> four of us would have reached very different conclusions. However, I believe that there would be true value in this type of "side-by-side" interdisciplinary work: If each of us had examined four different theories on meaning construction and reached four different conclusions, another interdisciplinarian could then take our four interdisciplinary papers and apply Repko's 10-step research process to our *interdisciplinary* papers. The interdisciplinarian would have then integrated 16 different theories on meaning construction. In this way, I believe that it is possible for interdisciplinary research to "build upon" itself, and this process might allow us to approach answers that we currently cannot even conceive.

A Narrative

A narrative is a written or spoken account or story. Narratives are powerful because humans naturally think in terms of narratives. Narratives are essential components to integrative learning and research, and are the most common way in which students and practitioners communicate the understanding. Narratives may be short or extended, depending on the complexity of the subject. Narratives are useful for describing any form of understanding and may be used in combination with them.

Examples of Narratives

This section includes two narratives. In the first example, J. Lewis (2009), an undergraduate student, has written a paper on why the U.S. public education system is failing to educate an increasingly diverse student population. In the second, Gary Blesser and Linda-Ruth Salter (2007), pioneers of the interdisciplinary field of aural architecture, provide a book-length study of this rapidly evolving field that is fully interdisciplinary. Following these narratives, lessons for readers are presented.

From the Social Sciences: J. Lewis* (2009), The Failure of Public Education to Educate a Diverse Population   Lewis's narrative is as follows:

> The interdisciplinary understanding that resulted from this integration is that it's going to take more than just those involved in education to begin the process of revitalizing public education. The massive veil that is held in place over the public education system must be removed to reveal how subtractive schooling and the increasing attrition rates are negatively impacting [the United States]. Sociological facets of education must be examined and given more attention to stop the blatant curtailing of innovative and adaptive teaching methods needed to satisfy the diverse needs of our children. Working together, change can

be implemented to avoid the bleak outlook that economists are predicting for the future. Their input should be valued as much as everyone else involved. The hegemony of the current public education system must be challenged by more than one discipline to create a more relevant and adaptive curriculum. New and integrative legislation is needed to ensure the problems created by current mandates are not allowed to continue to push our education system and its benefactors towards peril. (p. 1)

From the Interdisciplinary Field of Aural Architecture: Blesser and Salter (2007), Spaces Speak, Are You Listening?   Aural architecture refers to built environments such as an auditorium, a cathedral, or digital simulations of virtual spaces that are sonically complex. The concept of aural architecture, say Blesser and Salter, "is an intellectual edifice built from bricks of knowledge, borrowed from dozens of disciplinary subcultures and thousands of scholars and researchers." When integrated into a single concept, however, "the marriage of aural architecture and auditory spatial awareness provides a way to explore our aural connection to the spaces built by humans and those provided us by nature" (p. 8). Their comprehensive understanding of how aural architecture has and continues to influence social cohesion in different historical periods and cultures consists of three points:

- "Over the centuries, aural spaces have been created or selected to provide environments for a variety of groups and individuals. And the aural qualities of these spaces can either impede or support social cohesion over social distances that range from intimate to public" (p. 363).
- "Because the nature of social cohesion shifts as culture evolves, so, too, does aural architecture. Historically, small towns in warm climates actively encouraged cohesion by embracing aural connections through open windows, public commons, large churches, and outdoor living. Currently, modern advanced cultures embrace independence and privacy, supporting cohesion by means of the telephone and the Internet, the electronic fusion of remote acoustic arenas. The current generation frequently experience aural architecture with its visual spaces of manufactured music. The difference between then and now is nothing more than an evolution of cultural values" (p. 363).
- "Unlike other art forms, we cannot escape the influence of aural architecture because we live inside it. Whether intentionally designed or accidentally selected, our aural spaces influence our moods and behavior. Learning to appreciate aural architecture by closely attending to auditory spatial awareness is one way we can control, and thus improve, our personal environment" (p. 364).

Note to Readers

J. Lewis's (2009) undergraduate paper and Blesser and Salter's (2007) book conform, to varying degrees, to Boix Mansilla et al.'s (2009) criteria for quality disciplinary work:

1. Both build on a performance or practical view of understanding. In the case of Lewis, the understanding is a narrative describing a framework for a more comprehensive approach to curriculum design in order to solve the dropout problem. In the case of Blesser and Salter, the understanding is in the form of a detailed model grounded in theory (which they helped to develop) and field experience concerning how public spaces (both man-made and natural) should be developed. Lewis's paper was written as a class project with the goal of using it to support his candidacy for a teaching position in a particular public school with a primarily minority student body. Blesser and Salter have multiple specialized audiences in view: academics, technicians, and public officials who are involved in the design of public spaces.

2. Both are informed by disciplinary expertise and draw on the insights of relevant disciplines to create something new and more comprehensive. However, the disciplinary depth and breadth of the two projects varies considerably. J. Lewis, an undergraduate, was restricted to using a few disciplines and a handful of insights from each of them. By contrast, Blesser and Salter's research is exhaustive and draws on *all* relevant disciplines and utilizes *all* important concepts and theories, including the authors' own fieldwork.

3. Both integrate disciplinary views. J. Lewis follows the IRP described in this book and achieves partial integration, whereas Blesser and Salter compress many of the steps of the IRP (unconsciously so) and produce a fully integrated result.

4. Both projects lead to cognitive advancements, although to varying degrees. J. Lewis's understanding attempts to integrate important theories from sociology and education that, if applied, would add increased creativity and flexibility to the learning process. Blesser and Salter's understanding is a cognitive advancement in that it is the first attempt to produce a fully interdisciplinary approach to integrating the aural into the design of public spaces.

A New Process to Achieve New Outcomes

A process is a way of making the understanding immediately useful (and comprehensible) to practitioners. Processes include new approaches to solving particular sorts of problems or new modes of intellectual analysis that yield new insights.

Examples of New Processes

Two examples of new processes are presented here. In the first example, Delph (2005), an undergraduate student, presents a new integrative process that she believes will increase the success rate of homicide investigations and reduce the number of unsolved murders. In the second example, Bal (1999), a mature scholar, shows how using cultural analysis, an interdisciplinary mode of analysis that she pioneered, can be applied to an enigmatic note or letter painted in yellow letters on a red brick wall in Amsterdam.

From the Social Sciences: Delph* (2005), An Integrative Approach to the Elimination of the "Perfect Crime"   Criminal profiling, says Delph, could achieve its greatest potential if profilers from forensic psychology and forensic science would integrate their analytical techniques and share them with local criminal investigators. If adopted, she believes her approach would produce four likely outcomes: (1) quickly reduce the list of possible suspects, (2) predict the prime suspect's future behavior, (3) offer investigative avenues that have been overlooked by police, and (4) empower local law enforcement agencies to use these integrated profiling techniques themselves (p. 32).

From the Humanities: Bal (1999), "Introduction," The Practice of Cultural Analysis: Exposing Interdisciplinary Interpretation   Cultural analysis, as noted earlier, stands for an interdisciplinarity that is primarily analytical and seeks to discover new meaning in objects and texts that traditional approaches are unable to achieve. The note or short letter (i.e., "graffito") written on a wall, Bal says, is "a good case for the kind of objects at which cultural analysis looks, and—more importantly—*how* it goes about doing so" [emphasis added] (p. 2). The graffito, she says, is a letter both visually and linguistically. Though the literal translation of the opening from the Dutch is "Note," the more usual address that comes to Bal's mind is "Dearest" or "Sweety" (p. 3). "This implied other word fits in with the beginning of the rest of the text that says something like 'I love you'" (p. 3).

With the "discourse of the love letter" firmly in place, the graffito shifts to epistemic philosophy by continuing with "I did not invent you" or "I did not make you up" or "I have not thought you up." "The past tense, the action negated, the first-person speaking," observes Bal, "all indicate the discourse of narrative only to make a point about what's real and what is not" (p. 3). What is striking is that the address changes a real person, the anonymous writer's beloved, into a self-referential description of the note: A referential "Dearest" becomes a self-referential "Note" or short letter. "This turns the note into fiction," says Bal, and the addressee into a made-up "you," after all.

Yet, by the same token, this inscription of literariness recasts the set of characters, for the identity of the "you" has by now come loose from the implied term of endearment that personalized him or her. So, the passerby looks again, tripping over this word that says, "YOU! . . . Addressed as beloved and not as a guilty citizen, the city dweller gets a chance to reshape her or his identity, gleaming in the light of this anonymous affection. But is it real?" (p. 13).

One possible meaning of the note or letter, and one Bal considers plausible, is that the addressee is real even if the beloved cannot be found; "she or he is irretrievably lost, and the graffito mourns that absence" (p. 4). For Bal, the letter is an autographic note or letter. "Moreover, it is publicly accessible, semantically dense, pragmatically intriguing, visually appealing and insistent, and philosophically profound. Just like poetry" (p. 4).

Bal's understanding extends to linking the graffito to the interdiscipline of cultural analysis itself. It is the interest in more than the public self-exposure of the subject (author) and object (the lost beloved) of the note or letter that makes the exposition an exposure of the self. Such exposure, says Bal, is an act of producing meaning (1996, p. 2). Cultural analysis is also interested in moving from a literal meaning of the note or letter to its broader and metaphorical meaning. Exposing meaning, as Bal does, creates a subject/object dichotomy. The dichotomy enables the subject (in this case, the author of the note or letter) to make a statement about the object (in this case, the lost beloved). The object is there, explains Bal (1999), to substantiate the statement and enable the statement to come across (p. 3). There is an addressee for the statement: the reader. In expositions like the note or letter, a "first person," the exposer, tells a "second person," the reader, about a third person, "the object" or lost beloved, who does not participate in the conversation. But, Bal says, "unlike many other constative speech acts, the object, although mute, is present" (1996, p. 4). In this sense, the note or letter is a *sign*. A sign stands for a thing or an idea in some capacity, or for someone. In this instance, the note or letter is a sign for the writer's beloved, who is now lost. It is also a sign for the culture that produced it, the reader that reads it, and the field that examines it.

A New Product

Products are both immediately useful and comprehensible. They may be of two kinds: (1) a technological innovation or manufactured product and (2) works of art such as plays, poems, sculptures, paintings, or media productions. Technological innovations or manufactured products are the result of extracting relevant information from disciplines and applied fields and integrating their contributions (Blesser & Salter, 2007, p. x). Works of art operate differently, but are useful to communicate insights that are hard to express in words (insights that have an emotional or intuitive content).

A Critique of an Existing Policy and/or a Proposed New Policy

An interdisciplinary understanding can also take the form of a critique of an existing policy to show how it is failing to meet a societal need because of its disciplinary or conceptual narrowness. The critique may be followed by a proposed new policy, plan, program, or schema that, because of its inclusiveness, is more likely to solve the problem.

Examples of Critiques

This section includes two examples of understandings that critique existing policies on important issues. In the first example, Szostak (2009), a mature scholar, uses his integrative understanding of the causes of economic growth as a basis for critiquing government preference for a "one size fits all" approach to facilitate economic growth in underdeveloped countries. In the second example, Henry (2009), also a mature scholar, critiques narrow disciplinary policies that deal with the causes of school violence.

From the Social Sciences: Szostak (2009), The Causes of Economic Growth: Interdisciplinary Perspectives   In his statement of understanding (his "Concluding Remarks"), Szostak's main insight is that we should not expect our understanding of economic growth to yield "one true model" or "one secret formula for achieving growth everywhere, anytime" (p. 341). The reason, he explains, is because economic growth "is generated by a wide array of causes involving a host of economic and non-economic factors" (p. 341). He finds that insights "from diverse theories, methods, and disciplines into what causes growth can be integrated in order to produce more accurate and nuanced insights than could be generated by any one discipline" (p. 341). He identifies two policy implications of his understanding. The first is that scholars should jettison the "misguided presumption" that "the goal of scholarly analysis of complex questions is some simple grand theory" (p. 341). The second is that

> we should not give advice to any country without looking at its unique situation. What institutions has it inherited from the past? What is the fiscal capacity of its government? What is its infrastructure and education and health system like? Does the government have legitimacy? Does the culture favor hard work and thrift? . . . [T]he set of best policies depends very much on their answers. (p. 343)

From the Social Sciences: Henry (2009), School Violence Beyond Columbine: A Complex Problem in Need of an Interdisciplinary Analysis   In this threaded example, Henry presents his more comprehensive understanding of the causes of school violence.

> I have argued here that to understand the genesis of school violence, we need to adopt an interdisciplinary, multilevel analytical approach. In this way, we are able to better see the interconnected processes that produce school violence. Such an approach sensitizes us to the ways lower-level and more diffuse harm production can produce victims who, over time, can come to resent their victimization and react violently against it. In particular, social exclusion can occur in multiple ways that are both evident and concealed. In particular, they can be the product of social hierarchies in the social networks of peers, bolstered by societal-cultural discourses of masculinity and violence and

supported by school systems through their own hierarchies of power. Although we can examine the psychological processes and situational explanations for why students acted violently, we need to step outside of the microcontexts to explore the wider framing discourses of gender and power, masculinity and violence, and social class and race that produce social exclusion, victimization, anger, and rage. We need to see how these discourses shape the school curriculum, teaching practices, the institution of education, the meaning of "school," and its associated educational policy. How do parents, both in their absence and in their presence, harm the lives of students? We need to proactively engage in the deconstruction of hierarchies of power that exclude, and in the process create, a wasted class of teenagers who feel hopeless, whose escape from hopelessness is blocked, and whose only way out are violent symbolic acts of self-destruction and other destruction. We also need to challenge the ways in which the economic and political structure of American society reproduces and tolerates hierarchies of exclusion and structural violence. This needs to go beyond cultural causes of school violence to see how these cultural forms are integrated with structural inequalities. Any adequate analysis of school violence, therefore, has to locate the microinteractive, institutional practices and sociocultural productions in the wider political economy of the society in which these occur. Ignoring the structural inequalities of power in the wider system reduces the cause to local and situational inequalities of power, suggesting that policies can be addressed to intervene locally, such as at the level of peer subculture or school organization. Although these levels of intervention are important, they alone are insufficient. (pp. 16–17)

A New Question or Avenue of Scientific Inquiry

Because so much interdisciplinary work is conducted at the boundaries and intersections of disciplines, researchers are well positioned to detect gaps in existing knowledge. Detecting new lines of inquiry and pursuing these is part of normal research activity. The new understanding may include a new question or a new avenue of research that builds upon and extends the work just completed.

The Value of Communicating Back to Disciplines

There is value to communicating the product of interdisciplinary work back to the disciplines. Szostak (2009) says that this communication challenges the disciplines to do the following:

- Question (and hopefully abandon) certain misguided presumptions about how scholarship should be conducted: that it should be organized theoretically or that its purpose is to develop or defend simple grand theories.

- Appreciate the value of interdisciplinarity and of integrating disciplinary insights in order to gain a new insight into the problem, intellectual question, or object.
- Appreciate the value of theoretical and methodological flexibility.
- Appreciate that each theory has a particular range of applicability.
- Appreciate the value of integrating the widest array of empirical analysis within an organizing structure of causal links and emergent properties. (p. 344)

There are also challenges involved in communicating back to disciplines. Most obviously, one cannot communicate to a discipline unless one uses its terminology and publishes in its journals. Less obviously, one's communication will be ignored unless it is grounded in the discipline's literature, showing how the interdisciplinary insight is useful for the sort of question(s) the discipline investigates.

Chapter Summary

The last STEP in the research process is reflecting on the understanding produced in STEP 9, testing or assessing it, and communicating it. This chapter has argued that interdisciplinarians should be more reflective than disciplinary specialists, must demonstrate the ability to enter the specialized scholarly discourse (i.e., disciplinary literatures) on the problem in an interesting and persuasive manner, and must be willing to explain those elements of their own research that may cause concern among the intended audience. The four sorts of reflection that are called for in interdisciplinary work include what has actually been learned from the project, STEPS (of the IRP) omitted, one's own biases, and strengths and weaknesses of the insights, theories, and methods used, including the IRP itself.

In addition to detailing the cognitive abilities distinctive to interdisciplinarity, the chapter explained how these abilities can (and should) form the basis for testing the quality of the interdisciplinary understanding, identified four approaches to testing the quality of interdisciplinary work, and integrated these.

Finally, the chapter stressed the importance of communicating the understanding in multiple ways to multiple audiences depending on whether the author is a student or a mature scholar. The activity of communicating the results of integrative work is, in fact, another way of testing its coherence, unity, and balance, and thus whether it constitutes partial or full interdisciplinarity.

Note

1. For a basic introduction to rubrics and their utility for students, see Popham (1997).

Exercises

What Has Been Learned

14.1   Reflect on the project and ask, "What have I learned about (1) the content of the topic, (2) the process involved, and (3) whether or not the conclusions drawn indicate that understanding has been advanced by the integration of disciplinary views?"

STEPS Omitted or Compressed

14.2   If you decided to omit or compress some of the STEPS of the IRP, what was your reason for doing so? What was the cumulative effect of this/these decision(s) on the final product?

Self-interrogation

14.3   Reflect on your own bias at the outset of the project and ask how your view of the topic has changed as a result of examining views that conflict with your own.

14.4   Referencing the introduction to the paper, "The Ideal Manager: An Interdisciplinary Model," how might the paragraph be revised to eliminate personal bias while retaining the goal of the project: developing a model of the ideal manager?

Reflecting on One's Limited Understanding of the Relevant Disciplines, Theories, and Methods

14.5   Assuming you are at the apprentice level, consider the limitations of the relevant disciplinary understandings you used and explain how using an interdisciplinary approach has enlarged and strengthened your understanding.

Cognitive Abilities

14.6   How is the ability to engage in critical thinking developed differently in interdisciplinary contexts than in disciplinary contexts?

Testing for Quality

14.7   Of the five cognitive abilities that interdisciplinary learning fosters, which has been the most difficult for you to develop and why?

Holistic Approaches to Testing the Understanding

14.8   If the result of your research is policy-oriented, test it by applying either the Newell (2007a) or the Szostak (2009) test.

14.9   If the result of your research is not policy-oriented, test it by applying the Boix Mansilla et al. (2009) rubric, which features four defining traits of quality interdisciplinary work.

14.10   Referencing the four qualitatively distinct levels of student achievement (i.e., *naïve*, *novice*, *apprentice*, and *master)*, decide which level best describes your project. Why?

Metaphor, Model, Process, Product, or Avenue of Scientific Inquiry

14.11   Can you think of a metaphor or model that could depict your understanding visually?

14.12   If your understanding does not lend itself to either a metaphor or a model, write a narrative describing the new or improved process or product that you have created.

14.13   If your understanding is policy-oriented, use it as the basis for critiquing an existing policy.

14.14   If your work revealed a gap in knowledge, identify it and describe what steps need to be taken to address it.

Conclusion _____

Interdisciplinarity for the
New Century

This book invites researchers at all levels to practice interdisciplinary research in a more explicit, self-conscious, knowledgeable, rigorous, and nuanced way. It also asks them to think about eight interrelated issues: (1) the authoritative definitions of interdisciplinary studies introduced in Chapter 1 and the implications of these for education and research; (2) the ramifications of interdisciplinary studies having achieved the status of a maturing academic field; (3) the latitude and utility of the research model, which enable it to address complex problems that cut across multiple knowledge domains; (4) the body of theory that undergirds interdisciplinarity and the research model; (5) the refinement of our understanding of integration as a hallmark of interdisciplinarity; (6) the purpose and product of the interdisciplinary research process; (7) the cognitive outcomes fostered by interdisciplinary education and research; and (8) the variations in how the interdisciplinary research process plays out when disciplinary insights are drawn from the natural sciences, the social sciences, or the humanities.

_____ The Definition of Interdisciplinary Studies

The book dwells heavily on defining interdisciplinary studies and interdisciplinarity for two practical reasons. If interdisciplinary programs are fuzzy in their conception of what interdisciplinarity is, then they are unlikely to provide the distinctive educational outcomes that interdisciplinary education potentially offers. Developing a sustainable, rigorous, and coherent interdisciplinary studies program begins with having a clear notion of what interdisciplinarity is. Therefore, interdisciplinary programs should develop a local conception of the unique characteristics of their program (which might, for example, focus on complex problems of local interest). This conception should be informed by the authoritative and widely accepted definitions of interdisciplinarity from leading scholars and organizations presented in Chapter 1.

The second reason for dwelling at length on definition is that interdisciplinarity is still a widely misunderstood approach to education and research. Indeed, it is commonplace to hear well-meaning but uninformed academics claim, "It's in the air we breathe," and "We are already doing it." Perhaps this is true, but according to what standard and informed by what body of theory? Accompanying this claim is the occasional call to fold the local interdisciplinary program into disciplinary units now that interdisciplinarity is supposedly ubiquitous. These academics, it seems fair to say, are obliged to show how their discipline-based conception of interdisciplinarity is informed by their familiarity with the field's literature and theory. Without such grounding, their claim of "doing interdisciplinarity" is suspect.

One of the most promising developments in the academy at the undergraduate and graduate levels is the increase in border-crossing activity. This makes interdisciplinary programs more necessary than ever because they can provide the intellectual center of gravity for interdisciplinary education and research on campus. Even a cursory reading of the field's extensive literature shows that interdisciplinarity in all its breadth and complexity cannot be ignored or folded into narrow disciplinary structures.

Interdisciplinary Studies as a Maturing Academic Field

The book shows that interdisciplinary studies can rightfully stake its claim as a maturing academic field that deserves its place in the academy alongside the disciplines. The criteria necessary to substantiate this claim are already in place and identified in Chapter 1: There is a consensus understanding of what interdisciplinarity is; there is an integrated model of the interdisciplinary research process; there is a body of theory underlying the field's approach to education and research; there is a growing community of interdisciplinary experts; and there is an extensive and growing body of literature on best practices. This literature addresses administration, assessment, curriculum design, pedagogy, research process, theory, student learning, faculty development, and research on specific problems. Those claiming the mantle of interdisciplinarity should familiarize themselves, at least cursorily, with this literature.

The emergence of interdisciplinary studies as an academic field has far-reaching implications that can only be summarized here: (1) There now exists a paradigm of knowledge production of increasing sophistication that is compatible with, but essentially different from, that of the disciplines; (2) this paradigm is essentially incongruous administratively with the discipline-based structure of the academy; and (3) this paradigm's flexibility provides new and far-reaching opportunities to savvy administrators, innovative scholars, and enterprising students.

The Research Model

The book presents an integrated model of the interdisciplinary research process that rests on several assumptions: (1) Interdisciplinarians should identify such a process, (2) the disciplines are foundational to the interdisciplinary enterprise, (3) the accumulation of knowledge cannot and should not be limited to existing paradigms, and (4) integration is a cognitive process that is achievable.

By presenting the research model, the book addresses the sometimes contentious issue of what role the disciplines should play in interdisciplinary work. What we have in fact shown is that interdisciplinarians draw upon specialized research. The book does not establish that the disciplines are the only or the best way of organizing specialized research. The disciplines provide the depth while interdisciplinarity provides the breadth and the integration. Interdisciplinarity stands as a counterweight to the reductionist tendencies of the disciplines. This book is one way that interdisciplinarians can communicate to their disciplinary colleagues that interdisciplinarity is not about competing with the disciplines, or about replacing them, but rather about working with them to transcend their limitations. A proper understanding of interdisciplinarity might lead to more outward-looking disciplines. On this point, the literature is clear: Interdisciplinarity needs the disciplines, and the disciplines for relevance to complex issues need interdisciplinarity. This mutual dependence warns against an interdisciplinarity that is overenthusiastic, overconfident, and overwhelming.

Theory

The book presents the body of theory that undergirds the field and research model. This theory includes complexity theory, the theory of perspective taking, the theory of common ground, and the theory of cognitive interdisciplinarity. The field also draws on leader-member exchange (LMX) theory and critical theory as well as theories associated with learning, linguistics, and criminal justice. In addition, groundbreaking work has been done on the role of intuition and its connection to creativity and insight in understanding complexity, performing integration, and applying the interdisciplinary research process. Of particular importance is the development (under way) of a philosophically grounded theory of interdisciplinarity that fully situates interdisciplinarity in the history of ideas and establishes an epistemology of complexity.

Understanding Integration

In the controversy over integration, the book sides with "integrationists" who assert that integration is the key distinguishing characteristic of interdisciplinarity and that the goal of interdisciplinary work should be (ideally) full integration. Minimizing, obscuring, or eliminating integration from a conception of interdisciplinarity hollows out the concept of interdisciplinarity and makes it far easier for critics to argue that interdisciplinarity "is whatever we say it is." It also makes problematic the production and assessment of quality interdisciplinary work.

The book advances our understanding of integration in at least three ways. First, the book pries open a nebulous concept that has long resisted definition and shows it to be at root a cognitive process that is a native tendency of the human mind, allowing us to adapt to the complexities of reality. More particularly, the book introduces the concept and theory of common ground as a prerequisite for integration. After creating common ground between conflicting disciplinary concepts or theories using identifiable techniques, this common ground enables us to integrate a set of insights and construct a more comprehensive understanding or theoretical explanation of the problem. Second, as a cognitive process, integration is flexible and creative in its approach to problem solving. Third, since the process of integration is now transparent, it invites reflection, critique, and testing.

The Purpose and Product of the Research Process

The book explains the purpose and product of the interdisciplinary research process, which is to construct a more comprehensive understanding or cognitive advancement of the problem. This STEP of the research process and its underlying theory is of major importance to interdisciplinary research for two reasons. First, it makes possible a more rigorous and more granular assessment of interdisciplinary work through the use of rubrics based upon course and program learning outcomes. Second, the enlarged conception of interdisciplinary understanding effectively connects interdisciplinary work to the real world in new and creative ways because the products of the research effort include work that is practical, purposeful, and performance-oriented.

The Cognitive Outcomes of Interdisciplinarity

The book briefly discusses the cognitive abilities, outcomes, and underlying theory associated with interdisciplinary education and research. Students, academics, and administrators should be aware of how the interdisciplinary approach to problem solving and decision making involved in the research process differs from the learning that occurs in many traditional disciplinary contexts. A major recent finding of learning theory, for example, shows that with repeated exposure to interdisciplinary thought, students develop more mature epistemological beliefs, enhanced critical thinking ability, metacognitive skills, and an understanding of the relations among perspectives derived from different disciplines. These are critical cognitive abilities that students need when entering the professions or pursuing graduate study. The skills they have learned are useful in almost any job and in life more generally, and it is useful for them to consciously reflect on how to grapple with any complex problem that they may face in any situation in life.

The Variations in How the Interdisciplinary Research Process Plays Out

Lastly, the book explains the variations in how the interdisciplinary research process plays out when disciplinary insights are drawn from the natural sciences, the social sciences, or the humanities. Insights produced especially by the social and physical sciences generally rely on theories to explain the phenomena they study. Integration in these contexts involves presenting one integrative theory that combines elements of several competing theories to achieve the goal of full integration. Rather than providing one integration, scholars in the fine and performing arts, and often the humanities that study them, prefer setting up a range of alternative integrations for readers or viewers to consider. These scholars choose not to do fully interdisciplinary work and are "conscientious objectors," not failed interdisciplinarians.

Toward the Future

For interdisciplinary studies to fulfill its potential to advance knowledge in the new century, several developments need to occur, each of which this book encourages. One is the need to develop a course on how to do interdisciplinary research. This course should be included in each program's required core to be taken immediately *after* completing an introduction to interdisciplinary studies course and *before* taking advanced courses requiring substantive research. Such a course on the interdisciplinary research process (and its underlying theory) would show students how their interdisciplinary work differs from disciplinary work and prepare them for doing research and writing in advanced theme-based or problem-based courses. It would allow later courses to go into more depth about the nature of interdisciplinarity in various contexts and address conceptual, theoretical, and methodological issues with greater sophistication. Adding such a course would enhance the program's academic standing among disciplinarians who highly value research methods courses. At a minimum, focusing more intently on how to do interdisciplinary research would mute disciplinary criticism of interdisciplinary work for its lack of rigor and achieve balance between disciplinary depth and interdisciplinary breadth.

A second need is to inform faculty, undergraduate and graduate, who are new to the field or who have been doing interdisciplinarity on their own but have not had time to immerse themselves in the literature or to keep up with that literature. With a few exceptions (e.g., American studies), most graduate faculty teaching in interdisciplinary programs were themselves trained in a discipline and picked up an interdisciplinary approach later in their careers. Some may have developed their own idiosyncratic style of interdisciplinary research because the professional literature, until recently, had little to offer them. Some may not have reexamined the professional literature in recent years and may have missed its dramatic increase in sophistication, depth of analysis, and utility. Their graduate students, however, are likely to seek out the professional literature in conducting interdisciplinary research. Increasingly, some graduate faculty may be directing the research of students who are more familiar with the professional literature on interdisciplinarity than they are. This gap needs to close.

Finally, there is need for more research that is explicitly interdisciplinary and that creatively applies the research model presented in this book. This need is being met through the publication of journal articles and books, most notably *Case Studies in Interdisciplinary Research* (Repko, Newell, & Szostak, 2012). These publications demonstrate that a wide range of complex problems require the integrated efforts of many disciplines. Indeed, breakthroughs of lasting importance are increasingly the product of cross-fertilization between different knowledge formations and research cultures. What the interdisciplinarian brings to a complex problem is a tool kit of cognitive abilities and skills, a process to achieve integration, and techniques to construct a more comprehensive solution. It is hoped that the research model presented in this book will inform and challenge a new generation of students and scholars to engage in this much-needed work.

Appendix _____

Interdisciplinary Resources

_____ **Associations**

American Studies Association (ASA), www.theasa.net

For a current summary of the state of American studies as an interdisciplinary academic field, please refer to Bronner, S. (2008). "The ASA Survey of Departments and Programs, 2007: Findings and projections." *ASA Newsletter,* March. Retrieved July 14, 2011, from http://www.theasa.net/images/uploads/Final_Copy_Simon_Bronner_Article_PDF.pdf

Association of American Colleges and Universities (AAC&U), http://www.aacu.org/

The AAC&U is the leading national association concerned with the quality, vitality, and public standing of undergraduate liberal education. Integrative learning is a recurring theme in many of its conferences and publications.

_____

AUTHOR'S NOTE: Some of the information in this Appendix is adapted from Klein, J. T. (2003). Thinking about interdisciplinarity: A primer for practice. *Colorado School of Mines Quarterly, 103*(1), 101–114; Klein, J. T., & Newell, W. H. (2002). Strategies for using interdisciplinary resources across K–16. *Issues in Integrative Studies, 20,* 139–160; and Klein, J. T. (2010). "Resources." In *Creating interdisciplinary campus cultures: A model for strength and sustainability* (pp. 161–180). I have also drawn on Fiscella, J. B., & Kimmel, S. E. (Eds.). (1999). *Interdisciplinary education: A guide to resources.* New York: The College Board. I thank Julie Thompson Klein for making available her "Interdisciplinary Searching Module," and C. Diane Shepelwich, former interdisciplinary librarian at the University of Texas at Arlington, for providing the information on databases and online resources.

Association for General and Liberal Studies (AGLS), http://web.oxford.emory.edu/

AGLS is a community of learners—faculty, students, administrators, and alumni—intent upon improving general and liberal education at two-year and four-year institutions. AGLS identifies and supports the benefits of students' liberal education attained through general education programs. As an advocate, AGLS tracks changes in general education and liberal studies and sponsors professional activities that promote successful teaching, curricular innovation, and effective learning.

Association for Integrative Studies (AIS), http://www.units.muohio.edu/aisorg/

AIS is an interdisciplinary professional organization founded in 1979 to promote the interchange of ideas among scholars and administrators in all of the arts and sciences on intellectual and organizational issues related to furthering integrative studies. The website has materials that may be downloaded at no charge, including its journal, newer issues of the newsletter, peer-reviewed course syllabi, directories of master's and doctoral programs, guidelines for accreditation in interdisciplinary general education, interdisciplinary writing assessment profiles, and a list of core publications with tables of contents. The AIS journal *Issues in Integrative Studies* publishes articles on a wide range of interdisciplinary topics including assessment, pedagogy, program development, research process, theory, special reports on the status of and challenges to interdisciplinarity, and topics of current interest.

Interdisciplines, http://www.interdisciplines.org/

Interdisciplines is a project aimed at enhancing interdisciplinary research and exchanges in the humanities, but this project has evolved to embrace many scientific concerns. It sponsors conferences and seminars, each run by a specific team and sponsored by a different grant. Projects are selected by a scientific committee and supervised by Gloria Origgi. The overall project has been sponsored by the French National Centre for Scientific Research.

Network for Transdisciplinary Research (td-net), http://www.transdisciplinarity.ch/e/index.php

Funded by the Swiss Academy of Sciences, td-net is an organization involving scholars across Europe and beyond that supports the study of transdisciplinarity in both research and teaching. It defines transdisciplinarity in a way that is very similar to the definition of interdisciplinarity pursued in this book, but with an emphasis on involving people from outside the academy in collaborative research. The td-net website has many resources, including a useful bibliography.

Databases

Academic Search Complete

The world's largest scholarly, multidiscipline, full-text database, Academic Search Complete offers critical information from many sources found in no other database, including peer-reviewed full-text articles for almost 4,600 periodical titles in more than 100 scholarly journals dating back to 1965, or the first issue published (whichever is more recent). Areas of study include social sciences, humanities, education, computer sciences, engineering, language and linguistics, arts and literature, medical sciences, and ethnic studies.

ERIC

The ERIC (Education Resources Information Center) database is sponsored by the U.S. Department of Education to provide extensive access to education-related literature. The database corresponds to two printed journals: *Resources in Education* (RIE) and *Current Index to Journals in Education* (CIJE). Both journals provide access to some 14,000 documents and over 20,000 journal articles per year. In addition, ERIC provides coverage of conferences, meetings, government documents, theses, dissertations, reports, audiovisual media, bibliographies, directories, books, and monographs.

H-Net, www.h-net.org

H-Net is a self-described "international interdisciplinary organization" that provides teachers and scholars with forums for the exchange of ideas and resources in the arts, humanities, and social sciences. The database includes over 100 free, edited listservs and websites that coordinate communication in a wide variety of disciplinary and interdisciplinary fields as well as subjects and topics.

JSTOR

JSTOR (Journal Storage) is an archive collection of over 620 full-text scholarly journals primarily from university presses and professional society publishers. Subject areas include African American studies, anthropology, Asian studies, botany, ecology, economics, education, finance, folklore, history, history of science technology, language literature, mathematics, philosophy, political science, population studies, public policy administration, science, Slavic studies, sociology, and statistics.

ProQuest Dissertation Abstracts International

The ProQuest Dissertation Abstracts International database contains citations for dissertations and theses from institutions in North America and Europe. Citations for dissertations published from 1980 forward also include abstracts. Citations for master's theses from 1988 forward include abstracts. Titles published from 1997 forward have 24-page previews and are available as full-text PDF documents.

Web of Knowledge

Web of Knowledge contains abstracts and citations from Thompson Reuters's Science Citation Index Expanded, Social Sciences Citation Index, and Arts & Humanities Citation Index. The database allows for searches by subject term, author name, journal title, or author affiliation, as well as for articles that cite an author or a work. Along with an article's abstract, its cited references (bibliography) are listed for further searching.

WorldCat

WorldCat contains more than 32 million records describing books and other materials owned by libraries around the world.

Online Resources

Carleton Interdisciplinary Science and Math Initiative (CISMI), http://serc.carleton.edu/cismi/index.html

This site has compiled literature and resources to support interdisciplinary and integrative teaching activities, with an emphasis on science and math. Areas include research on expert interdisciplinary thinking and practice, assessing interdisciplinary work in college, strategies for interdisciplinary teaching, integrative learning, national reports, and books.

Integrative Learning: Opportunities to Connect, http://www.aacu.org/integrative_learning/index.cfm

Integrative Learning: Opportunities to Connect is a national project sponsored by the Association of American Colleges and Universities (AAC&U) and the Carnegie Foundation for the Advancement of Teaching. Aimed at promoting integrative learning in undergraduate education, this three-year project worked with 10 campuses to develop and assess advanced models and strategies to foster students' abilities to integrate their learning over time.

Interdisciplinary Studies Project, http://www.pz .harvard.edu/interdisciplinary/index.html

The project examines the challenges and opportunities of interdisciplinary work carried out by experts, faculty, and students in well-recognized research and education contexts. Building on an empirical understanding of cognitive and social dimensions of interdisciplinary work, the project develops practical tools to guide quality interdisciplinary education.

New Directions: Science, Humanities, Policy, http://www.ndsciencehumanitiespolicy.org/

This site focuses on interdisciplinary approaches to problems in research, education, and society.

Journals

There are many interdisciplinary journals, a few of the most useful of which appear here. Articles on interdisciplinary topics such as interdisciplinary resources and interdisciplinary curriculum design are scattered across professional journals, some of which periodically devote special issues to interdisciplinarity. Locating these requires searching databases using keyword searching and Boolean search strategy.

Academic Exchange Quarterly, http://www.rapidintellect.com/AEQweb/
History of Intellectual Culture, http://www.ucalgary.ca/hic/homepage
Issues in Integrative Studies, http://www.units.muohio.edu/aisorg/pubs/issues/issues.shtml
Journal of General Education, http://muse.jhu.edu/journals/journal_of_general_education/
Journal of Interdisciplinary History, http://muse.jhu.edu/journals/jih/
Journal of Research Practice, http://jrp.icaap.org/index.php/jrp
Science Studies, http://www.sciencestudies.fi/

Search Strategies

Locating resources for interdisciplinary purposes is typically not a straight-forward process for interdisciplinary students. A metaphor descriptive of the challenge of identifying and locating relevant resources is suggested in the title of a special issue of *Library Trends, 45*(2), "Navigating Among the Disciplines: The Library and Interdisciplinary Inquiry." Students must "navigate" across multiple knowledge forums to locate relevant information. Before using the following approaches, students must state the problem or question they are investigating as clearly and as concisely as possible.

There are three approaches or strategies to navigation. The first is to use the traditional method of keyword searching. The typical search box options are author, title, keyword, and subject. This approach works well when the author and title of the article are already known. If this information is not known, then keyword and subject searching should be used. For example, if the problem under investigation is "The Causes of Childhood Obesity: An Interdisciplinary Analysis," the primary search term is *obesity*. The search will identify numerous articles written by experts from several disciplines. The student must identify the disciplines these writers represent because interdisciplinary research projects typically involve analyzing a problem from three or more disciplinary perspectives.

The second approach is the Boolean search strategy. This strategy is useful when it is necessary to narrow the number of references to those that are most relevant to the problem. For example, a keyword search of the problem, "The Causes of Suicide Terrorism: An Interdisciplinary Analysis," would focus on *terrorism* and *suicide* because these terms are at the heart of the problem. However, navigating databases using just one, or even both, of them will yield an overwhelming number of references. The value of using the Boolean search strategy when faced with an abundance of resources is this: It refines the search by creating a "string" of terms that frame the search more precisely. The more one refines the search, the better the results.

The Boolean search strategy is based on the words AND, OR, and NOT. The basic formula for combining keyword and Boolean search strategy is as follows:

_____ AND _____ AND [OR] _____ *[Fill in your search terms.]*

Inserting the terms *suicide* and *terrorism* connects the two terms and narrows the number of relevant resources. A more refined search can be achieved by adding another term, say, *Islamic*, to the string.

Another way to narrow the number of resources is to use the NOT feature of the Boolean search strategy. For example, if the problem is youth gun violence, inserting the key terms *youth, gun,* and *violence* into the string will produce a substantial number of references. Adding a restrictive term, such as the name of a city, or a type of violence, such as homicide, into the string after NOT will produce a more precise result.

_____ AND _____ AND [OR] _____ NOT _____
[Fill in your search terms.]

Klein (2003) notes that different databases respond in different ways, so students should be prepared to "play" with the terms in the search string. If a particular term is not yielding good results, use a synonym, consult the thesaurus of a particular database, or check the list of common terms in the Library of Congress Classification (LCC) system. If the student encounters further problems, a librarian should be consulted.

The third approach is federated searching. This tool is a boon for interdisciplinarians because it enables access to multiple databases at a single keystroke. For example, the database ABI/INFORM allows for federated searching.

Regardless of the strategy used, achieving the most relevant results requires that students use precise keywords and Boolean logic, and this requires a clear statement of the problem or question.

Core Resources on Interdisciplinary Studies

This section identifies core resources under subject headings for ease of access. In a few cases, a publication may appear under more than one heading.

Assessment and Evaluation

Boix Mansilla, V. (2005). Assessing student work at disciplinary crossroads. *Change, 37,* 14–21.

Boix Mansilla, V. (2010). Learning to synthesize: The development of interdisciplinary understanding. In R. Froedeman, J. T. Klein, & C. Mitcham (Eds.), *The Oxford handbook of interdisciplinarity* (pp. 288–291). New York: Oxford University Press.

Boix Mansilla, V., Duraising, E. D., Wolfe, C. R., & Haynes, C. (2009). Targeted assessment rubric: An empirically grounded rubric for interdisciplinary writing. *The Journal of Higher Education, 80*(3), 334–353.

Huutoniemi, K. (2010). Evaluating interdisciplinary research. In R. Froedeman, J. T. Klein, & C. Mitcham (Eds.), *The Oxford handbook of interdisciplinarity* (pp. 309–320). New York: Oxford University Press.

Ivanitskaya, L., Clark, D., Montgomery, G., & Primeau, R. (2002). Interdisciplinary learning: Process and outcomes. *Innovative Higher Education, 27*(2), 95–111.

Klein, J. T. (2002). Assessing interdisciplinary learning K–16. In J. T. Klein (Ed.), *Interdisciplinary education in K–16 and college: A foundation for K–16 dialogue* (pp. 179–196). New York: The College Board.

Klein, J. T. (2006). Afterword: The emergent literature on interdisciplinary and transdisciplinary research evaluation. *Research Evaluation, 15*(1), 75–80.

Klein, J. T. (2008). Evaluation of interdisciplinary and transdisciplinary research: A literature review. *American Journal of Preventative Medicine, 35*(2S), S116–S123.

Popham, W. J. (1997). What's wrong—and what's right—with rubrics. *Educational Leadership,* October, 72–75.

Repko, A. F. (2008). Assessing interdisciplinary learning outcomes. *Academic Exchange Quarterly, 12*(3), 171–178.

Research Evaluation. (2006). [Special issue devoted to evaluating interdisciplinary research.] *15*(1), 1–80. Retrieved July 14, 2011, from http://www.ingenta connect.com/content/beech/rev/2006/00000015/00000001;jsessionid=72tg4b5q 5k61e.alice

Seabury, M. B. (2004). Scholarship about interdisciplinarity: Some possibilities and guidelines. *Issues in Integrative Studies, 22,* 52–84.

Wolfe, C., & Haynes, C. (2003). Interdisciplinary assessment profiles. *Issues in Integrative Studies, 21,* 126–169.

Bibliographies and Literature Review

Chettiparamb, A. (2007). *Interdisciplinarity: A literature review.* Southampton, UK: University of Southampton. Retrieved July 14, 2011, from http://www.heacademy .ac.uk/assets/York/documents/ourwork/sustainability/interdisciplinarity_literature_ review.pdf

Dubrow, G. L. (2007). *Interdisciplinary approaches to teaching, research, and knowledge: A bibliography.* Retrieved July 14, 2011, from http://www.grad.umn .edu/oii/Leadership/interdisciplinary_bibliography.pdf

Holly, K. A. (2009). *Understanding interdisciplinary challenges and opportunities in higher education. ASHE Higher Education Report, 35*(2). San Francisco: Jossey-Bass.

Klein, J. T. (2006). Resources for interdisciplinary studies. *Change,* April, 52–56, 58.

Collaboration

Amey, M. J., & Brown, D. F. (2004). *Breaking out of the box: Interdisciplinary collaboration and faculty work.* Greenwich, CT: Information Age.

Derry, S. J., Schunn, C. D., & Gernsbacher, M. A. (Eds.). (2005). *Interdisciplinary collaboration: An emerging cognitive science.* Mahwah, NJ: Lawrence Erlbaum Associates.

Stokols, D., Hall, K., Taylor, B. K., & Moser, R. P. (2008). The science of team science: Assessing the value of transdisciplinary research. *American Journal of Preventive Medicine, 35*(2S), S77–S249. Retrieved July 14, 2011, from http:// www.ajpmonline.org/article/S0749-3797(08)00408-X/abstract?refuid=S0749- 3797(08)00416-9&refissn=0749-3797

Comparative National Perspectives

Lenoir, Y., & Klein, J. T. (2010). Interdisciplinarity in schools: A comparative view of national perspectives. *Issues in Integrative Studies, Special Number 28.*

Curriculum Design

Augsburg, T. (2003). Becoming interdisciplinary: The student portfolio in the Bachelor of Interdisciplinary Studies Program at Arizona State University. *Issues in Integrative Studies, 21,* 98–125.

Linkon, S. (2004). *Understanding interdisciplinarity: A course portfolio*. Retrieved July 14, 2011, from http://www.educ.msu.edu/cst/events/2004/linkon.htm

Newell, W. H. (1994). Designing interdisciplinary courses. In J. T. Klein & W. G. Doty (Eds.), *New Directions for Teaching and Learning: Vol. 58. Interdisciplinary studies today* (pp. 35–51). San Francisco: Jossey-Bass.

Repko, A. F. (2006). Disciplining interdisciplinarity: The case for textbooks. *Issues in Integrative Studies, 24,* 112–142.

Repko, A. F. (2007). Interdisciplinary curriculum design. *Academic Exchange Quarterly, 11*(1), 130–137.

Szostak, R. (2003). "Comprehensive" curricular reform: Providing students with an overview of the scholarly enterprise. *Journal of General Education 52*(1), 27–49.

Vess, D. (2000–2001). *Interdisciplinary learning, teaching, and research*. Retrieved July 14, 2011, from http://www.faculty.de.gcsu.edu/~dvess/ids/courseportfolios/front.htm

Definitions of Interdisciplinarity

Committee on Facilitating Interdisciplinary Research. (2004). *Facilitating interdisciplinary research*. Washington, DC: National Academics Press.

Klein, J. T. (1996). *Crossing boundaries: Knowledge, disciplinarities, and interdisciplinarities*. Charlottesville: University Press of Virginia.

Klein, J. T., & Newell, W. H. (1996). Advancing interdisciplinary studies. In J. G. Gaff, J. L. Ratcliff, & Associates (Eds.), *Handbook of the undergraduate curriculum: A comprehensive guide to purposes, structures, practices, and change* (pp. 393–415). San Francisco: Jossey-Bass.

Domains of Practice

Science and Technology

Committee on Facilitating Interdisciplinary Research. (2004). *Facilitating interdisciplinary research*. Washington, DC: National Academies Press.

Culligan, P. J., & Pena-Mora, F. (2010). Engineering. In R. Froedeman, J. T. Klein, and C. Mitcham (Eds.), *The Oxford handbook of interdisciplinarity* (pp. 147–160). New York: Oxford University Press.

Weingart, P., & Stehr, N. (2000). *Practising interdisciplinarity*. Toronto: University of Toronto Press.

Social Sciences

Calhoun, C., & Rhoten, D. (2010). Integrating the social sciences: Theoretical knowledge, methodological tools, and practical applications. In R. Froedeman, J. T. Klein, & C. Mitcham (Eds.), *The Oxford handbook of interdisciplinarity* (pp. 103–118). New York: Oxford University Press.

Kessel, F., Rosenfield, P. L., & Anderson, N. B. (Eds.). (2003). *Expanding the boundaries of health and social sciences: Case studies in interdisciplinary innovation*. New York: Oxford University Press.

Klein, J. T. (2007). Interdisciplinary approach. In S. Turner & W. Outhwaite (Eds.), *Handbook of social science methodology,* (pp. 32–50). Thousand Oaks, CA: Sage.

Smelser, N. J. (2004). Interdisciplinarity in theory and practice. In C. Camic & H. Joas (Eds.), *The dialogic turn: New roles for sociology in the postdisciplinary age,* pp. 34–46. Lanham, MD: Rowman & Littlefield.

Humanities

Bal, M. (2002). *Traveling concepts in the humanities.* Toronto: University of Toronto Press.

Fredericks, S. E. (2010). Religious studies. In R. Froedeman, J. T. Klein, & C. Mitcham (Eds.), *The Oxford handbook of interdisciplinarity* (pp. 161–173). New York: Oxford University Press.

Klein, J. T. (2005). *Humanities, culture, and interdisciplinarity: The changing American academy.* Albany: State University of New York Press.

Klein, J. T., & Parncutt, R. (2010). Art & music research. In R. Froedeman, J. T. Klein, & C. Mitcham (Eds.), *The Oxford handbook of interdisciplinarity* (pp. 133–146). New York: Oxford University Press.

History of Interdisciplinarity

Klein, J. T. (1990). *Interdisciplinarity: History, theory and practice.* Detroit, MI: Wayne State University Press.

Klein, J. T. (1999). *Mapping interdisciplinary studies: The academy in transition series* (Vol. 2). Washington, DC: Association of American Colleges and Universities.

Moran, J. (2002). *Interdisciplinarity.* London: Routledge.

Information Research

Palmer, C. L. (1999). Structures and strategies of interdisciplinary science. *Journal of the American Society for Information Science, 50*(3), 242–253.

Palmer, C. L. (2001). *Work at the boundaries of science: Information and the interdisciplinary research process.* Boston: Kluwer Academic.

Palmer, C. L. (2010). Information research on interdisciplinarity. In R. Frodeman, J. T. Klein, C. Mitcham, & J. B. Holbrook (Eds.), *The Oxford handbook of interdisciplinarity* (pp. 174–188). New York: Oxford University Press.

Palmer, C. L., & Neuman, L. J. (2002). The information work of interdisciplinary humanities scholars: Exploration and translation. *The Library Quarterly, 72*(1), 85–117.

Palmer, C. L., Teffeau, L. C., & Pirmann, C. M. (2009). *Scholarly information practices in an online environment: Themes from the literature and implications for library service development.* Dublin, OH: Online Computer Library Center.

Integration

Newell, W. H. (2006). Interdisciplinary integration by undergraduates. *Issues in Integrative Studies, 24,* 89–111.

Newell, W. H. (2007). Decision making in interdisciplinary studies. In G. Morçöl (Ed.), *Handbook of decision making* (pp. 245–264). New York: Marcel-Dekker.

Pohl, C., van Kirkhoff, L., Hadorn, G. H., & Bammer, G. (2008). Integration. In G. H. Hadorn, H. Hoffman-Riem, S. Biber-Klemm, W. Grossbacher-Mansuy, D. Joye, C. Pohl, U. Wiesmann, & E. Zemp (Eds.), *Handbook of transdisciplinary research* (pp. 411–426). Berlin: Springer.

Repko, A. F. (2007). Integrating interdisciplinarity: How the theories of common ground and cognitive interdisciplinarity are informing the debate on interdisciplinary integration. *Issues in Integrative Studies, 27,* 1–31.

Sill, D. (1996). Integrative thinking, synthesis, and creativity in interdisciplinary studies. *Journal of General Education, 45*(2), 129–151.

Spooner, M. (2004). Generating integration and complex understanding: Exploring the use of creative thinking tools within interdisciplinary studies. *Issues in Integrative Studies, 22,* 85–111.

Literature and Resource Guides

Ackerson, L. G. (Ed.). (2007). *Literature search strategies for interdisciplinary research: A sourcebook for scientists and engineers.* Lanham, MD: Scarecrow Press.

Fiscella, J. (1996). Bibliography as an interdisciplinary service. *Library Trends, 45*(2), 280–295.

Fiscella, J. B., & Kimmel, S. E. (Eds.). (1999). *Interdisciplinary education: A guide to resources.* New York: College Entrance Examination Board.

Klcin, J. T. (2006). Resources for interdisciplinary studies. *Change,* April, 52–56, 58.

Klein, J. T., & Newell, W. H. (2002). Strategies for using interdisciplinary resources across K–16. *Issues in Integrative Studies, 20,* 139–160.

Newell, W. H. (2007). Distinctive challenges of library-based research and writing: A guide. *Issues in Integrative Studies, 25,* 84–110. Retrieved July 14, 2011, from http://www.units.muohio.edu/aisorg/PUBS/ISSUES/toc25.shtml

Palmer, C. L. (2001). *Work at the boundaries of science: Information and the interdisciplinary research process.* Boston: Kluwer Academic.

Palmer, C. L., & Neumann, L. J. (2002). The information work of interdisciplinary humanities scholars: Exploration and translation. *Library Quarterly, 72,* 85–117.

Pedagogy

Davis, J. (1995). *Interdisciplinary courses and team teaching: New arrangements for learning.* Phoenix, AZ: Oryx Press.

Haynes, C. (Ed.). (2002). *Innovations in interdisciplinary teaching.* American Council on Education. Series on Higher Education. Westport, CT: Oryx Press/Greenhaven Press.

Kain, D. L. (2005). Integrative learning and interdisciplinary studies. *Peer Review, 7*(4), 8–10.

Klein, J. T. (Ed.). (2002). *Interdisciplinary education in K–12 and college: A foundation for K–16 dialogue.* New York: The College Board.

Newell, W. H. (2001). Powerful pedagogies. In B. L. Smith & J. McCann (Eds.), *Reinventing ourselves: Interdisciplinary education, collaborative learning and experimentation in higher education,* pp. 196–211. Bolton, MA: Anker Press.

Newell, W. H. (2006). Interdisciplinary integration by undergraduates. *Issues in Integrative Studies, 24,* 89–111.

Repko, A. F. (2006). Disciplining interdisciplinary studies: The case for textbooks. *Issues in Integrative Studies, 24,* 112–142.

Seabury, M. B. (Ed.). (1999). *Interdisciplinary general education: Questioning outside the lines.* New York: The College Board.

Program Development and Sustainability

Augsburg, T., & Henry, S. (Eds.). (2009). *The politics of interdisciplinary studies: Interdisciplinary transformation in undergraduate American higher education.* Jefferson, NC: McFarland.

Carmichael, T. S. (2004). *Integrated studies: Reinventing undergraduate education.* Stillwater, OK: New Forum Press.

Chandramohan, B., & Fallows, S. (Eds.). (2009). *Interdisciplinary learning and teaching in higher education: Theory and practice.* London: Routledge.

Klein, J. T. (2010). *Creating interdisciplinary campus cultures: A model for sustainability and growth.* San Francisco: Jossey-Bass.

Smith, B. L., & McCann, J. (Eds.). (2001). *Reinventing ourselves: Interdisciplinary education, collaboration, learning, and experimentation in higher education.* San Francisco: Anker/Jossey-Bass.

Thew, N. (2007). *The impact of the internal economy of higher education institutions on interdisciplinary teaching and learning.* England: University of Southampton.

Seabury, M. B. (Ed.). (1999). *Interdisciplinary general education: Questioning outside the lines.* New York: The College Board.

Research Practice

Atkinson, J., & Crowe, M. (Eds.). (2006). *Interdisciplinary research: Diverse approaches in science, technology, health and society.* West Sussex, England: Wiley.

Boix Mansilla, V. (2006). Interdisciplinary work at the frontier: An empirical examination of expert interdisciplinary epistemologies. *Issues in Integrative Studies, 24,* 1–31.

Committee on Facilitating Interdisciplinary Research. (2004). *Facilitating interdisciplinary research.* Washington, DC: National Academies Press.

Hadorn, G. H., et al. (Eds.). (2008). *Handbook of transdisciplinary research.* New York: Springer.

Newell, W. H. (2007). Decision making in interdisciplinary studies. In G. Morçöl (Ed.), *Handbook of decision making* (pp. 245–264). New York: Marcel-Dekker.

Palmer, C. L., & Neumann, L. J. (2002). The information work of interdisciplinary humanities scholars: Exploration and translation. *Library Quarterly, 72,* 85–117.

Palmer, C. L. (2010). Information research on interdisciplinarity. In R. Froedeman, J. T. Klein, & C. Mitcham (Eds.), *The Oxford handbook of interdisciplinarity* (pp. 174–188). New York: Oxford University Press.

Repko, A. F., Newell, W. H., & Szostak, R. (2012). *Case studies in interdisciplinary research.* Los Angeles: Sage. (Note: This book provides several applications of the interdisciplinary research process described in Repko, A. F. [2008]. *Interdisciplinary research: Process and theory.* Thousand Oaks, CA: Sage.)

Rowe, J. W. (2003). Approaching interdisciplinary research. In F. Kessel, P. L. Rosenfield, & N. B. Anderson (Eds.), *Expanding the boundaries of health and social science* (pp. 3–12). New York: Oxford University Press.

Szostak, R. (2012). The interdisciplinary research process. In A. F. Repko, W. H. Newell, & R. Szostak (Eds.), *Case studies in interdisciplinary research* (pp. 3–20), Thousand Oaks, CA: Sage.

Szostak, R. (2009). *The causes of economic growth: Interdisciplinary perspectives.* Berlin, Springer. (Note: This is the only book-length application of the research process described in this book.)

Szostak, R. (2007). How and why to teach interdisciplinary research practice. *Journal of Research Practice, 3*(2), Article M17.

Weingart, P., & Stehr, N. (2000). *Practising interdisciplinarity.* Toronto: University of Toronto Press.

Theory

Boix Mansilla, V. (2006). Interdisciplinary work at the frontier: An empirical examination of expert epistemologies. *Issues in Integrative Studies, 24,* 1–31.

Newell, W. H. (2001). A theory of interdisciplinary studies. *Issues in Integrative Studies, 19,* 1–25.

Newell, W. H. (2001). Reply to respondents to "A theory of interdisciplinary studies." *Issues in Integrative Studies, 19,* 135–146.

Repko, A. F. (2007). Integrating interdisciplinarity: How the theories of common ground and cognitive interdisciplinarity are informing the debate on interdisciplinary integration. *Issues in Integrative Studies, 27,* 1–31.

Spooner, M. (2004). Generating integration and complex understanding: Exploring the use of creative thinking tools within interdisciplinary studies. *Issues in Integrative Studies, 22,* 85–111.

Szostak, R. (2004). *Classifying science: Phenomena, data, theory, method, practice.* Dordrecht, the Netherlands: Springer.

Szostak, R. (2007). Modernism, postmodernism, and interdisciplinarity. *Issues in Integrative Studies, 25,* 32–83.

Weingart, P., & Stehr, N. (2000). *Practising interdisciplinarity.* Toronto: University of Toronto Press.

Welch, J., IV (2007). The role of intuition in interdisciplinary insight. *Issues in Integrative Studies, 25,* 131–155.

Welch, J., IV (2009). Interdisciplinarity and the history of Western epistemology. *Issues in Integrative Studies, 27,* 35–69.

Welch, J., IV (forthcoming). The emergence of interdisciplinarity from epistemological thought. *Issues in Integrative Studies, 29.*

Other Works

Augsburg, T. (2006). *Becoming interdisciplinary: An introduction to interdisciplinary studies* (2nd ed.). Dubuque, IA: Kendall/Hunt.

Czechowski, J. (2003). An integrated approach to liberal learning. *Peer Review,* 5(4), 4–7.

Graff, G. (1991). Colleges are depriving students of a connected view of scholarship. *The Chronicle of Higher Education,* February 13, p. 48.

Overviews of the Field

Association for Integrative Studies, (2005). *Interdisciplinary studies today* [Teleconference and webcast]. Available from http://www.units.muohio.edu/aisorg/

Committee on Facilitating Interdisciplinary Research. (2004). *Facilitating interdisciplinary research.* Washington, DC: National Academies Press.

Froedeman, R., Klein, J. T., & Mitcham, C. (Eds.). (2010). *The Oxford handbook of interdisciplinarity.* New York: Oxford University Press.

Graff, G. (1991). Colleges are depriving students of a connected view of scholarship. *The Chronicle of Higher Education,* February 13, p. 48.

Huber, M. T., Hutchings, P., & Gale, R. (2005). Integrative learning for liberal education. *Peer Review,* 7(4), 4–7.

Kain, D. L. (1993). Cabbages—and kings: Research directions in integrated/ interdisciplinary curriculum. *Journal of Educational Thought/Revue de la Pensee Educative,* 27(3), 312–331.

Klein, J. T. (1999). *Mapping interdisciplinary studies.* Washington, DC: Association of American Colleges and Universities.

Klein, J. T., & Newell, W. H. (1997). Advancing interdisciplinary studies. In J. Gaff & J. Ratcliff (Eds.), *Handbook of the undergraduate curriculum: A comprehensive guide to purposes, structures, practices, and change,* (pp. 393–415). San Francisco: Jossey-Bass.

Lattuca, L. R. (2001). *Creating interdisciplinarity: Interdisciplinary research and teaching among college and university faculty.* Nashville, TN: Vanderbilt University Press.

Roberts, J. A. (2004). *Riding the momentum: Interdisciplinary research centers to interdisciplinary graduate programs.* Paper presented at the July 2004 Merrill conference, University of Kansas.

Walker, D. (1996). *Integrative education.* Eugene, OR: ERIC Clearinghouse on Educational Management.

Textbooks for Students

Augsburg, T. (2006). *Becoming interdisciplinary: An introduction to interdisciplinary studies* (2nd ed.). Dubuque, IA: Kendall/Hunt.

Repko, A. F. (2008). *Interdisciplinary research: Process and theory.* Thousand Oaks, CA: Sage.

Glossary of Key Terms _____

Abstract thinking: A higher-order cognitive ability that enables one to understand and express an interdisciplinary understanding or meaning of a problem symbolically in terms of a metaphor, or to compare a hard-to-understand and complex phenomenon to a symbol that is simple, familiar, and easy to understand. [2:62]

Academic disciplines: Scholarly communities that specify which phenomena to study, advance certain central concepts and organizing theories, embrace certain methods of investigation, provide forums for sharing research and insights, and offer career paths for scholars. [1:4]

Adequacy (in interdisciplinary sense): An understanding of each discipline's cognitive map sufficient to identify its perspective, epistemology, assumptions, concepts, theories, and methods in order to understand its insights into a particular problem. [2:60]

Analytical integration: The synthesis of theoretical perspectives on a highly complex process involving multiple factors such as metropolitan formation.

Analytical intelligence: Thinking that is required to solve problems and to evaluate the quality of ideas. [2:39]

Antidisciplinary: Preferring a more open understanding of knowledge and evidence that would include lived experience, testimonials, oral traditions, and interpretation of those traditions by elders. [2:53]

Applied fields: These include business and its subfields (e.g., finance, marketing, management), communications and its subfields (e.g., advertising, speech), criminal justice and criminology, education, engineering, law, medicine, nursing, social work. [1:5–6]

Association for Integrative Studies (AIS): A professional organization founded in 1979 whose purpose is to study interdisciplinary methodology, theory, curricula, and administration. [2:51]

Assumption: Something taken for granted, a supposition, a principle that underlies the discipline as a whole and its overall perspective on reality. This principle is accepted as the truth upon which the discipline's theories, concepts, methods, and curriculum are based. [4:120]

Base theory: One that incorporates both/and thinking in an interdisciplinary sense. [13:400]

Bilingualism: A popular, but inappropriate, metaphor for interdisciplinary work that implies mastery of or proficiency in two complete languages (comparing disciplines to foreign language), suggesting one cannot work in a new discipline without first mastering it, which is not the case. [1:28]

Border disciplinarity: That which exists when at least two disciplines focusing on the same problem create an overlapping area between them, each making a productive contribution to understanding the problem. [3:86]

Borrowing: Calls for borrowing from each relevant discipline the insights and theories and the information that they contain and carefully evaluating the material in terms of its credibility (is it peer-reviewed?), timeliness (is it time-sensitive?), and relevance (does it illuminate some part of the problem?). [7:196]

Boundary crossing: The process of moving across knowledge formations for the purpose of achieving an enlarged understanding. [1:26]

Bridge building: A metaphor connoting the borrowing of tools and methods from disciplines. [1:27]

Burden of comprehension: Having a minimum understanding of each relevant discipline's cognitive map necessary for borrowing from it. [7:196]

Categories of traditional disciplines: The natural sciences, the social sciences, and the humanities. [1:5]

Causal arguments: Examine the underlying cause for any particular situation or argument, and analyze in depth what causes a trend, an event, or a phenomenon. [13:387]

Causal or propositional integration: Refers to combining truth claims from disciplinary theoretical explanations to form an integrated theory—that is, a new proposition that is interdisciplinary and more comprehensive. [13:387]

Causal process: A change in the independent variable is presumed to cause change in the dependent variable. [12:361]

Causal relationship: Refers to how a change in one variable produces or leads to change in another variable. [12:358]

Classical division of knowledge: Aristotle's clear hierarchy of the different academic subjects with the theoretical subjects of theology, mathematics, and physics on top; the practical subjects of ethics and politics in the middle; and the productive subjects of the fine arts, poetics, and engineering at the bottom. [2:45]

Classification approach: The linking of all phenomena to particular disciplines, provided that one knows the discipline's general perspective and the phenomena it typically studies, to classify phenomena. [4:107]

Close reading: A fundamental method of modern criticism that calls for careful analysis of a text and close attention to individual words, syntax, and the order in which sentences and ideas unfold. [10:303]

Cognitive advancement: Using integrated knowledge to produce a more comprehensive understanding. [2:57–58]

Cognitive decentering: The intellectual capacity to consider a variety of other perspectives and thus perceive reality more accurately, process information more systematically, and solve problems more efficiently. The term *decentering* denotes the ability to shift deliberately among alternative perspectives and to bring each to bear upon a complex problem. [2:55]

Cognitive discord: Disagreement among a discipline's practitioners over the defining elements of the discipline. [4:99]

Cognitive fluidity: The phenomenon of boundary crossing and borrowing from other disciplines. [4:100]

Cognitive interdisciplinarity: The application of common ground theory to communication across academic disciplines, especially the natural sciences. [9:267]

Cognitive map: The defining elements of a discipline's perspective. [4:101]

Colleges, schools, or faculties: Clusters of related disciplines that form larger units within a university such as the college of science, the school of social sciences, or the faculty of arts. [4:93]

Common ground: That which is created between conflicting disciplinary insights or theories, preparatory for performing integration and producing an interdisciplinary product. [2:56–57]

Common ground integrator: The one or more assumptions, concepts, or theoretical explanations by which conflicting insights can be integrated. [9:267–268]

Communicative competence: The ability to comprehend and translate terminology that is discipline-specific. [2:61]

Complex systems theory: Concerns the properties of complex systems in general, including how an overall pattern of behavior is generated, its characteristics, and how it evolves over time or in response to changes in its environment. [2:35]

Complexity: Descriptive of a problem that has multiple components studied by different disciples. [3:85]

Concept: A symbol expressed in language that represents a phenomenon or an abstract idea generalized from particular instances. [4:126]

Concept or principle map: A visual showing meaningful relationships between the parts of the problem, which requires thinking through all of the parts of the problem as well as understanding how these behave or function. [5:150–151]

Consilience: The jumping together of knowledge across disciplines to create a common groundwork of explanation. [2:36]

Contested space: The "in between" space among disciplines. [1:7]

Contested terrain: Problems, issues, or questions that are the focus of several disciplines. [1:7]

Contextualization: Process that connects disciplines that are epistemological neighbors by embedding any disciplinary material in the fabric of time, culture, and personal experience and is used to interpret cultural artifacts, such as art works, in order to uncover their meaning. [9:282]

Controlled vocabulary: A language of descriptors established by librarians to use in subject headings to minimize the use of disciplinary jargon. [6:174]

Creative breakthroughs: Often occur when different disciplinary perspectives and previously unrelated ideas are brought together. [2:43–44]

Creative intelligence: Thinking that is required to formulate ideas and solutions to problems. [2:39]

Creativity: A process that involves rethinking underlying premises, assumptions, or values, not just tracing out the implications of agreed-upon premises, assumptions, or values. Creativity involves iterative (i.e., repetitive) and heuristic (i.e., experimental) activity. [2:63]

Critical interdisciplinarity: A society-driven approach that interrogates the dominant structure of knowledge and education with the aim of transforming them, while raising questions of value and purpose. [1:22]

Cross-level or multilevel integration: Wherein different behaviors occur on different levels. [13:388]

Cultural analysis: A research method, dominated by postmodernism, seeking to understand a text or an object of inquiry by drawing on a specific set of collaborating disciplines that include disciplines from the humanities as well as from the social sciences: history, psychology, philosophy, literature, linguistics, and art history. [7:214]

Curriculum: A discipline's universally recognized core of knowledge that is subdivided into specific courses. [1:8]

Decision making: A uniquely human activity necessitated by the prevalence of complex problems, decision making is the cognitive ability to choose after considering alternatives. [3:69]

Defining elements of a discipline's perspective: The phenomena it studies and the kinds of data it collects, its epistemology or rules about what constitutes evidence or "proof," the assumptions it makes about the natural and human world, its basic concepts, its theories about the causes and behaviors of certain phenomena, and its methods (the way it gathers, applies, and produces new knowledge). [4:101]

Dependent variable: The effect in a cause-and-effect relationship. [12:358]

Dialectical thinking: The ability to view issues from multiple perspectives and to arrive at the most economical and reasonable reconciliation of seemingly contradictory information and positions. [2:62]

Disciplinarity: The system of knowledge specialties called disciplines. [4:94]

Disciplinary: Relating to a particular field of study or specialization. [1:7]

Disciplinary adequacy: Comprehending how a discipline characteristically looks at the world in terms of its perspective, phenomena, epistemology, assumptions, concepts, theories, and methods. [2:60]

Disciplinary bias: Using words and phrases that connect the problem to a particular discipline. [3:78]

Disciplinary breadth: Refers to disciplines, subdisciplines, and interdisciplines interested in the problem and whose experts have produced the most relevant insights into it. [9:279]

Disciplinary categories: Broad categories of related disciplines that typically include the natural sciences; the social sciences; the humanities; the applied and performing arts such as music, theater, and dance; the applied fields such as communications and business; and the professions such as architecture, engineering, law, nursing, education, and social work. [4:95]

Disciplinary depth: The intensive focus on a discipline or subdiscipline. [9:278]

Disciplinary inadequacy: The view that the disciplines by themselves are inadequate to address complex problems. [2:53]

Disciplinary insight: An expert view on a particular problem that is based on research. [1:16]

Disciplinary jargon: Using technical terms and concepts that are not generally understood outside the discipline. [3:78]

Disciplinary knowledge: The source of disciplinary depth that includes (1) an understanding of the overall perspective of each relevant discipline and (2) adequacy in each discipline's defining elements as they pertain to the problem. These elements and the discipline's perspective in a general sense are usually reflected in the discipline's literature, from which insights into particular problems are drawn. [9:278]

Disciplinary method: The particular procedure or process or technique used by a discipline's practitioners to conduct, organize, and present research. [7:204]

Disciplinary perspective (clarified definition): A discipline's view of reality in a general sense, which embraces and in turn reflects the ensemble of its defining elements that include phenomena, epistemology, assumptions, concepts, theory, and methods. [4:101]

Disciplinary perspective (in a general sense): Each discipline's unique view of reality in a general sense. [4:96]

Disciplinary specialization: The focus on a particular portion of reality that is of interest to the discipline. [2:42]

Disciplinary theory: Explains an event or behavior based on research and has a specified range of applicability. [12:356]

Disciplinary understanding: Using knowledge and modes of thinking in disciplines such as history, science, or the arts to create products, solve problems, and offer explanations that echo the work of disciplinary experts. [1:25]

Discipline: A particular branch of learning or body of knowledge such as physics, psychology, or history. [1:4]

Discourse: The dominant language (spoken and/or written) used by a community to discuss or transact business of any kind. The knowledge of a discourse—its vocabulary, concepts, and rules—constitutes power. [4:118]

Elements: The constituent parts of a discipline that provide its essential and formative character. [4:105]

Emergent property: A characteristic of a system that cannot be understood by reference to its constituent elements (phenomena and causal links) but only at the level of the system as a whole. [13:396]

Empiricism: Epistemological position that all knowledge is derived from our perceptions (transmitted by the five senses of touch, smell, taste, hearing, and sight), experience, and observations. [4:113]

Enlightenment: A seventeenth- and eighteenth-century Europe-wide intellectual movement that emphasized the progress of human knowledge through the powers of reason, provided justification for the movement known as modernism, and challenged the notion of the unity of knowledge. [2:47]

Epistemic norms of a discipline: Agreements about how researchers should select their evidence or data, evaluate their experiments, and judge their theories. [4:111]

Epistemological interpretivists: Those who view epistemology as totally arbitrary, being nothing more than a political power game to legitimize one's favored views. [4:113]

Epistemological pluralism: Refers to the diverse approaches that the disciplines use to know and describe reality. [4:112]

Epistemological positivism: A "law and order" approach that views any flexibility in matters epistemological as a guise for relativism or at least a mask for being weak or lacking conviction in expressing one's views. [4:113]

Epistemological self-reflexivity: Awareness of the advantages and disadvantages of different epistemological approaches and of the influence of epistemological choices upon the selection of research methods that in turn influence research outcomes. [4:119]

Epistemology: The branch of philosophy that studies how one knows what is true and how one validates truth. [4:111]

Explicit knowledge: That which is accessible to others. [14:420]

Extension: Involves addressing differences or oppositions in disciplinary concepts and/or assumptions by extending their meaning beyond the domain of the discipline that originated them into the domain(s) of the other relevant disciplines. [11:340]

Feedback: Corrective information about a decision, an operation, an event, or a problem that compels the researcher to revisit an earlier phase of the project. This corrective information typically comes from previously overlooked scholarship. [3:75]

Feedback loops: Descriptive of the process that requires the researcher to periodically revisit earlier activity. [3:75]

Full integration: When all relevant disciplinary insights have been integrated into a new, single, coherent, and comprehensive understanding or theory that is consistent with the available empirical evidence. [9:265]

Full-scale literature search: A process that is as interested in disciplinary breadth as it is in disciplinary depth and involves identifying all relevant expert insights and theories on a topic once it is deemed researchable in an interdisciplinary sense, immersing oneself in the scholarly conversations on the topic, and achieving mastery of the problem in all of its complexity. [6:183]

General education movement: A post–World War I reform movement that sought to solve the problems of the lack of national unity and eroding cohesiveness of general education by reemphasizing the arts and the values associated with classical humanism, which emphasized wholeness of knowledge and of human nature. [2:49]

Generalist interdisciplinarians: Understand interdisciplinarity loosely to mean any form of dialog or integration between two or more disciplines while minimizing, obscuring, or rejecting altogether the role of integration. [1:4]

Generative technologies: Those whose novelty and power not only find applications of great value but also have the capacity to transform existing disciplines and generate new ones. [2:39]

Heuristic: An aid to understanding or discovery or learning that places the student in the role of the discoverer of knowledge. [3:70]

Heuristics: Intuitive speculative strategies that sometimes work and other times do not work. [2:39]

Holistic thinking: The ability to think about the problem as part of a complete system. [2:63]

Horizontal or side-by-side integration: That which implies overlapping influences. [13:388]

Humanities: Express human aspirations, interpret and assess human achievements and experience, and seek layers of meaning and richness of detail in written texts, artifacts, and cultural practices. [1:5]

Hybridization: The integration of specialties across disciplines. [2:36]

Ideographic: Referring to a theory that is applicable to only a narrow range of phenomena and under a constrained set of circumstances. [7:205]

Ideographic theory: Posits a relationship only under specified conditions. [7:205]

Inclusive: In the context of the full-scale literature search, the term refers not to the quantity of disciplinary insights but to the quality and diversity of these published insights. [6:184]

Independent variable: The cause in a cause-and-effect relationship. [12:358]

Insight: A scholarly contribution to the clear understanding of a problem based on research. Insights into a problem can be produced either by disciplinary experts or by interdisciplinarians. [1:7]

Instrumental interdisciplinarity: A pragmatic problem-driven approach that focuses on research, borrowing (supplemented by integration), and practical problem solving in response to the external demands of society. [1:22]

Integration: A process by which ideas, data and information, methods, tools, concepts, and/or theories from two or more disciplines are synthesized, connected, or blended. [1:3–4]

Integration of knowledge: Identifying and blending knowledge from relevant disciplines to produce an interdisciplinary understanding of a particular problem or intellectual question that is limited in time and to a particular context and would not be possible by relying solely on a single disciplinary approach. [1:23]

Integrationist interdisciplinarians: Believe that integration should be the goal of interdisciplinary work and point to a growing body of literature that connects integration with interdisciplinary education and research. [1:4]

Integrative process: Involves creating common ground between conflicting insights from two or more disciplines into a specific problem. [1:7]

Integrative thinking: The ability to knit together information from disparate sources. [2:41]

Integrative wisdom: The synthetic interaction between inspiration, intellect, and intuition. [11:330]

Intellectual center of gravity: That which enables each discipline to maintain its identity and have a distinctive overall perspective. [4:100]

Intentional learners: Those who can integrate knowledge from different sources. [2:39]

Interdisciplinarity: The conceptual essence of interdisciplinary research practice. [1:3]

Interdisciplinary breadth: The required knowledge about all the relevant disciplines so that one can work with their theories and insights and integrate them in the second half of the research process. [9:279]

Interdisciplinary common ground: One or more concepts or assumptions by which conflicting insights or theories can be largely reconciled and subsequently integrated, thus enabling collaborative communication between disciplines. [11:322]

Interdisciplinary communication: That which occurs when differences in common ground are discovered as the partners of cooperation (the relevant disciplines) find out that they use the same concepts with different meanings, or that they use different codings (terms, symbol systems) for similar concepts. [9:267]

Interdisciplinary insight: Produced when the interdisciplinary research process (or some version of it) is used to create an integrated and purposeful result. [1:16]

Interdisciplinary integration: The cognitive process of critically evaluating disciplinary insights and creating common ground among them to construct a more comprehensive understanding. [9:263]

Interdisciplinary question: One that is open-ended and too complex to be addressed by one discipline alone and that is researchable. [3:77]

Interdisciplinary research: A decision-making process that is heuristic, iterative, and reflexive. [3:69]

Interdisciplinary research process (IRP): A practical and demonstrated way to make decisions about how to approach problems, decide which ones are appropriate for interdisciplinary inquiry, and construct comprehensive understandings of them. [3:69–70]

Interdisciplinary studies: A process of answering a question, solving a problem, or addressing a topic that is too broad or complex to be dealt with adequately by a single discipline, and draws on the disciplines with the goal of integrating their insights to construct a more comprehensive understanding. [1:16]

Interdisciplinary triangulation: The ability to keep in equilibrium disciplinary depth, disciplinary breadth, and interdisciplinary integration. [9:278]

Interdisciplinary understanding: Integrating knowledge and modes of thinking from two or more disciplines in order to create products, solve problems, and offer explanations, in ways that would not have been possible though single disciplinary means. [1:25]

Interdisciplines: Fields of study that cross traditional disciplinary boundaries and involve a wide variety of interactions ranging from informal groups of scholars to well-established research and teaching communities. [1:6]

Interpretivist approaches: Theories such as postmodernism, feminism, and critical theory that are challenging the bedrock assumptions of modernism (e.g., that there is an independent reality out there that can be perceived and measured), claiming that the perceptions and interpretations of what we perceive are filtered through a web of values, expectations, and vocabularies that influence understanding. [4:118]

Interpretivists: Those holding the epistemological position that the world is socially constructed, social phenomena do not exist independently of our interpretation of them, and objective analysis is impossible. [4:112]

Intervening variable: A step(s) in the causal process that leads from the independent to the dependent variable. [12:361]

In-text evidence of disciplinary adequacy: Expressions may be in the form of statements about the disciplinary elements that pertain to the problem, the disciplinary affiliation of leading theorists, and the disciplinary methods used if one is engaging in basic research and in the use of the most current and authoritative scholarship pertaining to the problem. In-text evidence demonstrates academic rigor and highlights the distinctive character of the interdisciplinary research project compared to that of disciplinary research. [7:219]

Intuition: The natural ability to understand or perceive something immediately without consciously using reason, analysis, or inference. [11:329]

Issues in Integrative Studies: The peer-reviewed journal launched in 1982 by the Association for Integrative Studies (AIS), a national voice for interdisciplinary studies. [2:51]

Iterative: Involving repetition of a sequence of operations yielding results successively closer to the desired outcome. [3:71]

Knowledge production: Scholarly research published in the form of peer-reviewed articles and books. [1:25]

Literature search: The process of gathering scholarly information on a given topic. [6:167]

Mapping: A metaphor based on the idea that the carving up of knowledge space is like the practice of cartography or mapmaking and involves using a combinational or integrative method to map or display information that is gathered from a variety of sources. [1:27]

Meaning: An important concept in the humanities often equated with the intent of the author or artist. [1:15]

Metanarrative: A comprehensive explanation or totalizing truth embedded in a culture that is created and reinforced by power structures and is therefore not to be trusted. [4:113]

Metaphor: A figure of speech in which a word or phrase, a story, or a picture is likened to the idea that one is attempting to communicate. An example of a metaphor to illustrate the product of the interdisciplinary research process is the smoothie. [1:25–26]

Method: Concerns how one conducts research, analyzes data or evidence, tests theories, and creates new knowledge. [4:128]

Model: That which serves to communicate a theory; a representation that is specific and clear. [12:357]

Modernist approach: Belief in objective, empirically based, rationally analyzed truth that is knowable. [4:113]

Monodisciplinarity: The tendency to view a problem primarily from the perspective of the discipline in which the researcher is grounded while discounting or rejecting other disciplinary perspectives. [9:274]

More comprehensive understanding: The integration of insights to produce a new and more nuanced whole. It is the integration that forms a new whole; the insights or theories merely contribute to it. [13:382]

Most comprehensive interdisciplinary theory: The one that requires the least possible modification so that it includes all variables. [12:366]

Most relevant disciplines: Those disciplines, often three or four, which are most directly connected to the problem, have generated the most important research on it, and have advanced the most compelling theories to explain it. More specifically, these disciplines, or parts of them, provide information about the problem that is essential to developing a comprehensive understanding of it. [5:159]

Multidisciplinarity: The placing side by side of insights from two or more disciplines without attempting integration. [1:16]

Multidisciplinary research: Involves more than a single discipline in which each discipline makes a separate contribution. [1:17]

Multidisciplinary studies: Merely bringing insights from different disciplines together in some way but failing to engage in the hard work of integration. [1:17]

Multiple causality integration: Wherein several variables combine to produce an effect. [13:388]

Narrative: A written or spoken account or story. [14:429]

Narrow interdisciplinarity: Draws on disciplines that are epistemologically close (e.g., physics and chemistry). [11:331]

Natural sciences: Tell us what the world is made of, describe how what it is made of is structured into a complex network of interdependent systems, and explain the behavior of a given localized system. [1:5]

New humanities: The developing trend in the humanities of a pluralistic and even conflicted set of assumptions that challenges the older assumption of unified knowledge and culture and is apparent in cultural studies, women's and ethnic studies, and literary studies where the epistemological and political are inseparable. [4:123–124]

Nomothetic: Referring to a theory that is applicable to a broad range of phenomena. [7:205]

Nomothetic theory: Posits a general relationship among two or more phenomena. [7:205]

Nonlinear thinking: Approaching a problem creatively, thinking about it "outside the box" without being influenced by solutions attempted in the past, and viewing it from different perspectives. [3:75]

Nonlinearity (of the interdisciplinary process): Along the way the researcher should reflect on, and may need to revisit, or even revise, earlier work. [3:75]

Organization: A technique that creates common ground by clarifying how certain phenomena interact and mapping the causal relationships. [11:346]

Paradigm shift: A profound and transformative change in the philosophical and theoretical framework that dominates a discipline or an approach to knowledge formation. [2:54]

Partial integration: When only some insights have been integrated and it applies to only some part(s) of the problem. [9:265]

Peer review: The subjecting of an author's scholarly paper or book manuscript to the scrutiny of experts in the field who evaluate it according to certain academic standards that are viewed as fair and rigorous by the discipline's members. [6:168]

Personal bias: One's own point of view on the problem. [3:79–80]

Perspectival approach: The relying on each discipline's unique perspective on reality to classify phenomena. [4:107]

Perspective taking: The use of multiple perspectives, which involves viewing a problem or topic or artifact from alternative viewpoints, including disciplinary-based viewpoints, to assemble new sets of potential solutions to a given problem. [2:56]

Phenomena: Enduring aspects of human existence that are of interest to scholars and are susceptible to scholarly description and explanation. [4:105]

Philosophical assumptions: Those underlying or inherent in philosophical theories (and thus disciplinary perspectives). [10:296]

Philosophical theory: One of two kinds of theory, this relates to epistemological, ethical, and other outlooks. [4:127]

Positivists: Those holding the epistemological position that the world exists independently of our knowledge of it, social phenomena exist independently of our interpretation of them, and objective analysis is possible. [4:112]

Postmodernism: Epistemological approach that offers a way to understand society by questioning modernism's notion of objective knowledge, a challenge radiating across the disciplines but more so in the social sciences and the humanities. [4:117]

Postmodernist approaches: Typically operate under the assumption that there is no such thing as objective truth, and that knowledge is explained discursively. [4:113]

Potentially relevant discipline: One whose research domain includes at least one phenomenon involved in the problem or question at hand and whose community of scholars may or may not have recognized the problem and published their research. [5:144]

Practical intelligence: Thinking that is needed to apply ideas in an effective way, whether in business or in everyday life. [2:39]

Pragmatic interdisciplinarity: Focused on the historically situated problems of society while holding to the notion that general education is the place where all the parts would add up to a cohesive whole. [2:49]

Premise of interdisciplinary studies: The disciplines (including interdisciplines) themselves are the necessary preconditions for and foundations of interdisciplinarity. [1:21]

Principle of least action: Making sure that the changes made in concepts and assumptions are the smallest possible to still create sufficient common ground on which to construct the more comprehensive understanding. [11:335]

Problem-based research: Requiring more than one discipline, a holistic focus on unresolved societal needs and practical problem solving that emphasizes usefulness, efficiency, and practical results. [3:86–87]

Problem solving: Process that uses critical issues of public debate, product development, or an intervention such as one designed to improve health and well-being as focal points for making connections between disciplines and is aimed at generating tangible outcomes and change. [3:70]

Process: Following a procedure or strategy that involves integration and entails moment-to-moment interactions as well as interactions over the course of the project. [3:70]

Proposition: That which makes a truth claim, generally involving an argument about how one or more variables affect one or more others, though they may refer only to the internal workings of a variable. [13:387]

Propositional integration: See causal integration. [13:387]

Qualitative approach: Method focusing on evidence that cannot easily be quantified, such as cultural mannerisms and personal impressions of a musical composition. [4:129]

Qualitative research strategies: Focus on the what, how, when, and where of a thing—its essence and its ambiance. Qualitative research refers to meanings, concepts, definitions, characteristics, metaphors, symbols, and descriptions of things or people that are not measured and expressed numerically. [7:208]

Quantitative approach: Method emphasizing that evidence can be expressed numerically over a specified time frame. [4:129]

Quantitative research strategies: Emphasize evidence that can be quantified, such as the number of atoms in a molecule, the flow rate of water in a river, or the amount of energy derived from a windmill. [7:208]

Range of applicability: Which causal links a theory addresses and under what circumstances the theory holds along those links. [12:358]

Receptivity to other disciplines: Being open to information from any and all relevant disciplinary perspectives as well as being willing, even eager, to learn about divergent fields of knowledge, gaining both an intuitive and intellectual grasp of them. [2:59]

Redefinition: A technique that involves modifying or redefining concepts in different texts and contexts to bring out a common meaning. [11:336]

Reductionism: The strategy of "dividing a phenomenon into its constituent parts and studying them separately in the expectation that knowledge produced by narrow specialties can be readily combined into the understanding of the phenomenon as a whole" (Newell, 2004, p. 2). [4:131]

Reflection in an interdisciplinary sense: A self-conscious activity that involves thinking about why certain choices were made at various points in the research process and how these choices have affected the development of the work. [14:410]

Reflexive: To be self-conscious or self-aware of disciplinary or personal bias that may influence one's work and possibly skew the evaluation of insights and thus the end product. [3:71]

Relevant information: That which pertains directly to the problem, that is indispensable to understanding the problem, and that offers distinctive insights into it. [6:184]

Research map: A visual of the problem or question that includes the purpose of the research, what disciplines are potentially relevant, the perspective of each discipline on the problem, the assumptions of each discipline, and nondisciplinary sources or interpretations. [5:149]

Researchable in an interdisciplinary sense: A problem is researchable if (1) it is complex (i.e., requires insights from more than one discipline) and/or (2) it is the focus of two or more disciplines (i.e., authors from at least two disciplines have written on the topic or at least on some aspect of it). [6:172–173]

Revolutionary insights: Those ideas that have the capacity to transform how we learn, think, and produce new knowledge. [2:38]

Role taking: A type of perspective taking used especially by interdisciplinary research teams who adopt a set of perspectives associated with a person or a culture. [9:275]

Scaffolding strategy: Mapping that helps structure complex problems to reduce the cognitive load for students while also making disciplinary, and interdisciplinary, strategies explicit. [5:157]

Scholarly knowledge: Knowledge that has been vetted by a discipline's community of scholars through its peer review process. [6:168]

Scholarly literature: Journal articles, books (published by academic or university presses), and unpublished conference papers produced by a discipline's community of scholars. [6:168]

Scholarship: A contribution to knowledge that is "public, susceptible to critical review and evaluation, and accessible for exchange and use by other members of one's scholarly community" (Shulman, 1998, p. 5). [1:11]

Scientific method: Method of producing new knowledge that follows steps: (1) observation and description of phenomena; (2) formulation of a hypothesis to explain the phenomena; (3) use of the hypothesis to predict the existence of other phenomena, or to predict quantitatively the result of new observations; (4) execution of properly performed experiments to test those hypotheses or predictions. [4:130]

Scientific revolution: A seventeenth- and eighteenth-century intellectual movement that emphasized greater specialization and heightened research activity, initially in the sciences and then in all the disciplines, and challenged the idea of the unity of knowledge. [2:47]

Scientific theory: One of two kinds of theory, this is about the world and corresponds to the root meaning of "theory." [4:127]

Scope: The parameters of what is included and excluded from consideration, how much of the problem will be investigated, and the limits of the investigation. [3:77]

Searching: Locating sources on a proposed topic or problem, which involves deciding where and how to look for information. [6:173]

Sequential or end-to-end integration: That which implies a sequential causal order. [13:388]

Silo perspective: Perceiving the university and the larger world through the narrow lens of the major. [2:38]

Skewed understanding: The degree to which an insight reflects the biases inherent in the discipline's perspective and thus the way the author understands the problem resulting from the author's deliberate decision or unconscious predisposition to omit certain information that pertains to a problem. [8:235]

Social sciences: Seek to explain the human world and figure out how to predict and improve it. [1:5]

Spatial integration: Wherein theoretical explanations of why the causes or effects of problems are not distributed evenly in space. [13:388]

STEP: The term used to clarify the point of decision or operation that one would normally take in almost any interdisciplinary research project and to differentiate a particular decision or operation from others. [3:71]

Studies: A wide array of knowledge domains, work, and educational programs that involve crossing disciplinary boundaries, including interdisciplinary programs that include a core of courses, established interdisciplinary fields such as area studies and materials science, and newer fields such as environmental studies, urban studies, sustainability studies, and cultural studies. [1:9]

Subdiscipline: A branch of an existing discipline. [1:6]

Successful intelligence: Thinking that balances creative, analytical, and practical thinking, and knowing how and when to use them. [2:39]

Synthesis: A synonym of integration that connotes creation of an interdisciplinary outcome through a series of integrative actions. [9:263]

System: Any group of interacting components or agents around which there is a clearly defined boundary between it and the rest of the world, but also clearly definable inputs from the world and outputs to the world that cross the boundary. [3:85]

System map: A visual that shows all the parts of a system or problem and illustrates the causal relationships among them to help one visualize the system or problem as a complex whole. [5:152]

Systems thinking: A method for visualizing interrelationships within a complex problem or system by breaking it down into its constituent parts, identifying which parts different disciplines address, evaluating the relative importance of different causal linkages, and recognizing that a system of linkages is much more than the sum of its parts. [5:152]

Tacit knowledge: That which is not directly accessible to others. [14:420]

Taxonomy: A systematic and orderly classification. [4:104]

Theory: A generalized scholarly explanation about some aspect of the natural or human world, how it works, and why specific facts are related that is supported by data and research. [4:126]

Theory-based insights: Insights that are informed by or advance a particular theory or theoretical perspective. [10:296]

Theory extension: Calls for taking well-known facts normally treated as exogenous (i.e., external) to a disciplinary theory (such as organisms altering their environment) and making them endogenous (i.e., internal) to the theory and mutually interactive with it. [12:368]

Theory map: A visual that describes a theory's history, supporting evidence, importance, and similarity or competition to other theories. [5:152]

Traditional interdisciplinarity: Focused on the classical and secular ideals of culture and liberal education while holding to the notion that general education is the place where all the parts would add up to a cohesive whole. [2:49]

Transdisciplinarity: Concerns that which is at once between the disciplines, across different disciplines, and beyond all disciplines. Its goal is (a) the understanding of the present world, of which one of the imperatives is the unity of knowledge, and (b) the solution of mega and complex problems by drawing on and seeking to integrate disciplinary and stakeholder views on the basis of some overarching theory. [1:21]

Transformation: A technique used to modify concepts or assumptions that are not merely different (e.g., love, fear, selfishness) but opposite (e.g., rational, irrational) into continuous variables. [11:343]

Triangulation of research methodology: An approach to research that involves using multiple data-gathering techniques (usually three) to investigate the same problem/system/process. In this way, findings can be cross-checked, validated, and confirmed. [7:216]

Tribes: An anthropological metaphor used to describe the disciplines, each having its own culture and language. [2:50]

University: An institution of higher learning that provides teaching and research and is authorized to grant academic degrees. [2:46]

Variable: Something that can take on different values or assume different attributes—it is something that varies. [12:358]

Wide interdisciplinarity: Draws on disciplines that are epistemologically farther apart (e.g., art history and mathematics). [11:331]

References _____

Ackerson, L. G. (2007). Introduction. In L. G. Ackerson (Ed.), *Literature search strategies for interdisciplinary research: A sourcebook for scientists and engineers* (pp. vii–xvii). Lanham, MD: Scarecrow Press.

Adams, L. S. (1996). *The methodologies of art: An introduction.* Boulder, CO: Westview Press.

Agger, B. (1998). *Critical social theories: An introduction.* Boulder, CO: Westview Press.

Akers, R. (1994). *Criminological theories: Introduction, evaluation and application.* Los Angeles: Roxbury.

Alford, R. R. (1998). *The craft of inquiry: Theories, methods, evidence.* New York: Oxford University Press.

Alliance for Childhood. (1999). *Fool's gold: A critical look at computers in childhood.* Retrieved July 14, 2011, from http://www .allianceforchildhood.net

Alvesson, M. (2002). *Postmodernism and social research.* Philadelphia: Open University Press.

Alvesson, M., & Sköldberg, K. (2000). *Reflexive methodology: New vistas for qualitative research.* Thousand Oaks, CA: Sage.

American Sociological Association. (n.d.). *Society and social life.* Retrieved July 18, 2011, from http://www.asanet.org/employment/ society.cfm

Anderson, C. (2001). Knowledge, politics, and interdisciplinary education. In B. L. Smith & J. McCann (Eds.), *Collaborative learning, and experimentation in higher education* (pp. 454–465). Bolton, MA: Anker.

Anderson, J. R. (1982). Acquisition of cognitive skill. *Psychological Review, 89,* 369–406.

Anderson, L. W., Krathwohl, D. R., Airasian, P. W., Cruikshank, K. A., Mayer, R. E., Pintrich, P. R., et al. (2000). *Taxonomy for learning, teaching, and assessing: A revision of Bloom's taxonomy of educational objectives* (2nd rev. ed.). Boston: Allyn & Bacon.

Arms, L. A. (2005). *Mathematics and religion: Processes of faith and reason.* Unpublished manuscript, Western College Program, Miami of Ohio University.

Armstrong, F. H. (1980). Faculty development through interdisciplinarity. *The Journal of General Education, 32*(1), 52–63.

*Arthurs, A. (1993). The humanities in the 1990s. In A. Levine (Ed.), *Higher learning in America, 1980–2000* (pp. 259–272). Baltimore: The Johns Hopkins University Press.

Association of American Colleges. (1991). *Interdisciplinary studies* (Vol. 2: Reports from the field). Washington, DC: Author.

Association of American Colleges and Universities. (2004). *Greater expectations: A new vision for learning as a nation goes to college.* Washington, DC: Author.

Association of American Colleges and Universities. (2007). *College learning for the new global century.* Washington, DC: Author.

Atkinson, J., & Malcolm Crowe, M. (Eds.). (2006). *Interdisciplinary research: Diverse* approaches in science, technology, health and society. West Sussex, England: John Wiley & Sons.

Atran, S. (2003a, March 7). Genesis of suicide terrorism. *Science, 299*, 1534–1539.

Atran, S. (2003b). *Genesis and future of suicide terrorism.* Retrieved August 14, 2006, from http://interdisciplines.org/terrorism/papers/1

Atran, S. (2005, July 8). *Genesis and future of suicide terrorism: Discussion.* Retrieved July 18, 2011, from http://www.interdisciplines.org/archives.php

Babbie, E. (2004). *The practice of social research* (10th ed). Belmont, CA: Wadsworth/Thompson Learning.

Baca, J. F. (1994). Whose monument where: Public art in a many-cultured society. In R. M. Carp (Ed.), *Saber es poder/Interventions* (n.p.). Los Angeles: Adobe LA.

Bailis, S. (2001). Contending with complexity: A response to William H. Newell's "A Theory of Interdisciplinary Studies." *Issues in Integrative Studies, 19*, 27–42.

Bailis, S. (2002). Interdisciplinary curriculum design and instructional innovation: Notes on the social science program at San Francisco State University. In C. Haynes (Ed.), *Innovations in interdisciplinary teaching* (pp. 3–15). Westport, CT: Oryx Press.

Bakhtin, M. M. (1981). *The dialogic imagination: Four essays.* Austin: University of Texas Press.

*Bal, M. (1996). *Double exposures: The subject of cultural analysis.* New York: Routledge.

Bal, M. (1999). Introduction. In M. Bal (Ed.), *The practice of cultural analysis: Exposing interdisciplinary interpretation* (pp. 1–14). Stanford, CA: Stanford University Press.

Bal, M. (2002). *Traveling concepts in the humanities: A rough guide.* Buffalo, NY: University of Toronto Press.

Bal, M., & Bryson, N. (1991). Semiotics and art history. *The Art Bulletin, 73*(2), 174–208.

Baldick, C. (2004). *The concise dictionary of literary terms* (Reissue ed.). New York: Oxford University Press.

Baloche, L., Hynes, J. L., & Berger, H. A. (1996). Moving toward the integration of

professional and general education. *Action in Teacher Education, 18*, 1–9.

Bammer, G. (2005). Integration and integration sciences: Building a new specialization. *Ecology and Society 10*(2), 6.

Bandura, A. (1998). Mechanism of moral disengagement. In W. Reich (Ed.), *Origins of terrorism: Psychologies, ideologies, theologies, states of mind* (pp. 161–191). Washington, DC: Woodrow Wilson Center Press.

*Barnard, A., & Spencer, J. (Eds.). (1996). *Encyclopedia of social and cultural anthropology.* New York: Routledge.

Barnet, S. (2008). *A short guide to writing about art* (9th ed.). Upper Saddle River, NJ: Pearson Prentice Hall.

Baum, J. (2002, Fall). Toward a new integrative field: "Strategic organization." *Rotman Magazine,* 21–22.

Beauchamp, T. L., & Childress, J. F. (2001). *Principles of biomedical ethics* (5th ed.). Oxford, UK: Oxford University Press.

Becher, T. (1989). *Academic tribes and territories: Intellectual enquiry and the cultures of disciplines.* Milton Keynes, UK: Open University Press.

Becher, T., & Trowler, P. R. (2001). *Academic tribes and territories* (2nd ed.). Buckingham, UK: The Society for Research into Higher Education & Open University Press.

*Bechtel, W. (1986). The nature of scientific integration. In W. Bechtel (Ed.), *Integrating scientific disciplines* (pp. 3–52). Dordrecht, the Netherlands: Martinus Nojhoff.

Bechtel, W. (2000). From imagining to believing: Epistemic issues in generating biological data. In R. Creath & J. Maienschein (Eds.), *Biology and epistemology* (pp. 138–163). Cambridge, UK: Cambridge University Press.

Bell, J. A. (1998). Overcoming dogma in epistemology. *Issues in Integrative Studies, 16*, 99–119.

Bender, T. (1997). Politics, intellect, and the American University, 1945–1995. In T. Bender & C. E. Schorske (Eds.), *American academic culture in transformation: Fifty years, four disciplines* (pp. 17–54). Princeton, NJ: Princeton University Press.

Bennington, G. (1999). Inter. In M. McQuillan, G. MacDonald, R. Purves, & S. Thompson (Eds.), *Post-theory: New directions in criticism* (pp. 103–119). Edinburgh, Scotland: Edinburgh University Press.

Berg, B. L. (2004). *Qualitative research methods for the social sciences* (5th ed.). Boston: Pearson Education.

Bernard, H. R. (2002). *Research methods in anthropology: Qualitative and quantitative methods* (3rd ed.). New York: AltaMira Press.

Berthoff, A. (1981). *The making of meaning: Metaphors, models, and maxims for writing teachers.* Upper Montclair, NJ: Boynton.

Bishop, A. P. (1999). Document structure and digital libraries: How researchers mobilize information in journal articles. *Information Processing and Management, 35*(3), 255–279.

Bishop, M. (1970). *The middle ages.* New York: American Heritage Press.

Blackburn, S. (1999). *Think: A compelling introduction to philosophy.* Oxford, UK: Oxford University Press.

*Blau, J. R. (2001). Preface. In J. R. Blau (Ed.), *The Blackwell companion to sociology* (pp. x–xvi). Malden, MA: Blackwell.

Blesser, B., & Salter, L. R. (2007). *Spaces speak, are you listening?* Cambridge, MA: The MIT Press.

Bloom, B. S. (Ed.). (1956). *Taxonomy of educational objectives, handbook 1: Cognitive domain.* Boston: Addison Wesley.

*Bogdan, R., & Taylor, S. J. (1975). *Introduction to qualitative research methods.* New York: Wiley.

*Bohlman, P. V. (1996). Epilogue: Music and canons. In K. Bergeron & P. V. Bohlman (Eds.), *Disciplining music: Musicology and its canons* (pp. 197–210). Chicago: University of Chicago Press.

Boix Mansilla, V. (2002, October). *Approaches to ID inquiry.* PowerPoint presented at the Association for Integrative Studies Annual Convention, Springfield, MO.

Boix Mansilla, V. (2005, January/February). Assessing student work at disciplinary crossroads. *Change, 37,* 14–21.

*Boix Mansilla, V. (2006). Interdisciplinary work at the frontier: An empirical examination of expert interdisciplinary epistemologies. *Issues in Integrative Studies, 24,* 1–31.

Boix Mansilla, V. (2009). *Learning to synthesize: A cognitive-epistemological foundation for interdisciplinary learning.* Retrieved July 18, 2011, from pzweb.harvard.edu/interdisciplinary/pdf/VBM_Synthesize_2009.pdf

Boix Mansilla, V., Duraisingh, E. D., Wolfe, C., & Haynes, C. (2009, May/June). Targeted assessment rubric: An empirically grounded rubric for interdisciplinary writing. *The Journal of Higher Education, 80*(3), 334–353.

Boix Mansilla, V., & Gardner, H. (2003). Assessing interdisciplinary work at the frontier: An empirical exploration of "symptoms of quality" (GoodWork Project Report Series, Number 26). Retrieved July 18, 2011, from http://www.goodworkproject.org/wp-content/uploads/2010/10/26-Assessing-ID-Work-2_04.pdf

Boix Mansilla, V., Miller, W. C., & Gardner, H. (2000). On disciplinary lenses and interdisciplinary work. In S. Wineburg & P. Gossman (Eds.), *Interdisciplinary curriculum: Challenges to implementation* (pp. 17–38). New York: Teachers College, Columbia University.

Booth, W. C., Columb, G. G., & Williams, J. M. (2003). *The craft of research* (2nd ed.). Chicago: University of Chicago Press.

Borgman, C. L., Smart, L. J., Millwood, K. A., Finley, J. R., Champeny, L. Gilliland, A. J., et al. (2005). Comparing faculty information seeking in teaching and research: Implications for the design of digital libraries. *Journal of the American Society for Information Science and Technology, 56*(6), 636–657.

Boulding, K. (1981). *A preface to grants economics: The economy of love and fear.* New York: Praeger.

Boyd, I. (2006). Studying complexity: Are we approaching the limits of science? In J. Atkinson & M. Crowe (Eds.), *Interdisciplinary research: Diverse approaches on science, technology, health and society* (pp. 25–40). West Sussex, UK: John Wiley & Sons.

The Boyer Commission. (1998). *Reinventing undergraduate education: A blueprint for America's research universities*. Washington, DC: The Carnegie Foundation for the Advancement of Teaching.

Boyer, E. I. (1981). The quest for common learning. In *Common learning: A Carnegie colloquium on general education* (pp. 3–21). Washington, DC: The Carnegie Foundation for the Advancement of Teaching.

Bradsford, J. D., Brown, A. L., & Cocking, R. R. (Eds.). (1999). *How people learn: Brain, mind, experience, and school*. Washington, DC: National Academy Press.

Bressler, C. E. (2003). *Literary criticism: An introduction to theory and practice* (3rd ed). Upper Saddle River, NJ: Pearson Education.

Briggs, A., & Micard, G. (1972). Problems and solutions. In *Interdisciplinarity: Problems of teaching and research in universities* (pp. 185–299). Paris: Center for Educational Research and Innovation.

Brint, S. G., Turk-Bicacakci, L., Proctor, K., and Murphy, S. P. (2009). Expanding the social frame of knowledge: Interdisciplinarity, degree-granting fields in American colleges and universities, 1975–2000. *Review of Higher Education, 32*(2), 155–183.

Bromme, R. (2000). Beyond one's own perspective: The psychology of cognitive interdisciplinarity. In P. Weingart & N. Stehr (Eds.), *Practising interdisciplinarity* (pp. 115–133). Toronto: University of Toronto Press.

Brough, J. A., & Pool, J. E. (2005). Integrating learning and assessment: The development of an assessment culture. In J. Etim (Ed.), *Curriculum Integration K–12: Theory and practice* (pp. 196–204). Lanham, MD: University Press of America.

Brown, R. H. (1989). Textuality, social science, and society. *Issues in Integrative Studies, 7,* 1–19. Cited in S. Henry & N. L. Bracy (2012). Integrative theory in criminology applied to the complex social problem of school violence. In A. F. Repko, W. H.

Newell, & R. Szostak (Eds.), *Case studies in interdisciplinary research* (pp. 259–282). Thousand Oaks, CA: Sage.

Bruun, H., & Toppinen, A. (2004). Knowledge of science and innovation: A review of three discourses on the institutional and cognitive foundations of knowledge production. *Issues in Integrative Studies, 22,* 1–51.

Bryman, A. (2004). *Social research methods* (2nd ed). New York: Oxford University Press.

Burke, P. (1991). Overture: The new history, its past and its future. In P. Burke (Ed.), *New perspectives in historical writing* (pp. 1–23). University Park: Pennsylvania State University Press.

Businessweek. (2006, September 12). *Breaking down silos at Yale*. Retrieved December 14, 2009, from http://www.businessweek.com/bschools/content/sep2006/bs20060912_091596.htm

Caldwell, L. K. (1983). Environmental studies: Discipline or metadiscipline? *Environmental Professional, 5,* 247–259.

Calhoun, C. (Ed.). (2002). *Dictionary of the social sciences*. Oxford, UK: Oxford University Press.

Calhoun, C., & Marrett, C. (2003). Foreword. In F. Kessel, P. L. Rosenfield, & N. B. Anderson (Eds.), *Expanding the boundaries of health and social science: Case studies in interdisciplinary innovation* (pp. v–vii). New York: Oxford University Press.

*Capps, W. H. (1995). *Religious studies: The making of a discipline*. Minneapolis, MN: Augsburg Fortress.

Carey, S. S. (2003). *A beginner's guide to scientific method* (2nd ed.). Belmont, CA: Wadsworth.

Carlisle, B. (1995, June/July). Music and life. *American Music Teacher, 44,* 10–13.

Carp, R. M. (2001). Integrative praxes: Learning from multiple knowledge formations. *Issues in Integrative Studies, 19,* 71–121.

Caruso, D., & Rhoten, D. (2001, April). *Lead, follow, get out of the way: Sidestepping the barriers to effective practice of interdisciplinarity*. San Francisco: The Hybrid Vigor Institute.

Clark, H. H. (1996). *Using language.* Cambridge, MA: Cambridge University Press.

Colwell, R. (1998, September 3). *The National Science Foundation's role in the Arctic.* Retrieved December 14, 2009, www.nsf.gov/news/speeches/colwell/rc80903.htm

Connor, M. A. (2012). The metropolitan problem in interdisciplinary perspective. In A. F. Repko, W. H. Newell, & R. Szostak (Eds.), *Case studies in interdisciplinary research* (pp. 53–90). Thousand Oaks, CA: Sage.

*Coppola, B. P., & Jacobs, D. C. (2006). Is the scholarship of teaching and learning new to chemistry? In M. Taylor Huber & S. P. Morreale (Eds.), *Disciplinary styles in the scholarship of teaching and learning: Exploring common ground* (pp. 197–216). Stanford, CA: The Carnegie Foundation.

Cornwell, G. H., & Stoddard, E. W. (2001). Toward an interdisciplinary epistemology: Faculty culture and institutional change. In B. L. Smith & J. McCann (Eds.), *Reinventing ourselves: Interdisciplinary education, collaborative learning, and experimentation in higher education* (160–178). Bolton, MA: Anker.

Crenshaw, M. (1998). The logic of terrorism: Terrorist behavior as a product of strategic choice. In W. Reich (Ed.), *Origins of terrorism: Psychologies, ideologies, theologies, states of mind* (pp. 7–24). Washington, DC: Woodrow Wilson Center Press.

Creswell, J. W. (1997). *Qualitative inquiry and research design: Choosing among five traditions.* Thousand Oaks, CA: Sage.

Creswell, J. W. (2002). *Research design: Qualitative, quantitative, and mixed methods approaches* (2nd ed.). Thousand Oaks, CA: Sage.

Csikszentmihalyi, M., & Sawyer, K. (1995). Creative insight: The social dimension of a solitary moment. In R. Sternberg & J. Davidson (Eds.), *The nature of insight* (pp. 329–363). Cambridge: The MIT Press.

Cullenberg, S., Amariglio, J., & Ruccio, D. (2001). Introduction. In S. Cullenberg, J. Amariglio, & D. Ruccio (Eds.), *Postmodernism, economics and knowledge* (pp. 3–57). New York: Routledge.

Czuchry, M., & Dansereau, D. F. (1996). Node-link mapping as an alternative to traditional writing assignments in undergraduate courses. *Teaching of Psychology, 23,* 91–96.

Dabrowski, I. J. (1995). David Bohm's theory of the implicate order: Implications for holistic thought processes. *Issues in Integrative Studies, 13,* 1–12.

Davidson, C., & Goldberg, D. (2004). Engaging the humanities. *MLA: Profession,* 42–62.

Davis, G. A. (1992). *Creativity is forever* (3rd ed.). Dubuque, IA: Kendall/Hunt.

Davis, J. R. (1995). *Interdisciplinary courses and team teaching: New arrangements for learning.* Phoenix, AZ: American Council on Education, Oryx.

Davis, W. (1978). *The act of interpretation: A critique of literary reason.* Chicago: University of Chicago Press.

Delph, J. B. (2005). *An integrative approach to the elimination of the "perfect crime."* Unpublished manuscript, University of Texas at Arlington.

Denzin, N. K. (1978). *The research act.* New York: McGraw-Hill.

Denzin, N. K., & Lincoln, Y. S. (Eds.). (2005). *The SAGE handbook of qualitative research* (3rd ed.). Thousand Oaks, CA: Sage.

Derry, S. J., Schunn, C. D., & Gernsbacher, M. A. (Eds.). (2005). *Interdisciplinary collaboration: An emerging cognitive science.* Mahwah, NJ: Erlbaum.

De Saint-Exupéry, A. (2000). *The little prince.* New York: Harcourt.

Dessalles, J. (2007). *Why we talk: The evolutionary origins of language* (J. Grieve, Trans). Oxford, UK: Oxford University Press.

DeZure, D. (1999). Interdisciplinary teaching and learning. *Teaching Excellence, 10*(3), 1–3.

Dietrich, W. (1995). *Northwest passage: The great Columbia River.* Seattle: University of Washington Press.

Dogan, M., & Pahre, R. (1989). Fragmentation and recombination of the social sciences. *Studies in Comparative International Development, 24,* 56–73.

Dogan, M., & Pahre, R. (1990). *Creative marginality: Innovation at the intersections of the social sciences*. Boulder, CO: Westview Press.

Dölling, I., & Hark, S. (2000). She who speaks shadow speaks truth: Transdisciplinarity in women's and gender studies. *Signs, 25*(4), 1195–1198.

Dominowski, R. L., & Ballob, P. (1995). Insights and problem solving. In R. Sternberg & J. Davidson (Eds.), *The nature of insight* (pp. 33–62). Cambridge: The MIT Press.

Donald, J. (2002). *Learning to think: Disciplinary perspectives*. San Francisco: Jossey-Bass.

Dorsey, D., Campbell, G., Foster, L., & Miles, D. (1999). Assessing knowledge structures: Relations with experience and post training performance. *Human Performance, 12*(1), 31–57.

Dorsten, L. E., & Hotchkiss, L. (2005). *Research methods and society: Foundations of social inquiry*. Upper Saddle River, NJ: Prentice-Hall.

Dow, S. (2001). Modernism and postmodernism: A dialectical analysis. In S. Cullenberg, J. Amariglio, & D. F. Ruccio (Eds.), *Postmodernism, economics and knowledge* (pp. 61–101). New York: Routledge.

Dunbar, R. (1996). *Grooming, gossip and the evolution of language*. Cambridge, MA: Harvard University Press.

Easton, D. (1991). The division, integration, and transfer of knowledge. In D. Easton & C. S. Schelling (Eds.), *Divided knowledge: Across disciplines, across cultures* (pp. 7–36). Newbury Park, CA: Sage.

Education for Change, Ltd., SIRU at the University of Brighton, and the Research Partnership. (2002). *Researchers' use of libraries and other information sources: Current patterns and future trends*. London: Higher Education Funding Council for England. Retrieved January 25, 2010, from http://www.rslg.ac.uk/research/libuse/LUrep1.pdf

Eilenberg, S. (1999). Voice and ventriloquy in "The Rime of the Ancient Mariner." In P. H. Fry (Ed.), *Samuel Taylor Coleridge: The rime of the ancient mariner* (pp. 282–314). Boston: Bedford/St. Martin's.

Elliott, D. J. (2002). Philosophical perspectives on research. In R. Colwell & C. Richardson (Eds.), *The new handbook of research on music teaching and learning* (pp. 85–102). Oxford: Oxford University Press.

*Ember, C. R., & Ember, M. (2004). *Cultural anthropology* (11th ed.). Upper Saddle River, NJ: Prentice-Hall.

Engel, D., & Antell, K. (2004). The life of the mind: A study of faculty spaces in academic libraries. *College & Research Libraries, 65*(1), 8–26.

Englehart, L. (2005). *Organized environmentalism: Towards a shift in the political and social roles and tactics of environmental advocacy groups*. Unpublished manuscript, Miami of Ohio University.

Etzioni, A. (1988). *The moral dimension: Towards a new economics*. New York: Free Press.

Evans, J. (2008). Electronic publication and the narrowing of science and scholarship. *Science, 321*(5887), 395–399. Retrieved January 12, 2010, from http://www.sciencemag.org/cgi/content/full/sci;321/5887/395

Ferguson, F. (1999). Coleridge and the deluded reader: "The Rime of the Ancient Mariner." In P. H. Fry (Ed.), *Samuel Taylor Coleridge: The rime of the ancient mariner* (pp. 113–130). Boston: Bedford/St. Martin's.

Fernie, E. (1995). Glossary of concepts. In E. Fernie (Ed.), *Art history and its methods: A critical anthology* (pp. 323–368). London: Phaidon Press.

Field, M., Lee, R., & Field, M. L. (1994). Assessing interdisciplinary learning. *New Directions in Teaching and Learning, 58*, 69–84.

Fiscella, J. B. (1989). Access to interdisciplinary information: Setting the problem. *Issues in Integrative Studies, 7*, 73–92.

Fiscella, J. B., & Kimmel, S. E. (Eds.). (1999). *Interdisciplinary education: A guide to resources*. New York: The College Board.

Fischer, C. C. (1988). On the need for integrating occupational sex discrimination theory on the basis of causal variables. *Issues in Integrative Studies, 6*, 21–50.

Fish, S. (1991). Being interdisciplinary is so very hard to do. *Issues in Integrative Studies, 9*, 97–125.

Foisy, M. (2010). *Creating meaning in everyday life: An interdisciplinary understanding.* Unpublished manuscript, University of Alberta, Canada.

Foster, A. (2004). A nonlinear model of information-seeking behavior. *Journal of the American Society for Information Science and Technology, 55*(3), 228–237.

Foster, H. (1998). Trauma studies and the interdisciplinary: An overview. In A. Coles & A. Defert (Eds.), *The anxiety of interdisciplinarity* (pp. 157–168). London: BACKless Books.

*Frank, R. (1988). "Interdisciplinarity": The first half century. In E. G. Stanly & T. F. Hoad (Eds.), *WORDS: For Robert Burchfield's sixty-fifth birthday* (pp. 91–101). Cambridge, UK: D. S. Brewer.

*Frank, R. H. (1988). *Passions within reason: The strategic role of emotions.* New York: Norton.

Frankfort-Nachmias, C., & Nachmias, D. (2008). *Research methods in the social sciences* (7th ed.). New York: Worth.

Friedman, S. S. (2001). Academic feminism and interdisciplinarity. *Feminist Studies, 27*(2), 504–509.

Frodeman, R., Klein, J. T., Mitcham, C., & Holbrook, J. B. (Eds.). (2010). *The Oxford handbook of interdisciplinarity.* New York: Oxford University Press.

Frug, G. E. (1999). *City making: Building communities without building walls.* Princeton, NJ: Princeton University Press.

Fry, P. H. (Ed.). (1999). *Samuel Taylor Coleridge: The rime of the ancient mariner.* Boston: Bedford/St. Martin's.

Fuchsman, K. (2009), Rethinking integration in interdisciplinary studies. *Issues in Integrative Studies, 27*, 70–85.

Fuller, S. (1993). The position: Interdisciplinarity as interpenetration. In *Philosophy, rhetoric, and the end of knowledge: The coming of science and technology studies* (pp. 33–65). Madison: University of Wisconsin Press.

Fussell, S. G., & Kraus, R. M. (1991). Accuracy and bias in estimates of others' knowledge. *European Journal of Social Psychology, 21*, 445–454.

Fussell, S. G., & Kraus, R. M. (1992). Coordination of knowledge in communication: Effects of speakers' assumptions about what others know. *Journal of Personality and Social Psychology, 62*, 378–391.

Gaff, J. G., Ratcliff, J. L., & Associates. (Eds.). (1997). *Handbook of the undergraduate curriculum: A comprehensive guide to purposes, structures, practices, and change.* San Francisco: Jossey-Bass.

Galinsky, A. D., & Moskowitz, G. B. (2000). Perspective-taking: Decreasing stereotype expression, stereotype accessibility, and in-group favoritism. *Journal of Personality and Social Psychology, 78*(4), 708–724.

Gallagher, C., & Greenblatt, S. (2000). *Practicing new historicism.* Chicago and London: The University of Chicago Press.

Garber, M. (2001). *Academic instincts.* Princeton: Princeton University Press.

Gardner, H. (1999). *The disciplined mind: What all students should understand.* New York: Simon & Schuster.

Gardner, H. (2008). *Five minds for the future.* Boston, MA: Harvard Business Press.

Gauch, H. G., Jr. (2002). *Scientific method in practice.* Cambridge, UK: Cambridge University Press.

Geertz, C. (1980). Blurred genres: The reconfiguration of social thought. *The American Scholar, 49*(2), 165–179.

Geertz, C. (1983). *Local knowledge: Further essays in interpretative anthropology.* New York: Basic Books.

Geertz, C. (2000). The strange estrangement: Charles Taylor and the natural sciences. In C. Geertz (Ed.), *Available light: Anthropological reflections on philosophical topics* (pp. 143–159). Princeton, NJ: Princeton University Press.

Gerber, R. (2001). The concept of common sense in the workplace learning and experience. *Education + Training, 43*(2), 72–81.

Gerdes, E. P. (2002). Disciplinary dangers. *Liberal Education, 88*(3), 48–55.

Gerring, J. (2001). *Social science methodology: A critical framework*. Boston: Cambridge University Press.

Giere, R. N. (1999). *Science without laws*. Chicago: University of Chicago Press.

Giri, A. K. (2002). The calling of a creative transdisciplinarity. *Futures, 34*(1), 103–116.

Goldenberg, S. (1992). *Thinking methodologically*. New York: Harper Collins.

Goldsmith, T. E., & Johnson, P. J. (1990). A structural assessment of classroom learning. In R. W. Schvaneveldt (Ed.), *Pathfinder associative networks: Studies in knowledge organization* (pp. 241–254). Norwood, NJ: Ablex.

*Goldsmith, T., & Kraiger, K. (1996). Applications of structural knowledge assessment to training and evaluation. In J. K. Ford, S. Kozlowski, K. Kraiger, E. Salas, & M. Teachout (Eds.), *Improving training effectiveness in work organizations* (pp. 73–97). Mahwah, NJ: Erlbaum.

Goodin, R. E., & Klingerman, H. D. (Eds.). (1996). A new handbook of political science. New York: Oxford University Press.

Grace, N. (1996). An exploration of the interdisciplinary character of women's studies. *Issues in Integrative Studies, 14,* 59–86.

Graff, G. (1987). *Professing literature: An institutional history*. Chicago: University of Chicago Press.

Grayling, A. C. (1995). Introduction. In A. C. Grayling (Ed.), *Philosophy: A guide through the subject* (pp. 1–6). New York: Oxford University Press.

Graziano, A. M., & Raulin, M. L. (2004). *Research methods: A process of inquiry* (5th ed.). Boston: Pearson Education Group.

Gregorian, V. (2004, June 4). Colleges must reconstruct the unity of knowledge. *The Chronicle of Higher Education,* 12–14.

Griffin, G. (2005). Research methods for English studies: An introduction. In G. Griffin (Ed.), *Research methods for English studies* (pp. 1–16). Edinburgh, Scotland: Edinburgh University Press.

Gunn, G. (1992). Interdisciplinary studies. In J. Gibaldi (Ed.), *Introduction to scholarship in modern languages and literatures* (pp. 239–261). New York: Modern Language Association.

Hacking, I. (2004). *The complacent disciplinarian*. Retrieved July 18, 2011, from https://apps.lis.illinois.edu/wiki/download/attachments/2656520/Hacking.complacent.pdf

Hagan, F. E. (2005). *Essentials of research methods in criminal justice and criminology*. Boston: Allyn & Bacon.

Hall, D. J., & Hall, I. (1996). *Practical social research: Project work in the community*. Basingstoke, UK: Macmillan.

Halloran, L. (2009, May 31). *Gay activists, Black ministers seek common ground*. National Public Radio.

Halpern, D. F. (1996). *Thought and knowledge* (3rd ed.). Mahwah, NJ: Erlbaum.

Harris, E. (1997). The arts. In J. G. Gaff, J. L. Ratcliff, & Associates (Eds.), *Handbook of the undergraduate curriculum: A comprehensive guide to purposes, structures, practices, and change* (pp. 320–340). San Francisco: Jossey-Bass.

Harris, J. (2001). *The new art history: A critical introduction*. New York: Routledge.

Hart, C. (1998). *Doing a literature review: Releasing the social science research imagination*. Thousand Oaks, CA: Sage.

*Harvard University Committee on the Objectives of a General Education in a Free Society. (1945). *General education in a free society*. Cambridge, MA: Author.

Haskins, C. H. (1940). *The rise of universities*. New York: Peter Smith.

Hatfield, E., & Rapson, R. (1996). *Love & sex: Cross-cultural perspectives*. Boston: Allyn & Bacon.

Haynes, C. (2002). Introduction: Laying a foundation for interdisciplinary teaching. In C. Haynes (Ed.), *Innovations in interdisciplinary teaching* (pp. xi–xxii). Westport, CT: Oryx Press.

Hemminger, B. M., Lu, D., Vaughn, K. T. L., & Adams, S. J. (2007). Information seeking behavior of academic scientists. *Journal of the American Society for Information Science and Technology, 58*(14), 2205–2225.

*Hendershott, A. B., & Wright, S. P. (1997). The social sciences. In J. G. Gaff,

J. L. Ratcliff, & Associates (Eds.), *Handbook of the undergraduate curriculum: A comprehensive guide to purposes, structures, practices, and change* (pp. 301–319). San Francisco: Jossey-Bass.

Henry, S. (2005). Disciplinary hegemony meets interdisciplinary ascendancy: Can interdisciplinary/integrative studies survive and if so, how? *Issues in Integrative Studies, 23,* 1–37.

Henry, S. (2009). School violence beyond Columbine: A complex problem in need of an interdisciplinary analysis. *American Behavioral Scientist, 52*(8), 1–20.

Henry, S., & Bracy, N. L. (2012). Integrative theory in criminology applied to the complex social problem of school violence. In A. F. Repko, W. H. Newell, & R. Szostak (Eds.), *Case studies in interdisciplinary research* (pp. 259–282). Thousand Oaks, CA: Sage.

Hershberg, T. (1981). The new urban history: Toward an interdisciplinary history of the city. In T. Hershberg (Ed.), *Philadelphia: Work, space, family, and group experience in the nineteenth century* (pp. 3–42). New York and Oxford, UK: Oxford University Press.

Hirst, P. H. (1974). *Knowledge and the curriculum: A collection of philosophical papers.* London: Routledge & Kegan Paul.

Holmes, F. L. (2000). The logic of discovery in the experimental life sciences. In R. Creath & J. Maienschein (Eds.), *Biology and epistemology* (pp. 167–190). Cambridge, UK: Cambridge University Press.

Hopkins, P. (1992). Simulating Hamlet in the classroom. *Systems Dynamic Review, 8*(1), 91–98.

Horiuchi, Y. (2003). Alice in systems wonderland: A children's systems learning guidebook accompanying Alice's adventures in wonderland. *World Futures, 59*(1), 37–50.

Hoskin, K. W. (1993). Education and the genesis of disciplinarity: The unexpected reversal. In E. Messer-Davidow, D. R. Shumway, & D. J. Sylvan (Eds.), *Knowledges: Historical and critical studies in disciplinarity* (pp. 271–304). Charlottesville and London: University Press of Virginia.

*Houtz, J. C., & Patricola, C. (1999). Imagery. In M. A. Runco & S. R. Prentky (Eds.), *Encyclopedia of creativity* (Vol. 2, pp. 1–11). San Diego, CA: Academic Press.

Howell, M., & Prevenier, W. (2001). *From reliable sources: An introduction to historical methods.* Ithaca, NY: Cornell University Press.

Huber, M. T., & Hutchings, P. (2004). *Integrative learning: Mapping the terrain.* Washington, DC: The Association of American Colleges and Universities.

Huber, M. T., & Morreale, S. P. (2002). Situating the scholarship of teaching and learning: A cross-disciplinary conversation. In M. T. Huber & S. P. Morreale (Eds.), *Disciplinary styles in the scholarship of teaching and learning: Exploring common ground* (pp. 1–24). Stanford, CA: The Carnegie Foundation.

*Huffman, K., Vernoy, M., & Vernoy, J. (2000). *Psychology in action* (5th ed.). New York: John Wiley & Sons.

Humpreys, A. H., Post, T. R., & Ellis, A. K. (1981). *Interdisciplinary methods: A thematic approach.* Santa Monica, CA: Goodyear.

Hursh, B., Haas, P., & Moore, M. (1983). An interdisciplinary model to implement general education. *Journal of Higher Education, 54*(1), 42–59.

*Hutcheon, L., & Hutcheon, M. (2001). A convenience of marriage: Collaboration and interdisciplinarity. *PMLA, 116*(5), 1364–1376.

Hutcheson, P. A. (1997). Structures and practices. In J. G. Gaff, J. L. Ratcliff, & Associates (Eds.), *Handbook of the undergraduate curriculum: A comprehensive guide to purposes, structures, practices, and change* (pp. 100–117). San Francisco: Jossey-Bass.

Hyland, K. (2004). *Disciplinary discourses: Social interactions in academic writing.* Ann Arbor: University of Michigan Press.

Hyneman, C. S. (1959). *The study of politics: The present state of American political science.* Champaign: University of Illinois Press.

Iggers, G. G. (1997). *Historiography in the twentieth century: From scientific objectivity to postmodern challenges.* Middletown, CT: Wesleyan University Press.

Ivanitskaya, L., Clark, D., Montgomery, G., & Primeau, R. (2002). Interdisciplinary learning: Process and outcomes. *Innovative Higher Education, 27*(2), 95–111.

Karlqvist, A. (1999). Going beyond disciplines: The meanings of interdisciplinarity. *Policy Sciences, 32,* 379–383.

*Kassabian, A. (1997). Introduction: Music, disciplinarity, and interdisciplinarities. In D. Schwarz, A. Kassabian, & L. Siegel (Eds.), *Keeping score: Music, disciplinarity, culture* (pp. 1–10). Charlottesville: University Press of Virginia.

Katz, C. (2001). Disciplining interdisciplinarity. *Feminist Studies, 27*(2), 519–525.

Keestra, M. (2012). Understanding human action: Integrating meanings, mechanisms, causes, and contexts. In A. F. Repko, W. H. Newell, & R. Szostak (Eds.), *Case studies in interdisciplinary research* (pp. 225–258). Thousand Oaks, CA: Sage.

Kelly, J. S. (1996). Wide and narrow interdisciplinarity. *The Journal of Education, 45*(2), 95–113.

Klee, R. (1997). *Introduction to the philosophy of science.* New York: Oxford University Press.

*Klee, R. (1999). Introduction. In R. Klee (Ed.), *Scientific inquiry: Readings in the philosophy of science* (pp. 1–4). New York: Oxford University Press.

Klein, J. T. (1990). *Interdisciplinarity: History, theory and practice.* Detroit, MI: Wayne State University Press.

Klein, J. T. (1996). *Crossing boundaries: Knowledge, disciplinarities, and interdisciplinarities.* Charlottesville: University Press of Virginia.

Klein, J. T. (1999). *Mapping interdisciplinary studies.* Number 13 in the Academy in Transition series. Washington, DC: Association of American Colleges and Universities.

Klein, J. T. (2000a). A conceptual vocabulary of interdisciplinary science. In P. Weingart &

N. Stehr (Eds.), *Practising interdisciplinarity* (pp. 3–24). Toronto: University of Toronto Press.

Klein, J. T. (2000b). Voices of Royaumont. In M. J. Somerville & D. J. Rapport (Eds.), *Transdisciplinarity: Recreating integrated knowledge* (pp. 3–14). Oxford, UK: EOLSS.

Klein, J. T. (2001). Interdisciplinarity and the prospect of complexity: The tests of theory. *Issues in Integrative Studies, 19,* 43–57.

Klein, J. T. (2003). Unity of knowledge and transdisciplinarity: Contexts and definition, theory, and the new discourse of problem-solving. *Encyclopedia of Life Support Systems.* Retrieved July 15, 2011, from http://www.eolss.net/

Klein, J. T. (2005a). *Humanities, culture, and interdisciplinarity: The changing American academy.* Albany: State University of New York Press.

Klein, J. T. (2005b). Interdisciplinary teamwork: The dynamics of collaboration and integration. In S. J. Derry, C. D. Schunn, & M. A. Gernsbacher (Eds.), *Interdisciplinary collaboration: An emerging cognitive science* (pp. 23–50). Mahwah, NJ: Erlbaum.

Klein, J. T. (2010). *Creating interdisciplinary campus cultures: A model for strength and sustainability.* San Francisco: Jossey-Bass.

Klein, J. T. (2012). Research integration: A comparative knowledge base. In A. F. Repko, W. H. Newell, & R. Szostak (Eds.), *Case studies in interdisciplinary research* (pp. 283–298). Thousand Oaks, CA: Sage.

Klein, J. T., & Newell, W. H. (1997). Advancing interdisciplinary studies. In J. G. Gaff, J. L. Ratcliff, & Associates (Eds.), *Handbook of the undergraduate curriculum: A comprehensive guide to purposes, structures, practices, and change* (pp. 393–415). San Francisco: Jossey-Bass.

Klein, J. T., & Newell, W. H. (2002). Strategies for using interdisciplinary resources across K–16. *Issues in Integrative Studies, 20,* 139–160.

Kockelmans, J. J. (1979). Why interdisciplinarity. In J. J. Kockelmans (Ed.), *Interdisciplinarity and higher education* (pp. 123–160). University Park and London: The Pennsylvania State University Press.

Korazim-Korosy, Y., & Butterfield, A. K. (2007). Interdisciplinary community development from international perspectives: An introduction. In Alice K. Butterfield and Yossi Korazim-Korosy (Eds.), *Interdisciplinary community development: International perspectives* (pp. 1–12). Binghampton, NY: Haworth Press.

Kuhn, T. (1996). *The structure of scientific revolutions* (3rd ed.). Chicago: University of Chicago Press.

Kuklick, B. (1985). The professionalization of the humanities. In D. Callahan, A. L. Caplan, & B. Jennings (Eds.), *Applying the humanities* (pp. 41–54). New York: Plenum Press.

Lake, K. (1994). Integrated curriculum. In *School improvement research series* (Closeup #16). Retrieved September 9, 2007, from http://www.nwrel.org/scpd/sirs/8/c016.html

Lakoff, G., & Johnson, M. (1980). *Metaphors we live by.* Chicago: University of Chicago Press.

Lanier, M. M., & Henry, S. (2004). *Essential criminology* (3rd ed.). Boulder, CO: Westview.

Larner, J. (1999). *Marco Polo and the discovery of the world.* New Haven, CT: Yale University Press.

*Lasker, G. W., & Mascie-Taylor, C. G. N. (Eds.). (1993). *Research strategies in human biology: Field and survey studies.* Cambridge, UK: Cambridge University Press.

Lattuca, L. (2001). *Creating interdisciplinarity: Interdisciplinary research and teaching among college and university faculty.* Nashville, TN: Vanderbilt University Press.

Leary, M. R. (2004). *Introduction to behavioral research methods* (4th ed.). Boston: Pearson Education.

Lefebvre, H. (1991). *The production of space.* Oxford and Cambridge, UK: Blackwell.

Lenoir, T. (1997). *Instituting science: The cultural production of scientific disciplines* (writing science). Stanford, CA: Stanford University Press.

Leshner, A. I. (2004, February 6). Science at the leading edge. *Science, 303*(5659), 729.

*Levin, H. L. (2003). *The earth through time.* Hoboken, NJ: John Wiley & Sons.

Levy, F., & Murnane, R. (2004). *The new division of labor: How computers are creating the next job market.* Princeton, NJ: Princeton University Press; New York: Russell Sage Foundation.

Lewis, B. (2002, January). What went wrong? *The Atlantic Monthly, 289,* 1. Retrieved July 25, 2002, from http://www.theatlantic.com/doc/200201/lewis

Lewis, J. (2009). *The failure of public education to educate a diverse population.* Unpublished manuscript.

Li, T. (2000). *Social science reference sources.* Westport, CT: Greenwood Press.

Long, D. (2002). *Interdisciplinarity and the English school of international relations.* Paper presented at the International Studies Association Annual Convention, New Orleans, March 25–27.

Longo, G. (2002). The constructed objectivity of the mathematics and the cognitive subject. In M. Mugur-Schachter & A. van der Merwe (Eds.), *Quantum mechanics, mathematics, cognition and action* (pp. 433–462). Boston: Kluwer Academic.

Lyman, P. (1997). Liberal education in cyberia. In R. Orrill (Ed.), *Education and democracy: Re-imagining liberal learning in America* (pp. 299–320). New York: College Entrance Board.

Lyon, A. (1992, October). Interdisciplinarity: Giving up territory. *College English, 54*(6), 681–693.

Lyotard, J. (1984). *The postmodern condition: A report on knowledge.* Minneapolis: University of Minnesota.

*Mackey, J. L. (2001). Another approach to interdisciplinary studies. *Issues in Integrative Studies, 19,* 59–70.

*Mackey, J. L. (2002). Rules are not the way to do interdisciplinarity: A response to Szostak. *Issues in Integrative Studies, 20,* 123–129.

Magnus, D. (2000). Down the primrose path: Competing epistemologies in early twentieth-century biology. In R. Creath & J. Maienschein (Eds.), *Biology and epistemology* (pp. 91–121). Cambridge, UK: Cambridge University Press.

Maienschein, J. (2000). Competing epistemologies and developmental biology. In R. Creath & J. Maienschein (Eds.), *Biology and epistemology* (pp. 122–137). Cambridge, UK: Cambridge University Press.

Manheim, J. B., Rich, R. C., Willnat, L., & Brians, C. L. (2006). *Empirical political analysis: Research methods in political science* (6th ed.). Boston: Pearson Education.

Marsh, D., & Furlong, P. (2002). A skin, not a sweater: Ontology and epistemology in political science. In D. Marsh & G. Stoker (Eds.), *Theory and methods in political science* (2nd ed., pp. 17–41). New York: Palgrave Macmillan.

Marshall, C., & Rossman, G. B. (2006). *Designing qualitative research*. Thousand Oaks, CA: Sage.

Marshall, D. G. (1992). Literary interpretation. In J. Gibaldi (Ed.), *Introduction to scholarship in modern languages and literatures* (pp. 159–182). New York: The Modern Language Association of America.

Martin, R., Thomas, G., Charles, K., Epitropaki, O., & McNamara, R. (2005). The role of leader-member exchanges in mediating the relationship between locus of control and work reactions. *Journal of Occupational and Organizational Psychology, 78,* 141–147.

Mathews, L. G., & Jones, A. (2008). Using systems thinking to improve interdisciplinary learning outcomes. *Issues in Integrative Studies 26,* 73–104.

Maurer, B. (2004). Models of scientific inquiry and statistical practice: Implications for the structure of scientific knowledge. In M. L. Taper & S. R. Lee (Eds.), *The nature of scientific evidence: Statistical, philosophical, and empirical considerations* (pp. 17–31). Chicago: University of Chicago Press.

Mayer, R. E. (1995). The search for insight: Grappling with Gestalt psychology's unanswered questions. In R. E. Sternberg & J. Davidson (Eds.), *The nature of insight* (pp. 3–32). Cambridge: The MIT Press.

Mayr, E. (1997). *This is biology*. Cambridge, MA: Harvard University Press.

Mayville, W. V. (1978). *Interdisciplinarity: The mutable paradigm*. Washington DC: The Association of American Colleges and Universities.

McCall, R. B. (1990). Promoting interdisciplinarity and faculty-service-provider relations. *American Psychology, 45,* 1319–1324.

McDonald, D., Bammer, G., & Deane, P. (2009). Research integration using dialogue methods. ANU E-Press. Retrieved July 15, 2011, from http://i2s.anu.edu.au/i2s-publications/dialogue-book

McKeon, R. P. (1964). The liberating and humanizing arts in education. In A. A. Cohen (Ed.), *Humanistic education and western civilization* (pp. 159–181). New York: Holt, Rinehart, & Winston.

McKim, V. R. (1997). Introduction. In V. R. McKim, S. P. Turner, & S. Turner (Eds.), *Causality in crisis? Statistical methods and the search for causal knowledge in the social sciences*. Notre Dame, IN: University of Notre Dame Press.

Meadows, D. H. (1999). *Leverage points: Places to intervene in a system*. Hartland, VT: The Sustainability Institute.

Mehl, J., Gulick, W., & Cree, C. (1987, Fall). Open forum: Towards a functional definition of the humanities. *Humanities Education,* 3–15.

Mepham, B. (2000). A framework for the ethical analysis of novel foods: The ethical matrix. *Journal of Agricultural and Environmental Ethics, 12*(2), 165–176.

Merari, A. (1998). The readiness to kill and die: Suicidal terrorism in the Middle East. In W. Reich (Ed.), *Origins of terrorism: Psychologies, ideologies, theologies, states of mind* (pp. 192–210). Washington, DC: Woodrow Wilson Center Press.

Miles, M. B., & Huberman, M. (1994). *Qualitative data analysis: An expanded sourcebook* (2nd ed.). Thousand Oaks, CA: Sage.

Miller, A. I. (1996). *Insights of genius: Imagery and creativity in science and art*. Cambridge: The MIT Press.

Miller, R. C. (1982). Varieties of interdisciplinary approaches in the social sciences. *Issues in Integrative Studies, 1,* 1–37.

Minor, V. H. (2001). *Art history's history* (2nd ed.). Upper Saddle River, NJ: Prentice Hall.

Modiano, R. (1999). Sameness or difference? Historicist readings of "The Rime of the Ancient Mariner." In P. H. Fry (Ed.), *Samuel Taylor Coleridge: The rime of the ancient mariner* (pp. 187–219). Boston: Bedford/St. Martin's.

Monroe, K. R., & Kreidie, L. H. (1997). The perspective of Islamic fundamentalists and the limits of rational choice theory. *Political Psychology, 18*(1), 19–43.

Moran, J. (2010). *Interdisciplinarity* (2nd ed.). New York: Routledge.

Motes, M. A., Bahr, G. S., Atha-Weldon, C., & Dansereau, D. F. (2003). Academic guide maps for learning psychology. *Teaching of Psychology, 30*(3), 240–242.

Murfin, R. C. (1999a). Deconstruction and "The Rime of the Ancient Mariner." In P. H. Fry (Ed.), *Samuel Taylor Coleridge: The rime of the ancient mariner* (pp. 261–282). Boston: Bedford/St. Martin's.

Murfin, R. C. (1999b). Marxist criticism and "The Rime of the Ancient Mariner." In P. H. Fry (Ed.), *Samuel Taylor Coleridge: The rime of the ancient mariner* (pp. 131–147). Boston: Bedford/St. Martin's.

Murfin, R. C. (1999c). The new historicism and "The Rime of the Ancient Mariner." In P. H. Fry (Ed.), *Samuel Taylor Coleridge: The rime of the ancient mariner* (pp. 168–186). Boston: Bedford/St. Martin's.

Murfin, R. C. (1999d). Psychoanalytic criticism and "The Rime of the Ancient Mariner." In P. H. Fry (Ed.), *Samuel Taylor Coleridge: The rime of the ancient mariner* (pp. 220–238). Boston: Bedford/St. Martin's.

Murfin, R. C. (1999e). Reader-response criticism and "The Rime of the Ancient Mariner." In P. H. Fry (Ed.), *Samuel Taylor Coleridge: The rime of the ancient mariner* (pp. 97–113). Boston: Bedford/St. Martin's.

Myers, C., & Haynes, C. (2002). Transforming undergraduate science through interdisciplinary inquiry. In C. Haynes (Ed.), *Innovations in interdisciplinary teaching* (pp. 179–197). Phoenix, AZ: American Council on Education/The Oryx Press.

Myers, D. G. (2002). *Intuition: Its powers and perils.* New Haven & London: Yale University Press.

Nagy, C. (2005). *Anthropogenic forces degrading tropical ecosystems in Latin America: A Costa Rican case study.* Unpublished manuscript, Miami of Ohio University.

National Academy of Sciences, National Academy of Engineering, & Institute of Medicine. (2005). *Facilitating interdisciplinary research.* Washington, DC: National Academies Press.

*National Center for Educational Statistics. (2003). *The condition of education 2003.* Washington, DC: Department of Education.

National Research Council. (2002, April 17). *Connecting quarks with the cosmos: Eleven science questions for the new century.* Washington, DC: The National Academies Press. Retrieved October 3, 2007, from http://www.nap.edu/catalog.php?record_id=10079_

*Nehamas, A. (1997). Trends in recent American philosophy. In T. Bender, C. E. Schorske, & S. R. Graubard (Eds.), *American academic culture* (pp. 227–241). Princeton, NJ: Princeton University Press.

Neuman, W. L. (2006). *Social research methods: Qualitative and quantitative approaches* (6th ed.). Boston: Pearson Education.

*Newell, W. H. (1989). Strong sense critical thinking. *CT News, 8*(1), 1–4.

Newell, W. H. (1990). Interdisciplinary curriculum development. *Issues in Integrative Studies, 8,* 69–86.

Newell, W. H. (1992). Academic disciplines and undergraduate interdisciplinary education: Lessons from the school of interdisciplinary studies at Miami University, Ohio. *European Journal of Education, 27*(3), 211–221.

Newell, W. H. (1998). Professionalizing interdisciplinarity. In W. H. Newell (Ed.), *Interdisciplinarity: Essays from the literature* (pp. 529–563). New York: College Entrance Examination Board.

*Newell, W. H. (2000). Transdisciplinarity reconsidered. In M. Somerville & D. J. Rapport

(Eds.), *Transdisciplinarity: Recreating integrated knowledge* (pp. 42–48). Oxford, UK: EOLSS.

Newell, W. H. (2001). A theory of interdisciplinary studies. *Issues in Integrative Studies, 19*, 1–25.

Newell, W. H. (2004). Complexity and interdisciplinarity. In L. Douglas Kiel (Ed.), *Encyclopedia of Life Support Systems* (EOLSS). Oxford, UK: EOLSS. Retrieved October 20, 2006, from http://www.eolss.net

Newell, W. H. (2007a). Decision making in interdisciplinary studies. In G. Morçöl (Ed.), *Handbook of decision making* (pp. 245–264). New York: Marcel-Dekker.

Newell, W. H. (2007b). Distinctive challenges of library-based research and writing: A guide. *Issues in Integrative Studies, 25*, 84–110. Retrieved July 15, 2011, from http://www.units.muohio.edu/aisorg/PUBS/ISSUES/toc25.shtml

Newell, W. H. (2007c). Six arguments for agreeing on a definition of interdisciplinary studies. *Association for Integrative Studies Newsletter, 29*(4), 1–4.

Newell, W. H. (2012). Conclusion. In A. F. Repko, W. H. Newell, & R. Szostak (Eds.), *Case studies in interdisciplinary research* (pp. 299–314). Thousand Oaks, CA: Sage.

Newell, W. H., & Green, W. J. (1982). Defining and teaching interdisciplinary studies. *Improving College and University Teaching, 30*(1), 23–30.

Newman, D. M. (2004). *Sociology: Exploring the architecture of everyday life* (5th ed.). Thousand Oaks, CA: Pine Forge Press.

Newman, K., Fox, S. C., Harding, D. J., Mehta, J., & Roth, W. (2004). *Rampage: The social roots of school shootings*. New York: Basic Books.

Nicholas, D., Huntington, P., & Jamali, H. R. (2007). The use, users, and role of abstracts in the digital scholarly environment. *The Journal of Academic Librarianship, 33*(4), 446–453.

Nicholas, D., Huntington, P., Williams, P., & Dobrowolski, T. (2004). Re-appraising information seeking behavior in a digital environment: Bouncers, checkers, returnees

and the like. *Journal of Documentation, 60*(1), 24–43.

Nicolescu, B. (2007). *Transdisciplinarity as methodological framework for going beyond the science-religion debate*. Metanexus Institute. Retrieved July 15, 2011, from http://www.metanexus.net/magazine/tabid/68/id/10013/Default.aspx

Nikitina, S. (2002). "Navigating the disciplinary fault lines" in science and in the classroom: Undergraduate neuroscience classroom in mind, brain, and behavior at Harvard. *Issues in Integrative Studies, 20*, 27–44.

Nikitina, S. (2005). Pathways of interdisciplinary cognition. *Cognition and Instruction, 23*(3), 389–425.

Nikitina, S. (2006). Three strategies for interdisciplinary teaching: Contextualization, conceptualization, and problem-centering. *Journal of Curriculum Studies, 38*(3), 251–271.

Nissani, M. (1995). Fruits, salads, and smoothies: A working definition of interdisciplinarity. *Journal of Educational Thought, 29*, 119–126.

Novak, J. D. (1998). *Learning, creating, and using knowledge: Concept maps as facilitative tools in schools and corporations*. Mahwah, NJ: Lawrence Erlbaum Associates.

Novick, P. (1998). *That noble dream: The "objectivity question" and the American historical profession*. New York: Cambridge University Press.

Nussbaum, M. C. (1985). Historical conceptions of the humanities and their relationship to society. In D. Callahan, A. L. Caplan, & B. Jennings (Eds.), *Applying the humanities* (pp. 3–28). New York: Plenum Press.

Oblinger, D. G., & Verville, A. (1998). *What business wants from higher education*. Westport, CT: Oryx Press.

Organisation for Economic Co-operation and Development. (1972). *Interdisciplinarity: Problems of teaching and research in universities*. Paris: Author.

Palmer, C. L. (1999). Structures and strategies of interdisciplinary science. *Journal of the*

American Society for Information Science, 50(3), 242–253.

Palmer, C. L. (2001). Work at the boundaries of science: Information and the interdisciplinary research process. Boston: Kluwer Academic.

Palmer, C. L. (2010). Information research on interdisciplinarity. In R. Frodeman, J. T. Klein, C. Mitcham, & J. B. Holbrook (Eds.), *The Oxford handbook of interdisciplinarity* (pp. 174–188). New York: Oxford University Press.

Palmer, C. L., & Neuman, L. J. (2002). The information work of interdisciplinary humanities scholars: Exploration and translation. *The Library Quarterly,* 72(1), 85–117.

Palmer, C. L., Teffeau, L. C., & Pirmann, C. M. (2009). *Scholarly information practices in an online environment: Themes from the literature and implications for library service development.* Dublin, OH: Online Computer Literacy Center.

Palys, T. (1997). *Research decisions: Quantitative and qualitative perspectives.* Toronto: Harcourt Brace.

Pasler, J. (1997). Directions in musicology. *Acta Musicologica,* 69(1), 16–21.

Paternoster, R., & Bachman, R. (Eds.). (2001). *Explaining criminals and crime.* Los Angeles: Roxbury.

*Peck, J. M. (1989). There's no place like home? Remapping the topography of German studies. Special issue interdisciplinary theory and methods. *German Quarterly,* 62(2), 178–187.

*Peterson's College Search. (2006). *Four-Year Colleges.* Florence, KY: Author. Retrieved July 18, 2011, from http://www.petersons. com/college-search/college-guide-four-year. aspx

Petrie, H. (1976). Do you see what I see? The epistemology of interdisciplinary inquiry. *Journal of American Education,* 10, 29–43.

Pinnock, C. (1994). Feminist epistemology: Implications for philosophy of science. *Philosophy of Science,* 61, 646–657.

Pohl, C., van Kerkhoff, L., Hadorn, G. H., & Bammer, G. (2008). Integration. In G. H.

Harorn, H. Hoffman-Riem, S. Biber-Klemm, W. Grossenbacher-Mansuy, D. Joy, C. Pohl, U. Wiesmann, & E. Zemp (Eds.), *Handbook of transdisciplinary research* (pp. 411–426). Berlin Heidelberg: Springer.

Polkinghorne, J. (1996). *Beyond science: The wider human context.* Cambridge, UK: Cambridge University Press.

Popham, W. J. (1997). What's wrong—and what's right—with rubrics. *Educational Leadership,* October, 72–75.

Post, G. M. (1998). Terrorist psycho-logic: Terrorist behavior as a product of psychological forces. In W. Reich (Ed.), *Origins of terrorism: Psychologies, ideologies, theologies, states of mind* (pp. 25–40). Washington, DC: Woodrow Wilson Center Press.

Preziosi, D. (1989). *Rethinking art history: Meditations on a coy science.* New Haven, CT: Yale University Press.

Quinn, G. P., & Keough, M. J. (2002). *Experimental design and data analysis for biologists.* Cambridge, UK: Cambridge University Press.

Rapoport, D. C. (1998). Sacred terror: A contemporary example from Islam. In W. Reich (Ed.), *Origins of terrorism: Psychologies, ideologies, theologies, states of mind* (pp. 103–130). Washington, DC: Woodrow Wilson Center Press.

Rashdall, H. (1936). *The universities in Europe in the middle ages* (Vol. 1). London: Oxford University Press.

Reese, W. L. (1980). *The dictionary of philosophy and religion.* New York: Prometheus Books.

Reich, R. B. (1991). *The work of nations.* New York: Borzoi Book, published by Alfred A. Knopf.

Reisberg, D. (2006). *Cognition: Exploring the science of the mind* (3rd ed.). New York: Norton.

Remler, D. K., & van Ryzin, G. G. (2011). *Research methods in practice: Strategies for description and causation.* Thousand Oaks, CA: Sage.

Repko, A. F. (2005). *Interdisciplinary practice: A student guide to research and writing.* Boston: Pearson Custom.

Repko, A. F. (2006). Disciplining interdisciplinarity: The case for textbooks. *Issues in Integrative Studies, 24,* 112–142.

*Repko, A. F. (2007). Integration interdisciplinarity: How the theories of common ground and cognitive interdisciplinarity are informing the debate on interdisciplinary integration. *Issues in Integrative Studies, 25,* 1–31.

Repko, A. F. (2008). Assessing interdisciplinary learning outcomes. *Academic Exchange Quarterly, 12*(Fall), 171–178.

Repko, A. F. (2012). Integrating theory-based insights on the causes of suicide terrorism. In A. F. Repko, W. H. Newell, & R. Szostak (Eds.), *Case studies in interdisciplinary research* (pp. 125–157). Thousand Oaks, CA: Sage.

Repko, A. F., Newell, W. H., & Szostak, R. (Eds.). (2012). *Case studies in interdisciplinary research.* Thousand Oaks, CA: Sage.

Reshef, N. (2008). Writing research reports. In C. Frankfort-Nachmias & D. Nachmias (Eds.), *Research methods in the social sciences* (7th ed.). New York: Worth.

Rhoten, D. (2004). *Interdisciplinary research: Trend or transition.* Retrieved January 16, 2009, from http://www.ncar.ucar.edu/ Director/survey/Interdisciplinary%20 Research%20Trend%200r%20Transition. v2.pdf

Rhoten, D., Boix Mansilla, V., Chun, M., & Klein, J. T. (2006). *Interdisciplinary education at liberal arts institutions.* Brooklyn, NY: Social Science Research Council. Retrieved June 16, 2011, from http://www. teaglefoundation.org/learning/pdf/2006_ ssrc_whitepaper.pdf

Richards, D. G. (1996). The meaning and relevance of "synthesis" in interdisciplinary studies. *The Journal of Education, 45*(2), 114–128.

Rivkin, J. (2005). The strategic importance of integrative skills. *Rotman Magazine* (Winter), 42–43.

Rogers, Y., Scaife, M., & Rizzo, A. (2005). Interdisciplinarity: An emergent or engineered process? In S. J. Derry, C. D. Schunn, & M. A. Gernsbacher (Eds.), *Interdisciplinary collaboration: An emerging cognitive science* (pp. 265–285). Mahwah, NJ: Lawrence Erlbaum Associates.

Root-Bernstein, R. S., & Root-Bernstein, M. (1999). *Sparks of genius: The 13 thinking tools of the world's most creative people.* New York: Houghton Mifflin Co.

Rosenau, P. M. (1992). *Post-modernism and the social sciences: Insights, inroads, and intrusions.* Princeton, NJ: Princeton University Press.

Rosenberg, A. (2000). *Philosophy of science* (2nd ed.). New York: Routledge.

Saffle, M. (2005). The humanities. In M. K. Herndon (Ed.), *An introduction to interdisciplinary studies* (pp. 11–27). Dubuque, IA: Kendall/Hunt.

Salmon, M. H. (1997). Ethical considerations in anthropology and archeology: Or, relativism and justice for all. *Journal of Anthropological Research, 53,* 47–63.

Salter, L., & Hearn, A. (1996). Introduction. In L. Salter & A. Hearn (Eds.), *Outside the lines: Issues in interdisciplinary research* (pp. 3–15). Montreal: McGill-Queen's University Press.

Saxe, J. G. (1963). *The blind men and the elephant.* New York: McGraw-Hill.

Schatz , B., Mischo, W., Clole, T., Bishop, A., Harum, S., Johnson, E., et al. (1999). Federated search of scientific literature. *IEEE Computer, 32*(2), 51–59.

Scheurich, J. J. (1997). *Research method in the postmodern.* Washington, DC: The Falmer Press.

Schneider, C. G. (2010). Foreword. In J. T. Kline (Ed.), *Creating interdisciplinary campus cultures: A model for strength and sustainability* (pp. xiii–xvii). San Francisco: John Wiley & Sons.

Schoenfeld, K. (2005). *Customer service: The ultimate return policy.* Unpublished manuscript, Miami of Ohio University.

Schulman, L. S. (2002). Foreword. In M. Taylor Huber & S. P. Morreale (Eds.), *Disciplinary styles in the scholarship of teaching and learning: Exploring common ground* (pp. v–ix). Menlo Park, CA: American Association for Higher Education.

Seabury, M. B. (2002). Writing in interdisciplinary courses: Coaching integrative thinking. In C. Haynes (Ed.), *Innovations in interdisciplinary teaching* (pp. 38–64). Westport, CT: Oryx Press.

Seabury, M. B. (2004). Scholarship about interdisciplinarity: Some possibilities and guidelines. *Issues in Integrative Studies, 22,* 52–84.

Searing, S. E. (1992). How libraries cope with interdisciplinarity: The case of women's studies. *Issues in Integrative Studies, 10,* 7–25.

Seipel, M. (2002). *Interdisciplinarity: An introduction.* Retrieved July 15, 2011, from http://www2.truman.edu/~mseipel/

Sewell, W. H. (1989). Some reflections on the golden age of interdisciplinary social psychology. *Social Psychology Quarterly, 52*(2), 88–97.

*Shin, U. (1986). The structure of interdisciplinary knowledge: A Polanyian view. *Issues in Integrative Studies, 4,* 93–104.

Shoemaker, D. J. (1996). *Theories of delinquency: An examination of explanations of delinquent behavior* (3rd ed.). New York: Oxford University Press.

Shulman, L. (1998). Course anatomy: The dissection and analysis of knowledge through teaching. In P. Hutchings (Ed.), *The course portfolio: How faculty can examine their teaching to advance practice and improve student learning* (pp. 5–12). Washington, DC: American Association for Higher Education.

Silberberg, M. S. (2006). *Chemistry: The molecular nature of matter and change* (4th ed.). Boston: McGraw-Hill.

Sill, D. (1996). Integrative thinking, synthesis, and creativity in interdisciplinary studies. *Journal of General Education, 45*(2), 129–151.

Silver, L. (2005). *Composing race and gender: The appropriation of social identity in fiction.* Unpublished manuscript, Miami of Ohio University.

Silverman, D. (2000). *Doing qualitative research: A practical handbook.* London: Sage.

Simpson, D. (1999). How Marxism reads "The Rime of the Ancient Mariner." In P. H. Fry (Ed.), *Samuel Taylor Coleridge: The rime of the ancient mariner* (pp. 148–167). Boston: Bedford/St. Martin's.

*Sjoberg, G., & Nett, R. (1968). *A methodology for social research.* New York: Harper & Row.

*Smelser, N. J., & Swedberg, R. (Eds.). (2005). *The handbook of economic sociology* (2nd ed.). Princeton, NJ: Princeton University Press.

Smolinski, W. J. (2005). *Freshwater scarcity in Texas.* Unpublished manuscript, University of Texas at Arlington.

Snow, C. P. (1964). *The two cultures.* London: Cambridge University Press.

Society for Industrial and Organization Psychology. (1998). *Perspective-taking.* Retrieved July 18, 2011, from home.ubalt.edu/tmitch/641/LMX%20Theory.ppt

Sokolowski, R. (1998). The method of philosophy: Making distinctions. *The Review of Metaphysics, 51*(3), 1–11.

Somerville, M. A., & Rapport, D. J. (Eds.). (2000). *Transdisciplinarity: Recreating integrated knowledge.* Oxford, UK: EOLSS.

Somit, A., & Tanenhaus, J. (1967). *The development of American political science.* Boston: Allyn & Bacon.

Spanner, D. (2001). Border crossings: Understanding the cultural and informational dilemmas of interdisciplinary scholars. *The Journal of Academic Librarianship, 27*(5), 352–360.

Spooner, M. (2004). Generating integration and complex understanding: Exploring the use of creative thinking tools within interdisciplinary studies. *Issues in Integrative Studies, 22,* 85–111.

Squires, G. (1975). *Interdisciplinarity: A report by the group for research and innovation.* London: Group for Research and Innovation, Nuffield Foundation.

Stanford Encyclopedia of Philosophy. (2010). "Implicature." Retrieved July 15, 2011, from http://plato.stanford.edu/entries/implicature/

Steels, L. (2008). Is sociality a prerequisite for the emergence of language? In R. Botha & C. Knight (Eds.), *The prehistory of language* (pp. 36–57). Oxford, UK: Oxford University Press.

Steffen, W., Sanderson, A., Jager, J., Tyson, P. D., Moore, B., Matson, P. A., et al. (2004). *Global change and the earth system: A planet under pressure.* the Netherlands: Springer.

Stember, M. (1991). Advancing the social sciences through the interdisciplinary enterprise. *The Social Science Journal, 28*(1), 1–14.

Sternberg, R. J. (1996). *Successful intelligence: How practical and creative intelligence determine success in life.* New York: The Penguin Group.

Stoddard, E. R. (1991). Frontiers, borders, and border segmentation: Toward a conceptual clarification. *Journal of Borderlands Studies, 6*(1), 1–22.

Stoker, G., & Marsh, D. (2002). Introduction. In D. Marsh & G. Stoker (Eds.), *Theory and methods in political science* (2nd ed., pp. 1–16). New York: Palgrave Macmillan.

Stoll, C. (1999). *High-tech heretic: Why computers don't belong in the classroom and other reflections by a computer contrarian.* New York: Doubleday.

Stoller, P. (1997). *Sensuous scholarship.* Philadelphia: University of Pennsylvania Press.

Stone, J. R. (1998). Introduction. In J. R. Stone (Ed.), *The craft of religious studies* (pp. 1–17). New York: St. Martin's Press.

Struppa, D. C. (2002). The nature of interdisciplinarity. *Perspectives: The Journal of the Association of General and Liberal Studies, 30*(1), 97–105.

Sturgeon, S., Martin, M. G. F., & Grayling, A. C. (1995). Epistemology. In A. C. Grayling (Ed.), *Philosophy 1: A guide through the subject* (pp. 7–60). New York: Oxford University Press.

Swoboda, W. W. (1979). Disciplines and interdisciplinarity: A historical perspective. In J. J. Kockelmans (Ed.), *Interdisciplinarity and higher education* (pp. 49–92). University Park: Pennsylvania State University Press.

Szostak, R. (2002). How to do interdisciplinarity: Integrating the debate. *Issues in Integrative Studies, 20,* 103–137.

Szostak, R. (2004). *Classifying science: Phenomena, data, theory, method, practice.* Dordrecht: Springer.

*Szostak, R. (2006). Economic history as it is and should be: Toward an open, honest, methodologically flexible, theoretically diverse, interdisciplinary exploration of the causes and consequences of economic growth. *Journal of Socio-Economics, 35*(4), 727–750.

Szostak, R. (2007a). How and why to teach interdisciplinary research practice. *Journal of Research Practice, 3*(2), Article M17. Retrieved February 25, 2011, from http://jrp.icaap.org/index.php/jrp/article/view/912/89

Szostak, R. (2007b). Modernism, postmodernism, and interdisciplinarity. *Issues in Integrative Studies, 25,* 32–83.

Szostak, R. (2009). *The causes of economic Growth: Interdisciplinary perspectives.* Berlin: Springer.

Szostak, R. (2012). An interdisciplinary analysis of the causes of economic growth. In A. F. Repko, W. H. Newell, & R. Szostak (Eds.), *Case studies in interdisciplinary research* (pp. 159–189). Thousand Oaks, CA: Sage.

Taffel, A. (1992). *Physics: Its methods and meanings* (6th ed.). Upper Saddle River, NJ: Prentice Hall.

Taper, M. L., & Lele, S. R. (2004). The nature of scientific evidence: A forward-looking synthesis. In M. L. Taper & S. R. Lele (Eds.), *The nature of scientific evidence: Statistical, philosophical, and empirical considerations* (pp. 527–551). Chicago: University of Chicago Press.

Tashakkori, A., & Teddlie, C. B. (1998). *Mixed methodology: Combining quantitative and qualitative approaches.* Thousand Oaks, CA: Sage.

Tayler, M. R. (2012). Jewish marriage as an expression of Israel's conflicted identity. In A. F. Repko, W. H. Newell, & R. Szostak (Eds.), *Case studies in interdisciplinary research* (pp. 23–51). Thousand Oaks, CA: Sage.

Tenopir, C., King, D. W., Boyce, P., Grayson, M., & Paulson, K. L. (2005). Relying on electronic journals: Reading patterns of astronomers. *Journal of the American Society for Information Science and Technology, 56*(8), 786–802.

Thornberry, P. T. (1989). Reflections on the advantages and disadvantages of theoretical elaboration. In S. F. Messner, M. D. Krohn, & A. E. Liska (Eds.), *Theoretical integration in the study of deviance and crime* (pp. 51–60). Albany: State University of New York Press.

Toynton, R. (2005). Degrees of disciplinarity in equipping students in higher education for engagement and success in life long learning. *Active Learning in Higher Education,* 6(2), 106–117.

Tress, B., Tress, G., & Fry, G. (2006). Defining concepts and the process of knowledge production in integrative research. In B. Tress, G. Tress, G. Fry, & P. Opdam (Eds.), *From landscape research to landscape planning: Aspects of integration, education, and application* (pp. 13–25). Dordrecht, Netherlands: Springer.

Tress, B., Tress, G., Fry, G., & Opdam, P. (Eds.). (2006). *From landscape research to landscape planning: Aspects of integration, education, and application.* Dordrecht, Netherlands: Springer.

Trow, M. (1984). Interdisciplinary studies as a counterculture: Problems of birth, growth and survival. *Issues in Integrative Studies,* 4, 1–15.

University of Minnesota Libraries. (2006). *A multidimensional framework for academic support: A final report.* New York: Andrew W. Mellon Foundation.

*U.S. Department of Health and Human Services, National Institutes of Health. (2003, September 30). NIH announces strategy to accelerate medical research progress. *NIH News.* Washington, DC: Author. Retrieved July 18, 2011, from http://www.nih.gov/news/pr/sep2003/od-30.htm

USA Today. (2009). New push in Congress for common ground on abortion. Retrieved July 16, 2011, from http://www.usatoday.com/news/religion/2009-07-23-abortion-congress_N.htm

van der Lecq, R. (2012). Why we talk: An interdisciplinary approach to the evolutionary origin of language. In A. F. Repko, W. H. Newell, & R. Szostak (Eds.), *Case studies in interdisciplinary research* (pp. 191–223). Thousand Oaks, CA: Sage.

*Vars, G. (2002). Educational connoisseurship, criticism, and the assessment of integrative studies. *Issues in Integrative Studies, 20,* 65–76.

*Vernon, P. E. (1989). The nature-nurture problem in creativity. In J. A. Glover, R. R. Ronning, & C. R. Reynolds (Eds.), *Handbook of creativity* (pp. 93–110). New York: Plenum Press.

*Vess, D. (2004). *Explorations in interdisciplinary teaching and learning: A collection of portfolios by Dr. Deborah Vess Carnegie scholar 1999–2000* (pp. 1–10). Retrieved April 9, 2004, from http://www.faculty.de.gcsu.edu/~dvess/ids/courseportfolios/overview.htm

*Vess, D., & Linkon, S. (2002). Navigating the interdisciplinary archipelago: The scholarship of interdisciplinary teaching and learning. In M. Taylor Huber & S. P. Morreale (Eds.), *Disciplinary styles in the scholarship of teaching and learning: Exploring common ground* (pp. 87–106). Washington, DC: American Association for Higher Education and the Carnegie Foundation for the Advancement of Teaching.

Vickers, J. (1998). "[U]framed in open, unmapped fields": Teaching the practice of interdisciplinarity. *Arachne: An Interdisciplinary Journal of the Humanities,* 4(2), 11–42.

Wallace, R. A., & Wolf, A. (2006). *Contemporary sociological theory: Expanding the classical tradition* (6th ed.). Upper Saddle River, NJ: Pearson.

Walvoord, B. E. F., & Anderson, V. J. (1998). *Effective grading: A tool for learning and assessment.* San Francisco: Jossey-Bass.

Wasserstrom, J. N. (2006, January 20). Expanding the I-Word. *The Chronicle of Higher Education,* Section B, B5.

Watson, J. D. (1968). *The double helix: A personal account of the discovery of the structure of DNA.* New York: Simon & Schuster.

Weingart, P. (2000). Introduction. In P. Weingart & N. Stehr (Eds.), *Practising interdisciplinarity* (pp. xi–xvi). Toronto: University of Toronto Press.

Weingast, B. (1998). Political institutions: Rational choice perspectives. In R. Goodin & H. Klingerman (Eds.), *A new handbook of political science* (pp. 167–190). Oxford, UK: Oxford University Press.

*Weisgerber, D. W. (1993). Interdisciplinary searching: Problems and suggested remedies. A report from the ICSTI Group on Interdisciplinary Searching. *Journal of Documentation, 49*(3), 231–254.

Welch, J., IV. (2003). Future directions for interdisciplinarity effectiveness in higher education: A Delphi study. *Issues in Integrative Studies, 21*, 3, 5–6, 170–203.

Welch, J., IV. (2007). The role of intuition in interdisciplinary insight. *Issues in Integrative Studies, 25*, 131–155.

Wentworth, J., & Davis, J. R. (2002). Enhancing interdisciplinarity through team teaching. In C. Haynes (Ed.), *Innovations in interdisciplinary teaching* (pp. 16–37). Westport, CT: Oryx Press.

Wheeler, L., & Miller, E. (1970, October). *Multidisciplinary approach to planning.* Paper presented at Council of Education Facilities Planners 47th Annual Conference in Oklahoma City, OK. (ERIC Document Reproduction Service No. ED044814)

Whitaker, M. P. (1996). Relativism. In A. Barnard & J. Spencer (Eds.), *Encyclopedia of social and cultural anthropology* (pp. 478–482). New York: Routledge.

*White, H. D. (1996). Literature retrieval for interdisciplinary synthesis. *Library Trends, 45*(2), 239–264.

*White, L. M. (1997). The humanities. In J. G. Gaff, J. L. Ratcliff, & Associates (Eds.), *Handbook of the undergraduate curriculum: A comprehensive guide to purposes, structures, practices, and*

change (pp. 262–279). San Francisco: Jossey-Bass.

Wiersma, W., & Jurs, S. G. (2005). *Research methods in education: An introduction.* Boston: Allyn & Bacon.

Wilson, E. O. (1998). *Consilience: The unity of science.* New York: Knopf.

Wilson, L. O. (2006). *Beyond Bloom: A new version of the cognitive taxonomy.* Retrieved July 15, 2011, from http://www.uwsp.edu/education/lwilson/curric/newtaxonomy.htm

Wolfe, C., & Haynes, C. (2003). Interdisciplinary writing assessment profiles. *Issues in Integrative Studies, 21*, 126–169.

Worden, R. (1998). The evolution of language from social intelligence. In J. R. Hurford, M. Studdert-Kennedy, & C. Knight (Eds.), *Approaches to the evolution of language: Social and cognitive bases* (pp. 148–168). Cambridge, UK: Cambridge University Press.

Wyman, B. G., & Randel, J. M. (1998). The relation of knowledge organization to the performance of a complex cognitive task. *Applied Cognitive Psychology, 12*, 251–264.

Xio, H. (2005). *Research methods for English studies.* Edinburgh, Scotland: Edinburgh University Press.

Zajonc, A. (1993). *Catching the light: The entwined history of light and mind.* New York: Bantam.

Zeki, S. (2000). *Inner vision: An exploration of art and the brain.* New York: Oxford University Press.

Zerhouni, E. (2003). NIH roadmap of medical research, *Science,* New Series, *302*(5642), 63–64, 72.

Zetterberg, H. L. (1967). *On theory and verification in sociology* (3rd ed). Totowa, NJ: Bedminster Press.

Author Index _____

Ackerson, L. G., 191(n1)
Adams, L. S., 135, 222(n7)
Adams, S. J., 179
Agger, B., 100, 115, 127
Airasian, P. W., 262
Akers, R., 266, 372
Alford, R. R., 134
Alliance for Childhood, 246
Alvesson, M., 123
Amariglio, J., 122
American Sociological
    Association, 99
Anderson, C., 49, 416
Anderson, L. W., 262
Antell, K., 180
Arms, L. A., 344–345
Armstrong, F. H., 60
Association of American
    Colleges & Universities,
    52, 53
Atha-Weldon, C.,
    150, 151, 153, 156, 165
Atkinson, J., 271
Atran, S., 296, 301,
    305, 342

Babbie, E., 168
Bachman, R., 387
Bahr, G. S., 150, 151,
    153, 156
Bailis, S., 126, 277
Bakhtin, M. M., 269
Bal, M., 15, 83, 88–89, 126,
    135, 214–215, 221(n2),
    231–232, 237–238, 245,
    251, 253–254, 282, 295,
    299–300, 303, 315–316,
    318–319, 340, 384–386,
    432–433

Baldick, C., 140
Ballob, P., 329
Baloche, H. B., 56, 416
Bammer, G., 271, 351
Bandura, A., 235, 236, 367
Barnet, S., 116, 135, 214
Baum, J., 43
Beauchamp, T. L., 350
Becher, T., 50, 99, 101
Bechtel, W., 131
Bell, J. A., 113, 119
Bender, T., 50
Bennington, G., 21–22
Berg, B. L., 207, 208–211,
    221–222(n6)
Berger, H. A., 56, 416
Bernard, H. R., 115, 122, 133
Berthoff, A., 62
Bishop, M., 46
Blackburn, S., 125
Blesser, B., 37, 430–431, 433
Bloom, B. S., 261, 262
Boix Mansilla, V., 14, 15,
    23–24, 25, 57–58, 96,
    288, 407(n1), 411,
    414–415, 417–418,
    422–425, 426, 431
Booth, W. C., 191(n3)
Borgman, C. L., 180
Boulding, K., 345–346
Boyce, P., 181
Boyd, I., 85
Boyer, E. I., 49
Boyer Commission, 40
Bracy, N., 272, 336, 360–361,
    369, 370, 372, 387–392
Bradsford, J. D., 246
Bressler, C. E., 136
Brians, C. L., 123

Briggs, A., 46
Brint, S. G., 32
Bromme, R., 57, 58–59, 59,
    101, 140, 267–268,
    297, 326
Brown, A. L., 246, 336
Bruun, H., 94, 99
Bryman, A., 140, 222(n6)
Bryson, N., 135
Burke, P., 270, 277
Butterfield, A. K., 38

Caldwell, L. K., 9
Calhoun, C., 34, 44, 114, 126
Campbell, G., 417
Carey, S. S., 221(n4)
Carlisle, B., 60
Carnegie Foundation for the
    Advancement of
    Teaching, 52
Carp, R. M., 189, 255
Caruso, D., 37
Champeny, L., 180
Charles, K., 275–276
Childress, J. F., 350
Chun, M., 14, 414, 415
Clark, D., 56, 416, 417
Clark, H. H., 56, 57, 267
Cocking, R. R., 246
Columb, G. G., 191(n3)
Colwell, R., 36–37
Connor, M., 403–407
Cornwell, G. H., 415
Crenshaw, M., 334–335
Creswell, J. W., 222(n8)
Crick, F., 229, 252, 427
Crowe, M., 271
Cruikshank, K. A., 262
Csikszentmihalyi, M., 329

Cuban, L., 246
Cullenberg, S., 122
Czechowski, J.
Czuchry, M., 165

Dabrowski, I. J., 63
Dansereau, D. F., 150, 151,
    153, 156, 165
Davis, G. A., 61, 63
Davis, J. R.
Davis, W., 62
Deane, P., 271, 351
Delph, J. B., 82, 88, 230–231,
    338–339, 386–387, 432
Denzin, N. K., 216, 222(n8)
Derry, S. J., 140, 271
Dessalles, J., 401
Dewey, J., 246
DeZure, D., 37, 53
Dietrich, W., 43, 81, 87,
    194–195, 290
Dobrowolski, T., 180
Dogan, M., 36, 99, 264
Dölling, I., 30
Dominowski, R. L., 329
Donald, J., 121, 127,
    132, 139
Dorsey, D., 417
Dorsten, L. E., 134,
    221(n5)
Dow, S., 115, 133, 137, 138
Dunbar, R., 401–402
Duraisingh, E. D., 411,
    422–425, 431

Easton, D., 48
Eilenberg, S., 309, 312
Elliott, D. J., 111, 117, 118,
    119, 125, 136
Ellis, A. K., 416
Engel, D., 180
Englehart, L., 344, 350
Epitropaki, O., 275–276
Etzioni, A., 343, 347, 350
Evans, J., 179

Ferguson, F., 308, 312
Fernie, E., 253
Field, M., 415
Field, M. L., 415
Finley, J. R., 180
Fiscella, J. B., 174, 177, 178,
    188, 191(n2)

Fischer, C. C., 82, 86, 88,
    200–201, 202–203, 212,
    230, 240–244, 251,
    252–253, 256, 303, 307,
    310–311, 313–315,
    317–318, 319
Fish, S., 54
Foisy, M., 361–363, 427–429
Foster, H., 176, 180, 221(n1)
Foster, L., 417
Foucault, M., 50
Frankfort-Nachmias, C., 118,
    122, 221(n5)
Friedman, S. S., 54
Frodeman, R., xxiii
Frug, G., 406
Fry, G., 271, 419–420, 424–425
Fry, P. H., 201–202, 226,
    307–308, 311–312
Fuchsman, K., 264, 265, 266,
    290–291(n1)
Fuller, S., 26, 38
Furlong, P., 111
Fussell, S. G., 275–276

Gaff, J. G., 100
Garber, M., 139
Gardner, H., 23–24, 25, 41,
    96, 101
Gauch, H. G., 221(n4)
Geertz, C., 34, 58, 139
Gerber, R., 329
Gerdes, E. P., 323–324
Gernsbacher, M. A.,
    140, 271
Gerring, J., 118, 221(n5)
Giere, R. N., 140
Gilliland, A. J., 180
Giri, A. K., 54
Goldenberg, S., 250
Goldsmith, T. E., 416
Goodin, R. E., 115, 123,
    134, 335
Grace, N., 94
Graff, G., 49
Grayling, A. C., 111
Grayson, M., 181
Graziano, A. M., 134
Green, W. J., 4, 55, 139, 286
Gregorian, 41
Griffin, G., 116, 136
Griffin, J. H., 232
Gunn, G., 43, 60

Haas, P., 55, 59, 70, 71, 90
Hacking, I., 98
Hadorn, G. H., 271
Hagan, F. E., 221(n5)
Hall, D. J., 208
Hall, I., 208
Halloran, L., 323
Hark, S., 30
Harris, J., 116, 124
Hart, C., 191(n1)
Haskins, C. H., 46
Hatfield, E., 264
Haynes, C., 59, 77,
    78, 186, 298, 336, 411,
    422–425, 431
Hearn, A., 11, 139
Hemminger, B. M., 179
Henry, S., 58, 64, 272, 336,
    360–361, 369, 370,
    372, 387–392,
    397–399, 434–435
Hershberg, T., 48
Hirst, P. H., 45
Holmes, F. L., 131
Homan, G. C., 370
Horiuchi, Y., 152
Hoskin, K. W., 50
Hotchkiss, L., 134, 221(n5)
Howell, M., 116, 124,
    222(n7)
Huber, M. T., 4, 52, 139
Huberman, M., 222(n7)
Humpreys, A. H., 416
Huntington, P., 180, 181
Hursh, B., 55, 59, 70, 71, 90
Hutcheson, P. A., 49
Hutchings, P., 52
Hyland, K., 265
Hyneman, C. S., 134
Hynes, J. L., 56, 416
Hynes, J. L. Berger, H. A., 56

Iggers, G. G., 136
Innocent III, Pope, 46
Institute of Medicine, 6, 14
Ivanitskaya, L., 56, 416, 417

Jager, J., 121
Jamali, H. R., 181
Johnson, M., 26, 426
Johnson, P. J., 416
Jones, A., 35, 152, 154–159
Jurs, S. G., 221(n5)

Kain, D. L.
Karlqvist, A., 94
Kassabian, A.
Katz, C., 50, 51
Keestra, M., 165
Keller, H., 330–331
Kelly, J. S., 286
Keough, M. J., 121
Kimmel, S. E., 174, 191(n2)
King, D. W., 181
Klee, R., 264
Klein, J. T., 6–7, 9, 14, 19,
    20, 22–23, 24, 26, 27,
    28–29, 30, 32, 36, 43,
    46, 47, 48, 49, 51, 52,
    53, 59, 60, 62, 64, 71,
    72, 87, 90, 100, 101,
    119, 122–124, 127, 255,
    261–263, 278, 279, 280,
    353(n3), 414, 415
Klingerman, H. D., 115, 123,
    134, 335
Kockelmans, J. J., 322, 328
Korazim-Korosy, Y., 38
Krathwohl, D. R., 262
Kraus, R. M., 275–276
Kreidie, L. H., 367–368,
    392–395
Kuhn, T., 329
Kuklick, B., 6

Lake, K., 57
Lakoff, G., 26, 426
Lanier, M. M., 387
Lattuca, L., 29, 47, 112,
    127, 264
Leary, M. R., 115,
    122, 123, 134
Lee, R., 415
Lefebvre, H., 404
Lele, S. R., 141
Lenoir, T., 99
Leshner, A. I., 36
Levy, F., 34
Lewis, J., 429–430, 431
Lincoln, Y. S., 222(n8)
Linkon, S., 4
Long, D., 11
Longo, G., 114
Lu, D., 179
Lyman, P., 70
Lyon, A., 26
Lyotard, J.-F., 113

Magnus, D., 114
Maienschein, J., 112, 131

Manheim, J. B., 123
Marrett, C., 34, 44
Marsh, D., 111, 118
Marshall, C., 124, 222(n7)
Martin, M. G. F., 111, 117,
    125, 275–276
Martin, R., 275, 276
Mathews, L. G., 35, 152,
    154–159
Matson, P. A., 121
Maurer, B., 121
Mayer, R. E., 262
Mayr, E., 265
Mayville, W. V., 50
McCall, R. B., 55
McDonald, D., 271, 351
McKeon, R. P., 49
McKim, V. R., 249
McNamara, R., 275–276
Meadows, 158
Mepham, B., 350–351
Merari, A., 235, 236
Micard, G., 46
Miles, D., 417
Miles, M. B., 222(n7), 329
Miller, A., 330
Miller, E., 18, 25
Miller, W. C., 96
Millwood, K. A., 180
Modiano, R., 312
Monroe, K. R., 367–368,
    392–395
Montgomery, G., 56,
    416, 417
Moore, B., 121
Moore, M., 55, 59,
    70, 71, 90
Moran, J., 4, 16, 21–22, 29,
    44, 45, 46, 48, 50, 264
Morreale, S. P., 4, 139
Motes, M. A., 150, 151,
    153, 156
Murfin, R. C., 308, 309, 312
Murnane, R., 34
Murphy, S. P., 32
Myers, C., 59, 77

Nachmias, D., 118, 122,
    221(n5)
Nagy, C., 371–372, 427
National Academies, 17, 19,
    33, 34, 38, 84
National Academy of
    Engineering, 6, 14
National Academy of
    Sciences, 6, 14, 246

National Research Council
    (NRC), 246
Neuman, L. J., 186
Neuman, W. L., 176, 189,
    191, 191(n1), 221(n5)
Newell, W. H., 4, 7, 11, 12,
    15, 19, 30, 51, 53, 55,
    59, 61, 70, 71, 76, 85,
    90, 91, 131, 139, 152,
    153, 165, 167, 170, 172,
    173, 175, 177, 178, 179,
    186, 188, 189, 197, 226,
    234, 237, 244, 247, 255,
    268, 271, 273, 286, 288,
    291(n2), 294, 297–299,
    327, 335–337, 340, 343,
    345, 352–353(n2), 369,
    380(n1), 419, 421,
    424–425, 426, 444
Newman, D. M., 99
Nicholas, D., 180, 181
Nicolescu, B., 20
Nietzsche, F., 50
Nikitina, S., 19, 90, 140,
    269–270, 275–277,
    282–286, 328
Nissani, M., 17
Novak, J. D., 72, 126
Novick, P., 116
Nussbaum, M. C., 45

Oblinger, D. G., 34, 35
Organisation for Economic
    Cooperation and
    Development (OECD), 61
Ortega y Gasset, J., 48

Pahre, R., 36, 99, 264
Palmer, C. L., 3, 39, 173, 177,
    179, 180
Palys, T., 250
Paternoster, R., 387
Paulson, K. L., 181
Petrie, H., 139
Pinnock, C., 118
Pintrich, P. R., 262
Pirmann, C. M., 173, 177
Podolny, J., 40
Pohl, C., 271
Polkinghorne, J., 140
Popham, W. J., 436
Post, G. M., 368, 394, 416
Post, J. M., 235, 236
Prevenier, W., 116, 124,
    222(n7)
Preziosi, D., 99

Primeau, R., 56, 416, 417
Proctor, K., 32

Quinn, G. P., 121

Rapoport, D. C., 367
Rapport, D. J., 30
Rapson, R., 264
Rashdall, H., 46
Ratcliff, J. L., 100
Raulin, M. L., 134
Reisberg, D., 365
Remler, D. K., 216, 223(n13), 357–361
Repko, A. F., 12, 29–30, 74, 235–236, 263, 270, 271, 328, 341–343, 353(n3), 365–377, 392–395, 403, 444
Reshef, N., 167
Rhoten, D., 14, 37, 414, 415
Rich, R. C., 123
Richards, D. G., 29, 264, 265, 273
Rivkin, J., 34–35
Rizzo, A., 9, 139, 264
Rogers, Y., 9, 139, 264
Root-Bernstein, M., 40, 64
Root-Bernstein, R. S., 40, 64
Rosenau, P. M., 111, 117, 119, 128
Rosenberg, A., 113, 140, 141
Rossman, G. B., 222(n7)
Ruccio, D., 122
Ryzin, G. G., 216

Saffle, M., 46
Saint-Exupéry, A. de, 42
Salmon, M., 123
Salter, L., 11, 37, 139, 430–431, 433
Sanderson, A., 121
Sawyer, K., 329
Saxe, J. G., 98
Scaife, M., 9, 139, 264
Schatz, 181
Scheurich, J. J., 222(n7)
Schneider, C. G., 32
Schoenfeld, K., 339
Schulman, L. S., 4
Schunn, C. D., 140, 271
Seabury, M. B., 62, 288–289
Searing, S. E., 172
Seipel, M., 289–290
Sewell, W. H., 6
Shipman, B., 121

Shoemaker, D. J., 387
Silberberg, M. S., 131
Sill, D., 43, 330
Silver, L., 83–84, 89, 232, 338, 384–385
Silverman, D., 249
Simpson, D., 308, 312
Smart, L. J., 180
Smolinski, W. J., 82, 87–88, 200, 202, 229, 306, 309–310
Snow, C. P., 44
Sokolowski, R., 137
Somerville, M. A., 30
Somit, A., 123, 134
Spanner, D., 180
Spooner, M., 39, 63
Squires, G., 27
Standlee, L., 114
Steffen, W., 121
Steiner, R., 246
Stember, M., 222(n12)
Sternberg, R. J., 39
Stoddard, E. R., 27
Stoddard, E. W., 415
Stoker, G., 118
Stoll, C., 246
Stone, J. R., 117, 125, 137
Struppa, D. C., 38
Sturgeon, S., 111, 117, 125
Swoboda, W. W., 53
Szostak, R., 27, 28, 30, 55, 64, 73, 90, 96, 105–111, 126–130, 139, 140, 145–148, 173, 183, 184, 195, 204–206, 207, 210–214, 221(n3), 222(n12), 235, 247–251, 255, 265, 270–271, 322, 328, 330, 346, 348–349, 353(n3), 356, 362, 396, 407(n2), 410–412, 420–422, 434, 435–436, 444

Tabak, L., 19
Taffel, A., 114, 140
Tanenhaus, J., 123, 134
Taper, M. L., 141
Tashakkori, A., 208
Taylor, S. J., 291(n3)
Teddlie, C. B., 208
Teffeau, L. C., 173, 177
Tenopir, C., 181
Thomas, G., 275–276
Thornberry, P. T., 266

Toppinen, A., 94, 99
Toynton, R., 415
Tress, B., 271, 419–420, 424–425
Tress, G., 271, 419–420, 424–425
Trow, M., 59
Trowler, P. R., 99, 101
Turk-Bicacakci, L., 32
Turkle, S., 246
Tyson, P. D., 121

University of Minnesota Libraries, 186

van der Lecq, R., 400–403
van Kerkhoff, L., 271
van Ryzin, G. G., 223(n13), 357–361, 369, 377–379
Vaughn, K. T. L., 179
Verville, A., 34, 35
Vess, D., 4
Vickers, J., 53, 139, 189, 245

Walker, D., 237–238
Wallace, R. A., 100, 126, 370
Wasserstrom, J. N., 12
Watson, J. D., 212, 228, 238–239, 240, 251–252, 303, 313, 316–317, 319, 427
Weingart, P., 50, 51
Weingast, P., 352(n1)
Welch, J, IV, 90, 329, 330, 353(n3)
Wentworth, J., 61
Wheeler, L., 17–18
Whitaker, M. P., 122, 302, 305
Wickham, J., 132
Wiersma, W., 221(n5)
Williams, J. M., 191(n3)
Williams, P., 180
Willnat, L., 123
Wilson, E. O., 36
Wolf, A., 100, 126, 370
Wolfe, C., 78, 186, 298, 336, 411, 422–425, 431
Worden, 401–402

Xio, H., 222(n7)

Zajonc, 274–275
Zerhouni, E. H., 36

Subject Index _____

AAC&U (Association of American Colleges and Universities), 445, 448–449
AAHEA (American Association for Higher Education and Accreditation), 4
Abstract thinking, 62
Academic departments, 93–95, 440–441
  See also Disciplines
Academic Search Complete, 447
Acid rain example, 226–228, 232–233
Adequacies in disciplines
  bias based on, 414
  importance of, 75, 104
  integration and, 280
  in-text evidence of, 219–220
  knowledge, 193–198
  literature searches for developing, 169, 173
  methods understanding, 204–219
  theory identification, 198–204, 205
  willingness to achieve, 60, 76
Admission, Review, and Dismissal (ARD) meeting example, 337
AGLS (Association for General and Liberal Studies), 446
AIS (Association for Integrative Studies), 51, 446
Ambiguity, tolerance for, 59
American Association for Higher Education and Accreditation (AAHEA), 4
American Studies Association (ASA), 445
Analysis of problem. *See* Problem analysis
Analytical intelligence, 39
Ancient Greeks, 45
Anthropological metaphor of tribes, 50
Anthropology
  assumptions, 122
  epistemologies, 115
  methods, 133
  perspective, 103
  phenomena, 106

Applied/professional fields, 5–6
Appreciation of disciplinary perspectives, 43
Apprentice level, 424
ARD (Admission, Review, and Dismissal) meeting example, 337
Art and art history
  assumptions, 124
  epistemologies, 116
  methods, 135
  perspective, 98, 103
  phenomena, 106
Assessment
  faculty evaluation, 422
  integration, 272–274, 423
  interdisciplinary definition as critical to, 13
  during literature searches, 181–182
  quality testing, 414–418
  resources for, 451–452
  testing more comprehensive understanding, 418–425
Association for General and Liberal Studies (AGLS), 446
Association for Integrative Studies (AIS), 51, 446
Association of American Colleges and Universities (AAC&U), 445, 448–449
Associations, list of, 445–447
Assumptions of disciplines
  about, 120–126
  common ground, 334
  definitions, 120, 296, 370
  extending, 340–343
  modifying, 372–379
  research model and, 441
  theories and, 302–303, 309–313
  types, 298–300
Atmosphere example, 283
Aural architecture example, 430–431
Authoritative definitions, 14–15

Basic assumptions, 120
Bias
    of disciplines, 55, 226
    personal, 71, 233–234, 255, 276
    in problem definition, 79–80
    reflection on, 411–413
Bibliographies, 452
Bilingualism metaphor, 28
Biology
    assumptions, 121
    epistemologies, 114
    methods, 131, 217–219
    perspective, 102
    phenomena, 106
    problem analysis, 227, 228–229
    theories, 202
Black Like Me (Griffin), 232
Bloom's taxonomy, 261, 262
Boix Mansilla test, 422–425, 431
Book classification, 173–176
Boolean search strategy, 450–451
Border disciplinarity, 86
Borrowing from disciplines, 196
Boundary crossing, 26–27, 100
Bowl of fruit metaphor, 17
Breadth of knowledge, 194–197, 279–280
Bridge building metaphor, 27, 322
Broken window theory, 357–361
Browsing, 179–180, 182
"Bucket List" theory, 362–363
Burden of comprehension, 196
Bygone age of disciplines, 44–45

Carleton Interdisciplinary Science and Math
    Initiative (CISMI), 448
Case studies, 251, 427–429
Case Studies in Interdisciplinary Research
    (Repko, Newell, & Szostak), 444
Catching the Light (Zajonc), 274–275
Categories of disciplines, 94–95
Causal arguments, 387
Causal integration, 387–407
Causal loop diagrams, 154–155
Causal relationships, 358
    See also Variables
Checklists for literature searches, 187–188
Chemistry
    assumptions, 121
    epistemologies, 114
    methods, 131
    perspective, 102
    phenomena, 106
    problem analysis, 227, 228–229

CIJE (Current Index to Journals in
    Education), 447
CISMI (Carleton Interdisciplinary Science and
    Math Initiative), 448
Citation indexes, 188
Classification
    of books, 173–176
    of disciplines, 102–104
    of phenomena, 107–111, 126, 147–148
Close reading, 303
Cognitive abilities, 56–58, 415–418
Cognitive advancement, 57, 417–418
Cognitive decentering, 54, 55
Cognitive discord, 99–100
Cognitive fluidity, 100, 111
Cognitive interdisciplinarity, 267
Cognitive outcomes, 442–443
Cognitive psychology, 267–270,
    294–295, 296, 297
Cognitive sum of parts, 288
Cold War era, 49–50
Collaboration, 60–61, 452
College Learning for the New Global Century
    (AAC&U), 32
Color phenomenon, 270, 276–277
Columbia River ecosystem example
    adequacy development, 194–195, 217–219
    most relevant disciplines identified, 161
    phrasing of problem statement, 81, 87
Common ground
    definitions, 322–323
    importance of, 56–57, 267–269, 417
    summaries of, 385–386, 393,
        397–398, 400, 404
    See also Common ground between concepts;
        Common ground between theories
Common ground between concepts
    background, 321
    communication and, 267–268, 323–324
    conflicts between values and rights, 348–350
    ethics and, 348–351
    narrow versus wide contexts, 331
    process of attaining, 333–335
    requirements of, 324–331
    responsibility for, 332
    techniques for, 335–348
Common ground between theories
    critiquing theories, 369–379
    definitions, 355–356
    modifying theories, 364–369
    necessity of theories, 356–357
    relationship of models, variables and causal
        processes, 357–361

Communication
  common ground and, 267–268, 323–324
  competence in, 61–62
  importance of, 13, 419–420
  integration and, 425–436
Community development projects, 38
Comparative national perspectives resources, 452
Competing impulses, 21–22
Complexity of problems, 33–37, 44, 56–58, 85
Complexity theory, 401
Complex systems theory, 35
Computer-assisted education example, 246–247
Concept maps, 150–151
Concepts of disciplines
  about, 126
  definitions, 296, 370
  embedded in insights, 297–298
  modifying, 327, 371–372, 377–379
  more comprehensive understanding from, 384–387
  theories and, 198–204, 205, 302
  See also Common ground between concepts
Conceptual absorption approach, 372
Conceptual blending, 269
Conceptualization, 282–284
Conflicting perspectives, 265, 276–277
Conflict resolution, 289–290
  See also Common ground
Conflicts in insights. See Insight conflicts
Conflict theory, 391–392
Confrontation of differences, 24
Consequentialism, 348, 349
Consilience, 36–37
Content, reflecting on, 410–411
Content analysis, 249–250
Contested space, 7–8
Contextualization, 282
Controlled vocabulary, 176–178, 188
Core resources, 451–455
Costa Rican ecosystem example, 371–372, 427
Creative intelligence, 39
Creativity, 43–44, 63, 71
Critical interdisciplinarity, 22–23
Cross-level causal integration, 395–403
Cultural analysis example
  adequacy development, 214–215
  common ground, 340
  conflict identification, 315–316
  insight evaluation, 237–238, 253–254
  more comprehensive understanding, 385–386
  new processes, 432–433
  problem analysis, 231–232
Cultural anthropology, 296, 297

Cultural identity variable, 365–377
Current Index to Journals in Education (CIJE), 447
Curriculum and disciplines, 8–9
Curriculum design, 452–453
Customer service example, 339

Database cataloguing, 171–172
Databases, 173, 176, 177–179, 447–448
  See also Literature searches
Data tables, 185
Decentering, 54, 55
Decision-making process, 69–73, 348–349
Deductive approaches, 203–204, 205
Definitions of interdisciplinary studies, 12–16, 453
Delinquent behavior example, 397–399
Deontology, 348
Dependent variables, 358–359
Depth of knowledge, 194–197, 278–279
Development theory, 391–392
Dewey Decimal System, 174–175
Diabetes incidence example, 155–156
Dialectical thinking, 62–63
Disciplinary balance during literature searches, 182–183
Disciplinary bias, 78, 226, 275, 463
Disciplinary experts, 188–189
Disciplinary fragmentation, 264
Disciplinary grounding, 423
Disciplinary insight, 16
Disciplinary methods. See Methods
Disciplines
  categories of, 94–95
  communication back to, 435–436
  concepts of, 126
  epistemological positions, 111–120
  formation of, 45–48
  inadequacies of, 53–55, 86
  interdisciplinary critique of, 41–45
  interdisciplinary studies compared to, 9–10
  part of interdisciplinary studies, 4–7, 53
  phenomena, 105–111
  specialization of, 36
  structure of knowledge and, 93–95
  theories, 126–128
  See also Assumptions of disciplines;
    Identification of relevant disciplines;
    Perspective, disciplinary; specific
    disciplines
Dissertations, 448
Diversity, appreciation for, 60
DNA example
  conflict identification, 313

insight evaluation, 238–239, 240, 245, 251–252
methods, 211–212
problem analysis, 228–229
Domains of practice resources, 453–455
Drivers of interdisciplinary studies, 33–41

Earth sciences, 202, 306, 310
assumptions, 121
epistemologies, 114
methods, 132
perspective, 97, 102
phenomena, 106
theories, 200
Economic growth example, 434
Economics
assumptions, 122
conflict identification, 307, 311, 314
epistemologies, 115
insight evaluation, 252–253
methods, 133, 217–219
perspective, 103
phenomena, 106
problem analysis, 227–228, 228–229
theories, 200–201, 203
Education Resources Information Center (ERIC), 447
Elephant and blind men fable, 98
Elephant house fable, 17–19, 143
End-to-end causal integration, 388–389
Engineering problem analysis, 227, 228–229
Enlightenment, 46–47
Enterprise, 58–59
Environmental advocacy example, 344
Environmental studies problem analysis, 227, 228–229
Epistemological assumptions, 299
Epistemological barriers, 265
Epistemological interpretivism, 113
Epistemological pluralism, 112
Epistemological positivism, 113
Epistemological self-reflexivity, 119–120
Epistemologies, 111–120
limitations, 119
methods and, 129–130, 137–138
tables of, 114, 115, 116–117
theories and, 118
ERIC (Education Resources Information Center), 447
Ethics, 111, 348–351
Ethnographic fieldwork, 250
Evaluation. See Assessment; Insight evaluation
Experiments, 248
Experts' bias, 412
Explicit knowledge, 420
Extension technique, 340–343

Facilitating Interdisciplinary Research (National Academies), 14, 33
Faculty communication, 13
Faculty evaluation, 422
False consensus bias, 276
Federated searching, 451
Feedback loops, 75, 371
Feminist approaches, 118–119
Fine and performing arts, 5
Five Minds for the Future (Gardner), 40–41
"5 W questions," 241–244, 247–248
Flow theory, 362–363
Focus of research. See Problem analysis
Foreign language proficiency, 28
Foundations of interdisciplinary studies, 21
French National Centre for Scientific Research, 446
Freshwater scarcity example
conflict identification, 306, 309–310, 310
disciplines, 194
justification, 87–88
phenomena, 107
phrasing of problem statement, 82
problem analysis, 229–230
theories, 152, 200, 202
Full integration, 265, 273–274
Full-scale literature searches, 183–190

Gang examples, 370, 391–392
Gaps between disciplines, 43
Gender and race in fiction example. See Race and gender in fiction example
General Education in a Free Society, 49
General education movement, 49
Generalist critique of integration, 264–266
Generalist interdisciplinarians, 4
Generative technologies, 38–41
Global warming example, 44
Goal-setting theory, 362–363
Golden thread metaphor, 322
Graffito example
adequacy development, 215
common ground, 340
conflict identification, 295, 315–316
insight evaluation, 237–238, 245, 253–254
most relevant disciplines identified, 161
new processes, 432–433
phrasing of problem statement, 88–89
problem analysis, 231
Grants example, 345–346
Greater Expectations report, 40
Grooming and gossip theory, 401

Hallmark assumptions, 121–125
Handbook of Transdisciplinary Research, 271

Heuristic methods, 70–71
Historical development of problems, 169
History
    assumptions, 124
    conflict identification, 314
    as discipline, 5, 6
    epistemologies, 116
    insight evaluation, 245
    methods, 135–136, 217–219
    perspective, 103
    phenomena, 107
    theories, 203, 243
History of interdisciplinarity, 46–52, 454
H-Net, 447
Holistic test, 421–422
Holistic thinking, 63, 277–278
Horizontal causal integration, 389–390
Human cloning example, 146–147,
        160, 163–164, 286
Human Genome Project, 37
Humanities
    assumptions, 122–125
    as discipline, 48, 95
    epistemologies, 114, 116–117
    insight evaluation, 237
    methods, 135–137, 206–207, 212–215
    perspectives, 103–104
    phenomena, 106–107
    resources, 454
    theories, 201–202
    See also Cultural analysis example; Los
        Angeles metropolitan example; Race
        and gender in fiction example; Rime of
        the Ancient Mariner; Suicide terrorism
        example
Human world classification example,
        107–111
Humility, 61
Hybridization, 36

Ideographic theories, 205
Ideology, 50, 106, 109, 111, 116, 238, 271,
        308, 367, 394, 405
Ideal manager example, 413
Identification of relevant disciplines,
        143–166
    literature searches for, 170
    mapping, 149–159
    most relevant disciplines, 159–164
    potential disciplines, 143–149
Identity theory, 366, 367–368, 392–395
Independent variables, 358–359
Indexes, 177–179
Inductive approaches, 203
Information research resources, 454
Initial literature searches, 173–183

Innovation, 38–41
Insight conflicts
    communicating, 316–319
    importance of identifying, 293–295
    reasons for, 295–300
    theories as sources of, 300–316
Insight definitions, 16, 97–98
Insight evaluation
    checklists, 255
    data used for, 244–247
    by discipline perspective, 234–239
    methods and, 128–129, 247–251
    most relevant disciplines identified,
        160, 162
    phenomena, 251–254
    by theories, 239–244
    See also Problem analysis
Insights, need for, 38–41
Instrumental interdisciplinary, 22–23
Integrated definitions, 15–16
Integrating perspectives, 97–98
Integration
    about, 7, 23–24
    advantages of, 271–272
    assessing, 272–274, 423
    background, 442
    broad model of, 281–290
    common ground as integral to, 328
    conditions for, 274–280
    controversy about, 263–270
    definitions, 3–4, 261–263
    importance of, 417–418
    publications, 270–271
    resources, 454–455
    results, 285–289
Integrationist interdisciplinarians, 4
Integrative Learning: Opportunities to
        Connect, 448–449
Integrative thinking, 40–41
Integrative wisdom, 330
Intelligence, types of, 39
Interdisciplinarians traits/skills, 58–63
Interdisciplinary Education at Liberal Arts
        Institutions (Rhoten, Boix Mansilla, Chun
        and Klein), 14
Interdisciplinary research process (IRP)
    definitions, 24–25, 69–73
    integrated model of, 73–76
    methods, 215–216
    new models of, 270
    reflection on, 409–414
    STEP 1/2. See Problem definition/
        justification
    STEP 3. See Identification of relevant
        disciplines
    STEP 4. See Literature searches

STEP 5. *See* Adequacy in disciplines
STEP 6. *See* Insight evaluation; Problem analysis
STEP 7. *See* Insight conflicts
STEP 8. *See* Common ground
STEP 9. *See* More comprehensive understanding/theory
STEP 10. *See* Assessment; Communication; Reflection
Interdisciplinary studies
    assumptions, 52–55
    cognitive abilities and, 56–58
    competing impulses behind, 21–22
    critique of disciplines, 41–45
    current use of, 22–25
    definitions, 12–16, 94, 439–440
    disciplines compared to, 9–10
    drivers of, 33–41
    justification for, 84–89
    maturing academic field, 440–441
    methods and, 128–130
    multidisciplinary studies compared to, 16–21
    origins, 48–52
    parts of, 4–11
    premise of, 21
    theory and, 127–128
Interdisciplinary Studies Project, 449
Interdisciplines (project), 446
Internet. *See* Online resources
Interpersonal relations skills, 62
Interpretivism, 112, 118, 130, 215
Intervening variables, 361
Interviews, 250–251
In-text evidence, 219–220
Intuition and common ground, 329–331
Intuition and ethics, 348
Intuitive perspective, 323–324
Issues in Integrative Studies, 51–52, 446
Iterative process, 71

Jargon, 78–79
Job complexity, 33
Journals, 173, 176, 449
JSTOR (Journal Storage), 447–448
Justification for interdisciplinary research. *See* Problem definition/justification

Keller, Helen, 330–331
Keyword searches, 176, 177–179, 450
Knowledge
    advancement of, 443–444
    comprehending enough, 193–198
    developing, 416–417
    disciplinary and interdisciplinary, 25

explicit, 420
scholarly, 168
structure of, 93–95
system mapping and, 157–158
tacit, 420
See also Reflection
Knowledge production, 25

Lakewood Plan example, 405
Land-use example, 154
Language and common ground, 326–327
Language origins example, 377–379, 400–403
Law, 227, 228–229
Learned thinking process, 324–325
Learning outcomes, 415
Library cataloguing, 171–172
Library of Congress Classification, 174–175
Light waves example, 274–275
Lin, Maya, 426
Literature
    assumptions, 124–125
    epistemologies, 116
    insight evaluation, 254
    methods, 136
    perspective, 103
    phenomena, 107
    See also Rime of the Ancient Mariner example
Literature and resource guides, 455–458
Literature review resources, 452
Literature searches
    challenges, 170–172
    defining, 167–168
    full-scale, 183–190
    initial, 173–183
    journals, 449
    reasons for, 168–170
    relevant disciplines identified by, 144–147
The Little Prince (Saint-Exupéry), 42
Logotherapy, 362–363
Los Angeles metropolitan example, 403–407
Love of learning, 59

Macro-level variables, 359–360
Mapping exercises, 149–159, 233
Mapping metaphor, 27–28, 73–74
Marriage counselor role, 332
Marxism, 203, 243, 315
Mastery, 60, 424
Mathematics
    assumptions, 121
    epistemologies, 114
    methods, 132
    perspective, 102
    phenomena, 106
Mathematics and religion example, 344–345

Matrix for ethics, 350–351
Meaning, 15
Meaning Construction Model, 427–429
Meaning in everyday life example, 361–363
Metaphors, 25–29
    anthropological metaphor of tribes, 50
    bilingualism, 28
    boundary crossing, 26–27
    bowl of fruit, 17
    bridge building, 27, 322
    golden thread, 322
    integrative devices, 426
    mapping, 27–28
    musical chord as integration, 269
    smoothie, 17
Methods, 128–138
    adequacies in disciplines and, 204–219
    insight evaluation by, 247–251
    interdisciplinary position, 207–210
    strengths and limitations, 248–251
Micro-level variables, 359–360
Model, interdisciplinary, 441
Models to communicate integration, 426–429
Modern disciplines, 47–48
Modernism, 113, 117–118, 119, 212–214
Monistic perspective, 18–19
Monodisciplinarity, overcoming, 274–278
The Moral Dimension (Etzioni), 343, 347
More comprehensive understanding/theory
    assessing, 418–425
    definitions, 382–384
    modified concepts and, 384–387
    modified theories and, 387–407
    reflection on, 409–414
Most interdisciplinary theory, 366
Most relevant disciplines, 159–164
Multicausal integration, 390–395
Multidisciplinary studies, 16–21, 98
Multilevel causal integration, 395–403
Multiple integration, 265
Multiplicity of theories, 85–86
Musical chord metaphor, 269
Music and music education
    assumptions, 125
    epistemologies, 116–117
    methods, 136
    perspective, 104
    phenomena, 107

Naïve level, 423–424
Narratives, 429–431
Narrow interdisciplinarity, 286, 331
National Academies, 14
Natural sciences
    assumptions, 120–122
    categories of disciplines, 95

epistemologies, 113, 114
mathematics and religion example, 344–345
methods, 130–132, 206–207, 211
perspectives of, 102–103
phenomena, 106
See also Columbia River ecosystem example;
    Costa Rican ecosystem example; DNA
    example; Freshwater scarcity example;
    Language origins example
Natural thinking process, 324–325
Nature, problems of, 33–38
Network for Transdisciplinary Research
    (td-net), 446–447
Neutrality, 79
New Directions: Science, Humanities, Policy, 449
Newell test, 419, 420
New generalism, 123–124
New humanities, 123–124
"New" integration, 287, 289
New processes, 431–433
Niche construction theory, 400
Nomothetic theories, 205
Nondisciplinary sources, 189
Nonlinear thinking, 75
Northwest Passage (Dietrich), 290
    See also Columbia River ecosystem example
Novice level, 424

Occupational sex discrimination example
    adequacy development, 200–201,
        202–203, 212
    conflict identification, 307, 310–311,
        313–315, 314–315
    insight evaluation, 240–241, 252–253
    most relevant disciplines identified, 161
    problem analysis, 230
    theories, 241–244
Online resources, 173, 176, 177–179, 448–449
Ontological assumptions, 298, 299
Organizational challenges, 185–186
Organizations supporting integration, 271
Organization technique, 346–347
Overviews of field, 458

Paradigm shifts, 54
Paradox, tolerance for, 59
Partial integration, 265, 273
Participant observation (PO), 250
Partnerships, 38
Pedagogy literature/resource guides, 455–456
Peer-reviewed sources, 168, 420
Perfect crime elimination example
    common ground, 338–339
    more comprehensive understanding, 386–387
    new processes, 432
    problem analysis, 230–231

Performing arts, 5, 95, 266, 273–274, 289, 297, 384, 407, 443
Personal bias, 71, 233–234, 255, 276
Personality traits variable, 365–377
Perspective, disciplinary
  as voice, 269
  classification, 147–148
  common ground and, 372
  concept of, 96–104
  definitions, 145
  insight evaluation, 234–239
  relevant disciplines identified with, 159, 160–161
  table of, 102–104
  techniques, 416
Perspective taking, 56, 274–275
Phenomena
  classification, 107–111, 126, 147–148
  concept of, 105–111
  insight evaluation, 251–254
  relevent disciplines identified with, 145
  Szostak's categories, 106–107, 108–111, 176
Philosophers, 349
Philosophy
  assumptions, 125, 296
  epistemologies, 116–117
  methods, 137
  perspective, 104
  phenomena, 107
  theory, 127
Phrasing of problem statements, 80–84
Physics
  assumptions, 121
  epistemologies, 114
  methods, 132
  perspective, 103
  phenomena, 106
  problem analysis, 227, 228–229
Piaget example, 153
Policy critiques, 433–435
Political science
  assumptions, 123
  conflict identification, 296, 297
  epistemologies, 115
  methods, 134
  perspective, 103
  phenomena, 106
  problem analysis, 227, 228–229
  theories, 202
PO (participant observation), 250
Positivism, 112, 118, 129–130, 215
The Postmodern Condition (Lyotard), 113
Postmodernism, 113, 117–118, 119, 130, 213–214
Potentially relevant disciplines, 143–149
  See also Identification of relevant disciplines

Power, 55
Power seeking variable, 365–377
Practical intelligence, 39
Pragmatic interdisciplinarity, 49
Premise of interdisciplinary studies, 21
Prepositional integration, 387–407
Principle maps, 150–151
Principle of least action, 335
Probing in literature searches, 180
Problem analysis
  bias in, 233–234, 412
  disciplinary perspective in, 225–233
  "5 W" questions, 241–244, 247–248
  See also Insight evaluation
Problem definition/justification
  complexity of problems, 33–37, 44, 56–58, 85–89
  criteria for, 84, 89–90
  narrowing focus, 168–169
  phrasing statements, 80–84
  selection of problem, 76–84
  See also Literature searches
Problem solving approach, 284–285
Process, reflecting on, 410–411
Professional education, 5–6, 55
Professional societies, 48
Program development and sustainability literature/resource guides, 456
Propositions, 387
ProQuest Dissertation Abstracts International, 448
Psychology
  assumptions, 123
  conflict identification, 315
  epistemologies, 115
  insight evaluation, 235–237, 254
  methods, 134
  perspective, 103
  phenomena, 106
  theories, 203
  See also Suicide terrorism example
Publications about integration, 270–271
Public education failure example, 429–430
Purposefulness, 422
Purview, 97

Qualitative research, 129, 130, 208–210
Qualitative Research Methods (Berg), 208–210
Qualities of mind, 280
Quality testing, 414–418
Quantitative research, 129–130, 208
Questions
  by broad model of integration, 289–290
  by discipline, 227
  See also Problem definition/justification

Race and gender in fiction example
 common ground, 338
 more comprehensive understanding, 385
 phrasing of problem statement, 83–84
 problem analysis, 231–232, 232
Reading challenges, 186
Real-world problems, complexity of, 33–37
Receptivity to others, 59–60
Recognition of differences, 24
Redefinition technique, 336–340
Reductionism, 131
Reflection
 importance of, 59
 on IRP, 409–414
 on quality, 414–418
Reflexive process, 71
Reinventing Undergraduate Education
 (Boyer Commission), 40
Relevance-for-status theory, 401
Relevance of disciplines. See Identification of
 relevant disciplines
Religion, 26, 43, 94, 109, 125, 137, 164, 172,
 199, 236, 302, 344–345, 365, 367–368
Religious studies
 assumptions, 125
 epistemologies, 116–117
 methods, 137
 perspective, 104
 phenomena, 107
Renaissance Man ideal, 48
Research maps, 149–150
Research practice literature/resource guides,
 456–457
Resources in Education (RIE), 447
Results complicating integration, 265–266
Rights and values conflicts, 348–351
Rigor demonstrations, 220
Rime of the Ancient Mariner example
 conflict identification, 307–309,
 311–313, 312
 problem analysis, 226
 theories, 201–202
Role taking, 275–276

"Sacred" terror theory, 366, 367
Sacred values variable, 365–377
Saint-Exupéry, Antoine de, 42
Salmon population example. See Columbia
 River ecosystem example
Scaffolding, 157
Scholarly knowledge, 168
Scholarship, 11
School violence example, 397–399, 434–435
Sciences
 as discipline, 47–48
 problem analysis, 227, 228–229

resources, 453
 See also Natural sciences; specific sciences
Scientific inquiry, new avenues to, 435
Scientific method, 131–132
Scientific revolution, 46–47
Scientific theory, 127
Search strategies, 179–182, 449–451
Secondary data analysis, 249
Self-sanction theory, 366, 367
Sequential causal integration, 388–389
Side-by-side causal integration, 389–390
Signs, 433
Silo perspective, 35
"Situatedness," 215
Skewed understanding, 235
Skills of interdisciplinarians, 61–63
Skimming, 181, 182
Smoothie metaphor, 17
Social learning theory, 392
Social production of space theory, 404
Social sciences
 assumptions, 122–123
 categories of disciplines, 95
 Costa Rican ecosystem example,
 371–372, 427
 as discipline, 48
 environmental advocacy example, 344
 epistemologies, 114, 115
 grants example, 345–346
 insight evaluation, 240–241, 245,
 252–253
 justification examples, 88
 methods, 133–134, 206–207
 perspectives, 103
 phenomena, 106
 phrasing of problem statements, 82
 problem analysis, 230–231
 resources, 453–454
 theories, 200–201, 202–203
 See also Economic growth example; Gang
 examples; Los Angeles metropolitan
 example; Meaning Construction Model;
 Occupational sex discrimination
 example; Perfect crime elimination
 example; Public education failure
 example; School violence example;
 Suicide terrorism example
Society, problems of, 33–38, 86–87
Sociology
 assumptions, 123
 conflict identification, 314
 epistemologies, 115
 methods, 134
 perspective, 97, 103
 phenomena, 106
 theories, 203

Spatial and analytical integration, 403–407
Specialization of disciplines, 36, 42–43, 47, 48
Statistical analysis, 249
STEPS of research process. *See* Interdisciplinary research process (IRP)
Stock and flow diagrams, 154, 155–156
Strategies for literature searches, 186–188
Students
   communication, 13
   friendly process for, 72
   morale, 13–14
"Studies" part of interdisciplinary studies, 8–11
Subdisciplines, 6, 94
Subject headings (LCC), 175
Subject searches, 176–179
Substance, 11
Successful intelligence, 39
Suicide terrorism example
   assumptions, 334–335
   common ground, 341–343, 365–377, 373–377
   conflict identification, 294–295, 296, 297, 301, 302, 304–305
   insight evaluation, 235–237
   more comprehensive understanding, 392–395
Surveys, 249
Synthesis, 263
   See also Integration
Systems mapping, 152–156, 156
Systems thinking, 152, 156, 157–159
Szostak test, 421–422

Table of potentially relevant disciplines, 146–147
Tacit knowledge, 420
Taxonomy of disciplines, 102–104, 303–305
td-net (Network for Transdisciplinary Research), 446–447
Teaching settings, 47
Techniques
   of extension, 340–343
   of organization, 346–347
   of redefinition, 336–340
   of transformation, 343–346
Technology studies, 227, 228–229, 453
Temple Mount example, 287
Terrorism studies, 23, 43
   See also Suicide terrorism example
Tests. *See* Assessment
Textbooks, 458
Textual analysis, 249–250
Theories
   adequacies in disciplines and, 198–204, 205
   background, 126–128, 441

bias toward, 413
insight evaluation with, 239–244
literature/resource guides, 457
mapping, 152, 153
methods and, 210–211
modifying, 327
more comprehensive understanding from, 387–407
most relevant disciplines identified with, 160, 162
perspective and, 97–98
selecting types of, 203–204, 205
as sources of insights/concepts/assumptions, 300–305
Szostak's typology of, 204, 206
   See also Common ground between theories
Theory-based insights, 296
Theory competition, 266
Theory extension, 368
Theory map, 152, 153
Time-sensitive topics, 220, 248
Traditional disciplines, 5, 8–9, 94
Traditional interdisciplinarity, 49
Tradition and ethics, 349
Traffic example, 154–155
Traits of interdisciplinarians, 58–61
Transdisciplinary studies, 20–21
Transformation technique, 343–346
Trans-sector problem solving, 20
Tress et al. test, 419–420
Triangulation, 216, 278–280
Tribes, anthropological metaphor of, 50
Truth claims, 112–113

Unconscious mind, 329
Unconventional thinking, 324–325
University origins, 46
University reforms, 50–51
Utilitarians, 349
Utility test, 419, 421

Value assumptions, 299–300
Values and rights conflicts, 348–351
Variables, 358–361
Variations in process, 443
Vietnam Veterans Memorial, 426
Virtue, 348
Visual metaphors, 426
Volunteer case study, 427–429

Web of Knowledge, 448
Wide interdisciplinarity, 286, 331
Work of interdisciplinary studies, 23–24
Workplace changes, 41
WorldCat, 448